Cecil County Public Library
301 Newark Ave.
Elkton, MD 21921

NOV 1 2 2010

T5-BSJ-671

At the Head of the Bay

A Cultural and Architectural History of Cecil County, Maryland

Compiled and edited by Pamela James Blumgart
with contributions by
Mark Walston, Paul Baker Touart, and others

The Cecil Historical Trust, Inc., Elkton, Maryland
The Maryland Historical Trust Press, Crownsville, Maryland

Copyright © 1996 by Cecil Historical Trust, Inc.
Copyright © 2010 by Cecil Historical Trust, Inc.

Library of Congress Control Number: 2010921045

All rights reserved. No part of this work may be reproduced or used in any form or by any means—graphic, electronic, or mechanical, including photocopying or information storage and retrieval systems—without written permission from the publisher.
The scanning, uploading and distribution of this book or any part thereof via the Internet or via any other means without the permission of the publisher is illegal and punishable by law. Please purchase only authorized editions and do not participate in or encourage the electronic piracy of copyrighted materials.
"Schiffer," "Schiffer Publishing Ltd. & Design," and the "Design of pen and inkwell" are registered trademarks of Schiffer Publishing Ltd.

ISBN: 978-0-7643-3561-7
Printed in China

Cover illustration of the confluence of the Elk and Bohemia rivers by Geraldine McKeown, Elkton, Maryland

Title page illustration: Engraving of the mouth of the Susquehanna River after artwork by John H. B. Latrobe, printed in 1827 by Fielding Lucas
(Maryland Historical Society)

Schiffer Books are available at special discounts for bulk purchases for sales promotions or premiums. Special editions, including personalized covers, corporate imprints, and excerpts can be created in large quantities for special needs. For more information contact the publisher:

Published by Schiffer Publishing Ltd.
4880 Lower Valley Road
Atglen, PA 19310
Phone: (610) 593-1777; Fax: (610) 593-2002
E-mail: Info@schifferbooks.com

For the largest selection of fine reference books on this and related subjects, please visit our web site at
www.schifferbooks.com
We are always looking for people to write books on new and related subjects. If you have an idea for a book please contact us at the above address.

This book may be purchased from the publisher.
Include $5.00 for shipping.
Please try your bookstore first.
You may write for a free catalog.

In Europe, Schiffer books are distributed by
Bushwood Books
6 Marksbury Ave.
Kew Gardens
Surrey TW9 4JF England
Phone: 44 (0) 20 8392 8585; Fax: 44 (0) 20 8392 9876
E-mail: info@bushwoodbooks.co.uk
Website: www.bushwoodbooks.co.uk

Contents

Foreword	v
Preface	vi
Acknowledgments	viii

The History, by Mark Walston

Chapter 1	"What Manner of People These Strangers Be"	1
Chapter 2	From "A-tradeinge" to Settlement at the Head of the Bay	15
Chapter 3	Making a Plantation Out of the Woods	37
Chapter 4	"An Excellent Situation" for Manufacturer and Farmer Alike	57
Chapter 5	"Farming and Improvements...in Advance of the Average in the State"	103
Chapter 6	"The Marriage Capital of the East" in the Modern Period	139

The Architecture, by Paul Touart

Chapter 7	House Forms of Cecil County (1670-1900)	163
Chapter 8	Methods of Construction in Cecil County Dwellings (1670-1900)	193
Chapter 9	The Manners of Interior Finish (1670-1850)	227
Chapter 10	"Improvements" on County Farms	249

Notes	268
Inventory of Historic Sites	277
Index	483

Foreword

IN THE EARLY 1970S the Cecil County Committee of the Maryland Historical Trust embarked on the preparation of a manuscript and an inventory of historic properties concerning the history of Cecil County and its relationship to our sister states of Pennsylvania and Delaware. When I was appointed to the committee some years later, I was advised that this project was a priority item on our agenda. Since that time the Cecil County Committee has merged with and become the Cecil Historical Trust, Inc. The manuscript and inventory at the time of the merger were no closer to completion than they had been many years before. Now, with the aid and support of the Maryland Historical Trust, an agency of the Maryland Department of Housing and Community Development, the dream of many, who had almost lost hope, has come true and you are about to read the result of the long years of labor by members of the Cecil County Committee, who were later assisted by others on the board of directors of the Cecil Historical Trust, Inc. We are very proud of this work and hope it will help readers learn more about Cecil County and its heritage and encourage them to enlarge that knowledge.

It would be difficult to list all those who have devoted so much time and effort to the success of this project, but I think special recognition should be given to all the members of the Cecil County Committee of the Maryland Historical Trust; the board of directors of the Cecil Historical Trust, Inc.; J. Rodney Little, director of the Maryland Historical Trust, and his staff; and the various boards of commissioners of Cecil County. Thank you all.

Judge Kenneth A. Wilcox
Past President
Cecil County Committee of the Maryland Historical Trust
Cecil Historical Trust, Inc.

Cecil Historical Trust, Inc., 1993-96

Mrs. Audrey Edwards, *past president*
(current vice-president)
Cecil Historical Trust Book Committee
Mrs. Eloise H. Davis, *chairman*
Mrs. Caroline Coffay
Mr. Nelson H. McCall
Mr. George Reynolds
Mrs. Dorothy Robinson
Mr. Morton Taylor

Mrs. Diane Stackwick, *president*
Mr. Ulysses G. Demond, *treasurer*
Mrs. Jacqueline Upp, *secretary*
Mrs. Betty Eliason
Mr. William Stubbs
Mr. Ralph Young
Mrs. Jayne Foard, *representative*
　of the Board of the Maryland
　Historical Trust

Preface

LONG BEFORE the National Historic Preservation Act of 1966 mandated the creation of historic preservation offices across the nation, the State of Maryland had committed itself to recognizing and maintaining the physical embodiments of its rich and varied history. That commitment found its greatest expression in 1961 with the creation of the Maryland Historical Trust. As succinctly stated in its charter, the Trust's mission was and continues to be "to preserve, protect, and enhance districts, sites, buildings, structures, and objects significant in the prehistory, history, upland and underwater archeology, architecture, engineering, and culture of the state, and to encourage others to do so and to promote interest and study in such matters." All of the activities involved in the process—identifying, evaluating, protecting, interpreting, and educating—have been prominently featured in the work of the Trust since its founding. And each one rests squarely upon the crucial first step in any preservation project: the historic sites survey.

To begin to preserve the past with some sense and direction, those sites worthy of retention must first be identified. Toward that end, the Trust sends professional surveyors across the state, searching town and field, highway and byway, upland and underwater for significant sites and structures. Once located, these resources are recorded and researched and the results deposited in the Trust library for future reference.

To date, the Trust's survey program, operating in part with federal funding, has inventoried nearly 86,000 historical and archeological sites. On the surface, the inventory would seem to form an impressive and complete catalog of Maryland's past. And yet, the inventory accounts for less than 20 percent of the potential pool of resources. Across the state an estimated half million buildings constructed before 1940 remain to be visited, inspected, and recorded. Included in that figure are 330,000 housing structures, representing approximately 18 percent of the state's total housing units. Add to that figure hundreds of thousands of undocumented historic objects, landscapes, cultural traditions, and archeological sites, and it becomes clear that the past accounts for a larger percentage of the present than is generally recognized; that its preservation is a very real concern in the maintenance of community life; and that much survey work remains before a complete picture of the tangible and intangible remains of Maryland's heritage emerges.

The information on historical and archeological sites recorded by the Trust was never intended simply to gather dust on library shelves. Nor was it collected merely to satisfy an intellectual curiosity, although each year many students in scholarly pursuit of the past avail themselves of this invaluable architectural reference. Foremost, the inventory, by establishing an official index to the state's historical and archeological resources, makes it possible for decision makers planning public and private projects to take into consideration the impact those projects may have on historic sites. The purpose of this consideration is to ensure that Maryland's shared heritage is not summarily wiped from the landscape by ignorance of its existence or simple oversight and to prevent important landmarks from being severely affected by future development.

Sorting through the collected data to put the past into perspective, however, can be an overwhelming task for those charged with managing the built environment. To help bring the vast amount of information contained in the inventory into a manageable form—one that is applicable in diverse situations—the Trust created the Maryland Comprehensive Historic Preservation Plan in 1986. This landmark document was a management plan that not only directed the Trust's programs but was of critical importance to state and local agencies attempting to integrate cultural resource concerns into their own planning processes. The plan created a unique format for organizing inventory sites by "historic context," by development periods, and by broader "themes" that cover all areas of human activity, from agriculture to commerce, education to transportation. Most importantly, the plan brought attention to the need to focus statewide research and preservation efforts not only on the most imposing, most artistic, or most ancient pieces of the past but on a spectrum of historical remains, including such seemingly ordinary but socially significant resources as black communities, workers' housing, or agricultural outbuildings.

Ten years after the first state preservation plan was written, a new plan, *Preservation 2000: The Maryland Plan*, is nearing its expected completion date of January 1996. This plan will highlight five major goals and outline strategies to address them. It will also recommend historic context development, particularly for use as a database resource as part of the Trust's new Geographical Information System (GIS). The Trust GIS contains information on all inventoried architectural and archeological properties in Maryland, as well as historic districts and preservation easements. It will be an important source of information for determining priorities in the Trust's review, compliance, and planning activities.

Since the early 1970s Trust surveyors have traversed Cecil County, identifying and recording an array of historic sites. Their combined efforts have created a county inventory encompassing more than 1,400 sites covering 10,000 years of occupation, stretching from prehistory to the mid-twentieth century. The results of their work form the basis for this volume, one in a series of county-specific historic sites inventories produced from the survey records of the Trust. This volume, as those which precede it, is divided into two distinct parts. The opening section presents a brief overview of the county's history and architecture, in this case in the form of essays by two authors, and the remainder of the book offers a glimpse into the county inventory of historic sites.

The essay on history is essentially a contextual piece that presents the social, cultural, and economic context in which the material culture of the county was created. In organization, its chapters follow the development periods outlined in both the 1986 and 1996 versions of the state comprehensive preservation plan. The narrative attempts to touch on various themes, but by no means is it intended to be a comprehensive history of the county. Instead, the essay is meant to add dimension and perspective to the historic sites inventory. The architecture essay discusses, from a historical perspective, the form, construction, and interior detail of houses in the county and the agricultural and domestic outbuildings that accompanied them.

The inventory section distills the thousands of hours of intensive site survey work in the county into concise catalog form. The information contained in each entry has been abstracted from longer inventory forms, the originals of which are at the Trust library in Crownsville; for the convenience of researchers, microfilmed copies of the inventory have been deposited at the Maryland State Archives in Annapolis. The Trust currently is undertaking the computerization of this massive database.

Every attempt was made by the historic sites surveyors to create as inclusive an inventory as possible, to record all sites and structures believed to hold significant clues to the county's past. Because of the magnitude of the Cecil inventory, only about half the inventoried sites have been included in this volume. As in any endeavor of this dimension—whether creating the inventory or publishing it—some sites are bound to be missed. Many of the sites that were standing at the time the inventory was last worked on in the 1980s have been demolished by a variety of causes—and are so indicated in this volume. Storms, erosion, flooding, and fire destroy their share of historic resources every year, as do more pervasive human activities, from the development pressures that have escalated in Cecil in recent years—often pitting the past against the present—to wanton destruction by vandalism or arson. Many times, Trust surveyors in Cecil County arrived on the scene in a building's eleventh hour. Too often after their visit, an old building, weakened by years of abandonment and neglect, would tumble to the ground. Today, all that remains is the site's documentary history filed in the Trust library. But although the building itself may be gone, the memory of its existence remains secure in the records of the Trust, for succeeding generations to study, analyze, and admire.

This volume, a record of sites past and present, makes the inventory accessible to a wider audience. Those who read it—whether county resident, visitor, or others interested in architecture and history—should gain a new respect for the past and the material evidence of it that has survived until the late twentieth century.

Mark Walston

Acknowledgments

A COUNTY HISTORIC SITES SURVEY is best performed and evaluated by a single individual, who will then have a comprehensive knowledge of the historic sites in the county and be able to place them in context. Because of the wealth of resources in Cecil County (about 1,500 sites have been identified, two or three times the number found in some other Maryland counties), the survey was extended over many years and contributed to by many individuals. In the process of compiling and editing the information they collected, I have become indebted to numerous people, some for many reasons and others for a single piece of information. Together, they made this book possible.

The members of the Cecil Historical Trust book committee, ably headed by Mrs. Henry V. Davis of Chesapeake City, managed the project. Eloise served as my primary contact with the Trust and helped in innumerable ways. She organized other Cecil Historical Trust members by election district to help select sites for inclusion in the inventory section and to update the information about them. These volunteers reviewed the inventory in manuscript and pages, along with the photographs selected to illustrate the sites. Their knowledge of local buildings proved invaluable. From the First Election District were Jackie Upp, Caroline Coffay, and William Manlove; from the Second District, Eloise Davis and Bill Stubbs; from the Third, Anne Copley and Anne Wilcox; from the Fourth, Geraldine McKeown and George Reynolds; from the Fifth, Ulysses G. Demond, Rebecca Phillips, and Nelson H. McCall; from the Sixth, Ron and Audrey Edwards; from the Seventh, Morton Taylor, Glen Longacre, George Hipkins, and Diane Stackwick; from the Eighth, June Reasin, Kerry Wheatley, and Frances Taylor; and from the Ninth, Edward Plumstead and Frances Hubis. George Reynolds photographed Indian artifacts he had found over many years, providing unique, county-specific illustrations for the prehistory chapter. He also wrote captions to accompany his photographs.

Geraldine McKeown, a member of the Cecil Historical Trust and a watercolorist of some renown, painted the watercolor that appears on the dustjacket. She chose the view, the confluence of the Elk and Bohemia rivers, because it is the "head of the bay," as well as a picturesque view of rolling hills meeting the water, a sight typical of many places in Cecil County.

Audrey Edwards served as president of the Cecil Historical Trust for most of the time I worked on the book. Her encouragement and support throughout the process were much appreciated. Ron Edwards, Caroline Coffay, and Nick Demond successively served as treasurer for the Trust and thus for this project.

The Maryland Historical Trust staff, under the guidance of State Historic Preservation Officer J. Rodney Little, administered the state grant given to the Cecil Historical Trust to help fund this book and facilitated my work in many ways. Jack Ladd Carr, Michael Day, Rebecca Hutchison, Orlando Ridout V, and Evelyn Cohen all helped this book on its way. Mary Louise de Sarran and Barbara Shepherd gave me free run of the Trust library and files, without which I could not have illustrated the inventory section or architecture chapters. Archeologist Maureen Kavanagh kindly reviewed the prehistory chapter. Marcia Miller, Michael Bourne, and the late Ron Andrews each contributed nuggets of valuable information, and Marcia and Ron spent time unearthing photographs. Lillian Wray contributed marketing knowledge and cheerleading in the home stretch, and Joan Arnold faithfully passed on messages. Orlando Ridout offered much encouragement and many helpful suggestions. He also reviewed portions of the manuscript.

Beyond those associated with the two Trusts, the list of those who helped with this project is lengthy, but chief among them is Paul Touart, who worked as a historic sites surveyor in Cecil County from 1978 to 1981. During that time, he wrote an architectural history of the county, which appears in revised form in this volume. Paul spent many hours rewriting these chapters, improving them significantly. He reviewed the text of the entire inventory section and unearthed floor plans and sections he had drawn many years ago. Most of all, Paul encouraged all my efforts in producing this volume. My brother, Anthony O. James, agreed to ink the drawings for the architecture chapters, and his fine work appears there.

Thanks for help with the architecture chapters also goes to Mary and Mike Scheeler and William H. Mechling, owners of Greenfields and Bohemia respectively, and to Sam Tull and Muriel Hall, residents of Rose Hill. All of them made their homes available to Paul Touart and me to examine and photograph so Paul could write knowledgeably about these important county houses. Thanks also to Bill Mechling for helping us measure Bohemia.

Mark Walston started me off right by sending his manuscript on a computer disk, which he had held onto hopefully for seven years. Staff members at the Maryland Historical Society; Maryland State Archives (especially Mame Warren); and Historical Society of Cecil County (especially president Mike Dixon and summer intern Jenifer Dolde) all helped immensely as I searched for illustrations for the history chapters. Thanks to Mike Dixon also for letting me copy items from his postcard collection. Bill Short, history professor at Cecil Community College, gave me access to the wonderful archive of historic photographs copied in a college project about a decade ago. These images add immeasurably to the presentation of county history in chapters 4 to 6. Individuals at the Winterthur Museum Library; the Chester County (Pa.) Historical Society; the Mariners' Museum in Newport News, Virginia; the Library of Congress; and the Peale Museum in Baltimore all helped in the search for images. Others who contributed to the book include Elizabeth Booth, Ronald A. Guns, Geoffrey Henry, Nancy Kurtz, George Lutz, Osbourne Mackie, Richard D. Mackie, Marion Warren, Christopher Weeks, James T. Wollon, and Gale Yerges.

Charlene Edwards of Whitney·Edwards Design in Easton, Maryland, tackled this huge book with enthusiasm and ably designed it to showcase the illustrations yet make the text accessible. Nan Terry proofread most of the book, asking sharp questions about style and consistency, and Richard Edwards provided support. My friend Janet Rumbarger contributed proofreading services and much sound advice.

In attempting to thank individually those who helped me with this project I have taken a risk. More than likely I have omitted some people. If you are one of these, I apologize.

My family and friends were very supportive during the two years I worked on the book. In particular, I thank David, Jake, and Molly for putting up with me while I engaged in this undertaking. It kept me very busy—sometimes busier than they liked!

Pamela James Blumgart
Mount Rainier, Maryland
October 1995

The Indian artifacts illustrated here were all found on Indian village sites near Big Elk Creek, the Elk River, and the Bohemia River. Some are tools used in everyday life, such as the mortar and pestle for grinding grain. Some are ornaments, such as the small fish carved from red slate with three holes for attaching it to an article of clothing. The flat, hollowed out tube may have been used for medicinal purposes or in religious ceremonies. All of these objects were found in association with spear points, knives, and arrowheads. (George M. Reynolds, Sr.)

CHAPTER 1

"What Manner of People These Strangers Be"

IN 1524 the sea-weathered ship of explorer Giovanni de Verazzano hove to off the Atlantic shore; from the deck the captain and his crew looked out upon a land of shimmering beaches and stately forests. Verazzano, an Italian by birth but sailing under French sponsorship, had journeyed from the Old World to North America, searching the coastline for the fabled western route to China. Instead of the elusive passage, he and his men happened upon a provocative land they poetically christened "Arcadia" in tribute to its rustic beauty.

The explorers disembarked for a closer look, pulling their small launch through the breakers and onto the shore, where they were startled by the sudden emergence of a man from the woods. He moved closer cautiously, Verazzano wrote, to see "what manner of people these strangers be":

> Watching us, he did not permit himself to be approached. He was handsome, nude, with hair fastened back in a knot, of olive color. We were about twenty in number....Coaxing him he approached to within two fathoms, showing a burning stick, as if to offer us fire. And we made fire with powder and flint-and-steel, and he trembled all over with terror, and we fired a shot. He stopped as if astonished and prayed, worshipping like a monk, lifting his finger toward the sky, and pointing to the ship and sea, he appeared to bless us.[1]

Verazzano's "Arcadia" was probably Maryland's Eastern Shore, and what the explorer set down in the account of his New World journeys, published in 1566, was the first recorded encounter between Europeans and the native inhabitants of Maryland. More important, perhaps, because of its lasting effect, was the ethnocentric interpretation of the native culture that Verazzano initiated with his description of a trembling, supplicant Indian. Nearly seventy-five years later, Captain John Smith evoked the same attitude in describing his first encounter with the Susquehannock Indians, near what later became Cecil County. Despite the formidable appearance of the native warriors, who, Smith remarked, "seemed like giants to the English," these Indians to European eyes "yet seemed of an honest and simple disposition, [and] with much adoe restrained from adoring us as Gods."[2]

This image suggested by the meeting of two cultures so dissimilar was irresistible for Europeans, in particular self-obsessed explorers extolling themselves as gods come down upon a childlike people of Eden, naive and awed by things beyond the narrow parameters of their culture, cowering under the might of even such simple European technology as gunpowder. Circumstances soon altered their view, however. Bloody conflicts between the disparate tribes, and between whites and Indians, tempered the European perception of native character, transforming the image from an unspoiled people of Eden to "the Noble savage." This equally persistent view of the native population found one of its earliest and most complete readings in the noted Maryland pamphleteer George Alsop's interpretation of Susquehannock culture. In his *Character of the Province of Maryland*, first published in 1665, Alsop delivered with a surgeon's precision an account of the gruesome Susquehannock process of ritual dismemberment of prisoners of war. In the same breath, he declared the Susquehannocks to be "a people lookt upon by the Christian Inhabitants as the most Noble and Heroick Nation of Indians that dwell upon the confines of America."[3]

Children of Eden and noble savage—both images, whether applicable or not, served to cloud red and white relations for centuries. Both of these handy encapsulations denied for Maryland's earliest European settlers a deeper understanding of the actual Indian culture, which had an

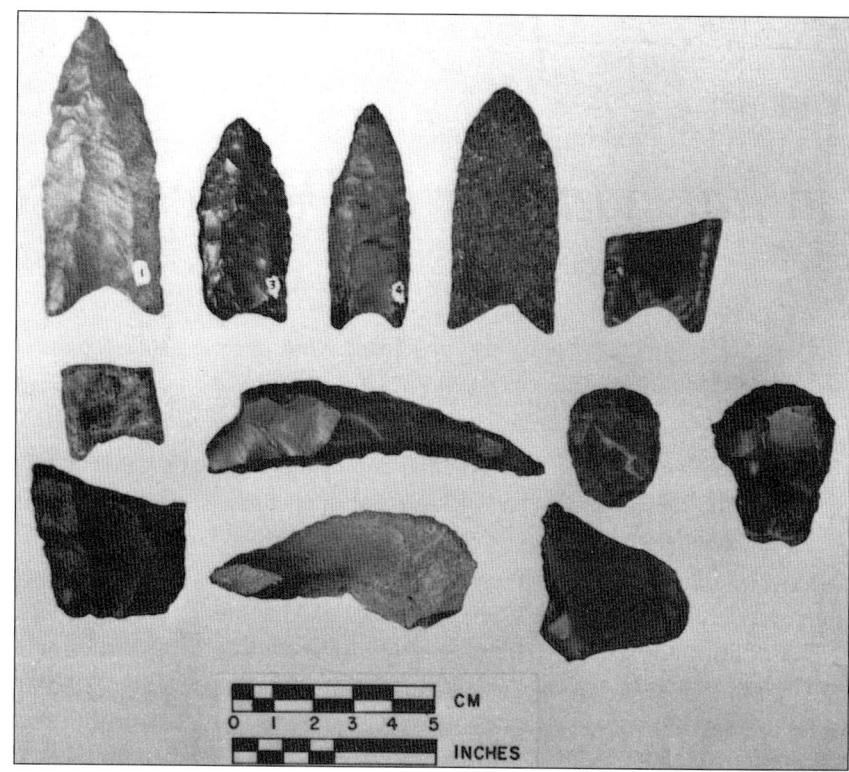

Archeologists have divided the native American culture before European settlement of America into several periods. The first of these is the Paleo-Indian, from approximately 9200 B.C. to 8000 B.C. Paleo-Indians survived by hunting the large animals of the time, including the mammoth, bison, and giant ground sloth. Their main hunting tool was a lance or stabbing spear tipped with a meticulously chipped blade in the eastern states called the Clovis fluted point. These points were made from high grade jasper, chalcedony, and chert. The points shown here, as well as the other artifacts illustrated in this chapter, were all found in Cecil County by George M. Reynolds. (George M. Reynolds, Sr.)

underlying complexity stemming from thousands of years of occupation in the Chesapeake region. Only now are these long-standing misconceptions being fully dispelled, due in large part to the systematic archeological investigation of the cultural resources of Maryland's Indian population.

No one is certain when the first Indians appeared in what is now Cecil County. Some archeologists have suggested that toward the end of the last Ice Age—perhaps as early as 13,000 years ago—groups of cold-adapted hunters from the west came to the mid-Atlantic region simply by following the roaming herds of big game animals on which they depended for food. Their presence in the area is indicated at a handful of sites by finds of the fluted spear points associated with their culture.[4]

The orientation of these earliest inhabitants, who were herd hunters in the true sense, was not to a specific locale but to movement, to the drift of the big game animals—mastodon and mammoth—that provided most of the group's needs. Where the herd went, the band went, and all its tools, habits, and lore were shaped and directed by this mobility and the taking of big game. When contact with one herd was lost, another had to be found. Conceivably their quests would have taken these groups over enormous distances, with winter camps and summer camps possibly hundreds of miles apart.

The archeological record indicates, however, that soon after their arrival in the Chesapeake region—from about 11,000 B.C. to 8000 B.C.—these herd hunters began to abandon their exclusively mobile way of life in favor of a seminomadic existence.[5] The shift was prompted perhaps in part by the hunters' growing familiarity with the new and varied natural resources that gradually emerged in the upper bay area during the waning years of the last Ice Age.

Environmental conditions when the nomads first arrived were markedly different than they are today. Huge ice sheets covering most of the northern United States as far south as Pennsylvania influenced the environment of the region. Temperatures were much colder, and for the most part the landscape below the glaciers comprised expanses of open grassland punctuated by thin forests of pine and spruce.

Slowly, over thousands of years, the glaciers rolled back, retreating northward with rising temperatures. Their movement caused significant changes to the landscape: water from melting glaciers filled deep gouges, forming expansive rivers and the Chesapeake Bay, and thick forests moved in on the grasslands. Large herds of grazing animals such as mas-

The Early Archaic peoples (8000 B.C. to 4000 B.C.) also lived a nomadic life, following the large herds of grazing animals and hunting them for meat and skins for clothing and shelter. They left no evidence of houses or cooking vessels. In general, their weapons and tools were crudely chipped from quartz or quartzite. It is likely that these people tamed the wild dog, the only domesticated animal in eastern North America. (George M. Reynolds, Sr.)

Although the nomadic lifestyle continued into the Late Archaic period (4000 B.C. to 2000 B.C.), these people moved within a more limited territory, learning and utilizing the places and times when fruits, berries, nuts, and grains were available. Their refuse pits have yielded the bones of animals, fish, and birds. Projectile points from this period were made of more flinty materials with an improved chipping technique. Hunters developed a spear thrower, termed an "atlatl," that allowed them to launch their spears over greater distances with greater accuracy. The full grooved hafted ax also appears in the archeological record during this period. (George M. Reynolds, Sr.)

todon and mammoth, dependent on the grasslands for their survival, had either to migrate northward with the glaciers or become extinct. The herd hunters who had drifted in with the game also had either to move on with the old sources of food or remain in the area and modify their lives and culture to survive in the changing conditions.

The increasing regional variation in food, resources, and environment that resulted from the end of the Ice Age eventually engendered considerable variation in native cultures throughout North America. The material expressions of the strategies these peoples adopted to contend with varying local conditions—the shelters built, clothes fashioned, food gathered—made each culture distinct and distinguishable from the others. For example, Indians in the American Southwest adjusted their lives to deal with an increasingly desert environment, while those in the Midwest perpetuated a culture oriented to ranging over miles of open grasslands.

The upper Chesapeake region lies astride the fall line where the massive Susquehanna watershed breaks out of the stony piedmont to spread onto the coastal plain. Here, thickening forests, slowly changing from pinewoods to hardwoods, eventually supported a varied animal community. In what would become Cecil County, an environment was developing that could furnish an abundance of plant and animal resources to suit the needs of any group. The location along the fall line provided opportune sites for both animals and people, moving north and south, to cross the numerous rivers dissecting the head of the bay. In addition, lithic resources in the area, thrust to the surface by the earth's upheaval, supplied a seemingly inexhaustible store of materials for stone toolmaking. These three elements—the varied plant and animal resources occupying both land and water, the river crossings afforded by the broken fall line, and the abundance of extractive materials—have shaped and directed the shifting cultures inhabiting Cecil County into the twentieth century. Over the years both Indians and Europeans created a lifestyle tailored to the region, a cultural system that efficiently made use of the great variety of ecological niches covering the land. Gradually the inhabi-

In the Transitional period (2000 B.C. to 1000 B.C.), the people became more sedentary and began to garden to supplement their diet. They developed the first known cooking vessels, which were carved of soapstone and shaped like a watermelon cut in half the long way. The ability to cook food resulted in a longer lifespan. Projectile points from this time, made of flint, jasper, chert, and rhyolite, are generally broad, flat, and thin. These people built fish weirs to trap fish and invented the canoe. (George M. Reynolds, Sr.)

The first evidence of houses appears in sites of the Early Woodland period (1000 B.C. to 500 B.C.). Other new items include clay ceramic pottery, sunflower seeds, and tobacco and pipes. Projectile points from this time are usually smaller and manufactured from flinty materials. Some are made of lithic materials from distant areas, suggesting that these people traded goods over long distances. (George M. Reynolds, Sr.)

tants organized their lives and societies to relate to their surroundings in ways required by the land and climate.

The archeological record of Cecil County has been only partially brought to the surface, but the evidence uncovered so far suggests the early Indian cultures were based around a territorially defined system of seasonally occupied camps. Each site was selected for a resource best obtained at that location and was associated with specific tasks and functions. The focal point of a camp may have been a preferred raw material for making tools or projectile points, such as extensive deposits of jasper or chert; watering areas and game trails of elk or deer; fish runs along water inlets; or dense patches of harvestable plants in the forest. These camps apparently were occupied according to a seasonal schedule of hunting, trapping, fishing, and gathering by small task-oriented bands. They stayed for several nights or weeks, periodically returning to a centrally located base camp. One theory suggests these bands were arranged according to kinship, perhaps by extended family, with the related groups providing only for their own needs. At certain times of the year, such as the ripening of fruits and nuts, the whole group would reunite to harvest a particular resource collectively.[6]

With the stabilization of modern climatic conditions, from about 6500 B.C. to 1000 B.C., the people of the upper Chesapeake began to build upon their adaptive strategies. Populations grew, promoted perhaps by the increasing availability of food resources, particularly such protein-rich staples as nuts, seeds, wild grains, fish, and shellfish. The social system still centered around bands moving among base camps and satellite sites, yet with the growing population and better definition of natural resources and territorial claims, the social structure became more complex.[7]

New features begin to appear in the archeological record at this time, suggesting this growing complexity. Stone mortars, cooking bowls, and querns or millstones—all heavy and cumbersome utensils not easily carried from place to place—indicate not only improvements in food production but a more sedentary way of life for at least a portion of the larger culture. Woodworking tools—including

Village life appeared in the Middle Woodland period (500 B.C. to A.D. 500), and clay pottery became more common, including decorations imbedded in the wet clay before baking. Burial rituals were more elaborate, the bow and arrow were invented, and trading occurred, via land and canoe, with more distant peoples. Evidence of corn or maize appears in the archeological record, and the arrowheads found are smaller, highly shaped, and much more efficient for killing game. (George M. Reynolds, Sr.)

The addition of corn, sunflower, squash, and other vegetables to their diet by the Late Woodland period (A.D. 500 to 1600 A.D.) resulted in a longer lifespan and a larger population. The people started to build towns surrounded by palisaded walls to protect themselves from animals and warlike neighbors. The increase in population engendered a struggle for territory that led to warfare with neighboring tribes. Travel and trade over long distances declined, and burial rituals became less elaborate. The projectile points from this period are predominantly triangular and highly chipped. (George M. Reynolds, Sr.)

stone axes, adzes, chisels, and gouges—are found with greater regularity at Archaic period sites throughout the county, suggesting that wooded areas were being cleared for settlement and timber was being dressed for shelters, containers, and water craft. Organic materials such as fiber mats and baskets and leather garments have not survived, but the presence at period sites of awls, needles, and punches made of stone and bone reflects their manufacture.

Toward the end of this period, during the first millennium B.C., the appearance of ceramics in the archeological record marks the beginnings of the Woodland period. A gradual shift toward incipient horticulture occurred during this period, with the cultivation of such locally known species as sunflower, goosefoot, marsh elder, and pigweed. By the ninth or tenth century A.D., domesticated strains of maize, accompanied by gourds, squash, and legumes, had found their way into the region, transported from Mexico along native trade routes. With the introduction of these crops, the shift to an agriculturally based economy was complete.[8]

The introduction of agriculture promoted a more sedentary lifestyle, altering an Eastern Indian cultural system that had remained relatively unchanged for thousands of years. Base camps, perhaps formerly established near naturally occurring harvestable foods and occupied only seasonally, now became agricultural villages specifically sited near favorable croplands and inhabited all year. Agriculture also reduced the amount of time and energy expended in obtaining an adequate food supply and thus created an environment that encouraged cultural developments. The introduction of agriculture also led eventually toward a sharper definition of labor based on gender, with men engaging in the hunt for game and women managing crop cultivation.

In the Late Woodland period there emerged in Cecil County a series of small agricultural villages inhabited by groups associated with the traditional Eastern Woodland society and apparently related to the Algonquian-speaking Indians occupying the Eastern Shore of Maryland. As noted above, archeological data uncovered in the county is incom-

Made of mats or bark attached to bent sapling structures, Indian houses were either round or long in shape. The latter, reserved for tribe members of the highest rank, are illustrated on Captain John Smith's map of Virginia, first drawn in 1608. The map also labels the areas inhabited by various Indian tribes, including the "Tockwoghs" along the Sassafras and the "Susqusahanoughs" above "Smyth's fales" on the Susquehanna. (detail from Smith, *Virginia*, Huntingfield Map Collection, Maryland State Archives, MSA SC G1399-101)

plete, but by combining what has been discovered with descriptive and excavative information from around the area, a general picture of the physical characteristics of these Woodland villages can be formed.

Captain John Smith provided the earliest descriptions of Indian housing in Maryland. In his *General Historie of Virginia*, Smith noted that the homes of the Maryland Indians most often were sited on riverbanks or close to fresh springs and were constructed of a framework of young saplings "bowed and tyed, and…covered with mats or the barkes of trees."[9] A hole in the top of the structure allowed the smoke from the interior campfire to escape. Although Smith made no reference to the size of these structures, on a map that accompanied the description of his journey to the Chesapeake he distinguished between two dwelling sizes: small, conical dwellings designated "ordinary howses," and longer houses marked as "king's howses." The presence of the longhouse may indicate the shift of native cultures away from the band society toward true tribal society, with the occurrence of a regency, social ranking, the tendency toward hereditary leadership within a particular lineage, and a more complex political system. While the dress of the leaders may have been indistinguishable from that of the rest of the tribe, their political standing eventually was codified in the "long house."

Later Maryland explorers and settlers verified Smith's description of native housing, repeating the distinction between small, conical dwellings and longhouses, the reported length of the latter varying from 30 to 100 feet. The width of the longhouse was recorded with more constancy at 12 feet. Colonel Norwood, among the shipwrecked passengers stranded somewhere near Assateague Island in 1650 and rescued by local Indians, gave a detailed description of the longhouse. The framework of the structure, called by Norwood the "king's palace," was constructed of sapling poles bent into an arch and tied off at the peak, with the skeleton covered with a skin of woven mats. In dimension, the house measured 60 feet in length and 18 to 20 feet in width. The interior was arranged in connecting apartments—Norwood counted fourteen hearth fires —with "the King's apartment…twice as long [as the others], and the bank he sat on…adorn'd with deer skins finely dressed, and the best furs of otter and beaver the country did produce."[10] In visiting a similar Maryland longhouse, the seventeenth century adventurer Henry Spelman reported that he had to pass through "many darke windinges and turnings before [arriving] where the Kinge is."[11]

It is unclear from the reports whether the longhouse was primarily a dwelling for the tribal leader and his extended family or a multiuse building type serving variously as dwelling, state house, and church. Ethnographers studying the Iroquois have found that culture's longhouses were built to serve the tripartite purposes of family dwelling, council meetinghouse, and religious sanctuary. In fact, the Iroquois developed a rather elaborate symbolism based on the longhouse, an indication of the importance of the structure to their confederacy. Descriptions of Iroquois longhouses correspond to those of the Maryland Indians: pole-framed, arched-roof structures covered with mats, ranging from 30 to 200 feet in length and 18 to 24 feet in width, and rising to a height of 18 feet. Each end of the house was pierced by a door. Running the length of the interior was a center corridor, where the fire hearths were

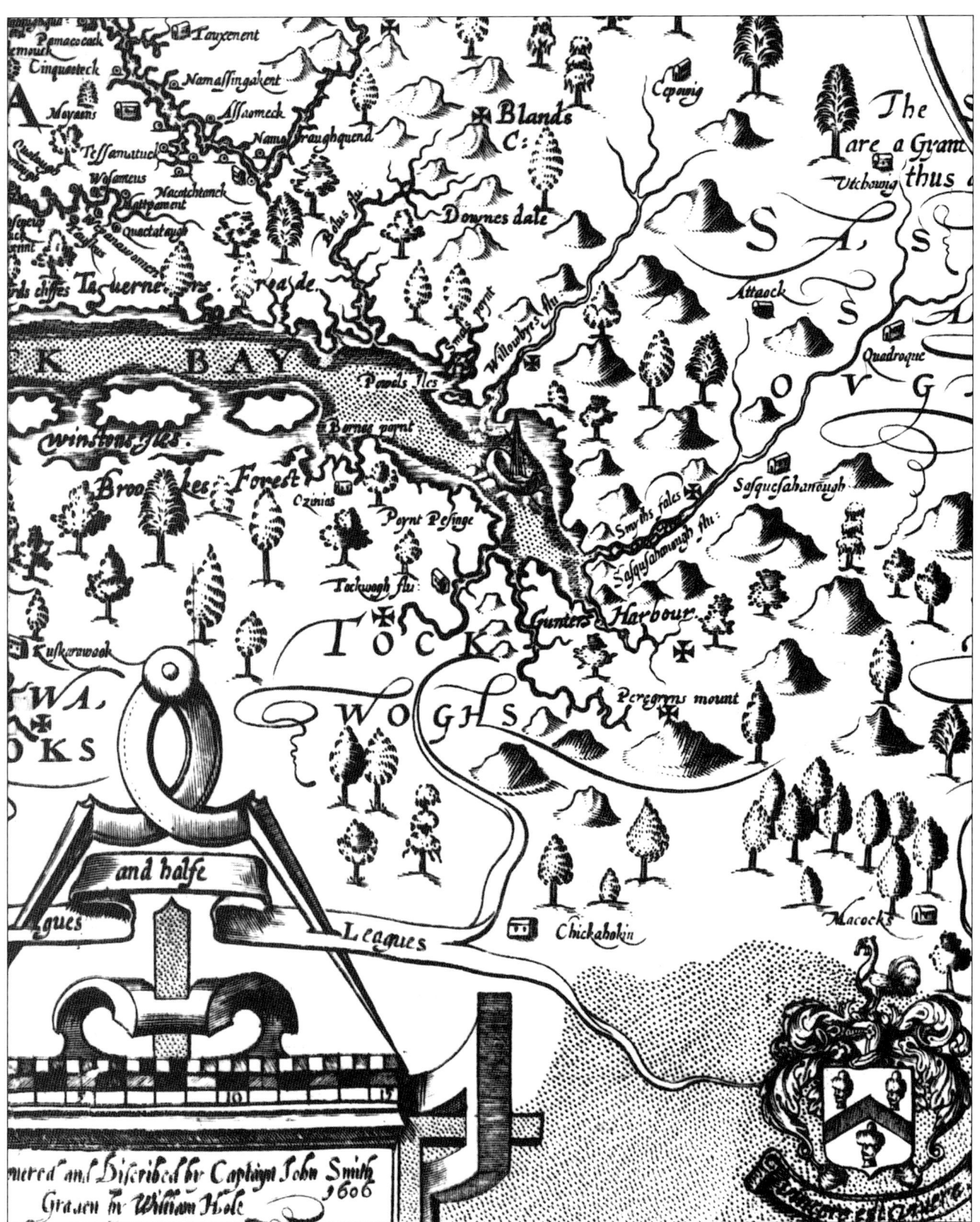

The importance of fishing in the Indian lifestyle was recorded in the many drawings carved in rocks by the fishing spots along the Susquehanna. Bald Friar, a mile and a half south of the Pennsylvania line, was an important fishing site as well as the only ford in the Maryland part of the river. (1880, from Persifor Frazer, Jr., Second Geological Survey of Pennsylvania, *The Geology of Lancaster County*, Harrisburg)

located, with corresponding holes cut into the roof. On either side of this corridor were "apartments" or partitioned spaces furnished with what were, in essence, bunk beds, five to six feet wide and six to twelve feet long. The lower bunk was positioned about a foot off the ground, the upper some five or six feet higher. While fire hearths may have been shared by a number of families, each apartment within the longhouse was occupied by a single family.[12]

Whether the longhouse was indigenous to the Maryland Indian culture or was a feature adopted from the Iroquois is a matter of speculation. Intertribal borrowing became increasingly common in the later Woodland period. The Maryland tribes were in contact with a variety of "foreign" Indians, and certain tribes may have incorporated this aspect of the Northern culture into their own. Daniel Brinton's account of life among the Delaware Indians suggests this pattern. He reports that communal longhouse life was not a feature of the Delawares' culture; rather, married couples lived in single-family dwellings constructed along conical lines.[13] On the other hand, Robert Beverly reported that, among certain tribes, he found both types of dwellings built and inhabited within a single village, a situation suggesting the cultural intermingling of dwelling types. The longhouse perhaps emerged along with the consolidation of power within particular lineages inside a tribe.[14] An equally plausible explanation for the appearance of the longhouse in Maryland is that, with the increase in tribal populations during the Woodland period and the unwillingness to abandon permanent village sites to accommodate the increase, some type of larger dwelling had to be created to shelter extended families within the limited land area of the village site.

In the northern bay country, most villages apparently held a mixture of communal longhouses and single-family conical houses. The population of the villages fluctuated with the seasons but remained inhabited by a portion of the tribe year-round; these were, after all, agricultural villages and were not totally abandoned unless the fields became unproductive. Between 80 and 100 acres of forest were slashed and burned in preparation for planting, and in the spring the women and children of the village took to the cleared fields, each armed with a dibble stick and a sack of seeds. A hole was poked into the charred earth with the stick, and then four or five kernels of corn and two beans were drawn from the sack and dropped together into the hole. Using the corn stalks as poles, the bean vines would climb, producing succotash in its natural state. Often, pumpkins and squash were also sown among the corn; Indian agriculture was not the regimented planting of its European counterpart.[15]

During the spring months, as the women and children prepared the fields, the men engaged in fishing, crabbing, and small-scale hunting. A common way of trapping fish was to build V-shaped rock structures—sometimes referred to as weirs—in river channels and streams. Some structures were designed to funnel the fish through a narrow chute from which they could be netted, scooped, or speared. Between the islands of the Susquehanna River, near Bald Friar, lay a series of these Indian fish weirs. Their significance to the Indians of Cecil County was indicated by a wealth of petroglyphs carved on the rock islands anchoring the traps. Among the various figures, the most common represented a fish; other types of marks—still undeciphered—included cup shapes and concentric circles. The islands, which rose out of the river between the northern falls and included the aptly named Indian Rock, may also have been the site of an Indian crossing. Some of the petroglyphs appeared to relate to the nearby ford, which crossed diagonally below what a 1695 land record referred to as "a great ffall called Connuagoe ffall."[16] Both the ford and the fisheries were later taken over by European settlers and continued to be sites of some importance to Cecil inhabi-

Many of the petroglyphs along the Susquehanna are now underwater, having been submerged when the Conowingo dam was built and the river above it flooded. The meaning of the concentric circles shown in this example remains a mystery. (1916, W. B. Marye, T. Milton Oler, Jr./Maryland Historical Trust)

Many of the petroglyphs along the Susquehanna depict fish, in one form or another. This one has a face inside a fish shape. (Maryland Historical Trust)

tants well into the eighteenth century. Sometime before 1769, a number of people living along this stretch of the river presented Maryland Governor Sharpe with a petition protesting a bill, then in the Assembly, that proposed a substantial penalty for "the making or Repairing of any Fish Dams & Pots on the River Susquehanna."[17] Since 1927 the Indian fisheries have been submerged by the lake impounded by the Conowingo power dam.

While the village may have been the main focus of Indian life during the spring and summer months, when fall came and the harvest was in, the hunting season began. The men left the village to journey to remote hunting camps, where they tracked deer and elk through the forest and trapped beaver and otter in the marshes and inlets. Cyprian Thorowgood, sailing the North East River in 1634, came across such a camp standing on the riverbank. He noted "beaver traps, and one quartering house, where the Indians use to bee in time of hunting."[18] All was done in preparation for the coming winter, at the height of which the men would return to the village and with their families await the spring thaw that brought life anew to the land.

The scattered settlements of Cecil Indians were separate, unfederated, and, for the most part, autonomous communities situated along the numerous rivers and streams crossing the county. They had created a pattern of life in tune and tow with their surroundings. They were content to plant, hunt, and fish, and apparently had little desire and less ambition to extend their political influence through conquest and territorial expansion. As such, they presented no threat to neighboring tribes as long as resources both inside and outside the village remained plentiful.

Sometime between 1200 and 1500 A.D. increasing pressures from outside the area forced the Cecil Indians into defensive positions. Stockades began appearing around the villages for protection, in particular against a small but aggressive tribe invading from the north: the Susquehannocks. With increasing regularity these formidable warriors, leaving their own families safe within palisaded villages along the Susquehanna valley in lower Pennsylvania, would paddle downriver to harass the northern Maryland Indians. Their aim is unrecorded. Perhaps it was to expand their territory through political rule; possibly it was to capture and adopt women and children to repopulate their own villages. Their influence, however, was unmistakable; the Susquehannocks brought many of the northern Maryland and Delaware tribes under both their control and protection and created a network of tributaries throughout the region. They had become the dominant Indian presence in Cecil County by the time of European contact.

In a broad sense the cultural landscape of the Cecil Indians anticipated the overlay of European settlement, with defined political boundaries encompassing compact agricultural settlements, a network of hunting and trading paths through the forests, fords at the river crossings, and "industrial sites" of fisheries and tool-making quarries dotting the countryside. Indian society was not the base, simplistic society implied in either the "children of Eden" or "noble savage" concept of the arriving Europeans. It was this very Maryland Indian system of land use and settlement, rather than the perceived inherent racial or ethnic inequality, that created the cultural conflict between the Indians and the English.

For Europeans, and in particular the English, who coveted the land inhabited by the Indians, the racially based images were necessary ammunition in an arsenal of usurpation. As early as 1609 Robert Gray, writing on the initial settlement of Virginia, rhetorically asked "by what right or warrant can we enter into [Indian] land, take away their rightful inheritance from them, and plant ourselves in their places, being unwronged or unprovoked by them?"[19] Gray had no intention of honestly addressing a question of such profound consequence to the settlement of the Chesapeake region. Instead, he, and a century of subsequent colonists, readily employed racial stereotyping to resolve the moral, legal, and practical problems presented by Indian land use patterns.

In Maryland, as elsewhere along the Atlantic seaboard, this stereotyping would eventually be reduced to the code of the two prevalent images. As the naturalistic, unspoiled "children of Eden," the Indians were blessed with a superabundance of fertile land but neither the knowledge nor the technology to put it to its fullest use. From this viewpoint, the English merely wanted to live in this earthly paradise with the Indians, sharing their land and, in return, sharing with the naive native the advantages of English culture and Christianity. Where tribes did not readily accept the cultural exchange program, the second image was invoked. As "noble savages," heroic individuals but nevertheless wild beasts somehow less than human, the Indians, to the English mind, forfeited their right to own land that was given by God to man, not to something less. Eventually, the image-in-practice, one way or another, forced the removal of the vast majority of Indians from the county and state, but not until the European settlers had extracted from them the means of making their replacement communities both secure and solvent.

Stockaded villages began appearing in the Chesapeake area between 1200 and 1500 in response to aggression from other tribes, particularly the Susquehannocks, from the north. Such a village is illustrated in the corner of this map, prepared by Ralph Hall. The map also shows Indian men carrying bows and arrows and some of the game they hunted. (1635, detail from Hall, *Virginia*, Huntingfield Map Collection, Maryland State Archives, MSA SC G1399-206)

Although it was executed in 1798, this watercolor of the mouth of the Susquehanna River gives a good idea of the scenery that greeted the English who first settled this part of Cecil County. Palmer's Island, settled before the *Ark* and the *Dove* brought Lord Baltimore's first colonists to Maryland, appears on the right, while the eastern shore of the Susquehanna is in the distance. This view is from a point just north of Havre de Grace, where the artist was catching the ferry northward to Philadelphia. (Benjamin Henry Latrobe, "View at Havre de Grace, the Mouth of the Susquehannah looking up the River," Sketchbook III-24, Maryland Historical Society)

CHAPTER 2

From "A-tradeinge" to Settlement at the Head of the Bay

FORAYS into the broad waters of the Chesapeake occurred throughout the earliest period of American exploration, but none came quite as high as the head of the bay. In 1525, the year after Verazzano's French-sponsored expedition, Pedro de Quexos, sailing under the Spanish flag, searched the Atlantic coast for safe harbors in which to establish settlements. Quexos recorded the existence of a large bay to the north of Cape Hatteras, but he never sailed into its waters.[1] Nearly half a century later, another Spanish explorer, Pedro Menendez, rescuing the remains of a Jesuit mission planted in North Carolina in 1570 and destroyed by Indians the following year, plied the mid-Atlantic coast. Intrigued by the numerous rivers and bays in the region, he sponsored a further survey of the area by his fellow countryman and explorer Pedro Menendez-Marques.

Menendez-Marques, searching for sites for Spain's third attempt to establish a mid-Atlantic stronghold, was one of the first Spanish seafarers to venture up the bay, exploring its shores, sand harbors, bountiful forests, and numerous rivers. The failures of previous Spanish settlement attempts, however, meant his home country's support for mid-Atlantic ventures was half-hearted at best, and Spain abandoned its Chesapeake explorations.[2]

Chesapeake Bay was thus left to the English, of whom the gentlemen speculators of the London Company sponsored the first full exploration of the great body of water. This effort was carried out in conjunction with the settlement of Jamestown and under the leadership of Captain John Smith, who enthusiastically promoted the Chesapeake real estate market, avowing that "heaven and earth seemed never to have agreed better to frame a place for man's commodious and delightful habitation!"[3] The 105 original settlers planting Jamestown in 1607 soon took exception to Smith's claims for this New World paradise; ceaseless suffering, sickness, and a devastating fire that destroyed many of the settlement's mud huts and stockades in January 1608, followed by a plague of rats that devoured most of the corn reserve, made Jamestown more of a living hell.

In the midst of these tribulations, in the summer of 1608, Captain Smith and a small crew of twelve, including six soldiers and six gentlemen (one of the latter a "chirgeon"), set out from Jamestown in a two-ton open barge on the second of Smith's voyages to "performe his discovery" of the "bay of Chisapeack."[4] The first journey had taken Smith and his crew around the lower region; the second led them nearly 200 miles from Jamestown, all the way to the "end of the bay." Smith and his crew thus became the first Europeans to visit Cecil County. In his account, published in 1624, Smith gives his impressions of the general lay of the land:

> At the end of the bay where it is 6 or 7 myles in breadth, it divides itselfe into 4 branches, the best commeth north-west from among the mountains, but though canows may go a dayes journey or two up it, we could not get two myles up it with our boat for rockes. Upon it is seated the Sasquesahannocks, neare it north and by west runneth a creeke a myle and a halfe: at the head whereof the Ebbe left us on shore, where we found many trees cut with hatchets. The next tyde keeping the shore to seeke for some salvages; (for within thirtie leagues sayling we saw not any, being a barren country,) we went up another small river like a creeke, 6 or 7 myle. From thence returning we met 7 canows of the Massawomeks, with whom we had conference by signes, for we understood

one another scarce a word: the next day we discovered the small river and people of Tockwhogh trending eastward.[5]

Smith traversed nearly the whole of the Cecil tidewater, exploring the Susquehanna, the North East, the Elk, and the Sassafras (Tockwogh) rivers. He roughly charted various landmarks and waterways and recorded Indian place names. The rocks in the lower Susquehanna he christened "Smyths fales" in his own honor, commemorating the spot where the explorers lost their grapnel when attempting to navigate the channels. Eventually, his rough notes were transformed into the first attempt at a definitive map of the Chesapeake region.

Smith also recorded his first impressions of the two principal tribes he encountered at the head of the bay. Clearly, he was intrigued by the Susquehannocks, "the strangest people of all these countries, both in language and attire." Smith's description of the Susquehannocks, and the portrait "of the greatest of them...signified on the mappe" accompanying his published history, became the pervasive image of the mighty New World warrior:

> Such great and well-proportioned men are seldom seen, for they seemed like giants...Their language [well becomes] their proportions, sounding from them as a voyce in a vault. Their attire is the skinnes of bears, and wolves, some have cossacks made of beares heads and skinnes, that a mans head goes through the skinnes neck, and the eares of the beare fastened to his shoulders, the nose and teeth hanging downe his breast, another beares face split behind him, and at the end of the nose hung a pawe, the halfe sleeves coming to the elbowes were the necks of beares, and the armes through the mouth with pawes hanging at their noses. One had the head of a wolfe hanging in a chaine for a jewell, his tobacco-pipe three quarters of a yard long, prettily carved with a bird, a deare, or some such devise at the great end, sufficient to beat out ones braines: with bowes, arrowes, and clubs, suitable to their greatnesse. The calfe [of the leg of the greatest of them] was three quarters of a yard about, and all the rest of his limbs so answerable to that proportion that he seemed the godliest man we ever beheld. His hayre, the one side was long, the other shorne close with a ridge over his crowne like a cocks combe. His arrowes were five quarters long, headed with the splinters of a white christall-like stone, in forme of a heart, an inch broad, an inch and a halfe or more long. These he wore in a wollves skinne at his backe for his quiver, his bow in the one hand and his clubbe in the other.[6]

These Susquehannocks, Smith continued, "inhabit upon the chiefe spring of these four branches of the bayes head, two dayes journey higher than our barge could passe for rocks," placing their village in the Susquehanna valley somewhere in present-day Lancaster County, Pennsylvania.[7]

Tradition has held that the Susquehannocks also occupied a palisaded fort at the mouth of Octoraro Creek, within the borders of Cecil County. Historical evidence for such an occupation, however, is both confusing and contradictory. Smith made no mention of a Susquehannock settlement on the lower portion of the river, and in fact noted that it took an interpreter three or four days to travel from the mouth of the river to the Susquehannock settlement to persuade the warriors to come visit with the English explorers. Nearly thirty years later, in 1634, Cyprian Thorowgood, journeying to the head of the bay in search of Indian trade, also noted in his journal that the Susquehannocks were "living in pallisadoe'd townes about 40 miles" from the mouth of the Susquehanna River. "They are commonly 2 daies in going home in their canowes, but can come downe in halfe a day, because of many falls which are in the river."[8]

The origin of the tradition appears to be testimony taken in 1740 before one of the many commissions established to determine the true boundary between Pennsylvania and Maryland. During this round of hearings, a parade of witnesses claimed that between 1690 and 1700 they had seen—or heard of—an Indian town of some forty cabins as well as the ruins of an Indian fort, both situated above Octoraro Creek near the angle formed by the creek and the eastern bank of the Susquehanna. Also, the deponents told stories of a great battle at the fort. One witness, Mar-

John Smith's drawing of the Susquehannock warrior on his map dated 1606 reflects the "noble savage" view of the native inhabitants held by Smith and other early travelers in the region. (detail from Smith, *Virginia*, Huntingfield Map Collection, Maryland State Archives, MSA SC G1399-101)

garet Allen, testified to having found "great numbers of human bones" along with "great numbers of stone arrowpoints and stone hatchets."[9] John Hans Steelman—a Dutch trader who organized Indian trading posts at Transtown (at the fork of Big Elk and Little Elk creeks) and at the mouth of the Susquehanna—claimed to have seen the rotted posts of the fort still in place around 1695.[10] John Henricks related that he had visited the adjacent Indian town about 1690 and was told by its inhabitants that the place was known as "Meanock," an Algonquian word translated by the Indians as "fortification."[11]

Outside of this testimony recorded nearly half a century after the supposed disappearance of both the fort and the town, there is no contemporary record of the Indian settlement's existence. An Indian town of some forty cabins and possibly a hundred people seems large enough to have left behind some account of contact, either official or informal, but none has been uncovered. Land records provide no clues, although patenting of the area between Octoraro Creek and Conowingo Creek was relatively late, with no lands surveyed before 1678.

Curious still is that not one of the witnesses testifying in 1740 offered the identity of the Indians who supposedly occupied the town and fort. The fact that the reputed Indians used the word "Meanock" to describe the place suggests an Algonquian association, rather than Susquehannock. The Penn family, embroiled in the continuing Maryland-Pennsylvania boundary dispute, seemed anxious to prove to the courts that this was, or had been, a Susquehannock fort. They asserted that, by some vague connection through William Penn's 1683 "purchase" of the mouth of the Susquehanna from a supposed Susquehannock by the name of Machaloha, Pennsylvania had a tenuous claim to ownership of the area. That a settlement of some type existed seems plausible enough; that it was occupied by the Susquehannocks during the seventeenth century seems unlikely, given the contemporary accounts of John Smith and others placing their village nearly thirty miles farther north.

Across the head of the bay from the Susquehanna, Smith and his crew sailed up the Sassafras River, where they encountered the Tockwoghs, whose village was seated "some seaven myles within the river." The Indians escorted the explorers to their

> pallizadoed towne, mantelled with the barkes of trees, with scaffolds like mounts, brested about with brests very formally. Their men, women and children, with daunces, songs, fruits, furres, and what they had, kindly welcomed us, spreading mats for us to sit on, stretching their best abilities to express their loves.[12]

Whether this settlement was located within the boundaries of Cecil County is unclear; if the map accompanying Smith's account can be considered an accurate indicator—which, in many instances, it cannot—the Tockwogh village was seated on the south side of the river, within the present borders of Kent County.

These people, "that can make 100 men," had apparently been made tributaries of the Susquehannocks, a subjugation they withstood for the sake of protection from a hostile tribe Smith notes as the "Massowomeks." From all indications, these warriors were members of the Five Nations, who at the time were subduing their Algonquian neighbors in upper New York. Their war parties—composed of either Senecas or Iroquois—are known to have come down the Susquehanna to attack the Susquehannocks.

Smith himself encountered a canoe fleet of Massowomeks as he crossed the head of the bay, who "signified unto us they had beene at warres with the Tockwoghes, the which they confirmed by shewing us their greene wounds." The Tockwoghs explained to Smith that these Massowomeks inhabited "a great water beyond the mountaines, which we understood to be some great lake, or the river of Canada." Then, in a truly vainglorious passage, Smith recounts how these Indians bowed down to him in adoration, draping him in bear skins and beads, laying tributes at his feet, "stroking their ceremonious hands about his necke for his creation to be their governour and protector…if he would stay with them, to defend and revenge them of the Mas-

This map of the Chesapeake adapted by John B. Homann in 1714 from an earlier map by Herman Moll shows present-day Cecil County as the home of the Tok Woghs and places "Caecil" County where Kent and Queen Anne's counties lie today. (detail from Homann, *Virginia, Marylandia et Carolina...*, Huntingfield Map Collection, Maryland State Archives, MSA SC G1399-193)

sawomeks." Smith declined, and the Indians "wept" at his departure.[13]

Other than a brief glimpse of their defensive architecture, Smith leaves us with few insights into the physical makeup of the Tockwogh settlement. Thereafter the tribe fades from the historical record, their settlement apparently wiped from the landscape by encroaching European plantations, and their people dispersed among the lost.

The Susquehannocks, however, were to have a profound effect on the early development of the county, an influence precipitated as much by the Europeans as by the Indians' own actions. First the Dutch, then the English enticed the Susquehannocks to alter their traditional lives in order to supply these newcomers with a precious trading commodity—furs.

In 1609, the year after Smith's initial exploration of Cecil County, Henry Hudson returned to Holland with glowing accounts of American forests abounding in fur-bearing animals and of thick, rich pelts had from the natives for a handful of trinkets. Dutch merchants were quick to act on Hudson's news. With government blessing and authorization, the Dutch West India Company was formed specifically to exploit the New World fur trade. The firm laid claim to the territory between the 40th and 45th degrees of latitude, from the Delaware River valley to the Hudson River valley, setting forth a movement to America of unimaginable consequence for the future development of Cecil County.

What lay behind this flurry of activity was the mania for furs that raged across northern Europe in the seventeenth century. Persons of wealth, importance, and royalty created fashion sensations with their fur-trimmed robes of white ermine, their felted beaver hats, muffs, wraps, coats for men and women, all made or detailed in any number of furs then in vogue. Satiating the demand for fur had created overhunting and near extinction of many native European fur-bearing animals, so when Hudson announced his discovery of a land teeming with beavers, otters, and foxes, it seemed to the Dutch as good as the fabled cities of gold for which Spain had searched so long.

By 1624 the Dutch had commenced settlement of the Hudson valley, followed shortly by attempts to establish trade outposts in the Delaware valley. The first Delaware colony, however, ended in disaster. Called Swanedndael, or "Valley of the Swans," it was seated by the patroons at the present site of Lewes in 1631. Less than a year later, the Sickoneysinck Indians attacked the outpost, burning the palisaded settlement to the ground and murdering every one of its thirty-two inhabitants. Despite this setback, within thirty years Adriaan Van der Donck reported the Dutch were shipping 80,000 beaver pelts annually from the New Netherlands settlements.[14]

The Dutch were not alone in tapping the lucrative beaver trade. Adventurers from the Virginia colony also struck out from the main settlement to establish trading posts from which to barter with the fur-rich Indians of the Chesapeake region. Along the lower Potomac River, Henry Fleet cultivated trade relations with various Southern Maryland tribes, and from a base on Kent Island, William Claiborne went farther up the bay to make contact with the Susquehannocks. A small island at the mouth of the Susquehanna River soon became the center of activity for the Indian trappers and English traders. The island had been claimed and named in the mid-1620s by Edward Palmer, a member of the Virginia Company who purchased the land with the intention of founding an academy "for the publick good" of Virginia colonists.[15] Palmer died in 1625 without realizing his dream, and Claiborne took over Palmer's Island as a trading post.

The Susquehannocks proved to be willing partners. Energetic and enthusiastic trappers long before the pressures of European trade, they followed the mid-Atlantic interior waterways as far as the Allegheny River in search of beaver. Eventually, to satisfy the increasing demand, the Susquehan-

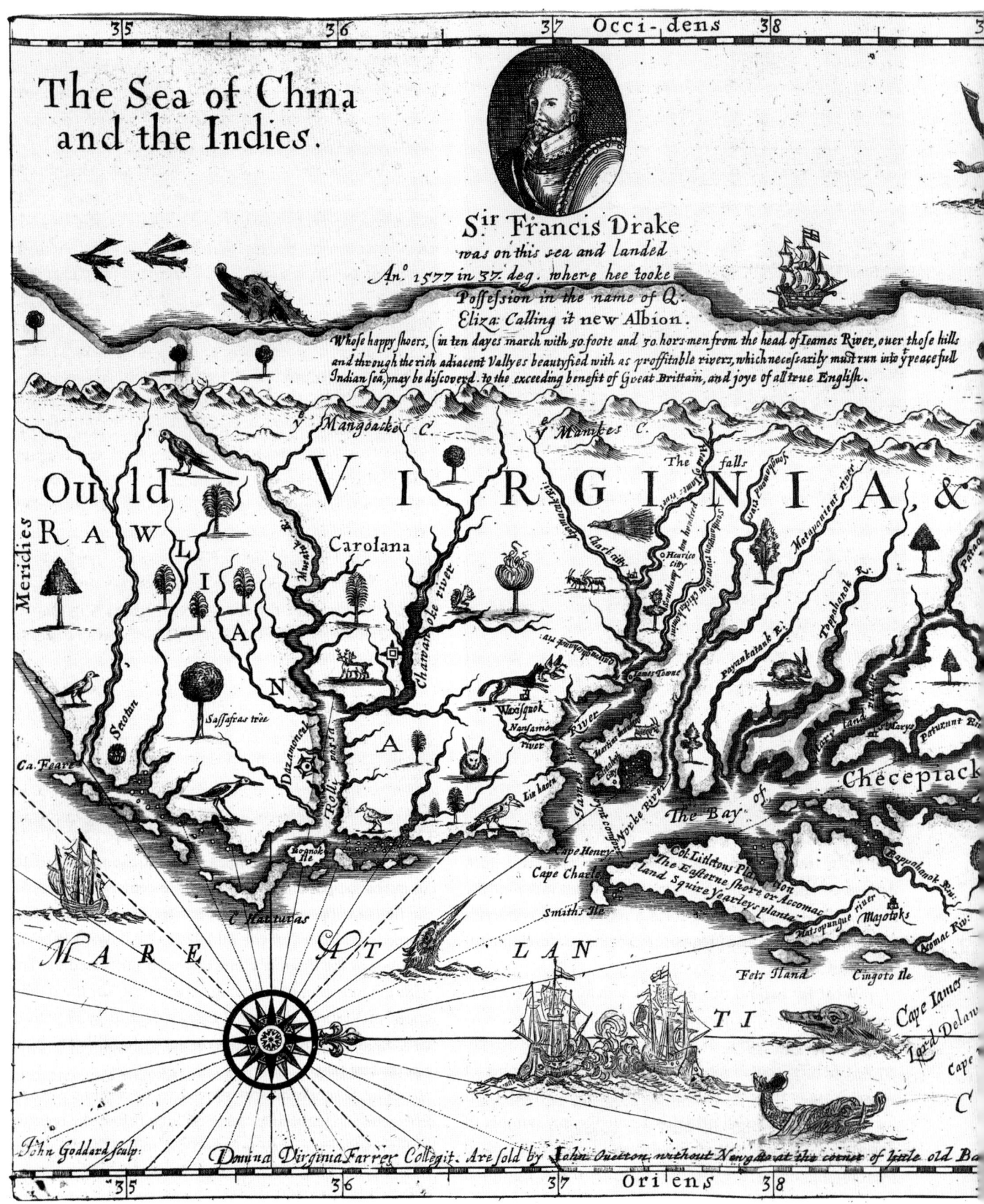

nocks spent the better part of the year trapping in the interior, usually from December to June, when the fur was thickest. The Susquehannocks' growing preoccupation with trading must have come as a relief to their tributaries, as the tribe's exactions from their neighbors lessened as English requisitions rose.

Claiborne already had staked out Cecil County as his trading domain when the *Ark* and the *Dove* sailed up the Potomac in 1634, landing the initial group of settlers under the Calvert proprietorship. These first Maryland colonists, however, were well aware of the burgeoning Chesapeake fur trade and were quick to make their entry. One month after arrival, as others attempted to make some semblance of a settlement at the seat of the new colony at St. Mary's, a small group of adventurers led by Cyprian Thorowgood set sail from the mouth of the Patuxent "a-tradeinge, in a small pinnace manned with seven men, with a nation at the head of the baye, called the Sasquasahannackes." On reaching Palmer's Island, they were discouraged to find "a boat of Clabornes in trade with the Indians which had gotten 700 skins, and 40 men loaden with beaver were sent a little afore to the Dutch plantation" in New Netherlands.[16] A tense confrontation between Claiborne's men and the intruding Maryland colonists ensued, apparently stopped short of physical force only by the Indians' unwillingness to enter the fray.

The sudden appearance of new traders on the scene caused Claiborne to tighten his grip both on Palmer's Island and on his share of the Susquehannock trade. In 1635 that defense turned violent when Thomas Smith, an "agent" of Claiborne's, attacked a pinnace from St. Mary's as it sailed "at the head of the bay neer Palmers Ileand," capturing the boat and "a great quantitie of trucking commodities from Jhon Tomkins and serjeant Robert Vaughan who had the charge of her and togeather wth. the sd. Pinnass and goodes

This map owes a lot to the imagination of its cartographer, Virginia Farrer, but, interestingly, it depicts a number of native American fur-bearing animals. Trapping was an important money-making venture on the early Chesapeake, and the first Cecil County settlement, on Palmer's Island, was a trading post from which the English traded with the Indians for furs. (1651 [1670], Farrer, *A mapp of Virginia...*, Hammond-Harwood Atlas Collection, Maryland State Archives, MSA SC G1213-269)

Mouth of the Susquehannah, passing Turkey point.

carried the sd. Tomkins and Vaughan prisoners to Kent [Island]."[17] Smith was later arrested and convicted of the first recorded incidence of piracy in Maryland.

In 1637 Claiborne further strengthened his hold on Palmer's Island by inducing the "king of the Susquehannoes" to grant the Englishman the Indians' rights to the island. Once done, according to one of Claiborne's servants, "the said king did cutt some trees upon the said Iland, and did cause his people to clear some ground for the said Claiborne to plant his corn upon that yeare, After which the said Claiborne did (by his servants) build houses and make a Fort for their better security upon the said Iland."[18] Claiborne's trading post thus became the first English settlement in Cecil County.

The enterprise was not in business long, however. Claiborne had been a continual thorn in the Calverts' side, with his outrageous claims of control over portions of the colony that, under the Maryland charter, the Lords Baltimore regarded as rightly theirs. Compounding the enmity were charges that Claiborne and his men performed despicable acts against the Maryland colonists and incited Indian attacks, as well as vague rumors of an impending coup against the government at St. Mary's. The animosity escalated in 1635 with a brief naval engagement in the Chesapeake between armed vessels of the rival factions. Sensing the rising heat of the Calverts' anger, Claiborne slipped off to Virginia and then to England for an extended stay. In his absence, Governor Leonard Calvert seized Claiborne's Maryland holdings, including Palmer's Island, which Calvert noted at the time was "already seated and fortifyed and a good stock of cattle to the number of thirteen head upon it." In relating the incident to his brother, Lord Baltimore, in 1638, Calvert wrote,

> I thought not good to supplant but understanding there were five men inhabiting it servants to Capt. Cleyborne and formerly under the command of Smith I sent serjeant Robert Vaugham and two others wth him from St. Maries to set downe there and to the sd: Vaugham gave the command of all the rest, and by reason Capt. Cleyborne had been attainted of ffelony in the last assembly at St. Maries by particular act and sentenced to forfeit all his estate in the Province I gave Vaugham authoritie to take the servants and other goodes and chattles belonging to Cleyborne upon the Ileand into his charge.[19]

The increasing English trading activity at the head of the bay, first by Claiborne and later by the St. Mary's colonists, not only increased pressure on the Susquehannocks to provide pelts but also forced the Dutch to step up the settlement of the Delaware valley, lest they lose a significant portion of the trade. To complicate matters, by 1638 the Swedes had arrived in the valley and, in an attempt to monopolize the Susquehannock trade, had begun constructing a series of fortified trading posts to guard the entrance of the Delaware and block the mouths of the tributaries that served as trade routes to Susquehannock territory. In that year Fort Christiana was founded on the site of present-day Wilmington. Five years later a two-story log governor's mansion was built for Johan Printz, newly appointed head of

This sketch by Benjamin Henry Latrobe shows Palmer's Island (now Garrett Island), Carpenter's Point, and Turkey Point from the Chesapeake. William Claiborne's trading post on Palmer's Island was the first European settlement in what is today Cecil County. (1806, Latrobe Sketchbook IX-6, Maryland Historical Society)

New Sweden, and a settlement was established on Tinicum Island in the Delaware River, strategically sited to give the Swedes an advantageous trading position. Poised between the English sailing from the southern settlements and the Swedes and Dutch exploring the interior from the east was Cecil County, occupying a pivotal position in the emerging trade system.

Maryland's relationship with the chief link in the chain of trade—the Susquehannocks—was not always one of peaceful cooperation. In the 1640s the colony was alarmed by reports of an impending uprising, and preparations were hastily made to defend the settlements. The Upper Council called for a company of men to be raised in 1643, to be ten in number and outfitted with "boat pvisions ammunition armes & all things necessary to seate & fortifie vpon palmers Iland." A small garrison apparently was established on the island, named "ffort Conquest."[20]

The anticipated Indian menace never materialized, but trouble in the Maryland colony did not end with the dissipation of the Susquehannock threat. The provinces were by no means immune from rising political dissension in England, which culminated in the Cromwellian succession. By 1652 the commissioners of Cromwell's new Parliament had wrested Maryland from the Calverts and dispatched instructions to loyal men in the colony to gain control of the proprietary government. Among those overseeing the change of administration in Maryland was none other than the Calverts' longtime nemesis, William Claiborne.

One of the first acts of the new government was the drafting of a peace treaty with the increasingly troublesome Susquehannocks. The Indians' trade activities had taken them farther and farther from their original territory; eventually, they were bartering for pelts with the Yadkins in the Carolinas and carrying them to the Dutch at Manhattan. By the 1650s they had cut a trail across Maryland, from the Susquehanna to the mouth of the Monocacy River, on the Potomac. Across the river, Virginia planters complained bitterly that the Susquehannocks were diverting the trade of the southern tribes to the Dutch in New Amsterdam. The Virginia Assembly expressed concern "that the Susquehannocks and other Northern Indians in considerable numbers frequently come to the heads of our rivers whereby plain paths may soon be made which may prove of dangerous consequence."[21]

A treaty enacted in 1652 attempted to sharply curtail the Indians' free-ranging expeditions by having them cede to the "English nation" all the lands lying from the Patuxent River to Palmer's Island on the western shore of the bay, and from the Choptank River to the North East River on the Eastern Shore. Within these ill-defined boundaries, the Susquehannocks retained the rights to the northern reaches of Cecil County. Excepted from the terms of the treaty was Palmer's Island, which, along with Kent Island, the new government conceded as rightfully belonging to William Claiborne. This acknowledgment of ownership was granted with the proviso that "Nevertheless it shalbe lawfull for… English, or Jndians to build a Howse or ffort for trade or any such like vse or Occasion at any tyme vpon Palmers Jsland."[22]

After the restitution of his outposts, Claiborne apparently found the fur trade did not have the same vitality it had had previously. In fact, the fur trade as a whole entered a period of decline at midcentury. Shifting tastes in European fashions lessened the demand, and overzealous hunting had begun to depopulate the region of its fur-bearing animals. Replacing the fur trade was a new commodity, which spread up the bay from the now-entrenched plantations of the lower tidewater. This new commodity was tobacco, and its cultivation and trade ultimately proved to be the inducement that was needed to instigate greater settlement at the head of the bay.

The export value of tobacco was first discovered in Jamestown in 1613, when John Rolfe—later to gain greater fame by marrying the Indian princess Pocahontas—imported seed from the West Indies and crossed it with local Indian-grown tobacco, producing a smooth smoke that dominated the world market. At once Virginia went tobacco mad; it was even grown in the streets of Jamestown. Stories of instant success abounded. One man, by his own labor, raised a crop that brought him £200 sterling in one season; another, with six hired men, netted £1,000. Samuel Argall, the last governor sent by the Virginia Company, arrived with "nothing but his sword" and left with more than £3,000 in his purse.[23]

Within five years of Rolfe's discovery, Virginia was trading 50,000 pounds of tobacco annually. Ships filled with choice Virginian criss-crossed the Atlantic, returning with European imports in exchange. Politically, the fledgling trade was almost snuffed out by King James, with whom tobacco was in ill repute. At his behest, Parliament would have prohibited the import of tobacco into England; shrewd lobbyists for the Virginia Company, however, eventually persuaded the House that such a move would ruin the colony.

The stories of New World fortunes founded on smoke did not escape the Maryland colonists, who soon after arrival set to cultivating what would become Maryland's cash crop for the next century and a half. By the 1730s more than 13 million pounds of tobacco were shipped annually from Maryland ports. Tobacco was the advertising hook found in Sir Edward Plowden's 1648 pamphlet *A Description of the Province of New Albion*, a spurious piece accompanying Plowden's unsuccessful scheme to bilk Englishmen out of their shillings in exchange for aid in settling them in "North Virginia," in actuality sections of Maryland and Delaware. In the pamphlet, Plowden extols the land around Cecil County as "rich black mould, with huge timber trees, most fit for Tobacco and Corn."[24]

Although Cecil land may have been some of the most fertile in the colony, a number of barriers blocked extensive settlement in the mid-seventeenth century. Prime land was still readily available around the emerging settlements in southern Maryland, and the pressure of population growth was insufficient to create much interest in lands that were, in essence, Indian country. Moreover, the not-so-slight matter of permanent liabilities placed on Maryland land by the proprietors prompted most potential landowners to patent only those tracts where a return on their investment could be realized reasonably quickly.

At the outset, the Lords Baltimore had hoped to establish a feudal aristocracy, but few true manors—replete with judicial and political trappings—were established in Maryland. Nonetheless, the colony's land system did incorporate some feudal elements, which for the most part lasted until the Revolution. As proprietors of a palatine colony, the Calverts held royal privileges within the domain of Maryland, foremost among them the ability to draw a permanent income from the land by subjecting it to the payment of annual quitrents, alienation fees, and escheat. While this arrangement made colonization a potentially lucrative venture for the Calverts, it made Maryland land much less attractive for settlers than land in other colonies where the terms were less burdensome.

At first, land in Maryland was apportioned on the basis of headright—the number of immigrants brought into the colony—according to the schedule set down in the prospectus *A Relation of Maryland*, published in 1634. Privileged Englishmen capable of fully outfitting—at an estimated cost of £20 per head—and transporting adventurers to the New World received as recompense 1,000 acres for every five men. This land was conveyed with the title of "manor" and "all such royalties and privileges, as are usually belonging to Mannors in England." A quitrent of 20 shillings per manor was due annually, along with "such other services as shall be generally agreed upon for publik uses, and the common good." Moving down the land grant ladder, a common adventurer received 100 acres for himself and every servant, if less than five in number, with a quitrent of 2 shillings per 100 acres. Families received 100 acres each for husband and wife and fifty acres for each child under 16, with a quitrent of 12 pence for every fifty acres. Those transporting women under the age of 40 received fifty acres per head. The inducements to settlement gradually diminished over the years, as population levels rose, and were finally replaced in 1683 by the payment of caution or purchase money.[25]

Once a headright had been secured or caution money paid and a piece of property scouted, selected, and given an appropriate name, a warrant was issued, giving the holder the right to survey the chosen acreage. Not until the survey and the certificate stating metes and bounds had been completed was full title to the land conveyed in the form of a patent, made official by the seal of the Proprietor. With patent in hand, the new citizen began payment of quitrent.

Unlike modern property taxes, apportioned according to the value of the land and its improvements, quitrent was a static tax bearing no relation to the value of the land. Desirable tobacco land in Anne Arundel County and untillable hills along the wilds of Cecil County carried quitrents in equal weight. Consequently, English adventurers seized with manorial notions found it could be costly to patent thousands of acres of unknown productivity on the remote frontier, especially if the land was held for any length of time without planting. With the quitrent itself amounting to three or four percent of the actual market value of the land, any speculative profit was substantially reduced in twenty years' time.

Adventurers with deep pockets could suffer yearly losses and hold out for the larger returns that came with time, comforted by the counsel of the English essayist Francis Bacon. Writing "Of Plantations" in 1625, Bacon warned that the "planting of countries is like planting of woods. For you must make account to lose almost twenty years' profit, and expect your recompense in the end."[26] Most speculators, however, realizing that quitrents did not become payable until the land was actually patented, preferred to deal solely in land warrants as vehicles for long-term land investment. With a warrant, an individual could stake claim to a property, block others from taking it up, and then renew the warrant for a period of years until patenting seemed advisable or until the warrant was sold for a profit. Speculating in warrants effectively tied up large, undefined tracts, impeding the survey and patenting of adjoining lands and forestalling the settlement of an area. For absentee speculators who proceeded with the patent process, the quitrent requirements ultimately encouraged the rise of tenancy.

The patenting of Cecil County land first began in the late 1650s. During this period the Calvert government was restored in an agreement that, among other things, stated Lord Baltimore would grant lands without favor to Puritan and Catholic alike. The earliest known patent was issued to William Carpenter in 1658 for a 400-acre tract named "Anna Catherine Neck" on Carpenter's Point Neck near Principio Creek.[27] While Carpenter and those who soon followed took up land in accordance with the cumbersome land grant process, a number of people appear to have settled in Cecil County without benefit of patent. By the 1650s a sizable group of former Delaware valley residents were encamped on Cecil County lands.

Conflicts between the Swedes and the Dutch, competing for settlement within the sharply circumscribed parameters of the Delaware valley, had increased by the 1650s. In 1651, in an attempt to check the spread of the northern Swedish settlements, the Dutch constructed New Amstel, a fortification on the site of present-day New Castle and within five miles of the Swedish Fort Christiana. New Amstel soon fell to the Swedes, who renamed it Fort Casimir. By 1655, however, the Dutch had emerged victorious in the struggle for the Delaware valley, capturing the two major Swedish strongholds. While the conflict raged, a number of people fled from the troubled territory, crossing the border and reestablishing themselves in the more tranquil confines of Cecil County.

The Calverts followed the Delaware situation closely, as both settlement and conflict occurred in what they considered part of Maryland. The governor and council feared the Dutch might ultimately lay legal claim to the Delaware settlements by right of adverse possession. Therefore, in 1659 they sent Colonel Nathaniel Utie, a council member who had settled on Spesutie Island near the head of the bay, to the Dutch to inform them they were occupying Maryland territory and should submit to its rule. Col. Utie apparently overstepped the bounds of his commission, threatening the Dutch with war if they did not acquiesce. Having just emerged from one war with the Swedes, the Dutch did not desire to engage in another, so two envoys were dispatched to St. Mary's in hope of negotiating a peaceful settlement of the dispute.

In the autumn of 1659 the Dutch delegation, accompanied by soldiers and Indian guides, set out from New Amstel for St. Mary's. They proceeded on foot westward across country, eventually striking the Big Elk Creek, where they turned to the south and "straight through the woods, without a path."[28] Eventually they took to the water, in a leaky and apparently abandoned boat noted by their Indian guides on a previous journey. The group covered the distance without seeing a single sign of settlement.

Paddling down the Elk River, they came to the Sassafras River, where they encountered their first settlement, the plantation of "one Mr. Jan Turner." Here they also

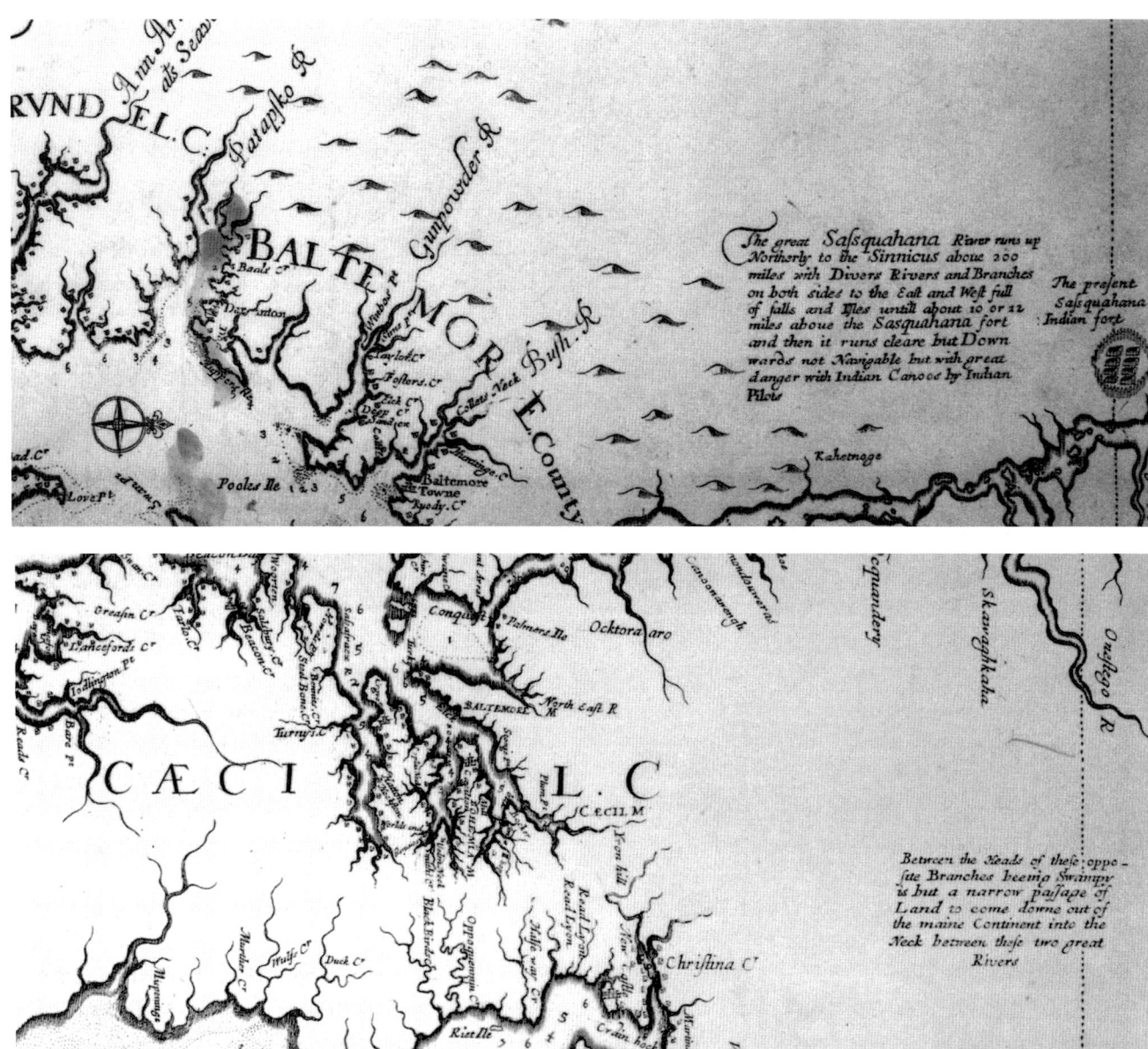

found "Abraham the Finn, a soldier who had run away from Christina" in the company of a Dutch woman whom he had brought with him from the Delaware valley. The envoys offered the pair "the General's [Peter Stuyvesant's] pardon, in case they would return to New Amstel within six months, and should they then be unwilling to stay there, they would be at liberty to go to the Manhattans." The woman, presumably an indentured servant, "accepted these conditions, having three months more to serve, when she would return." The soldier, however, refused the offer, more content with his new prospects than those he had escaped. The Dutch delegation briefly explored the surrounding area, looking for any information that might help their mission. Learning nothing, "as the only residents there were some Swedes and Finns, who had run away in the time of Governor Prins," the delegation continued on their way to St. Mary's.[29] The New Sweden fugitives, squatters along the Sassafras River, were among the first European residents in eastern Cecil County.

The negotiations between the New Netherlands envoys and the Maryland council failed to resolve the territorial dispute; both adamantly held to their positions of rightful ownership. But the mission to St. Mary's did bring about one result of consequence to Cecil County. During his journey

The Calverts commissioned Augustine Herman to map the Chesapeake region, granting him territory at the head of the bay in payment. It was Herman who suggested that the area where he lived be made a county named Cecil, after Lord Baltimore, and in fact he labeled it as such on his map before the county was founded. (details from 1673, Herman, *Virginia and Maryland*, Huntingfield Map Collection, Maryland State Archives, MSA SC G1427-43)

through the uncharted region, Augustine Herman, one of the Dutch envoys, concluded that a detailed and accurate map would be indispensable to future travelers. Soon after his return to New Amstel, he approached the Dutch administration with a proposal to make such a map. Unconvinced of its necessity, the Dutch rejected the offer. Undaunted, Herman turned to the Calverts, proposing again "an exact mapp" of the region; it was an offer they eagerly accepted. As down payment, in 1660 Lord Baltimore decreed Herman a resident of Maryland and in 1662 granted him a 4,000-acre tract along the eastern shore of Cecil County. The tract, which Herman named "Bohemia" after his homeland, was actually composed of two separate patents: Bohemia Manor, situated between the Elk and Bohemia rivers, and Little Bohemia, also referred to as "Middle Neck," adjoining to the south.

Sometime after 1660 Herman moved his family to Bohemia and set about the task of mapping the region. Initially he worked from notes taken during his earlier travels through the area, later supplementing these with further expeditions. Herman became increasingly involved in local affairs and eventually was appointed a justice of Baltimore County, in which Bohemia was then located. From the outset Herman envisioned his new homeland as a political body in its own right. As early as 1661, he had written to Lord Baltimore about the possibility of creating a new county at the head of the bay, to be called "Cecil" in honor of his new friend and protector, Cecilius Calvert.[30] Either prematurely or foresightedly, on Herman's map completed in 1670 the arc of land between the Susquehanna and Chester rivers is identified as "Caecil County." As final payment for his work, the Calverts granted Herman an additional tract, named St. Augustine Manor, an expanse of land connecting Bohemia Manor with Delaware Bay to the east.

Herman's map suggests that settlement of Cecil County had accelerated in the short time since he had first traveled through the largely uninhabited country. While the cultural markings on his map cannot be construed as exact representations, the chain of houses dotting the points and river banks of the southeastern section does indicate the planting of Cecil was on the rise.

Despite the increasing population, the character of Cecil remained largely frontier. The 1652 treaty with the Susquehannocks formally opened the bay coast and lower eastern shore section of Cecil County to settlement, but it created a neutral territory in the northern portion of the county. Indian hunting bands and white traders alike passed through this area, sometimes with disastrous results. In 1661 a group of Delaware Indians had a violent confrontation with planters along the Gunpowder River in Baltimore County. Mistaken for Susquehannocks and accused of the previous killing of a settler's wife, the Delawares were attacked by the planters; one Indian was shot to death as he attempted to swim ashore from his overturned canoe. The remaining Indians fled into the woods and struck out northeast for home. While crossing northern Cecil County, near Iron Hill on the Delaware-Maryland border, they encountered four white travelers. In an avenging rage they set upon the unsuspecting travelers, murdering all and stealing their clothes and belongings. The incident set off a minor war between the Maryland settlers and Delaware

Indians, climaxing in a battle on the banks of the Bush River in which one white man and five Indians were killed; among the Indian casualties was the brother of Pinna, chief of the Passayunk Delawares.

Fearful of escalation, Governor Philip Calvert quickly arranged a meeting with Pinna, at the village of Appoquinimink, near modern Odessa, Delaware. As a discerning opening gesture, Calvert admitted that the white planters had indeed provoked the initial incident and assured the chief the actions were in no way sanctioned by the governor of Maryland or his council. The two agreed to a treaty, made September 19, 1661, calling for "a perpetuall peace betwixt the people of Maryland and the Passayonke Indians." Underlying the terms of the treaty, however, was a rather unbalanced system of justice: If any white settler should find "any Passayoncke Indian killing either Cattle or Hoggs, that then it shall be lawfull for the English to kill the said Indian," but if any white settlers were found among the Indians, the Indians were to "bring them to Peter Meyors and there for every English man that they shall deliver they shall Receive one Matchcoate."[31]

That same year a treaty was entered into with the Susquehannocks. This document further curtailed their sphere of operations, stipulating they could not advance without permission beyond the Stockett estate in Baltimore County (on which the noted pamphleteer George Alsop was indentured). The treaty required that "for the prevencon of mischiefe that too often happens by misunderstanding and not distinguishing Sasquesahannoughs from other Indians, the Sasqueshannoughs shall not come ordinarily to any other howse, but the howse of Captin Thomas Stockett or of Jacob Caulson from when they shall have ticketts if they have occasion to come further among the English plantacons."[32]

In spite of the continuing conflicts, the Maryland authorities regarded the Susquehannocks as a "Bullwarke and Security of the Northerne parts of this Province." They were seen as protection against the equally warlike members of the Five Nations, in particular the Senecas, who had begun appearing with increasing regularity at the head of the bay. Consequently, every attempt was made to maintain the presence of the Susquehannocks as a buffer. Two disastrous occurrences, however, soon shook that security.

In 1661 an outbreak of smallpox ravaged the Susquehannocks, spreading to neighboring tribes and decimating village populations. Almost simultaneously, open warfare between the Susquehannocks and the Five Nations, simmering for years, finally erupted. For a time, the Maryland council imagined the two groups were in league, planning a full-scale attack against the Maryland settlements. But in 1674 the Susquehannocks, decimated by warfare and disease, were conquered by the Senecas. The military power of the Susquehannocks was gone, and the defeated tribe dispersed.

Only a handful of families remained at the settlement on the Susquehanna, near Lancaster; the remaining survivors drifted off, some absorbed by neighboring tribes, others fading into obscurity. Eventually, the Five Nations—becoming the Six Nations with the addition of the Tuscaroras—claimed the Susquehanna valley by right of conquest and attempted to repopulate the area with remnants of various displaced tribes seeking protection. One such tribe was the Shawnee, who, in their migration northward, reportedly settled for a while on Elk Neck; tradition ascribes the naming of Hance Point in honor of a Shawnee chief. Despite the late presence of migratory tribes, the native population in Cecil was on the wane following the fall of the Susquehannocks.

With the Indian presence reduced and a thirty-year period of government stability beginning at the end of the seventeenth century, the settlement of Cecil County proceeded apace. By 1674 a sufficient number of planters and traders had relocated to the head of the bay to warrant redistricting of the area. Cecil County was created as a separate political entity, following the boundaries previously proposed by Augustine Herman, from the Susquehanna to the Chester.[33]

Travelers passing through Cecil at the end of the seventeenth century were left with the impression of a rough-hewn community one step up from subsistence. Most who took up plantations in Cecil County from the late seventeenth century through the first half of the eighteenth century were in essence frontier farmers. They sought, through the employment of indentured servants—and increasingly of black slaves—to create a stable agricultural existence. The cultural landscape created by these frontier planters and the housing provided for their families and servants reflected this outlook.

Jasper Danckaerts, exploring Cecil County in 1679, recorded these frontier conditions. A member of the Dutch separatist sect called Labadists, Danckaerts and his fellow adherent Peter Sluyter had come to America searching for a suitable New World colony for the sect. Landing in New York, they chanced to meet Ephraim Herman, son of Augustine, who convinced the pilgrims to return with him to St. Augustine Manor, where Ephraim and his brother Caspar had settled on a section of their father's grant near Delaware Bay.

From the Hermans' Delaware plantations, Danckaerts and his companion followed a broad wagon road. Twenty-two miles in length, it had been cut by Caspar to reach his father's plantation along Bohemia Creek "in the uppermost part of Maryland, that is," Danckaerts commented, "as high up as it is yet inhabited by Christians."[34] After a seven-hour journey, the travelers reached Bohemia Manor, "a noble piece of land, in deed the best we have seen in all our journey south, having large, thick, and high trees, much black walnut and chestnut, as tall and straight as a reed." Here they found an enfeebled Augustine Herman, "miserable both in body and soul," his plantation "going much into decay, as well as his body for want of attention." The three men discussed the possibilities of the Labadists establishing their American colony at Bohemia. According to Danckaerts, Herman replied that he "would sell it to [the Labadists] cheap" if they were inclined to buy, but "he would never sell or hire it to Englishmen." Apparently some Dutch settlers in Maryland, as well as the Bohemian Herman, still felt a simmering resentment over the English usurpation of New Netherlands in 1664.

After a brief stay at Bohemia, the Labadists, armed with letters of introduction and credit signed by Herman, embarked on an exploration of the countryside. Danckaerts's account of his wanderings provides some insight into the cultural landscape of Cecil County during the last quarter of the seventeenth century. The innumerable rivers and creeks crossing the county served as the main transportation arteries, with small rowboats or Indian-style canoes essential to their passage. A system of horse paths and wagon roads was slowly emerging to connect the widely scattered plantations with developing villages and water landings. Paths through the woods were marked by "a piece cut out of the bark by an axe, about the height of a man's eyes." By this means, Danckaerts noted, "the commonest roads are designated through all New Netherlands and Maryland; but in consequence of the great number of roads so marked, and their running into and across each other, they are of little assistance, and indeed often mislead." Wider wagon or cart roads were being cut across the county, primarily to haul tobacco to the river landings. In general, the roads either took the form of private lanes, such as that connecting the Herman plantations, or semipublic roads, such as the cart road that led from Bohemia River to the Dutch village of Appoquinimink in Delaware.

Upon this latter road, Danckaerts remarked, "the goods which go from the South [Delaware] river to Maryland by land, are carried, and also those which pass inland from Maryland to the South river, because these two creeks, namely, the Apoquemene, and the Bohemia, one running up from Maryland, and the other from the Delaware river, as the English call the South river, come to an end close to each other, and perhaps shoot by each other, although they are not navigable so far; but are navigable for eight miles." As early as the 1660s the Dutch considered the possibility of connecting the two rivers by means of a canal. Their goal was to encourage Maryland planters to bring their tobacco to the Delaware, but the realization of such a waterway remained far in the future.

Significantly featured in this early road system were ferries, a number of which operated in the county, most notably near Ordinary Point on the Sassafras, where travelers were taken across the river for "an English shilling" each. Here, on the northern bank of the river crossing, the first Cecil County courthouse stood. The building was originally an ordinary, and it continued to serve that purpose after its designation as the seat of local administration.

Danckaerts's descriptions of late seventeenth century housing are wanting in detail. He and his traveling companion lodged and dined in a variety of private residences during their two-week stay in Cecil County but recorded little except whether the accommodations suited them. They visited "the plantation of Mr. Frisby, which stands upon an eminence and affords a very pleasant prospect, pre-

senting a view of the great bay as well as the Sassafras river." Here they were escorted into the house by slaves and "entertained well," served a "good meal," and given the use of the Frisby horses to complete their journey. Their comments suggest Frisby maintained a plantation of the better sort. At the other extreme, the travelers had spent the previous evening across the river with a family living deep in the woods. At this house they had been offered little to eat and given deer skins "dry and hard as a plank" to sleep on. Sluyter, sharing a bunk presumably with an indentured male servant, was "compelled to evacuate his quarters quickly" when heavy rains poured through the leaky house.

One evening, along the Appoquinimink-Bohemia road, the Labadists came upon two men at a work site; the encounter provides a rare glimpse into what may have been a typical pattern for building construction in late seventeenth century Cecil County. One of the men was a Quaker, "who was building a small house for a tavern, or rather an ale house, for the purpose of entertaining travelers"; the other man was an Irish carpenter, "who was assisting him on the house, and could speak good Dutch, having resided a long time at the Manathans." As a temporary residence at the work site, the Quaker had put up "a shed, made of the bark of trees, after the manner of the Indians, with both ends open, and little larger than a dog's kennel, and where at the best [three men] might possibly have been able to lie, especially when a fire was made…. He had nothing to eat but maize bread which was poor enough, and some small wild beans boiled in water; and little to lie on, or to cover one, except the bare ground and leaves."

The exigencies of providing for shelter while laying the foundations of a new enterprise in the wilderness, whether an ale house or plantation house, must have imposed a crude and hastily built quality on much of the first housing in the county. The Quaker's Indian-style lodge may have been the rudest type of housing imaginable, but its significance lies in the fact that it was intended to be an impermanent structure; once the carpenter-constructed tavern was completed, the temporary dwelling would be discarded. On plantations throughout the county, as throughout the colony, the same progression undoubtedly occurred: Subsistence housing—one-room log or frame houses with dirt floors and imperfect chimneys—was the norm on the frontier.[35] Time had to elapse before wealth would accumulate and plantations could move from frontier subsistence to agricultural stability; only then could conspicuous levels of "civilized" living and accompanying improvements in housing occur.

Danckaerts and Sluyter returned to the Labadist community in Wiewart, Denmark, with glowing reports of Bohemia Manor. Four years later, in 1683, they reappeared in Cecil County with a handful of Labadists to establish a new

Few roads crossed early Cecil County, and most travel was by water. The area's many rivers made ferries a must; this one across the Susquehanna, sketched by Benjamin Henry Latrobe, likely was typical of many. (1798, Latrobe Sketchbook III-26, Maryland Historical Society)

colony on Herman lands. Eventually, through the persuasion of Ephraim Herman, a recent convert to the Labadist sect, they obtained title to 3,750 acres along the Bohemia River. Here, with a disparate group of Old World and New World Labadists, some recruited from New York and some from the surrounding country, they undertook one of the first American experiments in communal living. Samuel Bownas, a Quaker preacher who visited the Labadist colony in 1702, described life in the austere community:

> [At supper] the women sat by themselves [in a separate room] and the men by themselves, having all things in common respecting their household affairs, so that none could claim any more right than another to any part of their stock, whether in trade or husbandry; and if any had a mind to join with them, whether rich or poor, they must put what they had in the common stock, and afterwards if they had a mind to leave the society, they must likewise leave what they brought, and go out empty handed. They frequently expounded upon the scriptures among themselves, and being a very large family, in all upwards of an hundred men, women, and children, carried on something of the manufactory of linen, and had a large plantation of corn, tobacco, flax and hemps, together with cattle of several kind.[36]

The Labadist community in Cecil County was silent, ascetic, and withdrawn from the world. Advocating strict separation from all nonbelievers, it was a tenuous experiment from the start. Under the shifting focus of its principal members, in particular Peter Sluyter, the colony soon fell apart. As the years progressed, Sluyter's leadership became less inspired by spiritual desires and more prompted by temporal pursuits. Finally, in direct opposition to the tenets guiding the community's founding, he seized control of the expansive Labadist tract, apportioned the property among a coterie of select members, and kept for himself the best of the lands, which he cultivated for personal gain. After Sluyter's death in 1726, the community disintegrated and dispersed.

While all types of settlements were springing up throughout southern Cecil County, the northern section remained a wilderness populated for the most part by hunters and traders until the 1680s. In that decade, the shifting gears of the great English land grant machine changed conditions in the Piedmont. William Penn, energetic defender of Quakerism and confidant of Charles II, had long regarded America as a safe harbor for English dissenters. In 1680 he called in a debt of £16,000 in back pay and loans to the royal exchequer that Charles II owed to his deceased father, Admiral William Penn. Penn asked the king for payment in the form of the American lands stretching west of the Delaware. The king's advisors initially counseled strenuously against granting this request.

Meanwhile, Charles Lord Baltimore, who inherited both title and province at the death of his father, Cecilius, in 1674, apparently caught wind of the Penn machinations. In an attempt to protect the unsettled northern border of Maryland from encroachment, he granted to his nephew George Talbot a sprawling 32,000-acre tract called Susquehanna Manor. This land lay between the Little North East Creek and the Octoraro River, reaching well into Pennsylvania. The reason for the grant, as set down in the conveyance, was that "George Talbot…hath undertaken, at his own proper cost and charges, to transport, or cause to be transported into this province within twelve years…six hundred and forty persons of British or Irish descent."[37]

In March 1681 Penn finally received the land he desired. He promptly tested Lord Baltimore's claim to the northern section of the province, dispatching letters on September 16, 1681, to the leading planters of Baltimore and Cecil counties—including James Frisby, Edward Jones, Augustine Herman, George Oulfield, Henry Ward, and Henry Johnson. In the letters, addressed to their "Plantations in Pennsylvania," Penn notified the planters that, according to the evidence of his newly granted charter, they now resided in what was legally Pennsylvania. Therefore, he went on, they "should not pay anymore taxes, or assessments by any Order or law of Maryland."[38] The contents of the letter spread across the two counties, causing a minor uprising among the inhabitants, who immediately ceased payment of all provincial levies. In response, Lord Baltimore ordered the military officers of both counties to help the sheriffs collect taxes from truculent landowners.

At the heart of the dispute between Penn and Lord Baltimore was the location of "the fortieth degree of Northerly Latitude from the Equinoctiall," as the original charter described the northern border of Maryland. Its exact location had not been conclusively proven in the first half century of the province's existence. Part of the problem stemmed from an early—and necessary—reliance on the less-than-accurate latitude lines appearing on the map accompanying John Smith's *General Historie of Virginia*. Leonard Calvert, lieutenant governor of Maryland, in a 1638 letter to his brother Lord Baltimore, refers to the fact that "the line of fortie by Smiths map by wch. the Lords Refferies lade out the bonds [boundaries of Maryland] lyeth right over the first falls [of the Susquehanna]," thus leading the Lords Baltimore initially to believe their province extended little beyond a few miles north of the head of the bay.[39] Later surveys radically redrew the line, pushing the fortieth degree well northward, some ten miles past the future site of Philadelphia.

Penn, for his part, was anxious to prove that the earlier placement of 40 degrees was the true location, thus giving him a much desired outlet on Chesapeake Bay. In addition to his letter to the Cecil and Baltimore planters, Penn dispatched William Haig to the head of the bay to take a few astronomical observations in hopes of bolstering his claims. Apparently, the latitudinal readings proved contradictory, for, according to William Markham, Penn's deputy governor, "it was then given out by the Quakers, that if the degree of forty did not afford William Penn a harbor, he would be forct to buy one of [Lord] Baltemore."[40]

Lord Baltimore, meanwhile, was equally anxious to resolve the boundary dispute and instructed his own commissioners to proceed to Cecil County. There they were to make, "for the lord's satisfaction," their own observations as to the area's relation to the fortieth degree. In addition, the survey party crossed over into Delaware, taking readings in New Castle with a precision sextant borrowed from a ship's captain. To Lord Baltimore's delight, they found "the lattitude of the place of observation which was in the towne, to be thirty nine degrees forty odd minutes." Thus assured, Lord Baltimore arranged for a meeting between himself, Markham, and the Maryland and Pennsylvania commissioners, to be held at Augustine Herman's Bohemia Manor.

Lord Baltimore and the Maryland contingent arrived at the appointed time—September 19, 1682—but Markham and the Pennsylvanians failed to show. After being advised that Markham "was gone up Delaware, and finding little room, and want of severall conveniences at Mr Herman's," the Marylanders pushed on to New Castle, then to Upland (Chester), Pennsylvania, where they finally caught up with Markham.[41] Despite Lord Baltimore's personal intervention, nothing productive resulted from the meeting, from subsequent meetings with Penn himself held at Colonel Thomas Tailler's plantation in Anne Arundel County, or, for that matter, in the next fifty years of discussion.

In the interim, as Penn realized his Chesapeake Bay outlet would not be so easily had, he turned for help to his father's former protector, the Duke of York. In 1682 Penn purchased the duke's Delaware holdings, thus assuring himself of an Atlantic outlet. Three years later, when the Duke of York ascended the throne as King James II, the Lords of Trade—at Penn's petition—invalidated Lord Baltimore's claim to the whole of the Delaware region, directing that the disputed peninsula be split down the middle, from a line drawn from the latitude of Cape Henlopen northward to the fortieth degree, with Lord Baltimore taking the western half and Penn the eastern.

Back in Cecil County, George Talbot, who had established his residence along Principio Creek, was busy trying to fulfill the terms of his grant of Susquehanna Manor, now renamed New Connaught and the surrounding region New Ireland, in honor of his homeland. Talbot pursued the notion of a northern Cecil Irish connection in 1683, when, as surveyor-general of Maryland, he laid out the 6,000-acre New Munster tract in the upper valley of the Big Elk Creek. This property, extending well into Pennsylvania, was surveyed for "Edwin O'Dwire and fifteen other Irishmen." For the settlement of his own manor, Talbot broadly interpreted Lord Baltimore's private directions "to give all

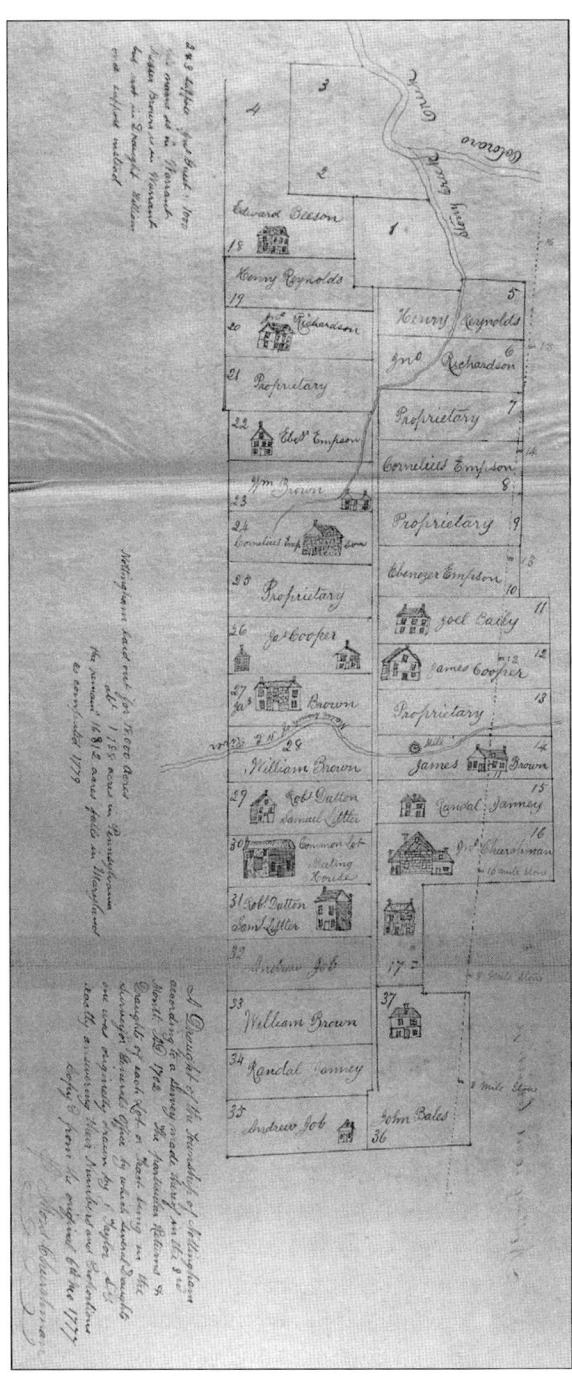

The Nottingham Lots were first settled in fall 1701 on land claimed by both William Penn and Lord Baltimore. This map, based on a plat drawn in 1702, suggests that by 1777 houses had been built on about half the thirty-seven lots. A mill is marked on the west bank of the North East River on James Brown's lot, and a Friends' meetinghouse stood on the lot reserved for community use. The dotted line through the northern half of the lots is the Mason-Dixon line, which clearly puts most of the Nottingham Lots in Cecil County, Maryland. (Chester County Historical Society)

Mercer and Hannah Brown built a house on one of the Nottingham Lots in 1746. A slate marker with their initials and the date stands as a testament to their efforts. (Maryland Historical Trust)

reasonable Encouragement to such persons as may be willing" to move to northern Cecil County. Venturing into Pennsylvania, he attempted to convince the resident Swedes and Finns that there was "better Land and Cheaper rents and greater Incouragements for poore men in Maryland than in Pensilvania." As an additional incentive to move, Talbot explained that Maryland levied no taxes for having children, while in Pennsylvania residents had to "pay a Crowne per Childe."[42]

Just how successful Talbot's campaign to populate northern Cecil County was is unknown. A significant number of Pennsylvania residents must have been enticed to leave for Maryland, as William Penn in 1684 called Talbot to a private conference to discuss his "interference...with the Government of Pennsylvania." Talbot's role in Maryland affairs came to an abrupt halt that same year, when he murdered Christopher Rousby, a collector of the king's customs. Although eventually pardoned for the crime, he left

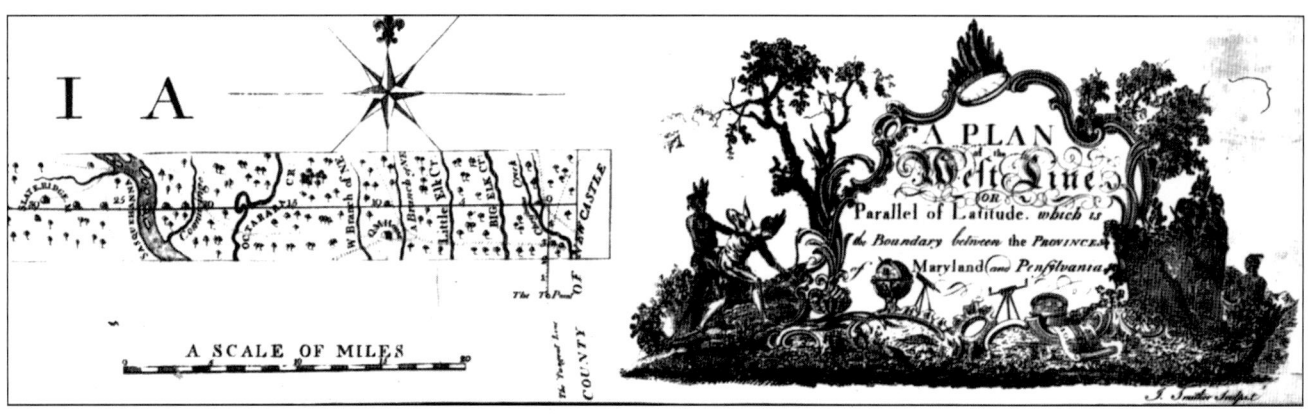

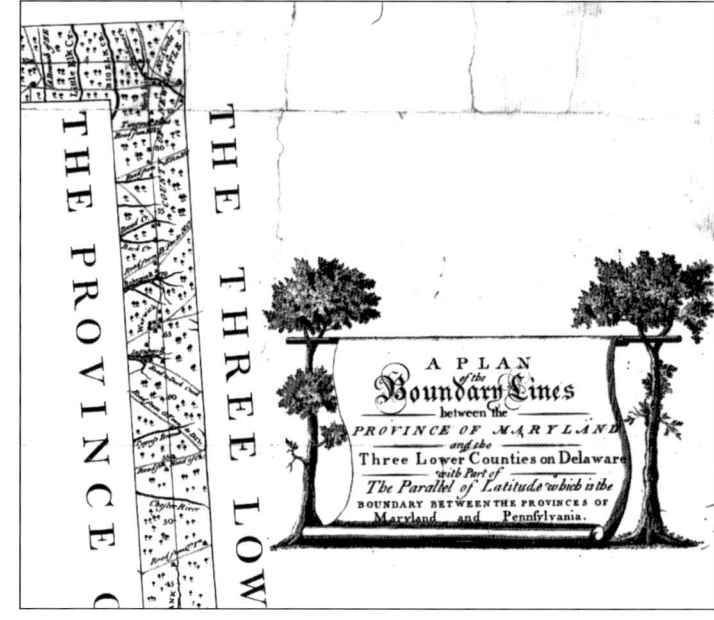

The boundary dispute between Maryland and Pennsylvania was finally settled through the survey work of Jeremiah Dixon and Charles Mason in the 1760s. Their 1768 maps of the so-called Mason-Dixon line show very little of the ground on either side of the line, but the Cecil waterways that cross the boundary are clearly enumerated. (portions of [Mason and Dixon], *A Plan of the Boundary Lines between... Maryland and Pennsylvania*, Hammond-Harwood Atlas Collection, Maryland State Archives, MSA SC G1213-293-1)

the province in 1687, his mission to settle northern Cecil County unfulfilled.

William Penn and Lord Baltimore sailed for England in 1684, hoping to resolve the ongoing boundary dispute, but to no avail. For both men, the political revolutions and shifting monarchies of the ensuing years resulted in the temporary loss of their American holdings. Maryland was declared a royal province in 1691, following the ascension of William and Mary and the end of the Catholic regency in Protestant England, and Lord Baltimore's proprietorship was not restored until 1715. Although Pennsylvania underwent a similar transformation in 1692, Penn was reinstated as proprietor only two years later.

Another five years of litigation and political maneuvering prevented Penn from returning to America until 1699. Upon his return he was confronted by a hostile Pennsylvania assembly in the process of stripping him and his council of all legislative authority. By 1701, with the establishment of the Charter of Liberties, as the assembly's plan became known, the Pennsylvania legislature essentially was running on its own, the Delaware counties had created a separate representative assembly, and Penn as proprietor was left only with the power of veto, exercised almost exclusively through his appointed governor.

With the government of the province effectively removed from his control, Penn directed his energies to the one area in which he still had the upper hand: the granting of lands remaining in his ownership. Immediately he turned his attention to the disputed lands along the Cecil County border. In 1701 he persuaded a group of Quakers near Philadelphia and Upland, Pennsylvania, to remove themselves to a tract called the Nottingham Lots, 18,000 acres of prime land bounded by Octoraro Creek on the west and extending about ten miles to the present Blue Ball on the east,

The new Mason-Dixon line was marked with boundary stones set a mile apart along its entire length. Many of these markers survive *in situ*. (Historical Society of Cecil County)

Every tenth boundary marker along the Mason-Dixon line had the coat of arms of Lord Baltimore on one side and William Penn on the other. Here, Baltimore's arms appear on the left and Penn's on the right. (Historical Society of Cecil County)

well across the Maryland border and within the absent Talbot's holdings. Penn himself accompanied the Quaker leaders to the new settlement and, upon arriving at the site, he "then and there set apart and dedicated forty acres of land to them and their successors forever for the combined purpose of public worship, the right of burial ground and the privilege of education."

Payment to Penn for the land to be settled was to consist of "the yearly rent of two bushels of good winter wheat for every hundred acres to be paid yearly at some navigable water—a landing place in Delaware."[43] Penn, still stinging from his inability to wrest a Chesapeake landing from the Lords Baltimore, saw to it that at least a portion of the crops produced in the disputed lands would find their way to a Delaware port, even if they had to travel three times the distance to reach a landing. Also in 1701, along the Delaware border, Penn granted a group of Welsh Baptist miners a huge 30,000-acre parcel surrounding Iron Hill and known as the Welsh tract.

These two grants of Penn's, which infringed upon Cecil County, were of questionable validity and seemingly more vindictive than substantive. They were among his last acts in the province, as later that year Penn returned to England. The Maryland-Pennsylvania border controversy, which had created the first impetus for the settlement of northern Cecil County, continued well after Penn's death in 1718. It was not fully resolved until the 1760s, when the English engineers Charles Mason and Jeremiah Dixon, following the final decision of the Lord Chancellor, laid out their eponymous line and established once and for all the county's northern and eastern borders.

Samuel Lewis's map of Maryland shows five towns in Cecil County in 1794—Frederick Town, Head of Elk, Charlestown, Nottingham, and Warwick. The sunburst mark in the far northwestern corner of the county represents Patrick Ewing's mill. It is not clear why his mill and no other is indicated. (detail from Lewis, *The State of Maryland*, Huntingfield Map Collection, Maryland State Archives, MSC SC G1399-1-195)

CHAPTER 3

Making a Plantation Out of the Woods

WELSH MINERS, Labadist separatists, Swedish refugees, Quaker transplants, Indian remnants, English planters, African slaves—Cecil County at the turn of the eighteenth century seemed anything but a homogeneous society. Despite this variety, the population was scant. Settlement came neither fast nor steady to the head of the bay. By 1712, of the thirteen Maryland counties then established, Cecil had the lowest enumerated population. The census of that year found 2,097 inhabitants, including 504 "masters and taxable men," 435 white women, 873 children, and 285 black slaves. Together, they accounted for only four percent of the colony's population.[1]

The county's cultural diversity at this time, though apparent, was deceptive. Across tidewater Cecil and into the north county there was one link that connected the disparate settlements to each other and to the rest of Maryland: tobacco. Too much and too little can be attributed to the role of tobacco in the early establishment of Cecil County. Agricultural diversification had always been understood as crucial to Maryland's eventual success; even before the end of the seventeenth century planters were warned about the economic consequences of relying upon tobacco as the sole staple crop. In an attempt to encourage diversification, the Assembly issued edicts requiring those who planted tobacco to plant at least two acres of corn. Nonetheless, tobacco remained the bait by which many a family was hooked and landed in Cecil County. These settlers hoped that by setting out a few seasons of the "golden token," they would accrue enough wealth to raise them above the level of subsistence. Settlers with such a frame of mind came to southern Cecil throughout the early eighteenth century, eventually establishing a plantation culture that spread in a verdant arc from the Sassafras to the Susquehanna.

By its very nature the Cecil tobacco culture created a disjointed and decentralized landscape characterized by scattered plantations. These properties were not the plantations of the South described in twentieth century popular culture; in general the improvements on these farms were minimal, consisting of tobacco houses, crude landings, and the most basic of homesteads. Corncribs held what was to become a mainstay of most farm tables, along with meat from the free-range hogs many farmers kept. The intricate process of establishing and cultivating a new plantation thus directed the pattern and tenor of life in southern Cecil through the first half of the eighteenth century.

With or without the aid of slaves, getting in the first season's crop was of the utmost importance to the new plantation; it was hoped that crop would give the planter the wherewithal to continue and thus the harvest took precedence over all other activities, including home construction. The steps involved in establishing a foothold differed little throughout the southern colonies. Thomas Nairne, in a *Letter from South Carolina*, published in 1710, offers one of the earliest and most typical accounts of the process of hewing a new plantation out of the fringes of civilization:

> If anyone designs to make a Plantation in this Province, out of the Woods, the first thing to be done is, after having cutt down a few Trees, to split Palissades, or Clapboards, and therewith make small Houses or Huts, to shelter the Slaves. After that whilst some Servants are clearing the land, others are to be employed in squaring or sawing Wall-plats, Posts, Rafters, Boards, and Shingles for a small House for the Family, which usually serves as a Kitchin afterwards, when they are in better Circumstances to build a larger.[2]

Once the land had been staked out and cleared and a temporary shelter erected, the long, arduous, labor-intensive process of planting the tobacco began. It culminated in the harvest, which continued over a period of weeks as whole

Tobacco was a vital cash crop in early Cecil as it was in other English settlements around the Chesapeake. Dried leaves were packed tightly in hogsheads with a tobacco prise. The pressure of the large weighted beam continued for days until the hogshead was filled and headed. Sealed hogsheads were sent to Europe and sometimes the Caribbean, where the crop was sold and items not available in the colonies were purchased. (This tobacco prise, now at Mt. Harmon in Cecil County, was originally from St. Mary's County.) (Maryland Historical Trust)

fields rarely ripened together. Second cuttings were common after the new leaves had matured; on fresh lands a third cutting was sometimes possible. Each successive cutting lessened the quality of the leaf, and eventually such practices were curtailed by legislation in an effort to maintain the marketability of Maryland tobacco.

The tobacco was hung to dry on wooden scaffolds, first outdoors and then, later in the process, in the tobacco house. This structure consisted of an integral scaffold, or series of beams, erected in regular gradations from bottom to top. Once the tobacco was sufficiently cured, the leaves were stripped from the stalks and tied into "hands." These were packed into hogsheads and pressed down into the huge wooden casks with the help of a tobacco prise. Once full, the sealed hogsheads were either rolled overland or lashed to a boat and floated downriver to market.

Cecil planters, like those throughout the colony, sent their tobacco to Britain under the consignment system. Restrictive trade legislation, designed to ensure Parliament its share of revenues from the burgeoning tobacco trade, prohibited Maryland planters from selling directly overseas. Instead, the Cecil planter was required to ship hogsheads to a merchant in Britain, who would receive the tobacco, clear it through customs, pay the duties, and market the crop, receiving a sizable commission for his services. Meanwhile, under the planter's instructions, the merchant would purchase cloth, tools, and other goods not obtainable in the colonies. The trade system, populated by brokers who all too readily extended credit to meet—or exceed—the planter's material requirements, created a state of perpetual debt for many with lesser business acumen.

The rigorous demands of planting, coupled with the vicissitudes of the weather and the world tobacco market, often impeded the Cecil settler's climb to success. The constant attendance required by the crop made labor a critical factor in the tobacco economy; this need was filled by the

St. Mary Anne's Episcopal Church was built in 1742 in North Elk Parish, which had been established in 1706 to accommodate the increasing population in the county. (1985, Maryland Historical Trust)

importation of indentured white servants and, increasingly in the eighteenth century, of black slaves. Ironically, the growing supply of labor helped worsen the economic situation. Tobacco surpluses expanded, prices fell, and depression lingered. By the turn of the eighteenth century the British market was so inflated with colonial tobacco that nearly two-thirds of it had to be reexported to the Baltic countries, Holland, France, Spain, and other European markets.

The international trade network was always delicately balanced, and any number of political or economic circumstances could—and usually did—weight the scales against Maryland planters. Between 1702 and 1713 trade was effectively curtailed by the escalation of the War of the Spanish Secession—Queen Anne's War. France, Spain, Flanders, and the Baltic area were lost as markets, and Holland began growing as much as 20 million pounds of her own tobacco yearly. Parliament, in a desperate attempt to salvage the American tobacco industry, began issuing rations of tobacco to the British military and petitioning neutral ships to deliver tobacco directly to France. Such artificial stimulants, while bringing temporary relief, only masked the greater problems to come.

Despite these problems, tobacco continued to dominate Maryland and Cecil agriculture until the mid-eighteenth century. As a result, those in the county who most vigorously pursued its cultivation—planters in the southern end of the county, mostly English and Anglican in orientation—emerged as the dominant force in Cecil's political and economic affairs. This growing coterie of tidewater planters, in other counties as well as Cecil, established Anglican parishes that played a central role in the political and social life of the colony.

Soon after the ascension of William and Mary in 1688, the Church of England became the official church of Maryland. By 1693 the General Assembly had divided the colony into thirty Anglican parishes, each to be managed by a select group of vestrymen and funded not by charitable tithing but by a tax. Forty pounds of tobacco was to be levied against each taxable person within the parish boundaries, regardless of belief or adherence.

Two parishes were established in Cecil County. North Sassafras Parish encompassed the North Sassafras, Bohemia, and Elk hundreds, and South Sassafras Parish took in Worton and South Sassafras hundreds, which became part of Kent County in 1706. Both parishes were first attended by the Rev. Mr. Vanderbush. As more and more Anglicans began populating tidewater Cecil, petitions increased for the establishment of a network of chapels of ease. In these, the parish rector could hold services every few weeks for

the convenience of distant parishioners. One such chapel was formed at Bohemia Manor in 1695 to serve members of the North Sassafras Parish in that vicinity. The first St. Stephen's, the central church of the parish, was built in the first decade of the eighteenth century.

As new plantations continued to open and the population grew, petitions were presented to the General Assembly for the establishment of separate parishes. The North Elk Parish was created in 1706, embracing the lands between the Elk and Susquehanna rivers. St. Mary Anne's in North East served as the parish church. Later, St. Mark's, near the Susquehanna, was established as a chapel of ease for North Elk Parish, and in 1744 St. Augustine Parish was carved out of North Sassafras Parish and centered around the former chapel of ease at Bohemia Manor.

The establishment of the Church of England and the enforcement of English law put Roman Catholics in the English colonies under serious disabilities; churches were forced to subsist on a private, almost clandestine basis, while individual Catholics were constantly threatened or visited with legal actions. Since there were probably no more than 3,000 Maryland Catholics in 1708, survival was a serious question.[3] However, because many Catholic adherents were landed and moderately wealthy, as a group they possessed sufficient social prestige to withstand the seductions of conversion provoked by eighteenth century circumstances, guaranteeing the continuity of the Roman Church in Maryland.

In Cecil County the Society of Jesus—familiarly known as Jesuits—had initiated missionary activities at Bohemia Manor as early as 1704. In fact, the Jesuit enclave in the county was one of the best developed in the colony, with a vast tract of land in the brothers' possession amounting to nearly 1,200 acres. Cultivating their fields and planting extensive orchards and gardens with the help of slaves and tenant farmers, the brothers also built a rectory and chapel, grist- and sawmill, brick kiln, blacksmith shop, still, and loading wharf on their property.

In 1745 the Jesuits at Bohemia founded a secondary school more substantial and long-lived than those previously founded in Maryland at Saint Mary's (1650) and Newtown (1670), although those were both established in times more favorable to the Catholic Church. At the Cecil institution several of the colony's most distinguished leaders—including John Carroll, first Catholic bishop in America, and Charles Carroll, a signer of the Declaration of Independence—received part of their education.[4] The school at Bohemia is thought to have been the forerunner of Georgetown University.

The Cecil Quaker community, centered around the Nottingham Lots, never experienced the vicissitudes of the Roman Catholics in the county. Nevertheless, from the time of the first Friends' meeting held at James and William Brown's log house in 1704, they remained an isolated community distinct from the Anglican planters of the southern tidewater. Their geographic and spiritual orientations tied them to the pacifist communities of Pennsylvania, which in general had nonslaveholding, nontobacco traditions.

Shortly after its settlement, the Quaker community on the Nottingham Lots was prospering. The itinerant Quaker minister Thomas Chalkey noted that by 1709 a new meetinghouse had been built here, "which is a large meeting,

Quakers from Pennsylvania founded a sizable settlement on the Nottingham Lots at the disputed border with Pennsylvania. Brick Meeting House was built in 1724 to serve this community, replacing an earlier log structure. It was enlarged later in the century with a fieldstone addition. (1902, Maryland Historical Trust)

and greatly increases."[5] Upon this site in 1724 a substantial two-and-a-half story brick meetinghouse, known today as Brick Meeting House, was constructed to replace the earlier log meetinghouse. Increases in the Friends' population necessitated the enlargement of Brick Meeting House in 1752 and the creation of additional meetings, one in West Nottingham in 1730 (replaced with a brick structure in 1811) and, by the first half of the nineteenth century, one near Octoraro Creek and another in Colora.

One factor that lessened the prospects for unimpeded growth of the Quaker community in Cecil County was the influx of a vigorous non-Quaker element around the lots, in particular the arrival of wave upon wave of Scots-Irish Presbyterians. For half a century England had sought to attract Scotsmen to the Irish plantations in Ulster, and by the 1660s had succeeded in bringing in 100,000 or more. After 1660, however, the enactment of various repressive measures put the Scots-Irish to flight. A few departed late in the seventeenth century, but the eighteenth century saw this trickle swell to a tide.

Resentment over conditions in Ireland, in combination with the tempting lure of opportunity in the new world, drew thousands of Scots-Irish to America. Many entered by way of the Delaware valley, and sometime before 1708 a Presbyterian church was organized at the Head of Christiana, just across the Cecil border in Delaware. By the 1720s sufficient numbers had migrated into the county to warrant the creation of Rock Church, in the valley of the Little Elk Creek. Around that time George Gillespie, pastor at the Head of Christiana, noted "there are a great many congregations erected, and now erecting; for within the space of five years by gone, near to two hundred families have come into our parts from Ireland, and more are following."[6] In 1723 an Anglican missionary at New Castle complained "the church [here] is environed with greater number of Dissenters than ever, by reason of these fresh recruits sent us of late from the North of Ireland."[7]

All was not to be peaceful within the transplanted Scots-Irish Presbyterian community. The arrival of the evangelist George Whitefield in 1739 brought to a boil a simmering antagonism between revivalist and nonrevivalist factions within the church. Eventually their differences culminated in a split of the Cecil congregations into New Side (revivalist) and Old Side groups. In 1744 the New Side faction built a church near Rising Sun and called upon the Reverend Samuel Finley to lead their new congregation. Finley, reflecting the New Side's sense of responsibility for the future of Presbyterianism in America, immediately founded the West Nottingham Academy "to educate young men for the gospel ministry."[8]

During the eighteenth century the academy boasted a

Built in 1762, this church, the second Rock Church on the site, symbolized the reunion of two Presbyterian factions in Cecil County. (c. 1973, Maryland Historical Trust)

The poor conditions of the roads in 18th and 19th century Cecil made travel slow and arduous. Taverns by the side of main roads were a necessity for travelers who could not be certain of reaching the next town before dark. Many farmhouses were used as taverns at one time or another. Several of the county's best-known taverns are illustrated here. Clockwise from bottom left: early inn formerly on the site of the courthouse, Elkton (1936, E. H. Pickering, Historic American Buildings Survey); Fair Hill Inn, Fair Hill (George M. Reynolds, Sr.); Blue Ball Tavern, on one of the Nottingham Lots (1936, E. H. Pickering, Historic American Buildings Survey); Indian Queen Tavern, Charlestown (1926, collection of Mrs. William Henry, copied by M. E. Warren, Maryland Historical Trust); Rodgers Tavern, Perryville (Maryland Historical Trust)

number of distinguished alumni, including Dr. Benjamin Rush, physician and Revolutionary patriot. So great was Finley's success at West Nottingham that in 1761 he was elected president of the Presbyterian College of New Jersey, later to become Princeton. The same year Finley left Cecil County the two rival Presbyterian factions were reunited, and in a symbolic coming together constructed an impressive stone church at the site of the original Rock Church.

The Quaker and Presbyterian congregations in Cecil increased throughout the eighteenth century and were later joined by Methodists. Nonetheless, the self-perpetuating Anglican vestries remained the preserve of the county's socially and economically privileged, whose influence extended well beyond the sanctuary walls. The reins of the county were in their hands, and the county court was essentially an Anglican court. The court had been moved in 1719 from Oldtown, located on the north bank of the Sassafras and then known as Jamestown, to a place closer to the population center of the county—the spot "where a certain William Thomas lived on Elk River known by the name of Long Point on Bohemia Manor," later renamed Court House Point.[9]

The county court had no small power in shaping the pattern of county life throughout the century. In it rested nearly all the functions of government. The court sat four times a year to hear both civil and criminal cases; the justices of the court also sat as the board of county commissioners. By midcentury their dual roles as judges and commissioners authorized them to perform most local government functions: they levied county taxes, assessed parish rates, fixed and regulated parish boundaries, annually appointed the constables, and in general administered justice upon the actions of guardians and orphans; runaways, servants, slaves and masters; and executors and other matters relating to cases testamentary, civil, and criminal. Only civil suits involving more than £100 and capital crimes were required to go directly to the General Court in Annapolis.

Of no small consequence to Cecil residents, it was also the county court that decided who should receive a license to operate a tavern or ferry. As the century progressed, the county's location between the expanding Pennsylvania and Maryland settlements—in particular the growing market centers of Philadelphia and Baltimore—took on greater economic significance. Often these two travel-oriented services, catering to the needs of those who passed through the county on their north-south journeys, were connected. For example, Stevenson's tavern lodged a constant stream of travelers who crossed the river at nearby Susquehanna lower ferry. By 1788 John Rodgers had acquired both the tavern and ferry, which later became a major stopping point on the Baltimore and Philadelphia post road.

Some farmers living along better traveled Cecil roads may have petitioned for tavern licenses simply to avoid putting up wayfarers at their own expense. The description of one eighteenth century traveler suggests little distinction between a farmer's house and a formal tavern: Every ten miles or so there appeared a tavern, "all built of wood, and much in the same stile, with a porch in front the entire length of the house [where] all sorts of people, just as they happen to arrive, are crammed together into the one room, where they must reconcile themselves to each other the best way they can."[10]

The great number of jury presentments for retailing spirits or cider without a license indicates taverns were much in demand. Throughout the eighteenth century a number of them sprang up along major cross-county stage and post routes. On the roads to and from Lancaster County, New Castle, Philadelphia, and Baltimore, the names of Cecil taverns and tavernkeepers became familiar to frequent travelers.

In addition to the justices of the county court, a host of lesser officials carried out the daily operations of county government. The sheriff acted primarily as the chief executive officer, serving writs, arresting criminals, levying taxes, paying bills, and supervising elections. Since both the county levy and the parish levy were paid in tobacco, it was the sheriff's responsibility to see that the tobacco taken in was sold at a good price.

Perhaps the most problematic task in all the county belonged to the road overseers. These individuals had the particularly burdensome responsibility of keeping assigned stretches of the public highway in repair. Overseers received no pay for the work but paid a heavy fine for failure of duty. As a result, the job was rarely held by the same person for more than one or two years in succession. The upkeep of roads was particularly important to Cecil County because of its key role in the colony's north-south transportation sys-

"Making a Road" in Eighteenth Century Cecil

In discussing the condition of Cecil County roads in 1795, Isaac Weld left a telling description of road building at the time:

> ...the best cultivated parts of the county are not seen from the road, which passes chiefly over barren and hilly tracts called "ridges." The reason for carrying the road over these is, because it is found to last longer than if carried over the flat part of the county, where the soil is deep, a circumstance which people of Maryland always take into consideration; for after a road is cut, they never take pains to keep it in good repair....Whenever they attempt to mend these roads, it is always by filling the ruts with saplings or bushes, and covering them over with earth. This, however, is done only when there are fields on each side of the road. If the road runs contiguous to a wood, then, instead of mending it where it is bad, they open a new passage through the trees, which they call making a road. It is very common in Maryland to see six or seven different roads branching out from one, which all lead to the same place. A stranger, before he is acquainted with this circumstance, is frequently puzzled to know which he ought to take. The dexterity with which the drivers of the stages guide their horses along these new roads, which are full of stumps of trees, is astonishing, yet to appearance they are the most awkward drivers possible....

Quoted from G. E. Gifford, Jr., *Cecil County, Maryland, 1608-1850, as Seen by Some Visitors and Several Essays on Local History* (Rising Sun, Md.: Calvert School, 1974), pp. 114-15.

tem. Despite this, highway overseers seem to have regularly neglected their duties; presentments by the jury for failure to carry out the work properly were made every year. In 1795 Isaac Weld noted the dire condition of Cecil roads:

> The roads in this state are worse than in any one in the union; indeed so very bad are they, that on going from Elkton to Susquehannah ferry, the driver frequently had to call to the passengers in the stage, to lean out of the carriage first at one side, then at the other, to prevent it from oversetting in the deep ruts with which the road abounds....[11]

The market importance of roads in the county was invariably stressed in petitions to the county court for their establishment, repair, and maintenance. Many roads began as private lanes commonly enjoyed by the public, but as settlement progressed it became increasingly necessary either for the county to assume public ownership of the lanes or to open up new roads. In 1729 Scots-Irish settlers in the Octoraro region petitioned the court for a road "leading unto the Quaker meeting house at the west end of Nottingham," citing as their reason that the intervening section of the countryside was filling so fast the old road was about to be closed up.[12]

The creation and sustenance of new towns was an area of Cecil's physical development shared by the county court and the General Assembly. In 1730 Ceciltown was laid out at Broxen's Point, on the south side of the Bohemia River. A complete town never appeared, and the development, languishing into the nineteenth century, eventually amounted to but a handful of houses. Fredericktown, created by an act of Assembly in 1736, encompassed sixty equal lots imposed in a grid upon thirty acres along the north banks of the Sassafras. Lot holders in the town were required to pay one pence per lot per annum in quitrent to Lord Baltimore. In 1744 a man anchored off North East wrote in his diary that the town was "composed of two Ordinaries, a Grist Mill, Bakerhouse, and two or Three Dwellings."[13] Town development was slow in coming, however; only subsequent legislative measures assured its continuance.

Perhaps the most ambitious new town enterprise was Charlestown, established by the General Assembly in 1742

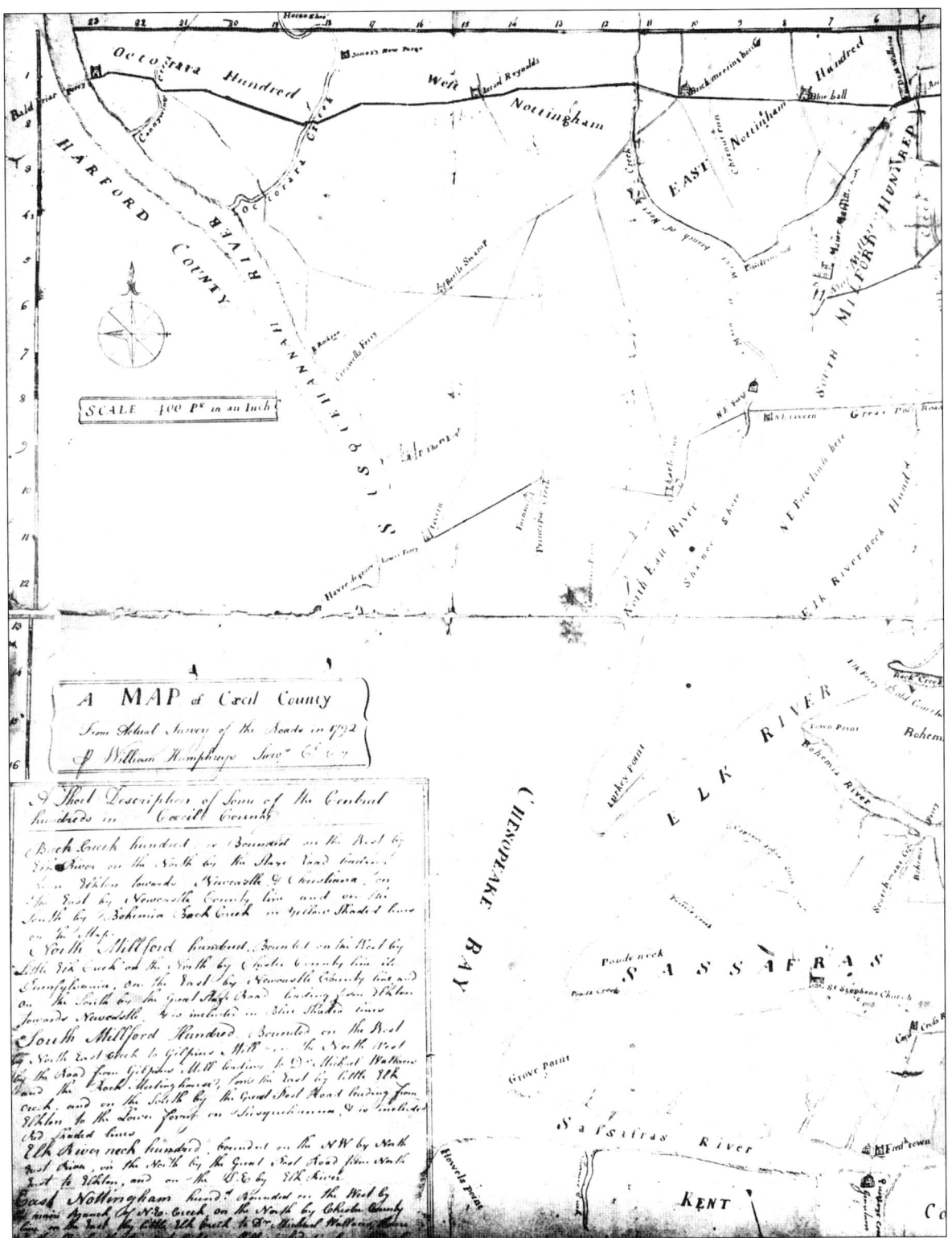

By 1792, the year this map illuminates, a network of roads had spread over Cecil County. Traveled by foot, horse, or wagon, these muddy, poorly maintained thoroughfares served not only county residents but travelers between the cities of Baltimore and Philadelphia as well. (William Humphreys, "A Map of Caecil County…," Maryland State Archives Map Collection, MSA SC G1427-1-209)

and envisioned as a full-service port rising out of Long Point on the west side of the North East River. Named in honor of the fifth Lord Baltimore, Charles Calvert, the town was laid out on a 200-acre tract, with 300 adjacent acres designated as a common. A number of inducements were built into the town plan in an attempt to encourage growth. Squares were marked and reserved in anticipation of the county court relocating to the new town, with additional space held for the construction of public wharves, warehouses, market buildings, and other facilities. The quitrent was set at two pence per lot, twice the amount of Fredericktown, presumably for twice the amenities. Building codes for new home construction were enacted to ensure only the finest of streetscapes. Twice-yearly market fairs were immediately instituted to establish the town as a trade center. And, as a final incentive, the Reverend William Wye, rector of North Elk Parish, excused residents from the yearly tobacco tax for support of the clergy.[14]

Despite these grand plans, the town never fully materialized. Thirty years after its founding one critic remarked, "What, I beseech you, is Charles town?—a deserted village, with a few miserable huts thinly scattered among the bushes, and daily crumbling into ruin."[15] Perhaps one explanation for Charlestown's failure to mature is that, ultimately, its founding proceeded less from social or economic need for a town at this location and more from a political need on the part of both Maryland and British authorities to devise a means of controlling the burgeoning Cecil wheat trade.

(above) By the time Benjamin Latrobe made this sketch on September 29, 1813, Charlestown had lost the county court to Elkton and many resident merchants to Baltimore. Latrobe labeled the buildings shown in his sketchbook. Included among them are dwellings that originally housed several Marylanders well-known in the early history of the United States: John Paca, father of signer of the Declaration of Independence and later Gov. William Paca; Francis Key, grandfather of Francis Scott Key; Nathaniel Ramsey, Revolutionary hero and brother-in-law of Charles Willson Peale; and Gov. Thomas Bladen. Other houses belonged to craftsmen such as saddler John Smith, cooper David Davis, and carpenter Edward Tully. The market house is pictured, as well as the still house, where sugar cane products from the West Indies were made into rum, and the fairground, where the first twice-yearly fair was held in 1744. Slightly fewer than half the buildings pictured remain in the 20th century. [Latrobe Sketchbook XII-5, Maryland Historical Society; information in this caption is from *Latrobe's View of America, 1795-1820*, ed. E. C. Carter II et al. (New Haven: Yale University Press for the Maryland Historical Society, 1985), p. 308.]

(right) Named in honor of the fifth Lord Baltimore, Charlestown had an ambitious beginning, as shown by this plat. Four lots were reserved for the county court, headquartered here until it moved to Elkton in the 1780s. The map shows the common set aside for the use of town residents, as well as busy traffic on the river. (17[42], Geography and Maps Division, Library of Congress)

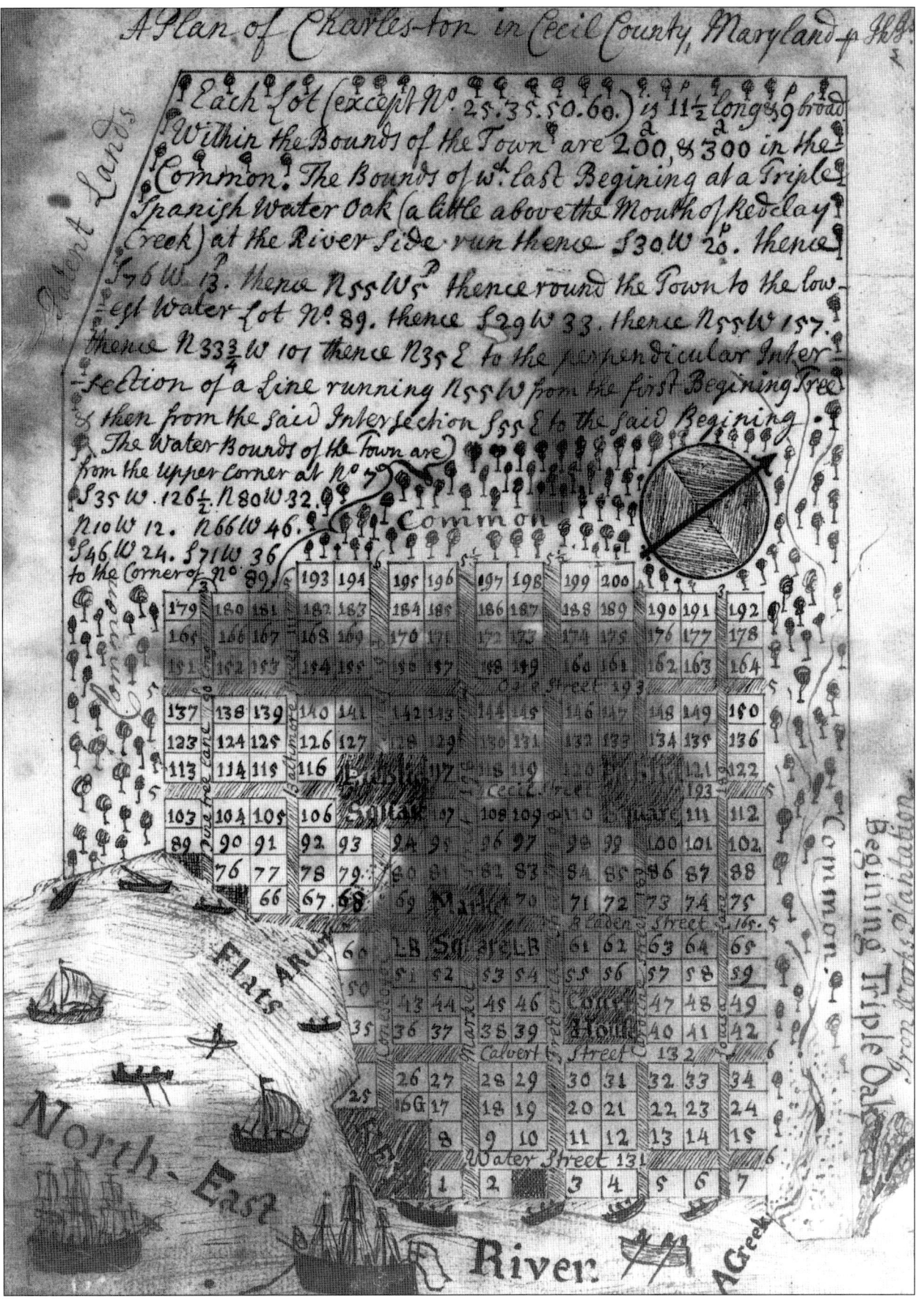

Flour had long been one of Parliament's enumerated items, controlled by the countless trade and navigation acts issued from Great Britain from the seventeenth century onward. Flour, however, had never enjoyed as profitable a trade as tobacco and consequently was never as closely monitored. For most of the eighteenth century, tobacco continued as Maryland's principal export commodity and, due to the lack of hard currency, its primary domestic medium of exchange. Debts were contracted in terms of tobacco, and taxes were payable in cured leaf; merchant, mechanic, and minister alike took their fees in the form of tobacco.

With this dependence on tobacco as currency, its overabundance constantly played economic havoc. With too much in circulation in the colony, tobacco began to lose its value. In 1724 one Marylander wrote, "Tobacco, our money, is worth nothing, and not a Shirt to be had for Tobacco this year in all our country."[16] As prices fell, planters began packing trash tobacco into their hogsheads, extending the harvest by cutting the quality, much to the ire of English and Scottish merchants who received the poor quality leaf. Maryland tobacco fell into disrepute, and the depressed state of affairs brought on by poor prices caused rioting in tobacco areas all over Maryland.

By the 1740s Maryland, following Virginia's lead, had realized that controlled inspection would be the only salvation. As one Marylander bluntly informed Lord Baltimore in 1743, no improvement in the state of the colony's tobacco industry was possible without inspection regulations that "will prevent the sending to market Such trash as is unfit for any other use but Manure."[17] By 1747 a system of government-controlled inspection had been established by the General Assembly. Public inspection stations were set up at Fredericktown on the Sassafras and at John Holland's at Bohemia Ferry under one inspector and at Charlestown under the authority of a separate county-appointed official.

By the time Joshua Hempstead visited Charlestown in 1749, the inspection station was up and running; at the town wharf he found "a good Storehouse for goods & Weights and Scales, for Tobacco & Press for it."[18] The paid public inspector, usually himself a skilled planter, was

Milling was an industry eminently suited to the terrain and economy of Cecil County, which sits astride the fall line between the coastal plain and the piedmont, making its many north-south waterways fast-running and suited to producing power. Rock Run Mill in Port Deposit, a merchant mill built in the early 18th century, ground local grain for export. (George Hipkins)

charged with examining each hogshead that passed out of the port, opening each cask, analyzing the contents to determine if they were "good and merchantable," weighing both tobacco and cask at the public scales, marking the inspected hogsheads, and stowing them away in the public warehouse to await shipment. Once past inspection, the planter received a crop note that listed hogsheads by number, recorded the gross weight, and specified the grade and type of tobacco, whether sweet-scented or oronoko, stemmed or leaf. The planter then could either consign his tobacco to England or mark it for sale in the colonies. At the station smaller planters could turn in tobacco by the bundle, receiving a transfer note entitling them to the same type and quality tobacco.

The Inspection Act guaranteed both Charlestown and Fredericktown a share in the tobacco trade. By the time of the act, however, the orientation and products of Cecil farms had shifted significantly, bringing a new type of trader to county wharves. Increasing demands for American wheat to feed the overpopulated West Indies, replace the lost harvests of war-torn Europe, even to supplement shortages in New England, encouraged the expansion of grain cultivation in Maryland. Although variable, the market possibilities were encouraging enough to prompt many to eschew tobacco in favor of wheat.

In northern Cecil, a grain-oriented community had already been firmly established by the Quakers in the first quarter of the eighteenth century. By the 1740s, converts to grain cultivation, better suited in any case to the soil in the county, had increased significantly, as had attendant flour production. The General Assembly, responding to the shifting economy, began allowing certain taxes to be paid with grain, issued the colony's first paper currency for the exchange benefit of farmers no longer involved in tobacco cultivation, and instituted a flour inspection system similar in intent and execution to that of tobacco. Charlestown became the designated flour inspection station for the northeast region, with every cask of flour milled in the area required to pass through the port for inspection.

Some county residents looking for ways to free themselves from dependence on fluctuating tobacco prices found milling a profitable solution. Combining the emerging grain culture and the ready supply of water, these individuals constructed grist and merchant mills everywhere in the county, although many fewer were established in the south. Provisions for gristmills—in the true sense of the word, holding one or two small runs of stone and grinding grain primarily for home or plantation use—had been made from the earliest years of settlement. In 1687 George Talbot transferred to Jacob Young a tract of land called "Clayfall," in Susquehanna Manor, in consideration of Young's promise "to make to me and my heirs forever for 5 s. sterling of ye seat of a mill that he formerly caused to be built at the head of Pony Creek vulgarly called Mill Creek."[19] At least as early as 1706 William Smith owned a mill at Head of Elk; in 1711 Isaac Van Bibber was operating a mill on a branch of Bohemia River; and by 1734 Jeremiah Brown, Sr., miller, and William Coale, millwright, in "joynt and equall partnership" had constructed a mill at the Nottingham Lots.[20] True merchant mills—holding multiple runs of stone and grinding for export markets—had appeared in the county by the 1730s in response to the increase in grain cultivation. Rock Run Mill along the Susquehanna was specifically designated a "merchant mill" in a 1731 road petition.[21]

In addition to the mills, a number of other entrepreneurial enterprises were attracted to eighteenth century Cecil by the ample natural resources available in the county, especially the abundant water power. Iron ore deposits discovered in the area of Principio Creek engendered one of the county's—and the colony's—most notable early industries. As early as 1716 Robert Dutton had established a bloomery near the "bottom of the main falls of North East."[22] In the same year Stephen Onion and William and Thomas Russell, with the backing of English financiers, organized the Principio Company to exploit the Cecil ore deposits.

Iron ore found near Principio Creek led to the early 18th century construction of a bloomery, the first of several enterprises named Principio that stood on the site. The iron furnace built at Principio in 1722 operated until the 1750s. (Maryland Historical Trust)

Ironworks were of great interest to the Maryland General Assembly, and in 1719 it enacted legislation to assist fledgling companies such as Principio. The act cleared the way for any person desiring "to set up [a] Forging-Mill, and other Conveniencies for the carrying on such Iron-Works" simply to request from the Assembly a writ to purchase unimproved lands from private owners.[23] As a result, the Principio Company took 12,000 acres, apparently enough to guarantee a sufficient supply of iron ore and timber for charcoal to stoke the furnaces.

By 1722 construction of the Principio Company's first blast furnace had begun. Work progressed slowly, however, and when John England, a seasoned British ironmaster, arrived in 1723 to oversee the operations, he found "ye furnis which, according to they information when at London was very near Ready to blow, is but 18 inch above ye Second Cuplings."[24] He also learned that no iron deposits of continuing value had been secured for the company's use. England finished the furnace the next year, directed the construction of a forge, and located additional iron deposits along the Patapsco. In 1726 he struck an agreement with Augustine Washington to transport ore from his Accokeek, Virginia, property to Principio for smelting. A year later the company decided to erect a separate furnace at the deposit site in Virginia.

By the time England died in 1734, the Principio Company had become one of the most successful in America, producing high-quality iron that was well received on the London market. William Black, visiting the complex in 1744, called it "as complete a work as any on the continent."[25] Five years later, Joshua Hempstead described the operations of the furnace:

> The furnace I suppose is 20 feet high or more & is fed with oar & Coal &c at the Top as if it were the top of a Chimney…There they bring in Horse Carts the oar the Coal & oyster Shells & there stayed two men Day & night. The top of ye Furnace is about breast high from the floor where they Stand to Tend it & yet flame Jets out continually.[26]

In the 1750s the Principio Company closed down the furnaces at Principio and Accokeek due to the expense of transporting iron ore and sufficient charcoal to these sites. The successful forge at the Principio site, as well as a second Cecil forge established at North East in 1735, continued in operation. By the eve of the Revolution, nearly 25,000 tons of pig and bar iron had issued from the company's furnaces and forges at Principio, Accokeek, Kingsbury, Lancashire, and North East.[27] Principio iron accounted for nearly half of total colonial exports. Others attempted to set up forges in Cecil County, including the Elk Forge Company, organized in 1761 along the Big Elk Creek, and John Evans, whose bar iron and nail factory and copper rolling mill also stood along the Big Elk. None, however, matched the success of Principio.

While entrepreneurial enterprises caused ripples in eighteenth century Cecil society, it was the inexorable rise in grain cultivation that brought about the most significant changes. The differences were not only in the landscape—with the emergence of large field cultivation, bank barns, and attendant milling industries—but in the labor force as well.

The wheat farmer had no need for the continuing presence of the large numbers of field hands that dominated tobacco culture, hands employed throughout the year in seeding, transplanting, topping, suckering, spearing, stripping, and prizing. In contrast, wheat was only labor-intensive during the harvest season, when a full crew was needed to cradle, shock, thresh, and winnow the grain. For the wheat farmer to provide for large numbers of laborers during the growing season would have been an inordinate economic drain. For them, it was more expedient to hire only during harvest. As a result, Cecil's dependence on slave labor declined in the last half of the eighteenth century, and its white population increased accordingly. By the end of the century, Cecil had the largest white population of any Eastern Shore county. The county slave population, however, did not disappear overnight. By the 1790s, 24 percent of the population remained enslaved, with less than 2 percent free black. Although significant, the numbers were well below those of Eastern Shore neighbors—Kent, Queen Anne's, and Somerset were each more than 40 percent enslaved—and nowhere near the percentages found throughout Southern Maryland—with Prince George's, Charles, and Calvert nearly 50 percent enslaved.[28]

Poised between the two classes in eighteenth century Cecil was a variable group of laborers, neither landed nor enslaved, who broadly fell under the heading of tenancy. Tenancy in Cecil, as elsewhere around the Chesapeake, rose with the increasing predominance of wheat culture, with its need for a temporary class of workers, but it was by no means restricted to grain cultivation. From the earliest days of settlement, particularly during the doldrums of the tobacco market, many planters found they could do as well with tobacco raised by tenants and paid as rent as with tobacco raised by their own servants. Overall, long-term leases held a real advantage for the larger landowner; the tenant was often obligated to make certain improvements, clearing so many acres, planting orchards, and fencing fields. When the lease expired, the landowner could bring the acreage into cultivation himself, without incurring any of the labor or expense of clearing it.

Tenancy always held out to the tenants the promise of establishing a foothold in the county, eventually becoming landed themselves. Indeed, in the 1750s and even later some of the better land in Cecil had yet to be patented. As late as

the 1780s it was still possible for a man to take a land warrant and certificate of survey to Annapolis and obtain title to twenty acres of farmland. Yet the mere presence of untilled or unpatented land in no way suggested land was available to every man in the county. Patents for new lands most commonly went to the owners of neighboring tracts, since the land was often of value only as an adjunct to an existing plantation. Patents issued to previously landless tenants became exceedingly rare as the eighteenth century progressed; if land had been so easily had, at such a low price, it would not have been profitable for landowners to continue to lease farms. Moreover, the continuing presence of large tracts held by speculators worked to keep land out of the reach of the ordinary man. The opportunities that seemed so ripe at the opening of the century became increasingly limited as the years progressed.

But whether tobacco planter in the south, wheat farmer in the north, or tenant in between, most who moved from longer settled regions into the hinterlands of Cecil County had to be satisfied, of necessity, with bare subsis-

Those planters who rose to the top of the economic scale in 18th century Cecil County often served also as merchants, marketing their neighbors' crops as well as their own and purchasing goods from England and the Caribbean for their own use and to trade with others. These men used their profits to build houses such as Bohemia, built at midcentury by George Milligan, to exhibit their wealth and status. (1970, Maryland Historical Trust)

tence when it came to improvements. Indeed, most who took up new plantations in Cecil, from the late seventeenth century up to the time of the Revolution, were in essence frontier farmers, seeking through the employment of a handful of hired laborers, indentured servants, or black slaves to reach a stable agricultural existence.

The exigencies of building shelter while establishing a new enterprise necessarily imposed a crude and hastily built quality upon all housing. But even in the most primitive of surroundings, the social, hierarchical order of landowner and tenant, master and slave, was maintained and built into the landscape. Often size or framing was the only difference between "mansion house" and tenant or slave dwelling, but it was difference enough.

In 1789 on the estate of Joshua George there stood the home of a tenant farmer, "one round log dwelling house, nineteen feet long by sixteen feet covered with oak shingles in bad repair."[29] At the same time, on the Etherington estate, there was "one negro quarter hew'd poplar logs eighteen and a half by sixteen in very bad repair."[30] The descriptions of tenant house and slave quarter seem interchangeable; often they were. Nonetheless, there are significant differences in the comparison, not in the buildings themselves but in the relationship between building and inhabitant.

Many tenants could select the type, style, and location of the house themselves; most slaves had the one-room log house thrust upon them, with little choice in the matter. Most important is the difference in mobility. Tenants were free to abandon their housing conditions; they could eventually move up from the one-room log house to a larger, two-story structure. The slave, on the other hand, was tied to his condition, to his little log house, in perpetuity. Encapsulated in that quarter was the basic concern of slavery: to create a static laboring class unable to move up the social ladder and therefore unable to pose a political or economic threat to the dominant position the planter class held in Maryland society.

For the landed class, as the century progressed and the county moved from frontier subsistence to agricultural stability, there was an accompanying improvement in housing. Of course, not everyone felt compelled to improve either his own house or that of his servants once the plantation had begun producing a stable income. Even after economy was no longer necessary, many families who had grown accustomed to the old ways of housing continued them.

For some southern Cecil planters, however, life on the plantation by the 1750s was changing from one of limited conveniences to one of relative comfort. At the beginning of the century their holdings may have been comparatively small, their servants few, their houses simple and unassuming. Yet, as their knowledge of agriculture grew, their ability to master the intricacies of the market became more complete, their profits increased accordingly, and their houses grew larger and more nearly complete.

Much of the charm of the "manor houses" of Cecil can be attributed to their location and setting. As is true of Bohemia, the mid-eighteenth century Milligan home along the Bohemia River, the "Big House" was located on an elevation above the river, from which it commanded a view of the plantation wharf. Between house and river was an expanse of ground, framed by hardwoods, that imparted a feeling of spaciousness and dignity to the estate that was largely missing from landlocked northern county homes. The houses themselves exuded solidness: thick masonry piles, brick in the south, stone to the west, two rooms deep, accentuated by projecting courses and well-framed openings. Near the main house stood the several outbuildings housing the household servants and the summer kitchen, dairy, laundry, and other services enjoyed by well-to-do planters of the time.

Although in many ways the mature architectural

John Churchman (1705-75) was an elder of East Nottingham (called Brick) Meeting by the time he was 26. He built a stylish, expensive brick house—a rather strong statement for a Quaker leader—on one of the Nottingham Lots in 1745. (Maryland Historical Trust)

expressions of the tidewater planters seem vastly different from those encountered in Cecil's northern communities, in many respects they were alike. The later homes of the Nottingham Quakers similarly expressed the growth and development of a mature agricultural community. Life among the Friends may have originally been guided by a strict moral code reflected in a certain plainness of dress, manner, and architecture. Yet by the mid-eighteenth century a subtle transformation of the Quaker spirit had occurred, a change the more cynical among the congregation noted as a shift in concern from the meetinghouse to the countinghouse. As one aged Quaker minister in Philadelphia lamented in 1764, in the early days of the community

> Friends were a plain lowly minded people and that there was much tenderness and Contrition in their meetings and That at the end of twenty years from that time the society increasing in wealth and in some degree conforming to the fashions of the World, true Humility decreased and their meetings in general were not so lively and Edifying That at the end of Forty years many of the Society were grown rich, that wearing of fine costly Garments and with fashionable furniture, silver watches became customary with many and with their sons and daughters. And as these things prevailed in the Society and appeared in our Meetings of Ministers and Elders; so the powerful overshadowings of the Holy Spirit were less manifested amongst us....[31]

The meetinghouse itself may have retained the original humble spirit that infused the community. When the Brick Meeting House at Nottingham was enlarged in 1752, the stone addition mirrored the earlier block, and when the meetinghouse burned in 1810 it was rebuilt inside the original walls. But the homes of the Quakers became sumptuous reflections of their growing preoccupation with the temporal side of life, none perhaps more so than the house of the minister himself, John Churchman. His substantial brick home fairly drips with Georgian excess: glittering glazed headers, molded water table, projecting pent roof wrapping from front to gable end, boldly underlining the date "1745" marked out in dark headers. Inside were the finest of paneled interiors; thus did the minister instruct the meeting in the ways of the world.

Such pretensions, however, were for the privileged few. The overall social order of eighteenth century Cecil County remained a conservative one, unmoved by any great leveling forces that may have been shortening the distances between classes in New England on the eve of the Revolution. In Cecil, as throughout Maryland, the chasms still yawned wide and unbridged long after the struggle for national independence was over.

A town stood on the site of Frenchtown from the 17th century through the 19th. Originally named Thompsontown or Transtown, in the 18th and early 19th centuries the town was a busy port serving as a transfer point on the trade route between Philadelphia and Baltimore. The first steamboat on Chesapeake Bay, the *Chesapeake*, sailed on her maiden voyage from Baltimore to Frenchtown, where goods were loaded for overland travel to New Castle, Delaware. The town went into decline in the mid-19th century, when it was bypassed by the main railroad lines. (1806, Benjamin H. Latrobe, "Rough Sketch of French town…," Sketchbook IX-3, Maryland Historical Society)

CHAPTER 4

"An Excellent Situation" for Manufacturer and Farmer Alike

CECIL'S location on the main route between Pennsylvania and Virginia guaranteed the county its share of troop activity during the war for independence. In August 1777 British General William Howe sailed into the bay with a fleet of 300 war vessels, throwing the Maryland tidewater into a frenzied panic. The fleet first hove to off the mouth of the Patapsco, but then proceeded to the head of the bay. Cecil County was not its final destination, however. Philadelphia was the target, and an overland route the plan of attack. General Howe did, however, leave some soldiers behind in Cecil County to keep communication open with the fleet in the bay.

Disembarking several miles south of Head of Elk, two brigades of British soldiers marched through the county with little resistance, although their movement did not go undetected by the American commanders. From the top of Gray's Hill above the Elk, George Washington watched intently as the red-coated columns headed north. The British are said to have burned a number of buildings along the way, including a grain warehouse in Elkton, and damaged the ironworks at Elk Forge. A contingent, crossing at Courthouse Point, reportedly removed some court records but left the courthouse intact. Despite desperate fighting by Washington's troops at Brandywine Creek near Chadds Ford, Pennsylvania, by September Howe had crossed the Schuylkill and taken Philadelphia. One last effort by Washington to dislodge the British troops from their Germantown encampment proved fatal, and the Americans retreated ingloriously to Valley Forge. During the brutal winter of 1777-78 many sick and dying soldiers were transported to Nottingham, either for treatment or burial, and the Brick Meeting House was pressed into service as a hospital.

In 1781 Cecil again was overrun with soldiers, as the combined troops of Washington, Lafayette, and the Comte de Rochambeau marched through the county en route to Yorktown and eventual victory. Heavy artillery and baggage wagons crossed the Susquehanna at Bald Friar. Rochambeau's aide-de-camp, Baron von Clausen, cursed the ford as "diabolique" due to the slippery rocks and potholes that disabled many a horse and wagon as they crossed.[1]

A generation later British troops returned to Cecil County during "Mr. Madison's war," the War of 1812. In April 1813 a squadron of small vessels under the command of Rear Admiral George Cockburn appeared at the head of the bay, armed with orders to cut off the enemy's supplies and destroy any foundries, stores, and public works aiding the American war effort. In particular, they were directed to proceed to Frenchtown on the Elk, which informants had reported was an important depot for military stores.

Since 1806 Frenchtown had been a transfer point on the packet route between New Castle and Baltimore. Accordingly, on the evening of April 18, 1813, Cockburn moved his squadron into the Elk as far as the ships' drafts allowed. Under cover of night, lighter boats carried 150 marines and five artillerymen from the fleet toward their target. Navigating through unknown waters in the dark, the British mistakenly entered the Bohemia River instead of staying in the Elk, and the boats did not reach Frenchtown until late the following morning. The delay allowed alarmed citizens along the Elk to make hasty defensive arrangements.

By the time the British reached Frenchtown, a six-gun battery had been thrown up along the bank, and heavy fire was opened from shore as soon as the boats came within range. British shipboard artillery returned the fire as the marines streamed ashore. The stunned American militia fled from the battery to the adjoining woods; a second group of defenders, made up largely of stage drivers, momentarily

held the advancing marines at bay but were also repulsed. The British troops set fire to the warehouses, the wharf, and five vessels lying at anchor and destroyed the guns of the battery. The casualties were one British seaman, wounded in the arm by grapeshot, and one American, killed by a rocket.

The British continued up the river, making for Elkton. Accurate fire from the guns at Fort Defiance, a heavy chain across the river, and an earthen battery erected at Elk Neck turned them away. The British then attempted to approach the town from the opposite side of the river, blundering into Fort Hollingsworth, where they were again repulsed. Elkton, however, was merely a side excursion for the British; their main objective, the military supplies at Frenchtown, had been successfully reduced to ashes.

Admiral Cockburn next turned his attention to the Sassafras River. On the night of May 5, a party of British marines and artillerymen again embarked in light boats, proceeding upriver toward Georgetown and Fredericktown. They had arrived within a mile of the town, closing ranks to sail between two projecting points, when heavy fire was opened from field pieces and 300 American militia entrenched on either side of the river. Again the fire was returned; again the defenders beat a hasty retreat, this time before the fixed bayonets of the British marines. In retribution for the audacious American attack, the British burned nearly every building in the two towns, sparing only those "whose owners had continued peaceably in them, and had taken no part in the attack."[2]

By now every community in Cecil County feared similar treatment at the hands of marauding British marines. Contemplating the fate of Fredericktown, the citizens of Charlestown sent a peace party out to greet Cockburn as his fleet lay in the Sassafras, "to assure the rear-admiral that the place was considered at his mercy."[3] After an unopposed landing, the British destroyed the cannon factory at Principio. Satisfied that Cecil was sufficiently subdued for the moment, Cockburn gave the order to weigh anchor, and his light squadron retired from the head of the bay.

(right) One of the first steamboats to ply the waters of the Chesapeake was the *Eagle*, built in Philadelphia in 1813. It served the Elkton Line for several years beginning in 1815, leaving Baltimore for Elkton at 4 pm on Tuesday, Thursday, and Sunday. Passengers took a stage from Elkton to Wilmington, where they caught another ship to Philadelphia. (Eldredge Collection, The Mariners' Museum)

(left) This large brick house at Frenchtown landing was built circa 1800 as an inn. It survived the attack of the British in the War of 1812 but was destroyed by fire in the 1960s. It is visible in the sketch of Frenchtown by Benjamin Latrobe on page 56. (1930s, Writers Project Administration Collection, Maryland State Archives, MSA SC 908-570)

On June 21, 1813, barely two months after the British marines had burned the public stores at Frenchtown, the first commercial steamer to ply the bay pulled up to the reconstructed wharves along the Elk; the steamboat *Chesapeake* had arrived in Cecil County on its maiden voyage out of Baltimore. Since 1806 regularly scheduled sloops had carried the products of Cecil industry from the Frenchtown depot to the burgeoning warehouses of Baltimore. The age of steam travel advanced these market connections, and in the wake of the side-mounted paddle wheeler came a golden period in Cecil economic life.

In many ways the turn of the nineteenth century marks the beginning of modern Cecil culture. Many practices emerged from this period that were to have a lasting effect on the technological, agricultural, and social manifestations of Cecil life through the early twentieth century. Three-cornered cocked hats, embroidered coats, sack-backed dresses with stomachers, and wigs belonged to the older generation. In with the new century came long trousers, round-brim hats, simple chemise dresses, flat soles, and powder-free hair, the essential elements of modern dress.

Until the first decades of the nineteenth century, Cecil progressed slowly in the adaptation of technology to work and home life. Since the arrival of the first settlers in the county, homes had been heated by fireplaces and illuminated by candles. The land had been tilled with the crudest of tools and the crops harvested with centuries-old methods and implements. Cloth had been woven on hand looms, and metals forged on the anvil. Travel by horse or foot continued to be the most common means of road transportation at the end of the eighteenth century.

An Outline History of Turkey Point Light

The beacon at Turkey Point light tower still shines from Turkey Point, now in Elk Neck State Park. The keeper's house and other buildings were torn down after World War II. (c. 1942, J. Frank Holt Collection, Historical Society of Cecil County)

The lighthouse at Turkey Point in Cecil County has guided local fishing boats and ships traveling to and from the C & D Canal for more than 160 years.

1831 Congress authorized construction of a lighthouse on Turkey Point at the mouth of Elk River.

1832 The Lighthouse Board purchased a site from John B. and Juliana Paca in December.

1833 John Donahoo completed the lighthouse and keeper's quarters in July 1833. The brick tower had an interior stairway of wood to reach the lantern. The brick house was one and a half stories and had an attached kitchen. James Geddes supplied and installed the lighting system, a lantern consisting of eleven lamps, each with a reflector. In August Robert Lusby, the first keeper, began operating the light.

1844 As often happened when a married keeper died, Elizabeth Lusby was appointed keeper of Turkey Point light after the death of her husband. She served until her own death in 1861.

1855 A newfangled Fresnel lens was installed in the old-style lantern at Turkey Point as part of a program to upgrade the lanterns of all the lighthouses on the Chesapeake. The Fresnel gave a brighter, more reliable light than that provided by the smaller, less durable Argand lamps used previously.

1867 A new lantern, better able to accommodate the Fresnel lens, was finally installed at Turkey Point.

1888 The addition of a fog bell increased the services of Turkey Point light.

Fannie Salter, keeper of Turkey Point light from 1925 until 1947, was the last female lighthouse keeper on the Chesapeake. (c. 1942, J. Frank Holt Collection, Historical Society of Cecil County)

1889 The keeper's house received a second, board-and-batten story, and a porch added across the front.

1925 Mrs. C. W. Salter took charge of the light after the death of her husband.

1933 The lamp in the lens was changed from an oil lamp to an incandescent oil vapor lamp.

1942 Turkey Point light station was converted to electricity.

1947 Mrs. Salter retired, after which the light was automated and the house and outbuildings torn down. Now on state park property, the lighthouse continues to guide vessels safely around Turkey Point.

Information in this sidebar comes from a manuscript on the history of Maryland lighthouses by Ross Holland, Silver Spring, Maryland, 1992.

Beginning in 1800, in the short span of fifty years came a rapid series of technological innovations that profoundly affected the county's development. In that time steamboats and passenger trains began to encroach on the place of sailing vessels and stagecoaches. The regulated glow of oil lamps took the place of flickering candle flames, and by midcentury cast-iron stoves were rising before bricked-in fireplaces. Also just past midcentury, mechanical reapers and threshers removed some of the manual drudgery from farmwork; large-scale cotton and woolen mills eclipsed home industry; and rolling mills, rather than hammer forges, converted Cecil iron into bars and nails.

Under the influence of the relative peace and prosperity that followed the War of 1812, the attention of Cecil County residents increasingly became directed outward. The popular and political movement for internal improvements that swept the nation in the first half of the nineteenth century found its Cecil proponents. With market possibilities expanding along the Atlantic coast and the outlets for Cecil goods increasing accordingly, the need for an efficient transportation network was heightened. Waterborne commerce remained the mainstay of the Cecil economy, so quite naturally the attention of the business community turned first to improving and enhancing the county's waterways. As a result, those communities founded on continuing water access and adequate harbor facilities were destined to prosper in the first half of the nineteenth century.

Yet, as the contrasting fortunes of Charlestown and Elkton make readily apparent, suitable docking facilities alone were not enough to ensure a town's prosperity. At Charlestown, every possible commercial amenity had been planned and, to varying degrees, implemented. Warehouses, wharves, even a shipyard had sprouted along the banks of the North East River. The much ballyhooed arrival of the county court in 1781 to many minds presaged the coming of greater things. But natural catastrophe and demographic happenstance combined to undo the grand plans. A severe hurricane that swept up the coast in 1786 radically altered shipping lanes at the head of the bay. Havre de Grace, in neighboring Harford County, now found itself propitiously endowed with a newly cut deep water channel, thus drawing a significant portion of the shipping trade away from more northerly Charlestown. As well, the steadily

Charlestown had declined in importance by the early 19th century but still was a center of local business and trade. Taverns such as this one welcomed traveler and local alike. (Maryland Historical Trust)

increasing population in the northeastern corner of the county, directing its commerce to the Elk River landings, drew away the lifeblood of commerce on which the continued growth of Charlestown relied. By 1787 the convenience of combining trade centers with government centers had forced the removal of the county seat from Charlestown to Head of Elk, now renamed Elkton. Gone with the courts went any last hopes of a booming economy in Charlestown.

By the end of the eighteenth century Charlestown had resigned itself to the quiet life of a wayfaring town, populated by individuals catering to wagoners traveling overland from Philadelphia and Baltimore, sporting a handful of industries of local interest only—cobblers, tanners, brick makers, and the like. Indeed, the major export industry of the town depended on the continuing presence not of people but of the teeming masses of herring that made their annual run up the North East River. By the 1790s 16,000 barrels of salted herring were leaving the town docks each year, the great percentage headed for the plantations of the West Indies.[4] There the herring would be exchanged for, among other commodities, sugar cane molasses, to be brought back to the small distillery in Charlestown, converted into rum, and served as a favorite libation of the travelers who frequented the local taverns.

Charlestown was not alone in exploiting the abun-

(top) Depicted here is the "residence, fishery, and farm property of George W. Barnes, Esq., Carpenters' Point." This drawing from the 1877 Lake, Griffing, and Stevenson atlas of Cecil County demonstrates that fishing was often used as a means of boosting an income largely made in other ways. (Historical Society of Cecil County)

(bottom) Fishermen stayed in huts by the side of the river from March until June so they would lose none of the short season traveling to and from their homes. Fish were cleaned on tables in front of the huts, then salted and packed in barrels for shipment. The fishing house at Carpenter's Point shown on the far right belonged to Harry Barnes. (c. 1910, E. McMullen/Cecil Community College)

dance of fish populating county waters. In fact, the spawning frenzy of shad and herring each spring turned the Cecil shores, from the Susquehanna to the Sassafras, into a riot of fishermen all competing for what until the end of the nineteenth century was a major county commodity. From ramshackle huts hugging the shores the seasonal workers crowded the waters with nets, baskets, whatever could be used to land the fish. By the 1820s huge rafts, floated out to midstream and set with long seine nets, allowed catches in prodigious numbers. One Thomas Stump, fishing the Susquehanna near the Pennsylvania line in 1827, reportedly netted fifteen million shad in a single day, amounting to more than 100 wagonloads.[5]

In the wake of this overfishing, catches in Cecil rivers, as throughout the bay, dropped off significantly in the last half of the nineteenth century. Accompanying this was a decline in many fishing communities. Despite various attempts by private industry and the General Assembly to

Fishermen wield a net from a float in the Susquehanna River during spawning season. These rafts, first employed by Cecil fishermen during the 1820s, remained in use into the 20th century. The huge numbers of fish caught by this and other methods vastly reduced the population of herring, perch, sunfish, catfish, shad, rockfish, carp, and pike in the upper bay, severely damaging the local fishing industry. (c. 1905, Historical Society of Cecil County)

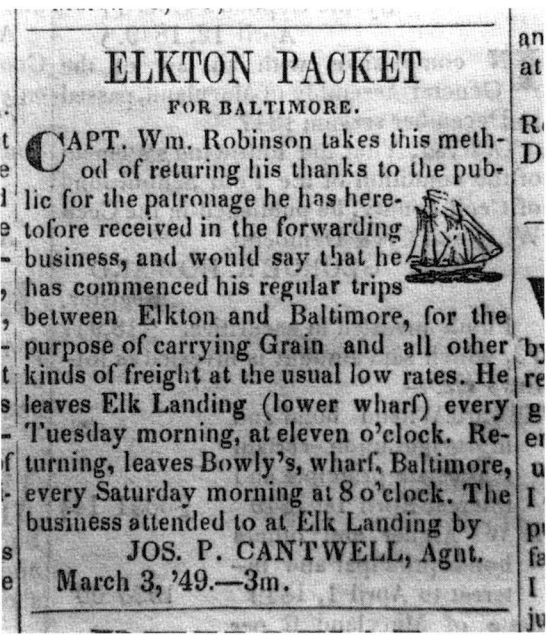

Water trade between Elkton and Baltimore was brisk during the first half of the 19th century. The packet advertised in this piece carried in the May 12, 1849, edition of the *Cecil Democrat and Farmer's Journal* was one of many ships that carried goods and passengers between Elkton and Baltimore. (Historical Society of Cecil County)

control the ravages of overfishing, the shad and herring populations continued to decrease.

Even in bountiful years, the seasonal nature of the Cecil fishing industry imposed a rough-hewn quality on many fishing villages. The small huts thrown up to house the temporary workers gave the enclaves "every aspect of poverty and ruin," as James Kent described the fishing village of Charlestown in 1793.[6] Meanwhile, in those communities where more stable year-round industries arose, the appearance of the town reflected the solid economic foundation of its commerce.

By the early decades of the nineteenth century, Elkton in particular had surrounded itself with a number of manufacturing concerns that took the raw materials spilling out of the countryside and transformed them into marketable products. Because of the early diversity of Elkton's enterprises, its fortunes were not heavily tied to the fluctuations of one particular product, in direct contrast to the tobacco-dependent communities of the eighteenth century and the herring-based markets of the nineteenth century.

Elkton harbor at the head of the tidal Elk River's navigable waters gave rise to the town's market importance. At the turn of the nineteenth century it had been called "one of the greatest wheat markets in America," with an estimated 150,000 bushels of that crop sold out of its granaries each year.[7] Although the phenomenal growth of Baltimore as an international port cut into Elkton's share of the wheat trade, other industries were simultaneously being established that gave the town a varied economic base that would assure continuing productivity. In 1807 Joseph Scott described the diverse nature of Elkton life:

> Elkton contains 120 dwellings, some of which are handsomely and well built, the public buildings are a neat court house, an academy and market house, in which markets are held every Tuesday and Saturday and fairs four times a year, viz. April, June, October, and December, for the sale of cattle, horses and all kinds of American produce and manufactures.
>
> About 1,000 castor and wool hats are annually manufactured; besides hat making, there is a number of other mechanical trades carried on. It is an excellent situation for mechanics and manufacturers, being situated on a navigable river…

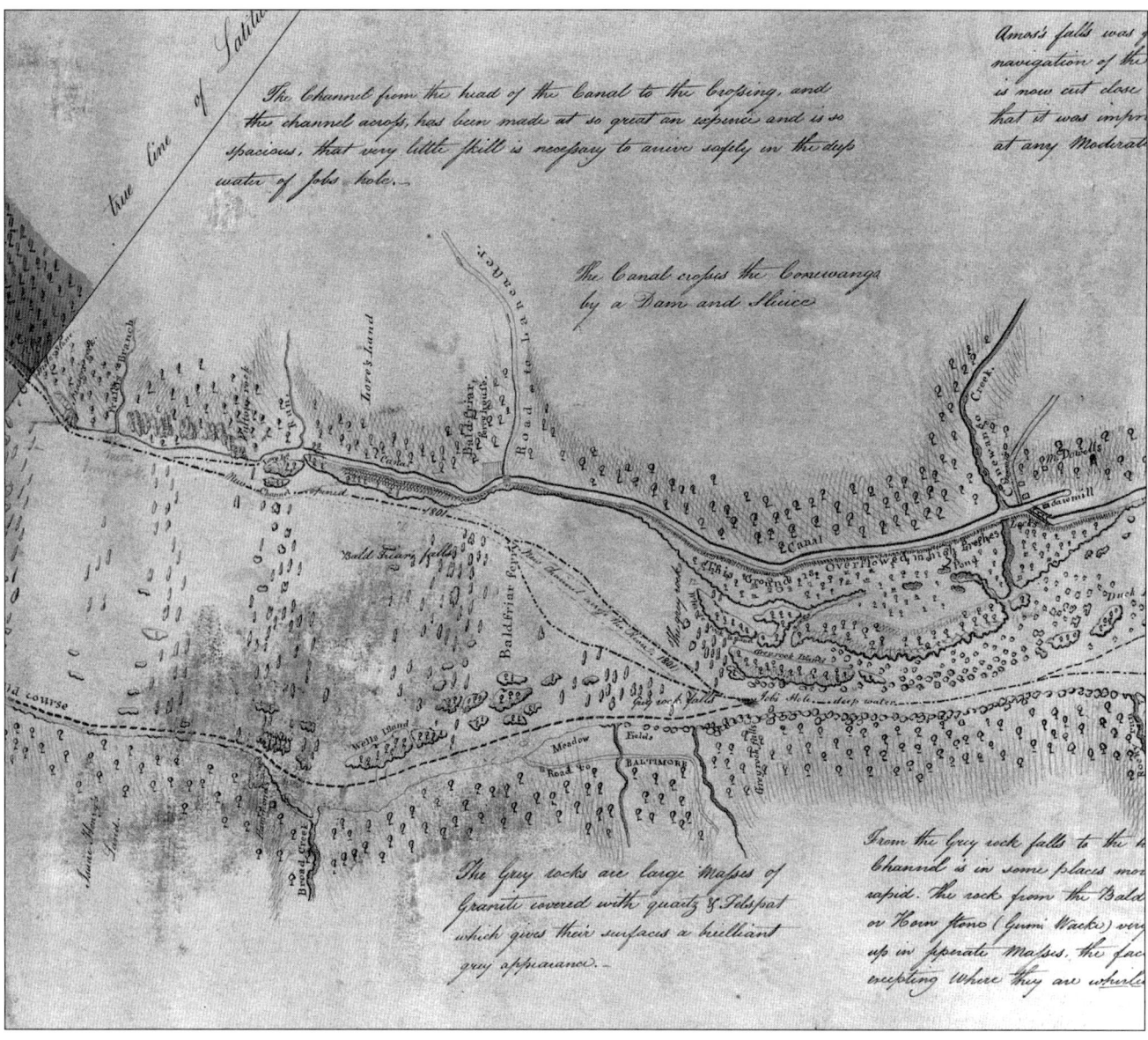

besides having in its vicinity several furnaces, forges, and a great many grist and saw mills, and at the distance of about three miles, a large woolen factory.[8]

The liveliness of the trade in early nineteenth century Elkton is given voice in the account books of the Hollingsworths, a family whose business acumen was intricately linked to the town's rise to preeminence. These records show their boats departing from Elk Landing loaded with Cecil flour, nails, bar iron, lumber, pork, and other supplies and carrying them down the bay to Baltimore, from whence they returned with coal, molasses, coffee, whiskey, and other items.[9]

The connection between a town's commercial prosperity and its water access led to the first attempt at river enhancement in the county, the Susquehanna Canal. Chartered by the State of Maryland in 1783—the first canal charter of its kind issued in the United States—the project was intended to broaden the navigability of the Susquehanna River. The idea was to cut a channel around the treacherous falls that had stymied ships since Captain John Smith first lost his grapnel on the rocks in 1608. Construction of the canal, however, was neither swift nor sure. To begin with, the northern terminus never extended beyond the Maryland border; Pennsylvania authorities, naturally protective of native commerce and hesitant to fund a feature that would obviously siphon products away from

The Susquehanna Canal was conceived as a way of improving transportation along the Susquehanna River. Benjamin H. Latrobe took charge of the Pennsylvania portion of the canal, working in conjunction with Sebastian Shade and Christian Hauducoeur in Maryland. This portion of a diagram of the river below the Pennsylvania border, executed by Latrobe, clearly shows the location of the ford and ferry at Bald Friar, as well as that of the planned canal. (detail of 1801-02, Benjamin H. Latrobe, "Susquehanna River Survey Map," Maryland Historical Society)

Philadelphia, refused to charter the extension of a canal into their territory. As an alternative, the Pennsylvania legislature in 1799 entered into a cooperative agreement with the Susquehanna Canal Company for the simple improvement of navigation along the lower portion of the river in both states.

Eventually, noted architect and engineer Benjamin Henry Latrobe assumed supervision of the Pennsylvania section of the project. He worked in conjunction with the Susquehanna Canal Company engineer, Sebastian Shade, and his assistant, Christian P. Hauducoeur, to survey and plan the clearance of major obstacles along the lower portion of the river. By 1802 most of the more manageable ones had been removed, allowing safe downstream travel for low-draft vessels during the spring freshets. Construction of the canal itself, however, limped along.

Twenty years after it had begun, construction along the canal route, running in its entirety from a point near Luff's Island south to the highest point of navigation just below Smith's Falls near Creswell's Ferry, had yet to be completed. Few things seemed to go as planned, and those that did turned out wrong. Not only was the canal shorter than originally intended, but once it was opened to traffic in 1805 it was discovered the engineers had designed a canal that was narrower than practicable. The width of both the ditch and the locks prohibited passage of the larger barges, eliminating its usefulness for transporting greater amounts of grain and produce. Five years later the canal was widened, but its effectiveness as a mode of transportation never matched its builders' expectations.

In the end, waste and bad management prevented the canal project from getting anywhere. As Hezekiah Niles, editor of the *Baltimore Evening Post* commented, "More money than water is being poured into the Port Deposit Canal."[10] As the promoters became less and less willing to invest money in the canal, progress came to a halt, and in 1817 the undertaking finally collapsed. The wisdom in conceiving the project, however, was borne out twenty years later, with the success of the Susquehanna and Tidewater Canal on the west side of the river, in Harford County, in operation after 1839.

Regardless of its efficiency as an improved means of transportation, the construction of the canal, along with the clearing of the Susquehanna, did spur along one development of lasting importance to the county: the founding of a new town. In 1812 Philip Thomas, owner of most of the land near the southern terminus of the canal, gridded a stretch of property precariously perched between the riverbank and the granite precipice jutting above it. The following year the community was officially christened "Port Deposit," in anticipation of its eventual livelihood. Unlike the traditional pattern of other canal-oriented communities up and down the East Coast, Port Deposit was not an overnight boomtown. The community's importance as a port of deposit was still too inconsequential to attract the attention of the invading British in 1813, who bypassed the newly named town in favor of burning a warehouse across the river.

Within the span of a quarter century, however, Port Deposit matched its founder's vision, rising to a place of prominence among Cecil towns, even rivaling the county seat for the vitality and diversity of its commerce and population. Contributing significantly to the market importance of the town was the construction in 1816-17 of the first in a series of bridges crossing the Susquehanna near Port Deposit. This impressive piece of engineering provided wagoners and cattle drovers with a welcome alternative to the ferries it replaced. The bridge was rebuilt after a fire in 1829, and again in 1854 following destruction by a particularly unruly mob of cattle.

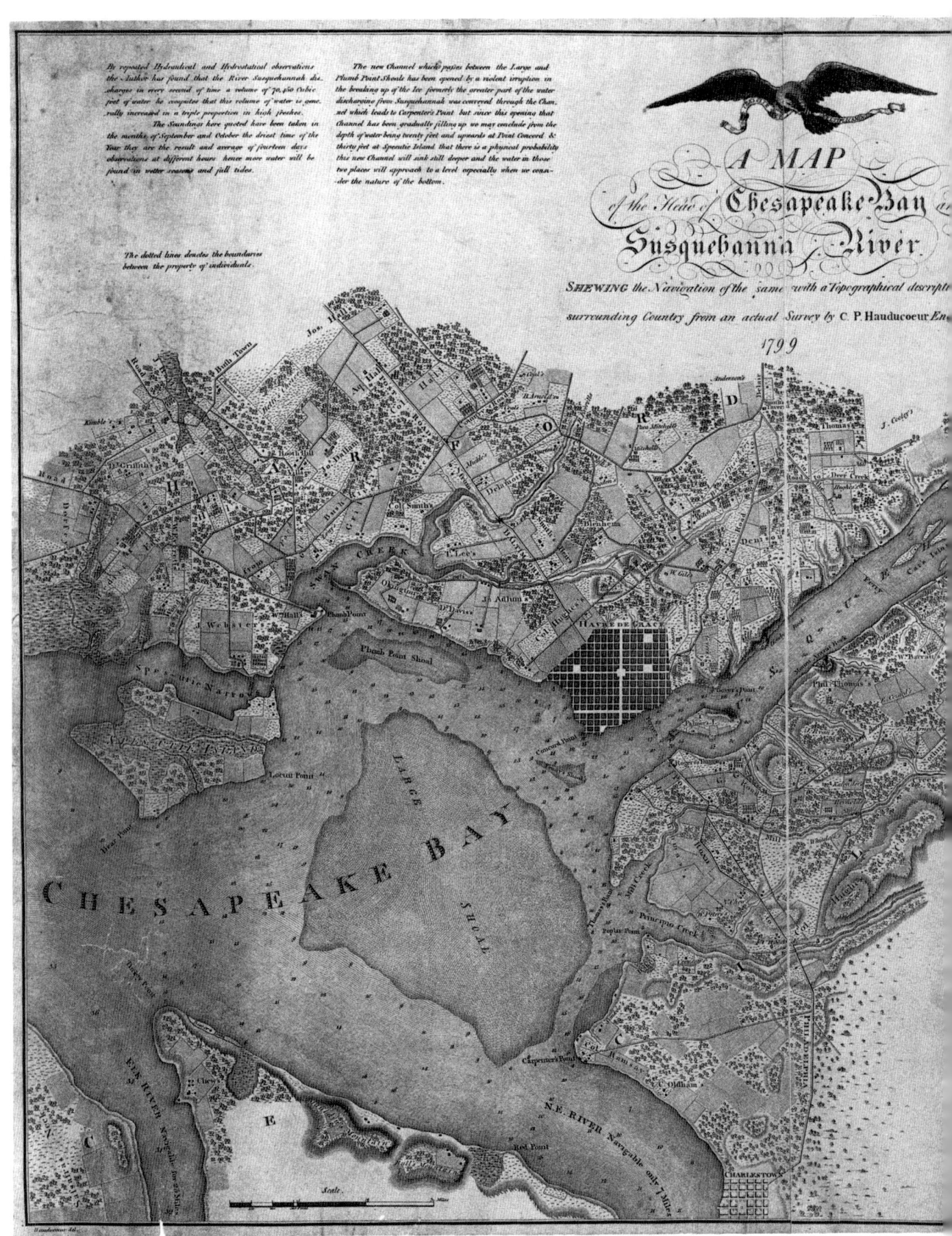

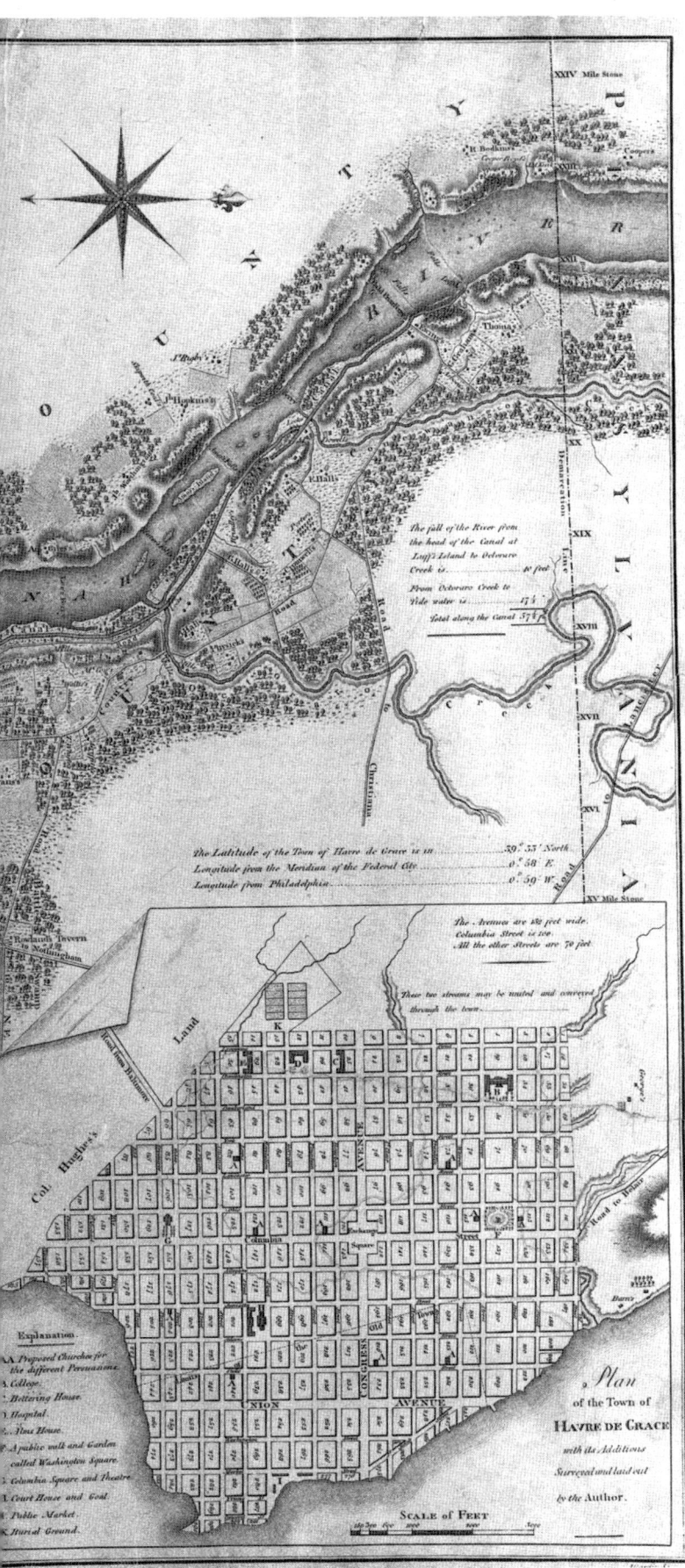

Christian P. Hauducoeur, assistant to the engineer responsible for the Maryland portion of the Susquehanna Canal, mapped the geographical features along the shores of the river. His map is one of very few that show land use at this time. It also shows the location of the canal, which ultimately was completed on the west bank of the river, in Harford County. (1799, Hauducoeur, *Map of the Head of Chesapeake Bay and Susquehanna River*, Maryland Historical Society)

In 1822 nearly $1.5 million worth of materials and commodities passed through Port Deposit. Great wooden rafts, lashed together in arrangements flexible enough to withstand the ripples and rapids of the river, floated downstream from the north, loaded with grain and flour, iron and slate, pork, and other products. At Port Deposit, the cargo was reloaded on ships waiting at the wharves; by the 1820s nearly 1,000 rafts and barges came down the river and canal each year, and more than 100 commercial ships entered and cleared the port annually.[11]

The raft lumber itself became an important part of local industry. Upon reaching Port Deposit, the rafts were disassembled and the floating lumber herded into private holding ponds, such as that of the Round Island Lumber Company. Here the lumber was inspected; measured; graded into common grub plank, select grub plank, or best grub plank; and marked for resale. In 1835 Round Island Lumber purchased from Hugh Fullerton one such raft, which contained raw lumber ranging in length from 25 feet to 60 feet and totaling 4,350 feet, along with a parcel of cut two-inch planks and joists.[12] Often the raft lumber bore the marks of the logs' long sojourn in the holding ponds. Many planks became encrusted with freshwater barnacles and urchins, requiring the lumber to be scrubbed and cleaned before use.

Port Deposit companies acted as wholesalers to retail lumber dealers throughout the county. For example, Bennett and Karsner, lumber merchants of Chesapeake City, ran this advertisement in 1848:

> The subscribers have just received from Port Deposit a fresh supply of lumber of every description, embracing pine boards of all quantities, one-half inch siding, pine and hemlock joists and studding, pine and cypress shingles of all lengths, hemlock fencing boards, &c., which they offer to the public on the most accommodating terms.[13]

While the lumber floating downriver from Pennsylvania and northern Cecil forests provided a steady stream of construction materials for home builders throughout the county, one of Port Deposit's own industries as well pro-

Although the location of this photograph is not known, rafts such as the one pictured played an important role in the economic life of Port Deposit. Logs shipped down the barely navigable Susquehanna were tied into rafts or made into arks to transport other goods from Pennsylvania to the Cecil County town. The rafts and arks were taken apart at Port Deposit and the logs sold to lumber merchants. Barnacle-encrusted boards found in one Cecil County house stand testament to this trade. (Marie Collins/Cecil Community College)

Building at the foot of steep cliffs, the founders of Port Deposit carved a terrace from the rock above the main street to accommodate more houses. (1976, George Hipkins)

duced building material of unmatched quality. Beginning at the end of the eighteenth century, the granite deposits that extended 200 feet up from river level had been quarried sporadically, usually on a local, project-specific basis. By the early nineteenth century, however, the use and reputation of Port Deposit granite had expanded considerably and quarry operations had expanded to meet the rising demand. Joseph Scott noted in 1807, "On the sides of hills, bordering on the Susquehanna are large quarries of black and grey stones, excellent for building. Large quantities of them are sent by water to Baltimore."[14]

From an engineering standpoint, Port Deposit granite had few rivals. Among other structural uses, the stone was featured prominently in the bridge abutments of the Susquehanna River crossing of 1816-17. It was, however, the tone and texture of the stone, in combination with its lasting qualities, that made it a favorite aesthetic choice for area

(right) This sidewalk and wall demonstrate the widespread use of granite in the physical fabric of Port Deposit. (1976, George Hipkins)

(below) Local granite was used at least for basements in Port Deposit in order to protect the buildings from frequent ice gorges. When the spring thaw came, the frozen Susquehanna frequently ended up in the streets of the town. (c. 1904, Robert G. Merrick Collection, Maryland State Archives, MSA SC 1477-5799)

The local granite, well-known in the region in the 19th century, appears in profusion in the buildings of Port Deposit. (1976, George Hipkins)

house builders. The public square in Port Deposit, laid out in a hollow of the cliff dominating the town's main streetscape, soon could boast a number of houses of local stone rising in sculptured echoes of the ragged cliff faces. Eventually, the cliff itself was terraced to accommodate a second row of houses. Many of the buildings rested on high stone basements, testament to the danger of spring floods and winter ice gorges that annually threatened residents.

At the same time the builders of the Susquehanna Canal were grappling with that increasingly doomed project, across the county the directors of the Chesapeake and Delaware Canal Company struggled to bring to fruition the long-imagined link between those two great bays. The man-made waterway, a scant fourteen miles long, would shorten the water route between Baltimore and Philadelphia by 296 miles. Operating under a 1799 charter from the Maryland General Assembly that was subsequently altered and agreed to by the legislatures of Pennsylvania and Delaware, the directors called upon Benjamin Latrobe to undertake the task of laying out a route.

Working intermittently in 1803 and 1804, Latrobe traversed the area between the bays, making sketches, taking notes, and searching for an appropriate route and—most important for Cecil fortunes—for a suitable deep water location for the western terminus of the canal. He finally settled

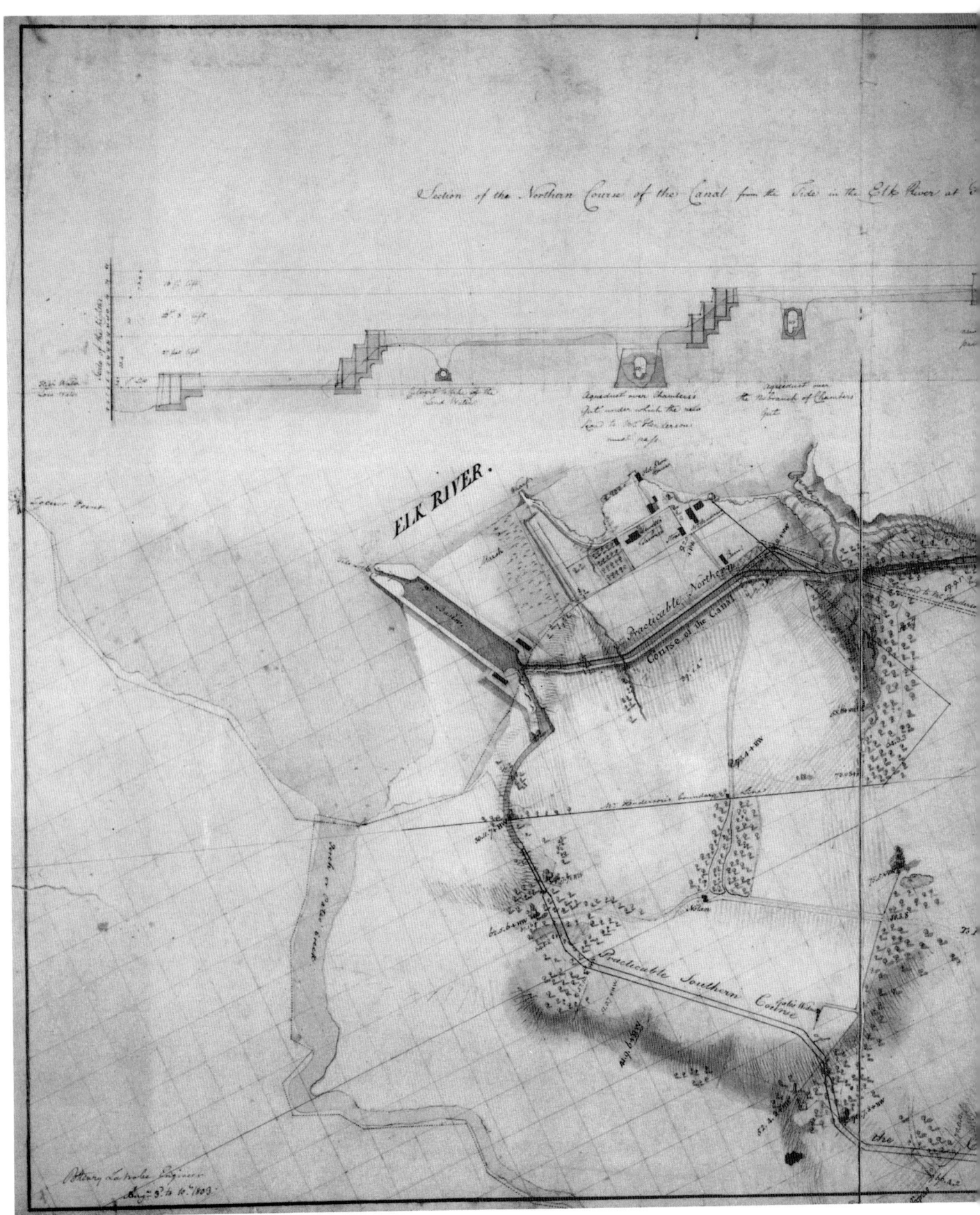

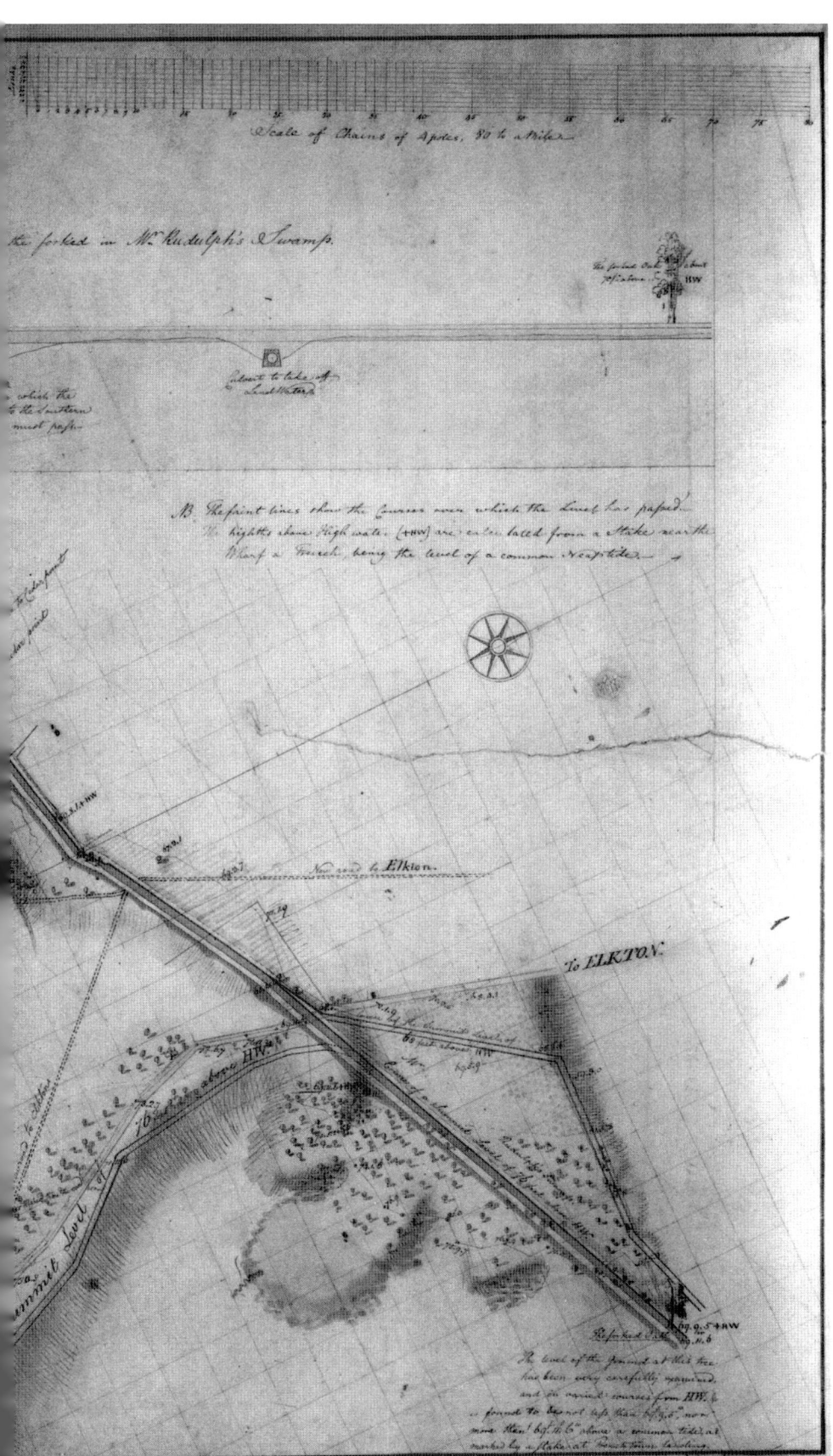

As a result of the survey work of Benjamin Latrobe and a number of others investigating a route for the C & D Canal, the canal company considered two routes for the canal—an "upper" and a "lower." Shown in this watercolor map is the western terminus of the upper route, which ran east from the Elk River at Frenchtown to Christiana, Delaware, and from thence either to the Delaware River at New Castle or into the Christina River. The lower route was shorter and ran from Back Creek in Cecil County to St. Georges Creek in Delaware. (1803, B. H. Latrobe, map showing proposed courses of the C & D Canal, Library of Congress)

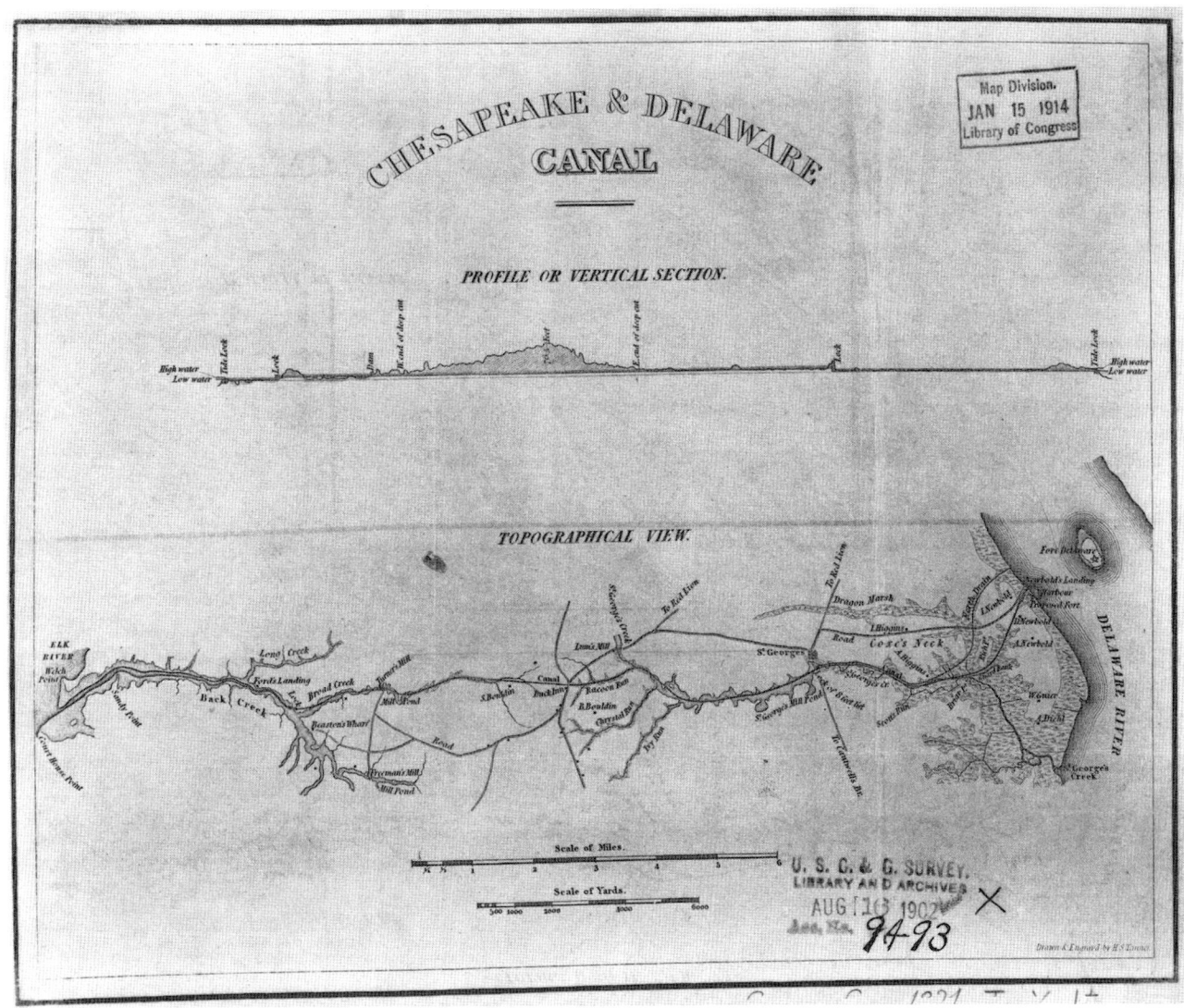

(left) The construction of a canal connecting the Chesapeake and Delaware bays was a project years in the making. Of interest to residents of both Maryland and Pennsylvania, the idea was first discussed in the 17th century and further developed in the 18th century. The canal's board of directors put Benjamin Latrobe, later chief engineer of the canal company, in charge of the survey work that would determine where the canal should be built. Latrobe recommended Welch Point, so named because of a party of Welsh settlers who died and were buried there, as a suitable entrance from the bay to the canal. These views, from the sketchbook he carried on his travels, show Welch Point from the water, both close up and from a distance. At the top is a view of Frenchtown landing.
(1806, Benjamin H. Latrobe, "View of Welch point…," 45.105.8, Maryland Historical Society)

(above) Arguments in Congress about the suitability of federal funding for regional improvement projects held up that body's financial support of the C & D Canal project. Private investors provided enough funds to restart construction in 1824, this time along the lower route, which still began in the west at Back Creek. This map shows not only the route of the canal but a section through the landscape indicating the location of locks and the deep cut needed through the center of the peninsula between the Chesapeake and Delaware bays.
(1824, Henry Schenck Tanner, map from the *Fifth General Report of the C & D Canal Co.*, Library of Congress)

The water supply for the C & D Canal as it was first built proved inadequate, particularly at the summit, and in 1848 the canal company announced a contest "for the best design of a steam pump" to move water into the canal at Chesapeake City. Construction began on the pumping station in 1851, and a second engine was added in 1854, resulting in the building shown here. (c. 1916-18 postcard, Maryland Historical Society)

on Welch Point, a narrow promontory along the Elk River that formed the north cape of Back Creek. As an aside to the copious engineering measurements recorded in his project journal, Latrobe noted the origin of the name Welch Point. It was, he wrote, reportedly "derived from the Circumstance of a Ship, in which many Welch were passengers, having landed them here while a great mortality prevailed among them, and a great number were buried at this place."[15]

Construction of a feeder canal that would carry water from the upper Elk to the C & D Canal was begun in 1804. Financial and labor difficulties stopped this work before it was completed, and despite the efforts of those who supplied capital and direction for the development of the canal—both Pennsylvanians and Marylanders—construction along the approved route languished until 1824. The year before, enough subscriptions to the canal company had been sold to fund construction anew. This success led to a much needed infusion of working capital from the federal government, when in 1825 Congress authorized a $300,000 purchase of canal company stock, followed by a second government purchase of half the size four years later.[16]

Before construction of the canal began again, the route chosen earlier was carefully reexamined. The sites and the old survey work were studied by William Strickland, who agreed with Latrobe's conclusions as to route and the necessity of building a lock canal, and John Randel, Jr., who favored the lower route and the idea of a sea-level canal. At the request of the canal company, other civilian engineers and engineers from the army Board of Engineers studied Strickland and Randel's reports and recommended a route. The result was a lock canal built along the lower route.

Once again, the opening of a canal presaged the cre-

(opposite above) The design chosen for the Chesapeake City pumping station was offered by Philadelphia engineers Samuel V. Merrick and John H. Towne. Their plan called for a lifting or scoop wheel operated by a steam engine; it was chosen because it was cheaper to construct than the other proposals but just as efficient. A second engine was added on the other side of the wheel after construction to improve performance, and in 1856 a new, sturdier wheel was installed. The resulting facility operated with some renown, being the only one of its kind in the country, until the locks were removed from the canal in 1927. (Historic American Engineering Record, Prints & Photographs Division, Library of Congress)

(opposite below) The C & D Canal as it was first built has been described as a "meandering cut." Thirty-six feet wide and ten feet deep, it wound its way from the Delaware Bay at Delaware City to the Elk River below Chesapeake City. This view of Deep Cut in Delaware, with the bridge at Summit in the background, gives a good idea of the nature of the canal in the 19th century. (Marie Collins/Cecil Community College)

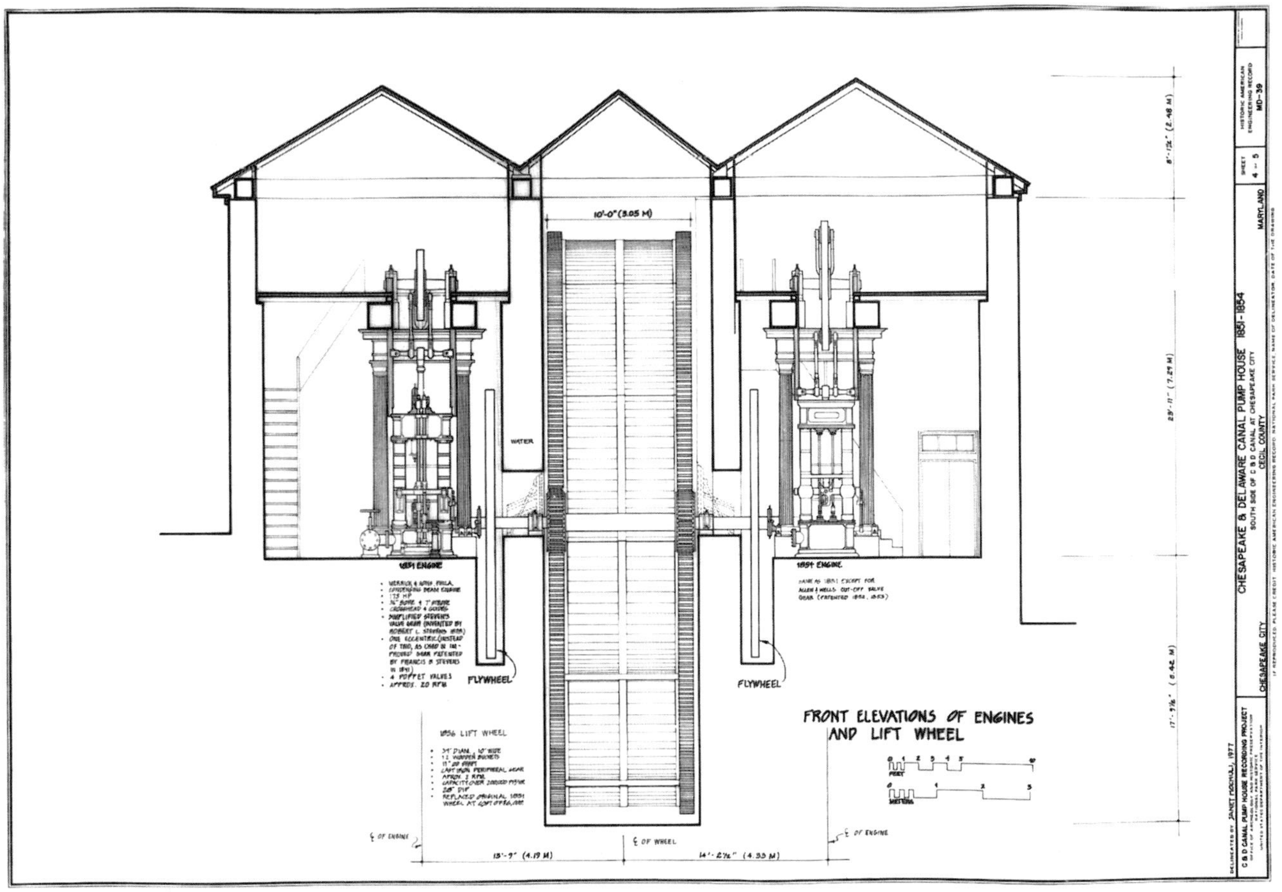
10'-0" (3.05 M)
WATER
1851 ENGINE
1854 ENGINE
FLYWHEEL
FLYWHEEL
1856 LIFT WHEEL
FRONT ELEVATIONS OF ENGINES AND LIFT WHEEL
℄ OF ENGINE
℄ OF WHEEL
℄ OF ENGINE
13'-9" (4.19 M)
14'-2½" (4.33 M)
CHESAPEAKE & DELAWARE CANAL PUMP HOUSE 1851-1854
SOUTH SIDE OF C & D CANAL AT CHESAPEAKE CITY
CHESAPEAKE CITY
CECIL COUNTY
MARYLAND
SHEET 4 - 5
HISTORIC AMERICAN ENGINEERING RECORD
MD-39
DELINEATED BY JANET MOCHUL, 1977
C & D CANAL PUMP HOUSE RECORDING PROJECT

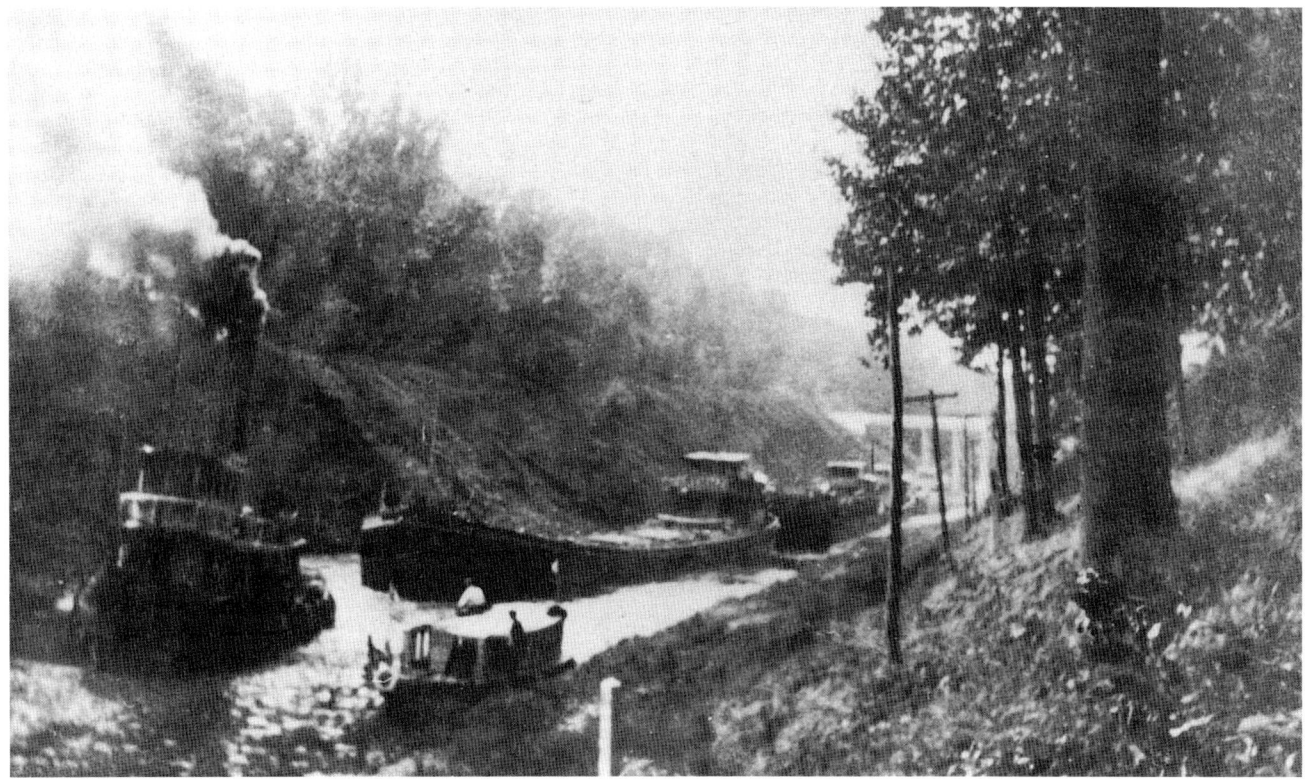

(above) The C & D Canal was ten feet above sea level, requiring locks to move boats through it. Sailboats loaded with fruit in the lock at Chesapeake City show how narrow the locks were. (1898, George Barrie, Jr., The Mariners' Museum)

(opposite above) The entrance gates to the lock at Chesapeake City opened into Back Creek. (F. R. Webb, The Mariners' Museum)

(opposite below) The functions of the buildings flanking the lock at Chesapeake City were described by Walter Cooling in 1981: the small building at the far left housed the gas engine that operated the drop gate, the building the man is leaning on housed the wheels that raised and lowered the drop gates, and the building on the far right was the waiting house with a small coal shed attached. In the lower left of the picture is a work raft, and behind the waiting house is the waste basin. The buildings in the distance belong to the Southern Transportation Company, a shipping line and employer of many Chesapeake City residents. (postcard, Marie Collins/Cecil Community College)

ation of a new Cecil town, this time the aptly named Chesapeake City. The town sprouted along the north and south banks of the canal in the years following the passage of the first ships through the locks in 1829. At the same time the first barges laden with timber, iron, and other South Jersey products were making their way through the new route to the bay, plans were afoot just north of the canal for an entirely different type of transportation system.

In 1815 the New Castle and Frenchtown Turnpike Company, first chartered in 1809, had opened their privately maintained toll road along the old overland route from New Castle on the Delaware to Frenchtown, from which packets carried goods on to other Chesapeake ports. In 1827, inspired by the technological triumphs of English engineers experimenting with new types of motive power, the company directors took a completely modern turn and incorporated themselves as the New Castle and Frenchtown Turnpike and Railroad Company. The Frenchtown Railroad was one of the earliest in the nation, and plans for it

Crossing the Creek in Early Cecil

Commerce and travel by land in Cecil County were complicated by many small creeks. Ferries were operated at many sites, particularly crossing the wide Susquehanna, but smaller waterways were sometimes spanned by bridges. In the eighteenth century these often consisted of a single timber, but as time passed and traffic increased more durable bridges were constructed. Dr. John Ricketts, one of the supervisors for North Milford Hundred, apparently contracted John Gilpin in 1794 to build a log bridge. The bill (see below) accounts each day's work, the labor involved and the pounds, shillings, and pence charged.

to 2 carts and 3 hands, 2 days halling stone,	2..7..6
to 1 team and 4 hands, 1 day halling a log 66 feet long to put over creek,	1..6..3
to 2 hands, 2 days hewing,	..15..
to 2 carts and 3 hands, 2 days halling stone,	2..7..6
to 2 carts and 5 hands, 2 days,	3..2..6
to 2 teams and 3 hands, 1 day halling stone,	1..3..9
to 1 hand, 1 day ditching,	..3..9
Total	£ 11..6..3 [a]

Often, a bridge more substantial than this log one was required to span a river or ravine. In 1806 Theodore Burr recommended the following specifications for a one-arch bridge to be built over Principio Creek:

> I evaluate [it] will cost about one thousand dollars allowing the distance of the span of the arch to be ninety feet, the arch to be built either with timber plank or boards and the ends to be filled up with stone or earth to make it easy to get on and off and to have the arches land with boards to protect them from weather.[b]

Owing to the expense of such bridges and the condition of the early roads, water travel was often easier for residents of Cecil County as well as for travelers passing through from Philadelphia to points south. Much short distance travel was accomplished in small personal boats, as evidenced in Thomas Burnside's 1836 journal:

> April 15th, this morning I got in an old boat and went to Hancis Point. The boat had like to have sunk. The wind blew hard and the waves were high, but I made it out to get across.... I returned home in the evening and the boat had nearly sunk before I noticed it. I had to make for a vessel as soon as I could cork her and bail her.[c]

In the first half of the nineteenth century railroads and steamships were added to the transportation network in Cecil County, offering residents other options for transporting goods. Nonetheless, roads remained an important network for local travel, despite the difficulties involved in keeping them up, which were not really solved until the age of the automobile.

Information in this sidebar is substantially taken from a 1981 manuscript by Paul Touart on the urban life of Cecil County.

The *Penn* was one of two "large and fast new steamers" built to serve the passenger trade through the C & D Canal in the early 20th century; the other was the *Lord Baltimore*. These two, which operated only in the summer months, and their sister ships, which also carried freight and operated all year, were especially designed to just fit through the locks on the canal, giving them an odd tall, narrow look. (Marie Collins/Cecil Community College)

were based primarily on the century-old British system of horse-powered tramways used over short distances to connect inland industrial sites with various canals and ports. Like its more famous Maryland counterpart, the Baltimore and Ohio Railroad, chartered in the same year, the Frenchtown Railroad was created as a technological response to growing concerns over protecting older market routes from increasing competition.

For Baltimore, which in 1827 numbered 80,000 people, maintenance of its western business connections was imperative to retaining its rank as the third largest city in the Union. The city's bankers had already financed the construction of a road that connected at Cumberland with the National Pike, opened to traffic as far as Wheeling, Virginia, since 1818. Now Baltimoreans were disturbed by the loss of business to the Erie Canal in New York State, completed in 1825. Fewer and fewer ships were entering the Chesapeake, while more and more coastal vessels were finding their way into New York harbor. Furthermore, Pennsylvania businessmen, undismayed by the towering altitude of the Allegheny mountains, were planning to supersede their stone-surfaced turnpike to the West with a combination canal and level-and-inclined plane railroad running between Philadelphia and Pittsburgh.

Goaded into action, leading Baltimore citizens laid plans for the organization of the Baltimore and Ohio Railroad, chartered by the Maryland legislature on February 28, 1827. Only a horse-drawn railroad was considered practicable at that date, as steam locomotives were still in the experimental stage, even in England. On January 7, 1830, travel began on the B & O, with passengers carried to the far side of the stone-arch Carrollton viaduct.

Similarly, merchants in Cecil and surrounding Delaware looked to the laying of a railroad as a way of assuring their continuing share of market products. On July 4, 1831, the Frenchtown Railroad line opened, with horses pulling cars over the wooden rails between New Castle and Frenchtown. Less than a month later, the B & O replaced all its horses with steam locomotives; a year later, the Frenchtown system unveiled its first steam locomotive. Named the *Delaware*, the locomotive got underway on September 19, 1832, pulling two cars.

With the proven success of steam-powered rail lines, discussion of further canal and river enhancement projects subsided. Soon the drive was on to link all sections of the county, state, and nation by iron rail. The connective power of railroads, both physical and psychological, was immediate and unmistakable. Nowhere in Maryland was the effect of the railroad on the community more apparent than on the Eastern Shore. There, in one of a series of determined change for goods. april 9.

Philadephia, Wilmington and Baltimore

RAIL ROAD LINE.

THE TRAINS between Philadelphia and Baltimore, will run for the present as follows:

For Baltimore.		*For Philadelphia.*	
1st train,	$10\frac{3}{4}$, A. M.	1st train,	$10\frac{3}{4}$, A. M.
2nd "	$3\frac{1}{4}$, P. M.	2nd "	$1\frac{1}{2}$, P. M.
3rd "	$10\frac{1}{2}$, nig't.	3rd "	$9\frac{3}{4}$, nig't.

☞ A regular passenger car will be attached to the through freight train for the accommodation of way passengers, to leave Wilmington for Elkton at half past 6 o'clock P. M.

BENJAMIN WELLS,
Agent.

Feb. 26.

SAFETY FLUID LAMPS.—A new article just invented, warranted not to ex-

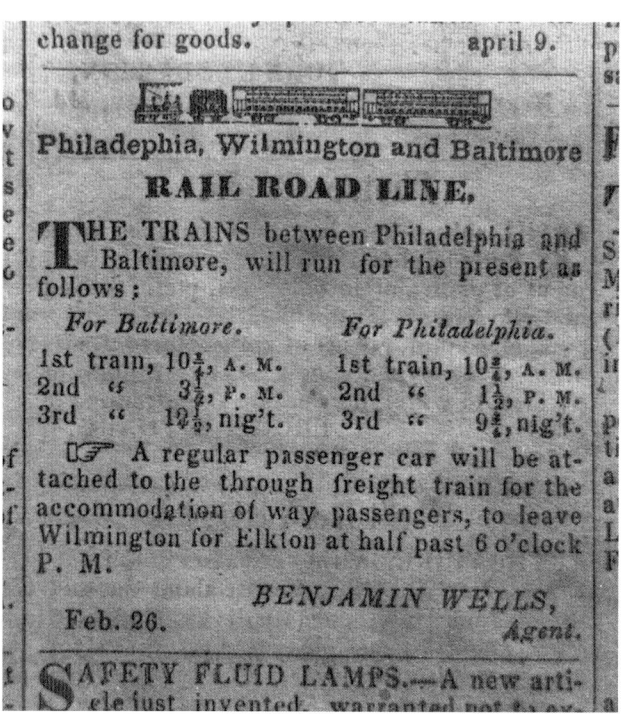

(above) Elkton became a stop along the Wilmington and Susquehanna Railroad in 1837. This line gave the town its first rail link to the Atlantic coast. (1835, Huntingfield Map Collection, Maryland State Archives, MSA G1399-658-1)

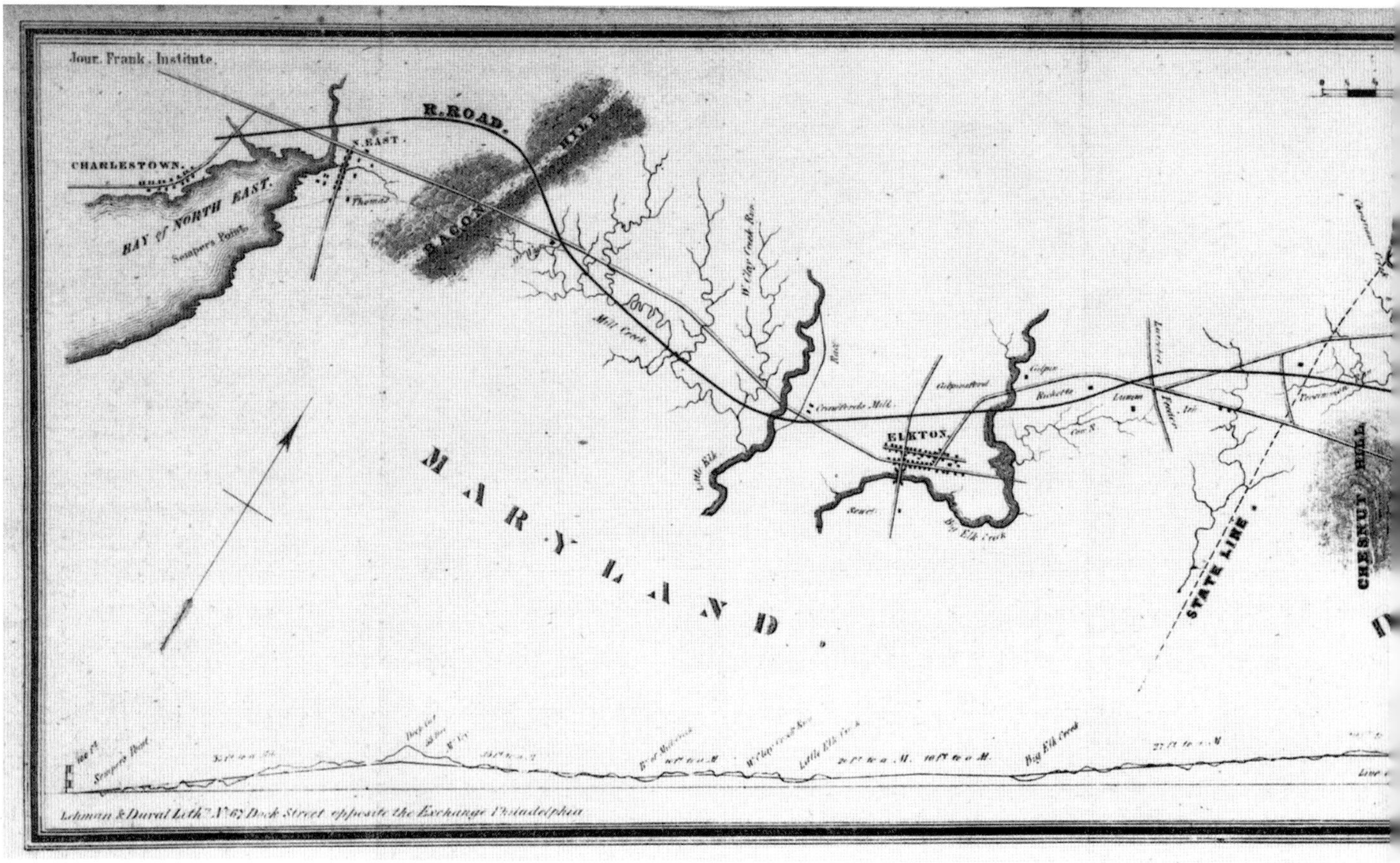

(left) The year after it reached Elkton, the Wilmington and Susquehanna was taken over by the Philadelphia, Wilmington, and Baltimore Railroad. In the June 4, 1853, edition of the *Cecil Democrat*, that company advertised three trains a day along the line. (Historical Society of Cecil County)

attempts, agitators tried to secede from the rest of Maryland and become part of Delaware or a separate state. They were headed off only with the General Assembly's appropriation of $1 million to fund a railroad between Elkton and Crisfield, thus pledging both in symbol and structure to finally link the Eastern Shore to the rest of Maryland.

The rail construction project crashed, however, in the severe economic depression that beset the nation in 1837.

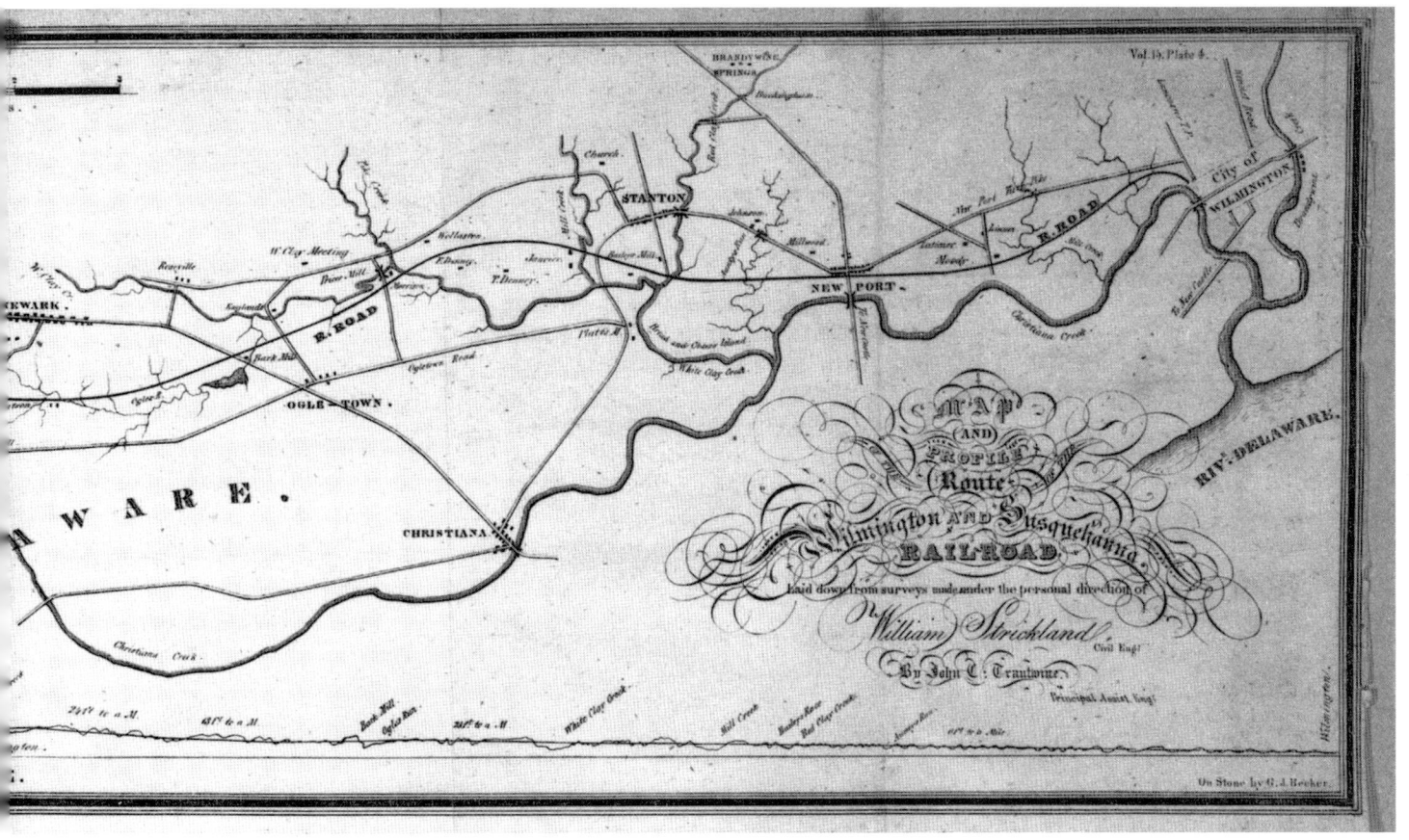

When a railroad was eventually completed in the region, it was primarily a Delaware line, with feeders linking that state to the Eastern Shore. Consequently, commerce in the area, formerly tied to the western shore by water transport across the bay, became increasingly bound to Wilmington and Philadelphia.

While Elkton's vision of itself as the commercial center of the Eastern Shore dissipated with the financial panic, it nevertheless received its rail link to the rest of the Atlantic coast. Instead of being a major terminus, though, the town found itself an intermediate point along the line. First was the Wilmington and Susquehanna Railroad, completed through the town in 1837 and ending initially at Perryville. Later came the longer Philadelphia, Wilmington, and Baltimore Railroad, which took over the shorter line in 1838. Although it brought new vigor to the Elkton economy, the new railroad spelled the end of the limited Frenchtown and New Castle line, which made its final run in 1854.

Within thirty years of the opening of the Frenchtown line, Cecil, except for the area below Elkton, was crisscrossed by rail. In 1866 the Columbia and Port Deposit Railroad opened a new line, symbolically destroying the old Susquehanna Canal in the process. By the 1870s main lines and spurs of the Baltimore and Ohio Railroad and the Philadelphia, Wilmington and Baltimore Railroad (incorporated, along with other locals, into the larger Pennsylvania Railroad in 1881) ran east and west through the heart of the county and north along the banks of the Susquehanna. Unlike the canals, which generally had only a limited effect on the development of Cecil County, the railroads led to the growth and creation of a number of communities, much to the chagrin of those bypassed by the modern methods of transportation.

The village that is now Perryville, from its eighteenth century beginnings as a stopping place for travelers crossing at the lower Susquehanna ferry, had passed quietly into the nineteenth century with little change to its river and post road orientation. The arrival of the Philadelphia branch in

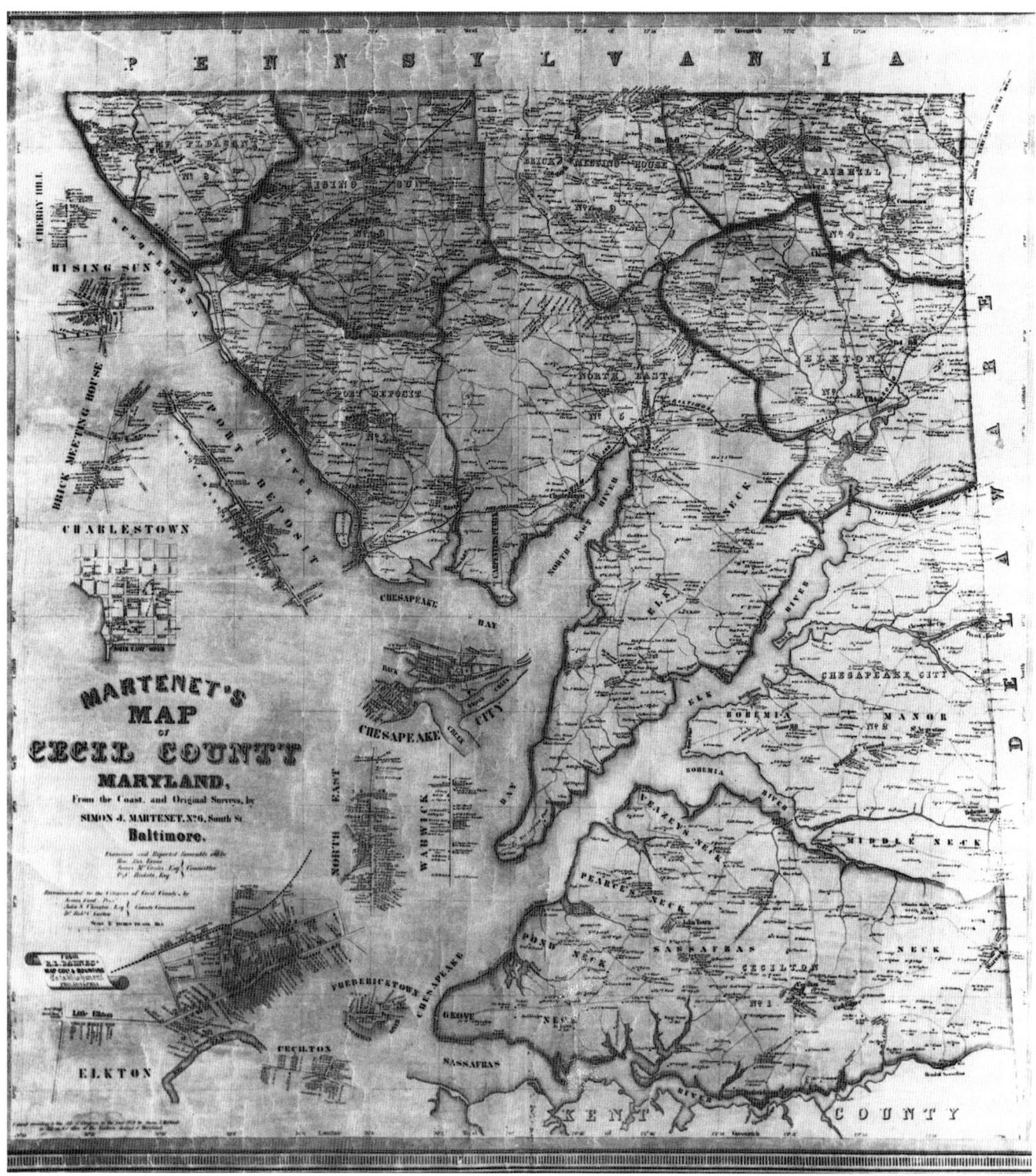

The Cecil County map published by Simon J. Martenet in 1858 shows the county crisscrossed by railroad lines. The small companies that built them frequently merged with other small lines or were absorbed by larger, regional railroads. (Cecil Community College)

In 1866 the Baltimore Central Railroad passed through Rising Sun, changing the sleepy little village to a bustling railroad town. Those towns without a direct rail link suffered during the 19th century railroad boom. (collection of William McNamee)

1837, with a steam ferry transferring railroad cars across the river, eradicated the older pace of life. Railroading now dominated town affairs; its concerns were the town's concerns. During the winter of 1852-53, when the Susquehanna froze so hard and so long the steam ferry became inoperable, all of Perryville fretted, and everyone celebrated the solution of laying the tracks across the solid ice. Fittingly, by the 1870s, the central village green at Perryville was not a quaint picture of broad store windows and white picket fences but a mosaic of sinuous tracks and burly railroad buildings.

Up north, the small hamlet of Rising Sun also found itself transformed by the railroad. Before the completion in 1867 of the Philadelphia spur connecting the Susquehanna line, the town was little more than a handful of dwellings clustered around the intersection of the post roads from Elkton to Lancaster County. The arrival of the railroad made it the commercial and social center of north central Cecil.

In contrast, other crossroads communities—including Cecilton, Brick Meeting (renamed Calvert in the 1880s), and Warwick—settled into periods of quiescence. Bypassed by the railroads, they remained dependent on the local post office commission, the loyal patronage of the farmers in the immediate vicinity, or the operations of an adjacent mill for continued vitality.

Milling remained an important industry in many Cecil communities. At the turn of the nineteenth century, fifty-three grist and merchant mills, fifty sawmills, four fulling mills, and two oil mills catered to the needs of Cecil residents.[17] The diversity of the milling enterprises in the county was noted by John Partridge, who surveyed the dif-

Milling grain and sawing boards were important industries in Cecil County from the 18th through the 19th century. A prosperous mill often spawned a small commercial center, as in the case of Jackson, which sprang up around the Jackson grist- and sawmills. (c. 1900, Mildred McGuirk/Cecil Community College)

ferent falls along the Little Elk Creek in the 1840s. He noted the existence of

> Purnell's grist mill, Hollingsworth old mill, no longer in operation, Sewall's saw mill, Mackies' grist, saw and clover mills, an old forge now owned by Mr. Robert Carter, who erected a paper mill, which we are told will be the most extensive one in the state, and which will soon be in operation; Rock Spring Mill, owned by Mr. Carter, worked by Mr. Lewis, a paper mill, the New Leeds Factory, owned by Mr. Harlon, a cotton factory; the Cecil paper mills, the homestead of the Carter's two paper mills, grist mill, saw mill; Fulton's fulling mill, now in operation; Providence Paper Mill, owned by Mrs. Hannah Meeter, a large paper mill 100 feet long 45 feet wide by four stories high; a paper mill belonging to Dr. Richard Brookings and Mr. Cristie; this is the last improved falls in Cecil County, higher in Pennsylvania there are two grist mills and a saw mill.[18]

The scores of mills operating throughout the county sustained many local economies, in some instances provid-

This steam sawmill and lumberyard in Chesapeake City, owned by H. Burgett, was illustrated in the 1877 Lake, Griffing, and Stevenson atlas of the county. (Historical Society of Cecil County)

ing the impetus for the creation of villages. These towns ranged in size and importance from small crossroad mill villages such as Liberty Grove and Bohemia Mills to the larger industrial-based Rowlandsville, the nucleus of which was formed by an iron rolling mill and a merchant mill at the crossing of the Octoraro Creek and a major road from Lancaster to Port Deposit. The McCullough Company, which assumed ownership of the sheet metal works in 1859, supplemented the small cluster of existing buildings with several company-built workers' houses. Eventually independent cooper and blacksmith shops and general stores were built, and a variety of dwellings perched on the hillside above the mill buildings.

At the other end of the mill village continuum stood Elk Mills, a planned company town built along Big Elk Creek. Founded in 1846 by Daniel Lord, a cotton manufacturer from Litchfield, Connecticut, the enterprise transformed the earlier Elk Forge property into a full-scale cotton factory village. At its start this consisted of a five-story, gambrel-roofed stone mill, various forge buildings adapted for use as weaving mills, two rows of stone tenements, and Daniel Lord's residence. Similarly, at Principio, where the ruins of the eighteenth century establishment had been taken over by the Whitaker Iron Company in the 1830s, a new industrial village emerged around the reconstructed furnaces, with workers' tenements, managers' houses, company offices, and a depot of the Philadelphia Railroad.

(right) Weaving mill at Elk Mills (1877 atlas, Historical Society of Cecil County)

(below) Elk Mills was a company town built by Daniel Lord, who had established a cotton factory there in 1846. The complex consisted of a large, five-story stone mill; a one-story weaving mill converted from an earlier forge on the site; and workers' housing, including two rows of connected stone houses. (1927, Louise Baldwin/Cecil Community College)

Much of the mill workers' housing at Elk Mills consisted of frame duplexes such as those shown here. (1981, Maryland Historical Trust)

While the increasing industrialization of Cecil created and profoundly affected the lives of many communities, agriculture remained the predominant occupation in the nineteenth century. Farming was the foundation of Cecil prosperity, and farms were the dominant feature of the landscape.

By the turn of the nineteenth century the land on most Cecil farms had been depleted of nutrients, as had happened throughout Maryland. Thomas Johnson, writing in the 1790s, described the ravages that a century and a half of destructive farming methods had brought to once-fertile lands:

> It has been generally tended that the first two years in tobacco, the third in Indian corn, and sown down in wheat. As common throughout the State the tobacco is planted three feet distance each way, the corn about six; so that it has become a general estimate, that 4,800 tobacco plants, or 1,200 corn hills, take up an acre. The produce of tobacco is so various, as from four to ten plants to the pound, nor is that of Indian corn more certain. Such land as I have described, may be expected to yield for the first four crops, according to the seasons, a pound of tobacco for every six or seven plants planted, for some will fail. From 15 to 10 bushels of Indian corn, and from nine to 12 bushels of wheat, to the acre.

> After this destructive course, the land is often again planted the next year with Indian corn, and sown down again with wheat or rye, without any assistance. The crops accordingly lessen, till the land becomes so exhausted that its produce scarcely pays for the ploughing.[19]

John Beale Bordley blamed grains as much as tobacco for wearing out the soil. "On the Maryland course," he wrote in 1784, "the great Exhausters Maize and Wheat, with an intermission of eighteen months of Rest, constantly follow each other—and what is this Rest?—a barely momentary cessation from uninterrupted courses of exhausting corn crops."[20]

This time looking to reverse the declining fortunes of their farms, Marylanders once again turned to Great Britain for inspiration. In late eighteenth century England, scientific agriculture had become the fashion among wealthy gentleman farmers, who could afford to experiment with new kinds of livestock and crops, new methods of cultivation, and newly invented agricultural machinery. This enthusiasm for agriculture, this passion for improvement and experimentation, was not confined exclusively to the British nobility, however. Farm periodicals, popular books, agricultural societies, and private exhibitions of livestock or sheep shearing stimulated a ferment of ideas and brought them to the attention of a wider audience. Unlike the cost-prohibitive preoccupations of the industrialists, the concerns of the

gentleman farmers were the concerns of farmers of all classes. Consequently, events such as sheep shearing demonstrations found an interested audience encompassing all types of farmers and gave publicity to the latest agricultural improvements.

In Maryland John Beale Bordley, Harry Dorsey Gough, and others caught the spirit of the British movement. Bordley began by sending to England for the latest works by leading British writers on the subject of agricultural enlightenment. He then compared the most advanced English methods with those of Maryland in a significant study of his own, published in 1784. His conclusions were a less than favorable commentary on the conditions of agriculture in the state. In 1785, to facilitate an exchange of ideas by "gentlemen improving farmers," Bordley helped form the Philadelphia Agricultural Society.[21] Patterned after English models, and including many Marylanders among its members, the society was intended to encourage farmers with larger properties to test new ideas.

One of the first series of tests conducted involved devising means of replacing the minerals taken from the soil by successive crops of tobacco and corn, including dressing the soil with plaster of paris and sowing clover. One farmer who tried plaster in 1784 reported better crops, "but the use of this sand, as it was called, produced from my neighbors a great deal of ridicule."[22] The use of plaster greatly increased the yield and quality of both wheat and corn, especially when combined with the manure needed to prevent too much stiffening of the soil. An agricultural treatise published in 1803 reported that "farmers make three or four times the wheat that they did prior to using [plaster]…the greatest complaint at present is against its luxuriant growth."[23]

The founders of an agricultural society begun in Tal-

By the 1830s, the property of the Principio Company belonged to the Whitaker Iron Company, and in 1880 it continued producing iron under the hand of George P. Whitaker. A village grew up around the busy ironworks, housing workers and providing opportunities for storekeepers and others looking for a prosperous community in which to do business. (1850s, William H. Rease, lithograph, Merrick Collection, Maryland Historical Society)

bot County in 1805 outlined the purposes of such organizations, stating they hoped to achieve, "by communication…related to systems of husbandry,…the improvement of soils by particular cultivation, and the employment of peas, beans, and other pulse." By 1810 many such societies had been formed in Virginia but few in Maryland. The period from 1817 through the early 1820s saw a surge in interest in the groups in both states. In 1820 Martha Ogle Forman of Rose Hill in Cecil County recorded in her diary that her husband went to Savinton to "assist in forming an agricultural society." A month later she wrote that he again traveled to Savinton, now renamed Cecilton, "to attend the agricultural society, and much against his inclination was chosen President."[24]

Information was also disseminated through papers, some devoted solely to agricultural issues but others simply local or statewide newspapers that published columns about farming methods of interest to their readers. The Reverend David Wiley began the *Agricultural Museum* in Georgetown in 1810, but one of the loudest voices of progressive farming in Maryland was *The American Farmer*, a magazine published in Baltimore by John S. Skinner, beginning in 1819. "I have found the spirit for internal improvement and for a thorough amelioration of all our agricultural habits and practices, very far surpassing what I had supposed to exist," editor Skinner told his audience in the first issue.[25] In Cecil County the *Elkton Press*, a general newspaper published from 1823 to 1832, ran a column called the "Farmers' Register" in nearly every issue.

In the first year the column consisted of articles reprinted from other newspapers; a letter written by an anonymous contributor; an article by a "Delaware man"; and "remarks by a North-Carolina farmer." Subjects addressed were hemp, cider, preparing seed wheat to prevent disease (in "a mode which is successfully practiced in England"), a remedy for Hessian fly and other insects, the management of cows, and rearing and fattening swine. Articles reprinted from the *American Farmer* discussed such particular subjects as "cheat—named barley—field pea—grape, and other vines," the management of calves, and seed corn. One column was tagged "Advice to Young Farmers" and imparted much information about "The Horse."

The *Elkton Press* also reported an agricultural exhibition in its issue of November 8, 1823. The "first exhibit by the Agricultural Society," it was held in Chester County, Pennsylvania. The correspondent reported that the weather was fine and "several thousands" attended the event, where they saw "new-fashioned ploughs, moles, cultivators, and driths." On the last day "the Address was delivered," the plowing matches performed, and the "premiums awarded." The subject of the address was not reported, although many details were given about the plowing competition, including the times of the winners.

In November 1822 Martha Ogle Forman noted the "day of the Cattle Show" in her diary. Premiums were also given to the winning exhibits at this event, and she recorded that the prize steer won a "ladle for soap." The following day the "domestic manufactures" were exhibited, and an acquaintance of Mrs. Forman's won the premium for butter—a butter knife.[26] Cecil County farmers also traveled to Delaware to see agricultural exhibitions. In 1836 Phoebe George Bradford, a Cecil native and part-time resident, attended an exhibition held by the "Agricultural and Horticultural Society of Delaware…in the City Hall.…The fruits were excellent, vegetables fine, flowers poor."[27]

Despite the interest demonstrated by agricultural societies, exhibitions, and papers, improved farming methods caught on slowly, even among gentleman farmers who could afford to experiment with the latest improvements. Some men, however, like Sidney George Fisher, owner of Mount Harmon on the Sassafras River, were fascinated by the results that could be achieved. Fisher was a vigorous proponent of enlightened farm management during the early nineteenth century. A gentleman farmer, he lived part

(right) In 1788 Sidney George built a house at Mt. Harmon that was later inherited by his nephew Sidney George Fisher. That house is gone but its walls contain a reconstruction of the original. (Danny Justice, Elkton, Maryland Historical Trust)

(below) Before Sidney George Fisher inherited the Mt. Harmon property in the early 19th century, the house stood empty and the land uncultivated for nine years. Fisher, a Philadelphian who resided at Mt. Harmon part-time, experimented with the latest farming methods, improving his crops with the use of fertilizer and clearing the overgrown landscape to make it more beautiful. (c. 1971-73, Action! Photo, Wilmington, Maryland Historical Trust)

Sidney George Fisher often spent his country evenings at Mt. Harmon reading works from his library and writing in his journal. His record of life at this county estate offers a glimpse of life and agricultural practices in early 19th century Cecil County. (Maryland Historical Trust)

of the year in Philadelphia but still directed the farming of his Cecil County property. When he first took over the farm at Mount Harmon, the house had been vacant for nine years and the farm not cultivated in that time. He addressed himself to improving the property and took much interest in the appearance of the fields and woods.

A man named Rickards farmed the land at Mount Harmon, and in his journal Fisher often mentions discussions between them about the work to be done. It appears the two men generally agreed on an approach to improving the property, although Fisher's remarks indicate Rickards sometimes had to be convinced of the efficacy of his employer's novel ideas. Fisher's journal entry for July 8, 1837, gives some idea of the efforts being made to improve the farm at Mount Harmon:

> Rickards came home from Smyrna whither he went yesterday. Sees nothing like his crop anywhere he says, & seems full of the spirit of improvement. Agrees with me *now* that we ought to have six tillages, & says he will divide the prize-house field. We shall then have each field 3 successive years in grain & three in grass…The grain fields will then be smaller, & we shall soon be able to cover one each year completely with barn yard manure.[28]

Fisher did not return to Mount Harmon until that fall, and in October 1837 he made the following entry in his journal:

> When I arrived found Rickards getting out the wheat & the hum of the threshing machine resounded over the place. He has this year a famous stack-yard, and the enormous ricks of straw, the numerous stacks of grain, hay & fodder, & the busy laborers presented a very gratifying picture of industry, prosperity and abundance which was doubly pleasing from the contrast which it afforded to the scene here in former years. He seemed glad to see me, & in excellent spirits about the farm. Says there will be at least 1000 bus: wheat & 1200 oats, which at $1.80 or $2.00 for the first & 35 or 40 cts. for the last will do pretty well.[29]

The next day he recorded the arrival of a load of lime, and then commented on another case in which his modern methods had to be proved to his farm manager:

> I find that the reason the clover did not take well on the sandy field this year, was that it was not harrowed in. Part of the field was harrowed & there the clover was excellent but where it was not harrowed there was scarcely any. Rickards is now convinced that it is the best plan.[30]

A little more than a year later, Fisher walked around the farm, looking things over, discussing them with Rickards, and trimming trees. After complaining that Rickards had cut too many trees, he commented in his journal, "I have not much cause to complain of him, as he is very obliging

The Greek Revival style of architecture, which became popular in the 19th century in Cecil County as elsewhere around the young nation, was most notable in new towns of the period such as Chesapeake City. Franklin Hall, built circa 1870 by the Conrey family, is a good example. (1976, Maryland Historical Trust)

and willing, and an excellent tenant." He was satisfied as well with the appearance of his property, observing that

> the farm has certainly improved in an extraordinary manner, and the work and capital applied to it during the last four years, has not only trebled its value but completely altered its whole aspect. It may now compete with the best Penna. farms and in beauty far surpasses any that I ever saw there.[31]

From the beginning of his farming enterprise in Cecil County, Fisher compared his efforts to those of farms he was familiar with in Pennsylvania. The following journal entry records his interest in progressive farming methods and demonstrates that he was not alone in his opinions:

> In Pennsylvania, clover, plaster, and lime have only been introduced within the last 10 or 20 years, a start has been made here, its palpable success is the best argument in its favor, my wheat crop speaks more eloquently than a thousand theories, the agricultural papers, particularly *The Cultivator*, which circulates very extensively through the country, are calling attention to the subject, the exhausted condition of their farms demands a different system of cultivation, and I have no doubt that in 10 years, a very great change will be produced in the appearance and prosperity of the country.[32]

Change did gradually occur. Each successful agricultural experiment led to newer methods and technologies that eventually were used to revitalize Maryland farming. The stiffening of the soil from increased use of plaster gave rise to more efficient plow models and wider use of manure to lighten the soil. Increased yields in field crops resulting from proper crop rotation and use of various fertilizers— including Peruvian guano—led to the development of new harvest machines, chief among these the mechanical reaper.[33]

The first half of the nineteenth century was a vital and dynamic period in the development of Cecil County. Industry, trade, and agriculture collaborated in the development of a prosperous county. On Cecil farms, the revolution in agricultural practice and the healthy harvests that ensued were the catalysts for a major rebuilding on farm properties that continued into the third quarter of the nineteenth century. In place of the tobacco houses of the eighteenth century rose the barns, granaries, silos, and dairy houses needed to accommodate the grain harvests and dairy herds that took the place of tobacco in the agricultural economy.

As far as domestic architecture went, eighteenth century traditions held their own well into the nineteenth century, especially in the older communities. This adherence to established trends reflected the conservative nature of many county residents, who continued to find the forthright styles of earlier periods satisfactory for the construction of houses. This popularity did not yield easily to new architectural movements, but during the first decades of the nineteenth century, many in the county turned from the older traditions of Roman-based classicism to a new fashion of classically based architecture, this time inspired by ancient Athens. Although this movement, which came to be known as "Greek Revival," gained acceptance throughout the county, the style became a more conspicuous adornment in towns that developed during the second quarter of the nineteenth century, such as Chesapeake City. In the older parts of the county, the new classicism often mingled comfortably with the old traditions.

The details of the Greek Revival style were interpreted differently in various parts of the county, but a plethora of Greek-inspired architecture handbooks exerted a unifying influence in design approach. The early and influential *Antiquities of Athens*, printed in England in 1762, was followed by the American works *The Architect, or Prac-*

tical House Carpenter by Asher Benjamin between 1830 and 1845 and *The Beauties of Modern Architecture* by Minard Lafever, the latter published in 1835.

Despite its variations—and its stylistic freshness when set beside the older traditions—the Greek Revival was in general a superficial, ornamental style reflected in varying degrees not only in the architecture of the period but in literature, art, costumes, and manners as well. Though popular, it ultimately proved largely unrelated to the realignment of domestic needs occurring at the time. Despite this, for years

(right) Essex Lodge, near Earleville, an Italianate brick dwelling, exemplifies the popularity of revival styles in the mid- to late 19th century. Well-to-do county residents looking for a bit more decoration than that offered by the simple Greek style experimented with styles based on many other periods of history. (1968, Maryland Historical Trust)

(below) The cross gable was the architectural feature most commonly adopted from the flurry of revival styles popular in the 19th century. This example, from the 1877 atlas of the county, even has a cross gable on the barn. (Historical Society of Cecil County)

A number of 19th century Cecil farmhouses such as this one from the 1877 county atlas were built in the Greek Revival style. Today the clapboard walls of many of these structures have been covered with later forms of siding that save on maintenance but camouflage the characteristics of the style, particularly features such as the pilasters at the corners of the house and the dentil molding around the top of the walls. The nearly flat roof, small third story windows, and Greek-inspired columns supporting the porch roof have proved more durable. (Historical Society of Cecil County)

This example of a farmhouse sporting the cross gable also shows a bit of Gothic Revival influence in the pointed-arch window in the gable. (1980, Maryland Historical Trust)

Greek Revival remained part of the repertoire of builders and architects catering to the desires of prosperous property owners.

The very prosperity that encouraged the use of the Greek Revival style in Cecil County, as throughout Maryland, brought about its descendant popularity. Those who had grown stylishly comfortable on the strength of Cecil commerce were not long contented with the simplicity of the Greek Revival style as public evidence of their new-found social and economic status.

Their aspirations more readily found expression in the revival styles that began to appear as the nineteenth century progressed. American designers on Old World grand tours scoured the European countryside in a frenzied search for the next important style, returning from England with the Gothic, from Paris with the Second Empire, from Provence with the Romanesque. Throughout the mid-nineteenth century, their mixtures of European-inspired designs were popularized in countless illustrated journals and pattern books published by architects of varying degrees of competence. Among the most accomplished, the most popular, and the most widely distributed were Andrew Jackson Downing's *The Architecture of Country Houses* and Calvert Vaux's *Cottages and Villas*.

The plates of picturesque house plans contained between the authors' discussions of "good taste in architecture" gradually found a range of material manifestations throughout Cecil County, from the Italianate derivation of Essex Lodge, near Earleville, to the Renaissance-inspired alterations along Elkton's Main Street, to the fully developed Gothic of the Coulson house near Port Deposit, with its board-and-batten frame construction, center cross gable, and clay chimney pots.[34] But ultimately it was the requisite cross gable of the latter style that became the most accepted feature of the countless elements put forth by the succession of revival architectural styles. The center-gable Gothic cottage became the ubiquitous choice of the middle class throughout the county until the early twentieth century.

Beyond the obvious exterior massing and ornamentation, what stood the new style-conscious houses in marked contrast to their predecessors was the use of uniform building materials and standardized lumber sizes and the new construction methods that accompanied these materials. As the nineteenth century progressed, building practices became increasingly streamlined, moving farther away from early timber framing methods. The sawmills of Cecil County were well situated to supply the materials for the new construction methods, which eventually resulted in the modern balloon frame. First used in the 1830s, this framing method was not fully employed in Cecil County until later in the century. Such framing techniques facilitated the construction of complex angles, intersecting slopes, polygonal spaces—a whole range of design devices unimaginable to earlier builders. By the end of the century, the builders' growing proficiency with flexible balloon framing had led to the complex structures commonly associated with the Victorian era.

Not everyone in nineteenth century Cecil County was concerned with keeping up with the latest styles in architecture, nor was everyone financially able to express their interest in high culture publicly. A significant percentage of the Cecil population remained firmly pinned to the lower echelons of the class structure. The houses of tenant farmers, landless laborers, and slaves remained relatively unchanged from their eighteenth century counterparts and ranged in size from the smallest one-and-a-half story, two-room plan to slightly larger, two-story center hall houses.

Slavery itself was well on the wane in the county long

before emancipation. While slave labor dominated in the 1790s—with 3,407 slaves, as opposed to 163 free blacks—by the 1850s these figures had reversed, with the Cecil slave population dropping to 844 and its free black population increased to 2,623, accounting for nearly 14 percent of the total population.[35] Free black labor was integral to the success of many of the industrial and commercial enterprises sprouting up around the county during the first half of the nineteenth century. Significantly, by the 1850s the greatest concentrations of free blacks were to be found in Port Deposit, where they constituted 21.8 percent of the population, and Elkton, where they made up 20.6 percent.[36]

With all the work available in the mills, factories, fisheries, and lumberyards of Port Deposit and Elkton, these towns grew into prominence. On the eve of the Civil War, they were respectively the eighth and tenth largest cities in all of Maryland, making Cecil the only county to post more than one city among the ten most populous in the state.

Most Cecil County men who fought in the Civil War joined the Union Army. These men were recruited in Elkton by the Fifth Maryland regiment in 1862. (Robert G. Merrick Collection, Maryland State Archives, MSA SC 1477-5811)

CHAPTER 5

"Farming and improvements generally… in advance of the average in the State"

THE CIVIL WAR YEARS witnessed the unleashing of forces in Maryland that eventually brought about significant shifts in the character of Cecil society. Despite its strategic location as a passage for Northern troops marching south toward Washington and war, Cecil was spared the assault upon person and property experienced by other Maryland communities thrust to the center stage of a theater of war. The forces that led to change in Cecil were political and economic ones.

Cecil's closest military encounter came in July 1864, when a ragtag collection of Union defenders scurried into the county from Wilmington, Delaware. Hastily dispatched to points along the Susquehanna, they were responding to the advance of a guerilla group of Confederate cavalry under the command of Maryland's own Major Henry Gilmor. Gilmor had been sent into northern Maryland as part of a last-gasp attempt by General Robert E. Lee to divert the attention of the Union forces under General Ulysses S. Grant from their assault on Petersburg.

Gathering together a force of some twelve to fifteen thousand men, Lee sent a small army under General Jubal Early in a wide swing up the valley, across the Potomac, and down into Maryland. They reached Frederick by July 9, and from there Early dispatched Colonel Bradley T. Johnson's cavalry toward Baltimore, with instructions to destroy the railroads linking Washington and Philadelphia as part of an effort to free the Confederate prisoners at Point Lookout, at the tip of Southern Maryland. Toward that end Johnson dispatched Major Gilmor and a small force to disrupt communications as much as possible between Baltimore and the North. Passing through Harford County, Gilmor's men cut telegraph lines and at Magnolia Station captured a train from Baltimore carrying a coterie of Union officers, including Major General William B. Franklin.

Meanwhile, at Wilmington, Major Henry B. Judd, the post commander, acutely aware of Confederate forces moving toward his sector, frantically scraped together what counterforces he could. Hastily, he dispatched 100 convalescents and veteran reserves to Cecil County. There they were to guard the railroad ferry linking Perryville and Havre de Grace and secure the Conowingo bridge, which they were either to defend or destroy. Every available vessel capable of passing through the Chesapeake and Delaware Canal was rounded up and sent to Perryville, there anchored to serve as emergency troop transports if the Confederates should take the ground north of the town.[1]

A small detachment sent farther down the line, to Magnolia Station, discovered Gilmor and his men in the process of dismantling a second captured Union train. A brief skirmish ensued, during which the Confederates backed an uncoupled section of their captured train out onto the Philadelphia railroad bridge crossing the Gunpowder River and set it ablaze; the span was destroyed as the burning cars crashed through to the river below. Their mission accomplished, Gilmor and his men retired toward Washington.

While the Union army's control of the Cecil countryside may have been contested in 1864, there was no question about the Union party's control over the political life of the county, nor their firm grip on the Maryland General Assembly. It was the forces of the Union's political body that brought about the greatest wartime changes to Cecil and the rest of Maryland. The first, and unquestionably greatest, change was the unfettering of every black man, woman, and child from the shackles of slavery. President Lincoln had issued his landmark Emancipation Proclamation in 1863, but it extended only to territories under Confederate control, leaving Maryland as an anomaly: Loyal citizens of Maryland, including some of the staunchest Union

A leader of the Republican Party in Maryland after the Civil War, John A. J. Creswell served in the U.S. Congress from 1863 to 1969, during which time he worked for voting and other rights for the newly freed black population. (reprint of *Men of Mark in Maryland*, Historical Society of Cecil County)

men, could and did continue to own slaves. It was clear that slavery was doomed, however, and in response the framers of the 1864 state constitution abolished the institution of slavery. For Cecil County, the passage gave legal voice to a movement that had begun years before.

Unlike those in Maryland's southern counties, the slave population in Cecil had declined steadily in the years before statewide manumission. Even so, the future of the free black in Cecil remained unclear. Would they simply no longer be threatened with the prospect of enslavement, or would they be citizens blessed with the full rights of their white neighbors? For Elkton lawyer John A. J. Creswell, Cecil's leading political light and the acknowledged head of the postwar Republican Party in Maryland, the answer was clear: They should be not only be free, but equal. Creswell served as Cecil's representative in Congress from 1863 to 1865 and later as U.S. senator from 1865 until 1869, when he was appointed postmaster general in Grant's administration. During his time in Congress, Creswell fought unceasingly for increased rights for the newly freed blacks, upholding suffrage and supporting the creation of the Freedmen's Bureau.

The wartime passions for freedom and equality that impelled the Union party dissipated when the war ended. In 1867 the Democratic Party took control of the General Assembly and forced through a second state constitution, denying both citizenship and voting rights to Maryland blacks. The new constitution could not reverse the verdict of the war, however, and after ratification of the Fourteenth and Fifteenth amendments to the U.S. Constitution, Maryland could no longer prevent blacks from voting or claiming other rights of citizenship. Blacks began voting in Cecil elections in 1870, when the amendment took effect.

Despite the constitutional initiatives, the movement of blacks in Cecil County was sharply curtailed for some time to come. "Jim Crow" restrictions kept blacks in separate enclaves at the edge of town or in isolated communities, such as Mt. Zoar in the county's northwestern barrens.

The second great movement set in motion by the Maryland Constitution of 1864 was the establishment of the state's first comprehensive school system. Public education in Maryland was slow to emerge. In fact, Maryland was one of the last states to create a statewide school system, second only to South Carolina. It was not that education was deemed a frivolous, unimportant component of society. In fact, the earliest proposal for schools actually predated the creation of the province. Rather, the scattered settlement pattern and the recognized power of an educated populace—and its perceived threat to the political elite of provincial Maryland—impeded the establishment of "free" schools until long after the colonial period.

Early in the seventeenth century, Edward Palmer, owner of the strategic trader's island at the mouth of the Susquehanna, planned to erect an academy there, perhaps in imitation of the College of Henrico, established by the settlers at Jamestown. Proposals for public schools were put before the provincial government of Maryland as early as 1671; in that year there was read before the Assembly "an Act for the Founding and Erecting of a School or College within this Province for the Education of Youth in Learning and Virtue."[2] Although it passed the Lower House, the act was rejected by the Upper House. Later, under Assembly acts of 1694 and 1695, provisions were made for funding "free" schools with taxes levied on tobacco, furs, Irish Catholic indentured servants, and black slaves. From these, the first public school in Maryland, King William's School—later St. John's College—was founded in Annapolis in 1696. The masters of King William's School were required to teach as many poor children as the trustees determined, but the school was mostly filled with the children of the planter and merchant classes in the Annapolis area. Little room was left for the children of the less well-to-do or those from such remote sections of the province as Cecil County.

Later, "free" schools were established in some areas in the more populous counties of Maryland. These were not actually free but required payment of a daily rate for each child, limiting their availability. In any case, creation of such schools was not strenuously pursued. By 1722 Colonel Samuel Young, then treasurer of Maryland, was compelled to report to the Assembly that a considerable portion of the sum accrued from taxes for funding "free" schools in the counties remained unspent.[3] An act of 1723 attempted to encourage the construction of schoolhouses in the various counties, and a few new schools were erected as a result. Among these was the first free school in Cecil, set up on a 100-acre tract on Sassafras Neck and administered by a board of trustees. For the most part, however, the school funds went unexpended, and the Cecil school closed after only a few years of operation.

Gradually the colony's original plan of maintaining a large number of "free" schools was abandoned by the General Assembly in favor of concentrating on the development of one or more colleges. In 1754 the Lower House, by a vote of 38 to 13, resolved that the "Fund, now appropriated for the Several County Schools, and the Money which may arise on the Sale of the Lands, and Houses which appertains to the several County Schools, be applied towards the Erection of One Public Seminary of Learning."[4] Essentially, the Assembly intended to leave the task of elementary and secondary education in the counties to private or community enterprise. In so doing, they established a pattern that Cecil County schools were to follow for the next hundred years.

Schools did arise in Cecil County in the eighteenth century, but for the most part they were established either in affiliation with a religious denomination or were private subscription schools. West Nottingham Academy, founded in 1744, was a Presbyterian institution, and the Bohemia Academy, founded the following year, a Jesuit one. The Old Stone School, established near Rising Sun around the time of the Revolution, charged a 2½-cent daily rate. Because of the cost, these schools were not available to most county children.

Throughout the early nineteenth century, efforts to establish public-supported education in Cecil were at best spotty and disorganized. In 1812 the General Assembly offered the first of a series of state assistance acts to Cecil and other counties with the passage of the Bank Road bill, which incorporated companies to build turnpikes and extend banking services, provided the companies paid an

Before 1859 even "free" Cecil schools charged a subscription fee, making them inaccessible to much of the population. It was not until later in the 19th century that more standardized schoolhouses such as this one—Locust Hill Academy, built in 1881 at Fredericktown—became commonplace. (1973, Maryland Historical Trust)

(opposite above) Beginning relatively early in the colonial period, education for the elite was offered in private Cecil schools that often were run by religious groups. One such school was West Nottingham Academy, founded by the Presbyterians in 1744 and still educating students in the late 20th century. The oldest school building on the campus is this brick structure built circa 1865. (Historical Society of Cecil County)

(opposite below) Before a county school system was established, some industrial companies made education available to the children of their employees. Eight Corner or Carter's School, built in 1820 by mill owner Robert Carter, was used until 1886. It stood at the intersection of Black Snake and George Kirk roads, near Providence. (c. 1914, Historical Society of Cecil County)

assessment to help educate poor children. Under the bill, the money accrued was to be distributed evenly to the various counties, regardless of population. Around the state, most of these funds were not spent because of a lack of commitment to education for the less well-to-do, and the funds eventually reverted to the comptroller. Similar acts and amendments passed during the 1820s and 1830s did not yield any better results.

By 1850, however, the first countywide effort to establish a true free school system had been launched by a handful of enlightened local leaders, including Francis Ellis, James McCauley, and Samuel Maffit. At their urging a convention was called that year in Elkton, which resulted in the draft of a bill for a workable free school system. This was sent to the Cecil delegation at the General Assembly, who recognized the political sensitivity of the issue and agreed to sponsor the bill on one overriding condition: Before the law could become operative, it had to be approved by the voters of Cecil. Accordingly, in May 1851 the law was submitted to the people for their approval.

The voters soundly rejected the legislation. Their objection focused not on the precepts of the system but on the taxes needed to support it. Many in the county viewed the new county school tax as a burdensome addition to the other taxes they believed had already risen alarmingly. Others questioned how equitable the school system would be, asking whether it was right to tax a man who had no children to educate to help pay for the man who had.[5] Cecil's free school advocates were not easily dissuaded, and by decade's end they had once again brought their proposal before county residents. This time the proponents won, aided in part by the growing recognition by political leaders across the state that an educated populace was better able to contend with the increasing complexities of American life.

In 1859 the first countywide comprehensive school system was put into operation. Under its structure, a county board of commissioners of public schools was empowered with full authority to employ teachers, set a course of studies, buy and sell school property, and build or lease schoolhouses. Accordingly, the new board assumed control of a handful of old schoolhouses built under the previous subscription system. Former private schools, such as the "Old Stone" schoolhouse near Rising Sun and the Leeds School,

After the Civil War, the question of educating black children became a topic of some controversy. It was not until 1872 that the General Assembly required the expenditure of government funds for "schools for colored children." Before that, black schools were built and run with private funds. Mt. Zoar, a black community established in the first half of the 19th century, built a school, at one point known as Conowingo School No. 5 (1980, Maryland Historical Trust)

first opened in 1816 by the Reverend John Wilson, were adopted as part of the new county system. Many of the schools, however, met in buildings that were little more than poor frame shacks, destitute of suitable desks, seats, and other furniture. The board authorized the construction of new schoolhouses, and in communities where no schoolhouses existed or were immediately planned, buildings were leased to serve the purpose until a proper schoolhouse could be built.

A significant boost to the county's fledgling public school system came from the State Constitution of 1864, which established Maryland's first state superintendent of public education and its first department of education. Under their guidance, a uniform, statewide system of public education was finally adopted, providing Cecil and the other counties with the tools necessary to forge an effective public education system. In 1872 the state legislature extended that aid to all segments of society with the passage of Chapter XVIII of the school law, "Schools for Colored Children," providing the impetus for the creation of the first public-supported black schools in Cecil. Under the provisions of the constitutional amendment, one black school was to be established in each election district.

Black schools existed in Cecil before the passage of the 1872 act, but, being excluded from the 1859 free school system, they were funded solely with private monies. Often they were set up as an adjunct of community church outreach and self-support programs. Initial efforts to take advantage of the legislative mandate for public-supported black education were severely hampered by outrage from certain segments of the white community in Cecil. Education was regarded as a powerful tool for achievement, and many in the county perceived an educated black populace as a potential threat to the white community. As a result, many district leaders repeatedly ignored petitions for the creation of black schools. When black schools finally were established, many conducted classes under continuing threat of attack. In fact, arson destroyed a number of black schools in Cecil County, as it did throughout the state.[6] Despite these perils, the black schools survived, segregated and less well funded than their white counterparts. "Separate but equal" remained the political dictum for black schools throughout the county and state well into the 1950s.

By the 1880s the Cecil school system boasted seventy-six white and thirteen black schools. Each building was a simple affair, devoid of ornamentation and reduced to just those materials essential to providing adequate shelter for the budding scholars within. Indeed, it was apparently a policy of the school board to spend the least amount necessary to

Jacob Tome opened a school for Port Deposit children in 1894. The first building was Washington Hall (on the left), constructed across the street from Tome's home (mansion on the right). Washington Hall first housed the intermediate grades and later served as the girls' high school. (c. 1894, Maryland Historical Society)

build a new schoolhouse. Politicians were hesitant to raise the school tax, creating a scarcity of funds. As a result repairs were often performed gratis by community members and furniture and textbooks were recycled from school to school. At the bottom of the rung, the black schools used furnishings and instructional materials deemed unusable in the white schools and continually had the school year shortened from lack of funds.

Progress in public education was slow, much too slow for one Port Deposit citizen in particular. The industrialist Jacob Tome was an outspoken critic of a county school system he deemed woefully inadequate. In 1889 Tome acted upon his dissatisfaction by endowing the town with a substantial part of his amassed fortune to establish a separate free school for area youth. Like the hero of a Horatio Alger novel, Tome's life was a rags-to-riches story. Arriving in town in 1833 on a log raft from York County, Pennsylvania, penniless but ambitious, Tome joined with men of greater capital and entered the lumber business. He quickly prospered, invested and reinvested his profits, and expanded his timber holdings as far west as the Great Lakes. Eventually he became one of the wealthiest men in the state.

Tome never forgot the town of his beginnings, and in his later years, reflecting upon the cultural condition of Port Deposit, he decided his greatest gift to the town would be a source of good education for its children. Accordingly, he created the Jacob Tome Institute, with an initial endowment of $1.5 million and the mandate to establish a series of free schools far superior to the county's public schools. Incorporated in 1889, the Jacob Tome Institute first opened its doors to Port Deposit children in 1894. Washington Hall, a staid brick-and-brownstone building, was constructed along Main Street as a substantial announcement of the school's educational mission. Within four years more than 600 area children attended school in the various buildings composing the institute.

(top) The legacy Jacob Tome left to the Tome Institute when he died in 1898 was used to found a boys' boarding school on the bluffs overlooking the Susquehanna. The dozen Beaux Arts buildings constructed to house the school centered around Tome Memorial Hall, pictured here. (1911, Maryland Historical Society)

(bottom) The Tome boarding school was an elaborate facility, including this Italian garden, a destination of Sunday steamboat excursions from Baltimore. Income from the boarding school helped support the Tome Institute's free schools. (c. 1915, Maryland Historical Society)

At Tome's death in 1898, another sizable amount was bequeathed to the school system bearing his name. The school's trustees used this second endowment to establish a boarding school for boys on the high bluff overlooking the town and the river. By 1905 twelve Beaux Arts buildings perched on the hill, the largest and most prominent being Tome Memorial Hall, a building of Port Deposit granite and Indiana limestone designed by the New York architecture firm of Boring and Tilton, whose other commissions included the Ellis Island complex in New York harbor. As a boarding school, the Tome School for Boys was open to students outside the Port Deposit area; consequently, the school acquired a reputation that extended beyond the banks of the Susquehanna. Income from the boarding school supported the free schools of the Tome Institute.

The success of the Tome Institute initially came at the expense of the county schools, as it offered area families an alternative to the woeful inadequacies of most one-room schoolhouses. The early years of the twentieth century, however, brought a period of substantial growth and significant development in the county school system, which eventually resulted in declining enrollment in the Tome schools. The emerging science of educational instruction witnessed increased experimentation in all areas of public schooling. In particular, a movement had been inaugurated at the state level to standardize both one- and two-room schoolhouses. Circulars issued from the state department of education addressed all physical aspects of public education, from playground landscaping—with separate play areas for boys and girls—to the appropriate tinting for schoolhouse walls—gray, a soothing neutral tone school officials had determined most conducive to a good educational environment.[7]

As prescribed by state officials, the interior of the ideal schoolhouse featured two cloakrooms immediately flanking the entrance—again, boys and girls—in which the students deposited slickers and lunch pails. Near the rear of the room was the wood stove, squat on a fireplate and wrapped in an iron jacket to prevent accidental burning. Students ranging in age from six to sixteen years of age, from grades 1 through 7, would take their place in the rows of double desks, lifting the lids to store books and materials. At the front of the room, on a raised platform, was the teacher's desk. Behind it, running the length of the wall, was a slate blackboard; to the side, a globe for geography lessons and a bookshelf to hold the school's small library. Wainscoting protected the plaster of the lower walls from the ravages of roughhousing, and the windows were placed high enough to discourage daydreaming.[8]

A peculiar aspect of the state standardization program was the adoption of the unilateral lighting system, developed in part by German educational researchers at the turn of the century. According to their theory, all light within a schoolroom should come from the students' left side, so that no shadows would be cast across the papers of the predominantly right-handed students seated and writing at their desks. As a result, the windows of many of the county's one-room schoolhouses were boarded over on one side.[9]

From meager beginnings, the Cecil public schools grew to be a symbol of pride for the community, imparting as they did the great precepts of American democracy in addition to the rudiments of reading, writing, and arithmetic.

This photograph of Perryville High School students and their teacher demonstrates the amenities available in schools after the school reform movement of the late 19th century, including light streaming in from what must have been large windows and a radiator to provide heat. (c. 1910, Mildred McGuirk /Cecil Community College)

Students learned the virtues of patience, perseverance, and obedience; their fundamental rights as Americans; and their role in the business of American democracy.

By the last quarter of the nineteenth century, the business of America was, quite literally, business. It was the emerging age of the American businessman, whose main concern was to provide a favorable climate for industrial expansion. This concern was shared enthusiastically by most of the public and political sector alike. The benefits brought by industry were apparent to all, and no one wanted to disturb its growth. High tariffs, artificially reducing the threat of foreign competition; government concessions; and favorable laws regarding common carriers, labor, and immigration found immediate legislative support in Congress and the White House. What the industrialists looked for and received was a reasonably free hand with which to develop their own enterprises. The political philosophy of the 1870s was congenial to the requested lack of interference, and anyone who suggested government regulation of business was dismissed as somehow anti-American. In this environment, industry moved relentlessly forward.

The impact of the industrial age might be thought

remote from Cecil County, but the explosive growth, unfettered by federal control, spelled the end of the smaller industrial concerns that had dotted the Cecil landscape since the eighteenth century. Likewise, the small family farms in the county were threatened by the staggering yield of the Midwestern wheat fields. With their newly developed combines—heavy, cumbersome machines first hauled by forty-horse teams and later by steam tractors—the western farms contrasted sharply with their older Cecil counterparts. The combines cut, threshed, and bagged the crop all in a day's operation, and the grain was shipped by railroad out of Chicago and Moline. In contrast, by century's end Cecil farms —averaging little more than 100 acres each—remained firmly rooted in the tradition of horse-drawn reapers and binders.[10] Not until World War I, with its shortages of food, men, and horsepower and the accompanying demand for increased production, did the tractor become a general feature of county farms.

With the shift of the nation's center for wheat production went the bulk of its milling enterprises, now dominated

Despite the increasing use of farm machinery, in Cecil County, as in the rest of the nation, less than 25 percent of all hay was baled before World War II. (c. 1910, collection of Lloyd Balderston III, Nancy Conrad/Cecil Community College)

By the end of the 19th century, many Cecil industries were losing ground to larger ventures located closer to the vast natural resources in the West. The county's quarries remained successful, however, and the largest of these was the McClenahan granite quarry in Port Deposit. (c. 1904, Roberta White/Cecil Community College)

by the hulking, steam-powered roller mills of the Midwest.[11] The older, smaller, water-powered Cecil mills, their three or four runs of stone unable to compete with the cheaper output of the Midwestern concerns, began to fold, one by one.

Even harder hit among Cecil's original industrial mainstays was the long-standing iron industry. By the end of the nineteenth century, it was practically a thing of the past, its demise also caused in large part by changes in technology. After the Civil War cheaper iron was needed to feed the railroads and other iron-hungry enterprises, and a radical change in the iron industry came about to meet this need. The output of county furnaces was replaced by that of the large iron and steel furnaces that rose in western Pennsylvania, Ohio, and Indiana. Furnished with an abundant supply of ore from Lake Superior and Alabama, these coke-burning furnaces were able to manufacture huge amounts of iron at relatively low cost. The price of pig iron fell to such an extent it was no longer profitable to mine Cecil iron ore, and the small production charcoal-burning furnaces closed one by one.[12] By the 1890s the McCullough Iron Company complex at Rowlandsville had switched production from galvanized sheet metal to roofing paper, and the pioneering Principio Furnace had been forced to abandon its founding site.

Of all Cecil's native industries, only quarrying remained on a firm footing in the face of growing western competition. The quarries in Port Deposit continued to yield the

This photograph of Tome School students visiting the McClenahan quarry dramatizes the size of the operation and the blocks of stone cut from the cliff face.
(1907, Harris & Ewing, The Jacob Tome Institute)

lion's share of the income derived from working the mineral resources of the county. The largest and most successful Cecil quarry was the McClenahan Granite Company of Port Deposit. It had been founded by Ebenezer McClenahan, who in the 1830s annually increased the run of cut stone from the rock walls. By 1837 nearly 15,000 perches (or 371,250 cubic feet) of Port Deposit granite were shipped from his works.[13] By the turn of the century the business, then owned by McClenahan's sons, had been aided immeasurably by two convenient sources of transportation. The railroad that passed by the quarry connected it with the markets of Philadelphia, Baltimore, Washington, and Harrisburg, and the light-draft vessels tied up at the town wharf provided shipment to points as far away as Richmond at a fraction of railroad rates.

Various attempts at opening new quarries to rival the McClenahan operations were made throughout the end of the nineteenth century. Following the Civil War, a small operation was opened at the eastern end of the B & O suspension bridge over the Susquehanna, initially to provide

Cecil forests supported a burgeoning pulp and paper industry beginning in the mid-19th century.

(left) The Radner Pulp Mills had a high profile on the Elkton skyline. (collection of Michael J. Dixon)

(below) George Childs, owner of the Philadelphia *Ledger*, took over the Marley Paper Mill after the Civil War to supply his newspaper company. (c. 1907 postcard, Kermit DeBoard/Cecil Community College)

(opposite top) This early 1890s view of the Cecil Paper Mill at New Bridge shows the brick engine room, a large white building that housed the sorting room and beaters, the paper loading room in the building on the left, and the "Bailey Room" in the building on the right. The coal wagon suggests the source of the mill's power. (Horace and Louise Witman/Cecil Community College)

(opposite bottom) The Elk Paper Company is reflected in the settling pond. (Elizabeth Coyle/Cecil Community College)

By 1902 tomatoes and corn had long been important crops in north central Cecil County, and the region was a prominent tomato-canning district until the early 20th century. Wagons carried tomatoes to market or the cannery. The latter were small facilities relatively close together and operated only a few months each year. (1909, Richard Mead Balderston, Nancy Conrad/Cecil Community College)

stone for construction of the railroad bridge. The quarries languished until 1894, when they attracted the attention of William Gray and Sons of Philadelphia. This firm, with a capital outlay of $8,000, pushed the quarries into expanded operations, and within two years increasing contracts encouraged further opening. Frenchtown rock from the Gray quarries was featured prominently in such Philadelphia buildings as the Cold Storage Warehouse and the extension of the Baldwin Locomotive Works.

Other industries across the county continued to provide a varied economic base in turn-of-the-century Cecil, although none came close to rivaling the scope of the Port Deposit quarries. The Cecil, Green Hill, and North East fire brick companies turned fireclay into stove brick. White fireclay dug in Cecil was shipped to R. Remey and Son in Philadelphia for the manufacture of stoneware. The Maryland Clay Company, situated along the railroad line southwest of North East, mined and washed kaolin clay for use in coated paper. The numerous quartz outcroppings of the Conowingo area were quarried for flint, ground fine at a series of small mills and shipped to potteries in Trenton, New Jersey. Similarly, feldspar dikes along Octoraro Creek near the state line were quarried for spar for use in pottery works in Liverpool, Ohio.

The forested sections of Cecil—which at the turn of the century ranked with Allegany, Garrett, and Calvert as the best wooded counties in the state—gave rise to a series of pulp and paper mills. The Marley Paper Mills were taken over by George Childs after the Civil War for the use of his Philadelphia *Ledger*, and the Providence Paper Mill was

By the end of the 19th century, railroads had taken over a large proportion of the county's shipping business, but a track on Cole Pier at Perryville demonstrates the continued link between water and rail transportation. (early 20th century, Ward Abrahams Collection, Historical Society of Cecil County)

operated by William Singerly, owner of the Philadelphia *Record*. The Kenmore Pulp and Paper Company of Elkton consumed 12,000 cords of wood each year, primarily white poplar.[14]

The serpentine barrens of the northwestern county, home of quartz and feldspar quarries, also spawned a brief gold rush. Prospectors told wild stories of large pockets of the precious metal there for the taking, and toward that end a number of small concerns staked out mines. The largest of these was the Klondike Gold Company, formed to control the mineral properties and operate mines on a tract in the extreme northwestern corner of Cecil. The promoters of the project, in ferreting out gullible investors, touted scientific analyses reportedly showing the rock to be encrusted with valuable ore. But, as the Maryland Geological Survey warned, "the promised return for the investment in land and the unusual prices offered for property produced temporary demoralization, and in a few instances when the disappointing failure came, produced more or less suffering…There is no more profit in mining small quantities of gold at large expense than in farming poor land with large amounts of fertilizer for a small crop."[15]

At the turn of the century, farming remained Cecil's main industry, and wheat still occupied pride of place in a large corridor stretching across the county. Nonetheless, the nearness of urban markets had begun to work changes in county agriculture. Truck crops in the north and fruit culture in the south had become important adjuncts, as had fattening feeder calves for city butchers. Dairying became more and more integral to the northern and central sections, due to the presence of the two main railroad lines. The branch line of the Philadelphia railroad furnished an easy outlet for the northwestern section, while in the southern part of the county water transportation remained the main line to urban markets.

By the last quarter of the nineteenth century, the volume of waterborne commerce had been eclipsed by the rising dominance of the railroads. With the completion of the northern lines after the Civil War, the 1866 construction of a railroad bridge over the Susquehanna at Perryville, and the consolidation of existing short lines, the railroads in Cecil assumed an unassailable economic position in the county. For a time, competition from the canals for wheat shipments helped keep rates on the railroads fairly low. Once completed, however, the rails were never in any real danger from the canals, although many rail carriers offered rebates to their larger shippers to foster the illusion of continued competition.

Cecil's major canal-oriented community, Chesapeake City, found its fortunes fluctuating with the rise and fall of the Chesapeake and Delaware Canal. The C & D continued to be a significant economic link between the major ports of Philadelphia and Baltimore, and early in the twentieth century it proved strategically important for the emerging

U. S. defense network. The canal provided a sheltered southern passage for troop and cargo transports, eliminating the necessity of exposing them to an Atlantic route. Consequently, in 1919 the federal government purchased the entire canal from the canal company for $2.5 million, a mere $250,000 more than the entire cost of construction when the canal was completed ninety years earlier. Soon after, the U. S. Army Corps of Engineers began a radical reworking of the canal bed, removing the lock system and lowering the entire channel to sea level. At Chesapeake City this engineering feat required the demolition of two bridges. These were replaced with a single bridge with a lift span in the center, which engendered a reorientation of the town's main street.

The canals were not the only transportation system to suffer from the domination of the railroads. For years the state legislature had extended cash advances and bond subscriptions to finance private canals, railroads, and turnpike companies. Even so, the General Assembly never conceived of Maryland's main public transportation system—the thousands of miles of roads that linked town and country, county seat and capital—as an obligation of the state. It remained, in their minds, strictly a local affair. While millions of public dollars were poured into the railroads in the second half of

(above) The bridge shown here, crossing Back Creek, was one of two bridges connecting North and South Chesapeake City. It pivoted in the middle, each half swinging in opposite directions, to allow boats past. (early 20th century, Marie Collins/Cecil Community College)

(opposite top) Although less than fourteen miles long, the C & D Canal was vital to the economic and military affairs of the region and, during wartime, of the nation. Chesapeake City, home to many who worked on the canal or the ships that sailed it, bloomed on either side of the waterway at its eastern terminus. On the left in this photograph is the home of the lock tender and in the center the office of J. Steele, a grain and feed dealer. The large brick building, later the Masonic hall, was a store at this time. (early 1920s, Joseph Savin/Cecil Community College)

(opposite bottom) The federal government bought the C & D Canal in 1919 and soon embarked on a program of improvement. Early goals were to reduce accidents and better accommodate modern shipping, first by lowering the canal to sea level so the locks could be removed and then by straightening and widening the canal. The lock at Chesapeake City was removed circa 1926-27. (Marie Collins/Cecil Community College)

(right) The C & D Canal as it was rebuilt by the federal government converted the waterway from a small barge canal to a ship canal that permitted use by modern seagoing vessels. Compare this view to that of the 19th century canal, shown on page 79. (1941, A. Aubrey Bodine, The Mariner's Museum)

(below) A lift bridge was built to span the C & D Canal at Chesapeake City in the early 1920s. The central portion, here in the raised position to allow passage of the Bull Line steamer *Jean*, moved the roadbed up and down to accommodate the height of the large ships that could fit through the rebuilt canal. (A. Aubrey Bodine Collection, The Mariner's Museum)

In the 1880s several attempts were made to improve the county road system. One of these involved replacing deteriorating wooden bridges around the county with iron spans. This bridge across the Bohemia was part of that program. (c. 1908 postcard, Georgia Robinson/Cecil Community College)

the nineteenth century, relatively little money was expended on maintaining the public highways. As a result, Cecil roads were in more dire straits in the 1870s than they had been a century earlier.

The problems of repairing and maintaining the roads were charged to the county commissioners, a legacy they inherited from the earlier levy court.[16] The eighteenth century system, under which the county justices appointed overseers to maintain public roadways in their communities at their own expense, was superseded in the late nineteenth century by various acts of the General Assembly. These authorized the county commissioners to survey and plat new roads, to purchase private lanes for public use, to alter or improve the course of existing roads, and to employ engineers and road supervisors to maintain the county's public roads. By the end of the century, Cecil County employed ninety road supervisors, each paid $1.25 a day and supervising from two to ten laborers, usually only a few weeks each year, at a wage of $1.12 a day. To perform the work, the county maintained twelve road-scrapers and rollers and a stone crusher.[17]

In the 1880s the county commissioners initiated several attempts at improving the county road system, with varying degrees of success. Commissioners William Potter, Wilson Pierson, and Ellis Sentman contracted Charles H. Latrobe in 1884 to prepare plans and specifications for rebuilding or replacing several bridges crossing Octoraro and Conowingo creeks. Latrobe proposed a series of iron, Pratt truss bridges, with sixteen-foot roadways and wooden decks for existing crossings near Elk Forge, Richardsmere, Pilot Town, and a spot along the Conowingo that later gave rise to the aptly named community of New Bridge. The new iron spans replaced decaying wooden bridges that had been used for decades, including the covered Porter's Bridge crossing the Octoraro near Richardsmere.

Despite the new system of allocating responsibility and money for their upkeep, at the end of the nineteenth century roads in the county remained in deplorable condition.

Of the ninety-one miles of major roads on which the majority of county residents depended, ten miles were loose gravel, two miles were crushed shell, five miles carried a hard-packed stone surface, and the rest were of dirt.[18] A state geological survey report on Cecil County published in 1902 remarked that "no systematic efforts have been made to equip the county with roads built on scientific principles."[19] In fact, the longest stretch of the hard-packed stone road between Elkton and Providence was primarily the result of the private initiative of William Singerly, publisher of the Philadelphia *Record*, who in 1881 had acquired the paper mills at Providence and a pulp mill at Elkton. Completed in 1897, the road consisted of two layers of stone, the first coarsely and the second finely broken, covered with a thick

(above) Farmers depended on county roads, often in terrible condition, for hauling their crops to market. In the late 1890s residents in Cecil and elsewhere around the state finally petitioned the General Assembly for help in improving local roadways such as Calvert Road, on which C. W. McKinney is shown hauling corn. (c. 1912, Helen E. Harding/Cecil Community College)

(right) Wagons hauling coal for local industries were among the vehicles adding wear and tear to local roads, helping to make them too rough for the first cars. Here two six-mule teams stand in the road by the Cecil Paper Mill coal house. (early 1890s, Horace and Louise Witman/Cecil Community College)

layer of cinders, which helped smooth the road surface when ground by the passing wheels. Even this, the best road in the county, sometimes offered poor road conditions; eventually the cinders became ground to a fine dust that sent up choking clouds in dry weather and turned to a sticky quagmire in wet weather.

Beyond the main roads, the supervisors and their crews had 683 miles of roads to maintain that were no better than rutted dirt paths. Typical was the road leading from Elkton to North East, described in an 1899 survey report as "practically impassable" during "the winter months and wet weather."[20] Periodically, road crews made an effort to improve the road surface, simply

> throwing clay from the sides to the center, but the rains soon wash it back into the ditches. To put this piece of road into passable condition would require the construction of deep side-ditches, thorough underdrainage, and a filling in of the roadway with good gravel.[21]

The desperate state of the county's roads was a source of continuing frustration for Cecil farmers away from the railroad lines, for they depended on the county roads for hauling produce both to the station and to market. Their cry for better roads was soon taken up by other community and county leaders across the state, and together they petitioned the General Assembly to address the condition of the public roadways. In 1898 the legislature directed the Maryland Geological Survey—formed two years earlier—to conduct a thorough investigation of the state of road construction in Maryland. The resulting report, prepared under the supervision of Arthur Johnson, the state's first professional highway engineer, fully documented for the first time the sorry con-

Maintaining Cecil roads was problematic from early settlement until after World War I. By the time the first cars came along, roads such as the one pictured (between Port Deposit and Rising Sun, now Route 276) were "muddy and slippery when it rained, dusty and rough in summer, and when the frozen road thawed in the spring, the cars were almost buried in quagmire holes." (Roberta White/Cecil Community College; quote from Norman R. Touchton, "Dick the Country Storekeeper," Zion, 1982)

dition of a county road system developed by amateurs and maintained at best in a lackadaisical manner.[22]

Despite the dismal portrait painted by the report, it was not until 1904 that the General Assembly enacted the first in a series of legislative moves that resulted in significant road improvements. Under that first act, $200,000 in state funds was to be apportioned annually to each county on a matching basis for the construction of modern hard-surfaced roads. Proposed road designs were to be submitted to the Geological Survey. Once designs were approved, state surveys were to be conducted, plans and specifications drawn up, and the construction opened to competitive bidding. It was to be a state aid program only; the roads would remain the province of the individual counties, which would retain responsibility for their upkeep.

While such state programs may have instigated the upgrading of Cecil roads, it was the convergence of two dynamic forces in the first decade of the twentieth century that brought the "good roads" movement to full fruition. The first—and undoubtedly the most important—was the rise of the automobile. By 1905 the "horseless carriage" had

Situated along the "Newark & Conowingo Route," the H. C. Davis Service Station took advantage of Americans' new mobility, selling gasoline and, as advertised on the back of this postcard, "home made pies & cakes, a specialty." (Historical Society of Cecil County)

ceased to be an experiment and was well on its way to becoming an integral part of American life. This fact produced the second force affecting the condition of roads around the country: Americans began to travel rather extensively in their new vehicles and demanded roads suitable for their use.

Although the automobile quickly advanced from the position of technological toy it held in the 1890s, in 1900 motorcars remained a mixed lot—an amalgam of steam-, electric-, and gas-powered machines restricted principally to the wealthy due to prohibitive prices ranging from $3,000 to $12,000 each. Industry output for 1900 totaled 4,192, the vast majority of which were steamers.[23] By the middle of the decade, preference had shifted to the internal combustion engine because fuel for it was inexpensive and the motor needed less care and operating skill than did steamers or electrics. Standardization set in, and Henry Ford retooled the four-year-old Ford Motor Company for mass production in 1907, shifting the industry into high gear. With a revamped, assembly line approach, the factory turned out 14,887 cars in its first year of production. The popularity of Ford's Tin Lizzie was increased by its affordability. By the outbreak of World War I, the retail price of a Ford four-cylinder model varied from $345 to $645.[24]

With the widespread use of the automobile, overland travel began to exert a set of demands greatly different from those of the horse-powered days. Modern, automobile-oriented roads required longer curves, lower gradients, smoother pavement, multiple lanes, and elaborate patterns for controlling access. As a result, the new roads had a different impact on the landscape than their antecedents. Where an old wagon road may simply have followed the contours of the land, the new automobile roads often required a dramatic reworking of the landscape. The very nature of these new roads made them a more pervasive, more conspicuous feature of the landscape.

Most important from an administrative standpoint, the construction of automobile roads could not depend upon the amateur endeavors of community farmers. Expert engineering, imparting durable and dependable surfaces, played a major part in building the new roads. As a result, the growing

(above) The construction of the first Route 40 made a trip across Cecil, for long distance travelers and residents alike, an easier journey. County residents remember Circus Park as a popular wayside stop on the new highway (now Route 7). (1930s, Carol Smith/Cecil Community College)

(right) Governor Austin Lane Crothers, a Cecil County native, was elected to office in 1907 on a platform calling for reform. One of the first acts of his administration was to create the State Roads Commission, which developed a plan for a state highway system connecting Baltimore and the twenty-three county seats. (Maryland Historical Society)

coalition of automobile enthusiasts across the state began lobbying the legislature to create a professional organization to handle new road construction. Their call for government regulation of the public roadways was joined with that of the rising chorus of Maryland "reformists," who sought to influence the involvement of state government in a broad range of public affairs.

Once Ford and Chevrolet began making more affordable cars, the number of vehicles in the county gradually increased. The needs of drivers, who used their cars for recreation as well as business, ultimately forced the county and state governments to institute a serious program of road building and maintenance. Here Murray J. Ewing and friends stop to make a record of a pleasure trip. (c. 1917, Helen Ewing Harding/Cecil Community College)

The legislative excesses of the end of the nineteenth century, doling out perquisites to private industries often at the expense of the individual, came under increasing attack in the first decade of the twentieth century. Maryland progressives, like their counterparts across the nation, had come to realize that positive action and direct intervention by the state government was needed, not only to foster private industries but to provide public services for all citizens. Leadership of the state's progressive movement was provided by Austin Lane Crothers, a native of Cecil County, who was swept into the governor's office in 1907, along with a Democratic majority in both the Senate and the House of Delegates. Crothers's administration was able to move quickly to achieve a number of reformist programs, including the establishment of a Public Utilities Commission, a direct primary elections law, and a corrupt practices law.

One of the administration's first acts in 1908 was the creation of a State Roads Commission to oversee the development of a modern highway system. Under the act, Governor Crothers was authorized to appoint three salaried and

Fire Protection in Elkton

Members of the Singerly volunteer fire company of Elkton enjoy showing off their two 19th century hand pumps during a city parade. (Historical Society of Cecil County)

Like many other towns in the late nineteenth century, Elkton experienced several disastrous fires. Earlier interest in starting a fire company had resulted in the town's acquisition of two hand engines but, despite no fewer than three attempts, had failed to yield an organization responsible for them. The fires of 1890-91 and a concurrent interest in developing a town water system changed that, and in 1892 the William M. Singerly Steam Fire Engine and Hook and Ladder Company No. 1 was born.

In April 1891 Richard Thomas called a meeting to organize a fire company. Interim officers were elected, and plans were made for the fledgling company to purchase a steam pumping engine. The transaction brought Elkton an Amoskeag engine and 500 feet of hose sold by a Wilmington fire company for $1,000.

The Singerly charter was signed in January 1892 and a board of directors promptly elected. This body had twelve members, including Richard Thomas as president, Osborn R. Chaytor as third vice-president, and Samuel B. Enos as secretary, all of whom had served as interim officers. Adam Meisel was the first chief and Herman Jeffers the first chief engineer.

Coming up with money to purchase and maintain equipment was a major difficulty for the company in the first several decades. This problem was finally solved circa 1920, when the company began holding a yearly carnival to raise funds. This project provided enough money to purchase equipment and begin saving for future needs. F. H. Leffler, a member of the Maryland legislature, further secured the fire company's future by having a bill passed requiring the town of Elkton to pay the fire company two cents on each dollar assessed in property tax. The county commissioners later made their own contributions to the company's coffers, ending worries about funding.

In the beginning the company used the Hydraulion "Waterwitch," a hand engine with hose reel built in 1818 and purchased by Elkton in 1827; an 1859 suction engine "Arrow"; and the Amoskeag steam engine to fight fires. Motor equipment was first used in 1916, when the company purchased a GMC truck equipped to carry a hose and ladders. A small pump was added to complement this vehicle in 1920. In 1919 an Ahrens-Fox pumping engine was purchased to replace the steam engine, which was lost in a fire in a shop where it was being painted. A Hale engine was purchased in 1925 to replace the GMC truck. The Historical Society of Cecil County has taken custody of the two nineteenth century hand trucks—the Hydraulion (one of only twelve built) and the suction engine. These two old warhorses still occasionally appear in parades proudly displayed by current members of the company.

The Singerly volunteer fire company continues to provide fire protection in Elkton in the late twentieth century, and its history corresponds to that of volunteer fire companies in other Cecil towns.

Adapted from John J. Denver, "Short History of the Singerly Fire Co., 1892-1942," in the collection of the Historical Society of Cecil County, Elkton, and "Way Back When," *Maryland Magazine* (Winter 1985).

two unsalaried commissioners. Included in the first commission were John M. Tucker, one of Cecil's political leaders; Francis Clopper Hutton, a civil engineer; and William B. Clark, state geologist. Under their guidance, Maryland became a notable pioneer in the conception and implementation of one of the nation's first planned state highway systems. The system was originally designed to connect each of the state's twenty-three county seats with the city of Baltimore and secondarily to interconnect the county seats. Within seven years of the commission's founding, a total of 1,305 miles of hard-surfaced, concrete or macadam roads had been constructed.[25]

More than fifty miles of new state roads were built through Cecil County before the outbreak of World War I. Stretching out in a fourteen-foot-wide concrete and macadam ribbon, tying Perryville to Elkton to Fredericktown, these thoroughfares had an immediate effect on both town growth and county agriculture. No longer was development compelled to follow the lines of the railroad. Communities that had languished during the last half of the nineteenth century found their fortunes reversed by new links to the urban centers and by the liberating effect of the automobile. The property values of those whose land fronted hard-surfaced highways began to increase rapidly.

The development of the modern highway system and the growing availability of motor trucks at reasonable cost led to a veritable revolution in agriculture across the county. Now nearly all of Cecil had direct access to Baltimore, Philadelphia, and Wilmington and their rapidly expanding suburbs, with their constant demands for dairy products, beef, pork, fruits, and vegetables. For many years Cecil had had a reputation in the Baltimore markets for the fine quality of hay it produced. Now that reputation was enhanced by a flood of new market products. To the south, the fruit industry flourished, with quantities of peaches and pears trucked to market. Near Rising Sun, almost every field held several acres each year in tomatoes, with late crops grown for the canning industry.

Small, independent canneries operated during the late summer and early autumn months, putting up tomatoes and corn. Gradually, however, the profitability of these scattered canneries lessened in the face of growing competition from larger, better equipped canning factories in New Jersey and the Midwest, with their extended runs from early spring to late fall. The inability of the smaller Cecil concerns to consolidate ultimately crippled the local industry in the early twentieth century.[26]

Not every section of the county enjoyed the agricultural renaissance. At Charlestown, on Elk Neck, and near the western part of Gray's Hill, the soils had declined to such a state that many considered them too worthless to pay for the cost of clearing. The few attempts made at cultivation had proved decidedly discouraging, and scrub pine thickets eventually moved in to reclaim the fields. Unfortunately for the county image, both the Pennsylvania and the B&O railroads passed through some of the most unproductive sections of Cecil. The scenes unfolding from the passenger windows painted a picture of poverty for out-of-town travelers, who all too often wrongly supposed the impoverished landscape was indicative of the entire county.

Rather, the quality of the soils in the county ranged widely, from absolutely barren to most productive. In 1880 the *Maryland Business Directory* had described the county as "one of the most thriving in the State":

> The character of the land is mixed, the part above the Bay being mostly rolling and quite hilly, like the Western Shore, and below Elkton, quite level and similar to the adjoining Eastern Shore counties. The soil comprises every variety, a considerable portion centrally situated, called the "Barrens," being pure sand and gravel (though this section has of late been improved) whilst other parts have heavier clayey soil, mixed rocky, and the lower part an excellent light clay loam. The County is well populated, and farming and improvements generally are in advance of the average in the State.[27]

It was true that the poorer farming sections, in the gravel and clay hills of the central county, were characterized by ragged, dilapidated fences, crudely patched barns and sheds, and tumbled-down dwellings. But throughout the better farming sections and in the established towns and villages, the prosperity of the period was reflected in a pervasive spirit of rebuilding. Comfortable and stylish farm dwellings, well-

Telephone Service Comes to Cecil

Early in the twentieth century residents of the Rising Sun area wanted local telephone service. Members of the Cecil Farmers' Club obliged them by establishing the Cecil Farmers' Telephone Company around 1904. Five years later the local lines were hooked up with those of the Diamond State Telephone Company, making the long distance service of the Bell Telephone Company available to Cecil residents. The stock of Cecil Farmers' Telephone was held largely by local residents, and by 1919 the company had more than 400 subscribers.

Once the telephone exchanges were automated, all calls made in Cecil County went through Elkton. Before that, however, when an operator still handled every call, calls were reported to telephone exchanges in Perryville, North East, Chesapeake City, and Elkton.

Cecil Farmers' Telephone Company advertisement in Celia D. Mitchell, ed., *Cecil Whig: Historical and Industrial Edition, 1841-1919* (reprint of 1919 ed., Elkton: Cecil County Round Table, 1991).

---

ance of the progressive generation. Cecil society—and American society—was settling into the conspicuous cultural and social patterns of modern times, with each segment intricately linked in a hierarchical order. At the top stood the aristocracy of money and of intellect, enjoying the full range of benefits accrued from the industrial and technological innovations of the period. Next was the bulging middle class, with its various gradations; and at the bottom, the poor in both wealth and education. More than ever the homes of each class in Cecil County became a visual index of the family's individual status, from the suffusive ornamentation of the houses of the wealthy, parlors filled with handcrafted woodwork and drawing rooms displaying imported sculptures and original oils, to the severity of the tenant farmers' houses rising starkly amidst the scrub and stubble of marginal land.

It was the class between the extremes, the ever-broadening middle class—the diversified farmer, the small-scale industrialist, the well-connected merchant, the skilled contractor, the doctor, the lawyer—that composed the greater part of Cecil society, and it is in their homes that a picture of domestic life brings greater understanding of the period. Working under new conditions, and living according to the influences of new developments in science and industry, the lives of the middle class were more closely attuned to the pace of American culture than those of the wealthy, for whom the choices were endless, or the poor, who had few choices.

Dominating the pace of American culture was the machine, in all its permutations, which brought about the inexorable replacement of the wash basin and pitcher with the bathroom sink and faucet, of the kerosene light with the electric bulb, of the wood stove with the gas range. The machines of transportation and communication, from railroad to automobile and telegraph to telephone, all but eliminated the final vestiges of provincialism from the lives of the Cecil middle class.

Together, the machines had penetrated the isolated areas of the country and finally brought the United States together, not only as a political unit but as an interdependent economic unit. Few areas of the United States remained completely removed from the influence of the rest of the country. More and more, idiomatic customs, clothing, and housing began to disappear, replaced by a standardization

kept barns and outbuildings, in-town houses bordering on pretentiousness, and neatly trimmed hedges made up the picturesque domestic scene.

Reflected in the hard scrabble of Elk Neck and the fertile fields of Rising Sun, Cecil at the dawn of the twentieth century had become a land of contrasts, of wealth and poverty, of now and then, of the hand-hewn simplicity of the earlier generation and the machine-produced exuber-

A Matter of Public Safety

The Victorian Singerly mansion in Elkton was the first home of Union Hospital. (c. 1909, postcard collection of Michael J. Dixon)

By 1902 a movement was afoot to build a hospital to serve the citizens of Cecil County, who until then had to travel to Baltimore or Wilmington when they required the services of a hospital. A public meeting held in October of that year yielded a resolution, stating that a local hospital was a necessity, and a chairman, who was authorized to appoint a committee to get the project underway. Chairman George A. Blake, Esq., was to choose one clergyman, one attorney, one doctor, one businessman, and one newspaper man to serve with him.

The Hospital Building Committee held another public meeting in December, where a number of doctors spoke about the need for a hospital that would serve all county residents, rich and poor, and about their belief that there were enough interested people to provide the support needed to succeed. Ways of raising money to open a hospital were discussed as well. Twelve incorporators—doctors from Elkton, Chesapeake City, Rising Sun, and Port Deposit—were chosen to formalize the process of founding a hospital.

Articles of incorporation for the Union Hospital of Cecil County were signed by a judge at the end of January 1903 and recorded in the courthouse several days later. An article in the March 14, 1903, edition of the *Cecil Whig* discussed how the hospital would accommodate patients who could not pay and the terms under which doctors would practice there. The article firmly stated, "We intend to build the Hospital.... It is a matter of not only public pride, but public safety."

Although the inspiration for the hospital's name has been lost to time, it seems to stem from the idea that people from all over the county would have to work together to establish such an institution. This cooperation was represented by the union of doctors from a number of towns who got the incorporation off the ground.

The next step was to find a site for the hospital. After some investigation, the *Cecil Whig* reported in May, the "fine Singerly residence at Cathedral Street and Singerly Avenue" was chosen. John S. and Annie E. Byers sold this large Victorian mansion, built in 1888, to the Union Hospital that same month. Several adjacent parcels were purchased as well, and work was begun to convert the house to a hospital.

In November 1908 the *Whig* reported the hospital would open on December 1st. A new three-story wing had been dedicated several days earlier. At first one nurse took care of the professional needs of the patients, while practical nurses fed and bathed them, cleaned the premises, and fired the coal furnace. Surgery was performed by doctors who came on the train and returned to Baltimore after the operation was completed. A nursing school was begun at Union Hospital in 1911 and operated until 1929. A ladies' auxiliary was formed to supervise housekeeping tasks at the hospital; this group, which also organized fund-raising efforts for the hospital, has continued its efforts over the years. In 1912 a one-story addition was built to house a kitchen, pantry, and refrigerator. In 1913 another three-story wing was constructed, giving the hospital an L shape. This enlarged facility served the Cecil community well until World War II.

The influx of people who came to work in the munitions plants in Elkton during the war severely strained the facilities of Union Hospital. A new hospital was begun on the hospital grounds in 1943 and completed in 1944. Further advancements in technology and county population growth required replacement of this facility in 1973. The four-story hospital built at that time still serves the community.

Adapted from George M. Reynolds, "Union Hospital of Cecil County," *The Bulletin of the Historical Society of Cecil County* (September 1993).

not only of material concerns but of ideas and interests. Mass production and modern advertising sold all Americans a shared vision of domestic life. Families in Elkton gathered around the same dining room table and enjoyed food prepared on the same kitchen range as families in Chicago or St. Louis. As a result, Main Street Elkton became in essence Main Street America.

Despite these changes, the new houses that appeared along that main street beginning at the turn of the century were hardly a homogeneous lot. They reflected the gamut of historical and contemporary influences, from the traditional homes of the colonial frontier to those of the machine-driven industrial city. Indeed, to some extent the architectural complexity and diversity that dominated the building scene in industrial American cities intruded upon Cecil streetscapes. As a result, these became melting pots of style, materials, approach, and attitudes.

Continuing the game of architectural free association initiated by the preceding generation—and aided immeasurably by readily available, mass-produced elements—professional and amateur house builders alike drew inspiration from 2,000 years of Western design to produce a restless architecture seemingly unencumbered by any restraining philosophy. Old World images continued to be reworked into American main street counterparts. Increasingly, toward the end of the century, the United States turned for inspiration to its own architectural heritage, brought to the forefront of the nation's consciousness by the Centennial Celebration of 1876.

Historical purity of form and detail was by no means every builder's guiding principle, nor was there a strict sequential appearance of any of the designs inspired by the past. Rather, loose interpretations of Gothic cottages, French minor chateaux, Italian villas, and Queen Anne manor houses appeared concurrently with colonial-inspired farmhouses and machine-cut hybrids, creating a riot of towers, turrets, balconies, oriels, broken pediments, and mansard roofs across town and country. Often, various styles converged and combined in a single house, the exuberance of the design and the mixture of elements curtailed only by the financial and creative resources of the builder.

Few Cecil communities were immune from at least one example of machine-driven architectural excess. Even Charlestown, which had reached the apex of its economic and cultural vitality years earlier, found its streetscape enlivened by such adventurous builders as the McKown brothers. In 1897, anxious to display their modernity—and their newly acquired fortune, made from operating gambling houses during the Alaskan gold rush—the McKowns built a flamboyant house incorporating visual references to nearly every architectural style then in vogue.

Many professional architects began to decry the profusion of styles and, using the occasion of the World's Columbian Exposition held in Chicago in 1892-93, set out to artificially impose some restraining order on the architectural confusion. Their solution was to reinsert a studied classicism as the desired architectural order, an approach advocated in America by graduates of and adherents to the teaching of the Ecole des Beaux-Arts in France. Such self-conscious movements had only a tangential effect on the design and construction of domestic architecture in Cecil County. Most private house builders blithely continued to mine the architectural past. By World War I they had introduced a whole host of American apparitions, from New England Cape Cods to gambrel-roofed Dutch colonials, from antebellum Georgian plantation houses to southwestern Spanish missions.

Nowhere was this profusion of acceptable architectural types made more apparent than in the pages of America's great style follower, the Sears, Roebuck catalog. By the early twentieth century, readers flipping through the mail-order catalog could find, tucked among the pages of clothing, hardware, and other mass-produced merchandise, ready-to-build houses. These ranged in size from a modest two-bedroom bungalow for $700 to a grand $6,000 Colonial Revival mansion featuring columns, porticoes, and servants' quarters. These "kits" arrived from warehouse to building site in parts, from rafters to nails to the kitchen sink. By the 1920s Sears offered 450 different house models, encompassing the entire spectrum of popular styles.[28]

No American architectural movement of the seventeenth, eighteenth, or nineteenth century appears to have escaped being copied, adapted, and modified for early twentieth century homes. Little regard was given to the geographical provenance of the original house forms; east and west freely exchanged once-indigenous architectural styles

(left) Wealthy Cecil residents who wanted to flaunt their riches sometimes chose to do so by building a stylish dwelling. The "Klondyke" house in Charlestown exhibited a flamboyant combination of styles and was paid for with money its owners, the McKown brothers, had made from the Alaska gold rush. (Maryland Historical Trust)

(below) The Colonial Revival structure with Victorian tower built by Howard Bratton at 237 East Main Street, Elkton, exemplifies the combination of styles in one house often found just before the turn of the 20th century. Despite architects' efforts to set standards in the 1890s, such popular enthusiasm for combining styles continued into the next century. (1985, Maryland Historical Trust)

From the late 19th century until World War II, the Sears, Roebuck Company sold house kits through its mail-order catalog. Everything required to build these houses, available in every conceivable style and many sizes, was shipped by rail and transported from the nearest terminal to the building site. The Henry Hager house on Bohemia Avenue in Chesapeake City, was constructed in 1914 from a Sears kit. (1995)

and forms. Thus, by the 1920s, on estates within the confines of old Bohemia Manor, were constructed two buildings as disparate as the Bayard family's new mansion and the neighboring house built by the Sharp family. The textbook-derivative Georgian Revival Bohemia Manor is a hulking brick re-creation of the golden era of tidewater tobacco plantations, while the caretaker's house built near Cayot's Corner by Rodney Sharp is a provincially anomalous Mission Revival structure, with stuccoed walls, corrugated red pantile roof, and bell tower recalling the romance of old California.

Not every house builder in Cecil County during the period opted for a new style house. Indeed, the traditional two-story, three-bay frame house continued to be a popular house form well into the early twentieth century—often only thinly disguised for the times with a modicum of applied ornamentation. This form may, in fact, better represent the typical period house than its more elaborate contemporaries. While the exterior forms of the new style houses may have reflected styles in favor when they were built—whether renaissance, romanesque, classical, or colonial—their floor plans retained a certain flexible and informal soundness that had been integral to Cecil dwellings for a century or more. The houses of the period were built from the inside out; they were conceived and executed within the framework of what constituted a house—center hall or side passage, large interconnecting social areas on the first floor, sleeping chambers on the second—developed long before the explosion of style consciousness at the turn of the century. Such arrangements remained satisfactory until changing economic conditions between the world wars rendered them obsolete.

(left) The house today called Bohemia Manor was built in the early 20th century in the Georgian Revival style. Its scale is larger than that of an 18th century house, but its details are textbook examples of Georgian stylistic features. (1995)

(below) The diversity in the architectural styles considered suitable for dwellings in the early 20th century is demonstrated by the Spanish Mission caretaker's house built by Rodney Sharp around the same time and in the same vicinity as the revival Bohemia Manor. (1979, Maryland Historical Trust)

(above) The Atlas Powder Company manufactured explosives at its Perry Point site for several years during World War I. The power plant (on the right) constructed as part of that work continued in operation for several years after the war. (September 1918, Clifton Lewis/Cecil Community College)

(right) The federal government bought the Perry Point estate near Perryville at the outset of World War I, leasing it to the Atlas Powder Company. The military has used the property for various activities since the 1920s. (1968, Maryland Historical Trust)

CHAPTER 6

The "Marriage Capital of the East" in the Modern Period

THE MASSIVE MILITARY OUTPOURING of the United States during World War I, first in materials and then, after America's formal entrance in 1917, in manpower, provided the impetus that propelled Cecil County fully into the modern era. The two-edged sword of war cut both ways, however. The escalation of war-related activities along the Eastern seaboard, with new camps and new munitions plants springing up seemingly every month, eventually came to Cecil County. The federal government purchased the Perry Point estate near Perryville, long the home of the Stump family, and leased it to the Atlas Powder Company. The huge powder plant built at the site produced both explosives and job opportunities. At the war's end the government converted the plant into a medical and psychiatric facility for the rehabilitation of returning veterans.

Greater changes in the county were wrought by the

Cecil World War I veterans, marching by the Howard Hotel in Elkton, participate in a parade. (1924, Robert G. Merrick Collection, Maryland State Archives, MSA SC 1477-5797)

movement of nonmilitary personnel. Population levels in Cecil, as throughout the Eastern Shore, declined as able-bodied workers left field and farm for the higher wages of city industries. Baltimore and Philadelphia swelled with the ranks of laborers imported from surrounding rural areas and thrown into the steel mills, shipyards, factories, and countless smaller enterprises turning out supplies destined for the front. In fact, by the end of the war the combined populations of the nation's urban centers, growing steadily since the 1870s, finally eclipsed the population of the rural communities. Henceforward, more people would live in the cities than in the country.[1]

The increased density of urban dwellers created an increased demand for the agricultural products of Cecil fields. The combination of decreasing farm labor and calls for increased agricultural production led to the further mechanization of county farms, accelerating a process begun at the turn of the century. On farm after farm, in the period between World War I and World War II, the old horse and sulky plow were replaced with the gasoline tractor and gang plow. Mule-drawn corn cutters gave way to mechanical cornpickers, and with the older method went the armies of corn shocks marching into the distance. The sight of men forking and stacking hay in the fields gave way to hulking hay balers pulled through the timothy by a solitary tractor driver; transporting the large amounts of hay demanded at home and abroad was much easier in baled rather than loose shipments.[2] Creaking farm wagons yielded to open-bed and panel trucks carrying products to market.

(left) This steam-driven tractor required a water wagon in order to generate steam. The belt hooked up to the tractor's engine is part of an operation to thresh grain. (c. 1920, Catherine Short/Cecil Community College)

(below) Increased demand for crops and a smaller available labor force encouraged the mechanization of Cecil farms between the world wars. Pictured is the first known tractor in Elk Neck, at Piney Creek Farm. The farmer stands proudly beside his new acquisition. (1920, Howard Henry/Cecil Community College)

Before the small companies sprang up that first offered electricity on a larger scale to Cecil residents, some wealthy families acquired their own electrical supply systems. This small brick building was built to house the electric generator at Bohemia Manor, the Georgian Revival house built by U.S. Senator Thomas F. Bayard of Delaware in 1920. (1995)

The world of county dairy farmers began to change to meet modern demands fueled by sanitary considerations. Calamitous outbreaks of typhoid fever and particularly of tuberculosis—linked to contaminated milk—swept American cities in the early twentieth century. As a result earthen floors and wooden milking stalls were labeled disease promoters and replaced with concrete slabs, metal stanchions, and block wall construction in dairy barns and silos. In 1918 New Yorker Edgar P. Young bought the Kershaw farm at Elk Mills and planned "extensive improvements" typical of the new ways. Carpenters and masons were hired to repair the buildings and add "concrete work." A water system operated by air pressure and an "electric light plant" were to be installed and the house and barn wired for electricity. This work was intended to achieve the owner's purpose of establishing "a thoroughly modern dairy farm in every particular."[3]

Electricity proved to be another new force of change in Cecil, one that was sometimes subtle and sometimes dramatic. After 1886, the year Nikola Tesla conceived of the first practical alternating current system capable of transmitting power over long distances, more and more communities across the nation began going electric. Many county farmers at the turn of the century recognized the value of electricity but were outside the reach and scope of either the Baltimore or Philadelphia companies then supplying power to their primarily urban customers. To meet their needs, some farmers, like Mr. Young, constructed their own small-scale electric systems. Power produced by gasoline-driven or windmill-driven generators or self-contained battery systems provided enough electricity to light milking parlors, pump water into cisterns, and illuminate the home.

Others in the county had a larger vision. William Warburton was an Elkton attorney seized by the dream of bringing electricity to the county. In 1895 he began purchasing property along the North East Creek and set about constructing a hydroelectric plant to harness the power of Gilpin's Falls, with its 106-foot drop in the span of 2,000 feet. By 1905 Warburton's dream, incorporated as the Elkton Electric Light and Power Company, was supplying area homes with power. By 1919 another enterprise, the Home Manufacturing Light & Power Company of Cecil County, was also offering customers electric service available all day every day of the year.

An even greater boost to the electrification of Cecil County came in the 1920s, this time from a Pennsylvania interest. The untapped power of the Susquehanna falls near Conowingo had attracted the attention of the Philadelphia Electric Company, then searching for a suitable location for a new hydroelectric facility. By the 1920s the company had entered protracted negotiations with the State of Maryland to construct the plant. Engineering such a massive project proved formidable, but an even greater obstacle came in the form of the Baltimore power interests, who were concerned about encroaching competition. By way of appeasement, the state handed the Baltimore utilities a guarantee

24 HOUR SERVICE

The Home Manufacturing Light & Power Co. of Cecil County

If you have an Electric Washer, Cleaner, Iron, Toaster, Percolators, etc., you will need our 24 HOUR SERVICE. We are the ONLY ELECTRIC COMPANY in the County that gives such service the year round.

We are exceptionally well equipped to supply current for large motors.

We can supply your needs.

WM. STERLING EVANS, Sec'y & Mgr.

(left) Several Cecil County entrepreneurs started companies to make electricity available in the county before Baltimore and Philadelphia firms grew large enough to reach outlying areas. This 1919 advertisement for the Home Manufacturing Light & Power Co. of Cecil County outlines the company's services. (C. D. Mitchell, *Cecil Whig: Historical and Industrial Edition*, reprint of 1919 ed.)

(below) This covered bridge crossed the Susquehanna at Conowingo in the 19th century. By the time it was demolished to make way for the Conowingo dam, only some spans remained covered. (Machean Collection, Maryland State Archives, MSA SC 1751-4)

(above) Cecil County came fully into the modern age when the Philadelphia Electric Company built the Conowingo dam in 1926-28. (c. 1928, Lewis Hevrin/Historical Society of Cecil County)

(left) Construction of the Conowingo dam changed the Cecil landscape, particularly above the dam, where the Bald Friar ford and Indian fishing grounds were flooded. This view of the spillway from the window of the turbine hall suggests the force of the water held back by the dam. (Theodor Horydczak Collection, Prints & Photographs Division, Library of Congress)

that the planned Conowingo facility would be prohibited from extending its lines toward the city for a period of fifty years. Under such constraints, construction of the sprawling dam across the Susquehanna began.[4]

The $20 million dam contract was awarded to the Arundel Corporation, a Baltimore-based concern headed by businessman and Democratic boss Frank Furst. Many Maryland Republicans eyed the award suspiciously; Furst was a close friend of then-governor Albert Ritchie and had helped launch Ritchie's political career. It was not the first Cecil project award tainted with charges of cronyism. During the Austin L. Crothers administration, the old Pennsylvania Railroad bridge crossing the Susquehanna at Perryville had been given free of charge to a consortium of area businessmen that included the governor's brother. The group spent a paltry $700 to plank the bridge for vehicle passage, charged a toll for all trucks and cars, and collected more than $370,000 before selling it to the state for $585,000. The charges of cronyism against the progressive-minded Crothers were only whispered; those leveled against Ritchie in the award of the Conowingo project were shouted in the press. The charges did not stick, however, and the Arundel Corporation proceeded with construction.[5]

By 1926 nearly 4,000 workers had poured into Harford and Cecil counties to build the dam and accompanying power plant. The project called for a radical reworking of the landscape; stretches of the adjacent railroad had to be rerouted, fifty spillways constructed, and the old Baltimore Pike—now known as U. S. Route 1—run atop the 4,648-foot length of the dam. The impounded lake, filling up behind the completed dam in 1927, eventually contained more than 150 billion gallons of river water, stretching behind the dam for fourteen miles and measuring a mile across at the widest point. This deluge reshaped the riverbanks, inundated long familiar landmarks, and brought to a final close Port Deposit's river connection to the north. The power plant was completed and began operations in 1928. Constructed on the Harford side of the river, it was one of the largest power plants in the world when it opened.

More than any other structure, the Conowingo Dam heralded the modern age in Cecil County. Sprawling and powerful, a stunning example of the ability of man and technology to harness hitherto untamed forces, it was a harbinger of the future. Within a year, however, the bright prospects of the electric age were dimmed by the utter blackness of the Depression. In 1929 the stock market, stretched to the limits by rampant speculation, crashed, signaling the beginning of catastrophic circumstances for the national economy. Agricultural and commodity prices soon plunged, and the national income collapsed. By January 1930 nearly 4 million Americans had been laid off or unemployed; by the

> ## "Marriage" Names World War II Plan after Elkton
>
> Elkton's renown as a marriage capital named a naval operation during World War II. In the midsummer of 1943, the joint chiefs of staff drew up a plan to isolate the large Japanese naval and air bases at Rabaul, New Britain. This plan, for the first time, required the cooperation of both the Southwest Pacific forces under General MacArthur and the South Pacific forces under Admiral Halsey. This "marriage" of the two forces caused the joint chiefs to name their plan "Operation Elkton."
>
> With reference to William Breuer, *Devil Boats, The PT War against Japan* (Novato, Ca.: Presidio Press, 1987).

(opposite top) During the wedding boom, many Elkton residents turned the town's location into an economic opportunity. As the first stop in Maryland for trains coming from the north, where it was more difficult to obtain a marriage license, Elkton became part of the history of many out-of-town couples. The courthouse issued licenses, and local entrepreneurs such as W. F. Hopkins offered other services. (postcard collection of Michael J. Dixon)

(opposite bottom) Weddings were big business in Elkton roughly from 1913 until 1938, when Maryland adopted a 48-hour waiting period for getting a marriage license. (The Aubrey Bodine Collection, Peale Museum, Baltimore)

end of the year more than 1,300 banks had closed their doors.[6]

Cecil did not remain unscathed by the economic turmoil. Business and trade declined throughout the county. Tenant houses were abandoned, fields left untended, farms went under. Within five years of the crash, nearly 200 family farms were lost to hard times.[7] By 1932 a state report revealed that nearly two-thirds of Elkton's black laborers were out of work.[8] Many people—black and white alike—left for Baltimore in hopes of finding employment.

In the midst of the hardship, however, one peculiar Elkton industry seemed somehow depression-proof: the wedding business. This was a local affair that had grown out of the fortuitous combination of the looseness of Maryland's marriage law, which required no waiting period for licenses or blood tests, and the county seat's position as the first Maryland courthouse encountered by lovestruck couples traveling by rail or highway from New York, New Jersey, and eastern Pennsylvania. Elkton by the 1920s had become the self-proclaimed "Marriage Capital of the East," and everyone in town seemed to own a piece of the business. Taxi companies—sometimes merely any car owner—lined up at the station, waiting to take the anxious couples on their rounds. Hotels and inns offered honeymoon specials, and local merchants carried an assortment of ready-to-wear wedding bands. Main Street was littered with the signs of "marrying parsons" posted outside their homes, advertising quick ceremonies conducted in the convenience of a front parlor.

As the trade increased, cab drivers began offering couples an array of package deals that included a trip to the courthouse, to the chapel or parson, to the honeymoon suite at a hotel, and back to the station, all for $25. As a further inducement, some would throw in a wedding ring — no additional charge. Many in town derived a comfortable living from the wedding brigades; in a single year, Baptist minister W. R. Moon performed 4,000 weddings.[9] The Cecil County courthouse, on the other hand, found its aging facilities overtaxed by the constant stream of couples and the mountains of marriage licenses issued and recorded. In 1933 Cecil began petitioning the General Assembly to appro-

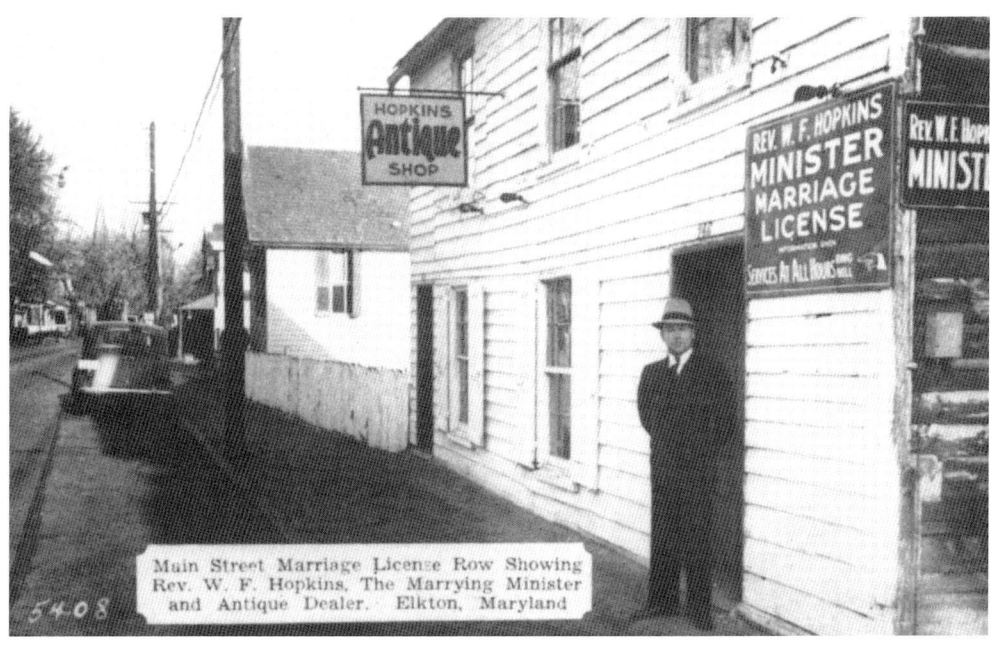

HOPKINS
Antique
SHOP
REV. W. F. HOPKINS
MINISTER
MARRIAGE
LICENSE
SERVICES AT ALL HOURS
Main Street Marriage License Row Showing
Rev. W. F. Hopkins, The Marrying Minister
and Antique Dealer. Elkton, Maryland
5408

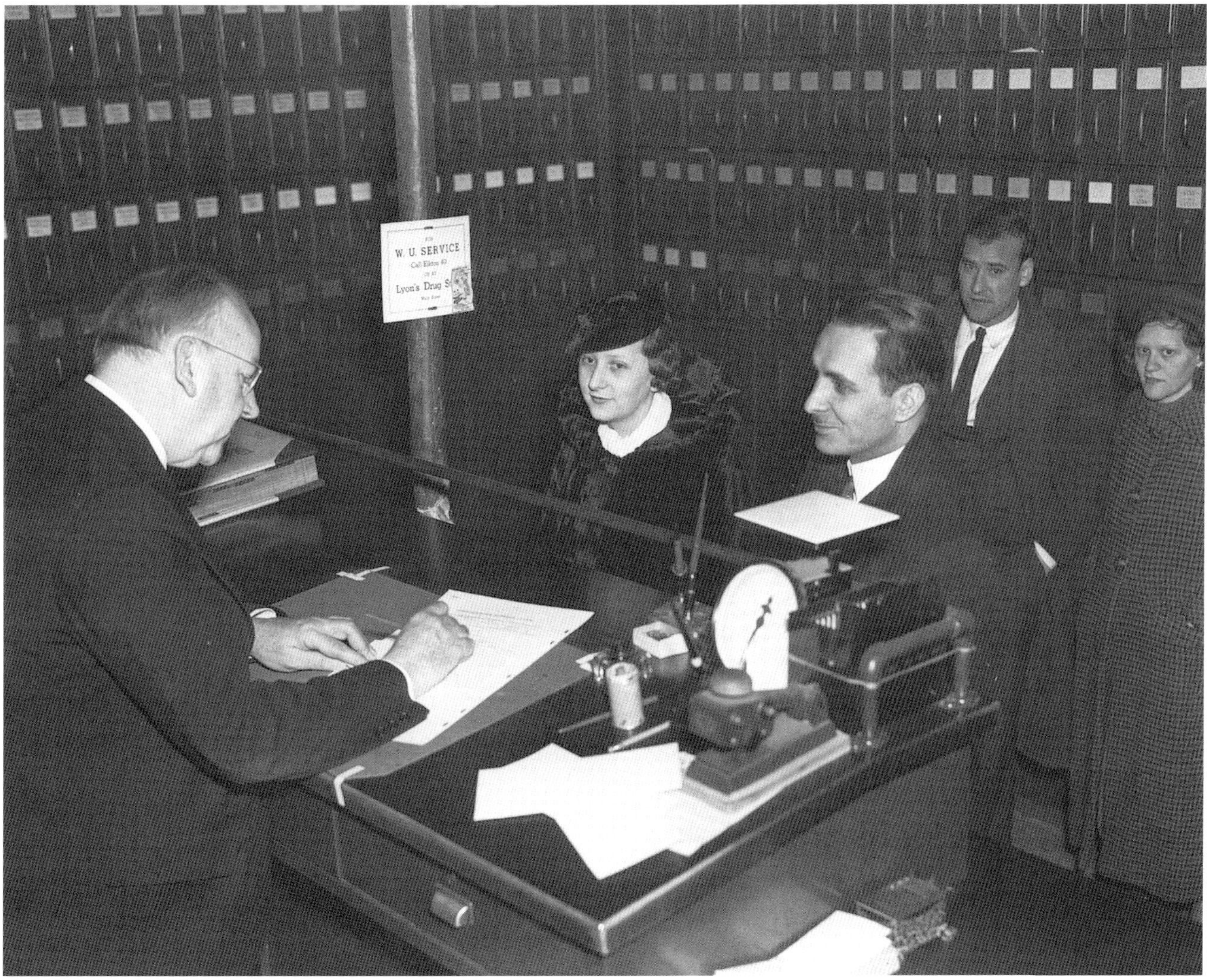
W. U. SERVICE

By the early 1930s, the marriage trade in Elkton had outgrown the facilities of the Cecil County courthouse. When this stylish new building opened in 1940, it seemed very stark and unattractive to many residents. (postcard, Maryland Historical Society)

priate the funds necessary to build a new facility to expand its cramped court offices.

Maryland was still caught in the throes of the Depression and struggling to mend the seams torn open in its economy, but in 1933 help arrived. The tailor's name was Roosevelt, and the needle and thread were called the New Deal. Only one day after his inauguration in 1933, President Franklin D. Roosevelt issued a proclamation declaring a nationwide four-day "bank holiday," bringing a halt to the depletion of the nation's gold reserves; placing an embargo on the export of all gold, silver, and currency; and effectively stopping the panic-stricken run on the banks. In his next move Roosevelt by executive order reduced federal salaries, pensions, and other benefits netting a savings of $400 million. Then, turning his attention to the armies of unemployed, Roosevelt pushed through Congress the National Industrial Recovery Act. Enacted in June, it authorized $3.3 billion for public works. From this came the Works Progress Administration, which was created and authorized to disburse money to federal, state, and local agencies for modernization projects "of public benefit." The National Recovery Act also prescribed maximum working hours and minimum wages for industry and trade, guaranteeing workers a basic living, and released additional millions in federal loans and grants into the economy, including $400 million to the states for highway construction.[10]

Ultimately, Cecil County benefited from these and other New Deal programs, as did many communities across Maryland. The NRA road funds brought about the construction of Route 40 and a new Susquehanna bridge. The Rural Electrification Administration, created in 1935 to provide low-cost loans to cover the costs of constructing power lines and other facilities, brought central station service from the Conowingo plant to farmers throughout the county. The Public Works money released into the state finally brought

Elkton a new courthouse, high school, and post office. Public Works funds were also used to widen, straighten, and deepen the C & D Canal.

The county commissioners opted to build the new courthouse on the site of the old Fountain Inn, some 200 yards up Main Street from the facility it replaced. The architecture firm of Malone and Williams of Salisbury was contracted to design the new building, and plans proceeded apace. Meanwhile, the General Assembly was working on plans of its own that would significantly curtail the number of future patrons of the Cecil courthouse. In 1938 Maryland adopted the forty-eight-hour waiting period for the issuance of marriage licenses; exceptions could be made only under special circumstances such as the overseas transfer of military personnel. Although Elkton remained a traditional destination for eloping couples, little by little its marriage trade slowed.

In May 1939 the cornerstone of the new courthouse was laid with much pomp, circumstance, and talk about the dawning of a new and glorious day for the county. When the completed building formally opened the following year, however, the light reflecting off the new bronze trim appeared a little too glaring for many people's eyes. Hubert Footner perhaps spoke for a sizable number of people both in and out of town in his criticism of the new courthouse:

> The building stands directly upon Main Street without a tree or a bit of grass to grace it. The material is handsome enough, being the native stone of Cecil county, but the bronze trimmings seem strangely out of place and the design, inclining to L'Art Moderne, hopelessly out of character with the simple, pleasant American town that surrounds it. The desire to be up-to-date leads men into strange aberrations.[11]

Architecturally, the new Cecil courthouse did mark a sharp break with the older courthouse, reworked in 1896 with a turreted addition, and with the earlier buildings of downtown Elkton, many of which followed the revival styles popular for both commercial and residential architecture. The designers of the new courthouse and the county officials who approved the design had eschewed traditional designs for a thoroughly modern style—lean, muscular, and reflective of Elkton in the twentieth century.

Perhaps the courthouse design was intended to drag the county, however reluctantly, into architectural modernity. The so-called Art Moderne movement—a term in many instances interchangeable with the more popular "Art Deco"—indeed had begun in the early twentieth century as a conscious reaction by both European and American designers against the strangulating ornamentation and mangle of intersecting planes and angles that characterized the recent past. Art Deco and its later offshoot, Streamline Deco, were decorative and modish, happily incorporating modern materials such as plastic, formica, black glass, and chrome. This combination of style and materials was thought to symbolize the dynamic industrial and technological twentieth century, with its speed and machines, fast cars, trains, airplanes, and steamships. Drafting-table geometrics and sleek mechanical curves appeared everywhere in the designs.

Such '30s architectural designs were outgrowths of other modern design movements beginning to stir after the changing of the order at the end of World War I. In the visual arts the picturesque sentimentality long espoused in painting and sculpture was being replaced by the hard-edged, often cynical vision of cubism and its allied movements. These approaches eliminated the lush realism with a surreal reduction of modern life to a juxtaposed series of angles, planes, and surfaces. Commercial designs as well, from automobiles and railway cars to kitchen equipment and bathroom fixtures, were undergoing stylistic changes aimed at simplifying surface contours and introducing new color schemes. With such a design revolution going on all around, it was only natural for new buildings of the period, whether commercial, public, or domestic, to be as up-to-date as the art on the wall, the cars in the garage, or the coffee pot on the kitchen counter.

Social critics and architectural theorists of the time, from Le Corbusier in the Old World to Frank Lloyd Wright in the New, sought through the use of new materials, methods, and manners to break from the restraints, or rather the unrestrained traditions, of architecture. Some, like Le Corbusier, would take their imaginings to the extreme, proclaiming that houses were no longer houses but, in the

The modern style was popular for commercial buildings such as this diner, which stood at the intersection of present-day Routes 40 and 213 just outside of Elkton. On the back of this postcard, the restaurant is advertised as a "Modern De Luxe Diner" with "Counter and Booth Service; Never Closed—Air Conditioned—Good Parking; Modern Wash Rooms." (postcard collection of Michael J. Dixon)

spirit of the times, "machines for living in." By extension, commercial buildings became "machines for selling" and public buildings "machines for administration," with the emphasis on machine—each efficient, impersonal, based on function, symbolized by the basic box, with plain walls, large expanses of glass, flat roofs, and projections supported by straight iron columns.[12]

To a certain extent, the dictums of the modern styles found adherents in public and commercial buildings in Cecil County. The allusions are apparent in the Susquehanna River Bridge Administration Building, built in 1940 as part of the construction of Route 40. The building features the curving walls and ornamental banding typical of many modern designs of the period. Often, however, there was a greater economic reason, overriding the design philosophy, for the acceptance of the modern look of the 1930s. The Depression had forced developers to count every penny spent on construction and equipment. Architects as well developed deeper commitments to economical buildings and low-cost construction. Despite stylistic disagreements, everyone was convinced of one thing: There was no room left for the pretentiousness of easier, earlier times and buildings that were overly decorative, labor-intensive, handmade, and suffused with costly ornamentation. The modern style, drastically stripped of surface ornamentation and happily employing ready-made, mass-produced architectural elements, was perfect for cost-conscious clients.

But while the modern style became popular and ubiquitous for chain stores and other commercial and public buildings popping up in Cecil County during the 1930s, it was not readily embraced by home builders or buyers. The shock of the new for many was just too stark, too cold, too alien. The blank box seemed more engineering feat than comfortable dwelling. Granted, the profuse ornamentation of the earlier revival and eclectic styles was no longer appropriate, given the economic vicissitudes of the times. But most builders in Cecil County could not or would not turn their backs on the past. Instead, they sought to align the traditional, past-inspired house with the present by stripping away the accretions of preceding periods until they eventually reduced—and returned—the house to its basic form, whether square or rectangular, one-and-a-half stories or two. What resulted was a small house architecture with an affinity to the American colonial period, farmhouses and Cape Cods, sometimes harkening back to their European cottage antecedents. There was an economy of materials and of space, to be sure, but tempered with a modicum of tradition.

In many ways, the reductionist tendencies of traditional builders brought on by the Depression paralleled the streamlined spirit. If left unhampered to run their logical course,

Built in 1940 to house the operations of the new bridge across the river at Perryville, the Susquehanna River Bridge Administration Building reflected the times. Its Art Deco style was sleek, modern, and stripped of expensive (to build and maintain) ornament. (1980, Maryland Historical Trust)

(right) In 1941 the campus of the Tome School for boys at Port Deposit was taken over as a naval training facility. Sailors were a common sight on the streets of the town during World War II. (postcard collection of Michael J. Dixon)

(below) The 1942 collision of a German-built tanker with the lift bridge at Chesapeake City caused much difficulty. The bridge was not replaced until after the war, and residents rode a ferry back and forth between North and South Chesapeake City. (1942, collection of Lewis A. Collins)

Bainbridge Naval Training Center, established on the grounds of the Tome School for Boys, prepared both officers and seamen for war. (postcard collection of Michael J. Dixon)

they ultimately may have led to a wider acceptance of the more severe modern styles, including the so-called International style advocated by European architects. But the exigencies of World War II, with its material and manpower shortages and its intense return to Americanism, brought a halt to any further experimentation. Once again, a nation prepared to go to war. Once again, communities across Maryland found their populations declining as men and women left to join the effort, in factories at home and in service overseas.

For Cecil County the war was brought right to its doorstep with an incredible influx of war activities and personnel perhaps unmatched by any other county in the state. During the war years the Cecil population almost tripled, as the county was literally commandeered by the American war effort. In 1941, only a year after the Tome School for boys at Port Deposit had closed its doors, the sprawling campus was taken over by the U. S. Navy as a training ground for the thousands of seamen needed to man the fleets. Named for Commodore William Bainbridge, commanding officer of the historic U. S. F. *Constitution*, the Bainbridge Naval Training Center was the principal training center on the East Coast. It grew to enormous proportions, with hundreds of barracks, training halls, classrooms, gymnasiums, and mess halls quickly raised on the 1,000-acre property. At its peak, the center housed nearly 35,000 recruits; by the war's end, more than half a million servicemen and women had passed in and out of its gates.[13]

Across the county, Chesapeake City also geared up for the war, taking on a strategic importance from its location along the C & D Canal. The constant stream of ships, barges, and tankers following the inland route to escape the threat of German submarines off the Atlantic coast brought an occasional burst of excitement to the town. In 1942 a passing tanker crashed into the lift bridge across the canal. Crews worked overtime to repair the damage, to ensure the vital channel remained clear and open for wartime shipping, and within a week the canal was back in operation.

While Port Deposit and Chesapeake City saw their share of wartime activities, neither found its entire life caught up in such a dramatic fashion as Elkton. The catalyst for the complete transformation of the county seat was Triumph Industries, a small factory that, until the war, had mainly produced firecrackers. In 1940 the company received an order from Finland for signal flares, which Triumph's 200 workers quickly filled; that order was soon followed by a request from England for gunpowder. Recognizing the profits to be made from the war, the company shifted its production lines to include a variety of explosives, from detonators to land mines.

Following the escalation of the American war machine in the months after the bombing of Pearl Harbor, Triumph Industries found itself besieged with federal contracts for

In 1940 Triumph Industries, an Elkton firecracker manufacturer, began making explosives for military use, beginning with signal flares but soon moving to antiaircraft shells and incendiary bombs. (1937, Guy Rhoades/Historical Society of Cecil County)

munitions. The increased demands soon proved too much for the company's managers; making antiaircraft shells for Navy warships was, after all, a great leap from making firecrackers for Fourth of July festivities. By this time, however, the U. S. armed forces were too far committed to Triumph, and too dependent on its products, to pull the contract and shop elsewhere. So, in 1942 the federal government confiscated the Triumph plant by executive order and turned the company's management over to a group of Pittsburgh businessmen, who invested $4 million in federal funds in the facility. Nearly 1,000 small, self-contained buildings were constructed at the plant site, each one holding a separate shell-packing operation and located a sufficient distance from its neighbor to avoid the disastrous possibility of a chain reaction of explosions should one of the buildings blow.[14]

While the buildup was going on, company recruiters were out scouring the region, hiring the workforce needed to get the plant underway. Using the resources of the Federal Manpower Commission, representatives traveled to Pennsylvania, West Virginia, Virginia, and North Carolina to search for people willing to move to Elkton to pack shells

Nearly 100 two-family dwellings were built at Hollingsworth Manor in the early 1940s as part of the effort to house the defense workers who flooded Elkton. (postcard collection of Michael J. Dixon)

Main Street Elkton saw many new faces during the defense buildup of World War II. The town population was almost quadruple its pre-war size during the six years Triumph Industries kept up wartime production. (1944, postcard collection, Historical Society of Cecil County)

at a minimum wage. Ads were placed in hundreds of local newspapers, and in March 1944 fifty thousand job announcements were dropped from airplanes over the West Virginia hills.[15] Women and minorities became the target audiences, not only because most white male laborers had joined the services, but because plant managers believed them best suited to the tedious chore of packing munitions.

By March 1943, 11,500 workers—nearly 80 percent of them women—had invaded Elkton, more than three times the town's permanent population, which totaled 3,518 in 1940.[16] To provide housing for the newcomers, both federal agencies and private businesses hastily built wooden barracks, and almost 100 small dwellings were put up in a development known as Hollingsworth Manor. In addition, many local residents, in town and out, offered room and board to workers from out of the area. Eventually, 6,000 more people arrived in town, following family members employed at the plant or simply hoping to profit from the opportunities presented by a new city literally springing from the ground overnight.

Citizens responded gamely to the demands of the time, but despite their best efforts the town of Elkton was ill-

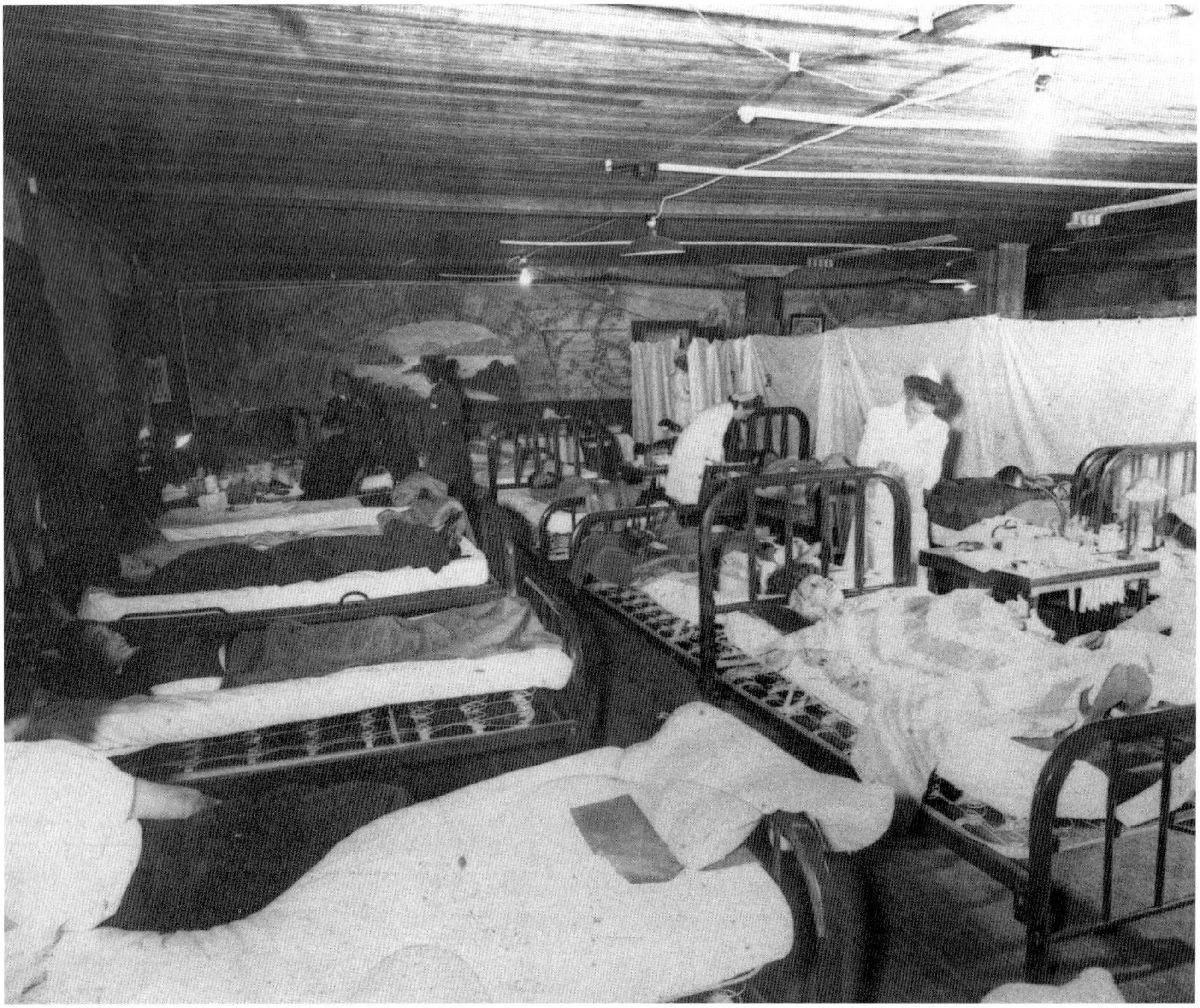

(right) In World War II Elkton, the USO functioned at a level far beyond its usual role of entertaining the country's armed forces. The influx of workers hired by Triumph Industries put a heavy strain on local services, and the USO stepped into the breach. Serving as liaison between government, industry, and community, USO staffers found people jobs and places to live, acquired public funds for housing and town water and sewer facilities, and helped the town establish playgrounds, among many other activities. From the five branches they operated in the Elkton area, including one at Triumph and one for blacks, the USO helped bring order to the wartime community. (1943, postcard collection of Michael J. Dixon)

(above and right) Elkton turned out to celebrate the end of World War II. (Historical Society of Cecil County)

(left) Blood donors make their contribution to the war effort at the Red Cross facility in the basement of the Catholic church in Elkton. The dangerous work of manufacturing explosives resulted in accidents, but more pervasive health problems were caused by the chemicals used in the process, which turned skin yellow and hair red, among other side effects. (Historical Society of Cecil County)

equipped to handle these overwhelming circumstances. The town's water and sewage system was stretched to the limit, its stores and shops depleted of stocks, and its police unable to control the off-hours crowds roaming the streets looking for entertainment. The latter situation was continually exacerbated by the hundreds of recruits from the Bainbridge Center and nearby Aberdeen Proving Ground and New Castle Air Base who came into town for relaxation. At times, relations between workers, residents, and recruits became so volatile that the Bainbridge commander was forced to dispatch the military police to Elkton to assist the local police.

Compounding the problems in Elkton was the unending turnover of Triumph employees, at a rate exceeding 100 percent annually.[17] The job was not without its hazards. Women working day in and day out with the explosive chemicals watched their hands and faces slowly become stained a mottled yellow, their hair dyed a hideous red. The danger of explosion was constant, and small accidents were continually reported. The worst explosion of all occurred in 1943, killing fifteen people and injuring more than 100.

Once a peaceful, slow-paced town, Elkton had become an occupied city, a boisterous encampment beyond local control. Into this situation stepped the Elkton United Service Organizations, or USO. Set up in 1942 as a joint effort of the Cecil County Council of Defense, local clergy, and the Federal Security Agency, this group eventually returned some semblance of order and harmony to the town. Mustering the full force of its federal connections—and federal funding—it established itself as a buffer between the interests of the town and those of Triumph Industries and the military.[18]

USO officials took on many of the tasks that were handled by town administrators in peacetime. All newcomers had to first report to the USO, where staff members recorded their arrival and issued approval slips for both housing and employment. As a conduit for federal supplies and funding, the USO dispensed monies for the construction of new utilities, approved water and sewer hookups, and allotted war-restricted materials to both public and private enterprises. In

As Americans acquired more leisure time and more spare cash in the prosperous period after World War II, marinas sprang up on many Cecil waterways. These pleasure craft at Fredericktown were owned by families from nearby Pennsylvania and Delaware as well as Cecil and Kent county residents. (c. 1960, Marion E. Warren Collection, Maryland State Archives, MSA SC 1890-MI-1169)

addition to these activities, the group continued to perform its more familiar duties of providing leisure activities for both servicemen and civilians. From five branch buildings, both in Elkton and in surrounding communities, the USO staged the dances and diversions that ultimately proved to be the key to defusing the tensions.[19]

Only with the end of the war did the frenzy of activity that had gripped both Triumph Industries and the town of Elkton truly subside. Gradually, the thousands of workers who had come to town were laid off. Some who had come to the county with the war remained, pushing the Elkton population from 3,518 in 1940 to 5,245 by 1950.[20] Most, however, moved on, helped by the USO to return home or find employment elsewhere. The temporary housing was pulled down and the hundreds of shell-packing buildings either demolished or converted to peacetime uses. At the Bainbridge Center, Navy officials slowly phased out the facilities, and by 1947 the recruit-training section had closed. Thereafter, the center was used only sporadically, alternately serving as the site of a WAVES training center, the Service School Command, the Naval Academy Preparatory School, and a storage facility for the Navy Bureau of Personnel. By 1976 the Navy no longer used the center.

Slowly, Cecil returned to a state of normalcy. The postwar flood of material goods to a rich and hungry market and the need to make up for the wartime building blackout led to increased productivity all around the county. Grains and dairy products, beef cattle and hogs issued from Cecil farms, but more indicative of the future of county agriculture were the fruit orchards that once flourished across the lower county. Ravaged by blight, these were replaced by the westward shift of production centers, and as the period progressed more Cecil farms gave way to the new industries and new developments spreading across the land. Over the next twenty years, the percentage of Cecil land in cultivation steadily declined, from 77.8 percent in 1940 to 56 percent by 1960.[21]

Increasingly, light industries appeared on the landscape. In Elkton and Port Deposit, in North East and Perryville, these ranged from apparel factories and electrical supply companies to chemical plants and crushed gravel operations. New employment opportunities in auto works across the border in Newark strengthened the ties between Delaware and the east end of the county. Along the bay and rivers the focus remained on the water, with marine works at Port Deposit and boatyards at Fredericktown and Chesapeake City not only serving commercial industries but catering to the owners of the growing number of pleasure craft that cruised Cecil waters.

In the southern part of the county, a new enterprise appeared: horse breeding. By the 1960s the area around Bohemia Manor had become home to some of the most renowned breeders and thoroughbreds in the nation. Kelso, five times honored as horse of the year, ran in the fields at Mrs. Richard du Pont's Woodstock Farm, while Northern Dancer, winner of the 1964 Kentucky Derby and Preakness Stakes, was quartered at nearby Windfields Farm. Northern Dancer sired 106 stakes winners and twenty champions, helping to make Windfields Farms and Cecil County one of the leading producers of champion thoroughbreds in the nation.[22]

By the 1960s the volume of overland transports rumbling in and out of the county had exceeded the limits of the older roads, in particular the heavily traveled Route 40. Eventually, a parallel route was constructed, superseding the older highway. In November 1963 President Kennedy presided over the opening of I-95, which ran straight through the heart of the county. At the same time, the U.S. Army Corps of Engineers had begun its massive expansion of the Chesapeake and Delaware Canal, lowering the waterway to a depth of 35 feet and widening it to more than 400 feet. The decade of the '60s also saw the Susquehanna River Basin Commission commence the equally formidable task of clearing the river, from its headwaters in New York to

its mouth at the bay, of damage caused by many years of sewage, runoff, and industrial waste pollution.

Steadily the county population grew, from 33,356 in 1950 to 53,291 by 1970. To accommodate the nearly 20,000 new residents, new types of development began to appear more frequently across the county.[23] Large-scale subdivisions crept over the land, as developers took advantage of the new interstate system connecting workers with the expanding commercial centers around Baltimore, Philadelphia, and Wilmington. The first townhouse and apartment complexes built in the county appeared in response to the need for moderately priced rental housing. These were soon followed by the shopping center, ranging from small clusters of a few convenience stores to the larger neighborhood and regional centers that would dominate the postwar commercial scene. The role of the automobile influenced these patterns of development, which eclipsed the older crossroads and in-town commercial centers. The new road and building construction continued to take its toll on farmland, and by 1980 Cecil farms accounted for only 39 percent of all land use.[24]

Despite these changes, Cecil remained a county largely characterized by quiet residential communities of detached, single-family houses. Multiunit complexes were a minor and relatively late addition to the county building scene and by no means matched the volume and intensity of the new communities rapidly changing the housing characteristics of the Washington-Baltimore corridor. Throughout the last half of the twentieth century, the image of Cecil as a haven of homes in the country has enticed people to settle here; it is an image that persists.

Nonetheless, in many regards, the whole notion of home had changed dramatically in the years following the successive upheavals of the Depression and World War II, both in Cecil County and throughout the nation. Architecturally, the traditional colonial-inspired house remained a stalwart

After World War II horse breeding in Cecil County achieved national status as several county horse farms became known as producers of champion thoroughbreds. One of these was Kelso, of Mrs. Richard du Pont's Woodstock Farm. This postparade photograph with jockey Ismael Valenzuela was taken in 1964 after they won the International. (Jerry Frutkoff)

of new developments, although the style was continuously redefined in terms of modern materials and construction methods until only the basic shell remained identifiable with its historical antecedents. The radical design philosophy of the modern styles touted so heavily before the war was softened in the comforts of postwar America and transformed into the ubiquitous style for 1950s and '60s developments—the ranch house or rambler. A product of California architects and perfectly suited, with its large ground coverage, to the sizable tracts available to builders, the ranch house was, in general, an informal treatment of modernism that, when replicated in wood, brick, or stone, was appropriate for the times. The style resulted in simple, unpretentious houses, usually one story in height, two if built on a sloping site; modern, but not too modern; traditional, but not too traditional. If an extra story was required, the ranch easily became a split-level, with a forward facing gable perched on one end.

Inside the new houses, the patterns of social life had changed as well. The large, formal double parlors that had once held the grand private affairs of the community were displaced by hotels and private clubs, eliminating the need for large social spaces in the home. Recreation was also found at movie theaters, public parks, and other commercial agencies. The advent of television had a further revolutionary effect on both domestic activities and household arrangements. Modern Americans required five, rather than four, distinct spaces in their homes: space for cooking and space for eating (although kitchen needs could now be compressed into a narrow passageway through which food quickly passed from supermarket to dining room table); space for sleeping, traditionally separated from other spaces; space for quiet living—the older parlor, shortened and now renamed the living room; and a new space for more raucous gatherings and for the higher noise levels of the television and the hi-fi set—variously termed the family room, the "rec" room, or the rumpus room. There was, as well, a sixth area of the modern home unknown to earlier houses, a space devoted to one of the most important members of the modern American family—the automobile. Built to accommodate the family cars, garages grew to enormous proportions in relation to the house; often the wide expanse of the paneled track door of a two-car garage, either attached or integral, dominated the street side of the house.

But there was a deeper difference between the houses of postwar America and those of preceding generations, a difference that went beyond the superficialities of appearance and arrangement and cut to the critical roles housing played in the overall lives of their inhabitants. No longer were houses expected to be a family homestead, passed down from generation to generation. The dynamism of postwar America, the shifting emphasis away from the land and toward the office and factory, created a population more transient than earlier generations. The individual who once worked the ancestral land now more often moved from job to job, from employment center to employment center, from apartment to house, trading up, trading out. In the process, families were scattered to new opportunities far away from the home community. More and more, houses were designed for the convenience of construction crews, regardless of site or skill. They were styled for the comfort not of individuals but of demographic groups. And they were bought with the same thought and attention given to selecting a new car.

Despite the transient, impersonal aspects of the modern house, in Cecil and countless other American communities the sentimental attitude toward the home remained as strong as at the century's start. The tree-lined lane, the white picket fence, the dormer window looking down on the rose-covered gate persisted amidst conspicuously modern settings; such attachments are not so easily discarded. When connected to the present, objects suggesting the past offer their owners a sense of security—not necessarily physical, but psychological—in the face of a disorienting world. They impart a sense of stability in an ever-changing landscape, and they preserve in physical form the hopes of generations past, perhaps rekindling those desires for generations to come.

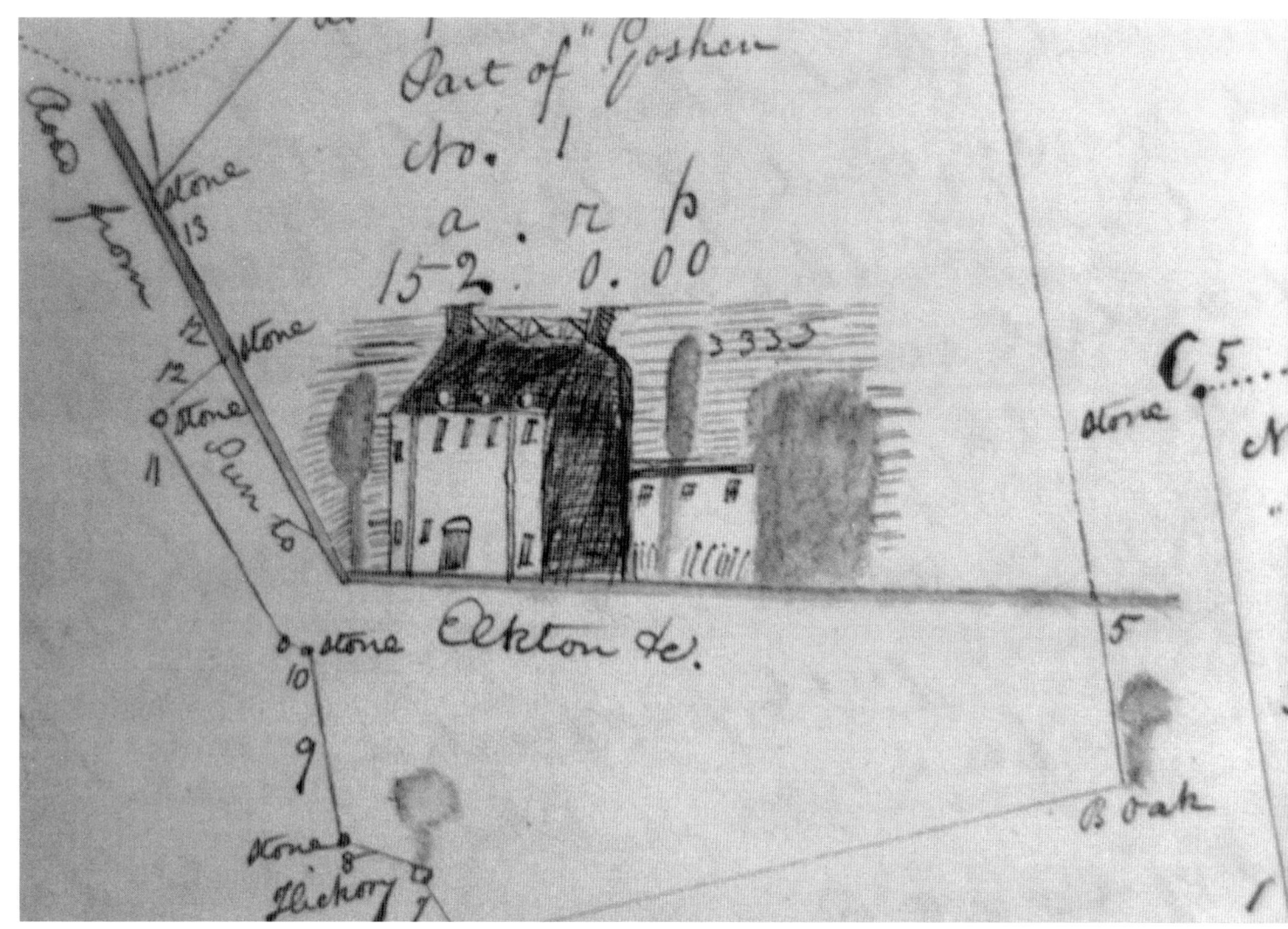

Sketch of a house on "Part of 'Goshen'"
(Cecil County Land Records)

CHAPTER 7

House Forms of Cecil County *(circa 1670-1900)*

EUROPEAN EXPLORERS, traders, trappers, and colonists quickly realized the land at the head of the Chesapeake was fertile ground, well-watered and well-suited to colonial settlement and cultivation. Settlers of a variety of faiths and pasts arrived in Cecil County with varied plans for carving out new lives in a new world. The earliest Anglo-American settlers probably came by the most obvious route, sailing up the wide Chesapeake and following any one of a half-dozen hospitable Cecil tributaries. Some, such as Bohemian Augustine Herman, first arrived in the county by an overland route from ports on the Delaware River. Several decades after Herman's first visit in 1659, settlers, principally the Scots-Irish, settled the New Munster and Susquehanna Manor tracts. Later yet was a large influx of Quaker settlers, who came to populate the Nottingham Lots, laid out in 1701-02 by William Penn as part of a plan to expand his Pennsylvania colony to the south.

Whether of English, Scots-Irish, or continental European nativity, most Chesapeake settlers were beset by unending hardships. Early life on the peninsula was probably much like that described by Jasper Danckaerts on his trip to visit Augustine Herman in the late fall of 1679. After landing at New Castle, Danckaerts traveled overland across the top of the peninsula. His impressions upon finding the plantation of John Moll are telling:

> This plantation of his is situated about fifteen miles from Newcastle…We passed through a tolerably good country, but the soil was a little sandy, and it was three o'clock in the afternoon when we reached the plantation. There were no persons there except some servants and negroes, the commander being a Parisian. The dwellings were very badly appointed, especially for such a man as Mons. Moll. There was no place to retire to, nor a chair to sit on, or a bed to sleep on.[1]

Several days later Danckaerts and his companions entered the extensive landholdings of Augustine Herman at Bohemia Manor to find that "he was sick when we arrived at his house…. His plantation was going much to decay, as well as his body for want of attention."[2] During his exploration of Herman's property and the southern parts of Cecil County, Danckaerts met several settlers who were trying to gain a foothold in the new land:

> One of them was a quaker who was building a small house for a tavern, or rather a ale house, for the purpose of entertaining travelers, and the other was the carpenter who was assisting him on the house, and could speak good Dutch, having resided a long time at the Manathans….The quaker, who had put up a temporary shed, made of the bark of trees, after the manner of the Indians, with both ends open, and a little larger than a dog's kennel, and where at best, we three might possibly have been able to lie, especially when a fire was made which would have to be done, offered us his lodgings, if we wished, and as good accommodations as he had, which were not much.[3]

Danckaerts's passages describing plantations and temporary shelters in the northern Chesapeake parallel those in numerous other travel accounts of the time. All speak of a hardscrabble colonial life, at times desperately difficult even for wealthy men like Augustine Herman and John Moll, who counted indentured servants and slaves as well as hundreds if not thousands of acres their own. Seventeenth century plantation dwellings, as Danckaerts implied, were often unremarkable and in need of repair.

By the early eighteenth century some Cecil County planters had accrued a fair profit, mainly through tobacco

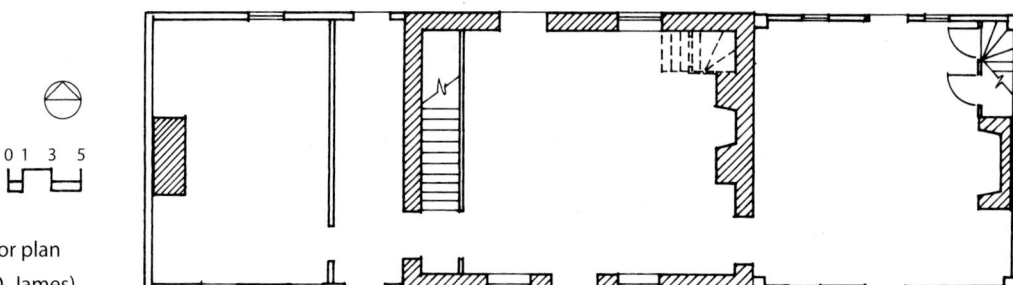

Fisher-Wilson house floor plan
(Paul Touart, Anthony O. James)

cultivation and later a grain-based agriculture. These planters took advantage of their prosperity to improve their living conditions, constructing more permanent types of houses, either brick or stone buildings or log or frame structures on substantial masonry foundations. Certainly not all planters could afford to rebuild in more expensive materials, but the impermanent nature of much early house construction in Maryland meant that inevitably houses were replaced, whether with lasting materials or again with impermanent ones.

The causes and effects of rebuilding are varied and complex, but in Cecil County, as on much of the Eastern Shore, one major result of this process has been the almost complete disappearance of lower class housing of the eighteenth and early nineteenth centuries. This distinct change in the landscape has permanently biased the architectural record toward the most expensive structures, as those are generally the ones that have survived. To reconstruct a fuller picture of the range of building types that once populated the Cecil County landscape, it is necessary to turn to the written record for evidence.

European immigrants to the new world brought with them specific ideas about how a house was to function and be assembled. The foreign building materials they found in the colonies forced the settlers to rethink some aspects of house construction, and contact with other groups provided a climate ripe for architectural exchange and adaptation. As evidenced by the variety of eighteenth and nineteenth century house types that still dot the Cecil County landscape, planters, merchants, and yeoman farmers could choose from a number of different house forms according to their needs, aspirations, and societal status.

House form is defined by the most basic aspect of a house—its plan, including the disposition of rooms on the first and second floors, the location of the fireplace(s), and the position of the stair(s). These elements are inextricably linked to the ways in which a house was intended to function and thus reveal much about how former occupants lived. In Cecil County a general conservatism, common to the Eastern Shore as a whole, led to the use of various floor plans over many generations.

House forms common to preindustrial society fall into two primary groups in Cecil County: single-pile (one room deep) and double-pile (two rooms deep). A house falls into the single-pile category if the primary living space extends the full depth of the structure, whether or not an auxiliary space is divided. It is important to remember that these basic house forms are not strict models. Individual plans vary from house to house according to individual preferences and interpretations. The following discussion is organized according to complexity of house type and is not strictly chronological or developmental.

The most basic house forms found in Cecil County involve dwellings with one or two rooms. These houses are often thought of as the earliest and perhaps crudest colonial dwellings, but this view prevents a complete understanding of these forms. Surviving one- and two-room plan houses are not always the earliest structures in an area, and they certainly are not always the crudest. One- and two-room plan dwellings have experienced a long history of use on almost every economic level in all parts of the county, and they were fashioned of all available local materials.

Various daily activities took place within the confines of a single room, with distinct functions often separated by placement of furniture and other objects. In most surviving one-room plan houses in Cecil County, working and sleeping spaces were placed on different floors and a corner, boxed winder stair, or perhaps a ladder, connected them. The overall dimensions of one-room houses vary, but more often than not they have a squarish shape. Most extant one-room houses have been expanded in some manner or another and no longer retain their original form. By the fourth quarter of the eighteenth century, it was common to have separate structures—a range of outbuildings or perhaps

CE-983, Fisher-Wilson house (1979)

an addition—to house the variety of daily domestic labors.

Information from travelers' accounts, supported by systematic reviews of Orphans Court evaluations and tax records, reveals that one-room dwellings were the most common house type in Cecil County at the close of the eighteenth century. When Zebulon Hollingsworth and Ebenezer Booth, officials of the county orphans court, assessed the estate of orphans Abraham and Benjamin Miller in August 1796, they found a selection of one-room structures among the improvements:

> [We] did find thereon as follows....first the old mansion house, where James Camlin lives, is about eighteen feet square, a frame two storeys high, one brick chimney, with two floor tolerable good...2d dwelling house is one that Andrew Hall lives in, a log house about eighteen feet by sixteen, brick chimney and two oak floors and good roof, in good repair...3rd dwelling is one that John Holliday lives in about 22 feet by 18 with two brick chimneys, log house, the chimneys, logs and roof are good, the floor above and below are laid down with oak—boards loose, the boards indifferent, there is about ten feet of the floor at the east of the house, well laid with good pine boards....4th dwelling house occupied by James Stewart is a log house, 16 feet square with brick chimney good roof, plank floor, above and below, laid with boards loose.[4]

A yearly valuation of £80 indicates the deceased Benjamin Miller left an estate that supported a standard of living well above the average at the close of the eighteenth century. The label "mansion house" identifies the two-story, 18 foot by 18 foot frame house as the principal dwelling on the property. True to extant contemporary examples, the cooking chores were not accomplished in the house but in an attached 32 foot by 17 foot log kitchen, in this case served with a clay chimney topped with brick.

One-room plan dwellings were easily enlarged when additional space was required. These alterations were designed to meet the needs of a particular family at a particular time, thus they vary enormously. The Fisher-Wilson house (CE-983), which stood southeast of Warwick until it was destroyed in the late 1980s, was erected during the last decade of the eighteenth century as a two-story, one-room

CE-50, Cherry Grove (1968)

plan dwelling of Flemish bond brick. It measured 24 feet 3 inches by 18 feet 10 inches. A kitchen wing of post and hewn plank was attached to the east gable end of the brick house in the early nineteenth century. Later in the nineteenth century another addition extended the house to the west. Included in each alteration was an additional stair, rendering the original winder stair in the eighteenth century house obsolete. It was removed, but scars on northeast corner walls—as well as a second floor stair directly above, which leads to the attic—indicated its former position. The second floor of the one-room plan house had been partitioned to create multiple bedrooms, but its earliest arrangement would have repeated the one-room plan of the first floor. The brick house did not have an excavated basement or a large first floor hearth, suggesting meal preparation was originally conducted in a detached structure.

Similarly expanded by gable end additions are two gambrel-roofed houses in the vicinity of Earleville—Cherry Grove (CE-50) and the log portion of the William Knight tenant house (CE-240). The longtime residence of the Ward family, Cherry Grove was recorded by the subscribers of the Cecil County Orphans Court on October 19, 1791, in an effort to document and value the lands of orphan Thomas Ward Veazey.[5] The officials of the court, Benjamin Porter and John Ward, found the following structures on the Veazey plantation:

> dwelling house fifty-two feet long by sixteen feet three inches of which twenty feet is logs and thirty-two feet frame with a frame shed twenty by twelve. The whole divided into three rooms and a passage on the lower floor with a fireplace in each room, and three rooms on the upper floor and a fireplace in two of them with cedar shingles and is in tolerable repair with a frame pantry and log kitchen adjoining, the pantry twelve by seventeen feet and the kitchen twenty by seventeen feet, the whole weatherboarded with pine plank and covered with oak shingles in good repair.[6]

CE-1094, George Grant house (1980)

At the heart of the gambrel-roofed, log-and-frame dwelling is the one-room log structure that was the original Veazey house. Each later addition preserved a segment of this structure. In the full cellar under the log section is a remnant of a former bulkhead entrance, which was covered when the frame addition was attached to the north end around 1780. The late eighteenth century shed-roofed addition that enlarged the one-room house to the rear protected part of the original roof, preserving what today is a rare example of hand-split oak shingles fastened with wrought nails.

Similarly expanded by a gable end addition was the William Knight log house, a gambrel-roofed, one-room plan dwelling erected around 1810. Standing in the midst of a plowed field north of Earleville, this full dovetailed log structure measured 18 feet across by 16 feet deep. An interior brick chimney rose through the north end. Fixed in the northwest corner was a winder stair. An early nineteenth century gable-roofed, log-and-frame addition tripled the size of the original house. (This house is illustrated in Chapter 8.)

As the nineteenth century continued, one-room houses were often expanded to provide a larger, more formal type of dwelling. The desire for private entrance halls and parlors and integral service wings required the transformation of many one-room plan structures, including the George Grant house (CE-1094) on Little Egypt Road north of Fair Hill. Built into the slope of a hill, this two-story fieldstone dwelling built around 1820-30 originally contained a single room on each floor. An enclosed winder staircase in the northeast corner, across from the west wall fireplaces, provided access between floors. This stone structure was enlarged during the third quarter of the nineteenth century with the addition of a two-story frame section. Set perpendicularly to the earlier house, the addition has a front porch and center entrance that face the road, subordinating the original fieldstone structure, which now serves as a rear service wing.

As these extant examples and court records affirm, the one-room plan dwelling was a basic house type used across Cecil County. Whether of log, frame, brick, or stone walls, essential features of the house remained the same, with only slight modifications made to suit a particular owner. The house type met the modest aspirations or needs of many Cecil County residents for many years. By the mid-nineteenth century, however, the space limitations of one-room dwellings had caused a decline in their use as a principal residence for the middle and upper classes.

Paralleling the history of the one-room plan is a house form that included two rooms on the first floor. Commonly called the hall/parlor plan—and sometimes referred to as one of several "cross passage" plans—this room disposition is represented by some of the oldest extant dwellings in Cecil County. Its popularity was long-lived, however, and use of the floor plan in the county can be traced in modified form until the third quarter of the nineteenth century.

The physical dimensions of hall/parlor houses—often

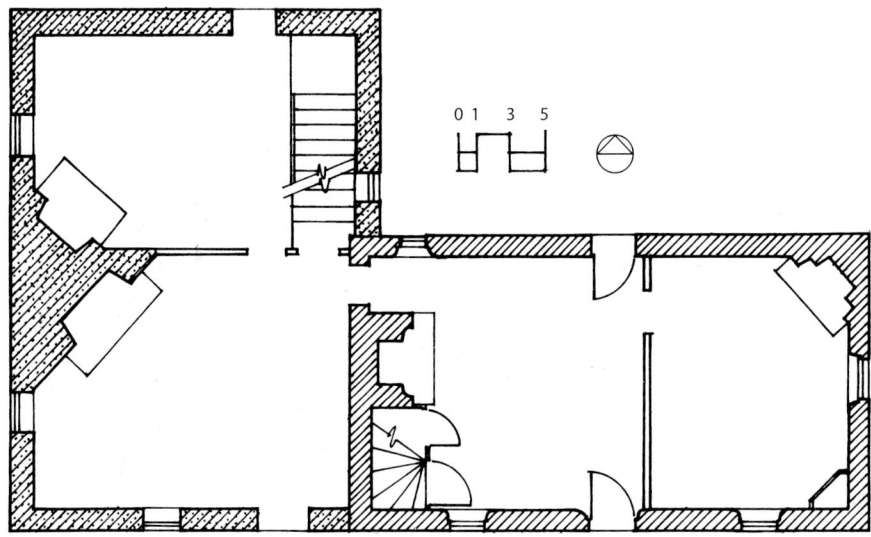

CE-187, John Churchman house; floor plan (Paul Touart, Anthony O. James)

measuring around thirty feet across by sixteen feet deep—were not much larger than their one-room contemporaries, but the inclusion of a second room on the first and second floors afforded the family a measure of privacy and comfort unavailable in a one-room plan structure. A main feature of the hall/parlor plan is the large room that runs the full depth of the house and has two doors, one on the front wall and one on the rear. These doors, which face each other, led to the term "cross passage."

Early among the surviving hall/parlor dwellings in Cecil County is the brick portion of the John Churchman house (CE-187), firmly documented by the glazed brick date "1745" masterfully laid in the east gable end wall. The house was erected on "Lot 17" of the Nottingham Lots—north of the meetinghouse lot—for Quaker minister John Churchman (1705-75).

The front and rear doors of the Churchman house open into the "hall." In the same tradition as the one-room plan dwellings, this room served as the principal living space. A large, four-foot wide fireplace is flanked on the south side by an enclosed winder stair. The stair and an adjacent closet are encased in a finely crafted raised panel

CE-1100, Tyson Mill house (1980)

wall. Divided from the hall is a smaller, more private space entered through a single door in the middle partition. Known in general terms as the "parlor," this space may have served a variety of functions as a parlor, chamber, or dining room. Without any exterior doorways, entrance into this part of the house could be limited to family and invited friends. Enhancing the comfort of the Churchman parlor is a corner fireplace and a finely crafted corner cupboard, signs of a better built, more expensive dwelling, as many parlors did not have a direct source of heat or expensive raised panel furniture.

The hall/parlor plan, with its two rooms, was favored across much of northern Cecil County. The Quakers who settled the Nottingham Lots used it, as well as the Scots-Irish and English immigrants who populated the New Munster tract and Susquehanna Manor. The plan was also used by the English who settled the southern portions of Cecil County, but extant examples there are relatively few.

Representative of the early nineteenth century hall/parlor houses that survive in the county is the fieldstone house built into a bank on the Tyson Mill property (CE-1100) around 1800-20. This five-bay house (meaning it has five openings across its front elevation) was assembled in two distinct stages within a period of twenty to thirty years. The earliest section is the three-bay eastern block, which faces south. The main level of this portion contained the principal living space—the hall or cross passage, which was divided from the rest of the first floor by a partition (now missing). Front and back doors provided access to the nearly square cross passage, which was heated by an east end hearth. In this case, the smaller, western room was left unheated and used as a formal parlor or first floor bed chamber. An enclosed winder stair next to the hearth in the southeastern corner of the hall connects the floors. The second floor is divided into more chamber spaces, and the cellar or ground floor housed the cooking facilities. As is true of many hall/parlor houses in northern Cecil County, the house is set into a bank to take advantage of the natural protection and warmth the surrounding earth could provide. Scars from a former two-story porch remain on the south wall; an exterior stair built within the porch probably eased movement between floors.

A southern Cecil example of the hall/parlor house survives in the Reuben Lake house (CE-1046), built circa 1830-50 east of Chesapeake City. This two-and-a-half story, three-bay example, like the Tyson house, is supported by an exposed fieldstone basement kitchen with an enclosed winder stair in the northwest corner. The main first floor space is divided by an off-center partition with the larger hall or cross passage segregated from a smaller, unheated room. This frame dwelling, with its taller elevation and late Federal style pilastered dormers, assumes a different archi-

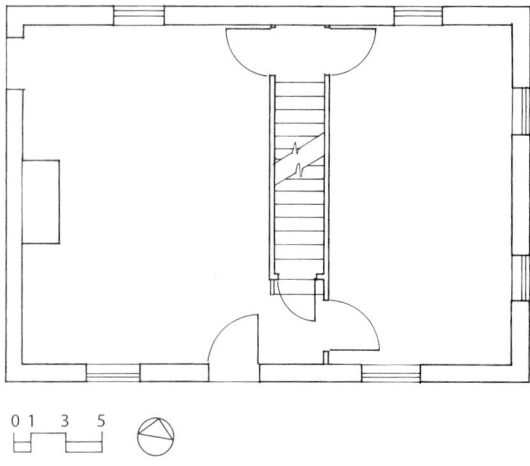

CE-900, McNamee log house (1978);
floor plan (Paul Touart, Anthony O. James)

tectural character than the more natural or organic aspect of the bank-sited, fieldstone Tyson Mill house. Despite contrasts in stylish decoration, the floor plan and essential organization of the two houses are traced to a common source in the vernacular building traditions of Cecil County's Anglo-American immigrants.

By the middle years of the nineteenth century, influences from American society as a whole were reshaping the way people lived in urban as well as rural environments like Cecil County. The popular desire for more formal entrance into a house precipitated a distinct alteration in the concept of the cross passage entrance. One result of this rethinking of the arrangement of house elements was shifting the stair to the center of the rectangular form so that visitors would step into a small stair hall with partitions and doors to each side.

The beginnings of this rearrangement of the hall/parlor floor plan are reflected in the McNamee log house (CE-900), constructed on a raised fieldstone foundation around 1840-50 near Rock Springs. The plan of this hall/parlor log structure includes at its center a staircase built with a straight run of steps more hospitable than the narrow pie-shaped treads of the earlier winder stair. Despite the new position of the staircase, the room arrangement of the McNamee log house differs little from earlier hall/parlor dwellings, continuing the direct entrance into the "hall," although the door in the rear wall was excluded.

The Tosh-Basham house (CE-1121), a slightly later example of a hall/parlor dwelling erected around 1840-50 in the vicinity of Harrisville, demonstrates the full development of the revised plan. As in the McNamee house, the stair is fixed between the two rooms, but in this case a small entrance hall has been defined by a second partition that blocks direct entrance into the principal first floor room. In addition, the kitchen space was moved from the cellar to the first floor and incorporated into a rear service wing.

The formal entrance into the house by way of a center passage and the convenience of an attached kitchen were by no means new ideas in Cecil County. Wealthy Chesapeake planters had employed these features since the early to mid-eighteenth century, although they did not become common in a broader range of American households until the turn of the nineteenth century. Architectural historians view the need for enhanced privacy, the change in stair placement, and the convenience of an attached first floor kitchen as some of the most significant developments in the planning and construction of both rural and urban dwellings in the early nineteenth century. By midcentury technological and societal changes, ushered in with the gradual industrialization of the building trades and the mass production of house parts, were clearly influencing the houses built in Cecil County.

Paralleling the development and modification of the two-room, hall/parlor plan house were similar changes that shaped another dominant Cecil County house form—the three-room/cross passage plan. This type of house is found largely in northern Cecil County, especially in the Nottingham Lots and peripheral areas of Quaker settlement, although a few examples have been located in southern Cecil and even farther south in Somerset County, Maryland.[7]

CE-1121, Tosh-Basham house (historic photograph)

The popularity of this plan among the residents of the Nottingham Lots is not entirely surprising since a 1684 flyer, signed by William Penn, recommended this well-established British house form as a type suitable for new settlements in the colonies: "To build then, an House of thirty foot long and eighteen foot broad, with a partition neer the middle, and an other to divide one end of the House into two small Rooms."[8] These exact dimensions and the framing directions outlined in the tract are not repeated in any house known in Cecil County. However, the many close parallels erected throughout northern portions of the county point to an overall familiarity with the three-room plan that extended beyond the limited circulation of Penn's promotional literature.

County examples of the three-room/cross passage house type date from the early decades of the eighteenth century through the mid-nineteenth century. Over the course of that century and a half, the plan did not remain constant. Like most early forms, it was subjected to formal alterations in room orientation and exterior appearance that mirrored larger societal changes.

The earliest examples are the closest to the published formula. The Roger Kirk house (CE-209), dated by a "1719" scratched in a rafter, stood in the vicinity of Brick

Meeting House until 1980. Measuring approximately 28 feet across and 22 feet deep, the first floor was originally divided into three rooms. A partition near the center of the house separated the cross passage from two smaller rooms of equal size. Entered through a front or rear door, the cross passage contained the sole source of heat, a stone chimney at the west end. Beside the chimney stack was an enclosed winder stair that led to the cellar kitchen and to the chambers in the upper half-story. Although the uses of the smaller first floor rooms are undocumented, part of the space may have served as a weaving room, the occupation by which Roger Kirk earned his living. The steep pitch of the roof allowed for a garret above the second floor chambers.

Another early three-room/cross passage plan structure is buried in the enlarged, L-shaped Haines house (CE-216), also known as the "Poor House," erected around 1720-30. Standing just north of Rising Sun, the braced timber frame structure, with its ogee-curved post heads, was enlarged in 1767 and remodeled and enlarged again during the mid- to late nineteenth century. The original three-room plan structure has been modified, but the off-center partition that divided the cross passage from two rooms east of the front door survives. A second partition once divided the current dining room into two segregated rooms, each entered from a doorway into the cross passage. (The doorway that provided access to the southeast room has been blocked.)

The original timber frame house measures 30 feet 6

CE-209, Roger Kirk house (1979)

inches by 20 feet 6 inches and rests on an excavated fieldstone cellar. Although the large fireplace in the cross passage has been covered over, its generous size is evident in the chimney mass that rises through the gable end. True to other early cross passage plans, a winder stair rises against the chimney stack to connect the cellar, first and second floors, and attic.

Built in a more permanent fashion is the Joseph Haines house, also known as Willowdale (CE-218), erected in 1774 of fieldstone and formerly encircled with pent eaves. At Willowdale the cross passage is somewhat narrower than that found in the Haines house, and the two smaller rooms were formerly heated by corner fireplaces. By the third quarter of the eighteenth century much more attention was devoted to finishing interior spaces with elaborate raised panel carpentry. In place of the tight winder stair of the

CE-216, Haines house (1995); floor plan (Paul Touart, Anthony O. James)

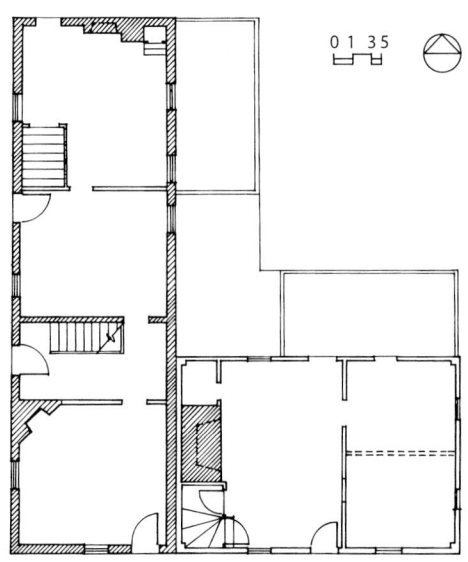

CE-98, Evan's Choice (1980)

Poor House is a more open, expensively crafted turned baluster railing. An arched passage that passes underneath the staircase provides access to the west gable end doorway, which opens into a later stone addition. The face of the arched passage is finished with a molded arch surround and carved keystone, raised paneling, and a bold baroque cornice. (See Chapter 9, "Manners of Interior Finish," for a lengthier discussion of interior woodwork traditions for this period.)

A variation in the cross passage floor plan featured two front doors instead of one. The large stone dwelling in northwestern Cecil County known as Evan's Choice (CE-98) is the earliest surviving example of this form. Erected around 1751, this solidly built fieldstone dwelling follows

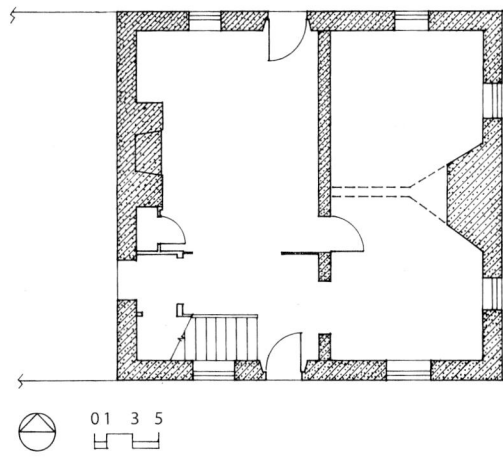

CE-218, Willowdale (1983);
floor plan (Paul Touart, Anthony O. James)

CE-38, Old Fort Smith house (1978)

the cross passage plan with three-bay front but here the bays incorporate a single window and two doors, rather than a door flanked on each side by a window. One of the front doors opens into the cross passage and the other provides access to the smaller front room, probably a parlor.

The presence of two front doors has instigated endless discussion among homeowners and architectural historians alike. In fact, this arrangement is a characteristic feature of houses in adjacent Pennsylvania, where many dwellings have a distinct Germanic background. Two doors are found there in both three- and four-bay elevations combined with a variety of two-, three-, and four-room Germanic plans.

German building traditions include a three-room plan dwelling—not too dissimilar from the cross passage plan—known as the *flurkuckenhaus* or hall-kitchen house. It is not surprising that the buildings of northwestern Cecil County, an area settled in part by Pennsylvanians moving south across the border, reflect a strong tie to Germanic forms. Although Cecil County did not experience a large influx of German-American immigrants as western Maryland did, the construction of hybrid forms of the *flurkuckenhaus* dwelling by Anglo-American immigrants shows a definite exchange and borrowing of ideas between neighboring cultural groups.

The two-door elevation provided family members with more choices for controlling access to formal and less

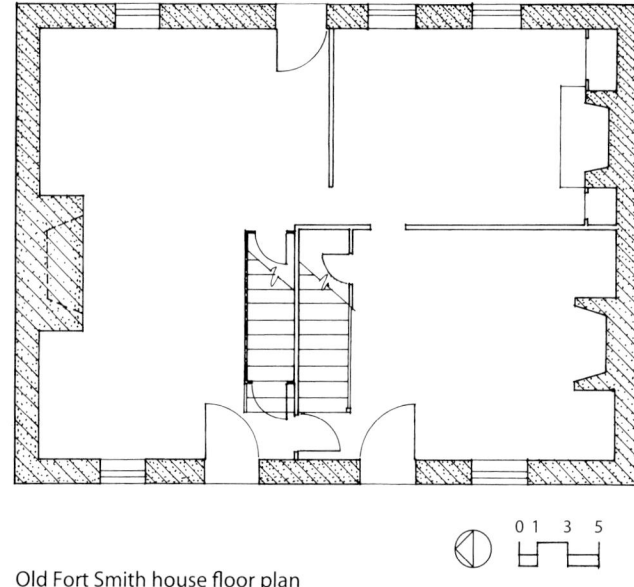

Old Fort Smith house floor plan
(Paul Touart, Anthony O. James)

formal spaces. Everyday use of the front door into the cross passage of the Evan's Choice house was much the same as that in a dwelling with a single front door. The second front door, on the other hand, gave the residents the option of restricting entry into the working core of the house. On more formal occasions, family and friends could be guided through the centrally positioned door into the smaller room. The family probably furnished this space, which was

CE-39, John Swisher house

served by a corner fireplace, more formally than their everyday living space in the cross passage.

The builder of Evan's Choice apparently perceived the functional flexibility of the two-door elevation as a convenience and was willing to replace one window of the three-bay facade with a door. After the mid-eighteenth century, the asymmetrical fenestration that resulted from this arrangement was no longer acceptable stylistically. The strictly balanced Georgian design formulas that became popular with most cultural groups, whether in rural or urban situations, during the third and fourth quarters of the eighteenth century led builders of this house form to reconfigure the two-door elevation. To achieve a symmetrical elevation for the three-room/cross passage plan house, a fourth bay was added so the front of the house had two doors in the center flanked by a window on each side. Although the desire for bilateral symmetry proved persuasive enough for builders to alter the traditional exterior appearance of a house, it apparently was not strong enough for them to rearrange the asymmetrical interior spaces of this house form.

An early example of the three-room/cross passage plan with a two-door, four-bay elevation is a stone house that stands in the vicinity of Oakwood in northwestern Cecil County, where this form is especially prevalent. Known as the Old Fort Smith house (CE-38), this two-story dwelling measures 41 feet across by almost 32 feet deep and was built around 1780-90. The traditional cross passage is entered through the left door. In lieu of a corner winder staircase, a straight flight of steps rises against the middle partition. The south end of the house is divided into two rooms of unequal size with a second staircase rising in the front room or parlor. Built-in cupboards in the southeast room indicate it was probably a dining room.

Northwestern Cecil County was substantially subdivided during the late eighteenth and early nineteenth centuries when immigrants pushed south from more crowded Pennsylvania townships such as London Grove, New Garden, and Coleraine. The John Swisher house (CE-39), built in 1833, and its family history are representative of this southern movement of both family and house form. In March 1813 John Swisher, Sr. bought two tracts on the south side of Octoraro Creek from Stephen Rowland.[9] He subsequently named it "Father's Gift" and sold it to his son John Swisher, Jr. The land transaction indicates that the Swisher family had emigrated from Coleraine Township in Lancaster County, Pennsylvania. With this origin in the heart of an early German-American community, it is not surprising that John Jr. and his family built themselves a two-story stone house with a three-room plan. Mingling Germanic and English building traditions, the Swisher house had one large room heated by a single fireplace on

CE-229, Nathan and Susannah Harris house (1980)

the west side of the house and two smaller rooms with corner fireplaces occupying the east side. An enclosed staircase was built against the middle partition.

A dwelling that combines both three- and four-bay forms is the Nathan and Susannah Harris house (CE-229), built in 1798 at the Harrisville crossroads. Its slightly uneven south facade has four openings on the first floor, with two center doors, and three openings on the second floor. This variation in window and door placement signals formal changes within the house intended to accommodate specialized room functions. When Nathan and Susannah Harris built this house, they decided to include a formal stair passage to separate the cross passage kitchen from the more formal parlor and rear chamber at the east end of the house. The addition of a center stair hall necessitated another door in the main facade in this modified cross passage plan.

For the Harrises to make this change in plan required a formal reassessment of their social and cultural values. Their final response, as expressed in the house they financed, is clearly a reaction to the social and cultural pressures they experienced during the late years of the eighteenth century. Their needs were evidently strong enough to allow them to alter both the exterior fenestration and interior floor plan of a traditional house form. County residents continued to use the three-room/cross passage

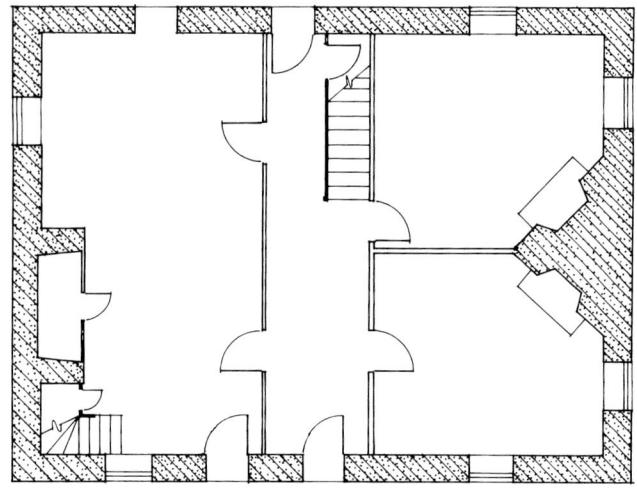

Nathan and Susannah Harris house floor plan (Paul Touart, Anthony O. James)

CE-27, gambrel-roofed portion of Rose Hill (1995)

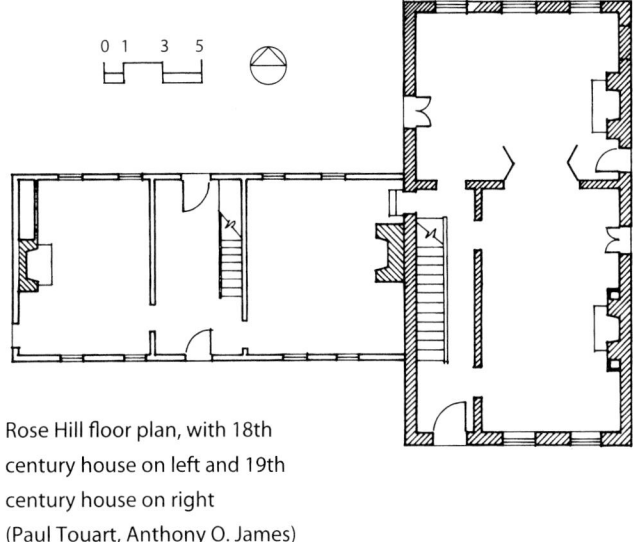

Rose Hill floor plan, with 18th century house on left and 19th century house on right (Paul Touart, Anthony O. James)

plan, modifying it for their needs, until the mid-nineteenth century.

The idea of a center stair hall was not new in 1798, for the Chesapeake gentry had experimented with center passages since the early eighteenth century in their attempts to define and order space in expanded plantation dwellings. Accrued profits from the commercial tobacco and grain agriculture of the seventeenth and eighteenth centuries allowed a small fraction of Maryland and Virginia planters to finance dwellings much more complex and pretentious than those of their ancestors or their contemporaries, signaling their elevated status in Chesapeake society. Coupled with the desire for larger, more expensively crafted houses was the gentry's conspicuous purchase of fine silver, china, glassware, and mahogany or walnut furniture to display in their new passages, parlors, and dining rooms.

As Chesapeake society became more stratified over the course of the eighteenth century, planters who could afford large new dwellings imposed an order on their households that touched almost every aspect of plantation life. Their desire to command complete control over entrance into and movement through the plantation house led to the adoption of the center passage plan, which allowed residents to achieve control simply by closing a door. By the mid- to late eighteenth century, a friend, visitor, or servant no longer walked through the front door of a wealthy family's house into a communal space devoted to working, eating, and sleeping. Instead, an entrance hall or passage provided a common or public ground in which a visitor could wait, either to be received there or escorted into more intimate parts of the house. Although the often generously dimensioned center hall, with doors at front and back, provided a cool, breezy retreat during the hot, humid Chesapeake summer, the passage primarily served as a place of reception with a direct path to the first floor rooms and a staircase leading to rooms above and sometimes below.

CE-55, The Rounds (1979)

CE-29, Rich Neck (1978)

Planters throughout Cecil County held slaves, but the largest concentration of slaveholding gentry in the county resided south of the Elk River along the Bohemia and Sassafras. In contrast to the largely self-sufficient, owner-operated nature of many northern Cecil County farms, which had few or no servants, these sprawling plantations spread over hundreds, if not thousands, of acres cultivated first by indentured white servants and then by enslaved blacks. Nowhere are the daily activities of a sizable Cecil County plantation better portrayed than in the diary of Martha Ogle Forman (1785-1864).

After her marriage to General Thomas Marsh Forman in May 1814, Martha Ogle moved to Rose Hill (CE-27) on the Sassafras. Here she found a single-story, gambrel-roofed frame dwelling (circa 1780-90) with a center hall/single-pile plan, a type of house much favored by Chesapeake planters. A center passage like that at Rose Hill often contained the principal stair, but more important, it separated a parlor on one side from a dining room on the other.

Despite the obvious working nature of the household as reflected in the hundreds of domestic labors Mrs. Forman recorded in her diary, it is clear that a few rooms of the main house were distinctly formal in contrast to the more public spaces inside the house as well as outside in the yard. The dining room was newly plastered on Mrs. Forman's arrival in 1814, and shortly afterward a new, imported marble mantel was installed.[10] Later that year General Forman and a man named Samuel Allen papered the dining room.[11] Not only do these improvements speak of a formal interior,

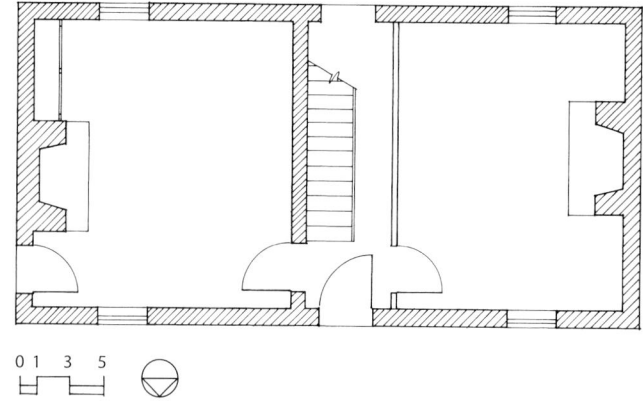

Rich Neck floor plan (Paul Touart, Anthony O. James)

but Mrs. Forman's frequent mention of the dining room in her diary points to the pivotal place this room held in the Forman household.

Houses with center hall/single-pile plans like that at Rose Hill are dotted throughout southern Cecil County. A prominent example is The Rounds (CE-55), a circa 1790 brick house on the south side of Little Bohemia Creek. The strictly symmetrical five-bay south elevation of the house, two stories carefully laid in Flemish bond, is marked by traditional Georgian brickwork conventions. An ovolo-molded brick cap tops the water table, and a four-row belt course marks the second floor level. The front entrance is enhanced by paneled reveals and a beautiful arched transom with intersecting muntins. The single-pile main block is twenty feet deep with a center stair hall flanked by a parlor to the

CE-40, Patrick Ewing house (1978)

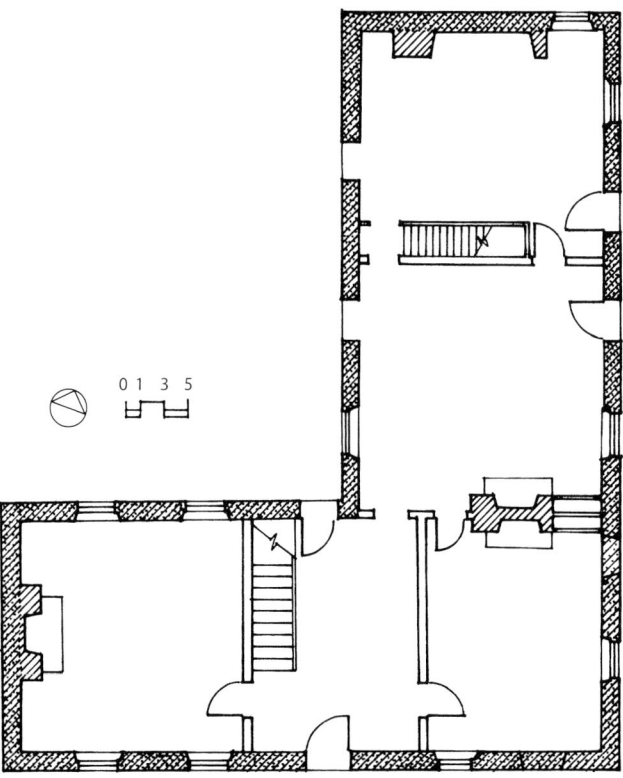

Patrick Ewing house floor plan
(Paul Touart, Anthony O. James)

west and a dining room to the east. A slight variation in the plan of The Rounds includes a third first floor room behind the dining room, which gives the main block an L shape. Attached to the east gable end is a kitchen wing.

The center hall/single-pile house type continued in favor during the early to mid-nineteenth century, and later examples show little modification to the traditional plan. Erected on a high bluff overlooking the Sassafras River is the Rich Neck plantation house (CE-29), also known as Frisby's Delight. It is a two-story, three-bay Flemish and common bond brick house dating from around 1820-30. The center stair hall is flanked on the west side by a parlor and on the east by a room fitted with built-in cupboards. Considering the cupboards and the room's proximity to the kitchen, the latter was probably used as a dining space.

Northern Cecil County is not without examples of this house form, and an outstanding early nineteenth century one is the Patrick Ewing house (CE-40), built in 1834 with a contemporary service wing. When Patrick Ewing erected his L-shaped stone house on the north side of Octoraro Creek, its overall classical balance was a major concern. In fact, architectural symmetry was so important that the construction program included a purely decorative east end chimney stack and four blind windows on the

CE-17, Bloomingdale (1981)

south and east elevations. The wide center stair hall separates a parlor to the west and a smaller sitting room to the east. Included as well in the stair hall is a door in the rear wall, which opens into the dining room in the rear ell. In the back of the service wing is the kitchen, designed with a large cooking fireplace. A second, service stair rises between the dining room and the kitchen.

Architecturally and politically, the revival of Renaissance ideals of classicism in seventeenth and eighteenth century Britain has been loosely labeled "Georgian" in honor of the four King Georges who ruled Great Britain from 1714 until the early nineteenth century. The designs of European architects—among them Andrea Palladio (1508-1580) and his disciples Colen Campbell (1673-1729) and Roger Morris (1695-1749), to name two—helped to inspire and promote a resurgence in neoclassicism that lasted through the eighteenth century in England and widely influenced Chesapeake plantation architecture. The bilateral symmetrical formula of the center passage house stems directly from this strong British influence. By the second quarter of the nineteenth century, this form was so well entrenched in the local building vocabulary that it remained popular even after the Civil War, a time when asymmetrical plans were widely publicized throughout the country by means of architectural trade literature. The construction of Bloomingdale (CE-17) around 1860 with Italianate features speaks of an outside architectural inspiration, but the three-story brick house follows a traditional center passage form.

The dwellings discussed thus far are single-pile structures. Adding the double-pile houses (those with a two-room depth) demonstrates further the diverse array of house forms built in eighteenth and nineteenth century Cecil County. In overall dimension and complexity, most double-pile houses outdistance their single-pile contemporaries. It is principally for this reason that most of these were created for the wealthiest members of the Cecil County populace.

For a very small group of Cecil planters living in the eighteenth and nineteenth centuries, the desire for formal passages and specialized room use was satisfied with the construction of lavish brick plantation houses. The dwellings of the planter elite in southern Cecil County include Worsell Manor, Bohemia, and Greenfields. The influence of English style books is quite evident in each of these examples, particularly Bohemia and Greenfields. In all three the double-pile main house was extended to each side with flanking wings that housed the domestic operations of the household.

Worsell Manor (CE-58), built circa 1760-70 and mea-

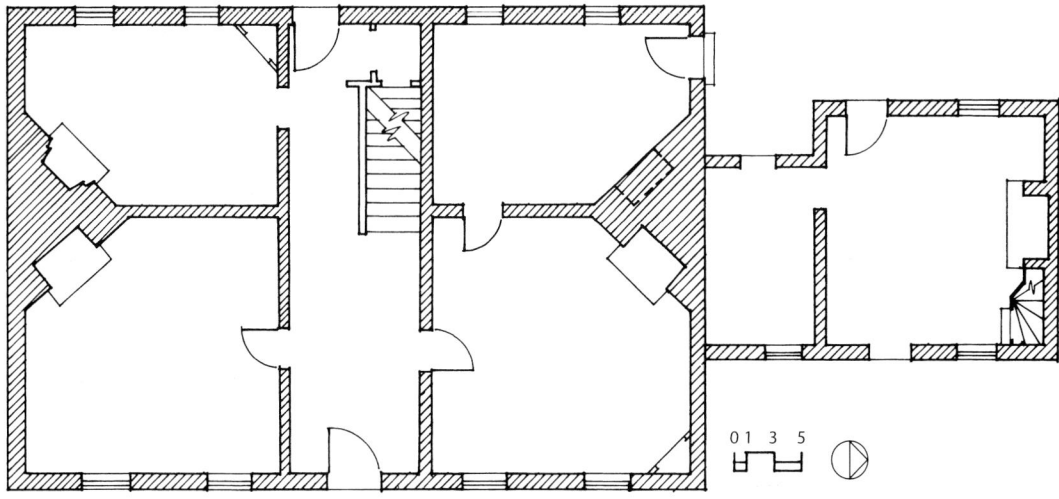

CE-58, Worsell Manor (1968); floor plan (Paul Touart, Anthony O. James)

suring 50 feet across by 33 feet deep, is a Flemish bond brick dwelling with a strictly symmetrical main (east) elevation. The principal entrance is centered exactly in the five-bay, fifty-foot facade. The front wall, with its horizontal emphasis and deliberate bilateral symmetry, is characteristic of the Georgian architectural formula. Large twelve-over-twelve sash windows light the four rooms that flank the spacious center hall, which contains the original turned baluster stair. Corner fireplaces were included in the design of each room. Contemporary service wings were attached to both gable ends, although only the north kitchen wing has survived. No room-by-room inventory reveals the functions of the first floor rooms at Worsell Manor, but the two large front rooms were probably used as a formal parlor and dining room.

The quintessential Georgian or Palladian-inspired plantation house in Cecil County is Bohemia (CE-32), on the south shore of Little Bohemia Creek. Believed to have been

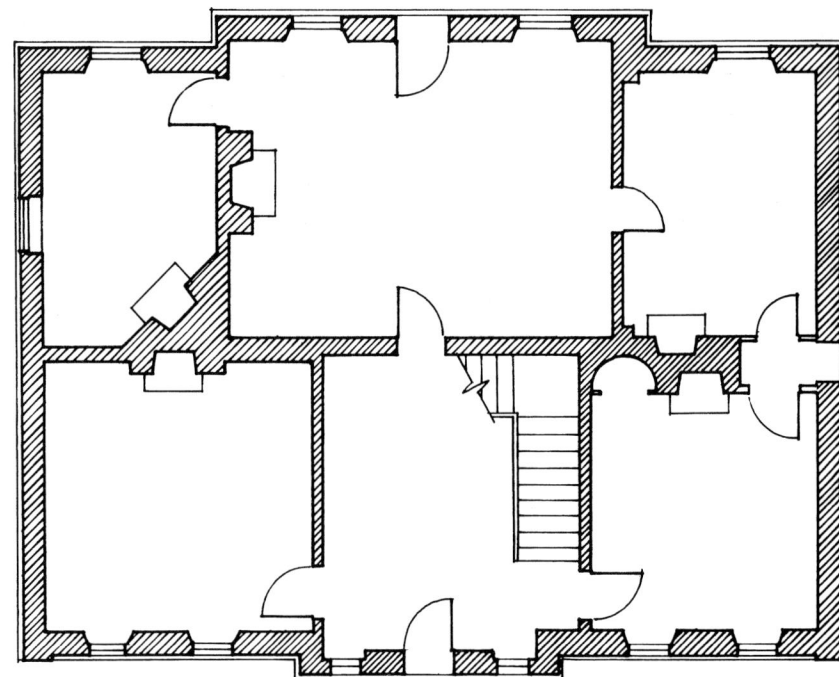

Bohemia floor plan
(Paul Touart, Anthony O. James)

started around 1751, the house has Flemish and header bond walls that rise to a broad hip roof. The river elevation is dominated by a templelike pediment, which draws attention to the center three-bay entrance wall. Likewise, the land approach is distinguished by a pediment that surmounts the projecting entrance bay. The floor plan of Bohemia is like none other in Cecil County, with a grand stair hall entered through the doorway on the land side. Featuring a masterfully crafted Chinese decorated staircase and intricate plasterwork ceiling and wall ornaments, the stair hall provided an elaborate entry intended to impress family, friends, and visitors alike.

Functioning in a manner similar to other center passages, the squarish stair hall at Bohemia clearly served as a reception area from which friends or other guests could be directed to one of three formal rooms obviously designed and decorated for entertaining. West of the stair hall is a squarish space usually referred to as the "music room" because of the distinctive lyre-shaped medallion that enhances the overmantel. East of the stair hall is the dining room, another squarish space, fitted with a built-in cupboard in the niche to the left of the fireplace. While refinements in plaster and woodwork ornament distinguish the "music room" and dining room, the largest space is the drawing room on the north side of the stair hall. Measuring twenty-three feet across and more than seventeen feet deep, this creekside room is enriched with a finely crafted chimney breast and wall moldings. The fireplace is framed by an intricately carved classical mantel of exceptional complexity, including an overmantel with a bold Doric order cornice composed of several layers of classical moldings and a row of triglyphs. The perimeter of this spacious room is trimmed with baseboard, chair rail, and cornice moldings. Two additional rooms, evidently intended for more private use, flank the drawing room. The impressive six-room plan is repeated on the second floor, although the wall finishes there were executed in a much less elaborate fashion. Bohemia, with its clear Palladian inspiration, was strictly balanced in elevation and in plan, exhibiting the builder's obvious desire to emulate the fine gentry dwellings of Georgian England.

Probably inspired by Bohemia, the impressive brick house known as Greenfields (CE-16) was erected around 1770 on the level plains north of the Sassafras River. This large hip-roofed, double-pile brick house has a broad center passage that divides the rooms to each side. Like that at Bohemia, the center entrance of the symmetrical five-bay front is contained within a projecting pavilion. However, the Greenfields doorway is enhanced by a triangular pediment and flanking pilasters. Also similar to Bohemia is the round or "ox-eye" window that pierces the center wall of the pediment, known as the tympanum.

Entrance through the pedimented front door at Greenfields provides access to a voluminous center passage,

CE-32, Bohemia (1936-37, Frances Benjamin Johnston Collection, Library of Congress)

which contains the principal staircase. The two large front rooms, the formal parlor on the left and the dining room on the right, contain the most elaborate Georgian woodwork finishes in the house. Crossetted surrounds frame the doorways and fireplaces, and each chimney breast features bold overmantel moldings. Both front rooms are enriched with baseboard, chair rail, and cornice moldings of various profiles and include such refinements as interior paneled shutters fitted into the window jambs. Although less elaborately detailed, the two rear rooms feature raised panel fireplace walls with built-in closets. A service stair rising in the northeast room provides direct access to the northeast chamber.

The generously dimensioned center passage/double-pile plan of the main block at Greenfields is extended by contemporaneous single-story wings that originally housed the cooking, cleaning, and wide array of other domestic chores necessary for the daily function of a large plantation. Detached flanking dependencies, symmetrically placed to each side of the wings, furthered the classically inspired balance of the plantation complex.

Greenfields, Bohemia, and Worsell Manor are particularly fine examples of the Georgian aesthetic as translated and adopted by Chesapeake planters who strove to create for themselves lives akin to the landed gentry of Great Britain. The ordered architectural spaces evident in the neo-Palladian dwellings of southern Cecil County were not repeated in the same fashion north of the Elk River. Nonetheless, the strong Anglo-American cultural base in northern Cecil also resulted in the construction of a wide variety of center hall/double-pile houses that demonstrate an interest in formal separation and segregation of interior spaces.

Built in 1791 of carefully laid fieldstone, Graystone Manor (CE-95) is a massive center hall/double-pile house situated among the gently rolling hills northwest of Rising

CE-16, Greenfields (1995)

Sun. The center hall and flanking rooms at Graystone Manor represent a distinct parallel to structures such as Worsell Manor. Although the center hall is not as wide at Graystone, this formal center entry served the same purpose of controlling access to adjacent rooms. Room use at Graystone Manor probably paralleled that at other center hall houses, with a formal parlor and dining room on the first floor, although a large fireplace in the northwest room apparently served as a cooking area before the gable end service wing was built. The southwest room has no open hearth, and it was evidently warmed by an iron-plate stove fed through the middle partition wall.

Not all double-pile houses with four rooms on a floor contain a full center passage. Hopewell (CE-172), built circa 1750-70 along the west bank of the Little Elk Creek, is important in a discussion of alternative center hall plan

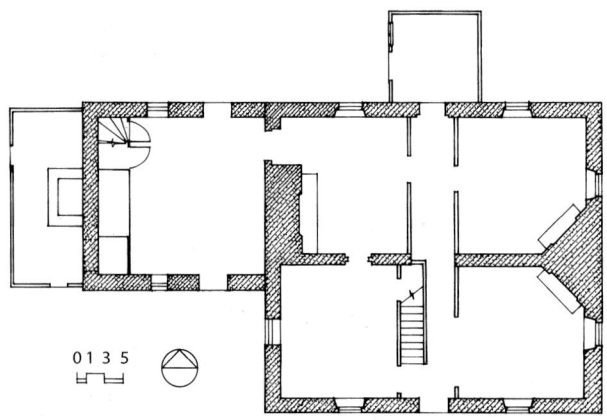

CE-95, Graystone Manor (1980);
floor plan (Paul Touart, Anthony O. James)

dwellings in Cecil County. On the first floor the center passage does not extend through the full depth of the structure; instead, the turned baluster staircase and passage are sandwiched between the two rear rooms. The two large front rooms could both be entered directly from the outside, but two front doors allowed for a measure of access control.[12] The southeast room, with a massive six-foot wide fireplace, is a space akin to the old common room, the "hall." The southwest room, with its smaller corner hearth and individual entrance, was probably a formal, less used parlor. The ownership history of Hopewell reveals a strong association with the Scots-Irish immigrants who populated much of northeastern Cecil County during the early eighteenth century, but the two-door front to the double-pile house points to the influence of nearby Pennsylvania and its Germanic residents.

A variation of the double-pile house erected when the

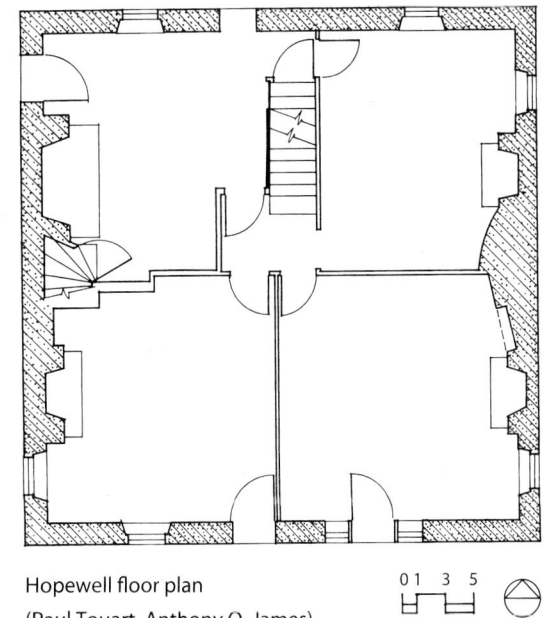

Hopewell floor plan
(Paul Touart, Anthony O. James)

CE-172, Hopewell (1968)

CE-76, Red Ball Tavern house (1980)

Scots-Irish settled the New Munster tract on the Big Elk Creek is the house thought to have been the Red Ball Tavern (CE-76). Erected of local fieldstone around 1820, it has four massive eighteen-inch thick stone walls that enclose four rooms separated by thin stud wall partitions. As at Hopewell, two doors arranged in a slightly asymmetrical elevation provide access to two large front rooms each served by a fireplace (in this case two end wall fireplaces). Fixed in the back (north side) of the house is the principal staircase, offering access to the second floor and the cellar. The northwest room, designed with an expansive six-foot hearth, provided the main living and cooking area in the house. Interestingly, a separate, segregated winder staircase fixed in the niche next to the large fireplace leads to third floor servant chambers but gives no access to the second floor rooms.

Asymmetry and alternative double-pile plans are not limited to the Scots-Irish houses of northern Cecil County. Great House (CE-65), circa 1750-70, stands out as one of the major early examples of a variation in the double-pile, four-room format. Standing on the old Labadist tract on

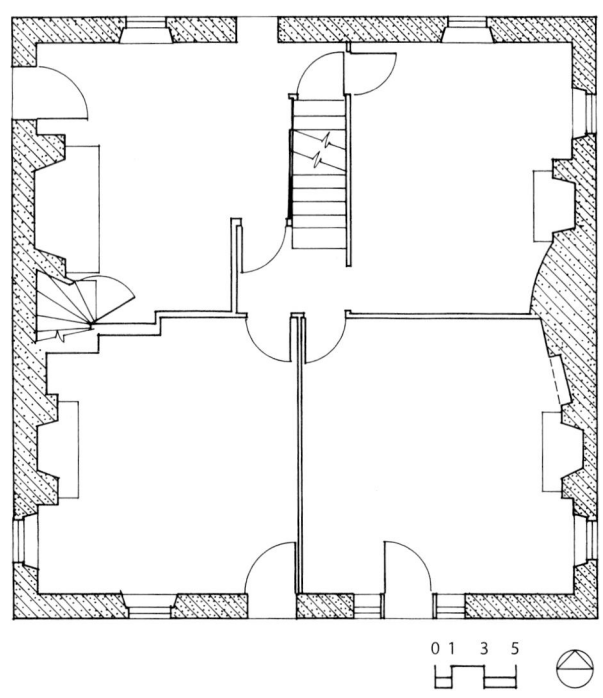

Red Ball Tavern house floor plan
(Paul Touart, Anthony O. James)

CE-65, Great House (1978)

CE-203, Jeremiah Brown house (1976)

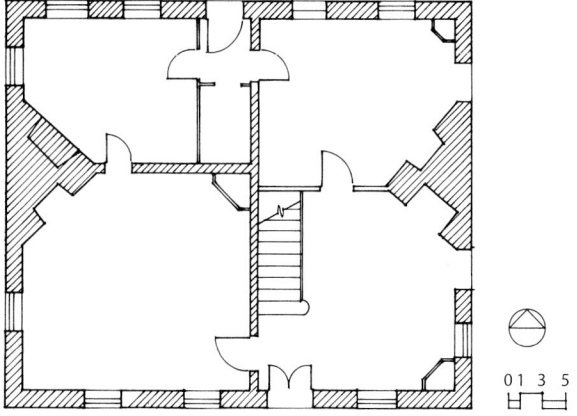

Great House floor plan (Paul Touart, Anthony O. James)

the north side of the Bohemia River, Great House has four rooms, each heated by a corner hearth. The major difference here, in contrast to nearby Worsell Manor and its center hall plan, is the absence of a broad through passage. In lieu of the center hall, the entire southeast corner of the house serves as the entrance and stair hall and is equipped with a corner fireplace. A "baffle" entrance on the north side of the house, opening into a small space between the rear rooms, provides a double-door system that had the dual function of providing a measure of privacy and protecting the back rooms from the direct entry of cold, harsh weather. General room use at Great House paralleled that at Worsell Manor, with a formal parlor to the left of the entrance and a dining room near the kitchen wing, in this case in the northeast corner. The fourth first floor room in Great House probably served as a first floor chamber or perhaps a plantation office.

Only a few of the landed gentry in Cecil County could entertain thoughts of financing a dwelling that resembled Great House or Bohemia during the mid-eighteenth century. Most planters, even most well-to-do planters, did with far less. One popular double-pile house form that offered some of the advantages of the center hall/double-pile plans but cost much less to build is the side passage/double-pile plan. An early dated example of this form is the Jeremiah Brown house (CE-203), erected in 1757 of local stone on the Nottingham Lots. Upon entering the front door of the house, visitors encounter a broad passage with a stair tucked in the far end. Acting in much the same way as a center hall, the side passage permitted control of access to the two first floor rooms, often a parlor and dining room. In many examples a door in the center partition allowed direct communication between the front and back rooms.

The popularity of the center passage forms in Cecil County ensured the widespread favor of the side passage form throughout the second half of the eighteenth century and much of the nineteenth century as well. In 1837-38, when Thomas and Martha Ogle Forman embarked on the construction of a new brick addition to their eighteenth century frame dwelling, they chose a form that resembled urban town houses they knew in Philadelphia, Baltimore, and elsewhere. The new structure at Rose Hill—an upright, two-and-a-half story side passage/double-pile dwelling—soared vertically above the low-slung, gambrel-roofed older house. The room arrangement of the new brick dwelling shows a slight modification in plan, with the stair hall reduced in size and importance. In exchange for a shorter, narrower hallway, the dining room was enlarged several feet to stretch across the entire back of the new house. (See floor plan on page 177.)

CE-222, Underwood house (1980)   CE-27, portion of Rose Hill built by the Formans in 1837-38 (1995)

The Formans chose to enlarge their new dining room to better suit their needs, as Martha Forman commented in her diary on November 25, 1837: "Saturday quite cold, began to plaster our new dining room…We have enlarged our dining room and my chamber 3 foot which will make them very comfortable."[13] Over the next few months Martha Forman wrote of adding refinements to her new dining room and drawing room. On the first of December she recorded, "The mantles [sic] for our drawing room and dining room arrived, they are very handsome."[14]

Entertaining and dining in the proper setting were clearly important to the Formans, and the couple chose a plan that allowed them to expand the first floor space easily. The parlor and dining room could be made into one large area simply by opening a set of double folding doors that divided the drawing room or parlor in the front from the dining room in back. On January 13, 1838, Martha Forman was pleased to write that her husband had just returned from Baltimore with a new carpet for the dining room and paper for the walls.[15]

A smaller, even more economical double-pile plan was built on a handful of Cecil County farms. Identified by architectural historians as the "double-cell" plan, this house type lacks a stair passage, having just two rooms, one behind the other. The double-cell form is especially easy to identify, with its narrow two-bay front elevation and full two-room

CE-127 Indian Queen (1968)

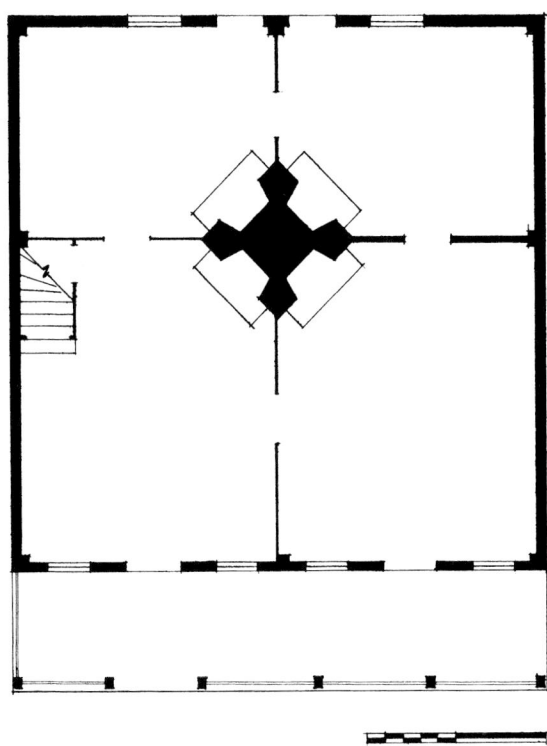

Indian Queen floor plan
(James T. Wollon, Jr., Anthony O. James)

depth. The two-room plan main block was often extended with a gable end kitchen wing, as at the Underwood house (CE-222), built around 1800-10 on the eastern edge of the Nottingham Lots near Fairview. The two first floor rooms are heated by end wall corner fireplaces, and the main stair is fixed in the northeast corner of the house, formerly separated from the back room by stud wall partitions. The Flemish bond brick structure was enlarged during the second quarter of the nineteenth century with a gable end, common bond kitchen wing.

Complicating the discussion of early Cecil County house forms is a small idiosyncratic group of dwellings built in an architectural tradition based on a central chimney plan rather than an end chimney plan. Archeological investigations of seventeenth century sites in the Chesapeake region reveal that center chimney dwellings were not uncommon. A wood or masonry stack rose near the middle of the house, often opposite a small lobby-type entrance. Parallels to this type of house are common in New England, but changing social priorities coupled with a hotter, more humid climate discouraged the long-term popularity of a center chimney plan in the Chesapeake region.[16]

In Cecil County the Indian Queen (CE-127), with its central stone-and-brick chimney stack, stands out as a distinct and significant alternative to the mainstream center hall, end chimney plans. Not only distinctive for its chimney construction, the Indian Queen is an anomalous structure without clear precedents within its own small group. Its odd plan, with large public rooms entered directly from the outside, most likely had to do with its early use as a tavern by innkeeper Zebulon Hollingsworth.

Dated circa 1750-60, the Indian Queen is a heavy, braced timber frame structure that exhibits exposed "gunstock" corner posts and brick nogging. Rising near the middle of the 30-foot-square structure is a massive brick chimney pile supported on a stone base. The chimney was designed to accommodate four corner fireplaces, one for each first floor room. Narrow vertical beaded board partitions divide the interior spaces. Meal preparation was accomplished in a detached structure that stands in the backyard.

Also prominent among the central chimney dwellings in Cecil County is the Woodrow house (CE-1214), built around 1800-20 along the south bank of Basin Run in the vicinity of Liberty Grove. The massive stone-and-brick chimney pile is supported by a triangular base that turns as it ascends through two floors and the attic to pierce the roof as a normal square stack. Similar to the Indian Queen, which may have served as its inspiration, the stuccoed stone house has a quartered plan with corner fireplaces serving the first and second floor rooms. Remnants of wrought-iron hardware and raised panel finishes are mixed with early and late nineteenth century woodwork and plan alterations that disguise the original room disposition. Nonetheless, the central chimney construction distinguishes the house as a distinct and rare variation from more common building practices in Cecil County.

A form of center chimney house found in northern Cecil County signifies another facet of the peripheral influence of the Pennsylvania German culture to the north. In general the southern migration of Pennsylvania Germans into Maryland, and the influence of their culture, was confined to the counties west of the Susquehanna River. However, major transportation and communication links arose during the late eighteenth century between Lancaster and Cecil counties. This development encouraged trade and, to a lesser degree, resettlement of Pennsylvanians in the less populated northwestern corner of the county between 1780 and the Civil War.

The presence of German-American building forms and construction practices in Cecil County is by no means obvious, for the characteristic Germanic house forms and building techniques had long been modified before their introduction south of the Mason-Dixon line. Despite the diagnostic subtleties, a small group of houses or construction techniques in northern Cecil County can be tied to a German-American influence. The Z.T. Rawlings house (CE-907) is one example.

This two-story, three-bay, rectangular log structure stands in the vicinity of Rock Springs. Erected around 1830, it is divided into two rooms of unequal size with a central chimney stack between. This plan, along with three- and four-room variations, was a well-established continental European house form. Characteristic of most Germanic houses is an asymmetrical placement of doors and windows, as seen in the center door and flanking windows of this example. A slightly off-center door opens into the main living/cooking space, similar to the English "hall" and known in German as the *kuche*. The second room of the Z. T. Rawlings house was probably a more formal parlor, in German the *stube*, or perhaps a first floor bedroom, or *kammer*.

Due to the acculturation of many continental European features by the early to mid-nineteenth century, the distinct Germanic aspects of this two-room house form had long been modified to conform more closely to its Anglo-American hall/parlor counterpart. The Lancaster County origin of the Rawlings family, the assumed builders, explains the construction of this foreign house form in northwestern Cecil County.[17] Other links to German-American cultural traditions are found in several building practices evident in a handful of Cecil County houses; these are discussed in Chapter 8, "Methods of Construction in Cecil County."

The wealth of diversity displayed by the surviving dwellings of Cecil County only hints at the broad array of house forms residents built during the eighteenth and nineteenth centuries. The surviving architectural record is heavily biased toward the longer-lasting stone and brick dwellings, but a combination of documentary research and

(above) CE-1214, Woodrow house

(below) CE-907, Z.T. Rawlings house (1978)

field study permits conjecture of a larger range of house types once covering the landscape. Each form was subjected to personal and permanent changes, both in exterior appearance and formal room arrangement, to suit the needs and interests of the family or individual for whom it was built. Toward the middle decades of the nineteenth century, use of many of these eighteenth century forms was generally discontinued in Cecil County, while others were modified to suit the new demands of the technological society ushered in with the Industrial Revolution. Citizens less interested in the past were able to turn to a host of new architectural forms inspired by Europe's past and carried to remote corners of the county through architects' style books and builders' trade journals. However, a strong conservatism in Cecil County, as across the Eastern Shore, led to extended use of the time-honored vernacular house forms, which county residents simply updated or modernized with stylish new woodwork. The building materials and stylistic decoration of the houses exhibiting these holdover house forms provide further insight into the technology and popular culture of the time and place in which they were built.

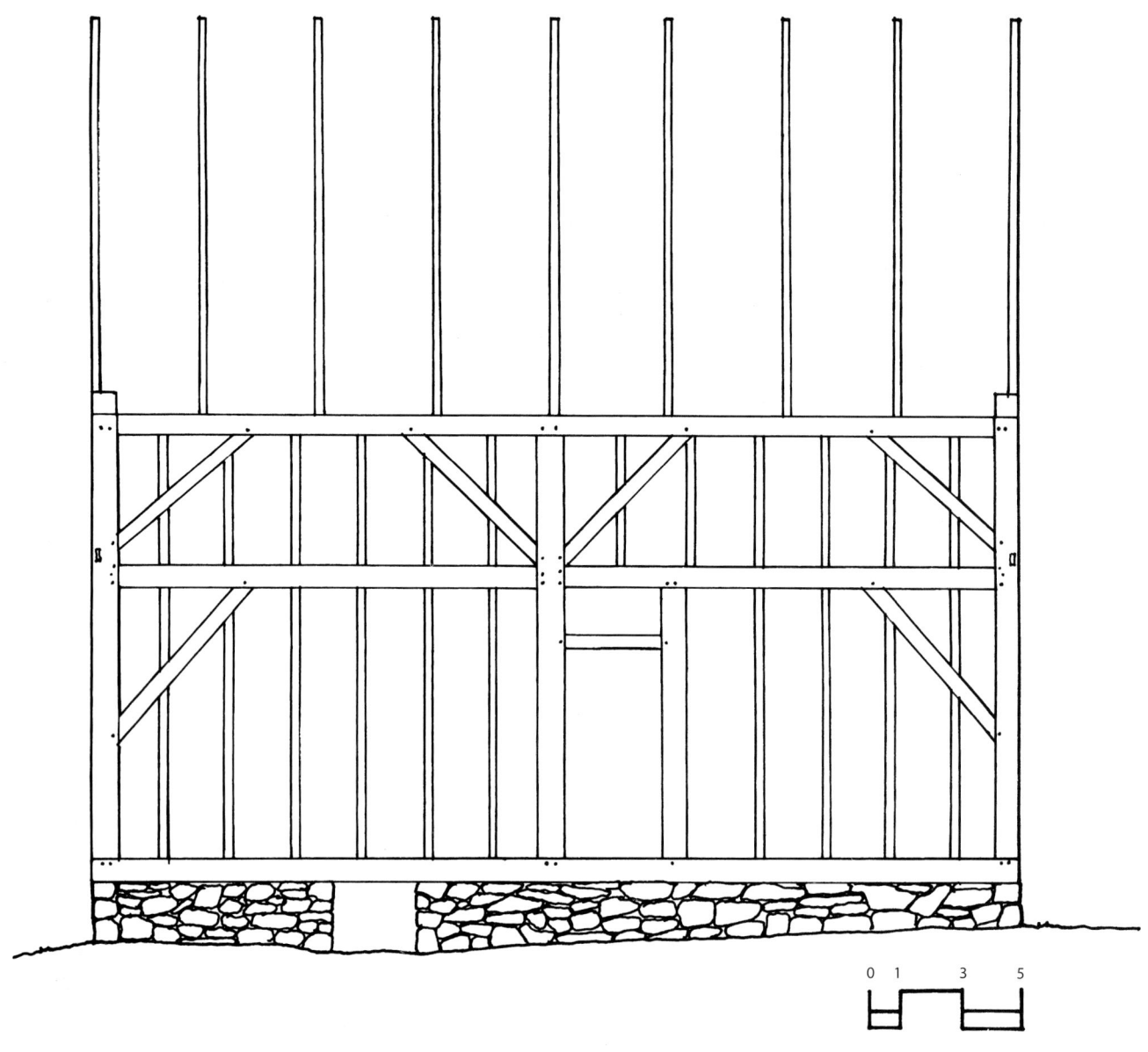

CE-209, framing elevation of the Roger Kirk house
(Paul Touart, Anthony O. James)

CHAPTER 8

Methods of Construction in Cecil County Dwellings (1670-1900)

INTEGRAL to any architectural history is a discussion of the materials and methods used to construct buildings. In Cecil County the list of construction practices is as complex as the array of house forms. Rich building traditions in timber and masonry reflect the variety of indigenous materials in the county and the diverse cultures from which immigrants came to the area. In Cecil, as elsewhere in the American colonies, European settlers adapted New World resources according to their native traditions, creating a distinctly American architecture.

Not long after the early settlement of Cecil County, the ethnic building practices of the first European residents were modified as individuals from different backgrounds came together and exchanged ideas. By the mid-eighteenth century, definitive signs of specific cultural traditions were well on the wane. By the early to mid-nineteenth century, the standardization of construction methods and practices brought on by industrialization had permanently erased any vestiges of older cultural traditions.

The technological and developmental histories of the varied building practices found in Cecil County are best illustrated with examples, using both artifact analysis and documentary records of particular buildings. It is fitting to begin with the earliest "dated" county structures, although the discussion that follows is not in strict chronological order.[1]

No standing Cecil structure can be comfortably dated before the first decades of the eighteenth century, and as a result the appearance and character of early Cecil architecture remain speculative. It is safe to assume, however, that the initial immigrants took advantage of the large stands of timber for house building, whether they were constructing a sapling hut or a carpentered timber frame or log dwelling. The presence of the several decades-old settlements around New Castle by Delaware Bay surely helped mitigate some of the problems that beset the first generation of immigrants to settle the northern reaches of the Maryland colony. Indeed, some of the first Quaker immigrants to populate the Nottingham Lots arrived by way of the port of New Castle, which was an easy day's journey distant. Rather than erecting quickly assembled impermanent dwellings, by the early eighteenth century some first generation settlers were building durable houses that have survived to the modern day.

The earliest dated Cecil County dwellings surviving today were built with Anglo-American braced timber frame construction practices. Comparable frame building traditions appear frequently in heavily settled Anglo-American regions such as New England.[2] The horizontal log walling techniques found in early Cecil County, on the other hand, were not part of the British building vocabulary. Rather, these were introduced by settlers of continental European descent. The mid-seventeenth century arrival of the Bohemian Augustine Herman and Dutch and Scandinavian refugees from the Delaware Bay settlements undoubtedly introduced log wall construction to the Chesapeake side of the peninsula.

During the seventeenth and eighteenth centuries much of Cecil County was planted by Anglo-American groups who carried with them strong traditions of heavy braced timber frame construction. Although it is unknown to what extent these methods were used in early county settlements, until the late twentieth century the framing practices were well represented in the Roger Kirk house (CE-209), built in 1719 and now destroyed, and the Haines house (CE-216), erected around 1720-30 and still standing near Rising Sun. William Penn presented a related method of framing a house in a 1684 tract he issued for prospective new settlers in the neighboring province of Pennsylvania:

…there must be eight Trees of about sixteen inches square and cut off, to Posts of about fifteen foot long, which the House must stand upon, and four pieces, two of thirty foot long, two of eighteen foot long, for Plates, which must lie on the top of the Posts, the whole length and breadth of the House, for the gists to rest upon. There must be ten gists of twenty foot long, to bear the Loft, and two false Plates of thirty foot long, Rafters of about twenty foot, to bear the Roof of the House, with several other small pieces, as Wind-beams, Braces, Studs, & c. which are made out of the Waste Timber. For covering the House, Ends, and Sides, and for the Loft, we use Clabboard, which is Rived feather-edged, of five foot and a half long, that well Drawn lyes close and smooth. The Lodging Room may be lined with the same, and filled up between, which is very Warm. These houses usually endure ten years without Repair.[3]

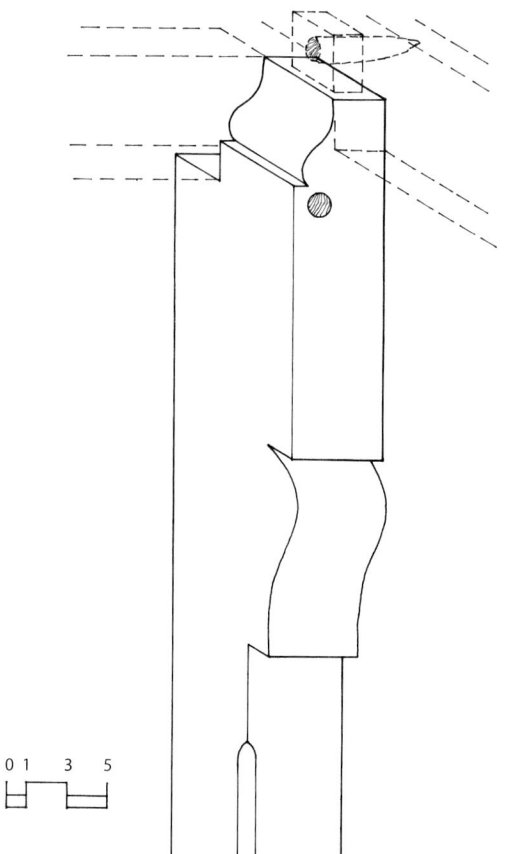

CE-216, post head, Haines house
(Paul Touart, Anthony O. James)

These dimensions and specifications portray a house type with its principal supportive posts set in the ground. Recognized today as part of a range of impermanent building practices common to seventeenth century architecture, houses, barns, and outbuildings of this hole-set post construction were erected across the Chesapeake region. Buildings with their main supportive posts set into the moist ground did not last many years without needing serious repair. Within the span of ten to fifteen years many hole-set buildings were replaced by more permanent structures, or at least raised off the ground on blocks or masonry piers.

Akin to the dwelling outlined in the Penn pamphlet is the Roger Kirk house, erected in 1719 with four stout corner posts fashioned with a flaring "gunstock" profile at the head. A more elaborately carved post head at the Haines house includes bold ogee curves and chamfered corners. The feature that made the Roger Kirk house better built than the earthfast dwellings described in the pamphlet was the continuous sill and fieldstone foundation on which the well-crafted timber frame rested. The four gunstock posts, along with several intermediate posts on each side wall, supported the primary horizontal framing members. The front and rear wall plates were fixed in place with tenons that extended from the top of the post head; the gable end tie beams were locked in place with a post tenon and dovetailed trench in the top face of the plate. Rafters that tapered on both faces were joined at the peak with a pinned mortise-and-tenon joint and on the front and rear plates with bird-mouthed joints. Collar beams, used to stabilize and strengthen the rafters, stretched between the rafter blades and were fastened with half-dovetailed lap joints. Between the main posts were smaller studs held in place by sill and girt mortises and used to support a uniform application of siding. The walls, as the pamphleteer suggested, were probably originally sheathed with riven clapboards.

The use of riven clapboards as an exterior wall sheathing is well documented in late eighteenth century Orphans Court records.[4] In 1792 the subscribers found on the property of Ephraim Logue "one old dwelling house thirty feet by eighteen, a frame weatherboarded with oak clapboards, covered on one side with oak shingles, the other side with cedar."⁵ The following year, on the property of Hyland Price, the subscribers found "a dwelling house 33½ feet long and 17 feet wide, of frame and logs, one half weatherboarded with pine plank the other half with oak clapboards."⁶

Evidently the Price and Logue plantation houses were covered with a range of building materials of oak, pine, and cedar. The distinction in the Price house between clapboards and weatherboards indicates that one side of the house was sheathed with riven boards four to five feet long, probably butted end to end with a tapered feather edge. The term weatherboard, on the other hand, referred to a longer piece of siding, which had been sawn instead of hand-split with a froe and mallet. Clapboards were a common siding material for most buildings during the seventeenth century, but only certain wood species, such as oak and cypress, split naturally to render the desired wedge-shaped boards. Timber suitable for making clapboards was valued for its marketability, and restrictions on its harvesting can be found in county land records. In a proprietary land grant executed on February 18, 1744, Lord Baltimore granted to Elihu Hall

> twenty acres of land lying on a run of water leading into Octoraro called Beeson's Branch… ten acres on the one side of the said run and ten acres on the other side there of with liberty to take fall cut down and carry away either by land or by water any wood or timber fit for building a mill other than timber fit to split into clapboards.⁷

Clapboards were also used for sheathing roofs and covering interior partitions and ceilings, although no surviving examples of this building practice have surfaced in Cecil County. By the early to mid-eighteenth century, well-built frame houses were sheathed with applications of long, sawn weatherboards or shiplap siding, often treated with a decorative bead. In contrast to the rough-hewn appearance of clapboards, the beaded siding signaled a level of craftsmanship often repeated inside with well-carpentered interior woodwork. Despite its waning use by prosperous residents during the eighteenth century, clapboard siding remained a practical option for poorer sorts of housing and outbuildings well into the nineteenth century.

Repeated references to cedar, cypress, and oak shingles in the Orphans Court records suggest these woods were favored for their durability, although few eighteenth century wood shingle roofs have survived to modern times. An early shed roof or lean-to addition is often responsible for preserving such materials, as at Cherry Grove (CE-50), where an eighteenth century shed addition to a log house provided cover for the rear slope of the gambrel roof. A full covering of sidelapped oak shingles, attached with wrought nails, gives some evidence of eighteenth century roofing practice. These eighteen-inch shingles were lapped by neighboring shingles on both the left and top sides to create a more secure, weathertight roof.

Another construction technique meant to yield a tighter and probably warmer house was the familiar English practice of filling the spaces between posts and studs with brick or perhaps stone. Brick nogging or fill is a traditional Anglo-American walling technique that was used repeatedly during the eighteenth and nineteenth centuries in Cecil County as well as throughout Maryland and other states. William Savin's plantation of "Green Spring," described by the Orphans Court officials on June 14, 1785, was improved by "one dwelling framed house filled in with brick, twenty feet long and sixteen feet wide with a plank floor above and below, a plain breast work, a brick chimney in the house one story high in bad repair, the roof entirely decayed."⁸ Very few examples of brick nogging remain both intact and exposed for illustration. One example was at the Ginn farmhouse (CE-778), an early nineteenth century dwelling (now demolished) in which an exposed brick-nogged wall survived under the shed roof of a kitchen addition. Bricks set between the large corner and intermediate posts were stabilized by smaller studs (see next page).

The interest in protecting the residents of a house from the cold is expressed as well by the practice of filling the spaces between the floor joists with a mixture of shaved sticks, mud, and straw. Surviving examples of this construction practice in Cecil County are found in a number of houses in the northwestern corner; use of such infill is more commonly found in Germanic houses in Pennsylvania, western Maryland, and the Shenandoah valley of Vir-

CE-778, brick nogging, Ginn house

CE-107, whitewashed interior of the Hamilton house kitchen (1936, Historic American Buildings Survey)

ginia.[9] In Cecil County this insulation method is represented in the late eighteenth century house called Bournes Forest (CE-414) in the vicinity of Richardsmere and the Gillespie log house (CE-1217) north of Port Deposit, built around 1820.[10]

Whether brick nogged or infilled with sticks, mud, and straw, cellar and attic spaces, as well as a variety of outbuildings, were often coated with a layer of whitewash. Used on both interior and exterior surfaces, whitewash provided a clean, orderly space for domestic functions. Multiple layers are often evident in kitchens and domestic outbuildings where repeated whitewashings built up a thick, flaky layer of paint. In her diary entry for April 20, 1838, Martha Ogle Forman mentioned "getting the house whitewashed and the chambers yellow washed."[11] Years earlier, on May 7, 1821, she had recorded a recipe for whitewash:

> Whitewash, a receipt obtained from Miss Anna Pearce: The proportions producing the whitest covering that will remain hard on walls are— 3 Gallons of white wash, 3 pounds of salt, and one pound of sugar, an increase of sugar will strengthen the cement but will injure the color. The wash should be made of the best lime, and slacked with enough water to cover the lime and make it of the consistence of good thick paint, if it thickens as you use it, thin with boiling water.[12]

Over the course of the nineteenth century, earlier timber framing practices in Cecil County were altered in favor of lighter weight posts and studs, which were usually hidden by layers of lath, plaster, and perhaps whitewash. No longer was it stylish to have any portion of the structural frame exposed. As uniformly dimensioned framing members became available from local lumberyards, the construction process was considerably eased.

Further streamlining of timber dimensions and construction practices in general characterizes the late nine-

CE-234, balloon framing, Pleasant View Farm (historic photograph in the collection of the F. Grove Miller family)

teenth and early twentieth centuries. The building technique known as balloon framing resulted in houses supported by a thin skeletal frame of smaller dimensioned lumber and nailed joints. Introduced in the United States as early as the 1830s, it was not widely used by Cecil County builders until the last decades of the nineteenth century. The slighter skeletons characteristic of this method were much easier to erect than traditional mortised-and-tenoned timber frame structures and made possible the rambling frame dwellings of the Victorian period, with their complex angles and shapes and scores of rooms. For example, construction in 1896-97 of the generously sized Queen Anne style house on Pleasant View Farm (CE-234), with its bay windows and multiple gable roof, was made practical by employing balloon frame construction.

In contrast to the well-established timber frame building traditions of Cecil County was the presence of a significant variant construction method known as plank framing. The most instructive example of this construction method was provided during the 1978 dismantling of the two-story Price-Murphy house (CE-51), built around 1820-30. This framing system involves stout vertical sawn planks that average 1½ to 2 inches thick and 15 to 20 inches wide. Set in a rabetted sill, the planks rise two full stories to the plate at the top of the wall. In some buildings, the planks serve as the main vertical support, while in other houses they are supported by an internal frame. The Price-Murphy house was an excellent example of this construction method because it employed both systems.

The main rectangular block of the Price-Murphy house was not supported by an internal frame. Instead, the structural elements included a continuous rabetted sill, front and rear girts, plates, and gable end tie beams to which the vertical planks were spiked with cut nails. These horizontal members were not supported by a corner post system. Two interior plank partitions divided a center stair hall from a

CE-51, Price-Murphy house (1968)

Plank framing gable end construction, Price-Murphy house (1978)

Price-Murphy house during demolition, showing plank exterior walls and room partitions (1978)

Engraving after artwork by John H. B. Latrobe, printed in 1827 by Fielding Lucas (Maryland Historical Society)

parlor on one side and a dining room on the other. Next to the dining room was a single-story, plank-walled gable end kitchen wing, which was supported by a braced internal frame. The difference in construction between the main block and the kitchen suggests the kitchen wing was erected first and served as partial support for the gable end of the larger main house.

On the exterior, the long planks of both house and wing were covered with plain weatherboards. The interior of the house was finished with lath and plaster. Small vertical spacers were nailed to the interior face of the planks and then a horizontal layer of split oak lath was nailed to these to hold the plaster. Both the first and second floor interiors were treated in this manner. The kitchen wing, on the other hand, was simply whitewashed, with the corner posts, braces, and second floor joists exposed. The attics of both sections were partly whitewashed as well.

Construction of vertical plank buildings is not peculiar to Cecil County or to Maryland, for examples of such building techniques are found from different periods in a variety of regions in North America.[13] The practice of vertical plank construction was relatively quick and cheap in contrast to the labor-intensive methods inherent in mortise-and-tenon carpentry. Use of this construction method appears to have been tied to two converging factors: the availability of an abundant source of long, straight timbers and the sawmill technology to produce uniformly straight planks. In Cecil County these factors meshed during the first half of the nineteenth century, supporting the estimated dates of local examples of plank frame construction.

During the early to mid-nineteenth century much of the building lumber used in Cecil County was floated down the Susquehanna from lumbering operations in eastern Pennsylvania. Tremendous lumber supplies and massive quantities of material goods arrived at Creswell's Ferry, known after 1814 as Port Deposit, the first navigable shipping point below Smith's Falls.[14] Port Deposit developed quickly and by midcentury was one of the most prosperous towns in Cecil County.

In order to be shipped on the Susquehanna and other waterways of the Chesapeake, lumber was fastened together in the form of arks or rafts. These vessels were subsequently disassembled and the lumber sold by county lumberyards. Nineteenth century Cecil County newspapers such as the *Elkton Press* ran many advertisements like this one, printed in 1848 for the Chesapeake City firm of Bennett & Karsner:

> The subscribers have just received from Port Deposit, a fresh supply of lumber of every description, embracing pine boards of all quantities, ½ inch siding, pine and hemlock joists and studding, pine and cypress shingles of all lengths, hemlock fencing boards, &c. which they offer to public on the most accommodating of terms.[15]

Although many lumber companies developed along accessible county waterways, Port Deposit became known as the "Great Lumber Mart." Raft lumber was first kept in the town's holding ponds, as evinced by county land records, which document both raft sizes and the appointment of Madison Rowland as one of the many inspectors, measur-

CE-51, holes from raft lumber visible in stair detail, Price-Murphy house (1978)

CE-170, holes from raft construction in Little Elk Farm outbuilding (1979)

ers, and markers of lumber for the town.[16] The account books of the Round Island Lumber Company of Port Deposit provide further evidence of the presence of rafts containing all shapes, sizes, and kinds of saleable lumber. In 1835 the company purchased from Hugh Fullerton one raft containing

    17 sticks 60 ft. long—1020'
    27 sticks 50 ft. long—1350'
    42 sticks 40 ft. long—1680'
    12 sticks 25 ft. long— 300'
                     4350'—$200
  17,035' two inch plank boards, rails and joices
                  $102.21[17]

In the same year the company sold to Robert Thompson 2,083 feet of "grub plank for stone ark." The term "stone ark" refers to the use of these rafts as transport, in this case for stone, probably quarried in Port Deposit itself. References to other grades of plank include "common grub plank," "select grub plank," and "best grub plank."[18]

The assembly of these planks into rafts for shipping materials is well documented, as is the dispersal of the raft lumber to distant parts of Cecil County and the Eastern Shore. The planks, or sometimes round logs, were attached with a device called a "raft auger," a large type of drill used to bore a pair of holes in both ends of each log. Cross-laid saplings were positioned over the holes and fastened in place with long wooden pins or staples.[19]

In her Rose Hill diary, Martha Ogle Forman mentions several times that her husband had purchased various grades of plank lumber. On May 29, 1818, she recorded the General's purchase "from Capt. Smith" of "10,000 feet, white pine inch[-thick] plank, 1250 feet panel at $24, 5000 feet common at $14 and 2750 feet call [cull] at $9," all of which had been scrubbed and cleaned at "long point."[20] The grades of lumber General Forman purchased agree with what was being sorted at Port Deposit, and the fact that the lumber had to be scrubbed and cleaned shows it had been submerged in local waters long enough to accumulate a crust of barnacles.

Sound physical evidence of the use of raft lumber as construction material was provided in the exposed planks of the Price-Murphy house, which formerly stood on Hacks Point, just north of Earleville and a short distance from Long Point. Some of the planks used in the house were spotted with whitish stains in the form of circular encrustations, remnants of waterborne travelers cleaned from the wood before construction. In order to achieve a tight, workmanlike fit, the boards had to be freed of any surface obstructions. Further evidence of their former use were the pairs of holes found every couple of feet along each board. These and the occasional larger holes in a chiseled recess were not associated with any system of attachment to the framing members of the house but with the drilling technique used to assemble the rafts. Pine plank raft lumber with paired holes appears as siding in the Spring Hills Farm barn (CE-1109) and was used for siding, flooring, and doorframes in other county barns and outbuildings.

In one form or another, frame building practices have

CE-1109, raft holes in siding of Spring Hills Farm barn (1979)

been in constant use since the founding of the county, ranging from early Anglo-American timber framing methods to late nineteenth century balloon framing techniques to peculiar variations such as plank construction. The continual move toward standardization of framing lumber and building techniques and the slow depletion of the county's vast timber resources were significant developments that kept skeletal frame construction vital.

In contrast, log wall construction, which played a dominant role in timber building in Cecil during the eighteenth and nineteenth centuries, had been fully replaced by frame construction practices by the late nineteenth century. It is not known when horizontal log wall buildings were first erected in Cecil County. The early English settlers were unfamiliar with log building techniques since extensive forests on the British Isles were gone by the seventeenth century, preventing such extravagant use of timber resources. However, settlers from Scandinavia and central Europe had long-established associations with horizontal log wall houses, which they certainly used in their timber-rich settlements in the New World.

The New Sweden settlement on Delaware Bay, established in 1638, and the arrival from Bohemia of Augustine Herman twenty years later undoubtedly served to introduce log wall construction to Cecil County by the early to mid-seventeenth century. In 1659 Herman came upon expatriates of the Swedish settlement as he explored the Elk and Sassafras rivers. At the plantation of one Jan Turner, Herman and his company found "Abraham the Finn," a soldier who had fled the rule of Governor Johan Printz.[21]

The first definitive record of a log structure in Cecil County refers to the 1702 construction of a two-story log house on William Brown's lot west of the common lot set aside for a meetinghouse at Nottingham. Nine years later, the first Nottingham Friends meetinghouse was erected with hewn chestnut and poplar logs. In 1719 Colonel E. A. Herman was ordered, for the sum of 1,000 pounds tobacco, to erect a prison 15 by 10 feet "at ye court-house, on Elk River, with hewed logs, and a substantial pillory and stocks near ye same."[22]

By the end of the eighteenth century log wall construction had been fully accepted across the region's cultural spectrum. Anglo-American settlers found log construction to be an efficient and practical way of using indigenous timber supplies and at the same time providing sound and durable dwellings. Thick, horizontal log walls chinked with clay and other materials afforded a much warmer shelter than a lightly framed dwelling covered with comparably thin boards. Log houses were favored particularly by the thrifty Scots-Irish immigrants, who settled northern Cecil County in large numbers during the mid- to late eighteenth century. When Joshua Hempstead visited his Maryland relatives in 1749, he commented on "old" Nottingham Presbyterian meetinghouse, established northwest of Rising Sun around 1724: "The ministers name is John Steel a Irishman & So are the greater part of the people, a Large old house, no workmanship no gallarrys."[23] Hempstead further observed that "the minister & people here are very modist in their apparel & in their houses mostly Log houses, Cribb fashion."[24] Earlier in his visit, during the last week of June 1749, Hempstead had recorded

Detail of Gillespie log house showing V notches, window frame construction, and sawn off supports for pent eave (1978)

that he "taryed at my kinsman a week & was one Day of it Invited to a Reaping & both my kinsman with me at Mr James Denorritees an Irish [man] that formerly was at my house & brot Letters & Carryed on to whom I Sold a Horse & c. very well Entertained after the Country manner in Cribb houses a Dozen or more, all Irish but wee."[25]

A review of forty-nine Orphans Court evaluations written between 1785 and 1797 indicates that during that time dwellings, barns, corn houses, and stables were far more likely to be built of logs than of frame, brick, or stone. Of the seventy-seven houses enumerated in the descriptions, 75 percent had log walls.[26] Log houses were so common in Cecil County by the end of the eighteenth century that in 1795 Irishman Isaac Weld, Jr., was prompted to observe:

CE-1217, Gillespie log house (1978)

> Elkton, twenty-one miles distant from Wilmington, and the first town in Maryland, contains about ninety indifferent houses, which are built without any regularity….In this neighborhood I first took notice of log houses; those which I had hitherto seen having been built either of brick or stone, or else constructed with wooden frames, sheathed on the outside with boards. The log-houses are cheaper than any others in a country where there is an abundance of wood, and generally are the first that are erected on a new settlement in America. The sides consist of trees just squared, and placed horizontally one upon the other; the ends of the logs of one side resting alternately on the ends of those of the adjoining side, in notches; the interstices between the logs are stopped with clay; and the roof is covered with boards or with shingles, which are small pieces of wood in the shape of slates or tiles, and

which are used for that purpose with few exceptions, throughout America. These habitations are not very sightly; but when well built they are warm and comfortable, and last for a long time.[27]

Numerous historical and architectural records contradict Weld's comment that log houses were not very "sightly" and provided cheap, or perhaps just ordinary, accommodations. These sources reveal that log houses were built in many shapes and sizes, from crude and cheap pole cabins to well-carpentered dwellings. Extant examples of log houses include one- and two-room plan structures but also more complex, three- and four-room plan dwellings equal in style and quality to many contemporary dwellings of brick, stone, or frame materials. The finish in these log houses ranged from plain whitewashed walls to interiors boasting expertly crafted raised panel woodwork.

That Isaac Weld was accurate in his description of log construction, at least, is well illustrated by the Gillespie log house (CE-1217), built around 1820 north of Port Deposit. Situated on a dramatically sloped site overlooking the former bed of the Susquehanna Canal, the house comprises a stone foundation supporting squared logs laid atop one another and fixed in place with V-notch corner joints. Specific methods of corner notching vary regionally, but in Cecil County the V-notch is dominant, although a few examples of the full dovetail method appear in southern sections of the county. As Weld described, the spaces between each log were filled with a mixture of clay and stone chinking to seal the walls. Visible on the west wall are the butt ends of the joists that support the second floor. Smaller sash of later date presently fill the window openings, but the vertical boards originally used to frame the rough openings remain. These two-inch thick boards are held in place by wooden pins driven through them into the butt ends of the adjacent logs. While the main body of the Gillespie house is of hewn log construction, the gable ends were enclosed with studs and horizontal weatherboards. The lack of corner notches above the cornice level usually dictated the need for a change in wall construction.[28] In order to protect the vital corner notches from decay, log houses were often covered with siding, although historic photographs and documentary evidence indicate many log walls remained exposed to the weather long after construction.

Certainly the best documented log structure in Cecil County, and perhaps one of the best finished for its time, is the two-story log dwelling (CE-583) that stands on the land known as "Bethel" south of Calvert.[29] Built by Samuel England for his son Elisha, to whom the property was left in Samuel's 1787 will, the log walls of the house were raised on June 25, 1785. Surviving invoices for the work completed by housebuilder William Cook document in detail the construction and finish of the log dwelling and a log barn, stable, and wagon house. Like the John Churchman house built forty years earlier, the two-story England house had a hall/parlor plan with chimneys rising through each end. Encircling the house were pent eaves, a distinctive mid-Atlantic feature that provided some protection from the weather. Cook framed the gable ends with studs and covered them with boards. Three doors and eight window openings were cut in the main body of the log house, including installation of what Cook referred to as "cheeks," or stabilizing boards, on each side of the openings. One of his last tasks, completed in 1785, was building a "fire door" in the roof, charged at 3 shillings.[30]

Inside the house, Cook laid an oak floor, which he planed on one side. He then assembled a vertical board partition and dressed it on both sides.[31] The second floor, on the other hand, was laid in poplar "plan'd on both sides," suggesting the joists were left exposed. Connecting the floors was a turned baluster stair. Cook charged Samuel England £1.6.8 for 64 balusters and £2.11 for framing the "balcony & putting in the ballisters." In addition to this decorative stair treatment, the windows were framed with an "Architrave" molding and a "wash board" was fitted

CE-583, Bethel (historic photograph)

around the perimeter of the rooms. Further room finish included "putting up a breast in the back room" for £1.5, which refers to raised paneling over the fireplace, probably in the parlor. A less elaborate "breast" and shelving were installed in an upstairs chamber for 17 shillings.[32]

A different type of log dwelling, labeled the dogtrot form and especially common in the American South, approximates the common center hall, single-pile house erected by countless Chesapeake planters around the bay in Maryland and Virginia. Standing on the property known as "Bristole," situated on Back Creek Neck between Elkton and Chesapeake City, is a dogtrot dwelling (CE-99) with woodwork dating from the late eighteenth century. The house form is characterized by two squarish log pens separated by an open breezeway. At Bristole the two 16-foot-square log sections of the main block, serving as the parlor and dining room, are separated by a nine-foot-wide hall, which contains the staircase. In the colder mid-Atlantic cli-

CE-99, Bristole (1995)

CE-1240, William Cosgrove house (1980)

CE-1078, Simpers log house (historic photograph)

mate of Cecil County, the center breezeway was enclosed with studs and a weatherboard covering.

A similarly built house was found on the Etherington plantation when the Orphans Court authorized Sidney George, James Morgan, and James Wroth to evaluate the property of John Etherington, deceased, for the benefit of his minor heirs, Elizabeth, John Ward, Susannah, and Bartholomew Etherington. The plantation house was described as

> one dwelling forty three and a half feet long containing three rooms sixteen and a half feet wide, two of the rooms hew'd logs and the middle room a frame covered with cypress shingles, not finished upstairs, gable end with poplar plank in bad repair, a kitchen fifteen and a half feet by sixteen and a half, hew'd poplar logs in good repair covered with oak shingles.[33]

Another atypical county log house stands near Principio, appearing as if it were transplanted from the piedmont of North Carolina or Virginia. However, the single-story, two-room or hall/parlor plan of the William Cosgrove house (CE-1240) is not as unusual as the large exterior stone chimney pile with detached brick stack.

One of the most vivid images of exposed log construction in Cecil County is a rare late nineteenth century photograph of the Simpers log house (CE-1078) near Union Church. In it, Mrs. Simpers sits on the threshold of her V-notched log home, within the confines of her picket fence. Her house illustrates yet another variation in log construction, following a form that has been termed the "saddlebag" house type. This label refers to the saddling of two structures around a central chimney pile. In this case, the right portion in the photograph is an addition to the portion on the left, and each room is heated by a separate fireplace. The saddlebag is another transplanted house form not particularly common to the Chesapeake region, and, like the dogtrot house, it is more common in the American South.

Horizontal log building traditions were not restricted to houses. Many farms and plantations included an array of outbuildings, many of these constructed of logs. In 1791 the two appraisers appointed by the Cecil County Orphans

(below) CE-240, William Knight tenant house (1979)

(right) Post and plank construction detail, William Knight tenant house (1979)

Court recorded the following description of the farm of Mary Price, orphaned daughter of Noble Price:

> We did find thereon, one sawed pine log barn fourteen feet ten inches by twenty six feet, oak roof and plank floor almost new, one old quarter hewed loggs sixteen feet by eighteen feet in bad repair, one corn house and stable sawed poplar loggs twelve feet by twenty-one feet, oak roof almost new, one meat house hewed logs nine feet nine inches by twelve feet, oak roof in good repair, one shadd [fish] house next to the dwelling house ten feet by twenty two feet four inches, one side cedar roof the other side oak, one hewed log kitchen eighteen feet four inches square.[34]

The reference to a sawn log stable in this evaluation was most likely to a structure erected with walls of narrower sawn logs, often three or four inches thick and sometimes referred to as plank walls. The logs or planks were probably joined at the corners with the common V-notch or dovetailed joint. In other cases, a vertical corner post, into which the planks were tenoned, provided structural stability.

The variation of log wall building labeled "post and plank" construction survives in a handful of examples in southern Cecil County around Earleville and Warwick. Clearest among them is the William Knight tenant house (CE-240) near Earleville. The modern use of the structure as a stable, with the walls fully exposed, clearly illustrates this construction practice. Both empty and filled mortises are visible where part of the east wall is missing. Another example of post-and-plank construction is found in the kitchen wing at nearby Cherry Grove (CE-50). Sheathed with exterior siding and finished inside, the wing reveals its construction in the unfinished closet under the corner winder stair.

Carefully fashioned corner notches or a mortised-and-tenoned corner post system provided stable support for horizontal log wall buildings, whether houses, kitchens, barns, or stables. Despite the evident craftsmanship with which many of these buildings were assembled, other log structures that surface in the written record speak of a poorer sort of building. A round log tradition involved peeled logs, unsawn or hewn, piled atop one another with a simple saddle notch at the corners. This type of structure, probably the cheapest sort of log building, appears in the Orphans Court record, such as Thomas Biddle's "round log stable" or Jesse Money's "20 by 16 dwelling of round logs." The round log walls were evidently exposed to the weather, and these structures, in general, did not last long without requiring substantial repair or replacement. As a result, no examples are known to have survived in Cecil County.

The plentiful supply of timber resources during the seventeenth and eighteenth centuries made frame or log houses a natural choice for most Cecil residents, and county Orphans Court and tax records of the time speak to the predominance of wooden buildings. Nonetheless, those who could afford more permanent materials turned to brick and stone construction. By the second quarter of the eighteenth century, the exploitation of sizable quantities of superior building stone and adequate deposits of clay, sand, and lime resulted in development of a significant masonry building tradition.

The fine qualities of the natural stone deposits in Cecil County were recognized early, certainly by the native inhabitants and later by European explorer and cartographer John Smith, who commented in 1608 that "the mountaines are of divers natures: for at the head of the Bay the rockes are of a composition like millstones. Some of Marble, & c. And many pieces like Christall we found."[35] Fieldstone, close at hand at the time of settlement, was used in building the first generation of Cecil houses. Roger Kirk's timber frame house, built in 1719, stood atop a full cellar that had been dug and walled with local fieldstone. The permanent nature of such a stone foundation afforded many houses, whether frame or log, a long life with some protection from the damage of moisture and decay.

Buildings completely assembled with stone walls were

erected primarily by the generation that followed the first settlers. When the East Nottingham meetinghouse (CE-82) burned during the mid-1740s, the 1724 brick structure was repaired and later enlarged with a stone addition. On July 4, 1749, Joshua Hempstead witnessed work on the building:

> I Set out for home between 9 & 10 having taken my Last farewell of my Sister Lucy. her 2 Sons & Daughters all Came with me to a Tavern about 5 miles a fine Brick house Mr. Mitchels hard by Nottingham Quaker meeting house, which hath been lately burnt down & now Enlarged. the Bottom of Stone is Laid.[36]

Several years later, in 1757, when Jeremiah Brown decided to expand his father William's 1702 log house, he financed the construction of a two-story, side passage/double-pile stone dwelling (CE-203). The year and Jeremiah Brown's initials were carved into a corner stone. Evident in the Jeremiah Brown house is the stonemason's craft of strengthening the walls by placing large, quoinlike stones at the corners, while the side walls are laid in rubble fashion. At this house the first floor door and window openings were spanned with tremendous single stones. Sometimes masons fitted these openings with a jack arch and center keystone or spanned them with a timber lintel, buried in the stone wall on each side for support. The latter practice is commonly found in nineteenth century buildings but appears in some eighteenth century structures as well.

Standing on the west bank of the Little Elk Creek is a testimonial to the stonemason's trade known as the "Beehive" (CE-72). This small commercial/industrial complex is dominated by a stone ruin with a massive exterior gable end chimney. Associated through tradition and research with the operation of a cooper's shop, the building displays a high level of stonemasonry skill. The semicoursed stone walls are put together with a minimum of mortar, and the massive relieving arch and shaped stone lintels are finely cut. Large stone quoins dominate the small building.

The northeast corner of the county is distinguished by a distinctively different building stone known as Wesahiggin schist, a superior stone ranging in color from a dense grayish shade to black. Large quantities of this stone were used

CE-82, stone portion of Brick Meeting House

to construct Rock Presbyterian Church (CE-73) in 1761 and the Mitchell house at Fair Hill (CE-74), erected around 1760-70. The large outcropping of Wesahiggin schist in front of Rock Church makes it highly probable the distinctive stone was quarried at the church site.

Houses of cut and finely executed stone were expensive to build. To defray masonry costs, many fieldstone walls were assembled in a rubble method in which closely set stones were laid in a heavy layer of mortar to compensate for their irregular surfaces. The early to mid-nineteenth century S. M. Jenness house (CE-1225) near Liberty Grove is an example of this rougher fieldstone building tradition. As seen in this house, the generously applied mortar is more evident than the stone. Rubble fieldstone construction practices were employed by many groups, but, like log construction, they were favored by the thrifty Scots-Irish, who erected numerous single-story or story-and-a-half fieldstone dwellings in pockets throughout northern Cecil County.

(left) CE-203, dated stone of the Jeremiah Brown house (1986)

(below) CE-72, The Beehive (1980)

CE-1225, S. M. Jenness house (1980)

CE-74, Mitchell house, Fair Hill (1985)

CE-291, stonework under stucco, the Paw Paw Building in Port Deposit before restoration

(opposite) CE-73, Rock Church (George Hipkins)

Irregular fieldstone walls were often made more uniform with a coat of whitewash or stucco. In some instances stucco may have been applied as a practical, moisture-proofing measure, but in other cases it was scored in a grid pattern to imitate more stylish, ashlar masonry. The rubble fieldstone walls of the Paw Paw Building (CE-291) in Port Deposit, erected in 1821, were stuccoed for the latter reason. The Gerry house (CE-271), located down the street from the Paw Paw Building, was built of uncoursed and coursed stone around 1813. The main block, built into a slope, has three floors exposed on the street facade. The first floor or basement is covered with a scored stucco, while the walls above are distinguished by finely jointed stonework. The side walls, on the other hand, were assembled in rubble fieldstone.

Despite the large collection of stone houses that dot the northern Cecil countryside, nowhere in the county was there a stronger stone masonry building tradition than in the western portion along the Susquehanna River and Octoraro Creek. Eighteenth century stone structures such as the Anchor and Hope farmhouse (CE-140) and Rodgers' Tavern (CE-129) parallel contemporaneous stone masonry in other parts of the county. By the first decades of the nine-

CE-278, McClenahan mansion in Port Deposit (1985)

McClenahan & Bros. granite quarry in Port Deposit
from the 1877 Lake, Griffing, and Stevenson *Atlas of Cecil County*

teenth century, however, commercial exploitation of natural stone deposits had led to the flowering of a particularly well-developed tradition of ashlar construction, which distinguished the prosperous merchant town of Port Deposit as well as some houses in the surrounding countryside.

Opened in 1829 with the construction of the Susquehanna Canal, granite quarries at Port Deposit provided material for numerous county houses as well as for structures much farther afield. Hemmed in by shear granite cliffs rising almost directly from the Susquehanna River, the town of Port Deposit developed along a narrow stretch of level floodplain situated at the northernmost navigable point on the river. The impenetrable granite walls, which physically limited town expansion, proved a tremendous natural asset when the proprietors of the Maryland Canal Company opened a quarry to extract building stone. The quarry operated from 1829 through the mid-twentieth century with few interruptions.

While Port Deposit granite has been shipped to distant places for major construction projects, nowhere is the stone more evident than in Port Deposit itself. The dwellings built by the McClenahans, who dominated the quarry business between 1865 and 1914; churches and schools; banks and stores; stables and even gas houses, as well as countless foundations, sidewalks, and retaining walls, were formed of the town's own bedrock. The most ambitious local building project to use the granite was the Jacob Tome Institute on the bluff above town, erected with an endowment left by Jacob Tome at his death in 1898.

The Thomas Patten house (CE-1223), erected outside Port Deposit in 1818 of granite quarried on the edge of town, exemplifies the masonry construction techniques used in the region. Shaped stones were laid in approximate rows, or courses, to produce a formal two-story ashlar facade. Large stone quoins, clearly evident on the outside edges of the five-bay facade, were laid in order to create a sound construction for the rectangular structure. A fine mortar joint accentuates the shape and color of each stone, emphasizing the stonemason's cutting skill. As well, carefully laid jack arches were crafted for the front window openings.

The Port Deposit region also boasts a collection of buildings with ashlar facades finely crafted of local sandstone. The Matthew Morrison house (CE-1181) near Rowlandsville is one of a small cluster of houses with stonework that suggests a single mason's craftsmanship during the second and third quarters of the nineteenth century. As is common

Jacob Tome mansion, Port Deposit
(1936, Historic American Buildings Survey)

CE-1223, Thomas Patten house

CE-1181, Matthew Morrison house (1980)

in stone construction, the use of finely shaped and coursed sandstone blocks is limited to the principal facade. The remaining sides were assembled in rubble fashion, with large stone blocks at the rear corners to ensure the stability of the walls. Large stone lintels more than three feet in length span the window and door openings on front and side elevations.

Just as the bedrock of Cecil County supplied the materials for countless eighteenth and nineteenth century stone structures, natural deposits of clay, sand, and lime provided the ingredients for a brick masonry building tradition. The solid, permanent appearance of brick dwellings stood in contrast to the need for constant maintenance and repair of buildings made of wood. In July 1762, when he stopped in Charlestown, Benjamin Mifflin recorded his impressions of the town. He found it

> agreeably Seated on a Hill reclining with an Easie Descent to the Head of Chesapeake Bay which yields a pleasant prospect, but…a Miserable forlorn place about 50 or 60 Houses built in a Scragling manner Mostly wood, but about 5 or 6 of Brick, no place of Worship in it, Court house nor Jail, which are all at a Distance from it.[37]

Brick buildings signaled to the outside world a strong sense of economic success and permanence. In 1724 the East Nottingham Friends chose brick when they replaced their original log meetinghouse. Quakers Mercer and Hannah

CE-88, bricks signed by those who helped build the Mercer and Hannah Brown house (1986)

CE-187, construction date spelled out in glazed headers, east gable end of the John Churchman house (1980)

CE-205, William and Elizabeth Knight house (1995)

Brown also chose brick for their finely appointed dwelling of 1746, evidently an addition to an earlier wood structure.

The exterior of the Browns' house (CE-88) is a singularly outstanding example of the mid-eighteenth century brick masonry craft. As well, a number of initials and names inscribed on the bricks provide rare insight into the construction of the house. The south wall, carefully laid in Flemish bond, is highlighted with a checkerboard glazed brick pattern. Distinctive to Flemish bond are alternating rows of stretchers (long side) and headers (butt end) in a horizontal as well as vertical line. The checkerboard pattern of the Flemish bond is further strengthened by the alternate placement of the glazed, or vitrified, headers, which attain a dark bluish-gray glaze when fired.

The narrow west gable end of the house is laid in Flemish bond and also features glazed brickwork. Above the second floor pent eave is a diagonal row of glazed bricks that parallels the roofline. The north wall and the east gable end were less important elevations and were built in a more utilitarian manner without elaborate brickwork decorations. Another striking feature of the Brown house is the tombstone-shaped datestone of slate on the south wall, fixed above the front door. Mercer and Hannah Brown's initials, along with the date 1746 and a trailing vine motif, detail this finely crafted emblem.

A series of incised initials at the southwest corner of the house evidently documents local residents who helped construct it. William White, identified by "WW," is recorded on a bill of sale to Mercer Brown for 500 bricks; Samuel England, "SE," also supplied bricks. "HR" probably stands for Hezikiah Rolls, a local cabinetmaker who was responsible for crafting the mid-eighteenth century interior of Brick Meeting House. Also present were John Day, "JD," a local tanner; miller Jeremiah Brown, "JB"; and Benjamin Chandlee, the famous Nottingham clockmaker, who carved his first initial and entire last name, wrapped around a brick on the corner.

Parallel examples of this elaborate decorative brick tradition are the John Churchman house (CE-187), with a glazed brick date of 1745 set in its east gable end; the William and Elizabeth Knight house (CE-205), also built in 1745, according to a datestone in the west gable; and a handful of other dwellings. Elaborate glazed header checkerboard brickwork also distinguishes St. Mary Anne's Episcopal Church, erected in 1742 in North East. The masonry practice of glazed header decoration diminished in popular-

CE-32, detail showing arch with keystone over first floor window on land side, belt course, and all header bond, Bohemia (1995)

ity after the Revolutionary War, but vestigial use of the tradition lasted until the second quarter of the nineteenth century.

As evidenced by the houses and meetinghouses mentioned, a fine school of brick masonry craftsmanship had been established in northern Cecil County by the early eighteenth century. But even more reliant on brick masonry were the planters of southern Cecil, who had fewer choices of building materials due to the lack of good building stone south of the fall line.[38]

Perhaps the finest and most diverse display of mid-eighteenth century brick masonry techniques in Cecil County is found at Bohemia (CE-32), erected around 1750 near the mouth of Little Bohemia Creek. The five-bay creek facade, with its projecting central pavilion, features a glazed header checkerboard pattern in Flemish bond, not unlike the glazed brick decoration on the Quaker-built houses in the Nottingham Lots. Similarly, segmental brick arches spanning the cellar and first floor windows are accented with glazed bricks. Defining the base of the house is a water table capped with molded ogee-curved bricks. While beautifully crafted, the creek elevation is clearly the less formal of the two principal facades. In contrast to it, the land approach was designed and built with additional brickwork details that accentuate its formality. Dominated by a projecting center pavilion like the creek side, the five-bay elevation features projecting brick pilasters at each outside corner and a belt course stretches across the facade between the first and second floors. Much of the wall is laid in all header bond, the only example in Cecil County of this relatively rare brick pattern. Interestingly, all header bond is found on a number of houses in Chestertown where George Milligan, builder of the house, operated as a merchant. The formality of the land approach elevation is further accentuated by the carefully crafted jack arches that highlight most of the window and door openings. Flared keystones of precisely cut rubbed bricks were fitted together and flanked by canted jack arch bricks separated by a thin butter joint of mortar. An unusual feature is the thin layer of off-white stucco on the jack arch bricks. The pargeted bricks frame the reddish-orange keystone and serve to distinguish the keystone as well as the arch from the adjacent wall surface.

Most masonry houses in Cecil County were designed with a wooden cornice that defined the base of the roof. In some cases the cornice was trimmed with elaborate classical features such as large modillion blocks, a more delicate dentil molding, or perhaps both. A fine example with decorated modillion blocks is found at Greenfields, a third quarter eighteenth century house near Cecilton. Several sizable

CE-246, Partridge Hill, a Hollingsworth family house in Elkton (1936, Historic American Buildings Survey)

brick dwellings in Elkton, including the prominent Hollingsworth family houses and the Mitchell house, have bold classical cornices that not only embellish the front of the house but stretch around the gable ends to form large pediments.

By the early decades of the nineteenth century, cornices were often made of molded brick. Bricks of various classical curves, with ovolo, cavetto, or ogee profiles, were used to define these features. The molded brick cornice that caps the Flemish bond walls of Frisby's Prime Choice (CE-12), built around 1810 near Earleville, is one of the earliest known county examples. Also evident in a 1930s photograph of the house are the well-defined rubbed brick arches over the second floor Palladian window and front entrance. These finely crafted brick arches emphasize the two central and most important openings in the five-bay facade.

As the century reached its second and third decades,

CE-16, wooden cornice at Greenfields. The cornice at Bohemia formerly had modillian blocks like these (some survive in storage). (1995)

CE-12, Frisby's Prime Choice (1979)

CE-27, 1837-38 brick town house addition with roof deck, Rose Hill (1995)

distinct changes were underway in brick construction that turned away from local traditions in lieu of more standardized practices common to the nation in general. When General Thomas Marsh Forman and his wife Martha Ogle Forman entered into a construction program for their 1837-38 brick addition at Rose Hill (CE-27), they drew on the skills of masons, carpenters, plasterers, and painters from a wide region reaching well beyond the boundaries of Cecil County. Some labor and materials were brought in by ship from as far away as Philadelphia via the eight-year-old Chesapeake and Delaware Canal.

Martha Forman's daily entries of progress on the addition offer a rare glimpse into the construction process during the early to mid-nineteenth century. She repeatedly mentions a Philadelphia carpenter, "Mr. Atmore," who presumably was the foreman of the construction project.[39] His arrival at Rose Hill during the evening of April 22, 1837, is the first mention of any specific activity associated with the building program. A month later, on May 21, stone for the foundation was delivered from the quarries of Port Deposit.[40] On June 4, Martha Forman recorded that "on my return from church I found three carpenters here from Philadelphia they brought all the wood on frames in the vessel."[41] Two Rose Hill slaves, Philip and Moses Antigua, started digging the cellar on June 26, and three days later, Mrs. Forman wrote, "All hands digging the cellar."[42] The building lime for the mortar was delivered three weeks later.

On July 12, six Philadelphia masons arrived at Rose Hill.[43] One of the men, whom Martha Forman called "Mr. Crispin," was probably the master mason. The laying of the foundation began the next day: "My husband had the corner stone of our new house laid this day he deposited under southwest corner a bottle of old spirits well corked and sealed and a bottle with a paper note telling by whom built and when."[44] Within two days Mrs. Forman remarked that the construction was going very fast, and on July 20 she mentioned, "the first joice put in our new house this day."[45] Nine days later, the masons had reached the second floor level.[46] Late in August the masons filled the spaces between the joists to help prevent the entrance of mice and rats.[47] By the second week in September the tinman was on the property attending to the roof. Midway in the construction of the gable roof the Formans decided to alter the pitch to include a flat peak that could accommodate an observation deck.

When the Formans' neighbor Sidney George Fisher visited the following April, he had this to say about the new addition, "[Forman's] new house is finished, tho not furnished. The rooms are comfortable, but it is ugly and inconvenient, being exactly a third rate city house, with a very narrow entry instead of a hall."[48] Although Fisher clearly disliked the floor plan of the town house addition he described his experience on the roof in glowing terms:

> On the top is a platform with a railing around it, to which we ascended. There are few finer prospects. As the country is not hilly but undulating, the view is very extensive, and the eye wanders over a wide region of wood and plain thro which wanders the broad winding Sassafras, which is indeed so very winding in its course runs up into so many nooks and bays, that even from this elevated point, it looks like three or four beautiful lakes in the landscape.[49]

While the exterior followed the Federal design of countless urban row houses, the appointments were solidly Greek in order to keep in step with the architectural fashion of the late 1830s. During the summer and fall months of 1837 the interior walls were raised, and by early October the plasterers had arrived.[50] The Formans had the exterior covered with a thin layer of stucco to provide a weathertight surface as well as to accentuate the solid massing of the structure.

While a stuccoed exterior was a stylish treatment during the second quarter of the nineteenth century, only a few houses were finished in such a manner. In lieu of the Flemish and English bonding patterns popular during the eighteenth century, a less expensive American or common bond was used, which involved three to fifteen rows of staggered stretchers for each row of headers. This bonding pattern was used consistently throughout the nineteenth

CE-69, Brantwood (1936, Historic American Buildings Survey)

century, although a slight variation included a single row of Flemish bond between multiple rows of stretchers.

An important common bond dwelling is Brantwood (CE-69), situated south of Elkton and erected during the middle years of the nineteenth century. Reflecting the popularity of Greek Revival design, the blockish L-shaped house is fronted by a formal elevation of finely jointed pressed bricks laid in common bond. The sides of the house, as well as the rear service wing, were assembled in typical common bond fashion without the more expensive pressed bricks found on the front of the house. The three-story common bond walls were capped by a bold brick cornice that defines the low-pitched roof. The cornice encircles the main block as well as the rear service wing.

By the time Brantwood was built at midcentury, construction of buildings was aided by the mass production of brick. Uniform sizes of common wall brick, as well as decorative molded or pressed brick, had become readily available from manufacturers that set up kilns around the region. Continued mass production of brick following the Civil War ensured that brick masonry would remain a vital construction practice through the balance of the nineteenth century and well into the next. By the late twentieth century, however, brick and stone, though still used in house construction, only appear in vestigial forms as a finish veneer for frame structures.

The historic timber frame, brick, and stone building practices in Cecil County all share a common tradition in timber roof construction. Distinguishing features in roof framing include the size and position of the rafter blades and the method by which they are supported. In Cecil two roof systems predominate—a common rafter roof and a principal rafter-purlin system.

By and large the medium to small dwellings in Cecil County were covered with common rafter roofs, which employ rafters of equal size. As represented by the Roger Kirk house, separate rafter blades are pinned at each apex, and each pair is reinforced with a supportive collar beam. The collar beam is usually fastened to each blade by a notched joint and pinned or nailed in place. When the principal members of the roof frame were crafted, the joints were normally scored with Roman numerals to ease fitting the frame together when it was raised. (See the framing elevation of the Kirk house on page 192.)

A principal rafter roof is more complex, consisting of a massive timber underframe on which a series of common rafters was placed. Usually required in double-pile dwellings with a longer roof span, like the Nathan and Susannah Harris house (CE-229), the principal rafter system involves three massive principal rafters held in place by horizontal butt-purlins. The butt-purlins span a ten-foot distance and are mortised and tenoned into the sides of the principal rafters.

(left) CE-82, king post truss roof, Brick Meeting House (1936, Historic American Buildings Survey)

(below left) CE-229, principal rafter roof, Nathan and Susannah Harris house (1980)

(below right) CE-229, principal rafter roof with through-purlin, Old Fort Smith house (1978)

The common rafters rest atop the outside face of each purlin and are pinned at the peak of the roof. In the Harris house roof frame, the common rafters are split in two sections with the top of one and the bottom of the other resting on the horizontal purlin.

A slightly different method of constructing a principal rafter system consists of supporting the common rafters with a through-purlin. In this case, the purlin is a continuous horizontal beam, in contrast to the staggered or broken series of purlins in the Harris house. Otherwise, the roof systems are very similar. A through-purlin system with some unusual features is found in the attic of the Old Fort Smith house (CE-38) near Oakwood. Here, a principal rafter, through-purlin truss supports a common rafter roof. The horizontal purlins are held in tension by collar beams and supported vertically by the principal rafters, which are notched over a false plate. The common rafters rest on the truss and their feet disappear into the mortared stone walls, rather than being nailed to the plate as well.

Large spaces were sometimes spanned by other roof systems that involved different methods of support. When Brick Meeting House was rebuilt in 1810, a series of massive king post trusses was crafted to span the brick and stone walls. Lateral diagonal braces rest on the flared sides of each

CE-218, outrigger for pent eave, Willowdale (1979)

king post and help support the large principal rafter trusses. Interspersed between the principal rafter trusses are stout purlins that support a layer of common rafters.

One characteristic feature of Cecil County roofing practices is the widespread use of the pent eave. Extensions of second and third floor joists through the exterior walls permitted the construction of a small shed roof at the second or third floor level. These roofs provided extra protection from weathering and helped to direct water away from the foundation. They also served as a stylistic device that visually continues the main cornice. Pent eaves are found across northern Cecil County and on a handful of dwellings south of Elkton. The feature appears as well in a larger geographic region that spans the Delaware valley.

In June 1794 when the subscribers of the Orphans Court visited the house of Andrew Malone, son of John, they found a mixture of outside appendages:

> There is part of two tracts of land, the one is called Sligo, the other Alexandria both in Back Creek Hundred…We did enter and find thereon, a brick dwelling house with a good cellar, the roof is bad, a porch on the south side of the house wanting a frame and posts to said porch and the roof of porch wants mending; there is a paint eave to the north of the house that wants a new roof….[51]

The pent eave was not used exclusively on masonry buildings, although almost all of the surviving examples are on brick or stone structures.

Although the pent eave had disappeared from practical use by the turn of the nineteenth century, the porch or "piazza" has been a vital part of domestic and public building from the seventeenth century until modern times. A porch has meant different things at different times, however. During the seventeenth century, a porch or more often "porch tower" was a squarish open or closed structure, covered by a gable roof, that sheltered the main entrance. In a porch tower, which had two stories, a loft or room under

Pent eave, Mercer and Hannah Brown house

the roof served as a sleeping or storage space. The more familiar single-story open structure, supported by columns or posts, did not become common in the Chesapeake region until the mid-eighteenth century.[52]

While the term "porch" appears in Cecil County Orphans Court descriptions, so does the term "piazza." Such a feature was recorded by Benjamin Porter and Joshua Ward in 1795, when they entered the farm of Thomas and John L. K. Jones. On the site they found

> one frame dwelling house forty three feet eight inches long by sixteen feet three inches wide with a Peaz on each side, the whole length of the said house weather boarded with poplar plank and covered with cedar shingles, two rooms and a passage on the lower floor and two rooms on the upper floor in very bad repair.[53]

The porch, piazza, or portico continued in popular use across Cecil County throughout the early to mid-nineteenth century. When Sidney George Fisher contemplated additions for his Mount Harmon plantation house in 1848 he wrote, "All that is now wanted to make it an elegant residence is some addition to the house. There ought to be

CE-41, Octorara porch (c. 1979)

piazzas and one or two other improvements. These I hope to accomplish before long."[54]

Two-story porches or porticoes like the one at Octorara (CE-41) served to extend the living space of the parlors on the first floor and the bedrooms on the second, with jib doors connecting the spaces. Although the two-story porch at Octorara is relatively plain, other examples display exact replicas of Greek columns of the Doric and Ionic orders topped with a wide classical entablature. Fixed between the columns of the early nineteenth century Gerry house in Port Deposit are cast-iron railings that incorporate sheaves of wheat.

Decorative ironwork had become readily available by the mid-nineteenth century, leading many homeowners to turn away from staid columns of Greek Revival taste. Instead, they purchased romantic cast-iron porches that exhibited organic forms, such as delicate trailing grapevines or cherubs eating out of fruit-laden urns.

At midcentury, however, much more than porch design was changing. Technology and mass production introduced many new materials and building practices to Cecil County, and, as a result, age-old traditions of hand craftsmanship began to fade. Factory-produced windows and doors, stairs and mantels, lighting and hardware streamlined construction processes. The mid-nineteenth century also brought a wave of new architectural inspiration in the form of trade literature for architects and builders. While foreign design influences introduced a host of new styles favored by the stylish, many Cecil residents remained loyal to the time-honored vernacular plans that had served past generations well.

CE-271, Gerry house porch, Port Deposit
(1936, Historic American Buildings Survey)

Original hand-painted wallpaper in the stair hall at Rose Hill, 1838 (1995)

CHAPTER 9

The Manners of Interior Finish (1670-1850)

THE METHODS used to finish the interior spaces of Cecil houses have developed in complex ways since the county's founding. During the first few generations of colonization and cultivation, interior treatments evolved from the basically utilitarian finishes common to settlement period dwellings to the finely appointed rooms distinctive to plantation houses designed and built during the mid- to late eighteenth century. Paralleling the changes in house forms and construction practices, interior finishes in Cecil County buildings of the eighteenth century exhibit a wide range of personal solutions. By the early to mid-nineteenth century, however, interior finishes reflected more standardized and established practices. This change was due in part to the influence of widely circulated builders' guides and architectural pattern books coupled with the mass production and distribution of building parts.

Only scant evidence remains of the carpenters and craftsmen who built Cecil County dwellings during the eighteenth and early nineteenth centuries. In a few instances the county Orphans Court records refer to the apprenticeship of young men as craftsmen, such as the June 11, 1799, indenture of Andrew McCologh "to learn the Carpenter trade." More revealing, but significantly more illusive, are documents such as William Cook's 1785-87 account detailing his work on the house, barn, and stable on Elisha England's Bethel farm.[1] Despite these tantalizing glimpses into the lives of eighteenth century craftsmen, little is known about the masons, house joiners and carpenters, plasterers, and painters who worked in Cecil County. What is clear is that local carpenters executed most of the interior elements and that their work displays their individual creativity.

Woodwork finishes, when linked with the hand-made or machine-made technologies that produced them, provide telling evidence of when a house was built. This dating tool must be used with caution, however, since applied woodwork is easily replaced and thus subject to alteration. Many house interiors display layers of woodwork that reflect changing priorities and attitudes in the finish of interior spaces. Periodic shifts in the style of finish, both interior and exterior, provide architectural historians with indications of when initial construction or later modifications took place. When a woodwork analysis is dovetailed with documentary research on a property, a fairly complete building history of a dwelling can be revealed. Occasionally, a house is inscribed with a specific date, which may appear in a prominent location on a date plaque or in an arbitrary spot on a wall, chimney, or structural beam. These "dated" houses serve as valuable benchmarks of building technology for a particular region and are useful in dating similar structures.

Although dwellings of the seventeenth century have not survived in Cecil County, documentary evidence indicates they were much like the settlement dwellings found throughout the Chesapeake region. For the most part, the first generation of Cecil County houses consisted of utilitarian structures erected to provide rudimentary shelter. When Jasper Danckaerts visited the area in 1679, he described the improvements on one of John Moll's properties, located on the road leading to Augustine Herman's Bohemia River plantation. Unimpressed with Moll's plantation, Danckaerts later wrote, "The dwellings were very badly appointed, especially for such a man as Mons. Moll."[2]

Utilitarian dwellings continued in use beyond the settlement period, as rough and unfinished houses dotted the Cecil County landscape throughout the eighteenth century as well. The records of the Cecil County Orphans Court make it clear that some dwellings remained only partially complete long after construction. When John Moody and Isaac Holt visited the Johnson plantation in 1793, these officials of the county court found

> One Dwelling House Twenty six feet long by twenty and a half feet wide the roof in bad order, two rooms above not finished, one with a fire

CE-216, carved post head in earliest section of the Haines house (c. 1979)

CE-127, exposed corner post on the second floor of the Indian Queen Tavern (1995)

place, three rooms below in good order, two with fire places—a kitchen in bad repair fourteen feet wide and twenty and a half feet long, the roof bad the walls stone, the loft half laid with plank."[3]

An evaluation recorded for the Etherington property mentions "a dwelling house forty feet long and sixteen feet wide three rooms on the lower floor, the upper all in one open space not having been laid off in rooms."[4] These and similar descriptions point to the uneven nature of the interior finishes that characterized Cecil houses in the late eighteenth century.

Although the southern tidewater region was the first part of Cecil County to be settled, the oldest surviving dwellings are located in the north, in the area surveyed in 1702 as the Nottingham Lots. Until the late twentieth century, the earliest dated structures in the county were two houses erected by first generation immigrants—the Roger Kirk house (CE-209), dated 1719 and now destroyed, and the Haines house (CE-216), dating from around 1720-30.

In contrast to the impermanent nature of houses erected by early settlers in other areas, which featured a foundation of hole-set posts or sills laid on the ground, these two timber-frame structures were assembled on durable fieldstone foundations, which protected the heavy braced timber skeletons from decay. The stout corner posts were exposed in both structures and treated as part of the interior finish of the house. A finished appearance was achieved by decorating the exposed edges with a chamfer (an oblique cut on an exposed corner), a bead, or perhaps a more elaborate treatment. Methods of decorative finish employed in Cecil County included beaded lower edges or chamfered corners. The tradition of exposed and decorated framing systems in domestic interiors was well-known to late seventeenth and early eighteenth century Anglo-American settlers arriving in Cecil County. Extensive documentation of structural decoration has been carried on in New England, where a wealth of buildings with these features survives.[5]

In Cecil County the most elaborate decorated post heads remaining are exposed in the Haines house. Here, the exposed edge of each post received a corner chamfer that ended in a tapered stop about two feet from the top of the post head. Above the chamfer is a double set of bold ogee curves, one on each exposed face of the post head. The upper curved surface gracefully expands the top of the post head, producing a larger area on which to rest the plate and gable end tie beam. Each of the horizontal members is locked into the corner posts by means of wooden pins or "trunnels" fixed in drilled holes. The Kirk house had flared or "gunstock" corner posts, similar to those in the Indian Queen Tavern (CE-127) in Charlestown, erected circa 1740-50.

In addition to the posts in these timber-frame interiors, in the principal rooms the floor joists and summer beam (if present) were usually exposed as well. At Maple Shade Farm (CE-212), a large summer beam stretches between the gable end walls, supporting narrow joists that extend to the front and rear walls and hold the floor boards on the second story. The exposed corners of the summer beam and each joist were finished with decorative beaded edges. Such exposed joist ceilings were used in small houses until the second quarter of the nineteenth century, but in general use the practice of exposing and decorating structural framing members had disappeared by the end of the eighteenth century, replaced with the practice of concealing posts and joists behind layers of lath and plaster.

It has been said that within the structural confines of a house, "few elements are as starkly functional as the stair."[6] The relative importance of the stair as an interior feature has evolved from completely functional medieval winder stairs or ladders, as this quotation implies, to the grand and decorated open balustered staircases of the second half of the eighteenth and early nineteenth centuries. In the large houses of the Cecil gentry, the stair had become one of the main focal points for architectural expression and elaboration by the second quarter of the eighteenth century.

Ladders undoubtedly provided access between floors in early Cecil dwellings, but their general inconvenience eventually demanded replacement. An eighteenth century ladder that has survived in the attic of Little Elk Farm (CE-170), built circa 1760-80, provided access from the second floor of the kitchen wing to the attic loft. Heavy oak stringers carry the treads, each of which is pinned in place with a through tenon.

Enclosed winder staircases, usually located to one side of the chimney stack, were common features in many

Enclosed winder stair, Haines house (1983)

houses, including the Haines house and the John Churchman house (CE-187). The tight spiral of steps occupied little more room than a ladder yet offered easier access to rooms above. The closeted stair also kept warm air from escaping through an open stairwell. At the Haines house corresponding stairways rise from the second floor to the attic and descend to the excavated cellar below. Positioned above one another, these stairs provided access to each floor in a minimum of space. Enclosed winder stairs remained in practical use in smaller houses and service wings through much of the nineteenth century.

The principal stair, however, did not remain encased in a claustrophobic box for long. In its stead, a more open form of balustered stair began to appear in larger houses by the second quarter of the eighteenth century. In its early forms, the balustered stair appeared as an addition to an enclosed winder stair. Although the balusters have been removed from the stair stringer in the Red Lyon Tavern in Charlestown (CE-128), the original form is apparent. The closed stringer stair previously supported a series of balusters, probably turned; a newel post; and a molded handrail. None of these elements remains intact, but the mortises in the stringer indicate where the balusters stood.

Completely open balustered stairs had begun to appear inside the houses of the Cecil County gentry by the mid-eighteenth century. Imposing interior flights rise in many

CE-187, raised paneling incorporating winder stair in the west room of the brick portion of the John Churchman house (1986)

Enclosed winder stair, John Churchman house (1986)

(above) CE-172, open balustered stair at Hopewell (1979)

(left) CE-246, open balustered stair at Partridge Hill (1936, Historic American Buildings Survey)

county houses, boasting the skills of local craftsmen whose artistry appears equal to any contemporary work in Maryland. An important early example of an open balustered staircase survives in the stone house (CE-172) built around 1740-60 on a tract of land known as "Hopewell." This closed stringer stair is dominated by a series of boldly turned balusters, a stocky square newel post, and a molded handrail. A second floor attic stair of stubbier proportions rises directly above the first. Both flights are supported by a scarfed vertical post that extends through the three floors. The space in the triangular area beneath the molded closed stringer is defined by deeply cut raised panels. Slightly later staircases of the 1760s and 1770s were often decorated with a scroll-shaped design similar to that found in Partridge Hill (CE-246), dated to 1764.

While different types of stairs eased movement between the levels of a house, a variety of interior wall construction practices defined the interior spaces in county houses. Partitioning was not always accomplished during initial construction but was undertaken as need and finances permitted. In the early domestic architecture of the Chesapeake region, the riven clapboards used to sheath the exterior were sometimes employed inside the house as well. William Penn's recommendations for settlement dwellings called for "Clabboard, which is Rived feather-edged, of five foot and a half long…The Lodging Room may be lined with the same."[7] The four- to five-foot long, hand-split boards were lapped and nailed to the studs; they were also used to floor lofts.

While no surviving example of a clapboard interior remains in Cecil County, the common practice of building partitions of vertical boards is still evident in a handful of

CE-1066, feather-edged vertical board partition, Samuel Taylor house (1980)

CE-1217, vertical board partition, Gillespie log house (1978)

early dwellings. At the Samuel Taylor house (CE-1066), built circa 1750-70, inch-thick, vertical, feather-edged board walls divide the second floor into three bedrooms and a hall. This wall construction technique involved the placement of vertical, planed pine boards next to one another in a line across the room. Each board was decorated with a tapered or feathered edge on one side and a grooved edge finished with a quarter round on the other. The feathered-edge surface of one board was set into the grooved edge of an adjacent board. This alternating pattern of feathered edges and quarter round moldings is repeated across the entire wall surface. Feathered-edge partitions are mostly associated with the interiors of early to mid-eighteenth century houses.

When house carpenter William Cook finished the interior spaces of the two-story, hall/parlor log house on the Bethel farm in 1785-87, he charged Elisha England 2 shillings and 13 pence for "raising the partition below stairs, plan'd on both sides." A second entry in his account included "raising the partition's in the chamber of poplar plan'd on both sides."[8] Vertical board partitions treated with decorated edges continued to appear in domestic spaces through the balance of the eighteenth and into the early nineteenth century.

A less finished method of room division involved overlapping sawn vertical boards with untreated corners, as found in the Gillespie log house (CE-1217), built north of Port Deposit circa 1800-20. On the first floor of this house, long overlapping inch-thick boards were toe-nailed into the floor and fixed to the corresponding floor joist above. Clearly exposed and covered with a whitewash finish, the board wall was later covered with layers of lath and plaster. The common practice of using board walls as room dividers in principal domestic spaces had disappeared from practical use by the early nineteenth century, although second floor bedrooms, attics, and cellars were partitioned with board walls well into the mid-nineteenth century.

Directly related to the feathered-edge craftsmanship of vertical board partitions is the practice of raised panel wall finishes, which enhance numerous Cecil County dwellings built in the eighteenth century. In the Thomas Mackie house, dated circa 1730-50, the second floor bedroom boasts a hearth wall finished with a combination of feathered-edge board partitioning and raised panel carpentry. A series of four rectangular and square panels covers the width of the stone chimney pile, while adjacent feathered-edge board partitions enclose recesses on each side for closets. The

CE-70, raised paneling in bedroom, Thomas Mackie house (1980)

hearth and door panels are surrounded by a mortised-and-tenoned grid of vertical stiles and horizontal rails. Each panel is tapered on its outer edge and set into the grooves of the corresponding frame. The feathered-edge boards on either side of the hearth are set into grooves in the outer hearth wall stiles.

By the time the Thomas Mackie house (CE-70) was erected in the second quarter of the eighteenth century, raised panel craftsmanship was well established as the preferred method for finishing the interior of both large and small houses. The framework of stiles and rails that held the raised panels was used not only to cover chimney stacks but also to craft doors and partitions or to enclose staircases, cupboards, and storage closets.

Raised panel carpentry varies significantly from house to house, with no rigid arrangement or patterned size of paneling. Although some similarities are evident in paneled walls on separate floors of the same house, in many dwellings the paneling exhibits considerable difference from floor to floor. The sizes of rooms often vary, and the second floor was normally treated in a less elaborate manner than the more public first floor space. An instructive comparison of raised panel carpentry between floors is found at the Red Lyon Tavern (CE-128) in Charlestown. Presumably designed and executed by the same craftsman during the mid-eighteenth century (circa 1740-60), the west end of each room is enhanced with expertly carpentered raised panel walls designed to fit each space. Both end walls include a fireplace, closet, and staircase. Despite the similarity in features, the second floor was not designed merely as a reduction of the first floor arrangement. Rather, an alternate solution that better suited the smaller space was employed for the second floor chamber.

(above) CE-128, raised paneling on first floor, Red Lyon Tavern
(below) raised paneling on second floor, Red Lyon Tavern

(left) CE-246, cupboard at Partridge Hill (1936, Historic American Buildings Survey)

(below) CE-65, cupboard in southwest room, Great House

Parlors and halls fitted with raised panel carpentry distinguish frame, log, brick, and stone houses that range from one- and two-room structures to more elaborate double-pile dwellings. Great House (CE-65), erected during the mid-eighteenth century, offers a wide range of raised panel woodwork overlaid with many references to baroque classicism. Distinguishing the southwest parlor is a corner hearth wall finished with overmantel raised paneling flanked by wide fluted pilasters that stretch from the floor to the heavily molded cornice, which extends around the entire room. A row of boldly executed Doric triglyphs embellishes the overmantel as well. The Great House parlor also exhibits a built-in architectural corner cupboard, labeled during the eighteenth century as a buffet. Often distinguished by masterly craftsmanship, the buffet was a place where fine china and silver plate could be displayed prominently. The Great House cupboard has fluted sides that simulate columns; the principal face is marked by a large arched door of glass and raised panels. Surmounting the corner cupboard is a heavy baroque cornice that steps outward in a dramatic fashion to draw attention to this built-in piece of furniture as well as to the valuable contents within.

While not a particularly common feature in Cecil County dwellings of the eighteenth century, architectural corner cupboards appeared more frequently after 1750. The corner cupboard photographed at Partridge Hill by the Historic American Buildings Survey repeats some of the features of the Great House cupboard, albeit in a different manner. In this composition the craftsman created rather stunted fluted pilasters, placing them atop high plinths. Springing from the pilaster capitals is a molded, arched surround interrupted by a carved keystone. As with the Great House cupboard, the pilasters and molded surround focus attention on the glazed door and the items stored inside. The cupboard is clearly treated as an integral part of the room, with continuous cornice and baseboard moldings running uninterrupted across the top and bottom.

The fluted columns and classical details applied to chimney breasts, corner cupboards, and cornices alike point to the pervasive influence of English taste in America during the eighteenth century. Architects of Georgian England authored a wide range of style books that publicized current fashions for dwellings of the gentry. In the Chesapeake region, the gentry embraced baroque classicism as manifested in Georgian England as a sign of material wealth easily recognized by family, friends, and passersby. The Georgian style, as it has been labeled, was a dominant force throughout the American colonies. The published academic designs, however, were most often used as sources of inspiration, rather than models to copy. Local carpenters experimented with design elements, attempting to create their own expressions in a recognizable idiom.

The use of expensive classical woodwork in the eighteenth century dwellings of Cecil County was often restricted due to the cost of installation. Elaborate woodwork was usually confined to the parlor, dining room, and entrance hall. The parlor of the Fountain Inn, erected in Elkton around 1790, was embellished with a classically inspired mantel with a crossetted fireplace surround, a plain frieze with ogee-curved ends, Wall of Troy bed molding, and a molded mantelshelf. The overmantel was plastered and topped with a heavy cornice that did not extend around the room.

Parlor mantel, Fountain Inn, Elkton
(1936, Historic American Buildings Survey)

Without any question the ultimate expression of eighteenth century, pattern book-influenced interior design is found at Bohemia (CE-32), designed and finished over a period that may have spanned as many as ten years between 1750 and 1760. The five-room first floor contains some of the most sophisticated carpentry and plasterwork finishes found in any house in Maryland. After a visit to Bohemia in 1837, Sidney George Fisher, a Philadelphia attorney who owned Mount Harmon, observed in his journal, "I was delighted with the fine old-fashioned mansion, which has really the appearance of a gentlemen's residence of the last century; it is very large, has a beautiful hall, the walls of the rooms are colored and ornamented with various designs of stucco work & carving which are very pretty of themselves & are interesting as being associated with the past."[9]

CE-32, music room at Bohemia
(1936, Historic American Buildings Survey)

The center door in the land facade at Bohemia opens into a grand stair hall finished in a highly elaborate manner. A beautifully appointed Chinese-style staircase, perhaps the finest in the colonies when it was built, is joined with rare Rococo plasterwork, also known as composition ornament. The latter serves as a strong architectural focus, leading the eye upward through the second floor balcony of Chinese trellis railings. The graceful curves of the ceiling ornament feature delicate flower and foliage forms that undulate around a bird frozen in flight clutching a lantern hanger. The masterfully crafted staircase is distinguished by Chinese trellis panels, each with a different lattice design. Instead of the solid newel post found in other eighteenth century dwellings, the Bohemia stair posts are fragmented into four individual posts topped by a capital shaped like the roof of a pagoda. A molded and ramped handrail tops the newel posts and Chinese trellis railing. Also designed in trellis forms are the scrolled stringer decorations; an additional row of Chinese fretwork finishes the bottom edge of the stringer. The grand entrance hall is further enriched with bold classical cornices on the first and second floors and delicate composition ornament over the principal doorways. (For further discussion of the Chinese stair at Bohemia, see page 278.)

West of the entrance hall is another outstanding display of woodwork and composition ornament in what has been called the "music room." This squarish space features a mixture of Georgian woodwork and neoclassical Adamesque plaster decoration. The principal focus of the room is a baroque mantelpiece featuring scroll-decorated consoles to

(above left) A pattern book was probably the inspiration for the Chinese-style stair railing installed at Bohemia in the mid-18th century. William and John Halfpenny's was first published in London in 1750; in addition to this drawing of a stair, the authors included a variety of Chinese trellis designs. (Winterthur Museum Library)

(above right) CE-32, lower flight of stair, Bohemia (1936, Historic American Buildings Survey)

(right) plasterwork on hall ceiling at Bohemia (1936, Historic American Buildings Survey)

(opposite) stair hall at Bohemia (1936-37, Frances Benjamin Johnston Collection, Library of Congress)

CE-229, stair, Nathan and Susannah Harris house (1980)

(above) Detail of mantel in northeast room, and (below) detail of mantel in southeast room, Harris house (1980)

each side of the firebox. What distinguishes this mantel from others in Cecil County is the broken pediment that rests atop the console-embellished frieze. Multiple layers of classical enrichment, including rows of delicately carved Wall of Troy moldings, heighten the attention this architectural fixture commands. Defining the overmantel is a rectangular neoclassical panel featuring a round medallion impressed with a lyre framed by garland swags, the corners of which are gripped in the mouths of lion heads. Webbed corners and ribbed columns of plaster distinguish the relief decoration that forms the border. Additional panels, some with draped swags, embellish the side walls as well. Centered on the ceiling is a large lobed oval of geometrically placed acanthus leaves well-known in the vocabulary of Adam brothers plaster decoration. The music room is embellished further with an elaborate plaster cornice, chair rail, and baseboard.

The neoclassical plaster decoration installed at Bohemia foreshadowed stylistic changes in American architecture that followed the Revolutionary War. The Federal style began to appear in Cecil County around 1790, often mixed with baroque molding profiles popularly used in the preceding half century. The Federal style continued in popularity until the late 1820s and was characterized by a turn from the exuberant and robust curves of baroque woodwork to less three-dimensional, flat or planar surfaces. Federal proportions usually had a strong vertical emphasis, which was often enhanced by delicate gougework in a variety of finely carved geometric patterns.

Despite distinct interest in the neoclassicism of the Federal style, the proportions of Georgian architecture and the profiles of baroque woodwork did not disappear from Cecil County overnight. The stone house (CE-229) Nathan and Susannah Harris built in 1798 reflects the changing nature of interior design at the close of the eighteenth century. The staircase, rising in the center passage, features a turned baluster handrail of slighter, more attenuated pro-

CE-84, dining room mantel, Elisha Kirk house (1979)

portions than Georgian balustrades of a few decades earlier. In contrast to the stout, bulbous profile of the Partridge Hill stair balusters, those at the Harris house are long and slender like the newel post and feature a subtle ring molding. While the handrail is molded in the eighteenth century practice, the proportions are much narrower, and it is more finely shaped than the Partridge Hill railing.

Raised six-panel doors open into the rooms adjacent to the stair hall at the Harris house. The room to the left contains a large cooking fireplace finished with a tongue-and-groove beaded board wall and exposed floor framing, including a beaded summer beam and beaded joists, that supports a beaded plank floor above. The two rooms to the right, on the other hand, are finely finished with fully plastered walls and corner fireplaces framed by mantels of expertly crafted Federal design with an undercurrent of bold baroque profiles common to Georgian woodwork.

The front parlor mantel at the Harris house follows a basic formula for mantel design that is common to the Federal style. The organization of a Federal mantel characteristically follows a three-part system of projecting panels that define the frieze, the surface fixed between the fireplace surround, and the cornice. In many cases, the central panel or tablet is dominant either in size or decoration in contrast to the outer frieze panels. Fixed above the frieze is the mantelshelf, which often corresponds visually to the protruding panels with a "broken" shelf outline. Highlighting the mantelshelf are finely carved rows of Wall of Troy and rope moldings. The ogee-molded fireplace surround and the bold cove molding of the mantelshelf recall the deeply cut baroque profiles of Georgian woodwork. In other cases the frieze and shelf are visually supported by narrow classical pilasters highlighted in a variety of ways with delicate fluting, reeding, or other decorative treatments.

The Elisha Kirk house (CE-84), built around 1810-15 in the village of Brick Meeting House (later known as Calvert), was fitted with a wide variety of finely executed Federal woodwork. Each mantel in the house is embellished with a different decorative treatment in a clear effort to distinguish the rooms from each other. The dining room mantel is particularly outstanding, with oval recesses executed in the frieze tablets and a delicately carved oval and diamond pattern enriching the pilasters. The chimney breast is further enhanced with a reeded corner molding. Additional visual interest in the room is provided by a reeded chair rail and a built-in storage cupboard.

In the Federal style, decorated or reeded pilasters are often combined with intricately executed gougework pat-

CE-1057, detail of Federal mantel in west parlor of the Courthouse Point Farm house (1979)

terning, a woodworking technique in which sharp chisels and gouges are used to create stylized forms across the surface of the frieze panels. Mantels exhibiting complex gougework patterns are usually found in the principal rooms of the house, while less public secondary rooms were finished in a less elaborate fashion.

Outstanding in its Federal design and interior finish is Holly Hall (CE-131), erected circa 1802 on the south side of Elkton for James Sewall. The imposing two-and-a-half story Federal brick house surpasses most buildings of the period in its level of architectural sophistication. One of its most dynamic focal points is the front entrance. Here the delicately crafted doorway is framed by an elliptical transom featuring a classical shield and sidelights with alternating diamonds and ovals in the muntins. The fluted column portico is a restoration based on architectural evidence from

CE-131, stair, Holly Hall (1936, Historic American Buildings Survey)

Venetian window in second floor hall, Holly Hall
(1936, Historic American Buildings Survey)

First floor mantel, Holly Hall
(1936, Historic American Buildings Survey)

a historic photograph of the house. The gentle ellipse of the entrance fanlight is repeated in the front hall, where an arched opening divides the main passage from the stair hall in the southwest corner.

The staircase itself is a masterful display of Federal carpentry rising in a continuous, uninterrupted line to the third floor. Probably taken from an architectural design source such as Owen Biddle's *The Young Carpenter's Assistant*, published in Philadelphia in 1805, are the attenuated dimensions of the stair parts, the slender stick balusters, and the circular profile handrail that terminates in a spiral at the base of the stair. The stringer is embellished with a delicate scroll bracket common to early nineteenth century architectural style books. Minimal additional woodwork, including a baseboard molding, corner block window surrounds, and chair rail (now gone) finish the adjacent wall surfaces. The second floor contains the same L-shaped stair hall and passage with a similar segmental arch dividing the space. Particularly noteworthy on the second floor is the Venetian or Palladian window, which dominates the bay directly atop the front entrance. The interior finish of the Venetian window includes fluted pilasters flanking the center arched section, which is filled with a six-over-six sash window, paneled base, and compass-head arch encompassing a fan ornament. The narrow sidelights and center sash are fitted with interior louvered shutters.

The mantels at Holly Hall do not date from the original construction of the house but were probably installed around 1830-40. The imported, gray King-of-Prussia marble mantels represent the next major period of architectural design, the Greek Revival style. Inspired by the architecture of ancient Greece, Greek Revival design was based on exacting drawings and replications of actual structures. In contrast to the interest in flat and linear surface decoration typical of Federal design, introduction of the Greek Revival style during the 1830s marks a return to heavier, more solid forms in three-dimensioned massing. Surface decoration was usually limited to fewer, bolder moldings in order to achieve the desired effect. The Ionic columns of the Holly Hall mantel stand outward from the mantel itself and support projecting frieze blocks under a thin, molded shelf.

While importing materials for interior finishes was not particularly new in 1830, the practice had become much more common in Cecil County, where it was made more feasible by improvements in transportation. The New Castle and Frenchtown Turnpike, built in 1809-13, carried freight and passengers from the Chesapeake to the Delaware River. Goods and travelers who came by ship from Baltimore to Frenchtown were taken overland by wagon to New Castle, where they boarded another ship to sail to Philadelphia, or vice versa. In 1814, when General and Mrs. Forman decided to install a new dining room mantel in their eighteenth century gambrel-roofed house, they ordered one from Philadelphia. The special attention awarded this event was commented on by Mrs. Forman, who wrote on November 16, "a man came from Philadelphia to put our marble mantle in the dining room."[10] On December 1 she commented, "The man finished our marble mantle and the materials of the mantle, hearth slab, soapstone and workmanship cost $116.95."[11]

Twenty-three years later, the Formans once again turned to Philadelphia for inspiration, labor, and materials, this time to erect a stylish new brick addition. By 1837-38 the New Castle and Frenchtown Railroad, which paralleled the old turnpike, had quickened the trip considerably.[12]

During the spring and summer months the cellar was dug and the brick walls raised at Rose Hill. By early October Martha Forman mentions that "three plasterers came this afternoon, Mr. Handburg and his men."[13] Installing lath and plastering the entire house was accomplished over the course of the fall months, and Mrs. Forman recorded the completion of the new dining room on November 25 with the rest of the plasterwork finished four days later.[14] The two principal downstairs rooms, the parlor and dining room, were embellished with plaster cornice moldings and bold ceiling medallions of acanthus leaves rigidly formed in a repetitive circular pattern. The plastering of the house was followed by the installation of imported marble mantels and imported wallpaper in the dining room and hall and the crafting of the finish carpentry for the staircase. The carpenters left Rose Hill on February 21, to Mrs. Forman's relief.[15] Mr. Armitage, the painter, arrived a few days later to begin the final leg of work. Painting the house was spread over several months, concluding on April 25, 1838.[16]

In Cecil County the professional construction and finishing of the Rose Hill addition by Philadelphia masons, carpenters, and painters was by no means common during the second quarter of the nineteenth century. Most residents could afford only what local craftsmen and materials could produce. Nevertheless, Mrs. Forman's diary passages vividly reflect the changing nature of house building during the late 1830s, signaling what became a broad-based transformation in the building trades a few decades later.

The inspiration for new architectural designs was changing as well. No longer were homeowners, rich or middle income, limited by the familiar vernacular plans and finishes repeatedly used and modified over the previous two centuries. Poignantly indicative of the new influences in architectural design was an observation penned by Sidney George Fisher on May 20, 1846:

> In the morning walked & read Alison, thro whose prolix history I am slowly making my way and some chapters of Downing's Landscape Gar-

CE-27, plaster ceiling medallion in 1838 parlor at Rose Hill (1995)

dening, a very well written & most useful book. It exhibits taste and a true feeling for nature. Its suggestions & instructions are practical and adapted to the climate & habits of this country....This book has had immense influence throughout the North in introducing a superior style of adorning country residences & particularly in banishing the odious habit of building houses of Grecian architecture with high colonnades instead of Gothic & Elizabethan cottage style, which harmonizes so admirably with the surrounding natural objects & is so much more easily adapted to the purposes of a dwelling. His work & another more especially devoted to the subject, is full of designs and plans of houses suited to all fortunes from the plain farm house or picturesque cottage up to the costly & highly decorated villa."[17]

During the half century that followed Fisher's observations, Cecil County farms and small towns experienced a significant rebuilding of the older housing stock. New dwellings replaced old or worn out houses, and many older structures were wholly transformed with a new addition or alteration that conformed to a new style.

The rebuilding or restyling of houses inside and out was expedited considerably by the mass production of building parts and the quick distribution of supplies made possible by the expanding railroad systems. Waves of published European-inspired architectural forms, from Italianate villas and Second Empire town houses to Gothic-inspired farmhouses and romantic cottages, influenced rural design during the second half of the nineteenth century. As a result, a diverse array of building forms, both vernacular and academic in design inspiration, survive on the rural landscape of small towns and farms in Cecil County.

Parlor mantel, 1838, Rose Hill (1995)

CE-1218, interior of Maplewood Farm barn, Port Deposit vicinity (1980)

CHAPTER 10

"Improvements" on County Farms

AGRICULTURAL PURSUITS have dominated the Cecil County landscape and economy for three centuries. During this time, farming practices have grown from the hand labor and medieval toil of the seventeenth and eighteenth centuries to the highly mechanized practices of modern times. The history of agricultural change in the county is most evident in an analysis of the barns, stables, granaries, corncribs, and other buildings that mark the agrarian landscape. The written record adds much to this physical evidence as it documents the vanished buildings that once played a vital role on Cecil County farms and plantations.

From the outset of colonial exploration, the soil in Cecil County was described favorably. Captain John Smith commented in 1608 that "the vesture of the earth in most places doth manifestly prove the nature of the soyle to be lusty and very rich."[1] He described the soil profile for the most part as "a blacke sandy mould," although in other places he found "a fat slimy clay and in other places a very barren gravell." True to Cecil County is a diversity of soil types that ranges from light sandy loams to reddish orange clay to the dark brown loam of the piedmont.

In 1634, a few decades after Smith's visit to the head of the bay, Cyprian Thorowgood explored the Elk River and noticed distinct differences in Cecil County geography. "The country we judged to have a very riche soile," he wrote, "with a gravell bottome in some places, and in others a deep read clay, and toward the water very marshier...."[2] The diversity clearly evident in Cecil soil profiles and terrain has influenced a wide variety of agricultural pursuits since exploration and settlement.

The earliest Cecil colonists, following in the footsteps of many other Eastern Shore planters, tried their hands at cultivating tobacco with the illusive dream of quick and substantial profits in the volatile European markets. During his passage through the upper part of the peninsula in 1679, Jasper Danckaerts commented that tobacco "is the chief article of trade in the country."[3] While sound evidence exists to prove that Cecil planters pursued tobacco as their principal cash crop well into the eighteenth century, records also indicate a substantial number of planters and farmers turned away from the tobacco lure to grow a variety of cereal grains for local consumption and foreign export. When Dr. Alexander Hamilton passed through Cecil County in 1744, sixty-five years after Danckaerts's visit, he observed that "in this part of the country I found they chiefly cultivated British grain, as wheat, barley, and oats. They raise, too, a great deal of flax, and in every house here the women have two or three spinning wheels a going."[4]

Also reflecting the diverse nature of Cecil agriculture are the descriptions of plantations and specific improvements that were written for the purposes of the Cecil County Orphans Court. When Hyland Price and James Morgan visited the land of orphan Benjamin Walmsley (son of Benjamin) around 1790, they briefly delineated the physical nature of the improvements, beginning with "one hew'd poplar log house twenty-two feet and a half by seventeen and a half with a shingled oak roof in bad repair." A second house was of frame construction and covered with an oak roof. The officials went on to describe the plantation outbuildings:

> One hewed log kitchen eighteen feet by seventeen and a half with a oak shingled roof in bad repair. One quarter, maw'ld logs clabboard roof fifteen by twelve in bad repair, one corn house hew'd poplar logs clabboard roof twelve feet by eight tolerable good repair, one old tobacco house posts in the ground oak shingled roof thirty six feet long by eighteen wide part of the weather boarding off and part on, one granary hew'd poplar logs thirteen feet by ten shingled oak roof in

bad repair, one hen house twelve by eight clabboard roof in tolerable good repair. One peach orchard of about 80 old trees. One apple orchard of 47 trees the greatest part old. One pailed garden, one hundred and ten feet one way and ninety the other in tolerable good repair, the plantation divided into two fields exclusive of the orchards.[5]

Through the eyes of the county officials we get a fairly complete picture of the essential features of the Walmsley plantation. Descriptive records such as these enable historians to reconstruct the built environment of the late eighteenth century and to know with some certainty the types and condition of buildings that once dotted the Cecil County landscape.

As evinced by the Orphans Court evaluations, county farms were improved by a variety of buildings in varying degrees of repair. Clear as well in the descriptions written between 1785 and 1800 is the relative infrequence of tobacco houses in contrast to the numerous listings of corn houses and granaries. This written testimony demonstrates the variety of cash crops being grown on the Cecil landscape by the close of the eighteenth century. As late as the 1820s Martha Ogle Forman mentioned planting tobacco or shipping it to Baltimore with other Rose Hill crops and produce.[6] Despite the continued presence of tobacco among the market crops of some Cecil planters, tobacco had been diminished in importance to corn and wheat for more than half a century.

Other than the dwelling, the central fixture of most farms or plantations was the barn. Due to the security the barn provided the harvested crop and livestock, much thought and expense were devoted to its construction. No known barn standing in Cecil County dates from the colonial period, but the written record suggests barns at that time were generally part frame or log structures. If erected in a frame tradition, the principal corner posts, like the Walmsley barn, may have been placed in holes that were then backfilled. These hole-set posts provided the barn's structural stability.

The early frame barns were covered with a variety of siding from riven clapboards to rougher boards, and the

CE-918, Green's Delight barn (1978)

roof was sheathed with a range of materials that included clapboards, shingles, and thatch. As late as the early nineteenth century a thatch roof was mentioned in a description of the lands of Henry Hollingsworth. In 1806 Orphans Court officials found "a barn with a thatched roof in tolerable repair" on the property with "a large two story frame dwelling," the latter declared "out of repair but with some expense [could] be a comfortable house to accommodate a tenant."[7] On the same estate there was "a stable with a thatched roof."[8] The impermanent nature of buildings set in the ground and covered with thin boards or thatch explains why these early farming structures did not survive.

During the mid- to late eighteenth century the nature of barn building in Cecil County underwent a dramatic change. Due to the proximity of Pennsylvania and the strong Germanic tradition of a bank-sited barn, similar structures became commonplace south of the Mason-Dixon line. Enough roll to the land south of the fall line permitted the

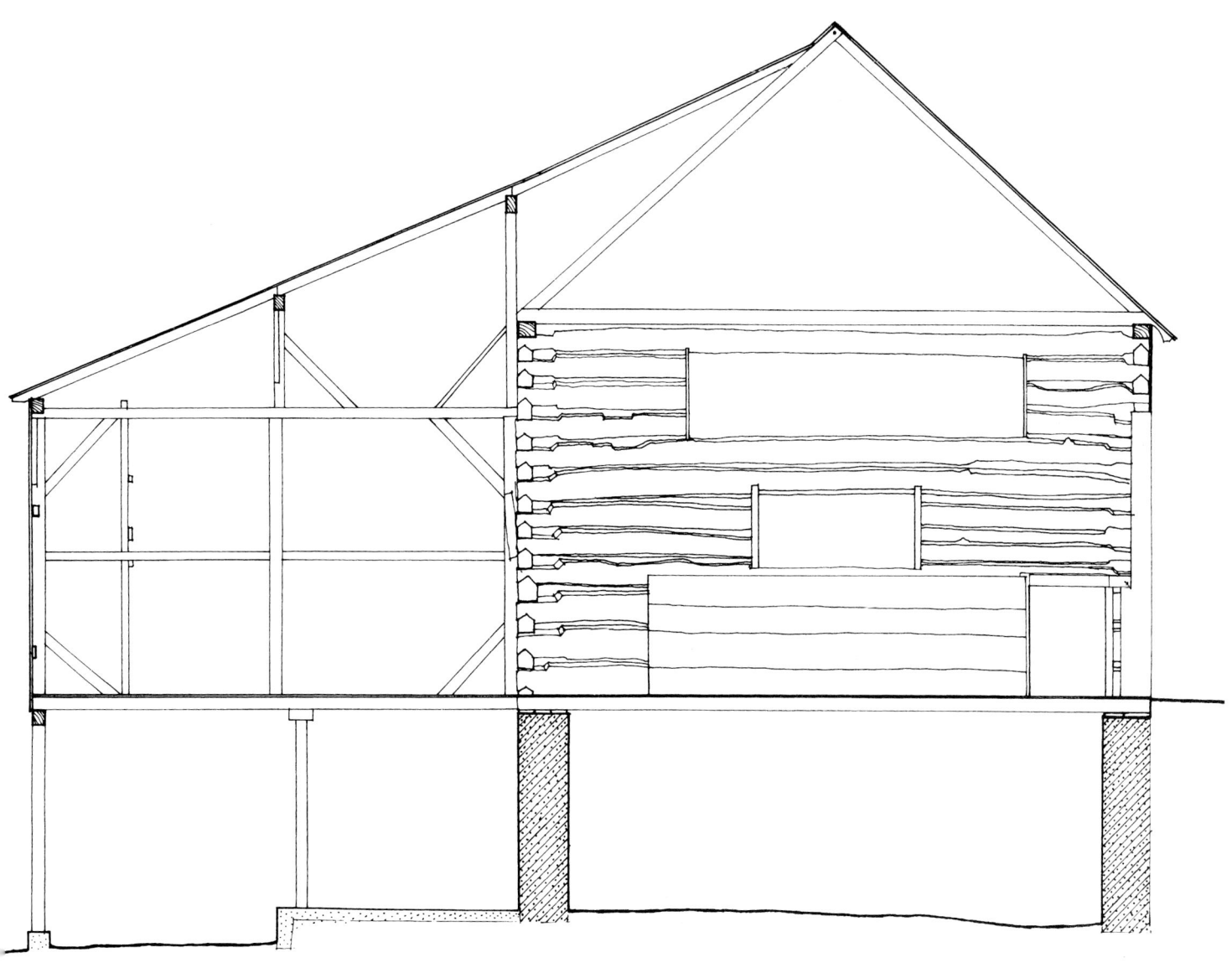

Green's Delight barn framing section
(Paul Touart, Anthony O. James)

construction of bank barns as far south as the Sassafras River, although they appeared on a much less frequent scale below Elkton.

Bank barns were erected in differing materials in a variety of forms. It is uncertain when the first ones were built in Cecil County, but they probably came into use around the time of the Revolution and were well established by the close of the eighteenth century. When Orphans Court officials visited William and James Young's plantation known as "Hog's Tract" in 1807, the improvements included "a good fraim barn with stone cellar, 28 x 34." The mention of a stone cellar indicates a belowground portion with the frame resting above.

An early double-pen log bank barn, dated by an inscribed stone to 1806, stands in northwestern Cecil County near Richardsmere. The Green's Delight barn (CE-918) is a rare and highly important survival of a once common building type. Here a center threshing floor and passage separates two unchinked, V-notched log haymows. Each log pen is loaded by means of a pulley system fixed within the apex of the rafters, which provides a way to carry the straw over the top of the inner log walls. Large rectangular openings in each log wall are used more for removing hay than for storing it. The Green's Delight barn rests on a fieldstone foundation with the entrance ramp on the north side and the barnyard to the south. This arrangement allows the bulk of the barn to protect the animals from harsh weather and at the same time exposes the livestock to the warmth of the sun.

In 1837, when planter Sidney George Fisher of Mount

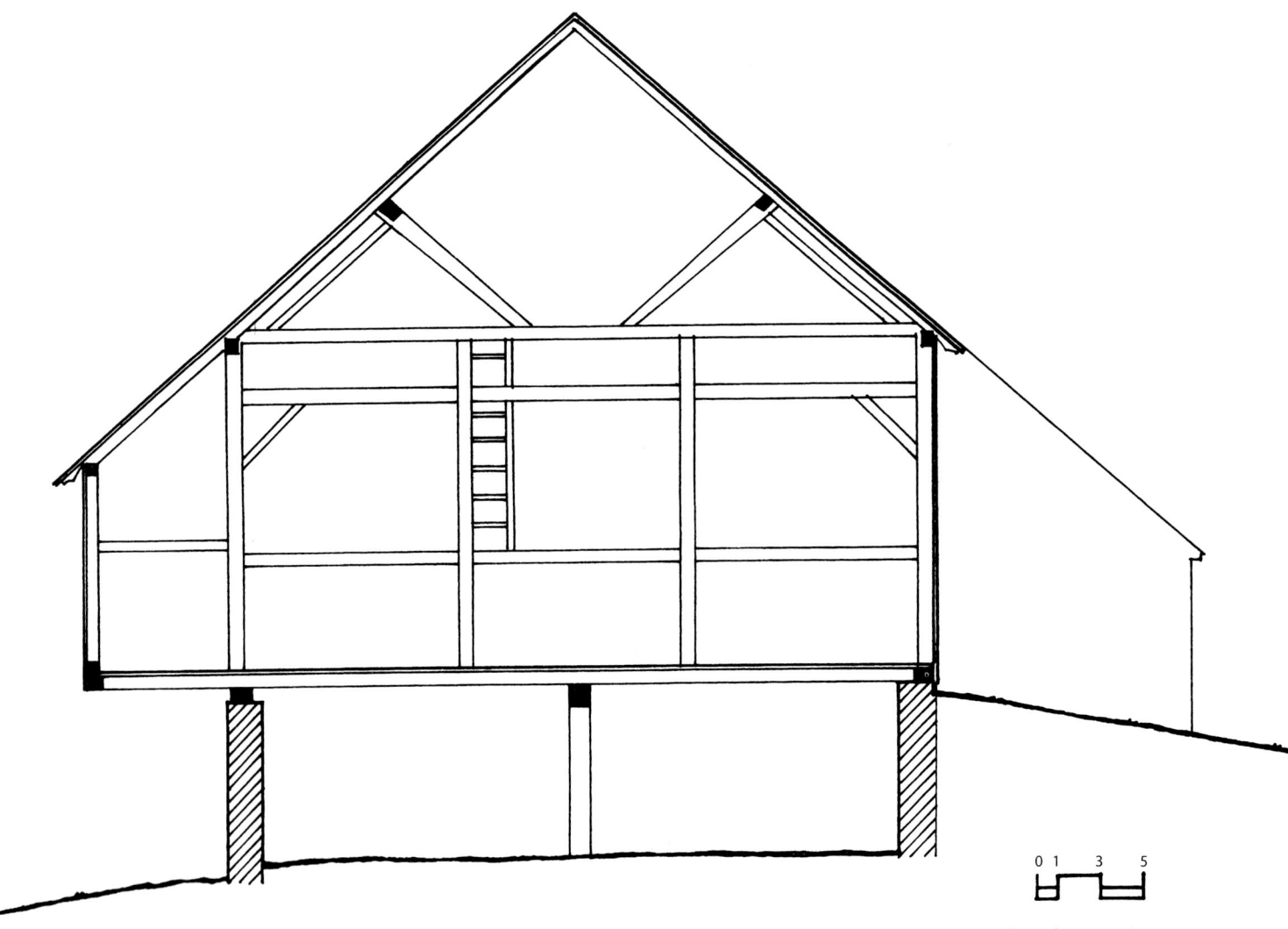

CE-41, Octorara barn framing elevation
(Orlando Ridout V, Anthony O. James)

Harmon decided to erect a new barn, he hired a barn builder from Delaware County, Pennsylvania, who had been recommended to him. Fisher made the following entry in his diary on November 3, 1837:

> On returning found Mr. Penrose McCullough, the carpenter whom Mr. Painter had recommended to build my barn, had arrived. He is a Delaware Co. mechanic and has just finished an excellent barn for Painter. After dinner went through part of the woods with him to see if there is any timber fit to use, and to select a site, which I have not decided on. Richards and he sat with me all the evening talking the matter over and making estimates. Find it will Cost $1500 probably more, a larger sum than I expected. I am determined to have a good one cost what it may. It will be a permanent and great improvement to the property, and I should think pay a fair interest on the money, in grain saved, and the superior condition in which it will keep manure, hay, and the cattle.[9]

The full dimensions of the Mount Harmon barn are not known, but Sidney Fisher does mention that after it was erected he wished it was twenty feet from sill to plate instead of sixteen feet.

The Mount Harmon tenant farmer, Mr. Rickards, asked that a modification be made to include a cellar under the "bridgeway" for rutabagas.[10] Also known as a "bridge house," the bridgeway spanned an open distance between the earthen entrance ramp and the barn itself. The space

Rear elevation of Evan's Choice barn showing "strawhouse" addition (1980)

beneath the bridge house served different purposes, from a place to park wagons, store implements, or, like the Mount Harmon barn, dig a root cellar. An additional feature of the Mount Harmon bridgeway was the incorporation of corn houses on each side. Carpenter McCullough was almost finished with the final details by the end of June 1838.[11]

More specific dimensions for the Mount Harmon bank barn are unknown. A common first floor plan for a bank barn has a central passage and threshing floor that provides access to the haymows on each side. In some cases, like the barn at Octorara (CE-41), the first floor joists are cantilevered over the foundation in order to achieve additional storage space and at the same time to provide a protective shelter for livestock housed in the cellar. The convenience of the two-level arrangement allowed for hay storage on the main floor and gravity-fed livestock below. Additions were attached to most barns as the need arose, but the most substantial extensions involved large "strawhouses," which usually projected on a perpendicular axis behind the main barn. As seen on the stone barn of the Evan's Choice farm (CE-98), the rear addition expanded the storage space for straw on the main floor and allowed room for an enlarged dairy herd on the ground level.

By the mid-nineteenth century the virtues of bank barns were well-known and promoted by writers like Lewis Allen, who wrote *Rural Architecture*, first published in 1852 and reprinted in 1863. In his introduction to barns he stated that the

> most thorough barn structures, perhaps, to be seen in the United States, are those of the state of Pennsylvania, built by the German farmers of the lower and central counties. They are large, and expensive in their construction; and, in a strictly economical view, perhaps more costly than required. Yet, there is a substance and durability in them, that is exceedingly satisfactory, and where the pecuniary ability of the farmer will permit, may well be an example for imitation.[12]

CE-216, Haines barn with bridge house and ramp (1979)

Mid-nineteenth century agricultural essayists discussed scores of topics relating to the management of the farm, often centering on better or more economical ways to erect farm buildings. Labor intensive structures such as the double-pen log barn, which required a good quantity of materials, were soon outdated, and the construction of bank barns and a host of other structures became more standardized. By the mid- to late nineteenth century the techniques for raising heavy, mortised-and-tenoned braced timber frames had reached a level of standardization unknown to the previous generation of barn raisers. The boxed, diagonally braced timber frame techniques, partially exposed in the Haines barn (CE-216) as it was dismantled in 1979 and on the interior of the Lincoln farm barn (CE-1115), are representative of methods used in barns around the county.

Although stone was used extensively for foundations, relatively few stone barns were built in Cecil County. The Evan's Choice barn and the Baldwin barn at Elk Mills (CE-166) are two of a handful of surviving examples. The front walls of the Evan's Choice barn and the two gable end stone

Interior of the Haines barn (1979)

CE-1115, Lincoln farm barn interior (1981)

(right) CE-166, Baldwin barn (1981)

(below left) CE-98, Evan's Choice barn from the west (1980)

(below right) CE-18, Indian Range barn (1979)

walls of the Baldwin barn are pierced by narrow vertical embrasures, which facilitate air circulation. This venting method is unusual in Cecil County barns and more indicative of central Maryland and Pennsylvania barn building traditions.

In some places in Cecil County the level terrain did not permit construction of a bank barn. In these areas barns were generally built on flat ground with a minimal stone or brick foundation, as seen on the Indian Range farm west of Cecilton (CE-18). Animal stalls fill a large portion of the ground floor, and the second floor is used for crop storage. Without a banked site, the two-story barn is nowhere near as convenient for storage, nor does it provide the same sort of berm protection for the livestock.

Equally important to many Cecil County planters who grew large amounts of wheat and corn were the storage buildings that protected these important cash crops. Although storage practices were by no means uniform, granaries generally held the processed wheat, while harvested corn was placed in corn houses or cribs. Evident in the written historic record are a variety of log or frame granaries not unlike those found on the land of Thomas and John Leach Knight Jones, whose property was visited by the officers of the Cecil County Orphans Court on April 15,

1795. The valuation included "one oak log granary twenty feet long by sixteen feet wide covered with cedar shingles in tolerable repair" and

> one frame granary two storey high twenty six feet four inches long by twenty feet wide weather boarded with cedar plank and covered with cedar shingles, one other frame granary two storey high thirty feet four inches long by twenty two feet four inches wide weather boarded with cedar plank and covered with cedar shingles in good repair.[13]

The presence of these sizable storage buildings clearly suggests that Thomas Jones, the orphans' father, had engaged in large-scale wheat production.

Corn, on the other hand, was largely stored in rectangular log structures by the close of the eighteenth century. Often measuring around sixteen feet by eight to ten feet, the logs were laid horizontally and notched at the corners. The sides of the log crib were left unchinked so that air passing through the walls would keep the corn dry. When new corn houses were declared necessary for the estate of Richard, William, and Joseph Richardson in March 1797, the officials of the Orphans Court recommended that part of the estate funds should be used to replace the "old one of no value." Their building instructions stated that "there is to be two pens, each twenty feet long and six feet broad in the clear, and nine feet to be kept between the pens, the whole under one roof and to be built with new oak logs."[14] Unlike the Richardson estate, most late eighteenth century farms were improved by single rectangular cribs such as Thomas Biddle's "sawed poplar log corn house 20 x 10 in good repair."[15]

While barns, granaries, and corncribs took different forms throughout the eighteenth and early nineteenth centuries, the standardization of building materials and the need to conserve timber resources soon outdated log construction in farm buildings. Paralleling new methods of fertilization, crop rotation, and careful land management were numerous ways to improve farm buildings for safer storage of crops and produce. Following this wave of new information, Cecil County planters and farmers not only returned nutrients to worn out fields but they engaged in an almost complete rebuilding of the agrarian landscape with more efficient dwellings, barns, and outbuildings. Sidney George Fisher noted these changes in his diary in 1838, writing, "New houses and barns are going up in all directions, everybody is liming and farming in the best manner, and the largest and best farms are held by men of capital able and anxious to improve them."[16]

Applying lime, plaster, and South American guano and rotating fields with various cover crops restored the soil, which ultimately led to larger yields. Larger quantities put extra demands on the older generation of farm buildings and farmers often opted to erect sizable additions or rebuild altogether. Mid-nineteenth century literature such as Lewis Allen's *Rural Architecture* or the New York agricultural periodical *The Plow*, which Allen quoted, stressed the construction of better designed, more efficient buildings. A section in *The Plow* that Allen used in his book describes a specific way to erect a "rat-proof" granary:

> If wooden posts are used, make them sixteen inches square, and set them in a hole previously filled, six inches deep with charcoal, or rubble stone and lime grouting, and fill around the posts with the same. The steps are hinged to the doorsill, and should have a cord and weight attached to the door, so that whenever it is shut, the steps should be up also; this would prevent the possibility of carelessness in leaving them down for the rats to walk up. The sides should be made of slates, with large cracks between, and the floor under the crib, with numerous open joints, no matter if shattered corn falls through, let the pigs and chickens have it. The circulation of the air through the pile of corn will more than pay for

CE-964, Gibson's Green farm double corncrib (1979)

all you lose through the floor. If you intend to have sweet grain, be sure to have a ventilator in the roof, and you may see by the vane on top of it, how the wind will always blow favorably for you.[17]

Few granaries employ all of these features, but a number of county examples, including the Gibson's Green farm corncrib (CE-964), closely resemble the model form.

Silos were introduced on Cecil County farms beginning in the mid-nineteenth century. These new structures for storing feed, with their voluminous vertical storage capacity, were a boon to farmers. The earliest silos in the county appeared in the third quarter of the nineteenth century, a date that coincides with the expansion of local dairy herds. Located next to the barn, early silos were constructed of wooden ribs secured with iron rod bands or fieldstone. The fieldstone silo on Stoney Batter farm (CE-1177) stands within a mile of three other stone silos near Colora. Their proximity to one another and their parallel, third quarter of the nineteenth century dates suggest the structures were erected by the same mason. Both subterranean and totally aboveground silos were built; subterranean silos, such as that

CE-1177, Stoney Batter farm stone silo (1980)

CE-1190, Ewing Mill property subterranean fieldstone silo (1979)

on the Ewing Mill property (CE-1190), are easily identified by their stunted appearance.

Other less important farm structures included wagon houses, chicken coops, and an occasional specialized structure. Many county farms had springhouses, usually placed some distance from the barnyard and obviously near a spring. Built of various materials, this outbuilding provided a measure of protection for a close source of fresh water. While frame springhouses are known to have existed, only masonry examples have survived. The small rectangular structure is usually covered by a gable roof with a door and small windows marking the sides. The eighteenth century Job farm springhouse (CE-584) was combined with the farm smokehouse, with the cool storage area and spring below the charred smoking room on the second floor. Many springhouses in the hillier northern areas were fitted with a water ram in order to drive the water a distance, sometimes up a steep grade. In the southern part of the county a stone structure houses the well at Red House Farm, homestead of the Hutton family.

Octorara springhouse (1978)

CE-584, Job Farm spring/smoke house

CE-1065, well house, Red House Farm

CE-106, Greenhill farm kitchen/slave quarter (left) and smokehouse (right) (1936, Historic American Buildings Survey)

Water storage tanks on county farms held a supply of water, often in a tank atop a frame or metal tower. The water storage tank on the Maplewood farm (CE-1218) is inconspicuously placed in a frame bell tower. On other farms the tanks were concealed in a rear wing of the house to provide an interior source of fresh water for the family.

Closely tied to the major farm operations and agricultural structures were the domestic outbuildings accompanying the house. On most farms, the domestic service buildings were set apart from the farm buildings, an arrangement tied to the male/female segregation of work. The domestic outbuildings were clustered close to the dwelling, while the structures associated with the farm's agricultural operations were sited some distance from the house.[18]

Before major kitchen operations were moved into the service wing of a house, the detached kitchen was an important outbuilding around which the daily activities of family life functioned. Because they became obsolete when the kitchen was fully incorporated into the house, few detached kitchens still stand in Cecil County. An important kitchen/slave quarter remains on the Greenhill farm (CE-106), perched on a high knoll overlooking the town of North East. The Flemish and common bond brick structure, dating from the late eighteenth century, stands directly east of the house. It is a rectangular brick structure with a two-room plan; cooking facilities were housed on the first floor with whitewashed and partitioned rooms above. The pres-

CE-1218, Maplewood farm tank/water tower/bell tower (historic photograph, Mrs. Hubert Ryan)

CE-543, Griffith-Smith smokehouse (1980)

CE-1222, Rawlings farm smokehouse (1979)

ence of two front doors allowed for some distinction in room use.

A large portion of the estates valued by the subscribers of the Orphans Court between 1785 and 1800 described a kitchen, either separate from the main dwelling or attached. The house of Benjamin Ellsbury and John Hyland Price was joined by "a kitchen 16 x 15 feet with a brick chimney, built of logs, a plank floor in the loft, covered with oak shingles about half worn."[19]

Unlike the detached kitchen, the meat house or smokehouse remained an important outbuilding throughout the nineteenth century, and a great number of these structures have survived to the present as handy storage sheds. Smokehouses in general tend toward square dimensions and are often covered by a gable roof. Frequently secured with a locked door, the smokehouse was the place where the family cured and stored its meat supply. In many cases it was one and the same with the meat house, although on larger plantations a second building of similar dimensions was used strictly for meat storage. Such may have been the case at Rose Hill.

In her Rose Hill diary Martha Ogle Forman repeatedly mentioned smoking, curing, washing, and storing meat. On February 10, 1824, she entered:

> I had all the meat hung up to smoke this day, there is 70 hams, 12 pieces of Midlings, 7 pieces of Chip beef, 8 boiling pieces of beef three tongues. I had the bacon washed in strong hot lye, 24 old hams of last year, 7 old hams know not how old but suppose some of them is 8 or 9 years old, two old shoulders of last year.[20]

Several years later, in April 1832, she spoke of having "packed away all the hams in salt to keep the fly from them in a hogshead in the meat house, 47 hams."[21] Another day, on January 15, 1838, she had "sausages hung up in the blacksmith's shop to smoke."[22] As these entries indicate, even on large plantations, meat was smoked or stored in a variety of structures, some erected specifically for the purpose and others not. Provisions for the control of a fire and the direct channeling of smoke were not normally made, except in a few isolated instances.

In the Rawlings smokehouse (CE-1222), built of fieldstone around 1860, a small hearth was fashioned in the northwest corner of the first floor. The meat was placed on the second floor, where the smoke would collect after traveling through the corner flue. A less elaborate example is found in the Griffith-Smith smokehouse (CE-543), where a hole was punched through the flue about six feet above the hearth so the smoke would exit into the room and cure the meat. A more common type of smokehouse is that found at the Seamon farm (CE-13), which has four log walls supporting a simple gable roof with a door in the east

CE-20, Swan Harbor, icehouse on the left, summer kitchen in the center, and meat house to the right (1979)

wall. The interior is appropriately blackened from years of curing meat.

The storage of milk products is not as well documented in local records as the storage of meat. Martha Forman occasionally mentions milk in her diary, mostly when they milked the cows. A few times, during unexpected cold snaps, she relates, "It has snowed all day, and is upon an average 4 inches. Our milk has froze in the safe, whilst the trees are all in bud, and the garden blooming with flowers."[23]

The milk safe or dairy, a single-story structure of frame, brick, or stone construction, usually stood in the yard around the house. Examples from the Orphans Court descriptions range in size from 4 feet 4 inches square to 12 feet square. The square, weatherboard-covered frame dairy on the Octorara farm is representative of many, including the slatted ventilators on each side and plastered interior. Milk was also stored in bilevel springhouses or subterranean vaults or perhaps an icehouse.

Icehouses have not survived in large numbers either. The building form used to house ice is immediately recognizable from a distance because of its peculiar appearance. In many cases the roof is all that is visible aboveground. The roof of the Swan Harbor farm icehouse is so close to the ground that it appears to have blown off an adjacent struc-

CE-27, Rose Hill dairy (1995)

CE-41, Octorara dairy (1980)

(left) CE-1191, Lloyd Balderston farm icehouse (1980)

(below) CE-28, Grove farm icehouse

ture. The roof covers a pit that extends ten to fifteen feet into the ground. A more unusual icehouse stands on the Grove farm. The stone-lined shaft is capped with a dentilled brick cornice and a conical slate roof.

Down Grove Neck Road Martha Forman recorded in her diary the winter chore of filling the icehouse on February 2, 1830: "finished filling the icehouse, it took 50 cart loads."[24] With the approach of warmer weather Mrs. Forman had the icehouse filled with snow. A late snow during the morning of April 15 caused her to comment, "Filled our Ice house with snow, began in the morning early to roll the snow in large balls, which prevented it from melting so fast. The sun broke out quite warm and altho the snow was quite deep there was no snow to be seen at night, except what had been rolled in large bodies."[25]

Martha Forman also recorded the frequent use of their gig or carriage, but specific reference to a carriage house does not appear in her diary. Carriage houses were not frequently found on rural farms, and their scarcity probably corresponds to the relatively few farmers who owned car-

riages. Those who did often stored them in a wagon house or addition to another outbuilding. In the case of Peter Bouchell's estate, a rather impermanent "gig house" was recorded by the subscribers of the Orphans Court in March 1832: "improvements belonging to this dwelling consists of an old log corn house covered with pine boards much decayed as also an apology for stable and gig house attached to corn house, built of old pine boards and thatched with corn tops."[26] A more substantial carriage house was erected on the Swan Harbor farm in 1864.[27] This two-story frame structure, combining a carriage house and stable, is distinguished by a pair of arched double doors and a cupola with a tapered spire (see page 265). The second floor is presently used for hay storage, but family tradition reports it earlier served as a schoolhouse. Small window openings above the double doors in the south gable end, although now blocked, support this tradition.

While the Swan Harbor carriage house incorporated three different activities in the same building, the Rawlings farm carriage house (CE-1222), erected around the same time in fieldstone and brick, was designed to provide space for carriages, a workshop, a springhouse, a wash house, and a storage area. The combination of so many functions in a single building had no particular precedent in the eighteenth or early nineteenth centuries. Its conception was part of the revolutionary thinking of the mid-nineteenth century, when architects and agricultural essayists presented novel ideas for improving rural life. Instead of maintaining three to four separate structures, the Rawlings family built a single, compactly designed masonry building to house various farm operations. By taking advantage of a sloping site, the building functioned on three levels, with the carriage house, wash house, and springhouse at grade and the workshop above the wash house and springhouse. A chimney in the west side of the building supplied a flue for the wash house hearth and a stove flue for the shop. A short ladder stair in the shop leads to the storage space above the carriage house bays. The building was trimmed with decorative bargeboards typical of the Civil War era.

Aside from the domestic outbuildings, an eighteenth and nineteenth century farm complex included a vegetable garden like the one described on Benjamin Ellsbury's estate: "a garden ninety feet by eighty feet done with rough oak pales newe and in good repair."[28] Almost every farmstead possessed some sort of fruit or nut trees—peach, apple, cherry, damson plum, or English walnut. Residents of eighteenth and nineteenth century Cecil County relied heavily on the produce grown in their own gardens and orchards. In the nineteenth century Martha Ogle Forman filled her diary with countless references to the bounty of her garden and her reliance on it as a source of food.

Despite a vagueness about the size of the orchard or the number of tilled fields, Orphans Court descriptions provide the best impression of the Cecil farm landscape at the close of the eighteenth century. The description of James Williamson's estate is representative of many:

> a small garden pailed in very bad repair, about 80 young apple trees and ten or twelve old ones and about one hundred peach trees, the plantation is divided into three fields and the fencing in tolerable repair, said guardian is permitted to cut oldest and most decayed timber to repair the fencing and for firewood....[29]

Many Cecil County plantations, large or small, depended on slave labor. General Forman had approximately fifty slaves at Rose Hill, and these individuals figured almost daily in Mrs. Forman's diary as she recorded the work she attempted. The Rose Hill slaves were spread over the 800 acres in various accommodations. Mrs. Forman documented the construction of new quarters at Rose Hill on December 1, 1830: "The General paid Thomas Hogan 30 dollars for sawing the logs for the people's new homes...."[30]

Documentary evidence, such as Martha Forman's diary, indicates that slaves occupied the kitchens, cellars, and attics of the main plantation dwelling as well as houses and cabins erected specifically for them. Early examples of slave quarters have not survived in Cecil County, largely due to the impermanent construction practices used to build them. Log or frame structures constructed close to the ground with dirt floors, few if any windows, and chimneys made of wood and mud did not last long beyond the lives of their occupants. This fact is supported by entries in the Orphans Court evaluations, which speak of the ruinously poor condition of many slave houses. Listed on the Etherington property in 1791 was "one negro quarter hew'd poplar logs eighteen and a half by sixteen in very bad repair."[31] The slave house at

(left) CE-1222, Rawlings combined carriage house/workshop/springhouse/storage shed (1980)

(below) Swan Harbor carriage house/stable/schoolhouse (1979)

(opposite above) CE-797, Longview Farm log slave quarter (historic photograph)

(opposite below) Swan Harbor "quarter" or tenant house (1979)

Cherry Grove, the land of orphan Thomas Ward Veazey, was described as "one quarter for negroes to live in 20 by 18 feet poplar logs and covered with oak shingles in bad repair."[32] A late nineteenth century image of Longview Farm (CE-797) captured a slave quarter standing next to a number of probable tenant houses. The log structure matches the Orphans Court descriptions, being approximately square with a single door opening on one side and two small window openings on the gable end wall; the upper window lights a loft. The heavy tilt of the quarter to one side demonstrates clearly why these buildings have virtually disappeared from the county landscape.

Many quarters intended for fieldhands were erected some distance from the main dwelling, often along a farm lane that led to the fields. Such is the placement of the frame "quarter" on Swan Harbor Farm. This two-story frame dwelling with shed kitchen dates from the third quarter of the nineteenth century, making it doubtful it was actually erected for slaves. In all likelihood, the house was used by a black family still resident on the farm following emancipation. The one-room plan of the main block contains a winder stair in the southeast corner.

Tenant farms have remained an important aspect of the county farming system to this day. Eighteenth century Orphans Court records document numerous examples of "tenements" on county farms. Joshua George's estate valuation alone contained at least three tenant houses:

> on one small tenement…one round log dwelling house, nineteen feet long sixteen feet covered with oak shingles in bad repair, on another tenament are one round log dwelling house, twenty-nine feet long by eighteen feet, two rooms on the lower floor, covered with oak shingles…on another tenament one round log dwelling house twenty-four feet long by twenty feet covered with oak shingles…one hew'd log dwelling house twenty-two feet six inches covered with oak shingles…[33]

Nineteenth century examples of tenant houses abound throughout the county and range in size from the relatively common two-story, one- or two-room houses to more substantial two-story center hall dwellings. The McLane-Knight tenant house (CE-965), built around 1850-70, is a two-story, side hall/parlor frame dwelling that was once a tenant farm belonging to neighboring Bohemia. William Knight, the owner of Bohemia through the late nineteenth century, rented ten other farms around Cecilton and Earleville to tenant farmers. William Wilson, a Kent County, Delaware, farmer, built three brick tenant houses along what is now called Edgar Price Road. The Wilson house (CE-985), built around 1850-60, was constructed as a tenant farmhouse, although the size and detail do not coincide with the popular image of a tenant dwelling. Two other houses of similar form and date stand along the same road in Delaware.

Farming practices rarely remain constant for long, and yesterday's vital farm buildings often are replaced by more efficient, lower maintenance structures. Just as eighteenth century barns, granaries, and corn houses were upgraded and replaced a century or so after their construction, mid-nineteenth century structures are now reaching levels of deterioration and impracticality that instigate replacement or extensive renovation. Because of the constant change inherent in such utilitarian structures, historic farm buildings must be recorded and studied before they disappear or are altered beyond recognition.

Notes

Chapter 1

[1] Harry F. Covington, "The Discoveries of Maryland, or Verazzano's Visit to the Eastern Shore," *Maryland Historical Magazine* 10 (1915): 202-209.

[2] J. Thomas Scharf, *History of Maryland*, vol. 1 (reprint of 1879 ed.; Hatboro, Pa.: Tradition Press, 1967), p. 12.

[3] George Alsop, "Character of the Province of Maryland" (1662) in *Narratives of Early Maryland, 1633-84*, ed. Clayton C. Hall (New York: Barnes and Noble, 1959), p. 365.

[4] C. Vance Hayne, Jr., "Fluted Projectile Points: Their Age and Dispersion," *Science* 145 (1964), pp. 1408-13; and Lois Brown, "Fluted Projectile Points in Maryland," paper distributed by the Council for Maryland Archeology (1979).

[5] William Gardner, "The Flint Run Paleo-Indian Complex: A Preliminary Report, 1971-73 Seasons," *The Catholic University of America Archeology Laboratory Occasional Publication*, No. 1 (1974); and William Gardner, "The Flint Run Paleo-indians Complex and Its Implications for Eastern North American Prehistory" in *Amerinds and Their Paleo-Environments in Northeastern North America*, ed. W. S. Newman and B. Salwen (New York: Annals of the New York Academy of Science, 1966).

[6] *Ibid.*

[7] Robert Humphrey and M. E. Chambers, "Ancient Washington: American Indian Cultures of the Potomac Valley," *G.W. Washington Studies* 6 (1977), p. 11.

[8] H. G. Ayers, "The Archeology of the Susquehanna Tradition in the Potomac Valley" (Ph.D. dissertation, The Catholic University of America, 1972).

[9] Reproduced in Scharf, between pp. 6-7.

[10] Col. Henry Norwood, "A Voyage to Virginia" in *Tracts and Other Papers Relating to the Colonies in North America*, vol. 3, ed. Peter Force (Washington: n. p., n.d.), pp. 143-70.

[11] Henry Spelman, "Relation of Virginia" (1613) in *The Travels and Works of Captain John Smith*, ed. Edward Arber (New York: Franklin, Burt, 1965), p. cvi.

[12] Harold Driver and William Massey, "Comparative Studies of North American Indians," *Transactions of the American Philosophical Society*, New Series, Part 2, 1957, pp. 299-300; and Barbara Graymont, *The Iroquois in the American Revolution* (Syracuse, N.Y.: Syracuse University Press, 1972), p. 9.

[13] Daniel Brinton, *The American Race: A Linguistic Classification and Ethnographic Description of the Native Tribes of North and South America* (New York, 1891), pp. 76-77.

[14] Robert Beverley, *The History and Present State of Virginia* (London: 1705), pp. 174-76.

[15] Christian Feest, "Nanticoke and Neighboring Tribes," in *Handbook of North American Indians*, ed. Bruce Trigger (Washington: Smithsonian Institution, 1978), p. 244; and Peter Thomas, "Contractive Subsistence Strategies and Land Use Factors for Understanding Indian-White Relations in New England," *Ethnohistory* 23 (1976), pp. 12-13.

[16] Certificate of Survey, "High Park," Patents, Liber C, No. 3, folio 378, Maryland State Archives, Annapolis.

[17] Proprietary Papers, 1703-69, No. 2, Maryland State Archives.

[18] G. E. Gifford, Jr., *Cecil County, Maryland, 1608-1850* (Cecil Co.: Calvert School, 1974), p. 13.

[19] "A Good Speed to Virginia" in W. F. Craven, "Indian Policy in Early Virginia," *William and Mary Quarterly* 3:1 (1944), p. 65.

Chapter 2

[1] L. D. Scisco, "The Discovery of the Chesapeake, 1525-73," *Maryland Historical Magazine* 40 (1945), p. 277.

[2] *Ibid.*, pp. 281-82.

[3] John Smith, *History of Virginia*, quoted in J. Thomas Scharf, *History of Maryland*, vol. 1 (reprint of 1879 ed.; Hatboro, Pa.: Tradition Press, 1967), p. 3.

[4] *Ibid.*, pp. 6 and 10.

[5] *Ibid.*, p. 12.

[6] *Ibid.*, pp. 12-13.

[7] *Ibid.*, p. 10.

[8] G. E. Gifford, Jr., *Cecil County, Maryland, 1608-1850 as Seen by Some Visitors and Several Essays on Local History* (Rising Sun, Md.: Calvert School, 1974), p. 12.

[9] *Pennsylvania Archives*, 2nd series, vol. XVI, pp. 522-25, 749.

[10] *Ibid.*; and George Johnston, *History of Cecil County, Maryland* (reprint of

[10] 1881 ed.; Baltimore: Regional Publishing Co., 1972), p. 48.

[11] *Pennsylvania Archives.*

[12] Scharf, p. 10.

[13] *Ibid.* p. 11.

[14] Adriaen Van der Donck, "A Description of New Netherlands," *New York Historical Society, Collections*, 2, 1 (1841), p. 210.

[15] Thomas Fuller, *The History of the Worthies of England* (London, 1662), p. 362.

[16] Gifford, pp. 11-13.

[17] Clayton C. Hall, ed., *Narratives of Early Maryland, 1633-84* (New York: Barnes and Noble, 1959), p. 154.

[18] William Hand Browne, ed., *Archives of Maryland: Proceedings of the Council of Maryland, 1667-87/8* (Baltimore: Maryland Historical Society, 1887), pp. 231-32.

[19] Hall, p. 154.

[20] William Hand Browne, ed., *Archives of Maryland: Proceedings of the Council of Maryland, 1636-67* (Baltimore: Maryland Historical Society, 1885), p. 134.

[21] *Archives of Maryland*, I, p. 407.

[22] *Archives: Council 1636-67*, p. 277.

[23] Samuel Eliot Morison, *The Oxford History of the American People* (New York: Oxford University Press, 1965), p. 52.

[24] Gifford, pp. 15-17.

[25] Hall, pp. 63-112.

[26] Quoted in Daniel Boorstin, *Hidden History* (New York: Harper and Row, 1987), p. xv.

[27] Johnston, p. 27.

[28] Augustine Herman, "Journal of the Dutch Embassy to Maryland," in Hall, pp. 314-15.

[29] *Ibid.*, p. 316.

[30] Perhaps this is an appropriate spot to mention the pronunciation of the name "Cecil." The Elizabethan pronunciation, current at the time of the county's founding, was "sissil." This pronunciation is still used in England, and long-time residents of southern Cecil County use it to refer to the county. The pronunciation "sessil" is today preferred in England and is used in addressing an individual named Cecil. "Seesil," used by most people to pronounce the name of the county, appears to be a nineteenth century pronunciation with origins in Webster's dictionary.

[31] *Archives: Council 1636-67*, pp. 412-16.

[32] *Ibid.*, pp. 420-21.

[33] In 1706, with the founding of Kent County, the southern border of Cecil became the Sassafras River. Johnston, pp. 246-47.

[34] Gifford, pp. 25-40.

[35] The impermanent nature of early buildings in Maryland is the reason that virtually no seventeenth century buildings survive in the state. In rare instances seventeenth century features are found at the core of a later house. Third Haven Friends Meetinghouse in Easton is the only seventeenth century building in Maryland to retain its early form.

[36] *Ibid.*, pp. 41-42.

[37] Johnston, pp. 111-12.

[38] *The Calvert Papers* 1 (Baltimore: Maryland Historical Society, 1889), p. 323.

[39] "Letter of Governor Leonard Calvert to Lord Baltimore, 1638" in Hall, p. 155.

[40] "Reports of Conferences Between Lord Baltimore and William Penn, and Their Agents, 1682, 1683, 1684" in Hall, pp. 414-44.

[41] *Ibid.*, p. 418.

[42] "Report of a conference between Coll Talbot and William Penn on various matters connected with his Government of Pensilvania and Coll Talbot's interference therein" in Hall, pp. 437-44.

[43] Gifford, p. 159.

Chapter 3

[1] "A Complete List of the Number of Christian Men, Women and Children, and also of Negro Slaves" in J. Thomas Scharf, *History of Maryland from the Earliest Period to the Present Day*, vol. 1 (1879; reprint ed., Hatsboro, Pa.: Tradition Press, 1969), p. 377.

[2] Quoted in Peter Wood, *Black Majority: Negroes in Colonial South Carolina* (New York: W.W. Norton, 1974), pp. 106-107.

[3] Joseph C. Cann, *History of St. Francis Xavier Church and Bohemia Plantation Now Known as Old Bohemia* (Warwick, Md.: Old Bohemia Historical Society, 1976).

[4] H. K. Carroll, *The Religious Forces of the United States* (New York: The Christian Literature Co., 1893), pp. 66-83.

[5] Quoted in G. E. Gifford, Jr., *Cecil County, Maryland, 1608-1850, as Seen by Some Visitors and Several Essays on Local History* (Rising Sun, Md.: Calvert School, 1974), pp. 43-46.

[6] John W. Christie, "Presbyterianism in Delaware," in *Delaware—A History of the First State*, ed. H. Clay Reed (New York: Lewis Historical Publishing Co., 1947), II, pp. 646-47.

[7] *Ibid.*

[8] Johnston, pp. 278-79.

[9] Morris Radoff, *The County Courthouses and Records of Maryland*, Publication No. 12 (Annapolis: Hall of Records Commission, State of Maryland, 1960), p. 56.

[10] Isaac Weld, *Travels through the States of America* (1795) in Gifford, pp. 114-15.

[11] *Ibid.*, p. 115.

[12] Johnston, p. 154.

[13] William Black in Gifford, p. 54.

[14] Johnston, p. 267.

[15] A correspondent of the Pennsylvania *Chronicle* quoted in Scharf, p. 415.

[16] Joseph Robert, *The Story of Tobacco in America* (Chapel Hill, N.C.: The Uni-

versity of North Carolina Press, 1967), p. 36.

[17] Daniel Dulany quoted in Arthur Middleton, *Tobacco Coast* (Newport News, Va.: Mariner's Museum, 1953), pp. 122-23.

[18] Gifford, pp. 67-71.

[19] Johnston, p. 130.

[20] *Ibid.*, pp. 186, 225, and 231.

[21] *Ibid.*

[22] *Ibid.*

[23] Clayton C. Hall, ed., *Archives of Maryland: Proceedings and Acts of the General Assembly of Maryland, 1717-20*, vol. XXXIII, (Baltimore: Maryland Historical Society, 1913), pp. 467-69.

[24] Edward C. Papenfuse et al., eds., *Maryland: A New Guide to the Old Line State* (Baltimore: Johns Hopkins University Press, 1976), p. 31.

[25] Quoted in Gifford, p. 55.

[26] *Ibid.*, p. 69.

[27] Michael Warren Robbins, "The Principio Company: Iron-making in Colonial Maryland, 1720-81," Ph.D. dissertation, George Washington University, 1972. The author of this paper examined the papers of the Principio Company.

[28] U.S. Bureau of the Census, *Historical Statistics of the United States, 1789-1945* (Washington: GPO, 1949).

[29] Cecil County Orphans Court Records, June 15, 1789, Orphans Court Record, Cecil County Courthouse, p. 45.

[30] *Ibid.*, 11 October 1791, pp. 122-23.

[31] Frederick B. Tolles, *Meeting House and Counting House: The Quaker Merchants of Colonial Philadelphia, 1682-1763* (Chapel Hill, N.C.: University of North Carolina Press for the Institute of Early American History and Culture, 1948), p. 123.

Chapter 4

[1] Evelyn Acomb, ed., *The Revolutionary Journal of Baron Ludwig von Clausen* (Chapel Hill: University of North Carolina Press, 1958).

[2] W. M. Marine, *British Invasion of Maryland, 1812-15* (reprint of 1913 ed.; Hatboro, Pa.: Tradition Press, 1965), p. 47.

[3] *Ibid.*

[4] D. M. McCall, M. D. Farrell, and L. E. Alexander, *An Early History of Charlestown, Maryland* (Charlestown, Md.: Colonial Charlestown, Inc., 1983), p. 19.

[5] Edward C. Papenfuse, Gregory A. Stiverson, Susan A. Collins, and Lois Green Carr, eds., *Maryland: A New Guide to the Old Line State* (Baltimore: Johns Hopkins University Press, 1976), p. 6.

[6] Quoted in G. E. Gifford, Jr., *Cecil County, Maryland, 1608-1850, as Seen by Some Visitors and Several Essays on Local History* (Rising Sun, Md.: Calvert School, 1974), p. 106.

[7] Joseph Scott, *A Geographical Description of the States of Maryland and Delaware* (Philadelphia: Kimber and Conrad, 1807), p. 116.

[8] *Ibid.*

[9] Nancy C. Sawin and Esther R. Perkins, *Backroading through Cecil County, Maryland* (Hockessin, Del.: The Holly Press, 1977), pp. 21-22.

[10] Quoted in U.S. Department of Transportation, *A Nation in Motion: Historic American Transportation Sites* (Washington, D.C.: GPO, 1976), p. 16.

[11] Papenfuse, et al., p. 7.

[12] Round Island Lumber Company Account Books, 1835, p. 38, Maryland State Archives; from the research of Paul Touart. See a further discussion of the use of raft lumber in construction in Paul Touart's chapter on house construction in this volume.

[13] Cecil *Democrat*, September 8, 1848.

[14] Scott, p. 113.

[15] Edward C. Carter II, John C. Van Horne, and Charles E. Brownell, eds., *Latrobe's View of America, 1795-1820* (New Haven: Yale University Press, 1985), pp. 260-61.

[16] Information about the history of the C & D Canal in the text and in the captions of accompanying pictures comes in part from Ralph D. Gray, *The National Waterway: A History of the Chesapeake and Delaware Canal, 1769-1985*, 2nd ed. (Urbana: University of Illinois Press, 1989).

[17] Johnston, p. 403.

[18] Partridge Papers, Manuscript Collection, Maryland Historical Society, Baltimore, Maryland.

[19] Thomas Johnson to George Washington, November 10, 1791, in *Letters from His Excellency George Washington to Arthur Young, Esq. and Sir John Sinclair Containing an Account of his Husbandry, with his Opinion on Various Questions in Agriculture and Many Particulars in the Rural Economy of the United States* (Alexandria, Va.: Cotton and Steward, 1803), pp. 32-39.

[20] John Beale Bordley, *A Summary View of the Courses of Crops in the Husbandry of England and Maryland* (Philadelphia: Charles Cist, 1784), p. 14.

[21] Olive Gambrill, "John Beale Bordley and the Early Years of the Philadelphia Agricultural Society," *Pennsylvania Magazine of History and Biography*, LXVI (1942), pp. 410-39.

[22] John A. Binns, *A Treatise on Practical Farming* (Fredericktown, Md., printed by John B. Colvin, editor of the *Republican Advocate*, 1803), pp. 16-17.

[23] *Ibid.*, p. 44.

[24] W. Emerson Wilson, ed., *Plantation Life at Rose Hill: The Diaries of Martha Ogle Forman, 1814-45* (Wilm-

ington: Historical Society of Delaware, 1976), pp. 105 and 107.

[25] *The American Farmer*, vol. I, no. 1, 1819.

[26] Wilson, *Martha Ogle Forman*, p. 151.

[27] W. Emerson Wilson, *Diaries of Phoebe George Bradford, 1832-39* (Wilmington: Historical Society of Delaware, 1976), p. 49.

[28] W. Emerson Wilson, ed., *Mount Harmon Diaries of Sidney George Fisher, 1837-50* (Wilmington: The Historical Society of Delaware, 1976), p. 18.

[29] *Ibid.*, p. 20.

[30] *Ibid.*, p. 21.

[31] *Ibid.*, pp. 42-43.

[32] Sidney George Fisher, *A Philadelphia Perspective: The Diary of Sidney George Fisher* (Philadelphia: Historical Society of Pennsylvania, 1967), p. 11.

[33] Avery Odelle Craven, *Soil Exhaustion as a Factor in the Agricultural History of Virginia and Maryland, 1606-1860* (Gloucester, Mass.: Peter Smith, 1965). The discussion of agricultural societies and experimentation with fertilizers in the text owes something to this work.

[34] See chapter 1 of Andrew Jackson Downing, *The Architecture of Country Houses* (New York: D. Appleton and Co., 1850).

[35] U.S. Census Service, *Seventh Census, 1850: Population* (Washington: GPO, 1853), pp. 220-21.

[36] *Ibid.*

Crossing the Creek in Early Cecil

[a] Manuscript 231, 1794, Cecil County Papers, Box 1 of 8, Maryland Historical Society, Baltimore.

[b] *Ibid.*

[c] Journal of Thomas Burnside, 1836-37, copy of historic document in the collection of Colonial Charlestown, Inc., Charlestown, Md.

Chapter 5

[1] *Official Records of the War of the Rebellion*, series I, vol. 37, part I (Washington, D.C.: GPO, 1887), pp. 225-30.

[2] M. P. Andrews, *Tercentenary History of Maryland* (Chicago: S. J. Clarke Publishing Co., 1925), pp. 382-85.

[3] *Ibid.*, p. 482; and J. Thomas Scharf, *History of Western Maryland*, vol. 1 (Philadelphia: Louis H. Everts, 1882), p. 432.

[4] Andrews, p. 482.

[5] Johnston, pp. 476-77; and W. D. Phillips, "History of Public Education in Cecil County, Maryland, Before 1876," M.A. thesis, University of Maryland, 1939.

[6] Robert Brugger, *Maryland: A Middle Temperament, 1634-1980* (Baltimore: Johns Hopkins University Press, 1988), p. 309.

[7] *Annual Report of the State Department of Education, Maryland, for the Year Ending July 31, 1905.*

[8] *Annual Report...Year Ending July 31, 1898.*

[9] *Annual Report...Year Ending July 31, 1915.*

[10] U.S. Census Bureau, *Compendium of the Tenth Census* (Washington, D.C.: GPO, 1883), p. 708.

[11] John McGrain, *Grist Mills in Baltimore County, Maryland*, a Baltimore County Heritage Publication (Towson: Baltimore County Public Library, 1980), p. 9.

[12] Joseph T. Singewald, Jr., *Report on the Iron Ore of Maryland with an Account of the Iron Industry*, for the Maryland Geological and Economic Survey (Baltimore: Johns Hopkins Press, 1911), pp. 135-36.

[13] Maryland Geological Survey, *Cecil County* (Baltimore: Johns Hopkins Press, 1902), pp. 196-203.

[14] *Ibid.*, pp. 305-308.

[15] *Ibid.*, pp. 222-23.

[16] In 1919 each county commissioner had "charge...of the roads in his...district, being limited in his expenditures to a certain percentage of the entire levy for maintenance of dirt roads." Reported in Celia D. Mitchell, ed., *Cecil Whig: Historical and Industrial Edition, 1841-1919* (reprint of 1919 ed., Elkton: Cecil County Round Table, 1991).

[17] Maryland Geological Survey, *Report on the Highways of Maryland*, vol. 3 (Baltimore: Johns Hopkins Press, 1899), pp. 226-28.

[18] *Ibid.*

[19] Maryland Geological Survey, *Cecil County*, p. 229.

[20] Maryland Geological Survey, *Report on Highways*, pp. 226-28.

[21] *Ibid.*

[22] Arthur Newhall Johnson, "The Present Condition of Maryland Highways," in Maryland Geological Survey, *Report on Highways*, pp. 187-261.

[23] American Association of State Highway Officials, *Historic American Highways* (Washington, D.C.: AASHO, 1953), p. 102.

[24] *Ibid.*, p. 103.

[25] *Fifth, Sixth, Seventh, and Eighth Annual Reports of the State Roads Commission for the Years 1912, 1913, 1914, and 1915 to the General Assembly of Maryland* (Baltimore: Kohn and Pollock, 1916), pp. 101-67.

[26] Maryland Geological Survey, *Cecil County*, pp. 228-29.

[27] *Maryland Business Directory* (1880), p. 129.

[28] Mark Walston, "Mail Order Houses," *Cobblestone* 9, 8 (1988): pp. 22-23.

Chapter 6

[1] U.S. Bureau of the Census, *1920 Census Abstract* (Washington, D.C.: GPO, 1925).

[2] U.S. Department of Agriculture,

Power to Produce: The Yearbook of Agriculture, 1960 (Washington, D.C.: GPO, 1960), p. 169.

[3] Celia D. Mitchell, ed., *Cecil Whig: Historical and Industrial Edition, 1841-1919* (reprint of 1919 ed.; Elkton: Cecil County Round Table, 1991).

[4] William Lloyd Fox and Richard Walsh, *Maryland: A History, 1632-1974* (Baltimore: Maryland Historical Society, 1974), p. 683.

[5] Sherry Olson, *Baltimore: The Building of an American City* (Baltimore: Johns Hopkins University Press, 1980), pp. 290-91.

[6] Mark Walston, *The Department of the Treasury* (New York: Chelsea House Publishers, 1989), pp. 82-83.

[7] U.S. Bureau of the Census, *1940 Census Abstract: Agriculture* (Washington, D.C.: GPO, 1943).

[8] Robert Brugger, *Maryland: A Middle Temperament, 1634-1980* (Baltimore: Johns Hopkins University Press, 1988), p. 520.

[9] Jacques Kelly, *A Pictorial History of Maryland* (Easton, Md.: Chesapeake Publications, 1984), p. 230.

[10] Samuel Eliot Morison, *The Oxford History of the American People* (New York: Oxford University Press, 1965), pp. 956-57; and Public Roads Administration, *Federal Legislation and Regulations Relating to Highway Construction through July 1947* (Washington, D.C.: GPO, 1947).

[11] Hulbert Footner, *Maryland Main and the Eastern Shore* (New York: D. Appleton-Century, 1942), pp. 249-50.

[12] For a detailed comparison of the vision of Wright and Le Corbusier, see Robert Fishman, *Urban Utopias in the Twentieth Century* (New York: Basic Books, 1977).

[13] Edward C. Papenfuse, Gregory A. Stiverson, Susan A. Collins, and Lois Green Carr, eds., *Maryland: A New Guide to the Old Line State* (Baltimore: Johns Hopkins University Press, 1976), p. 8.

[14] George H. Callcott, *Maryland and America, 1940 to 1980* (Baltimore: Johns Hopkins University Press, 1985), pp. 36-37.

[15] *Maryland in World War II* (Baltimore: War Records Division, Maryland Historical Society, 1951), vol. 2, *Industry and Agriculture*, p. 431.

[16] Ibid.; "The Girls of Elkton," *Harper's* (March 1943), pp. 347-54; and U.S. Bureau of the Census, *1940 Census Abstract: Population*.

[17] "Triumph's Tribulations," *Fortune* (March 1944), pp. 20, 30, 44.

[18] Callcott, pp. 37-38; and *Maryland in World War II* (Baltimore: War Records Division, Maryland Historical Society, 1958), vol. 3 *Home Front Volunteer Services*, pp. 55. The USO came out of a conference between the Office of Community War Services in the Federal Security Agency and the Joint Army-Navy Committee on Welfare and Recreation.

[19] U.S. Department of Labor, *Impact of the War on the Elkton Area, Cecil County, Maryland* (Washington, 1944); "How the War Ran Over Elkton," *Nation's Business* (October 1945), pp. 28-30, 131-32; and Callcott, p. 38.

[20] U.S. Bureau of the Census, *1950 Census Abstract: Population*.

[21] U.S. Bureau of the Census, *1960 Census Abstract: Agriculture*.

[22] Joseph B. Hickey, Jr., "The Thoroughbred: Maryland's Heritage," in *Maryland Our Maryland*, ed. Virginia Geiger (Lanham, Md.: University Press of America, 1987), pp. 253-60.

[23] U.S. Bureau of the *Census, 1970 Census: Population*.

[24] U.S. Bureau of the *Census, 1980 Census Abstract: Agriculture*.

Chapter 7

[1] G. E. Gifford, Jr., *Cecil County, Maryland, 1608-1850, as Seen by Some Visitors and Several Essays on Local History* (Rising Sun, Md.: Calvert School, 1974), p. 26.

[2] *Ibid.*, p. 29.

[3] *Ibid.*, p. 36.

[4] Valuation of the lands of orphans Abraham and Benjamin Miller, 14 October 1796, Cecil County Orphans Court Record Book 1785-97 (Register of Wills, Cecil County Courthouse, Elkton), pp. 421-22.

[5] Thomas Ward Veazey (1774-1842) later served as governor of Maryland, elected in 1836. Alice E. Miller, *Cecil County, Maryland: A Study in Local History* (Port Deposit, Md.: Port Deposit Heritage, Inc., 1949), p. 40.

[6] Valuation of the lands of Thomas Ward Veazey son of Edward, 19 October 1791, Orphans Court Record Book 1785-97, pp. 141-43.

[7] See Paul B. Touart, *Somerset: An Architectural History* (Annapolis: Maryland Historical Trust and Princess Anne: Somerset Historical Trust, 1986).

[8] [William Penn], "Information and Direction to Such Persons as are Inclined to America, more especially those related to the Province of Pennsylvania," [1684 pamphlet], from copy owned by the Historical Society of Pennsylvania and reproduced in the Massachusetts Historical Society's Americana Series #122 (Boston, 1919), appendix 2:23.

[9] Deed from Stephen Rowland to John Swisher Sr., March 1813, Cecil County Land Records JS 9/98.

[10] W. Emerson Wilson, ed., *Plantation Life at Rose Hill: The Diaries of Martha Ogle Forman, 1814-1845* (Wilmington: Historical Society of Delaware, 1976), p. 5.

[11] *Ibid.*, p. 12.

[12] The western front door in the south facade of Hopewell has been converted to a window.

[13] Forman diary, p. 389.

[14] Ibid., p. 390.

[15] Ibid., p. 391.

[16] Cary Carson et al., "Impermanent Architecture in the Southern Colonies," *Winterthur Portfolio* 16:2/3 (Chicago: University of Chicago Press, 1981).

[17] Release from Rebecca Rawlings to Robert M. Rawlings, 19 May 1849, Cecil County Records RCH 1/99.

Chapter 8

[1] The initial construction, or later expansion, of many buildings is documented with a construction date, either inscribed in a prominent place or scrawled on wall, beam, or some obscure location. These buildings with specific dates offer valuable information in the analysis of local building traditions.

[2] Abbott Lowell Cummings, *The Framed Houses of Massachusetts Bay, 1625-1725* (Cambridge, Mass.: Belknap Press of Harvard University Press, 1979).

[3] [William Penn], "Information and Direction to Such Persons as are Inclined to America, more especially those related to the Province of Pennsylvania," [1684 pamphlet], from copy owned by the Historical Society of Pennsylvania and reproduced in the Massachusetts Historical Society's Americana Series #122 (Boston, 1919), appendix 2:23; and Charles M. Andrews, *The Colonial Period of American History*, "The Settlements," vol. 3 (New Haven: 1937), pp. 241ff.

[4] During the 18th century, the office of the Orphans Court in Maryland evaluated the property of young children whose parents had died. Officials of the court, called "subscribers," visited the property for an assessment of the land and its improvements. Their specific descriptions of land and buildings have given historians one of the best sources of information concerning the houses and other buildings that defined the mid- to late 18th century Maryland landscape.

[5] Valuation of Ephraim Logue estate, 11 December 1792, Cecil County Orphans Court Proceedings 1785-97, p. 195.

[6] Valuation of Hyland Price estate, 11 June 1793, Cecil County Orphans Court, p. 215.

[7] Grant from Lord Baltimore to Elihu Hall, 18 February 1744, Cecil County Land Records MB 9/332.

[8] Valuation of William Savin estate, 14 June 1785, Cecil County Orphans Court, p. 2.

[9] Edward A. Chappell, "Acculturation in the Shenandoah Valley: Rhenish Houses of the Mansanutten Settlement," in *Common Places: Readings in Vernacular Architecture*, ed. Dell Upton and John Michael Vlach (Athens, Ga.: University of Georgia Press, 1986), pp. 35-36.

[10] The infill made of sticks, straw, and mud at the Gillespie log house was found during a renovation of the property circa 1979-80.

[11] W. Emerson Wilson, ed., *Plantation Life at Rose Hill: The Diaries of Martha Ogle Forman, 1814-1845* (Wilmington: Historical Society of Delaware, 1976), p. 395.

[12] Ibid., p. 124.

[13] Examples of plank framing techniques appear in early settlements of New England and in Canada in later periods. A considerable number of late 19th century examples have been identified in western Maryland.

[14] Port Deposit, formerly Creswell's Ferry, was laid out in 1812 by surveyor Hugh Beard for Philip Thomas. The name of the village was formally changed by the Maryland legislature in 1813. George Johnston, *History of Cecil County, Maryland, and the Early Settlements around the Head of Chesapeake Bay and on the Delaware River…* (Elkton: published by the author, 1881), p. 394.

[15] *Cecil Democrat*, September 9, 1848, Cecil County Historical Society.

[16] Cecil County Land Records JS 46/194 and RCH 1/651.

[17] Round Island Lumber Company Account Books, 1835, Maryland State Archives, p. 38.

[18] Ibid.

[19] Henry C. Mercer, *Ancient Carpenters' Tools…*, 3rd ed. (Doylestown, Pa.: Bucks County Historical Society, 1960), p. 45.

[20] Forman diary, p. 61.

[21] Augustine Herman, "Journal of the Dutch Embassy to Maryland," in *Narratives of Early Maryland, 1633-84*, ed. Clayton C. Hall (New York: Barnes and Noble, 1959), pp. 314-15.

[22] Johnston, p. 248.

[23] The congregation at Nottingham Presbyterian meetinghouse was established by Scots-Irish immigrants around 1724; this church was where Hempstead's brother-in-law and nephews were buried.

[24] Joshua Hempstead in *Cecil County Maryland 1608-1850 As Seen by Some Visitors and Several Essays on Local History*, ed. George Gifford, Jr. (Calvert, Md.: George E. Gifford Memorial Committee, 1974), p. 70.

[25] Ibid., pp. 68-69.

[26] Cecil County Orphans Court Evaluations, 1785-97, Register of Wills, Cecil County Courthouse, Elkton.

[27] Isaac Weld, Jr., in Gifford, p. 114.

[28] In a few rare instances the logs do extend up through the gable ends and are stabilized both by vertical pins set between the logs and by the roof structure.

[29] The Bethel farmhouse, initially erected in 1785-86, has undergone signifi-cant alteration during the 19th and 20th centuries.

[30] An account invoice from William Cook for "work at the house, stable, and barn propos'd for Elisha England at Bethel" in the years 1785, 1786, and 1787 was transcribed by Paul Touart from an original manuscript in the collection of Edward Plumstead, Calvert, Maryland.

[31] Cook invoice: An excerpt from 1786 specifies "to laying the lower floor of oak, plan'd on one side 5 square and 6 feet @ 10/ for square…£2.16.6; to raising the partition below stairs, plan'd on both sides 4 squr & 41 feet @ 12/ for square…£2.13."

[32] Cook invoice.

[33] Valuation of the estate of Elizabeth, John W., Susannah, and Bartholomew Etherington, children of John Etherington, 11 October 1791, Cecil County Orphans Court, pp. 122-23.

[34] Valuation of the estate of Mary Price, 11 March 1791, Cecil County Orphans Court, p. 100.

[35] John Smith in Gifford, p. 4.

[36] Joshua Hempstead in Gifford, p. 71.

[37] Benjamin Mifflin in Gifford, pp. 83-4.

[38] The fall line marks the transition from the floodplain around the Chesapeake to the piedmont above. It is characterized by waterfalls in the rivers that run south from the piedmont toward the bay.

[39] Forman diary, p. 381.

[40] Ibid.

[41] Ibid., p. 382.

[42] Ibid., p. 383.

[43] Ibid., p. 384.

[44] Ibid.

[45] Ibid., p. 385.

[46] Ibid. July 29: "They are putting on the joice on the second floor."

[47] Ibid., p. 386.

[48] W. Emerson Wilson, ed., *Mount Harmon Diaries of Sidney George Fisher, 1837-50* (Wilmington: Historical Society of Delaware, 1976), p. 38.

[49] Ibid., p. 38.

[50] Forman diary, p. 388.

[51] Valuation of the estate of Andrew Malone, June 1794, Orphans Court of Cecil County, p. 276.

[52] Carl R. Lounsbury, ed., *An Illustrated Glossary of Early Southern Architecture and Landscape* (New York: Oxford University Press, 1994), pp. 285-86.

[53] Valuation of the estate of Thomas and John L. K. Jones of Thomas, 15 April 1795, Cecil County Orphans Court, p. 331.

[54] Fisher diary, p. 230.

Chapter 9

[1] Account invoice from William Cook for "work at the house, stable, and barn propos'd for Elisha England at Bethel" in the years 1785, 1786, and 1787, transcribed by Paul Touart from an original manuscript in the collection of Edward Plumstead, Calvert, Maryland.

[2] G. E. Gifford, Jr., *Cecil County, Maryland, 1608-1850, as Seen by Some Visitors and Several Essays on Local History* (Rising Sun, Md.: Calvert School, 1974), p. 26.

[3] Valuation of the estate of Elizabeth, George, Jonathan, Charles, David, John, Tra., and Jacob Johnson of Jacob, May 1793, Cecil County Orphans Court Record Book 1785-97 (Register of Wills, Cecil County Courthouse, Elkton), p. 217.

[4] Valuation of the Etherington estate, 13 December 1797, Cecil County Orphans Court, p. 192.

[5] Abbott Lowell Cummings, *The Framed Houses of Massachusetts Bay, 1625-1725* (Cambridge, Mass.: Belknap Press of Harvard University Press, 1979), p. 158.

[6] Ibid., p. 162.

[7] [William Penn], "Information and Direction to Such Persons as are Inclined to America, more especially those related to the Province of Pennsylvania," [1684 pamphlet], from copy owned by the Historical Society of Pennsylvania and reproduced in the Massachusetts Historical Society's Americana Series #122 (Boston, 1919), appendix 2:23; and Charles M. Andrews, *The Colonial Period of American History*, "The Settlements," vol. 3 (New Haven: 1937), pp. 241ff.

[8] Cook invoice.

[9] W. Emerson Wilson, ed., *Mount Harmon Diaries of Sidney George Fisher, 1837-50* (Wilmington: Historical Society of Delaware, 1976), p. 16.

[10] W. Emerson Wilson, ed., *Plantation Life at Rose Hill: The Diaries of Martha Ogle Forman, 1814-1845* (Wilmington: Historical Society of Delaware, 1976), p. 5.

[11] Ibid.

[12] George Johnston, *History of Cecil County, Maryland, and the Early Settlements around the Head of Chesapeake Bay and on the Delaware River…* (Elkton: published by the author, 1881), p. 426. The railroad was finished initially in 1831 but was rebuilt in 1833 with the introduction of steam engines.

[13] Forman diary, p. 388.

[14] Ibid., p. 389.

[15] Ibid., p. 393: "They have finished this day, they have been here since the third of June. I am truly rejoiced they have finished and gone.

[16] Ibid., p. 396: "Mr. Armitage left this morning for the City, he has finished painting the new house, he has done it well and entirely to our satisfaction, he is a well behaved man."

[17] Fisher diary, p. 181.

Chapter 10

[1] John Smith in G. E. Gifford, Jr., *Cecil County, Maryland, 1608-1850, as Seen by Some Visitors and Several Essays on Local History* (Rising Sun, Md.: Calvert School, 1974), p. 4.

[2] Cyprian Thorowgood in Gifford, p. 13.

[3] Jasper Danckaerts in Gifford, p. 26.

4 Alexander Hamilton in Gifford, p. 61.

[5] Valuation of the estate of Benjamin Walmsley, c. 1790, Cecil County Orphans Court.

[6] W. Emerson Wilson, ed., *Plantation Life at Rose Hill: The Diaries of Martha Ogle Forman, 1814-45* (Wilmington: Historical Society of Delaware, 1976), 19 June 1820, p. 105: "Sending wheat, oats, rye, flaxseed, tobacco, and beans to Baltimore by Allen's Packet." 24 May 1821, p. 125: "It still continues to rain, a fine season for growing tobacco, we have planted all of ours. A fine rain after we had done planting."

[7] Valuation of the estate of Henry Hollingsworth, 18 March 1806, Orphans Court Record, p. 400.

[8] *Ibid.*, p. 402.

[9] W. Emerson Wilson, ed., *Mount Harmon Diaries of Sidney George Fisher, 1837-50* (Wilmington: Historical Society of Dela-ware, 1976), November 3, 1837, p. 26.

[10] *Ibid.*, p. 43.

[11] *Ibid.*, p. 46: "McCullough came last night, to attend to the completion of the barn. Spent an hour to two with him and Rickards inspecting the work & suggesting one or two slight alterations. The corn cribs are nearly finished, & the whole will be a very convenient building, better I suppose than any in the country, and I think worth the money to the property."

[12] Lewis F. Allen, *Rural Architecture…* (New York: C. M. Saxton, 1863), p. 286.

[13] Orphans Court valuation for Jones, 15 April 1795, p. 331.

[14] Valuation of the Richardson estate, 9 March 1797, Cecil County Orphans Court Record Book, pp. 439-40.

[15] Valuation of the estate of Thomas Biddle, 9 August 1796, Orphans Court Records, p. 401.

[16] Fisher diary, p. 54.

[17] Allen, p. 343-44.

[18] Henry Glassie, "Eighteenth-Century Cultural Process in Delaware Valley Folk Building," in *Winterthur Portfolio*, ed. Ian M. G. Quimby (Charlottesville, Va.: University of Virginia Press, 1972), pp. 50-51. The exact arrangements of buildings from farm to farm in Cecil County do not reveal any common plans that could be described as typical or atypical. This area of agrarian research needs more study.

[19] Valuation of the estate of Benjamin Ellsbury and John Hyland Price, 11 June 1793, Orphans Court Records, p. 215.

[20] Forman diary, p. 174.

[21] *Ibid.*, p. 315.

[22] *Ibid.*, p. 392.

[23] *Ibid.*, p. 100.

[24] *Ibid.*, p. 281.

[25] *Ibid.*, p. 250.

[26] Valuation of the estate of Peter Bouchell, March 1832, Orphans Court Record 1823-33, p. 8.

[27] Cecil County tax assessments for 1864 reveal that a new set of outbuildings had recently been completed on the Swan Harbor farm, listed under the heirs of Philip Thomas.

[28] Valuation of Benjamin Ellsbury's estate, 11 June 1793, Orphans Court Record, p. 215.

[29] Valuation of the estate of James Williamson, 3 March 1794, Orphans Court Record Book, p. 257.

[30] Forman diary, p. 293.

[31] Valuation of the estate of Elizabeth, John W., Susannah, and Bartholomew Etherington, 8 September 1791, Orphans Court Record Book, 1785-97, pp. 122-23.

[32] Valuation of the lands of Thomas Ward Veazey son of Edward, 19 October 1791, Orphans Court Record Book, 1785-97, pp. 141-43.

[33] Valuation of the estate of Joshua George, June 15, 1789, Orphans Court Record, p. 45.

Datestone in the south facade of the Hannah and Mercer Brown house in the 9th district (1995)

Inventory of Historic Sites

A COMPREHENSIVE historic sites survey of Cecil County was conducted by the Maryland Historical Trust from 1966 through 1986. Before this survey program, Cecil architecture was appreciated mainly by countless local residents and a few dedicated historians willing to search out the county's architectural gems. Isolated research and documentary efforts were either funded by the federal government's Historic American Buildings Survey or a few energetic private individuals. Since 1966, however, the Maryland Historical Trust has sponsored, often in conjunction with local governments or local nonprofit groups, a systematic survey of historical, architectural, and archeological sites throughout Maryland. In Cecil County, historic sites surveyors have identified nearly 1,450 sites, recording them with written descriptions, photographs, and, in some instances, documentary research or measured drawings. This comprehensive survey includes all types of historic structures from each region of the county.

The inventory as published in this volume comprises only about half the surveyed sites in Cecil County. The quality of the survey material ranges from minimal to exhaustive, and time, demolition, and alteration have all taken a toll on the recorded structures. The approximately 700 sites published here were selected to provide a comprehensive view of the amazing diversity of the surviving historic structures in the county.

The sites published here are presented in roughly chronological order by election district. These election districts have retained basically the same boundaries since the mid-nineteenth century (the Martenet map on page 86 delineates these) and seemed a logical tool for presenting the large number of sites in the county. Each site is identified by a county survey number as well as a name that reflects the historic ownership or historic name of the property when it is known and a distinguishing feature if it is not. (When documentary research had not been carried out, historic names were often taken from the 1868 Martenet map and the 1877 Lake, Griffing, and Stevenson atlas of the county.) Sites listed in the National Register of Historic Places are marked with "NR" in parentheses after the heading. Forty-three county sites, including eight archeological sites, are currently listed on the National Register, but many more are eligible for this distinction.

Historic sites surveyors who helped compile the Cecil County Historic Sites Inventory include Michael Bourne, Jean Ewing, George Lutz, Paul B. Touart, and Geoffrey Henry. Most of the photographs that appear in the inventory section were taken by these individuals and are part of the files of the Maryland Historical Trust, although a number were taken specifically for this book. Several members of the Cecil Historical Trust helped in this process, photographing sites that had been restored or altered or for which there were no photographs in the files: first district—Jackie Upp and Caroline Coffay; fourth district—Geraldine McKeown. George Hipkins provided a number of historic and recent photographs for sites in the seventh district. For the most part, other historic photographs that appear in the inventory section were copied, often from originals belonging to the owners, as part of the survey process by the surveyor who visited the sites.

Most of the properties listed in this inventory are privately owned. Readers should respect the privacy of these individuals and not use the information in this book to infringe on the property rights of others.

First District

Bohemia or Milligan Hall (NR)
c. 1750-60
Cecilton vicinity

Sited on a gentle rise of land well back from the south shore of Little Bohemia Creek is one of the finest examples of mid-18th century Palladian-inspired design in Maryland. Bohemia, also known as Milligan Hall, was conceived on an ambitious scale in its day, and its exterior and interior finishes have few parallels in the state. The fifty-foot by thirty-six foot, six-room plan main house was originally flanked by subordinate hyphens and wings. A fragment of the west hyphen wall, with a round-arched opening, remains standing.

The river elevation of Bohemia was designed with an impressive projecting pavilion and pediment, and the walls were laid in Flemish bond. True to well-established mid-18th century practice, the Flemish bond pattern was highlighted with glazed headers. Also distinctive to the river facade, and to the mid-18th century, are the segmental arches that span the first floor window openings. By contrast, the south front, or land entrance elevation, was assembled partially in header bond, a distinctive mid-18th century practice used selectively in a few dwellings in Chestertown and Annapolis. The window and door arches on the south front feature expertly crafted jack arches with projecting keystones. Other formal brickwork conventions include a molded water table and corner pilasters that frame the fifty-foot wall. The entrance is incorporated into a projecting pavilion, which is surmounted by a pediment pierced by a round or ox-eye window.

The south entrance opens into a generous stair hall, finished on the highest order for the time with a stylish Chinese-influenced staircase and a lavish display of ceiling and wall plaster decoration. Executed in two graceful flights, the quarter turn staircase was designed with a variety of Chinese trellis panels that support a ramped walnut handrail. The Chinese trellis railing continues around a second floor balcony allowing for an open view of the hall ceiling, which is enriched by undulating Rococo plaster decoration. Decorative plasterwork highlights the space above the stair hall door openings on both floors.

Although an exact date of construction has not surfaced for this impressive house, it was most likely designed and built during the 1750s by George Milligan, labeled a "merchant of Chestertown" in a 1751 transfer of "MacGregory's Delight" from his father-in-law, John Baldwin. The early 1750s date coincides with the printing of several English style books that introduced Chinese motifs for architectural applications. William and John Halfpenny's *Rural Architecture in the Chinese Taste*, to name one, appeared in 1750 and again in 1752. Due to Milligan's merchant activities and apparent desire to emulate current English taste, he appears to have closely followed a patternbook of this sort in building and finishing his impressive plantation residence.

At his death in 1784, George Milligan bequeathed "My Dwelling Plantation, sometimes called Milligan Hall," to his son Robert. Bohemia was later the residence of Louis McLane, who held many important political offices. He served in the Delaware House of Representatives between 1817 and 1827 and was Andrew Jackson's foreign minister to England from 1829 to 1831, Secretary of the Treasury from 1831 to 1833, and Secretary of State in 1833-34. His son Robert Milligan McLane was prominent as well, serving as foreign minister to China, Mexico, and France and as governor of Maryland. During the McLanes' periodic residency on the plantation, Sidney George Fisher of Mount Harmon made infrequent visits. On November 8, 1837, he related,

> Started at 10 oclk to go over to McLanes. The family have been at Bohemia since Sept. 2. Found the ladies at home, & was very graciously rec'd. McLane is in Baltimore, & comes to the place on Saturdays, returning on Monday. It is a handsome place, on the Bohemia, of 1000 acres, & the house is a large, fine old-fashioned mansion.

Throughout his diary Sidney Fisher made occasional comments about the McLanes, whom he greatly admired and counted as close friends. After a visit on November 17, 1849, he wrote these observations:

> At 11 started in the chaise to make a visit at McLanes. Found the family had gone to Baltimore a few days ago to remain a week. McLane is now permanently established at Bohemia. It is I fancy his only resource since he has been obliged to leave the Presidency of the railroad. He might be worse off, however, as it is a good farm of 1000 acres with an excellent house most beautifully situated. Had not been there since the autumn of 1845. Walked about to look at the grounds. The trees he has planted very numerous and well chosen have made a great growth since I saw them. The avenue of Tulips and Lindens is very fine. Some of the evergreens and magnolias are superb. A Norway fir near the hall door is the richest, most massey and beautiful I ever saw…. It is a noble looking old place with entirely the air of a gentlemen's residence. The approach is very

CE-32, Bohemia (1936-37, Frances Benjamin Johnston, Library of Congress)

CE-58, Worsell Manor (1978)

good, the view of the river beautiful and the extent of the ground, the clumps of trees—the masses of wood with occasional glimpses of water and the picturesque old fashioned house produce altogether an admirable effect. It is the handsomest place here.

Worsell Manor
c. 1760–80
Warwick vicinity

The plan of Worsell Manor consists of a wide center stair hall flanked on either side by two rooms, each with corner fireplace. The two-story, five-bay brick house is one of the best-preserved examples of Georgian architecture in Cecil County. The Flemish bond brick-work with random glazed headers was

CE-16, Greenfields (1936, Historic American Buildings Survey)

carefully mortared with grapevine joints. A three-string belt course and modillion block cornice embellish the exterior. The house retains nearly all its original woodwork. Especially unusual are the virtually untouched cellar storage rooms, which still have the original boarded window openings and a latticed door. A two-story brick wing laid in common bond stands at one end.

The house stands on land that was part of "Worsell Manor," a 1,000-acre land grant made in 1683.

Greenfields (NR)
c. 1770
Cecilton vicinity

Greenfields rises impressively from the level plain between Cecil County's two southern rivers, the Bohemia and the Sassafras. This remarkably well-preserved Revolutionary War-era brick dwelling survives as one of the Eastern Shore's best examples of a full Georgian plan expanded with subordinate hyphens and symmetrically balanced outbuildings. Conceived and built on a grand scale, it is a two-and-a-half story, Palladian-inspired dwelling, with pedimented front pavilion and broad hip roof. Although its design shows some influence from nearby Bohemia, erected a few decades earlier, Greenfields was designed with a slightly grander ambition. Raised on a full cellar, the two-story Flemish bond brick exterior is defined by a molded water table, belt course, and original Doric order cornice enriched with mutule blocks. Rare for Cecil County are the imported stone lintels that accent each window opening. Similar to Bohemia is the broad hip roof through which two massive brick stacks rise; here they serve a center hall/double-pile floor plan.

The interior spaces of Greenfields retain a high degree of architectural integrity, having survived with few alterations to the woodwork finishes. The two large front rooms, a parlor on the north and a dining room to the south separated by a grand center stair hall, are the most formal spaces. These rooms were clearly designed and crafted to impress visitors, friends as well as family. Each room is fitted with expensive Georgian woodwork, including fully developed chimney pieces boasting high crossetted overmantels that were styled after patternbook examples. Enriched cornices with dentiled or Wall-of-Troy bed moldings, as well as built-in paneled window shutters, add to the sophistication of each room. Rising in the east end of the wide center hall is the principal staircase, embellished with a turned baluster handrail and bold scroll brackets along the stringer. A second, more private service stair rises in the northeast study. Located next to one of the service hyphens, this tightly fitted corner stair

CE-8, Happy Harbor (1979)

CE-61, Quinn House

was probably used mostly by family servants for quick access to the second floor chambers.

Attached to each side of this large double-pile main house are single-story wings, each with a large cooking fireplace. Designed as an integral part of the original house, these subordinate rooms provided ample space for daily domestic chores associated with a large plantation. Unusual to these wings are wide double-door entrances encased in segmental-arched openings fitted with delicately crafted transom windows. The formal appearance of Greenfields was elevated further with flanking dependent brick outbuildings placed symmetrically on each side of the service wings.

Peregrine Ward II, grandson of Colonel John Ward, is credited with the construction of Greenfields. His ownership spanned the second half of the 18th century from 1759 to 1799. The Ward family retained ownership of Greenfields until the second quarter of the 19th century, when John Lusby acquired the plantation. When Sidney George Fisher visited the place in the fall of 1849 he commented:

> Drove afterwards to pay a visit to Miss Lusbie who lives on the road from Cecilton to Fredericktown. Her father is an eccentric old man, who leads the life of a perfect recluse and cares for nothing but fox hunting, never seeing any one but his own family if he can help it. He has a good estate, a pack of hounds and very good horses, but farms after the old Maryland fashion. His home farm is 800 acres of excellent land in very bad order. The house is the best in the neck and is a very handsome, large, well proportioned building, with numerous well kept offices and out houses, but the grounds totally neglected tho it is surrounded by large trees.

Quinn House
c. 1740-50, 1790s
Warwick vicinity

Situated on the outskirts of the quiet village of Warwick is the 18th century Quinn house with its fine Georgian interiors. Although neither the exact date of construction nor the builder is known, structural evidence indicates a three-stage sequence of construction. The first house was built in the early 18th century. In the mid-18th century a two-story, three-bay, gable-roofed brick structure with hall/parlor plan and gable end chimney was attached to the earlier house. Later in the 18th century, a four-bay brick structure containing the kitchen and dining room was built on the foundations of the original house. (The pedimented entrance on the mid-18th century portion is not original to the house but was acquired from the circa 1750 Lockerman house in East Providence, Rhode Island.) The interior retains most of its original woodwork.

Happy Harbor
c. 1780-1800
Fredericktown vicinity

Several county records attest that mills have stood on this property since the second quarter of the 18th century. A 1735 indenture transferred a parcel of land called "Happy Harbor by Drakes old mill" to Thomas Jones for £22 (ten of silver and gold). Successive owners continued the profitable milling business at this location until the mid-19th century.

A prosperous late 18th century miller undoubtedly built this dwelling. The severely plain, small brick house is two stories tall, two bays wide, and one room deep. Laid in Flemish bond, it was erected as a dwelling for the miller rather than a tenant. The interior corner fireplace paneling, molded and dentiled cornice, and chair rail point to a high level of craftsmanship and an owner of more than usual means. Additions have been made to the east end of the original house.

CE-55, The Rounds (1979)

The Rounds
c. 1780-1800
Warwick vicinity

Architectural details and the design of the interior woodwork suggest a late 18th century date of construction for this house. The L-shaped main block contains a central hall separating the two front rooms, and a third room is located directly behind the dining room on the east. The two-story kitchen wing extends from the east wall of this room. The L shape of the main block with its symmetrical main elevation is a form that was repeated often in early and mid-19th century Cecil County structures.

The property has been owned by various families, but the Rumseys, who owned the land from 1678 to 1807, were probably responsible for the construction of the house.

Strawberry Hill/Vulcan's Rest
c. 1780-1810 with additions
Warwick vicinity

Strawberry Hill is a side passage, two-room deep brick house with Flemish bond facade exhibiting random glazed headers, a molded water table, a four-string belt course, and segmental-arched dormers. This plan was particularly popular in urban areas because of its relatively narrow main facade and deep proportions. In most urban examples, lot shape led to additions extending to the rear. At rural Strawberry Hill, however, the one-and-a-half story, four-bay frame addition built circa 1850 was attached to the west gable end. (A two-story addition was added to the east end late in the 20th century.)

St. Francis Xavier/Old Bohemia Church (NR)
1792, 1825, 1912
Warwick vicinity

St. Francis Xavier Jesuit mission, more commonly called Old Bohemia, is an important site in the history of Roman Catholicism in the United States. Beginning in 1704, the Society of Jesus carried on missionary activities on this Bohemia River site, which was the second Jesuit mission in Maryland. The territorial responsibilities of Old Bohemia included the Eastern Shore of Maryland, Delaware, and southeastern Pennsylvania. To support their activities, the Jesuits acquired approximately 1,200 acres on which they managed a farm, grist- and sawmill, brick kiln, blacksmith shop, still, and loading wharf.

CE-60, St. Francis Xavier Church (1936, Historic American Buildings Survey)

In 1745, in accordance with the Society of Jesus's mandate to provide education, Bohemia Academy was established here. It is known for having educated both Charles Carroll of Carrollton, a signer of the Declaration of Independence from Maryland, and John Carroll, the first American Roman Catholic bishop and founder of Georgetown University. The latter fact, coupled with the Jesuits' role in parochial education elsewhere in Maryland, has created a local misunderstanding that Old Bohemia Academy was the predecessor of Georgetown University.

Today, Old Bohemia consists of a late 18th century brick church, an early 19th century brick rectory connected to the church with a brick hyphen, and a cemetery containing the graves of a number of prominent 18th century Jesuits. A 1912 fire gutted the interior of the church, and it was later remodeled in a manner inconsistent with its earlier appearance.

The Old Bohemia Historical Society, formed in 1953, maintains the property for the Catholic Diocese of Wilmington. Archeological work carried out in 1956 located the remains of Bohemia Academy.

CE-59, Strawberry Hill

St. Francis Xavier rectory

CE-983, Fisher-Wilson house (1979)

CE-50, Cherry Grove (1968)

Fisher-Wilson Brick and Frame House (site)
1790-1870
Warwick vicinity

"Painter's Rest," the tract on which this house stood, has had a long history as a tenant farm. The tract of 563 acres and the early two-story Flemish bond brick house with post-and-hewn log kitchen wing were first owned by Charles Henry Fisher, whose brother, Sidney George Fisher, owned Mount Harmon. By the mid-19th century William Wilson from Delaware had acquired this property as part of vast farm holdings. Wilson died in August 1879, and Painter's Rest, along with four other farms and a property in Warwick, was sold at auction in 1881. In that year Painter's Rest, described in the *Cecil Democrat* as having 223 acres divided into four fields, was leased to William Bland. The buildings consisted of a brick dwelling with two frame attachments, a brick meat house, a frame granary, and a stable.

These buildings survived until the late 20th century. The house was one of the earliest buildings in this area of the county. The 18th century brick section was a two-story, three-bay dwelling erected around 1790. About ten years later a log wing was added to the east gable end to provide an attached kitchen. In the late 19th century a frame addition was made to the other end of the brick house and the log portion was raised to two stories.

Linden Manor
c. 1790-1800 with additions
Warwick vicinity

The influence of two popular architectural periods can be seen on the exterior of this late 18th century, five-bay brick dwelling laid in Flemish bond. A Greek Revival front porch with fluted Ionic columns covers the three center bays. Later in the 19th century, the roof was replaced and a stylish central cross gable and two dormers were added. The interior, which has a one-room deep center hall plan, still displays fine examples of late 18th century woodwork. A two-story, three-bay brick addition is attached to the east gable end.

Cherry Grove
second half 18th century
Earleville vicinity

Very few houses reveal as much about vernacular building traditions as Cherry Grove, which exhibits three 18th century methods of construction: hewn log, timber frame, and post-and-hewn plank. Unusual building methods and details abound. An interesting account of the house is found in the 1791 Orphans Court description of the estate of Edward Veazey's son:

> one dwelling house fifty two feet long by sixteen feet three inches, of which twenty feet is logs and thirty two feet frame with a frame shed twenty by twelve the whole divided into three rooms

CE-56, Linden Manor (1968)

CE-3, Ben Price's Hotel (1994)

CE-973, Davis house (1979)

and a passage on the lower floor with a fireplace in each room and three rooms on the upper floor and a fireplace in two of them and covered with cedar shingles and is in tolerable good repair with a frame pantry and log kitchen adjoining, the pantry twelve by seventeen feet and the kitchen twenty by seventeen feet, the whole weatherboarded with pine plank and covered with oak shingles in good repair....

An addition was made to one end of the house circa 1975.

Ben Price's Hotel
early 19th century
Fredericktown

This two-story, Federal-style frame house is covered with beaded clapboards. Three bays wide and two deep, it has a steeply pitched gable roof. Six-panel doors open into the center bay front and back. The front door, flanked by two nine-over-six windows, has a transom window with remnants of the original diamond-shaped panes. The second floor openings contain six-over-six sash. The windows and doors are trimmed with ovolo and beaded backband moldings. Inside, the rooms have period trim, including chair rails and mantels.

The original wing on the east end of the building was dismantled early in the 20th century. The present one-and-a-half story wing, added in 1985, is covered in beaded clapboard to match the siding on the old section.

Frisby's Prime Choice
c. 1800-20
Earleville vicinity

This two-and-a-half story, L-shaped Federal house, laid in Flemish bond brick, dominates the farmland south of Earleville. Its main facade is enhanced by gauged brick arches over an elliptical fanlight and a second floor Palladian window; the entire ell is capped with an elaborate molded brick cornice.

Members of a Historic American Buildings Survey team documented extensive work done to this house in the mid-1930s, including recording an elaborate cast-iron front porch that was removed as part of the renovation. A new hipped roof added at this time undoubtedly saved this important example of early 19th century architecture. Further restoration is underway in the mid-1990s.

Davis House
c. 1800-30 with additions
Warwick vicinity

This is one of a small group of post-and-hewn log structures in Cecil County. The single-story, two-bay, one-room section predates the two-story frame addition by five or six decades.

CE-12, Frisby's Prime Choice (1979)

CE-1365, Carroll Short house (1985)

Carroll Short House
before 1818 and later
Cecilton

This large Federal house on West Main Street is two and a half stories tall and five bays wide. It features a handsome center door flanked by pilasters and topped with a three-light transom. The six-over-six sash windows have molded architraves and louvered shutters on the second story and paneled shutters on the first story. A one-story, two-bay wing with Victorian trim probably dates from the mid-19th century, as does the one-story wing to the rear.

Possibly dating from the 18th century and mentioned in a deed of 1818, the original house was probably raised to its present height somewhat later in the 19th century. A two-story addition was added on the north side in 1989.

Locust Thicket
c. 1820-30
Earleville vicinity

Although it does not possess an unusual house form, Locust Thicket has certain distinguishing architectural features that separate it from other houses of its type. Most unusual is the glazed header brick banding on each gable end. While this decorative brick patterning technique surfaces in other parts of the county, it is rare in this area.

Brick House Farm
c. 1820-30
Cecilton vicinity

In August 1821 Hyland B. Pennington, a merchant in Wilmington, purchased parts of three tracts—"King's Aim," "Bateman's Tryall," and "Frisby's Forest." The division of once-expansive tracts in the early 19th century was often undertaken by residents of the nearby urban centers of Wilmington, Philadelphia, and Baltimore. These speculators recognized the agricultural potential in the rich soil of southern Cecil County and the area's proximity to lucrative markets. Pennington assembled a 661-acre farm and built this two-story, three-bay Flemish bond brick house during his first decade of ownership.

Comparatively plain and basic, the house was not built for Pennington, the merchant, but for a tenant family who would manage his property. It does not match the popular conception of a tenant house, but viewed over the long term, construction of such a substantial dwelling was a wise investment. The house has been restored in the late 20th century.

CE-49, Locust Thicket (1968)

CE-11, Brick House Farm (1968)

CE-5, The Hideaway (1980)

Wickwire (site)
c. 1820-30
Earleville vicinity

An expansive view of the Chesapeake Bay spread out before the south elevation of this two-and-a-half story Federal brick house, which stood on Pond Neck until it was razed in 1990. The simple three-bay main block was laid in Flemish bond on the main facade and common bond elsewhere; it was flanked by single-story, three-bay wings. All three sections appeared to date from the same period, as they were trimmed with the same corbeled cornices and had similar interior woodwork. A brick meat house, also with corbeled cornice, stood south of the house, and several 19th century agricultural buildings stood to the east.

Seamon Farm
c. 1820-30
Cecilton vicinity

Located just west of Cecilton on Maryland Route 282 are the remains of an early 19th century telescope house. The term "telescope" has been broadly used to describe a structure of several parts with descending roof heights. Each telescope house developed in its own way, however, and it is not possible to extrapolate a sequence of construction from one to the next.

This particular dwelling began with a two-and-a-half story, side passage/parlor brick block laid in Flemish bond with a heavy corbeled cornice and two segmental-arched dormers. An early 19th century Classical Revival front porch retains half its Tuscan columns and diamond/lozenge pediment decoration. The two other sections that formed the telescope have been demolished, but the roofline formerly descended to a two-story, three-bay log addition with remnants of beaded weatherboard siding. The final section consisted of an even shorter two-story frame addition.

The Hideaway
1st quarter 19th century
Fredericktown

This important Federal frame dwelling stands south of Fredericktown's main street, facing east toward the Sassafras River bridge. The main block has a gable roof and is two-and-a-half stories tall, three bays wide, and two bays deep on a brick foundation. Portions of it are covered with original beaded clapboards, and an unusual double chimney rises from the south end. A narrow two-and-a-half story, gable-roofed wing is attached to

CE-30, Wickwire (1968)

CE-13, Seamon Farm (1979)

287

CE-1350, Wilson-Quinn house (1985)

CE-24, Mount Pleasant (1968)

the northwest corner of the main block.

The house has a side hall/double parlor plan and is notable for its exquisite Federal woodwork. A wide elliptical archway supported on piers with convex sides separates the entrance hall from the stair hall. The entire surface of the archway is reeded, with rope molding at the edges. The fireplace in the rear parlor is flanked by paneled pilasters and has a dentiled cornice with a reeded ledge and rope molding around the hearth opening. The mantel in the front parlor is even more sophisticated, with reeded pilasters, wall of Troy molding, and a frieze composed of a central panel with rope molding in a swag motif flanked by smaller oval panels. The two upstairs mantels are simpler but still impressive.

This house was possibly built on the foundations of an earlier house burned during the raid by the British in 1813.

Wilson-Quinn House
1st quarter 19th century
Warwick

Local tradition ascribes a date of 1825 to this two-and-a-half story, gable-roofed frame house with a chimney at each end. The house is four bays wide with doors in both center bays. A one-story, shed-roofed kitchen wing is located off the west end, and a one-story wing extends from the south facade. There are paired attic windows in each gable end, and the six-over-six sash windows with simple molded architraves are flanked by paneled shutters. In the 20th century the house was converted into two apartments, and the shouldered architrave molding around the kitchen fireplace has been restored.

Mount Pleasant
c. 1820-30
Earleville vicinity

The two-story, three-bay, center hall brick house that stands on a tract of land known as "Mount Pleasant" is similar in date, construction, plan, and stylistic detail to five other houses in the area: Brick House Farm, Grove Farm, Rich Neck Farm, Locust Thicket, and Scotchman's Manor. Laid in Flemish bond, this house differs slightly, with an arched fanlight over the front door and

CE-28, Grove Farm (1978)

CE-778, Ginn house (1979)

CE-29, Rich Neck Farm / Frisby's Delight (1936, Historic American Buildings Survey)

quarter-round, gable-end attic windows. The house underwent extensive preservation work in 1992.

Dr. John Thompson Veazey, who owned nearby Mount Harmon from 1820 to 1828, owned this property later in the 19th century.

Grove Farm
c. 1820–40
Earleville vicinity

The two-story, four-bay, single-pile brick house on Grove Farm, laid in Flemish bond, has distinct similarities to nearby Rich Neck Farm. Frame additions were made to the Federal house in the mid-20th century.
An unusual conical icehouse of fieldstone and brick survives on the property.

The map of this section of the county in the 1877 Cecil County atlas reveals a landlord/tenant relationship for the operation of this farm. At that time Harlan and Hollingsworth owned the property, but W. P. Rowan resided here.

Rich Neck Farm/Frisby's Delight
c. 1820–40
Earleville vicinity

Methods of construction and stylistic features date this two-story, three-bay, center hall brick house to the second quarter of the 19th century. The Flemish and common bond wall construction and corbeled cornices are features found in other houses on Sassafras Neck from this period. A brick kitchen wing similar to that at nearby Brick House Farm once stood at the east gable end; it was replaced by the present frame addition. The house underwent extensive restoration work in the 1980s.

According to 19th century land records, the individuals who owned this property lived outside the county for most of the period; several nearby farms have similar landholding histories.

Ginn House (site)
c. 1820–40
Warwick vicinity

This house was one of very few braced timber frame structures with brick nogging to be found in Cecil County. The bricks filled the spaces between the main framing members and studs, providing a measure of insulation not always found in old frame houses. Brick nogging was a common feature of many English dwellings, in which the bricks were stuccoed or plastered and the main framing members left exposed. In this house, the frame was always covered with an application of sawn weatherboards, some of which could still be seen in the room above the shed kitchen.

This farm is located at the northwest corner of Ginns Crossroads. Before it was razed circa 1980, the house was one of many Ginn family dwellings that once stood on the road leading to the head of the Sassafras River.

CE-19, The Anchorage (1936, Historic American Buildings Survey)

The Anchorage
c. 1800; 1835; and later
Cecilton vicinity

The Anchorage was built in three stages. Commodore Jacob Jones is credited with the 1835 construction of the massive two-and-a-half story, side passage brick structure laid in Flemish bond. The south elevation is dominated by twin chimneys, while the east elevation is distinguished by two segmental-arched dormers and an elliptical fanlight over the entrance. Jones's Federal addition dwarfs the earlier, center section, which was later lengthened by another addition, this time frame, of similar scale. The nine-bay house dominates this area of level fields just north of Cecilton.

A pyramidal icehouse, with roof nearly touching the ground, stands northeast of the house.

Stoney Battery
c. 1830-40
Hack's Point

Stoney Battery Farm is located on Hack's Point along the Bohemia River on what was originally part of the large landholdings of the Veazey family. The present farmhouse is a two-and-a-half story, five-bay stuccoed frame structure with a center hall plan. Of interest are the framing members in the house, all of which are of rough wood still covered with bark.

CE-52, Stoney Battery

CE-27, Rose Hill

Rose Hill (NR)
c. 1780; 1837-38
Earleville vicinity

Situated atop a ridge of land overlooking the Sassafras River, the Rose Hill plantation house is distinguished as much for its unusual architectural qualities as for being the home of General Thomas Marsh Forman (1758-1845) and his wife, Martha Ogle Forman (1785-1864). Mrs. Forman left a detailed diary of her life here between 1814 and 1845, and her writings of the daily activities at Rose Hill offer one of the richest sources of 19th century plantation life on the Eastern Shore of Maryland.

Built in distinct stages, the Rose Hill plantation house dates from several periods during the 18th, 19th, and 20th centuries. The oldest section, a story-and-a-half, gambrel-roofed frame dwelling, was built around 1780 following a center hall, single-pile plan. It survives with portions of stylish Georgian finish, including raised panel woodwork, enriched cornices and chair rails, and crossetted and kneed window surrounds.

In 1837-38, General and Mrs. Forman decided to finance a sizable brick addition, which completely dwarfed the 18th century house. Patterned after urban row houses common in Philadelphia and Wilmington, the two-and-a-half story brick addition, raised on an elevated foundation, combines Federal and Greek Revival architectural features. Martha Forman carefully chronicled the construction of the addition from the spring of 1837 until its completion during the spring of 1838.

On February 21, 1838, Mrs. Forman remarked, "Th[e carpenters] have finished this day, they have been here since the third of June. I am truly rejoiced they have finished and gone." The painting, papering, and furnishing of the addition continued through the balance of the winter and into the spring months. It is clear General and Mrs. Forman lavished great attention on the care of Rose Hill, creating one of the most envied plantations in southern Cecil County at the time. In June 1848, three years after the general's death, the Formans' neighbor, Sidney George Fisher of Mount Harmon, wrote the following in his journal:

> At 5½ in the afternoon drove over to Rose Hill....The avenue of Spanish chestnuts and silver pines along the road thro the estate planted by the old General is the handsomest I ever saw. It is nearly a mile long, the trees 30 feet high and full foliaged, and in full blossom. It shades the road and is worth a long drive to see.
> In ten years it will be magnificent. Found the old lady at home and spent an hour with her. Walked in the charming old garden of which I never weary. It is the full pride of its beauty now, all perfume, and bloom, and song and shade and varied colors. Never saw such a collection of exquisite and rare trees. Half a century of constant attention could alone create such a scene and I question whether there is anything comparable to it in the country. Where else can you see such splendid hedges of hornbeam, of English ivy, of box. Such a variety of evergreens, magnolia grandiflora, English yew, box trees 30 feet high, hemlock, black spruce, fir, silver pine, balm of gilead, and immense arbor vitaes, together with hundreds of rare deciduous trees and the ground covered completely with the dark rich green of the periwinkle in a mat a foot thick.

The Rose Hill house remained essentially as the Formans had known it until the mid-20th century when a gambrel-roofed frame

CE-994, St. Francis Xavier Church farmhouse (1979)

CE-359, Methodist parsonage (1973)

kitchen was attached to the east end and another wing was stretched from the west gable end of the 18th century section. The house is joined on the property by several 19th century outbuildings, including a smokehouse and icehouse.

Methodist Parsonage (site)
c. 1830s
Cecilton

This handsome late Federal dwelling with Greek Revival features had a bracketed cornice and an arched window on the center bay of the second story. An unusual feature was the use of flush siding on the front facade when regular clapboard siding was used on the other three sides. A two-story, gable-roofed wing extended from the rear. The house, razed in 1975, was one of a number of important buildings in Cecilton to be demolished in the late 20th century.

St. Francis Xavier Church Farmhouse
c. 1840
Warwick vicinity

This house was once part of the extensive holdings of the Roman Catholic Church in Cecil County. Father George Villiger, the priest in 1877, was listed on the patron list in the county atlas of that year with 1,100 acres. The only survivor of several structures built to house farm workers, the house is a two-and-a-half story, common bond brick dwelling typical of the period. It retains period woodwork; there is an addition at one end.

Swan Harbor
c. 1760-80; 1840-60
Earleville vicinity

A cursory analysis of the buildings at Swan Harbor suggests the structures date from the first half of the 19th century. The dwelling is a three-bay, side passage structure, two rooms deep with appropriately columned porch, six-over-six sash, and a kitchen ell. The mid-19th century date, however, applies to a major renovation of the house that included the construction of the accompanying outbuildings. The carriage house, summer kitchen, meat house, icehouse, tenant house, and privy form one of the best collections of auxiliary 19th century domestic structures in the county.

What was not new at midcentury was the front block of the dwelling, which had been constructed as a cross passage/three-room plan house in the 18th century. In the sec-

CE-20, Swan Harbor from the west (1979)

Swan Harbor from the east (1979)

CE-15, William G. Etherington house (c. 1915)

ond quarter of the 19th century, the plan of the early house was changed to incorporate a formal unheated hall with quarter-turn stair rising to the third floor. Corresponding mid-19th century woodwork abounds throughout the house; 18th century woodwork that was not replaced was grained.

William G. Etherington House
c. 1850-53
Cecilton vicinity

An early 20th century photograph shows how little this Greek Revival frame house south of Cecilton has changed. The imposing three-story elevation was a popular architectural form introduced in late 18th century Federal buildings and used continually through the mid-19th century Greek Revival period. The main block is typically framed by corner pilasters, which support a plain frieze and molded cornice. The same design is repeated on the five-bay front porch.

William G. Etherington appears responsible for construction of the house around 1850-53, when county tax assessments list a 267-acre farm with frame house and barn valued at $17,500. The property then passed to the Jones family through Etherington's son-in-law Daniel.

Biggs House
c. 1850
Earleville vicinity

Joseph Biggs, who came to the county from New Castle County, Delaware, in 1856, appears to have resided here in 1877. While he also owned an earlier brick house across what is now Route 282, the word "residence" is listed beside his name in the county atlas at this location. The traditional two-and-a-half story, five-bay frame house with center hall plan is here enlivened with a Palladian window on the second story. This feature may be a mid-19th century imitation of the Palladian window across the road at Frisby's Prime Choice. Interior woodwork typical of the period remains in place. A rear wing was removed from the house and replaced with a 20th century frame addition in which an 18th century Federal mantel from Middletown, Delaware, was installed.

Knight House
c. 1850
Earleville vicinity

Two exterior architectural characteristics make this house more unusual than most of the other two-story, five-bay, center hall frame houses in the county: The central second floor arched window with keystone adds variety to the main elevation, and the exposed brick fire walls in the frame gable ends are more characteristic of the lower Eastern Shore. The kitchen wing, though remodeled, also retains most of its mid-19th century quality.

This house was one of approximately a dozen in the vicinity owned by William Knight, a native of Queen Anne's County, in 1877. Also on the property is a mid-19th century granary; the flanking corn cribs are ventilated with panels of louvers rather than slats.

CE-954, Biggs house (1979)

CE-956, Knight house (1979)

CE-985, Wilson tenant house (1979)

McLane-Knight Tenant House
c. 1850
Cecilton vicinity

Severely plain, this house has none of the decoration that often adorned dwellings of the latter half of the 19th century; it likely served as a tenant house. The 1858 and 1877 county maps show it was owned by the two men who owned Bohemia Farm for much of the 19th century: Louis McLane and William Knight. The two-story, three-bay main block, which has a hall/parlor plan, has retained most of its period character. A two-story kitchen ell extends to the rear. Farm buildings on the property included a frame meat house, granary, wagon shed, and cow barns until a tornado in 1993 destroyed several of the structures.

Dr. Perkins House
c. 1850
Warwick vicinity

This two-story, five-bay frame house is exemplary of the many other mid-19th century houses of its type in Cecil County.

The center bay on the front is distinguished by an entrance accented with sidelights and transom on the first floor and a three-part window on the second story. The two-story "flounder" addition on the east gable end is an uncommon form.

Wilson Tenant House
c. 1850
Warwick vicinity

This is one of five Maryland farms William Wilson owned in 1877. A fruit and grain grower from New Castle County, Delaware, he purchased the property in 1840 and probably built the house in the following decade. The two-and-a-half story, five-bay, center hall brick dwelling, laid in common bond, is a typical mid-19th century house form that retains nearly all of its period detailing. The interior is a good example of the period, particularly in its demonstration of the Egyptian influence.

This house is very similar to two other brick houses owned by Wilson in nearby Delaware; the nearest of these is dated 1854. Although each of these structures is very substantial and might have been suitable for Wilson himself, each was built for tenants.

CE-965, McLane-Knight tenant house (1979)

CE-978, Dr. Perkins house (1979)

CE-960, Haynes house and store (1981)

CE-25, Woodlawn (1968)

Haynes House and Store (site)
c. 1850-60
Earleville vicinity

A single-story frame store building was attached to this two-story, five-bay, center hall frame house sometime after its construction in the mid-19th century. The store managers, who appear on historical maps, apparently rented the property from other landholders since the proprietors' names do not surface on 19th century land records for the property. The 1877 atlas shows William Haynes at this site, while George R. Van Sant was cited as the store's proprietor on the 1858 Martenet map.

Woodlawn
c. 1850-60 and earlier
Earleville vicinity

An examination of the exterior wall surfaces makes it obvious that Woodlawn experienced a major rebuilding in the mid-19th century. Remnants of a much earlier house appear in the brickwork on the gable ends, but for the most part the present house dates from the later period. The wide center hall, featuring a heavily turned mahogany balustrade and stair, divides a basic four-room plan. The rectangular brick house is capped with a heavy modillioned cornice and rooftop balustrade. Another midcentury feature is the single-story front porch with Doric columns. The surrounding garden, dating in part from the mid-19th century, is an excellent example of the picturesque ideal sought after in the early Victorian period.

William Price House (site)
c. 1853-60
Warwick vicinity

This elaborate Greek Revival/Italianate house built by William Price was important enough to be illustrated in the Lake, Griffing, and Stevenson atlas of 1877. Price was conscious of current architectural trends, and, while many structures of similar design are found throughout the county, most do not exhibit the amount of detail that was used in this example. It was torn down in the last quarter of the 20th century.

Gibson's Green Farm
1856 with alterations
Cecilton vicinity

This farmhouse, one of three known examples of a three-room plan in southern Cecil County, is an interesting example of how 18th century forms sometimes survived well into the 19th century in a predominantly Anglo-American region. While the roof slope has been changed and the interior remodeled somewhat, these alterations do not lessen the architectural significance of the house, which is a two-and-a-half story, three-bay frame dwelling with two-story

CE-995, William Price house (1979)

CE-964, Gibson's Green Farm (1979)

CE-1353, Mt. Olivet U.M. Church (1985)

kitchen wing. Also on the property are a log meat house, a granary, and other, more recent farm structures. The meat house, itself a rare survivor, exhibits half-dovetailed corner notching, a steeply pitched gable roof, and vertical board sheathing.

Cecil County tax records begin recording a new house on this tract in 1856, when it was valued at $600; the same figure was attached to the new barn on the property.

Warwick Academy
1859
Warwick

Warwick Academy, a one-room brick school laid in common bond with a datestone reading 1859, stands on the western fringe of the town of Warwick. When it was built, Warwick was a thriving crossroads community. After the railroad line was laid through Middletown, Delaware, rather than Warwick, the hamlet began a slow economic decline.

A small black community developed around this building after the Civil War. In 1890 a new school for white children was built on Main Street, and the old brick school was used by the black children. It has since been converted into a residence.

Mt. Olivet U. M. Church
c. 1859
Warwick

This simple church stands at the east end of the village of Warwick on the main road to Middletown. It is three bays long with a three-story bell tower at the center of the south gable end. The tower has a circular window above the double entrance and above this a shingle-covered roof with flared eaves. The third story consists of an open belfry decorated with jig-sawn woodwork.

Mt. Olivet is sometimes known as the "fox hunter's chapel" after a legend that the original funds for its construction were raised by local fox hunters making merry in the town's tavern.

Ward's Knowledge
c. 1830-60
Warwick vicinity

An intricate cast-iron porch with lyre motifs and iron bird and basket porch roof ornaments graces this three-story, side hall/parlor frame house built in the mid-19th century. The tract of land on which the house stands is known as "Ward's Knowledge" and was owned by the Davis family from the late 17th century until 1990. The front block was probably built by John Ward Davis, who was

CE-992, Warwick Academy (1979)

CE-57, Ward's Knowledge

CE-21, Essex Lodge (1994)

CE-1349, Gillespie Hotel (1985)

identified as the owner of the property in the Lake, Griffing, and Stevenson county atlas of 1877. The interior, with its grained woodwork and wallpaper with trompe l'oeil cornice and wainscoting in the front parlor, is largely original.

Essex Lodge
late 18th century; c. 1860
Earleville vicinity

Just north of Earleville on Veazey's Neck is this imposing three-story, five-bay brick house with center hall. Hidden behind large shrubs, the rectangular structure is capped with a low-pitched hip roof with heavy, bracketed cornice. Termed Italianate for its imitation of architectural features of 16th century Italian villas, this architectural form was popular in the mid- to late 19th century. The tall, narrow, segmental-arched openings and heavy molded woodwork are characteristic of the style. Hidden by this massive front block is a two-story Flemish bond brick dwelling that dates from the late 18th or early 19th century. (A photograph of the front of this house appears in chapter 4, "'An Excellent Situation' for Manufacturer and Farmer Alike.")

This house is more than an impressive mid-19th century residence, for it reflects an important development in the agricultural history of Cecil County. By the third quarter of the 19th century, improved soil management and crop rotation had greatly increased grain production in this part of the county, and the large yields enabled the Veazeys, Knights, Cruikshanks, and other families to build houses such as this to reflect their agricultural success.

Gillespie Hotel
c. 1860
Warwick

This three-story, five-bay frame building has a low-pitched hipped roof and paired Italianate brackets below the wide eaves. A chimney rises from each end, and the windows have six-over-six sash on the first two stories and three-over-three on the third story. The house is distinguished by corner pilasters, which rise the full three stories.

Constructed around 1860 as the Gillespie Hotel, this is the largest building in Warwick. In addition to the lobby and dining room, the first floor contained a saloon and the town post office. Behind the hotel was a small half-mile racetrack for trotting horses. The original owner, Samuel Gillespie, also operated a saddlery shop in the adjacent barn. The interior was altered when the hotel was converted to a private residence early in the 20th century.

St. Stephen's Rectory
c. 1860
Earleville vicinity

This building gained a new lease on life when it was raised off its foundations in the winter of 1978-79 and moved to its present location on Freeman's mill pond. The two-

CE-412, St. Stephen's rectory (1979)

CE-988, William T. Beeks house (1979)

story, three-bay, L-shaped Italianate frame house is dominated by a bracketed cornice that stretches around the entire building. The front block is framed by corner pilasters that visually support the cornice. The front porch, which repeats the cornice and column design, was also saved in the move.

William T. Beeks House
c. 1800, c. 1860
Warwick vicinity

This brick house dates primarily from the third quarter of the 19th century, although half the main block was part of an earlier two-story, three-bay, side hall/parlor brick structure. Apparently a fire gutted the early dwelling in the mid-19th century, and the old walls were used to rebuild the house. The early, three-bay main facade is laid in Flemish bond to the height of the second story windows; when the newer section was added, the roof was raised and the new portion of the walls was laid in common bond. A stylish mansard roof with bell curve was placed atop the rebuilt structure to unite the original portion with the new three-bay, common bond brick addition. A lower two-story brick kitchen wing stands at one end, and a brick meat house and typical 19th century frame barn building remain on the property.

William T. Beeks was probably responsible for the present appearance of the house, since he inherited the property from John L. Beeks in the mid-19th century and owned the place until his death in the 1890s.

Walworth House (site)
1860s
Fredericktown

This house was a notable example of the Second Empire style. The two-and-a-half story, five-bay dwelling had a mansard roof covered with fish-scale shingles, bracketed dormers, and two-story verandas on two facades.

Guenther Realty Building
late 18th century, 1860s
Cecilton

This tall five-bay Victorian building facing North Bohemia Avenue dates from the third quarter of the 19th century and was probably built by Dr. H. Cruikshank. Behind and perpendicular to the house is a much older two-and-a-half story log building sheathed in beaded clapboard siding with beaded corner posts. This structure features six-over-six sash windows, paired attic windows, and a roofing system with mortise and tenon joints. A one-story addition was added to the south side of the house in 1978.

CE-4, Walworth house (1973)

CE-1366, Guenther Realty building (1985)

CE-9, Herndon/Sealark farm (1978)

Herndon/Sealark Farm
c. 1864
Fredericktown vicinity

Francis B. Cruikshank built this imposing brick residence toward the end of the Civil War, and it reflects the revival architectural styles popular at that time. Although Herndon possesses a few Italianate elements on the exterior, including heavily bracketed front and side porches, clay chimney pots, and four-over-four window sash, the house generally follows architectural designs of an earlier period. The two-story, five-bay principal facade with central pediment and projecting pilasters imitates such Georgian period houses as nearby Bohemia and Greenfields. However, the interiors, with their marble mantels, mahogany woodwork, and elaborate plaster ceiling decorations, are in keeping with the styles of the 1860s.

B. J. Green House
c. 1864-67
Warwick vicinity

This is one of the few houses illustrated in the 1877 Lake, Griffing, and Stevenson atlas of Cecil County, undoubtedly because it was, and is, one of the most prominent buildings in the area. Cecil County tax assessments suggest Mr. Green built the structure between 1864 and 1867, for his 260 acres were assessed for $5,460 in 1864 and $14,300 in 1867. Such a large difference in amount, coupled with the architectural style of the house, fairly conclusively dates the house to this period, when its Second Empire style was popular.

The house basically follows the common mid-19th century form of two-story, five-bay frame farmhouses with a center hall plan seen around the county. This example is distinguished by its Second Empire details, most prominently the mansard roof, which accommodates a third story. As well, it has an intricate cast-iron porch; decorative arched dormers; and, in the center bay of the second floor, a three-part center window with fanlight above. The abundance of grained interior woodwork is an unusual survival. A two-story wing extends to the rear of the house, which was moved in 1988 to a site on Warwick-Cecilton Road.

Upper Wickwire
c. 1868
Earleville vicinity

Upper Wickwire is adjacent to Lower Wickwire, and the two farms were once associated. The mid-19th century Italianate structure on this property is the most elaborate of the three Italianate houses on Pond Neck Road. It is a two-story, five-bay frame structure with single-story porches on two sides and a large, two-story kitchen wing behind. The interior retains original

CE-989, B.J. Green house (1995)

CE-929, Upper Wickwire (1994)

woodwork. Also on the property are a number of mid-19th century outbuildings, including two barns, a granary, and a dairy.

Cecil County tax assessments date the construction of this house to 1868 and identify the builder as John H. Hessey. The 1877 county atlas reports that his family had come to Cecil County from Ohio around 1824.

Zion Methodist Church
1869 with additions
Cecilton

The original portion of this church is a two-story, gable-roofed brick building with lancet windows and a three-story bell tower. Tall Gothic Revival pinnacles rise at the four corners of the tower, which also features several decorative quatre-foil windows. Built on an L plan, the church has a large 20th century gable-roofed brick wing on the west side.

Husfelt House
c. 1870
Earleville vicinity

This house, along with numerous others of its type, provides substantial and undeniable evidence of the broad use of the two-and-a-half story, center hall, single-pile house type throughout the 19th century. The central cross gable with Gothic arch and the hip-roofed porch with sawn bracket ornament point to a construction date in the third quarter of the 19th century. The 1877 county atlas cites Daniel Husfelt as owner of the house.

School No. 7
c. 1870
Earleville vicinity

The substantial effort to better the county school system that began in the third quarter of the 19th century cannot be better illustrated than by listing the number of mid- to late 19th century schoolhouses that remain in Cecil County. Most of these structures have become residences, but they still demonstrate the increase in

CE-360, Zion Methodist Church (1985)

CE-921, Husfelt house (1978)

educational facilities made at that time. School No. 7 is exemplary of these single-story frame structures.

Cruikshank House
1870s
Cecilton

This large, three-story Victorian house with high mansard roof stands on the outskirts of Cecilton. It is L shaped with a porch along its length. The windows on the projecting wing are set within recessed molded circles and the dormer windows have unusual segmental heads. The wealth of jig-sawn trim on the porches, the bracketed cornice, and the roof with its decorative pattern in slate distinguish the house. Several original outbuildings survive, including one with a cupola and jig-sawn trim.

Wright House
1880s
Warwick

This well-maintained Victorian era residence is a two-and-a-half story, gable-roofed frame house built on an L plan with a rear wing. It features two-over-two window sash, Gothic lancet windows on the attic level, jig-sawn bargeboards, and one-story polygonal bays on the east and south facades. The house was probably built in the 1880s, soon after Lawrence Wright purchased the lot.

CE-31, Cruikshank house (1973)

CE-936, School No. 7 (1979)

CE-1354, Wright house (1980)

CE-22, St. Stephen's Church (1968)

CE-356, St. Stephen's Chapel (1980)

St. Stephen's Church (NR)
1874
Johntown

St. Stephen's Church was organized in 1692 in North Sassafras, one of the thirty original Anglican parishes in Maryland. The fourth structure to house the congregation, this building reflects the Gothic Revival design common to many 19th century church buildings. The architectural massing is typical of rural churches and consists of an axial orientation, rectangular sanctuary, and dominant front tower with broach spire.

Rebuilding of the church was completed in 1874 with designs and supervision from Thomas Dixon, a well-known Baltimore architect. The vestry minutes document the complete alteration of an earlier building:

> The roof and ceiling are to be taken off the present building, all of the doors and windows with their frames are to be taken out, the top part of the present walls are to be taken down to the height shown by the drawings, the end wall is to be taken down and the present stairs and fittings removed. The new additions are to be made agreeable to the dimensions shown figured on the drawings.

The new additions included a chancel, steeple, and much steeper roof. A major focal point for the farming communities of Earleville and Sassafras Neck, St. Stephen's has remained virtually unaltered since the 1870s.

St. Stephen's Chapel (site)
1879
Cecilton

This late Victorian brick structure designed by Philadelphia architect James Peacock Simms was built as a chapel of ease for St. Stephen's Episcopal Church in Earleville. It featured steeply pitched gable roofs, an expressed chancel, patterned slate shingles, and a small central belfry with jig-sawn woodwork. Insect damage and structural problems led to its demolition in 1980.

CE-6, Locust Hill Academy (1980)

CE-357, Blackway house (c. 1980)

Locust Hill Academy
1881
Fredericktown

This one-room school with attached vestibule is listed as "School No. 3" on the 1877 Cecil County atlas. Covered with German siding, the three-bay long frame building has large nine-over-nine sash windows. An earlier school at Fredericktown was destroyed by fire in 1880; the firm of Jackson Brothers built this one in 1881 at a cost of $634.

Blackway House
1890s
Cecilton

One of the largest residences in Cecilton, this house is a typical example of the late Victorian style. Asymmetrical and rambling in appearance, it is a two-and-a-half story frame house built generally on a T plan with steeply pitched gables on three sides. Notable for its wealth of exterior ornament, the house has Eastlake-style woodwork on a large wraparound porch, jig-sawn bargeboards, and corbeled chimney caps. Restoration work has been undertaken in the 1990s.

St. Paul's Methodist Church
1894
Johntown vicinity

The two structures standing on this property just west of Johntown until 1993 together offered an instructive architectural history of the Sassafras Neck Methodist church. The early church or meetinghouse, built in the late 18th century, was a single-story, weatherboard-covered frame building with steeply pitched roof and eight-over-twelve sash windows. In 1894 a second, larger church was built next door. The early building then served as a social hall until it was torn down because of deterioration in the spring of 1993.

While the 18th century church structure spoke of a congregation with sufficient size and funds to build a basic meetinghouse, the second church building suggests a stylistically conscious congregation who wanted to create more than just a larger space. The corner bell tower and exuberant late 19th century architectural features of the building signal their desire for change. The bell tower, corner buttresses, pointed-arch windows, and an application of richly patterned fish-scale shingles and sawn ornament clearly place the design of the building in the Queen Anne style, known for its dynamic use of sculptural forms and rich ornament.

During 1991-92 a second structure, a mirror image of the 1894 building, was added to its south side. The exterior was built with molding, siding, and windows imitating as nearly as possible those of the original structure.

CE-23, St. Paul's Methodist Church (1995)

Mount Harmon (NR)
c. 1963 and earlier
Earleville vicinity

Positioned on a 400-acre peninsular tract bounded by Forman and McGill creeks south of Earleville is a conjectural restoration of the 18th century plantation house that formerly stood on this point of land jutting out into a tributary of the Sassafras River. The Flemish bond walls of this two-and-a-half-story, center hall Georgian brick house, measuring 50 feet across by 32 feet deep, were reused in the effort to recreate the former residence of Sidney George, Jr., and his third wife, Mary Louttit. The exterior and interior finishes were based on Georgian-style designs copied from period houses in Delaware, Maryland, and Virginia. The craftsmanship of the Chinese decorated stair was based closely on the original staircase at nearby Bohemia. A tobacco prize house was also reconstructed on the property, with the prize and its parts brought in from St. Mary's County, Maryland. The rebuilding of the Mount Harmon plantation complex was accomplished under the ownership of Marguerite du Pont de Villiers Boden. (See photograph of the river facade of Mount Harmon in Chapter 4, "An Excellent Situation for Manufacturer and Farmer Alike.")

While the Mount Harmon house is an elaborate 20th century combination of Georgian period architectural elements, the basis of the property's historical significance remains largely in the diary left by one of its owners, Sidney George Fisher (1809–1871), who owned and managed the plantation. His detailed entries contain a wealth of information on farming practices and the changing nature of plantation agriculture during the second quarter of the nineteenth century. Fisher's descriptions of daily activities, his discussions of farming issues, as well as his interactions with his neighbors, provide a vivid picture of life in southern Cecil County between 1837 and 1850.

Lofland Farm
c. 1920
Warwick vicinity

This two-and-a-half story frame house is a sizable example of a house form popular in the early 20th century and later termed the "American foursquare." According to local residents, it was built on the site of an earlier structure, which burned around 1916. W. H. Lofland is listed as resident here in the 1877 atlas.

CE-26, Mt. Harmon

CE-1036, Scotchman's Creek bridge (1981)

CE-975, Lofland Farm (1979)

Scotchman's Creek Bridge (site)
c. 1931
Hack's Point

The Cecil County Commissioners ordered the bridge over Scotchman's Creek closed in March 1931. Soon after, the Luten Bridge Company submitted a competitive bid to replace the old bridge with a reinforced concrete span. This structure represented an unusual and distinctive form in Cecil County. Visually, the six open spandrel arches provided a light structural quality not often associated with the reinforced concrete bridges erected in the county. This aspect was especially evident in comparison to the neighboring Bohemia River bridge, a heavier, more typical structure.

This 1931 structure was replaced in the mid-1980s.

Second District

William Price IV House
18th and 19th centuries
Warwick vicinity

This house, part of which is the oldest dwelling still standing in Middle Neck, consists of two parts. The two-story, four-bay frame structure probably dates from the early 19th century and has been considerably altered. More interesting is the two-and-a-half story, two-bay stone section, in which heavy squared blocks were used as quoins. Probably dating from the early 18th century, this single-pile house originally featured a door on both the river and land sides and a steep dogleg staircase with simple square balusters and newel post. The first floor mantel has pilasters and early bolection moldings; the mantel on the second floor is later and probably dates from the installation of the adjacent closet. The attic shows evidence of early hand-split lathing.

Bristole
late 18th century, c. 1815, and later
Chesapeake City vicinity

Centrally located on Back Creek Neck, the property known historically as Bristole is improved by a singular example of an architectural form unusual in Cecil County. Identified by architectural historians as the dogtrot house form, the initial Bristole plantation house consisted of two squarish hewn log structures, a single room each in plan, separated by an open breezeway. True to other examples of this house type, the single-story log pens were joined by a continuous plate on which the roof rafters were nailed. Rising through each gable end were fieldstone chimneys with exposed backs. The interior finish of these rooms was relatively plain with open joist ceilings covered in whitewash. Access to the loft was probably by means of a ladder positioned to one side of a chimney stack. The construction date of this initial dogtrot house is not known but could be as early as the mid-18th century. Wrought-nail construction and the surviving woodwork date from the late 18th century.

Around 1815 the single-story dogtrot house was raised with a second story. The original roof was removed, and narrow four- to five-inch-thick hewn plank walls, dovetailed at the corners, were placed atop the stouter single-story log structure. A new common rafter roof was assembled, and new brick chimneys were laid atop the stone bases. The roof framing was assembled with a combination of mortise-and-tenon joints secured with pins and double-struck cut nails, a distinctive nail type used in the region during a narrow time period from circa 1805 to circa 1820. An enclosed winder stair was crafted in the center breezeway out of beaded board partitions. The front and rear walls to the breezeway were enclosed as well.

The siting of a dogtrot house in Cecil

CE-1331, William Price IV house (1985)

CE-304, Lana Wright house (1985)

CE-99, Bristole (1995)

County, as well as a number of examples located in the Delaware River valley, has generated conjectural explanations of the original derivation of this architectural form, now principally associated with the South. Although a distinct source for the antecedents of this form remains obscure, one theory suggests the dogtrot log house form was employed by Finnish settlers who moved into the Delaware River valley during the early to mid-17th century. Examples of two-room log houses incorporating a central passage or breezeway have been identified in Finland and offer a potential precedent for this distinctive house type in continental Europe.

Thomas Boulden, Jr., was constable of Back Creek Neck and served as a justice of the court, taking oaths of allegiance during the Revolution. He and later his cousin Noble Biddle, a lieutenant in the Continental army, resided on the Bristole plantation. Biddle is credited with establishing an iron foundry on the farm. A Boulden-Biddle family graveyard is located in a wooded area in front of the house. Two huge sycamore trees, one of them more than 400 years old, stand beside the house.

Lana Wright House
1750s with additions
St. Augustine vicinity

One of the oldest houses in this part of the Second District, the Lana Wright house is unusual for its brickwork, particularly the rare two-brick-wide belt course, which breaks upward at each corner. As was common in other well-built houses from the colonial period, Flemish bond was used on the front facade above the molded water table, English bond below. Further refinements include the use of Flemish bond on an additional facade, segmental-arched windows, and a bed molding and boxed cornice. A one-and-a-half story, three-bay stone kitchen, unusual for this area, is attached to the north gable end of the two-story main house. A two-story frame wing is a 20th century addition.

Although the first floor retains its hall/parlor plan and original chair rail, much of the interior woodwork dates from a later renovation. The kitchen still has a brick floor and the original hardware and mantel.

CE-65, Great House (1980)

Great House (NR)
c. 1750–80
St. Augustine vicinity

The mid-18th century structure on "Bohemia Manor" known as Great House is an unusual variation of a four-room house plan and contains some of the most exemplary mid-18th century woodwork in the county. Each room of the main block has paneled fireplace walls, architectural cupboards, molded cornices, and a chair rail. The paneling in the southwest parlor is an idiosyncratic interpretation of a classical entablature with fluted pilasters and oversized triglyphs. The heated stair hall to the southeast, with its heavily molded handrail and turned balusters, is another unusual survival in the tidewater area of Cecil County. Other uncommon architectural features include T-shaped chimneys, pent eaves, and gable end circular attic vents; the small round vent is a feature of several houses in nearby Delaware.

The farm property, known as Great House farm, is a small section of the 20,000-acre tract granted to Augustine Herman by Lord Baltimore in 1660 in exchange for creating an accurate map of Maryland. The farm is also part of the Labadie Tract, a 3,750-acre parcel Herman granted to Labadist settlers. The Labadists were a Dutch religious sect formed by John Labadie in the latter half of the 17th century. The parent community in Welward, Holland, began to dissolve in the late 17th century, about the same time the Bohemia colony in Maryland began to decline.

Randalia
mid-18th and mid-20th centuries
Chesapeake City vicinity

This imposing house, probably the oldest and certainly the best-known on the Randalia property, consists of three parts. A two-story, four-bay portion at one end was constructed of concrete block and dates from the mid-20th century. The two-story, three-bay center section was probably built nearly two centuries earlier and is constructed of fieldstone, an unusual building material in the Second District. On the other end is a one-and-a-half story, two-bay stone wing of the same or possibly earlier date. Both 18th century portions exhibit architectural features a typical for the time, including a cornice and bed molding, pegged door and window frames, and steeply pitched gable roofs.

The interior floor plan remains generally unaltered as does much of the fine mid-Georgian woodwork, including doors, chair rail, and a paneled cupboard. The one-and-a-half story section, now used as a kitchen, has an exposed brick floor and a fireplace with a simple mantel. The attic, probably once used as sleeping quarters by servants, is reached by a ladder.

The name "Randalia" dates from the 1830s, when the property was acquired by John Randal, Jr., a civil engineer from New York state and once an employee of the Chesapeake and Delaware Canal Company. When Randal was fired by the company in 1825, he sued in Superior Court in Delaware and received one of the highest civil damage awards in the state's judicial history.

Howard House
mid-18th century
Chesapeake City vicinity

Like nearby Randalia and built at about the same time, the old part of the Howard house consists of two sections. Both parts are built of fieldstone that has been stuccoed and feature paneled door jambs, six-over-six sash windows, and a boxed cornice with bed molding. The two-bay portion was raised a story at the same time the elevation of the first floor was raised to be even with that of the larger, three-bay section. Some original

CE-67, Randalia (1968)

CE-1057, Courthouse Point house (1979)

CE-54, Bohemia Manor ruins (1968)

18th century interior woodwork remains, although the chair rail has been removed. The one-story kitchen wing is a 20th century addition.

On the grounds is an unusual bank barn built on stone foundations. Because of the generally flat terrain found in the Second District, bank barns were only rarely built in this area.

Courthouse Point Farmhouse
c. 1770-1810
Chesapeake City vicinity

This frame farmhouse has experienced dramatic exterior change with the addition of a brick skin, but it retains its exterior telescope form, which is common on the Eastern Shore. At this house, the earliest section is a single-story timber-frame structure with exposed corner posts. A two-story hall/parlor addition was built around 1800.

The interior has been altered, but much late 18th and early 19th century woodwork remains. The two first floor mantels are especially fine examples of Federal design and craftsmanship.

The Cecil County courthouse was located here in the mid-18th century after its removal from Ordinary Point on the Sassafras River. The courthouse was moved again to Charlestown for five years and then to Elkton.

Bohemia Manor (ruins)
early 19th century
Cayots Corner vicinity

The effects of weathering often make ruinous walls appear older than they are. Architectural features and construction methods offer much more exact ways to date a building, and those seen here suggest an early 19th century date of construction.

Augustine Herman once owned this property, but the location and appearance of his 17th century manor house have not been determined. The Bayard family has owned this property for generations, and it is likely they were responsible for the construction of this farmhouse.

The property is of archeological importance as it may contain both the site of the original Bohemia Manor and the grave of Augustine Herman.

Old Brick House
c. 1800-25
St. Augustine

The crossroads at St. Augustine, sometimes known as Churchtown, grew up around the Episcopal church that sits at its center. This two-story, four-bay, one-room deep, hall/parlor brick house of the Federal period is the earliest remaining structure on the four

CE-68, Howard house (1985)

CE-63, old brick house (1968)

corners. Many local residents remember that Mr. Foard operated a store at this spot in the early 20th century; the house also served as the local post office.

Bayard House
early 19th century
South Chesapeake City

The earliest brick building in Chesapeake City, this house is essentially a vernacular structure, but the arched transom above the entrance is a common detail on Federal period buildings. Its location by the canal gives the Bayard House a prominent role in the visual quality of the town. The building for many years served as a hotel and inn for those traveling the canal.

Sara Beaston is the probable builder of this brick hotel. She and her husband Charles owned much property along Back Creek in the early 19th century. Sara sold the building to Richard H. Bayard in 1842. Around 1850 the hotel was known as the Maxwell house, and as such it appears on Martenet's Cecil County map of 1858. Captain Firman Layman operated the hotel as the Bayard House, with a livery stable behind it, until his death in 1881. Like his predecessors, he did a brisk business and advertised "bed and board for man and beast." Captain Layman apparently rented the building, for his name does not appear on the title. He did, however, own the furniture and fixtures in the hotel. At his death he devised these to his daughter—except for the furnishings in room number six, which went to his faithful housekeeper Eliza Ross.

In 1911 William Harriott bought the property, both stable and hotel, at the settlement of the John Smith estate. Harriott continued to keep a hotel with popular bar and dining rooms, catering largely to canal travelers and employees. A store selling tobacco and necessities was maintained on the ground level, beneath the main floor of the hotel. A dance pavilion Harriott built on the canal side of the hotel was a popular amusement center in the early 20th century. Later the pavilion was converted to a storehouse, and eventually it was torn down. The Harriott Hotel fell upon hard times partly because of the Depression, partly

CE-119 and CE-306, Bayard House and Layman house (1994)

CE-307 & CE-308, Cropper house and Slicher store (1994)

because of Prohibition, and partly because of change in traffic on the canal. In 1927 the U.S. Army Corps of Engineers opened the sea-level canal, which shortened the trip through the waterway and eliminated the stop at Chesapeake City.

Under the benevolent aegis of Mrs. Richard du Pont, the old hostelry was restored in 1984, revamped, and reopened; it now serves gourmet meals to tourists, boaters, and area residents.

Layman House
2nd quarter 19th century with additions
South Chesapeake City

This traditional two-and-a-half story, Federal frame house exhibits Victorian porch and trim. It has a side hall plan and sits on a stone foundation. A reminder of prosperous times when the C & D Canal operation was largely centered in Chesapeake City, the house was first owned by Firman Layman, keeper of the hotel next door.

Cropper House
1833 and mid-19th century
South Chesapeake City

This frame house, covered with beaded weatherboards, is now an L-shaped structure with a three-story, four-bay main block and a two-story, four-bay wing. It appears to date from the mid-19th century, but restoration work carried out in the early 1970s uncovered a smaller, one-room plan house underneath, apparently the house built in 1833 for Captain Kendall Cropper. The building later served at different times as a general store, tinsmith's shop, post office, and pool hall.

Slicher Store
c. 1840
South Chesapeake City

Recently restored, this small-scale, clapboard-covered frame house is four bays wide, with two doors alternating with two windows, and sheltered by a simple front porch. An interior chimney rises near the center of the house. This structure was probably built as a store during the town's canal-centered boom period. Residents of Chesapeake City in the 1980s remembered this building as a shoe store owned by Andrew Slicher.

Old Lock Pump House (NR)
1854
South Chesapeake City

The Old Lock Pump House was built in 1837 as part of the construction of the Chesapeake and Delaware Canal. Largely intact, it still retains the original machinery used to move water into the canal. The Army Corps of Engineers has long preserved the building and opened it to the public as a museum.

The idea of building a canal across the Delmarva Peninsula was proposed as early as the 17th century, when Augustine Herman recognized the attractiveness of such a project. Four attempts were made at constructing a canal in the first quarter of the 19th century, all of which were aborted (see index for references to C & D Canal history). By October 17, 1829, however, the Chesapeake and Delaware Canal was complete and the company announced it was "open and ready for business."

This pump house was built in 1854 to improve the operation of a key section of the C & D Canal at Chesapeake City. It contains a lift wheel, 38 feet in diameter and capable of pumping 20,000 gallons (130 tons) of water per minute in only one and a half revolutions. The two engines, installed in 1851 and 1854, were built by Merrick and Sons of Philadelphia. The gigantic wheel is encased in a stone trough 18 feet 8 inches wide and 22 feet deep into which water flowed through a tunnel from nearby Back Creek. The locks were rebuilt in 1853-54 following the installation of the lift wheel pumping plant at Chesapeake City. The pump house has not been used in its original capacity since the early 1920s.

(An early 20th century photograph of this building appears in chapter 4, "'An Excellent Situation' for Manufacturer and Farmer Alike.")

St. Augustine's Episcopal Church
1838, 1963
St. Augustine

St. Augustine's Church, built in 1838 as a chapel of ease for North Sassafras Parish, is the third such chapel to stand in this general area. A three-bay, one-story frame building with a steeply pitched gable roof, it is typical of many other simple rural churches built in Maryland during the 19th century. The Georgian-style cupola and porch and interior furnishings date from an extensive restoration carried out in 1963.

North Sassafras Parish was created in 1692, and the original chapel, known as "Bohemia Manor Chapel" or the "Mannour Chappel," was built in 1695. This log structure was replaced in 1735 by a larger

CE-124, Old Lock Pump House (1995)

CE-64, St. Augustine's Church (1967)

building described in the vestry records as a "brick structure 50 x 30 feet with a hipped roof" and a semicircular apse. The church was supposedly damaged by British and Hessian troops during the Revolution. The present building was constructed in 1838. St. Augustine's remained inactive between 1887 and 1964 but returned to active service as the parish church after the 1963 restoration.

Dr. Smithers's House
c. 1848
South Chesapeake City

This three-story house and several local counterparts exemplify an important house type in Chesapeake City. Clearly built by a more affluent class than the workers' houses that line George Street, its original owners nonetheless were less wealthy—or more conservative—than the people who built stylish structures such as the Davis house. Almost square, this three-story frame town house retains much of its original detail. A dentiled cornice decorates the house just under the eaves and the front porch exhibits some Victorian trim. The date 1848 appears on one of the downspouts.

CE-323, Dr. Smithers's house (1976)

Martindale-Hughes House
mid-19th century
South Chesapeake City

This two-and-a-half story, three-bay frame house has a side hall plan and a large rear wing built in several sections. It retains many of its original details, including segmental-arched dormer windows flanked with pilasters, and is representative of the types of dwellings built in the early years of Chesapeake City history. Also on the property is a small board-and-batten barn.

Martha Martindale leased this land from Richard Bayard in 1854. The Martindales probably built this house, on land then surrounded largely by meadow and woodland. At the turn of the 20th century, when many sea captains lived in Chesapeake City, this house was the home of Captain James Hughes and his family.

CE-318, Martindale-Hughes house (1976)

CE-321, Gassaway house (1976)

CE-69, Brantwood

Gassaway House
mid-19th century
South Chesapeake City

Built for workers on the C&D Canal, this structure has played a significant role in the history of Chesapeake City's black population. Early in the 20th century, it was the home of Robert Gassaway, police chief and the first black mayor. The small frame house resembles several others on George Street; it is a two-story, two-bay structure with rear wing and one-story front porch.

North Chesapeake City Row Houses
mid-19th century
North Chesapeake City

These four two-story, two-bay frame row houses on Biddle Street are characteristic of the houses of most 19th century Chesapeake City residents who worked on the C&D Canal. Many such houses were destroyed when the canal was widened in the 1930s. These houses have been greatly altered in the late 20th century.

Sartin Cottage (site)
mid-19th century
North Chesapeake City

Many C&D Canal workers who resided in Chesapeake City lived in row houses, but others lived in small cottages such as this one, which stood on the south side of Biddle Street. The two-story, three-bay house had narrow clapboard siding on the front, board-and-batten siding elsewhere, and a steep gable roof. A wing extended to the rear, and a porch with decorative Victorian trim graced the front. The house was razed in the late 20th century.

Brantwood
c. 1850-60
Elkton vicinity

David M. Taylor assembled a large estate in the mid-19th century that, by 1877, included eight tenant houses just below the New Castle and Frenchtown Railroad. His three-story brick residence was located in the middle of his holdings. The square, common bond brick mass was built all at once, as can be seen in the uniform brickwork and dentiled cornice that continues around all four sides. The house abounds with unusual architectural features, from the elaborate cast-iron front porch to the charred timbers and wrought-iron hooks of the third floor smokehouse.

CE-341, North Chesapeake City row houses

CE-342, Sartin Cottage

CE-1061, Boulden farm (1980)

CE-1051, DeCoursey house on Town Point Farm (1979)

Boulden Farm
c. 1850–60
Chesapeake City vicinity

William W. Boulden assembled a 167-acre property known as "Brick House Farm" from two adjoining tracts, parts of "Hispaniola" and "Bullens Range," in the mid-19th century. The house dates from the mid-19th century and, with its three-story elevation, low pitched roof, and exaggerated classical details such as the heavily dentiled cornices, belongs to the Greek Revival style. The property includes a common bond brick meat house and carriage house and a rare brick barn.

Reed House
c. 1855
St. Augustine vicinity

The Georgian formula of symmetrical facades and center passage houses was still popular when this house was constructed in the mid-19th century. In this example, the classical symmetry has been emphasized by the addition of a three-bay Colonial Revival hipped roof porch with Tuscan columns. A Mrs. Reed is listed as the owner on both the 1858 Martenet map of Cecil County and the 1877 Lake, Griffing, and Stevenson atlas.

Ebeneezer A.M.E. Church
1855
St. Augustine

The cornerstone of this simple one-story frame church is inscribed with the date 1855, and most of the exterior fabric, including the paneled window shutters, is original, although the louvered steeple and enclosed vestibule are probably later additions. On the grounds are a small board-and-batten caretaker's cottage from the 1850s and a few headstones from the mid- to late 19th century. Ebeneezer Church was once part of the small black community of Concord, of which only two houses survive.

DeCoursey House on Town Point Farm
c. 1855–63
Port Herman vicinity

The introduction of widely circulated architectural pattern books gave builders a choice of numerous architectural styles during the mid-19th century. This fact, coupled with the popularity of waterfront property, provided the circumstances for the construction of the DeCoursey-Foulks house on the Elk River peninsula of Town Point. Samuel W. DeCoursey and his wife purchased 99 acres from Jeremiah and Mary Ann Starr in December 1855 for $3,713.67. Eight years later they sold the same 99 acres to Colonel Joshua Clayton of New Castle County, Delaware, for $13,000. This $10,000 difference places the construction

CE-775, Reed house (1979)

CE-1329, Ebeneezer AME Church (1985)

CE-340, First Presbyterian Church

CE-125, Bohemia Hill (1979)

of the house between 1855 and 1863.

The DeCourseys were Philadelphians, and their house displays lively architectural design and applied detail that are atypical for Cecil County, implying that a design source other than a local builder influenced the construction of their house. Among the uncommon features are the lotus leaf capitals on the porch columns and the chain-link cornice decoration. The house once had a rooftop lantern.

First Presbyterian Church
c. 1859
North Chesapeake City

Presbyterianism had its beginning in the Chesapeake City area in 1723, well before the founding of the town. In that year, Richard Thompson leased an acre of land beside Broad Creek (later the Chesapeake and Delware Canal) to Samuel Alexander and Peter Bouchell. The rent was one ear of Indian corn per year. This congregation had disappeared from the records by 1740, but the graveyard was incorporated into that of the Bethel Methodist Church, erected nearby before 1790.

On April 28, 1857, an eight-member group held the first Presbyterian services in Chesapeake City. On November 1 of the same year, a committee of the Presbytery of Wilmington (now the New Castle Presbytery) organized a congregation, calling it the "first Presbyterian Church of Chesapeake City." This group built a church, dedicated on January 8, 1860, in the simple Greek temple style popular for rural churches in the 19th century; it remains basically unaltered.

Pennington Farm
c. 1860-70
Warwick vicinity

This two-and-a-half story, three-bay frame farmhouse on Middle Neck is a largely unaltered example of the common 19th century house form known as the I house; the original condition of the interior is particularly noteworthy. In this instance, the two-story, two-bay, one-room kitchen wing appears to predate the main part of the house. Seams in the foundation stone and weatherboards are exterior evidence of this, while an exposed corner sway brace in the wing appears to be a framing member left for support when the doorway was cut through to the new dining room.

Bohemia Hill
late 18th century, 1860-80
Port Herman vicinity

Located on a hill overlooking the Bohemia River, the house called Bohemia Hill has had a long history as a country residence for owners from outside Cecil County. The first nonresident was Benjamin S. Foulks, who bought the property in 1853 from William S. Foulks. Subsequent owners included many other residents of the Philadelphia area.

The addition of a mansard roof and a uniform coat of stucco and numerous interior alterations transformed the original, late 18th century house into a stylish residence of the mid-19th century. A small two-story kitchen wing is attached to the east side.

CE-1001, Pennington farm (1979)

CE-126, Elklands (1979)

CE-1044, James A. Lewis house (1979)

Elklands (Bohemia Vineyards)
c. 1862
Port Herman vicinity

Construction of this massive stone house is documented in the county tax records and the *Cecil Democrat*. The 1862 tax assessor listed Charles D. Knight as owner of thirty acres and a "new stone house" valued at $1,500. Fourteen years later the same property was owned by Edward Hipple, a Philadelphia photographer, and was advertised for sale in the *Cecil Democrat* on September 30, 1876. The advertisement described the property:

> Sale of a valuable farm, known as Elklands or Bohemia vineyards now occupied by Edward Hipple, Esq.... contains 156 acres more or less, the improvements consist of a splendid stone mansion house built a few years ago at a cost of $11,000, and containing 14 rooms together with a barn, stable, and shedding for cattle. There are also two tenement houses on the farm.
>
> The land is in a high state of cultivation ten acres of it in grapevines, six acres in peach trees, and four acres in apple trees, all in bearing. The grapes are known in the Philadelphia and New York markets as the best with which they are supplied....
>
> Noble T. Biddle, Trustee

James A. Lewis House
c. 1865
St. Augustine vicinity

The James A. Lewis house stands along Telegraph Road, at one time the main road from Elkton to Warwick. This two-and-a-half story, five-bay, single-pile, center hall house differs only slightly from others of its type by having a gable end shed kitchen rather than the more normal rear wing.

John Gilpin House/Fox Harbor
c. 1866-70
Chesapeake City vicinity

This picturesque frame house near Welch Point is an excellent example of the mid-century "country Gothic" style espoused by Andrew Jackson Downing. Downing popularized such board-and-batten houses in several books published in the mid-19th century.

The two-and-a-half story, five-bay structure faces the road and is covered with board-and-batten siding that employs unusual rounded battens. Above the line of the hipped roof are four symmetrically placed chimneys with corbeled caps and bases. The four round-arched dormer windows are topped by pediments with bracketed eaves and bargeboards. Paired Italianate brackets are situated below the second story cornice and along the eaves of the front porch. The interior was severely damaged by vandalism in the mid-20th century, but the tall, paneled sliding doors in the front rooms survive.

The house was probably built between 1866 and 1870 by John Gilpin, a lawyer from Kittanning, Pennsylvania. It, and a brick building farther down on Welsh Point that once served as a clubhouse, were described in a newspaper notice of 1878 when the land was auctioned to pay the mortgage debts of subsequent owner Peter Lyle.

Franklin Hall
c. 1870
South Chesapeake City

Easily the most substantial structure in Chesapeake City, Franklin Hall is impressive in both size and style: It is the only high-style Romanesque building in this part of the county, and the brickwork of the three-story, three-bay brick building is of superior quality.

Reference to the lot where Franklin Hall stands goes back to the earliest days of Chesapeake City, when a tavern was the town's only attraction. Mrs. Mary Chick ran a tavern here before 1800; in fact, the tavern probably existed during the Revolutionary War because several members of the family took the oath of allegiance in 1781. In 1799 Mrs. Chick willed the property to her son Peregrine, who carried on the business. When construction on the canal began in the 1820s, workmen settled here in quickly built, whitewashed houses along the banks of the canal; they also enjoyed the tavern, and "altercations," according to the local paper,

CE-1348, John Gilpin house/Fox Harbor (1985)

were not uncommon when the Irish laborers and black laborers started drinking together. Chick's Tavern and later the Bayard House were popular gathering places. Sailors coming here from ports to the north and south brought news of the world as well as of more local events, making Chesapeake City a hub of activity.

In 1870 Thomas Conrey, a builder, came into possession of the land and, it is believed, built the handsome brick building now known as Franklin Hall. There has always been a store on the street level. For many years the firm of Bowen and Boulden conducted a hardware and harness business here. On the lower level, in back, a stable housed horses for delivery wagons and other purposes. A stair in the center of the building led to the second floor, where merchandise was stored. Various parts of the building were used for meetings, dances, and band practices.

The year 1974 saw the beginning of restoration of Franklin Hall. The Chesapeake City District Civic Association bought the building and has restored it. The rear wing of the first floor houses a branch of the county library system. The Cecil County Arts Council opened its headquarters on the second floor in 1985.

CE-120, Franklin Hall (1995)

CE-121, J. M. Reed Store (1995)

CE-123, Thomas Conrey house (1976)

J. M. Reed Store
c. 1870
South Chesapeake City

This two-and-a-half story frame building once housed the Reed Store, established in 1861. On the first floor, two store windows with folding paneled shutters flank the entrance. A porch supported on square, chamfered columns extends across the facade. Architecturally, this is easily the best example of commercial architecture of the mid-19th century in Chesapeake City; it retains many original features found on other buildings of the period.

This site has been an important commercial property since the founding of the town. Kendall Cropper made arrangements to buy the property in 1832 but died before the deal was complete. His heirs carried out the agreement and transferred the title to Absalom Cropper, one of four sons. Absalom was a merchant and probably had a wharf and store building here. Other Cropper brothers were ship captains; William was also a merchant. The family apparently cooperated in their business ventures: Of the four daughters, one married Richard Bryan, a merchant, and one married James Schultz, a boat engineer.

In 1869 Charles A. Bryan transferred a "storehouse and lot of land" to one Alonza Boulden, who transferred the property in 1870 to John M. Reed, who built the present building. Reed's Store had the best selection of dry goods in town, according to advertisements, and the counters were piled high with merchandise shipped from Baltimore and Philadelphia on the Erikson Line steamboats.

For many years Frank Williams conducted a school on the second floor of Reed's Store. Williams was a highly respected teacher who went on to become a state senator. These quarters later became the office of Dr. Smithers, a dentist. Rooms on the second floor were made available for public meetings, and it was here that the Chesapeake City Fire Company was organized in 1911. Until this time the only defense against fire in the town was a bucket brigade or, with luck, the hoses of a steamer passing through the canal.

The present owners of Reed's Store

CE-316, Griffith house (1976)

CE-502, 205 & 207 Charles Street, Chesapeake City (1976)

CE-118, Davis house (1976)

opened the Back Creek General Store in 1985 and have carefully preserved the building.

Thomas Conrey House
c. 1870
South Chesapeake City

In form, this house is like many of the mid-19th century dwellings in Chesapeake City. Its brick construction, however, is unique to that form, and the mansard roof the only of its type in town. Thomas Conrey, builder of Franklin Hall, also was responsible for the construction of this house, where he made his home.

The house is a three-and-a-half story brick building, three bays wide, with an original two-story frame wing to the east. The west facade is laid in smooth stretcher bond brick with narrow mortar joints.

Griffith House
1870s
South Chesapeake City

Chesapeake City was prosperous throughout the Victorian era, as this spaciously comfortable, T-plan frame house evinces. The two-story, clapboard-covered house has a two-story bay window on the front and a side porch with posts with large, bracketed heads. The eaves of the wide, low-pitched gable roof sport bargeboards with unusual decorations including roundels at the gable ends and exposed rafters along the sides.

The house was built by Araminta Griffith in the 1870s.

205 & 207 Charles Street
1870s
South Chesapeake City

This house is a two-story, four-bay frame duplex covered with German siding. The duplex is another house form constructed in Chesapeake City for families who worked on the C & D Canal.

Early in the 1870s Harvey Burgett established a sawmill on the south side of Back Creek at the west end of Second Street. The mill was large, with drying sheds, offices, and the milling sheds spread over four acres. This house apparently was built on part of the "Mill Lot" and probably housed mill employees.

Davis House
1872 with additions
South Chesapeake City

One of the more elaborate and original dwellings in South Chesapeake City, the Davis house is a three-story frame Italianate structure, five bays wide and two deep with a two-story, four-bay wing extending from the rear. Built on a granite foundation, the house is sheathed with molded German siding, and a standing seam metal roof covers the low-pitched hip roof. The porch covering the three center bays of the George Street facade is decorated with pierced fret brackets and a pierced split balustrade. The windows on the front extend nearly to the floor and have six-over-four sash. The entrance, with sidelights and transom, is emphasized by a bracketed cornice.

The Davis house is important for its profusion of original and early detail, including the porches, weatherboard, window trim, and iron fence. The property also retains sections of old wooden fence and outbuildings. The structure remains as it was advertised in an 1879 handbill, a "large and elegant dwelling house."

The property on which this house stands was acquired in 1854 by Bohemia Lodge

#68 International Order of Odd Fellows. The lodge built a two-story frame building to be used as a school; one early resident remembered that the entrance to the schoolyard was through a stile in the picket fence, which made going in and out very difficult for the teacher in her wide skirts.

In 1872 the Bohemia Lodge sold the school building and lot to Joseph Hedrick, who had the front portion of the house built. Mr. Hedrick was an official with the Chesapeake and Delaware Canal and one legend has it that he misused canal funds, expending some on the construction of this house. When the scandal became known, Hedrick left the country and his property was sold at public auction to satisfy his creditors.

Joseph H. Steele bought the property at the auction in 1879 for $3,010. He built the elaborate iron fence, and his name is inscribed on its gate. For most of the 20th century, this was the home of Dr. Henry V. Davis and family.

Bethel A. M. E. Church
1873
South Chesapeake City

Long a focus of African-American religious activity in Chesapeake City, this one-story, gable-roofed frame church is an attractive late example of the Greek Revival style. Built almost like a small Greek temple, with a gable-end entrance, pedimented facade, and wide frieze, the church features paneled pilasters at the corners and flanking the door. It retains most of its original detail.

St. Rose of Lima Church
1874
North Chesapeake City

This brick church, dated 1874 according to its marble cornerstone, was built in a rural, vernacular interpretation of the Gothic Revival style. The walls are laid in common bond and the brick arch over the entrance projects slightly. Parishioners enter St. Rose through a doorway in the square tower topped with a steeple. The altar is fitted into a projection on the north gable wall. In 1976 a brick sacristy

CE-320, Bethel A.M.E. Church

CE-336, St. Rose of Lima Church (1995)

CE-122, Henry H. Brady-Rees house and office (1994)

Henry H. Brady-Rees House and Office
1876
South Chesapeake City

The Victorian Gothic style is best represented in Chesapeake City by this house. Built for his family by Henry H. Brady after he purchased the property from James A. Boulden in 1869, it is a two-and-a-half story, five-bay brick dwelling covered with German siding. The steeply pitched roof, broken by a wide cross gable on the front, is covered with decorative slate shingles. At the apex of the roof are two chimneys, one retaining an original terra-cotta chimney pot.

Adjacent to this house is the only 19th century private office surviving in Chesapeake City. Built for Henry Brady, owner of a fleet of tugboats essential to the operation of the C & D Canal, it later served Ralph Rees as an insurance and magistrate's office. The square structure has a low-pitched metal roof and a porch across the front. The framed walls are filled with brick nogging and covered with tapered weatherboard. The interior retains some oak wainscoting and other oak trim.

was built enclosing the altar area.

The church began as a Catholic mission established by Father Peter Epinette, a French Jesuit from Bohemia, to minister to the primarily Irish workers who built the Chesapeake and Delaware Canal. Later German Catholics who came to build the Frenchtown and New Castle Railroad constituted a majority of the Chesapeake City mission congregation, and services were regularly conducted in German. In the 20th century one last immigrant group swelled the ranks of St. Rose's congregation—a group of Ukrainian farm families, who built their own church, St. Basil's, ten years later on the other side of town.

The church was named for the only saint then canonized in the Western Hemisphere, St. Rose of Lima (Peru). An 1872 visit by Bishop Thomas Becker of Wilmington led to the selection of a building site and plan for a "handsome little Gothic church." Dedication Day was May 8, 1875. The *Cecil Democrat*, reporting on the occasion, wrote,

> Four years ago, a Catholic Church could not have been built in the place, owing to extreme prejudice....It is gratifying to see that as people...better understand the meaning of brotherly love and good will to their fellow-men, their prejudices soon vanish....

Bayard Farm
c. 1880
St. Augustine vicinity

The late 19th century saw not only the development of asymmetrical house plans and elevations but the continued use of the two-story, five-bay, center hall house form as well. Often these traditional structures were given fashionable trim with the addition of central cross gables, bay windows, and sawn porch brackets. This five-bay, two-and-a-half story house, with its period grained woodwork, is a good example of this common type. Another period feature seen here is the use of chimney stacks that rise from the center rather than the ends of the house; inside, the fireplaces flank the center hall.

The late 19th century farm buildings on this property, including a pressed metal garage, are uncommon survivors.

CE-1042, Bayard farm (1979)

CE-1043, DeCoursey frame house (1979)

CE-263, Church of the Good Shepherd (1976)

DeCoursey Frame House
c. 1880
St. Augustine

This, the last structure to be built at the four corners of the St. Augustine crossroads, at first seems totally different from its earlier neighbors. But, if one were to remove the Queen Anne-style features, including bay windows at each gable end, the fish-scale shingles, and corbeled brick chimneys, the house is not much different from a traditional two-story, five-bay house of fifty years earlier.

Church of the Good Shepherd
1883
South Chesapeake City

This handsome Victorian Gothic brick church was designed by Philadelphia architect Charles M. Burns, Jr., a well-known practitioner who specialized in ecclesiastical design. A very steeply pitched gable roof shelters the nave, and courses of glazed bricks accentuate the walls, which sit on a granite foundation. Gothic features include lancet windows and buttresses between the windows on the side elevations.

Mary Sophia Bayard, widow of Richard H. Bayard of Philadelphia, deeded the parish "a lot of sufficient dimensions for a church and rectory." The rectory was never built, but the church was and was consecrated by Bishop Layton on March 29, 1883. In 1887 Good Shepherd became the church of this parish, replacing the old church at St. Augustine. The parish house was finally built in the 1920s, largely through the efforts of James Adams, owner of a showboat that plied the Chesapeake. His boat made stops at towns along the way, and the show changed daily. Chesapeake City was a popular stop, where the boat tied up at the foot of Bohemia Avenue. After years of service in the early part of this century, Adams's showboat met with disaster and he and his family settled in Chesapeake City. The smell of the greasepaint lingered, and, when new, the Good Shepherd parish house boasted a stage and dressing rooms. In the less theatrical 1940s, these were converted into a kitchen and serving area.

Trinity Methodist Episcopal Church
1889
South Chesapeake City

The walls of this Gothic Revival church are laid in broken courses of rock-faced cut granite. Door and window openings are

CE-314, Trinity M.E. Church (1976)

CE-311, Chesapeake City Bank building (1976)

CE-327, Karsner-Wilsey house/office (1976)

outlined in brick and brick quoins decorate the bell tower, which is topped with an open belfry and octagonal spire. The stained glass windows that fill the pointed-arch window frames were donated by prominent 19th and early 20th century local families in memory of loved ones and preserve some of the congregation's history.

In 1846 a frame church was built on the site of this stone structure; it was the first permanent church building constructed in the seventeen-year-old canal town. In 1881 the first resident minister was assigned to the church, which had previously been served by circuit-riding preachers and, in their absence, lay readers called "extolers." The present church was completed in 1890 and has remained one of the community's most enduring institutions.

Chesapeake City Bank Building
1903
South Chesapeake City

Masonry—implying strength, stability, and security—has long been a popular construction material for banks. This one-story structure, built for the National Bank of Chesapeake City, is crowned with a mansard roof and has a two-story tower in the southeast corner. Entrance is gained through the tower under a semicircular masonry arch with masonry voussoirs. In 1922 the building was sold to the Elkton Bank and Trust Company; it has been donated to the town and now serves as the town hall.

Karsner-Wilsey House/Office
late 19th century
South Chesapeake City

Like its neighbors, this house is a three-story, three-bay frame dwelling with a rear wing. Standing on a stone foundation, it is covered with weatherboards. A one-story porch across the facade has square columns on pedestals with chamfered posts with lamb's tongue stops. The house is largely unaltered and is a good example of the use through the late 19th century of a house form established in the town thirty years earlier.

Dr. William C. Karsner probably built

CE-1054, road to Port Herman (historic photograph)

Elk River House at Port Herman (1979)

this house circa 1884; he served the people of Chesapeake City and the surrounding countryside until 1914. In 1915 Dr. Edward H. Wilsey opened his office here.

Port Herman
late 19th and early 20th centuries

The small community of Port Herman was laid out along the shores of the Elk River by Robert Thomas in 1849 on land that had been part of Augustine Herman's vast Bohemia Manor tract. Thomas was not the first to realize the potential of this waterfront property, however. Local tradition documents the operation of a vinegar mill on this site as well as a lumber mill and boatyard. These activities were located along the water's edge for access to ship transport. Local farmers also undoubtedly used these wharves to ship their crops to market. The mill and agrarian community gave way to summer cottages and a hotel in the 20th century.

The four Staats cottages are two-story, two-bay frame structures built circa 1860. The Elk River House, built in 1888, is a three-story, five-bay center hall frame house. The Hazel property has two two-story frame structures, one built in the second half of the 19th century, the other early in the 20th century. The Hadden double stone house was built circa 1845-50; the three-story, four-bay stuccoed fieldstone house was once two dwellings but now serves as one. The Biddle house is a two-and-a-half story, three-bay frame house built circa 1915. Port Herman Methodist Church was built of frame circa 1916 in a rectangular, rural church form. The 19th century Mansion House was altered in the early 20th century with the addition of clipped gable dormers and a hip roof typical of the 1920s. The Port Herman Store is a circa 1865, one-and-a-half story, three-bay frame structure. Many of these buildings have been altered over the years, but as a community Port Herman preserves a part of Cecil County history.

Boatyard Buildings
early 20th century
Chesapeake City

This group of early 20th century brick commercial buildings stands west of Chesapeake City near a cove used for mooring tugboats. These one-and-a-half story and two-story gable-roofed structures are laid in common bond with jack arches above the segmental-arched windows and doors.

Mackey House
c. 1904
South Chesapeake City

This two-story, two-bay frame house on George Street on the edge of town is representative of the form and scale of the majority of buildings in South Chesapeake City. It has a two-story wing and two porches, one across the front and one on the wing.

CE-1328, boatyard buildings (1985)

CE-473, Mackey house (1976)

CE-1052, Long property (1979)

Long Property
c. 1905–14
Port Herman vicinity

The abundance of accessible waterfront property in Cecil County enticed many nonresident investors during the 19th century. The Long family from Philadelphia was one such group of investors seeking property on the Elk River. According to a 1914 plat of this property, John Long reserved 32 acres out of Whiteoak Farm, which contained the four-story wood shingle beach tower house, tea house, and carriage house. The unusual shingled tower form is not unlike the popular shingled shapes found in Queen Anne architecture of the period. The eccentricities of late 19th century fashion and the flexibility of late 19th century architecture have joined to produce a fascinating example of turn-of-the-century recreational buildings.

Chesapeake City Firehouse
1911
North Chesapeake City

Volunteer Fire Company No. 1 of Chesapeake City was organized in 1911 after a fire occurred that destroyed three buildings and was only contained with the help of a ship passing through the canal. The city purchased a hand-pulled fire engine steamer, a suction hose long enough to reach from the creek or canal to any house in town, and 1,600 feet of hose. That same year, this two-story frame structure was built for $800 to house the equipment and offices of the fire company. It stood along the causeway on the south side of the canal on land leased from the federal government. The town offices were moved to the firehouse some time between 1915 and January 1918, when the old office was sold.

In 1922 the War Department revoked the lease on the land where the firehouse was located, and three years later it was moved by barge to Biddle Street on the north side of the canal, its present location. Twelve years later the fire company built a larger building, leaving this structure entirely for the use of the town government. The town office was moved to the old bank building in South Chesapeake City in the 1980s.

Rees's Store
after 1913
South Chesapeake City

Built by Ralph H. Rees after 1913, this store has an intricate pressed metal facade that rises a full two stories, although the building behind it is just one story tall. The metalwork was produced in Indiana.

Ralph Rees purchased the Brady house in 1913 and built this structure on the adjacent rose garden. He operated a hardware store here as well as one of the earliest Oldsmobile and Lexington automobile dealerships in the state.

Chesapeake City firehouse (1995)

CE-322, Rees's store (1995)

Hager-Kinter House
1914
South Chesapeake City

This frame house was built from a kit purchased from Sears, Roebuck & Company by Henry Hager, who operated a butcher shop in Chesapeake City from around 1900 until the 1930s. The three-story house is typical of houses built from Sears kits; that is, it is constructed of good quality materials and the style is the result of Sears' commitment to adapting popular designs with broad appeal. As in many Sears structures, this house combines features of several styles, in this case, Queen Anne and Colonial Revival.

St. Basil's Ukrainian Catholic Church
1919
South Chesapeake City

Although under the jurisdiction of Rome, the congregation of St. Basil's Ukrainian Catholic Church uses the Byzantine rite of worship rather than the more familiar Latin rite found in most Catholic churches in the West. This circumstance came about because the parishioners are almost exclusively descendants of immigrants from Ukraine, where the Roman Catholic and Eastern Orthodox churches meet.

Built in 1919 on land donated by Paul Wasyczuk, one of the original Ukrainian settlers, the church is a rectangular frame structure similar in form to many country churches of the 19th and early 20th centuries. However, its onion-domed bell and entrance tower and the choir's beautiful Byzantine chants speak of the origin of the congregation's founders.

St. Basil's Ukrainian Catholic Church (1995)

CE-1445, Bohemia Manor (1994)

Bohemia Manor
1920s
Cayots Corner vicinity

This large Colonial Revival mansion was built in the 1920s by Thomas F. Bayard, a U.S. senator from Delaware, on the supposed site of Augustine Herman's house. The brick house consists of a two-story,

CE-309, Hager-Kinter house (1994)

CE-1050, Bayard Sharp house garage (1979)

five-bay main block with flanking two-story wings set perpendicular to it to form a C shape. The drive approaches the open end of the C, while the river facade overlooks a long sloping lawn and the river. On the second story of the river facade are two concrete medallions, one marked with "AH" for Augustine Herman and the other with the patent date for Bohemia Manor.

Bradford House
1922
Middle Neck

Although sometimes known as "Little Bohemia," this elaborate Colonial Revival brick house bears little resemblance to the historic house that originally stood on this scenic point on the Sassafras River. Built by Henry Bradford in 1922 at a cost of $75,000, the Flemish bond brick house is an excellent example of the expensive country houses wealthy families built in the early 20th century. It also illustrates many of the differences between the Georgian Revival style and its supposed 18th century prototypes. For example, instead of facing the river as it would have in colonial times, the principal facade faces a wide circular drive. Many formal Georgian-style decorative features are used throughout the house, including the Adam-style doorway with fanlight, arched sash windows, and fine balustraded main stair with elaborate step ends. These details contrast with the generally informal plan and appearance of the house, especially the varied roofline and off-center entrance vestibule with its steeply pitched gable roof. The house has been completely restored and updated in the latter part of the 20th century.

Bayard Sharp House
1923
Cayots Corner vicinity

This is the only example in Cecil County of the Mission Revival style, a manner of building more common in the southwestern United States. The style is characterized by simple but very solid stuccoed forms, corrugated red tile roofs with exposed rafter ends, simple fenestration, and arched arcades. The bell tower, with its pyramidal red tile roof and arched openings, is another feature commonly found on such structures.

This house was built as a home for the caretaker of the Bayard Sharp estate, where the family had a large vacation cabin. (See chapter 6, "The 'Marriage Capital of the East' in the Modern Period," for a photograph of the house.)

CE-237, Bradford house (1994)

Third District

Friendship Stone
1681
Elkton

The easternmost lot in Elkton contains a pleasant two-and-a-half story, three-bay frame house. Also on the property is a boundary stone inscribed 1681 that marks the eastern corner of the tract that now makes up most of Elkton and was patented to Nicholas Painter by King Charles II. Painter later returned to England, and the property was passed on to his stepson and later divided. The Hermitage, which belonged to the Tory Robert Alexander, was the main house on the property during the American Revolution. The land extended from the stone to the "Hollow," roughly 100 acres.

Thomas Mackie House
c. 1740-50
Leeds vicinity

This mid-18th century stone house was tragically destroyed by fire in 1966 but has been partially restored. It retains several unusual interior features, including extensive original paneling.

The two-story, three-bay fieldstone house has an entrance in the center of both the front and rear facades. Segmental stone arches top the north entrance and the cellar door. There is evidence of a pent roof on all four facades; the existing pent on the south is a late 20th century reconstruction. At the west end, a frame kitchen has been built on the extended foundations of an old stone wing. The two small, square windows on the second story of each gable end light closets on either side of the chimney. A small window on the west end of the north facade opened into a cupboard between the large fireplace and the outside wall.

The house retains its hall/parlor plan, which originally included a winder stair leading to the second floor. (In the late 20th century, this was replaced with a stair that rises along the partition between the hall and parlor.) The west room on the first floor has a large open hearth surrounded by raised paneling that reproduces the paneling destroyed in the fire. The fireplace in the parlor is similar to that in the hall, although somewhat more elaborate. The paneling that once surrounded the fireplace has been removed. Most of the doors and hardware throughout the house are original. The east

CE-1311, Friendship Stone (1995)

CE-70, Thomas Mackie House (1980)

CE-181, Wilna (Maryland Writers Project Collection, Maryland State Archives, MSA SC 908-08-00585)

bedroom on the second floor retains its original chair rail and a fully paneled east wall, which includes two closets, one on each side of the fireplace.

Although neither the builder nor a definite date of construction is known, this house was probably built by a member of either the Wallace or the Alexander family, both prominent in 18th century Cecil County. Many members of the Scots-Irish Alexander family moved from Cecil to Mecklenburg County, North Carolina, and to western Pennsylvania beginning in the mid-18th century. The houses they built in Mecklenburg were very like Cecil County stone houses such as this one.

Wilna
c. 1740 and later
Childs

The house known as Wilna was twice destroyed by fire in the second half of the 20th century, making it nearly impossible to authenticate the 1740 date usually ascribed to it. The three-bay north half is probably older and had corner brick fireplaces on each floor, with a side hall/double parlor plan, an unusual arrangement for that early a date. The two-bay south wing had a single fireplace on each floor and a one-room plan. A four-bay kitchen wing, also built in two stages, extends from the east side of the house.

This house has had a long association with the Mackall family and nearby Cyclone (Wilna) Mill. Dr. Richard Mackall, born here in 1822, was educated as a dentist and served on the county school board and in the General Assembly. From 1873 to 1876 he was editor of the *Cecil Democrat*. His brother William was a general in the Confederate army and served as chief of staff to Generals Braxton Bragg and Joseph Johnston.

Wilna Mill/Cyclone Mill (site)
mid-18th century
Childs vicinity

Now reduced to ruins, this once-important mill on the Little Elk Creek was founded about 1740, when Richard Mackall migrated to Cecil County from southeastern Pennsylvania. Mackall, a Quaker who attended the Brick Meeting House in Calvert, used the mill to produce flour. It was a small, two-story gristmill built of fieldstone laid in rubble fashion with a one-story frame addition; it had an overshot wheel. All that remains are the foundation walls. The mill's popular name was coined after a cyclone allegedly ripped off the roof in the late 19th century.

Elk Landing Farm (NR)
c. 1750-75
Elkton vicinity

This two-story, three-bay stone house sits at the confluence of the Little and Big Elk creeks, south of Elkton. Its center hall/double-pile plan is one commonly used by Anglo-American residents of the region. Along with the plan, the fieldstone construction, approximately symmetrical massing, and interior detail of this dwelling are typical of the third quarter of the 18th century in northeast Maryland and adjacent parts of Pennsylvania. Two corner fireplaces share a chimney on the first floor of the south end; a less common feature is the corner fireplace in the northwest room.

Its advantageous location makes early development of this site unsurprising. William Price surveyed and patented the

CE-132, Elk Landing Farm (1936, Historic American Buildings Survey)

CE-255, Holly Inn/Hollingsworth Tavern (1984)

CE-246, Partridge Hill (1936, Historic American Buildings Survey)

tract on August 29, 1672, as "Price's Adventure." Swedish-American trader John Hanson Steelman occupied the site from 1693 until 1710. Local tradition suggests a log kitchen wing, razed in 1905, may have been his trading post. Hollingsworth family ownership of the property dates from the first decades of the 18th century, and this house was probably built by Zebulon Hollingsworth, who purchased this part of the old tract on May 20, 1735.

Holly Inn/Hollingsworth Tavern
c. 1760 and additions
Elkton

One of Elkton's few 18th century survivors, this important building is a contemporary of Partridge Hill and the Mitchell house. Originally called the Holly Inn, it was built as a hotel to serve travelers on the busy Post Road between Philadelphia and Baltimore. The road was busy, indeed: On August 17, 1777, George Washington slept here; two days later British General Howe was a guest, reportedly using the very room Washington had vacated.

The two-story, Flemish bond brick building still has its original stairway, window sash, and mantels. A large bay window has been added to the west side. Many of the windows still have their original jack arches and fine keystones; the east and west facades were given the further refinement of pedimented gable ends.

Partridge Hill
c. 1760
Elkton

This prominent two-story brick house was built as the Elkton residence of Col. Henry Hollingsworth. Like several of its 18th century contemporaries, the house was erected on the first appreciable rise of land above the Big Elk Creek and along the Old Post Road between Philadelphia and Baltimore. The three-bay brick building is flanked by two 20th century brick wings. The east wing replaced an early brick outbuilding that apparently dated from the same period as the house. Notable exterior features include fine examples of 18th century Flemish bond masonry construction, flared wooden lintels with projecting keystones, and a continuous dentiled cornice. The interior contains much fine woodwork, including cornices, mantels, cupboards, and raised paneling.

Col. Hollingsworth, who played a prominent role in the Revolution, raised the Elk Battalion of militia in 1775 and saw action at the Battle of Brandywine. He later became quartermaster and commissary of the Eastern Shore.

Ricketts House/Encatada
c. 1760-80 and later
Elkton vicinity

This ancestral home of the Ricketts family stands along the western bank of the Big Elk Creek just north of Elkton. The stuccoed brick dwelling has grown in several directions, but it began as a two-story, side passage, double-pile structure. The most

CE-232, Ricketts house/Encatada (1980)

CE-133, Kieffer brick house (1980)

CE-682, Mason-Dixon marker

CE-149, Mitchell house (1936, Historic American Buildings Survey)

prominent addition to the early house is the two-bay 19th century addition to the east. A modillioned cornice was faithfully copied to create a uniform five-bay facade.

The Ricketts family has long been associated with the county milling industry, especially with the grist- and sawmills that were located along the nearby creek in the 18th and 19th centuries. Ruins of a gristmill remain on the property, and a miller's house stands nearby.

Mason-Dixon Markers
1766
Various locations

The marker illustrated is one of 111 original milestones placed along the West Line surveyed by Charles Mason and Jeremiah Dixon in 1765 to define the boundary between Maryland and its neighbors. First set in place in 1766 and reset in the 1900-1903 resurvey of the Maryland-Pennsylvania boundary, seventeen of these milestones fall within Cecil County. Most of the stones have an "M" inscribed on one side and a "P" on the other; every tenth marker has the Baltimore coat of arms on one side and the Penn symbol on the other.

Kieffer Brick House
c. 1770-90
Elkton vicinity

This two-story, Flemish bond brick house is located just north of Route 40 close to Little Elk Creek. It has a slightly shorter two-story, brick-and-frame kitchen wing. A 1968 examination of the house revealed horizontal bands of glazed headers on the east gable end; these are now covered by paint. Other important architectural elements are the slightly asymmetrical main facade and original three-room plan, which was often used by early Anglo-American settlers in northern Cecil County. The front and rear doors allowed access into the main room, or cross passage, while the left half of the house was divided into two rooms, each with a corner fireplace.

Mitchell House (NR)
1769
Elkton

The two-story Mitchell house, a well-known landmark along Elkton's Main Street, is one of a handful of houses that remain as architectural evidence of the town's mid-18th century development. Other contemporaneous structures, like Hollingsworth's Tavern and Partridge Hill, were also built on the north side of Main Street with a view of Big Elk Creek. These three structures have important architectural similarities, most notably the use of dentiled cornices, pedimented gable ends, pent eaves, wooden keystone lintels, and narrow chimney stacks.

This house was the home of the well-known physician Dr. Abraham Mitchell and was probably built by him. Dr. Mitchell was an ardent supporter of the Revolutionary War and opened his house to serve the American forces as a hospital; Lafayette visited here in 1781. After the war Dr. Mitchell moved to the stone house he had built (perhaps as early as 1769) in Fair Hill, near the Pennsylvania state line.

CE-249, Reverend Duke's log schoolhouse (1984)

CE-131, Holly Hall (1985)

Reverend Duke's Log Schoolhouse
c. 1799
Elkton

In the 18th century Elkton had no shortage of interesting citizens; surely, however, the Reverend William Duke ranks *primus inter pares*. Duke was born in Baltimore (now Harford) County in 1757. He developed an ardent interest in religion and became a follower of Francis Asbury; unlike Asbury, however, Duke did not believe it necessary for Methodists to separate themselves from the established (Anglican) church. Duke believed reforms could be effected from within the existing religious order. Thus, he broke with the Methodists and became an Anglican priest.

Duke was made rector of North Elk Parish in 1795. That same year he wrote and published *Observations on the Present State of Religion in Maryland*. After much travel throughout the state, he returned to Elkton, and in 1799 opened a school for boys in this building. Duke conducted the first Anglican services in Elkton in this log house. The Historical Society of Cecil County had the structure moved to its present site on East Main Street from Bow Street and restored the structure in 1972, removing layers of asbestos siding.

Holly Hall (NR)
c. 1802
Elkton

James Sewall's Holly Hall was undoubtedly influenced by the published designs of well-known architects such as Asher Benjamin and Robert Morris. The basic two-and-a-half story, hipped roof form is a common feature of the Federal style in Maryland, but the recessed stuccoed panels and brick parapets are rare in the state. These features, along with a raised basement and large six-over-six sash windows, contribute to the towering, vertical appearance of the house. This emphasis on height would be increased if the rooftop balustrade that appears in early photographs were still in place. The front porch is a meticulous restoration of the Federal period original.

The interior of the house features a standard, double-pile Georgian plan with one notable exception: the graceful elliptical stair is on the side of the center hall against the two lefthand windows of the south facade. This arrangement is identical to that of the Zebulon Rudolph house in Elkton, which dates from no more than fifteen years after this house. The woodwork is in the typically delicate Federal style, mixed with some Greek Revival alterations. Especially noteworthy are the neoclassical marble mantels.

Arch across Feeder Canal for the C&D Canal
1804
Elk Mills vicinity

In November 1803 the directors of the Chesapeake and Delaware Canal agreed that Welch Point on the Elk River would be the western terminus of the canal. Built soon after, this arch near Elk Mills was part of a feeder canal meant to provide water to the main canal. The canal company ran out of money before the feeder was completed, and when construction resumed twenty years later it was in a different location.

One hundred thousand dollars was expended in constructing the feeder canal before the project was halted, yielding several arches of the aqueduct that was to carry the water of the feeder. The surviving arch was designed by architect and engineer Benjamin Henry Latrobe to carry a road across the aqueduct. According to county historian George Johnston, it was built so well that when Daniel Lord, owner of the cotton factory at Elk Mills, wanted to dismantle the arch and use the stone, his workmen determined it would be easier and cheaper to quarry new stone for their needs.

CE-247, Zebulon Rudolph house

CE-652, Harlan-Wilson mill (historic photograph, Elk Creek Preservation Society)

Zebulon Rudolph House
National Bank of North East
Between 1806 and 1817 and later
Elkton

This impressive Federal period brick residence, now a bank, stands prominently at the corner of Main and Bridge streets in Elkton. The original house was two stories tall with the front facade laid in Flemish bond. A mid-19th century expansion raised the house an additional story, added a bracketed cornice, and appended a three-story circular bay onto the rear and a two-story polygonal bay on the east elevation. Windows with six-over-six sash were used during both building periods.

The interior of the building reflects this evolution as well. The archway with reeded pilasters that separates the entrance hall from the graceful elliptical staircase, the paneling below the chair rail, and the two fireplaces on the west end of the house reflect refinements from the height of the Federal period. One mantel on the first floor features paired colonettes, corner blocks with oval panel insets, and a frieze decorated with carved swags and reeding. Another, simpler mantel is notable for its geometric reeded decoration. The window frames and some door surrounds probably date from midcentury, with the plaster Adamesque ceiling and elaborate fireplace mantel in the east parlor resulting from a refurbishing later in the century. The two-story portico and balcony on the front, as well as the shutters and fanlight over the door, were added after the house was converted to a bank in the 1960s.

There are several similarities in the interior features of this house and Holly Hall, built at approximately the same time south of Elkton. In particular, the design and placement of the elliptical staircase, the first floor archway, and some of the woodwork appear to be by the same workmen. The two houses were built by members of the same family, who may have employed the same designer. Holly Hall was built in 1802 by Maria Rudolph and her husband, General James Sewall; this house on Main Street was built by her cousin Zebulon sometime after 1806. A deed of partition in 1817 mentions "the New House built since the death of Tobias Rudolph," Zebulon's uncle, in 1806. Tobias was a prominent businessman, and Zebulon the grandfather of President James Garfield's wife.

Harlan-Wilson Mill (site)
1811 and later
Leeds

Destroyed with dynamite in the 1960s, this mill played a key role in the 19th century industrialization of the Little Elk Creek Valley. It was built by John Wilson in 1811 as a woolen mill and later sold to John Harlan, who ran it as a cotton mill until it burned in 1828. After it was rebuilt, Harlan produced matchbox paper. His sons, George and John, operated the mill, specializing in pasteboard for bookbinding, until the late 19th century.

Arch across C&D Feeder Canal (George Reynolds)

CE-152, Tyson-Torbert house (1985)

Tyson-Torbert House
c. 1812-17
Elkton

One of the oldest houses in the eastern section of Elkton is this two-story, three-bay, gable-roofed brick town house laid in Flemish bond on the main facade. Above the roof of the one-story front porch is a two-brick stringcourse and on each gable end is a one-brick stringcourse.

When it was bought by the present owner in 1965, the house was in deteriorated condition and required extensive remodeling. Nevertheless, the original floor plan and some Federal period woodwork remain. To the left of the stair hall are two rooms, each with a corner fireplace. The staircase, with its molded rail, simple balusters, and square newel post, and the chair rail that parallels it, appear to date from the Federal period. The window moldings with their paneled reveals and the door are of the Greek Revival period and could date from the time when the frame wing was added to the east end of the house.

The original portion of the house was probably built between 1812 and 1819 by Levy Tyson. On the property—which was part of lot 31 on the town plat of Elkton—when it was sold in 1819 were "a two story brick house, kitchen, stable and other outbuilding." The Greek Revival moldings and frame wing may date after 1846, when Martha Torbert purchased the house, which was subsequently occupied by her three daughters.

John Wilson House
1812
Leeds

This two-and-a-half story, three-bay fieldstone house has cut stone quoins and brick jack arches above the windows and a Georgian plan. The date 1812 is painted below the eaves on the west gable end. This substantial house was altered in the early 20th century by the addition of a Colonial Revival porch with pedimented entrance and a rear wing, which contains the present dining room.

According to most sources, this house was built in 1812 by John Wilson, who came to Cecil County from England to manage the Cecil Manufacturing Company. The company, formed in 1795 by Colonel Henry Hollingsworth and other prominent local businessmen, produced cotton broadcloth and reputedly provided the material for the suit worn by Thomas Jefferson at his second inauguration. Wilson, a native of Leeds, England, a city well-known for its textile mills, ran the mill between 1804 and 1811, when he left to build a new mill (later known as Harlan's Mill) farther up Little Elk Creek. This house was built at that time for Wilson's family.

Wilson was also responsible for building a store, the Old Leeds Church, and several of the stone workers' houses that still stand in the community he named after his native city. Among his children were the Reverend John Wilson (born in 1809), who succeeded his father as pastor of the Leeds Church, and Hannah Wilson, who organized the first Sunday School in Maryland.

Wilson Double House
c. 1815
Leeds

One of several stone workers' houses John Wilson built near his mill in Leeds, this dwelling is a two-story, six-bay double house with a center chimney. The two

CE-177 and CE-178, John Wilson house and Wilson double house (1968)

CE-266, Burbage-Brock house (1936, Historic American Buildings Survey)

doors on the south facade are each flanked by a window on either side, rather than the more usual arrangement of two doors placed next to each other in the center of the building. The windows have six-over-six sash on the first story and three-over-three on the second story. The interior woodwork is simple but recognizably from the early 19th century.

Wallace-Carter Mill
c. 1816
Providence-Walnut Valley vicinity

The fieldstone ruins of Robert Carter's Cecil Paper Mill are located in a forest along the Little Elk Creek. The extensive mill complex burned in 1900, was rebuilt to produce paperboard and later burned again, bringing its long history of paper production to an end. During the 19th century, the mill supplied paper to the Baltimore *Sun* and the Philadelphia *Public Ledger*, as well as other businesses in Baltimore, Philadelphia, Pittsburgh, and Boston.

Robert Carter, a native of Cartertown in Chester County, Pennsylvania, arrived in Walnut Valley in the early 19th century and bought Michael Wallace's gristmill in 1813, converting it to a paper mill soon thereafter. By 1813 Carter had achieved a respectable level of production and personal worth, for in that year he was assessed for $23,620 worth of land and buildings and for rags and paper valued at $3,000. In 1851 Carter sold the mill for $4,000 to his son Israel Day Carter, who operated it until 1888. Robert D. Carter, a physician, operated the mill until 1896, at which time Charles Lee Carter and George McQulkin formed a company.

Burbage-Brock House
c. 1820, with alterations
Elkton

Built as a residence and now serving as a wedding chapel, this two-and-a-half story, three-bay fieldstone structure is a fine example of how adaptive use can preserve historic buildings. The main door is surmounted by a round brick arch.

CE-71, Wallace-Carter Mill (1978)

Wallace-Carter Mill drying shed (historic photograph)

CE-1078, Simpers log house (1980)

Simpers Log House
1st and 2nd quarters 19th century
Mechanics Valley vicinity

The original portion of this house consists of an unsheathed, V-notched log building with a massive exterior stone chimney in one gable end; attached to the chimney end of the house is a one-room addition, resulting in an arrangement known as a "saddlebag." A late 19th century photograph (see Chapter 8) shows Mrs. Simpers sitting in front of her house before later alterations made it almost unrecognizable. These changes include the erection of a new roof with gabled dormers, a corbeled brick chimney, a frame wing built perpendicular to the older portion, and a wraparound front porch.

New Castle and Frenchtown Railroad
1830-32 and later
Elkton vicinity

The New Castle and Frenchtown Railroad originally crossed the Delmarva Peninsula from a wharf in New Castle, Delaware, to a wharf at Frenchtown on the Elk River. The Cecil County portion of the route no longer serves as a railroad bed, but parts of it accommodate country roads, including the long, curving roadbed that leads to the river. The most evident sections of the railroad bed are in stream valleys, where earth-fill embankments survive.

Like many early railroads, the New Castle and Frenchtown was first built on stone sleepers ten or twelve inches square. When this system proved unsatisfactory for carrying the strap-iron rails, the stones were replaced with wooden ties. Stone sleepers were salvaged from the railroad by local residents and may be seen today in the foundations of buildings near the right-of-way.

In 1830 John Randel, Jr., designer of the C & D Canal, became the chief engineer of the newly re-formed New Castle and Frenchtown Turnpike and Railroad Company. He laid out a route for a rail line from New Castle to Frenchtown and construction began that same year. The railroad opened for passenger service on February 28, 1832, using horse-drawn carriages because its temporary rails were too light for locomotives. By September 10 English-built steam locomotives were operating on the improved roadbed. The New Castle and Frenchtown Railroad was the first railroad in the United States to employ steam power to transport passengers. It was incorporated in part in various later, more extensive rail systems, until today only a part of its original route remains in service.

Joseph Scarborough House
c. 1830-40
Pleasant Hill vicinity

Joseph Scarborough's estate was settled in 1854, at which time a dower of 38 acres was set aside for his widow, Sarah. That parcel contained this two-story, three-bay, hall/parlor house of fieldstone. The slightly symmetrical placement of windows and front door is

CE-1081, Joseph Scarborough house (1980)

CE-1067, Andrew McIntire house (1980)

CE-537, Scarborough Mill house (1980)

CE-829, Watts house (1978)

CE-1325, Staples house (1985)

a common feature of houses with Scots-Irish builders. The fieldstone walls were covered with stucco circa 1980.

Andrew McIntire House
c. 1830-50
Elkton vicinity

Standing within a few hundred yards of the Delaware-Maryland line is this two-story, side hall/double-parlor Flemish bond brick farmhouse. The tract of land is a small part of the sprawling "Welsh Tract," part of which Andrew McIntire, Sr., bequeathed to his son Andrew McIntire, Jr., in November 1850. The main house extends to the west with a shorter two-story, three-bay kitchen wing with unusual single-story, brick outshut that was used as a washhouse. The outshut is incorporated into a single-story, shed-roofed porch on the south side of the wing. Similar porches of different materials are attached to the north and south sides of the main house. The porches date from the mid- to late 19th century; the south porch is graced with decorative ironwork.

Scarborough Mill House
c. 1840-60
Mechanics Valley

Built on an exposed fieldstone foundation, this modest, two-story, side passage/parlor frame house stands near the fieldstone ruins of the Scarborough Mill. These two structures, along with a store, post office, blacksmith shop, wagon shop, and several houses, comprised the mid- to late 19th century community known as Mechanics Valley.

Watts House
c. 1840-60
Elkton vicinity

This house is an extremely unusual combination of two fairly typical house and outbuilding types. The two-story, three-bay, one-room deep brick structure with corbeled cornices is typical of the mid-19th century and the square pyramidal-roofed structure is not unique, but the two structures are joined at their corners, which remains, in Cecil County at least, very unusual.

Staples House
c. 1851
Elkton

This nicely proportioned gable-roofed frame house is two-and-a-half stories high and five bays wide, with a door in the center of the street facade. The windows six-over-six sash with louvered shutters on the second story and paneled shutters on the first story. The windows have molded architraves and simple pedimented heads, and a dentiled cornice graces the street facade. The interior has been altered but retains its original mantels.

Archival research, substantiated by the architectural evidence, points to a construction date around 1851. Seth Staples bought the undeveloped property in 1849 and willed it in 1856 with "the house I built them about five years ago" to his daughter-in-law Louise.

The Hermitage
18th century with additions
Elkton

When originally built, the Hermitage stood outside of Elkton, but today it is surrounded by mid-20th century residential development. The masonry house, now completely stuc-

CE-764, The Hermitage (1985)

Italianate houses on East Main Street, Elkton
(top: 1995, bottom: 1936, Historic American Buildings Survey)

coed, was built in several stages from the 18th century onward and includes extensive mid- to late 19th century renovations. Much of the interior has been remodeled through the years, and no woodwork predates the early 19th century.

It is possible that part of the house was built by Robert Alexander, who owned a house in Elkton during the American Revolution. Alexander returned to England after the war, and his estate, which embraced much of present-day Elkton, was confiscated and subdivided. The house was given its present name in honor of Andrew Jackson by the Bratton family, strong Democrats who owned it in the 19th century.

The main section of the house is five bays wide and two-and-a-half stories high beneath an irregular roof (the front slope is steeper than the rear). An interior masonry wall parallel to and north of the ridge suggests the house was made deeper; this northern addition extends one short bay east of the conjectural original front section. Although it is not readily apparent, the front portion appears to be of two construction dates, exclusive of the northerly extension: Floor-to-floor distances in the center hall and west room are less than that in the east room.

The principal stair rises in the hall, with intermediate landings, to the third floor. Its round rail is supported by an oversized octagonal newel and by balusters that restate the same form. The north extension has two rooms on each floor with an enclosed straight stair rising between them.

Italianate Houses on East Main Street
1850s

Believed to have been erected by the same builder—Price Strickland—are four houses on East Main Street in Elkton; these serve as a transition between the dwellings of the colonial and Federal periods along the street, such as the Mitchell house at 131 East Main, and such Victorian extravaganzas as the Taylor house at 254 East Main. The house at 220 East Main, for example, is a three-story, three-bay brick structure with a superb one-story, cast-iron porch across its street facade, the elaborate ironwork formed into leaves

CE-1075, Antego (1980)

CE-262, Clayton Building (1985)

and flowers. Below the cornice is a metal downspout with an American eagle and the date 1853 stamped on it. It is believed that the house at 220 was built first and was followed, in order, by 215, 222, and 226 East Main Street.

Antego
c. 1850-70
Leeds vicinity

Located in a grassy wooded glen, this two-story, three-bay frame house has delicate bargeboard trim and a fanciful hip-roofed porch. The mid-19th century weatherboard-covered structure is still intact and stands on property known as Antego bordering Laurel Run. James McCauley is designated on the Martenet map as the owner of the property in 1858.

Clayton Building
1857
Elkton

Originally built as the Elkton Opera House and a meeting space for the International Order of Odd Fellows, this is one of the most vigorous Victorian structures in Elkton. Designed by the Baltimore architecture firm of Dixon and Davis, it provides evidence of the growth that Elkton experienced nearly a century after its founding.

The three-story brick building has a gable-end entrance facing North Street. Above the first story, the facade is divided into five recessed brick bays, each with a tall, round-arched opening on the second floor. These openings were all originally windows, but three of them have since been bricked in. Above these are five rectangular recessed panels; the center one has a datestone reading "I.O.O.F., 1857." Above the panels is a row of smaller, segmental-arched windows, and above them is a row of decorative brick corbeling.

CE-257, Elkton Methodist Church (1984)

CE-823, Otter Farm italianate house (1978)

Elkton Methodist Church
1859
Elkton

This two-story brownstone structure has a tower and a gabled entrance pavilion. The tower, which projects slightly from the south facade of the main body of the church, contains a tall, pointed-arch, stained glass window and a datestone. The spire above the tower is covered with butt-end shingles.

President Ulysses S. Grant visited this church while staying nearby with his friend Attorney General John A. J. Creswell.

Gilpin Manor
1760; 1860
Elkton vicinity

The Gilpin family's wealth and importance in Elkton society is demonstrated by this stuccoed brick house, which stands along the east bank of the Big Elk Creek. The two-story 18th century portion is three bays wide and two rooms deep. It is capped by a heavy modillioned cornice that forms a pediment on the east gable end and has a chamfered water table. The stucco surface was scored to imitate ashlar masonry. The 18th century structure is similar in size and detail to both the Mitchell house and Partridge Hill. Like these others, Gilpin Manor was enlarged by a 19th century addition, which in this case doubled the size of the house. The addition at Gilpin Manor is taller than the earlier house; a clerestory dormer was added to the original portion when the addition was made.

Otter Farm Italianate House
1860-80
Elkton vicinity

The Italianate form was a most appropriate one for this site if the builder had any intention of creating a statement of wealth and dominance. The height of the house is dramatically emphasized by its location on a hill, making the three-story structure loom over the surrounding farm. The five-bay, single-pile house with center hall plan retains most of its period details, including a heavy bracketed cornice. A one-story hipped roof kitchen wing extends to the rear. A log tenant house that predates it is located north of this house. Alfred Wetherill is listed at this site in the 1877 atlas.

CE-162, Gilpin Manor (1995)

CE-157, 221-23 Main Street, Elkton (1985)

CE-153, Henry Torbert house (1984)

221-23 East Main Street
c. 1865
Elkton

The ten bays of this long, two-and-a-half story brick duplex form one of the most prominent structures in the east end of Elkton. The building is two bays deep, but the windows have been filled in on the east facade. One-story, three-sided bay windows terminate each end of the main facade; the front is further enriched by a bold brick cornice and a one-story cast-iron porch.

Henry Torbert House
After 1867
Elkton

This urbane, sophisticated house is the best example of the popular French Second Empire style in Elkton and one of the best in the county. Built sometime after 1867 by Henry Torbert, it is a two-story, three-bay town house covered in stucco. It has projecting quoins and is topped by a steep mansard roof with a scrolled bracket cornice. The window architraves on the first story have a flat cornice and on the second floor a segmental-arched cornice. The paired dormer windows have gable roofs, bracketed eaves, and jig-sawn bargeboards. The oak double door at the entrance is notable for its deep molding and circular panels.

The interior of the house displays some of the finest Victorian period woodwork in Elkton. A marbleized Gothic wooden mantel adorns each of the two fireplaces in the front room. The ceiling has a deep cornice above a wooden molding in a floral design. Two large foliated plaster chandelier medallions add further decorative interest.

The right rear room has a fireplace on the east wall, which has a marbleized and mahogany veneer mantelpiece with a small roundel with a likeness of Mozart in the center panel. Elaborate Renaissance-style wood cornices top the two windows, one of which contains stained glass, and the ceiling panel is encircled by gilded egg-and-dart molding. In the center is a gilded lozenge medallion consisting of carved heads and flowers. The left rear room has been more extensively remodeled but retains a fine oak mantel.

Henry R. Torbert, born in 1834, was the grandson of the well-known Presbyterian minister William Torbert. A lifelong Republican, he twice ran unsuccessfully for Congress, was appointed surveyor for the Port of Baltimore, and served as clerk of the circuit court in Cecil County. In 1876 he assumed control of the *Cecil Whig*.

CE-1077, Union United Methodist Church (1980)

Union United Methodist Church
c. 1867
Pleasant Hill vicinity

The present Union Methodist Church stands across the road from the cemetery and site of the first church structure, a log building that measured 20 x 24 feet and was built in 1822. This larger, frame replacement measures 35 x 50 and is typical of rural country churches of the 19th century, with its rectangular shape, gabled roof, and small gabled vestibule. The stained glass windows date from the late 19th century and were installed as memorials to various members of the congregation.

Boulden Chapel and Cemetery
1871; 1938
Elkton vicinity

Small country churches and chapels dot the Cecil County landscape; this one was built in two stages. The earlier building is a square weatherboard-covered frame box with gable roof. The door in the gable end is flanked by six-over-six sash on either side. The same building proportions were repeated in the 1938 common bond brick replacement.

Harvey Frame House
After 1868
Childs vicinity

This two-and-a-half story frame house with Gothic Revival decorative trim stands on a hill overlooking the Harvey stone house. After its construction, this house was the main residence on the property, and the 18th century stone house served as a tenant house.

The frame house is five bays wide and three stories tall with a center gable containing a round-arched window. Two round-arched dormers flank the cross gable, as do four small three-light windows under the eaves. Carpenter Gothic woodwork with finials and pendants decorates the eaves and bargeboards as well as the flat-roofed front porch. A two-story wing extends to the rear.

Cecil County Jail
1872
Elkton

Victorians seemed fascinated by prisons, and the massive, fortresslike jails they built can still be seen in many Maryland cities: The castlelike Baltimore City jail and the Romanesque jail in Cambridge are classic examples. The brick-and-granite jail in Elkton is not as visually striking as those other structures, but it does make its own definite statement. Built of Port Deposit granite, it also once housed the sheriff's office and had several adjoining outbuildings, including a brick stable and carriage house. A garden, several acres in size, was cultivated by the prisoners.

CE-1080, Boulden Chapel and cemetery (1980)

CE-780, Gilpin house (1995)

CE-656, Harvey frame house (1985)

CE-1307, Cecil County Jail (1985)

Gilpin House

c. 1875
Elkton

Quiet and elegant, this house sits serenely back from East Main Street behind a privet hedge. The two-story, three-bay common bond brick building displays particularly fine mortar joints. All windows and doors are topped with segmental arches that were given a sense of rhythm by being finished with diminutive keystones. This rhythm is continued by the pairs of thin brackets carefully placed along the eaves. Although somewhat altered, the interior retains attractive semicircular niches in the two front parlors.

Elkton Presbyterian Church

1873
Elkton

The Scots have played a prominent role in the religious affairs of Cecil County since its settlement, as this impressive Presbyterian church suggests. It is a one-story brick structure with a two-story tower and spire on its east side; a gabled entrance pavilion stands opposite on the west side of the main facade. The brickwork of the church is echoed in the wall that encloses the adjacent lot.

This congregation was founded in Elkton in 1833 at this site. That first church was enlarged in 1858 and rebuilt in 1873.

CE-258, Elkton Presbyterian Church (1985)

Historical Society of Cecil County

2nd quarter 19th century, c. 1873, c. 1900
Elkton

The three-story, mansard-roofed brick structure on a stone foundation that serves as the headquarters of the Historical Society of Cecil County reflects several periods of construction. In the second quarter of the 19th century, it was built to accommodate a bank and cashier's quarters using a form and plan comparable to the regionally typical two-story, side passage/double-pile dwelling with rear service wing. It diverged from this model in that the main facade was four bays wide, with a second entrance between the windows that opened into the commercial space. The first floor plan has a large banking

CE-1355, Historical Society of Cecil County (1995)

343

CE-661, Childs store (1980)

CE-687, Childs Row 3 (1980)

CE-1308, *Cecil Whig* building (1985)

space in front, with an inner office or meeting room behind; masonry vaults open from each of these rooms. The side hall, to one side of the banking space, led to the residential space on the upper floors, used by the bank's cashier. Service functions were contained in a two-story rear wing.

In the second building phase, about 1873, the original roof was replaced with a mansard. The third period of construction occurred circa 1900 and encompassed moving the entrance to a brick vestibule added to the southwest corner of the front, wrapping an open porch around the southeast corner, and installing an elaborately decorated pressed metal ceiling in the banking room. A series of additions were made to the sides and rear of the building in the mid-20th century.

The interior of the building includes a combination of woodwork from the different construction periods.

Cecil Whig Building (site)
1841, 1876, 1882
Elkton

The *Cecil Whig* Building, home of one of Maryland's oldest surviving newspapers, was originally built in 1841 and rebuilt in 1876 after a disastrous fire. It was a two-story, two-bay brick structure that stretched far back from the sidewalk. The main facade,

CE-667 and 686, Childs Row 1 and 2 (1977)

facing the west side of North Street, was of particular interest. A tower built in 1882 on one side contained a Colonial Revival door on the ground floor and a multipanel window above; these two openings were set into a recessed panel that extended up the entire tower. The panel was corbeled at the top and inscribed with the dates 1841 and 1882. The other half of the main facade also had a recessed area with decorative carved brick in a floral design.

Childs Store
c. 1880-90
Childs

George W. Childs, owner of the Philadelphia *Ledger*, purchased the Marley Paper Mill from Robert Carter in 1866 and proceeded to develop his own mill community at the intersection of Cherry Hill and Blue Ball roads. Included in the development process were three frame tenements and this two-story frame store. The plain rectangular structure contains one large room on each story. While the first floor housed a store and for a time a post office, the second floor served as a meeting room for local community groups. A one-story lean-to addition crosses the rear of the building.

Childs Row
c. 1880-1900
Childs

George Childs, owner of the Marley Paper Mill, was responsible for constructing this row of buildings along Blue Ball Road and for enlarging and giving his name to the mill community.

First in this row is a two-story frame house with weatherboard siding, a stone foundation, a brick stove chimney, and a porch with bracketed columns. Next is a late 19th century frame duplex distinguished from other worker housing in the area by two bay windows with unusual triangular dormers. Its overall appearance suggests a single-family dwelling more successfully than most double houses in which separate front doors give away the two-family use. Third in this row is a relatively modest Queen Anne house that is slightly larger than the others. A gable end bay window and turned-post porch provide extra refinements. These architectural touches and the large side yard suggest a mill manager probably lived in this house.

CE-233, Elk Forge bridge (1968)

CE-422, George W. Childs Victorian house (1980)

Martha Finley House
c. 1883
Elkton

One of Elkton's most ambitious Victorian houses is this large, two-and-a-half story frame structure. It displays the asymmetry, irregular roofline, abundance of dormers, and porches typical of the Queen Anne style, enhanced with a variety of window treatments and sunburst designs in the hooded dormers of the main facade. (Aluminum siding added in the 20th century has obscured much of the fine detail.)

The house stands on one of the many lots created by the subdivision of the property of Daniel Bratton after his death in 1882. At the turn of the 20th century, the house was home to Miss Martha Finley, the well-known author of the Elsie books, favorites of generations of children. The building was converted to a funeral parlor in the mid-1930s and is today the Gee Funeral Parlor.

Elk Forge Bridge (site)
1884
Elk Mills

Photographed in 1968 before it was replaced, this single-span Pratt through truss bridge was similar to several bridges built in the county in the late 19th century during the term of commissioners W. S. Potter, W. D. Pierson, and E. S. Sentman. Attached to one of the diagonal tie rods was a date plaque that contained the commissioners' names and the date. The builder of the bridge was not recorded.

George W. Childs Victorian House
c. 1890
Childs vicinity

An abundance of steeply pitched gable, hip, and shed roofs; a variety of exterior siding materials; and an overall asymmetrical design place this house into the architectural style known as Queen Anne. One of several late 19th century styles, it developed as a contrast to the symmetrical and classically inspired dwellings of the late 18th and early 19th centuries.

When George W. Childs built this house, which is now hidden by mature trees, the hilltop site afforded an expansive view of the immediate neighborhood, including Childs's Marley Paper Mill.

Givens House
Last quarter 19th century
Leeds vicinity

Although its appearance has been altered by the application of asphalt brick siding, the Gothic Victorian features of this two-story frame house are still visible. The central three-story tower has hooded dormer windows, and an early 20th century shed-roofed porch crosses part of the front facade.

Black Rock Tavern
c. 1760 and alterations
Elkton

Behind the present, rather eclectic facade of this structure is an 18th century tavern. Such buildings once dotted the Old Post Road (now Main Street) in Elkton. The building is not without merit in its present form: Fish-scale shingles cover the third story,

CE-1310, Black Rock Tavern (1995)

CE-1082, Givens house (1995)

CE-1315, John Wirt house (1995)

CE-1309, Elkton Town Hall (1985)

adding a certain interest, as do the pendants that mark each corner. The old tavern is now an attorney's office.

John Wirt House
c. 1888
Elkton

Somewhat simpler in appearance than the houses on either side, this dwelling on Main Street in Elkton is a two-and-a-half story frame structure covered with clapboard on the first story and wood shingles on the second. Decorative half-timbering is used on the west gable and the cross gable on the front. Many of the windows have stained glass upper sash.

The interior is notable for four corner fireplaces executed in the late Victorian Art Nouveau style. The decorative treatment of the fireplaces includes the use of glazed majolica tile with floral moldings, ebonized woodwork, and elaborate grilles. The heavy newel post is topped by a metal cherub statuette holding an electric torch. Two stained glass windows light the stair hall: One is brightly colored in a stylized floral pattern; the other is painted with an elk's head, an appropriate subject in a town once named "Head of Elk."

John Wirt built the house shortly after 1888, perhaps as a delayed wedding present for his wife, whom he had married two years earlier. A prominent lawyer in late 19th century Elkton, Wirt was a Democratic state senator in the 1880s and was responsible for the introduction of the "Australian" or secret ballot in Maryland elections. He was also president of the *Cecil Democrat* during this period.

Taylor House
After 1888
Elkton

Elkton enjoyed one of several boom periods between 1880 and 1900. A new boatyard, fertilizer plant, and pulp mill were established in 1887. The pulp mill ranked as the third largest in the United States. The resulting prosperity took physical form in many of the houses at the city's extreme east end.

This house, an elaborate, three-story structure, dates from that prosperous time. It has an entrance on the east and a three-bay gabled pavilion that rises from the west, enlivening the main facade. There is a three-sided dormer in the roof above the entrance, and a porch, gabled and projecting farther at the entrance, stretches across the entire main facade.

Elkton Town Hall
mid-18th century, 1890s, 20th century
Elkton

Probably the oldest room in Elkton's downtown commercial district, Elkton's first courtroom, has been incorporated into the present town hall, built in the 20th century. The courtroom has an arched ceiling and brick floors. The brick building with tall tower that adjoins the city hall once served as the town's firehouse and was built in the 1890s. It has been integrated into the design of the present town hall.

CE-1317, Taylor house (1995)

Trinity Episcopal Church
1896
Elkton

The present church was erected after a circa 1867 building was destroyed by fire in 1896. The 1867 building itself had replaced a church erected in 1832. Displaying a vigorous design and an irregular roofline, Trinity is solidly constructed of dark Port Deposit granite with brick trim. Brick was used, too, in its steeple and chimneys. The building was designed by New York architect Henry Congdon, a specialist in ecclesiastical architecture.

The parish house behind the church was built in 1904 and is similar to the church in design and workmanship.

Plum Creek Bridge
c. 1890-1910
Elkton vicinity

The Warren truss bridge crossing Plum Creek near Elkton is a common bridge type for the late 19th and early 20th centuries. Each iron truss consists of five triangular divisions, which are strengthened by intermittent vertical supports. All the main structural members are joined by riveted connector plates and stiffened by small lattice braces. Additional support for each truss is provided by a series of lateral diagonal braces that extend outward from the vertical plane of the truss. No date plaque survives on the bridge, but the structural features and local history suggest a construction date at the turn of the century.

Bratton House
c. 1897
Elkton

This house, an interesting combination of the Queen Anne and Colonial Revival styles, was probably built by Howard Bratton after 1897. The two-story frame residence has a hipped roof with hipped roof dormers and is covered with wooden shingles on the second story. Below the dentiled cornice is a series of panels with carved garland swags in the centers; both are decorative features typi-

CE-256, Trinity Episcopal Church (1995)

CE-1037, Plum Creek bridge (1981)

CE-1320, Bratton house (1985)

CE-1035, Elkton Armory and war memorial (1985)

cal of the Colonial Revival style. There is an octagonal tower with a bell-cast roof at the southwest corner. The house is notable for its stained glass windows, some with oval frames above the porch and around the fine carved oak door. The interior, with its oak mantels, wide oak staircase, interior stained glass windows, and open floor plan, is a fine example of the architectural detail of the period.

Elkton Armory (NR)
World War I Doughboy Monument
1915
Elkton

The Elkton Armory, completed in 1915 at a cost of $39,000, was dedicated to the uses of Company E of the 115th Infantry, 29th Division of the National Guard. Subsequent reorganizations renamed the unit the 1729th Maintenance Company under the fifth regiment.

As part of the 29th Division, the Elkton unit shares in the honors bestowed upon the division at the close of World War II, most notably the distinguished unit citation and French *croix de guerre* with palm. Personnel of the unit are proud of its history and continuity, and a number of them have continued a family tradition of serving in the National Guard into a second and third generation.

Located near the town center, the armory emulates a medieval fortification, sporting towers, crenelated parapets, and strip buttresses. Faced with light gray granite, the T-shaped structure comprises a two-story "head house" parallel to the street with a one-story drill hall to the rear. It is one of at least eight similar structures in Maryland built during the reorganization and expansion of the National Guard in the early 20th century.

The Elkton Armory has housed numerous community events, including the first bowling alley in Cecil County, begun in the drill hall during the 1940s. The armory has also served as the staging area for community emergency operations resulting from natural disasters, particularly flood relief. It was used to provide temporary shelter for bodies of victims of a commercial airliner crash that occurred two miles outside of Elkton in 1963.

Erected on the southwest corner of the courthouse yard in 1921 was a monument to the men and women of Cecil County who served in World War I. Joseph H. Sloan of Elkton Marble and Granite Works received the contract to erect the monument, a Doughboy depicted as a sentinel and carved from Vermont marble. Monuments to the common soldier were popularized after the Civil War, when it was felt that the common soldier was as noteworthy

CE-1334, Peoples Bank Building (1985)

as the hero or leader and that monuments recognizing this symbolized the democratic ideal of equality. After the new courthouse was built in Elkton in 1940, the monument was moved to the armory grounds, where it remains.

Peoples Bank Building
1924
Elkton

The Peoples Bank Building on North Street is a large, well-preserved, two-story brick commercial structure with a gable end entrance. Notable features on the false-front facade are the corbeled brickwork below the steeply pitched eaves and, above the second story window, the brick entablature supported by terra-cotta brackets with decorative rosettes.

The bank is a rare example of early 20th century commercial architecture in Elkton. Most of the commercial structures along Main Street were built after several fires that devastated downtown Elkton in the 1940s.

Childs Pony Truss Bridge
1932
Childs vicinity

This bridge carries Maryland Route 545 over Little Elk Creek near Childs. It is a camelback pony truss bridge with a very short top chord, three panel divisions with diagonal tension members in the outer panels, and a pair of crosses in the very narrow center panel. Erected in 1932, this structure was built by Roanoke Iron and Bridge Works, Inc., of Roanoke, Virginia, using the specifications of the Maryland State Roads Commission, H. D. Williar, chief engineer.

U.S. Route 40 Bridge over AMTRAK
1939
Elkton vicinity

This bridge carries the eastbound lanes of U.S. 40 over the Amtrak main line near Elkton. A series of steel beam segments measuring 60, 71, 74, and 58 feet, respectively, rest at their junctures on three concrete bents of four arches each. The entire structure is sheathed in concrete. The bents parallel the railroad, and the highway crosses the cut at an angle, giving the bridge a parallelogram plan.

The bridge is notable for its lively Art Deco/Art Moderne ornament. The structure of the bridge is below grade (in the railroad cut), making the parapet walls the visible and highly decorated sections of the bridge. Above long horizontal panels that form the base of each wall are continuous bands of decorated concrete. The most striking features are the series of inset stepped zigzags and quarter circles within this band. A thin coping tops this section of the bridge walls and curved piers mark each end of the structure.

This bridge is one of only two historic concrete bridges in Cecil County and one of only nine of the same structural type in the state road network.

CE-999, Childs pony truss bridge (1979)

CE-998, U.S. Route 40 bridge over AMTRAK (1980)

Fourth District

CE-172, Hopewell (1994)

Hopewell (NR)
c. 1730–50
Rock Church vicinity

Hopewell is one of the earliest and most important buildings surviving in the Little Elk Creek Valley. Although the second front door was converted to a window in the late 20th century, it retains its original plan, much of its 18th century woodwork, and such masonry details as segmental arches over the windows. (See Chapter 8 for an unaltered photograph of this house.)

The Mackie family owned portions of the Hopewell tract in the 18th century and can be credited with building this ambitious uncoursed fieldstone house. The two large front rooms undoubtedly served as the main living and cooking areas, while the two rear rooms were probably first floor bed chambers.

Fixed between the rear rooms is the staircase, the most distinctive element of 18th century woodwork in the house. Rising clear to the attic, it has early turned balusters, a heavy handrail, and a square newel post that is beaded on each corner and has the remains of a molded cap. The triangular area below the stair is decorated with four raised panels. The four-panel door leading to the cellar is topped with two panels and a molded cornice with cyma curve profile. The stair pivots on a central vertical support, which is mortised and pinned at the second floor level. The turned balusters on the second floor stair are about half the size of the first floor balusters. On the second floor, the molding is not as elaborate and only a single raised panel is found below the stringer. The beaded newel post on this level has lost its cap. Two small rooms in the attic housed servants.

In the basement is one large room with a central stone pier supporting the main summer beam. Two corner fireplace supports rise in the center of the west wall; a large arched support on the east wall is joined by a corner support on the north. In the southwest corner of the room a set of stone steps leads into a sunken area with

CE-72, The Beehive (1994)

CE-191, Blue Ball Tavern (1994)

plastered stone walls that measures approximately eight feet square and eight feet deep. This area may have been used for cool storage of goods or ice. It is presently uncovered but originally was roofed.

Although the construction date of this house is uncertain, research has uncovered land transactions concerning Hopewell as early as 1714. In July of that year a tract of 544 acres called "Hopewell" was surveyed for Mathias van Bibber; he served as chief justice of Cecil County in 1719 at Courthouse Point. In 1725 van Bibber sold 423 acres of the tract to Stephen Hollingsworth, Robert Holy, and Robert Mackey, a Quaker from New Jersey. On October 31, 1731, Mackey secured from the governor and council of Virginia an order for 100,000 acres in the Shenandoah Valley; in May 1732, before going south to Virginia as one of the earliest white settlers west of the Blue Ridge mountains, he sold 100 acres of Hopewell to James Mackey, likely builder of this house.

Hopewell was the home of Captain James Mackey, who served in the Revolution in the 34th Battalion, Maryland Militia, and of Colonel David Mackey.

The Beehive
18th century
Rock Creek vicinity

This early industrial complex is popularly called the Beehive, an appropriate name for a center of busy commercial activity. Local tradition and research suggest the westernmost ruin was a cooper's shop, while the other stone buildings were three workers' houses and a store licensed to dispense alcoholic beverages. The two structures in the center were dismantled for their stone in the late 19th century for Franklin T. Mackie's house Highlawn. All that remains of these are weatherboarded gable end walls and stone foundations. The two-story, two-bay stone building at the right end of the complex was Michael Wallace's store.

Blue Ball Tavern
mid- to late 18th century
Calvert vicinity

The original Blue Ball Tavern is believed to have been housed in the building just north of the present tavern, which stands along Maryland Route 273 on the eastern edge of the Nottingham Lots. This building stands on lot 35, which was sold originally to Andrew Job. The exact date of construction is unknown, but strong architectural evidence indicates two 18th century building periods. The first, 1740-60, produced the western half of the stuccoed brick structure. A definite seam is evident in the slate roof where the second period (1780-1800) structure begins.

The juxtaposition of these two structures offers a rare chance to compare two 18th century vernacular floor plans in the same house. The western section, three bays by two with asymmetrical fenestration, had a cross passage/three-room plan. This plan was used by Anglo-American settlers throughout the area from the first years of settlement through the early 19th century. This three-room plan was eventually

CE-74, Mitchell house/Fair Hill Inn (1981)

replaced in popularity by plans influenced by the more formal, classically inspired Georgian style; one of these forms is the side passage/double-pile plan that can be seen in the eastern half of the tavern.

Mitchell House/Fair Hill Inn (NR)
before 1769 with additions
Fair Hill

Standing at the corner of two important colonial roads is the Mitchell house in Fair Hill. The stone portion is a fine example of a side hall/double-pile house form with several construction features distinctive to this region. Most interesting of these is the gable end pent eave, which deteriorated and was never rebuilt. The ends of the supports for it and the stone drip course are clearly visible.

The house is constructed of locally quarried Wesahiggin schist laid in rubble bond on the east and west facades. The south facade features cut stone, expertly laid with massive quoins. The similarity in the stonework of this house and of nearby Little Elk Farm and the Col. David Mackey house, combined with the roughly contemporary construction dates of the buildings, suggests the same builder for all three. All have unusually narrow mortar joints, indicating exceptional skill on the part of the stonecutter.

The interior of the Mitchell house retains much of its 18th century woodwork, although some had to be replaced during late 20th century restoration work. The paneled window reveals, chair rail, and stair are good examples of period craftsmanship. The stair features scrolled step-ends, a molded banister and corresponding half rail, and an unusual four-part open newel post.

No definite date of construction has been determined, although a fireback in the house bears the date 1764. More reliable evidence is the granting of a license in 1769 to John Strawbridge to operate a tavern here. Such licenses were often sought by owners of large houses along busy roads to relieve them of the onus of providing free food and drink to any traveler who stopped by.

The house is associated with two well-known members of the Mitchell family. Dr. Abraham Mitchell, a prominent physician during the Revolution, bought the house in 1781 and moved here from his town house in Elkton. His son Colonel George Edward Mitchell served in the War of 1812 and in the Maryland legislature and U.S. Congress. In 1824, while in Congress, Col. Mitchell introduced the resolution inviting Lafayette to visit the United States and later had the privilege of presenting him to Congress. In gratitude, Lafayette presented Mitchell with several cherry trees. An 1827 letter from Lafayette acknowledges receipt of "several kinds of corn from Fair Hill," sent by Mitchell in thanks for the cherry trees.

Mackey Farmhouse
c. 1770-90
Rock Church vicinity

This farmhouse, like many rubble fieldstone structures, has been covered with several coats of whitewash to create a uniform appearance. Architectural details and the side hall/double-pile form suggest a 1770-90 construction date.

At one time there was a datestone in the south gable end of this house; it fell out and has been removed from the property. The house is located on the old "Hopewell" tract and was probably built by a member of the Mackey family, possibly Sergeant James Mackey, who served in the Revolutionary War.

Little Elk Farm (NR)
c. 1775-1800
Rock Church vicinity

Nestled into a slope leading down to the Little Elk Creek, the stone house at Little Elk Farm stands on the "Little Venture" tract, patented to Robert Mackey on October 11, 1769. The house consists of two 18th century sections: a two-and-a-half story, gable-roofed main block and a two-story kitchen wing on the east gable end. The stonework of the south facade is exceptional and bears many similarities to that found at both the Mitchell house and

CE-170, Little Elk Farm (1979)

CE-173, Mackey farmhouse (1968)

CE-174, Col. David Mackey house (1968)

CE-533, William Fulton house (1994)

the Col. David Mackey house. The facade is laid in tight-fitting, finely cut, uncoursed fieldstone with queen quoins and keystone lintels over the windows.

Later owners made significant changes to the house in the mid- to late 19th century, adding dormer windows, front and back porches, and a slate roof with projecting eaves. Interior changes included the modification of the original floor plan. Instead of a small room with corner fireplace to the west and a long room across the north with corner fireplaces, the plan was altered to have one large room on the west with a fireplace on the west wall and a bath and cloakroom behind the center (or east) hall. The former kitchen, to the east and down two steps, was paneled and made into a dining room, leading to a remodeled kitchen and pantry.

Despite these changes, much of the exceptional 18th century woodwork remains, including the open main stair with its scrolled step-ends, molded handrail, paneled newel post, and parallel half-rail. The paneling in the second floor hall retains the original deep green stain. Also of interest is an 18th century ladder that once provided access to the sleeping loft in the east wing.

This was the home in the 18th century of First Lieutenant William Mackey, who served during the Revolution in the 34th Battalion, Maryland Militia, Captain James Mackey's company.

Col. David Mackey House
1784, c. 1830s
Lewisville, Pennsylvania, vicinity

This house exemplifies the way in which earlier houses were enlarged and remodeled in the 19th century. The 18th century house was a two-story, gable-roofed fieldstone structure with the entrance on the southeast corner. A 1784 datestone on the west facade has the initials of David Mackey, a returning Revolutionary War officer, who built this house on the "Hopewell" tract.

The stonework on the south or main facade of Col. Mackey's house exhibits the same high-quality masonry found in other houses in the immediate area, including the Mitchell house and Little Elk Farm. The cut stone is tightly laid with raised mortar joints and keystone lintels atop the doors and windows. The interior features a side hall/double-parlor plan and much later Georgian woodwork. The doors have shouldered architraves, and the stair features scrolled step-ends, a newel post with inset panels and molded cap, and a molded banister with corresponding half-rail. Other Georgian period features include the chair rail, beaded corners, and raised panel doors with HL hinges.

The location of the original kitchen is uncertain; it either stood to the right of the house and was reached through the door on the east facade, or it was the room to the north, now incorporated into a later wing.

The house was considerably enlarged, probably in the 1830s, with the addition of a third story and a two-story wing on the north side. The third story features windows with three-over-three sash, while the wing has a shed roof that slopes from west to east. The shed-roofed frame porch on the east facade is from the Victorian period.

The property is the probable site of the classical school moved to Cecil County from New London, Pennsylvania, in 1752. The school was housed in the home of the Reverend Alexander McDowell, pastor of the "Old Side" Presbyterians and operated until 1767, when it was moved to Newark, Delaware. Chartered by the Penn family two years later, the academy developed into present-day University of Delaware.

William Fulton House
1787
Providence vicinity

A datestone with the initials "WIF" and the year 1787 records the construction of this two-story, side passage, double-pile stone house along the west bank of the Little Elk Creek. William Fulton's will, probated in 1816, sheds further light on the construction of his house, noting that he left £20 sterling to his son Thomas "for his help as carpenter when I was building my house." The two-bay frame section, which extends from the passage end of the stone house,

CE-521, McCleary farm (1980)

CE 1100, Tyson Mill house (1980)

was built over an earlier foundation of unknown date; it contains evidence of a 12-foot hearth along the east end wall and a door and window on the south wall. The senior Fulton, who came to Maryland from Ayrshire, Scotland, via Lancaster, Pennsylvania, owned a nearby flax mill. He took the oath of allegiance to Maryland in 1778 and served as a first lieutenant in the Maryland militia during the Revolution.

New Munster Stone
1792
Big Elk Creek

On the west bank of the Big Elk Creek, a "pistolle shotte from the mouth of a rivulett called the Shure," stands a large gray stone that marks the beginning of a tract called "New Munster." Land records refer to property as located in New Munster up until the Revolution.

The tract was originally settled by Scots-Irish who had previously lived in Ulster, or northern Ireland. The 6,000-acre tract, which lay on both sides of the Big Elk Creek, was surveyed in 1683 by George Talbott for Edwin O'Dwire and other Irishmen by virtue of a warrant from Cecil Calvert as a defense against the encroachment of Penn's Quakers from the north. The tract extended about a mile into what is now Pennsylvania.

The stone replaced the poplar that first marked the beginning of the tract. In 1792 a boundary commission established the property rights of Matthew Wallace and set up the stone. On the east face is chiseled the letter B, for beginning; on the south, the letters WS are for "Wallace's scrawl" (his property formed a scroll, or U, around the base of the tract; scrawl was a variant of scroll); on the west was the date of the survey, 1683; and on the north NI atop NM, for New Ireland and New Munster.

McCleary Farm
late 18th through 19th century
Pleasant Hill

Architectural evidence in both the attic and the cellar of this two-story stuccoed log-and-fieldstone house records three stages of growth. The first was the two-story log half of the main block, which includes the central chimney pile; the second stage was the two-story, side passage/parlor fieldstone section; and the third consists of a wing extending to the rear of the log house.

The two front portions of the structure offer an interesting contrast in development. The early log house is a common three-bay cross passage/parlor form with direct entrance into the main room of the log house. In contrast, the newer section has a more private stair hall into which visitors enter before reaching the adjacent parlor. This more private room arrangement reflects the formalization of house plans in the late 18th and early 19th centuries.

Although it is not clear who built the log portion, most of the visible changes were executed by William, John, or Thomas McCleary, all of whom owned this 103-acre portion of "Consent" and "Chamber's Venture" in the early 19th century.

Tyson Mill House
c. 1800
Barksdale vicinity

This two-story fieldstone house, which stands on land known historically as the Tyson Mill property, has a two-room cross passage plan. This form was preferred by Cecil County's Scots-Irish settlers. The exposed fieldstone basement kitchen and bank location are typical features. Frame additions on front and back obscure a slightly later two-bay, one-room addition. The property is part of the extensive "New Munster" tract and was owned in

CE-1005, New Munster stone (1979)

CE-674, Carter's Mill workers' house (1979)

CE-76, Red Ball Tavern (1980)

the first quarter of the 19th century by Matthias Tyson.

Red Ball Tavern
c. 1800
Fair Hill vicinity

Research by local historians and architectural evidence both suggest this structure was built as a public house known as the Red Ball Tavern. Numerous tavern and ordinary licenses were granted to the owners of this property. The earliest one to mention the Red Ball specifically dates from 1793. A tavern is shown on approximately this site on local maps of 1792 and 1795.

The house is a massive two-story, double-pile structure built of fieldstone with an unusual stone cornice. The arrangement of rooms is also unusual, as is the presence of two staircases: a centrally located main stair and a back stair that offers direct access from the first floor kitchen to the third floor attic bedrooms. The presence of this stair is an obvious indication of a specialized use for the two attic bedrooms, possibly for servants. The overall floor plan is similar to that of the much older Hopewell, located nearby, which also contains four rooms with a stair dividing the two back rooms. Each of the two front rooms in the house has its own entrance. These separate entrances, coupled with extremely plain paneling, agree with the idea that this was a tavern. The unusual construction of this house has led some architectural historians to believe the house was built by an immigrant or artisans from Europe.

Carter's Mill Workers' House
1802, c. 1850-60
Pleasant Hill vicinity

Because of the rolling terrain of the Little Elk Creek Valley, many houses were built into the side of a hill. Such sites allowed for ground level access and more light in the excavated basement kitchens. This arrangement is clearly evident in both the dated 1802 stone portion of this house and in the later frame sections. Two-story porches like the one on this house are a common feature of these dwellings.

This house may have been built for mill workers but was later occupied by members of the Carter family.

Thomas Garrett House
1802
Appleton Crossroads

Construction of this two-story, four-bay stone house is credited to Thomas Garrett because of the very precise datestone that bears his initials and the date May 19, 1802. The dwelling, with its two separate doors, may have housed two families, perhaps workers at the nearby mill. However, in 1860 the property was sold to Joseph Warren, who apparently preferred farming. His 1863 inventory indicates he lived in the entire house: the cellar, front room, kitchen, and chamber. The inventory also lists a barn, corncrib, smokehouse, and assorted agricultural equipment and livestock.

This house is unusual in that the chimney is placed in the middle of the long south wall rather than at the gable ends. There are also several features characteristic of the 18th century, including evidence of a pent roof on the north facade and the raised mortar joints of the stonework. The fireplaces in the two first floor rooms are situated back to back; a steep winder stair connects one room to the second floor.

Underwood House
c. 1800-10
Fairview

The Underwood house is one of the best-preserved examples of a double-cell plan in Cecil County. The form is characterized by a single room width and double room depth. The adjacent one-room brick kitchen wing was apparently added soon after the house was finished. Each room in both sections had a corner fireplace and possibly its own stair as well. The current stair is in the northeast corner of the older

CE-715, Thomas Garrett house (1980)

CE-222, Underwood house (1980)

CE-790, Cowen brick house (1985)

portion, adjacent to the wing. It is a very well-crafted Federal closed-string stair with simple turned newel and reeded square balusters. The farm has been in the Underwood family since John G. Underwood acquired the property in 1849.

Fulton Flax Mill
1811
Providence vicinity

William Fulton, a clothier, carder, and fuller of wool, came to Cecil County before the Revolution and later established a fulling mill on his creek property. John Partridge's circa 1835-40 scrapbook listed "Fulton's fulling mill—not now in operation, advertised in this paper, Fall 7 Feet." Local tradition has pinpointed this relatively small two-bay stone structure, with its 1811 datestone, as Fulton's mill building.

Cowen Brick House
1st quarter 19th century
Cowentown

Although it is often said to have been built by Benjamin Cowen in the 1840s, this house appears earlier because of its Flemish bond facade, stringcourse on the front (possibly the remnant of a pent roof), and the brick jack arches above the six-over-nine sash windows. The door, set at the southwest corner, features a semicircular fanlight that bears comparison with the Greek Revival elliptical fanlight of the circa 1840s house across the street, also a Cowen property.

This brick house stands on Lot No. 2 of the estate of William Cowen and was involved in several legal disputes between his heirs before it was sold in 1841 to Samuel Kilvington.

Evans House
c. 1730-45, 1810-30
Cowentown vicinity

The success of the Evans family in both the tanning business and the manufacture of iron and copper is reflected in their large stone house along the west bank of Big Elk Creek. The two sections of the house mark two different periods in the family's history: The two-story, hall/parlor house was probably built by Robert Evans, who inherited the property from his father, John Evans (1680-1738), who had purchased it in 1730. The taller, side hall/double parlor section to the west was built by Robert's son John (1760-1823). The difference in floor plans illustrates a change in lifestyle reflected in house form: The front door of the older house gave direct access into the main living space, while the side entrance to the early 19th century section

CE-535, Fulton flax mill (1994)

CE-77, Evans house (1968)

CE-709, McCracken house (1980)

opened into a more private stair hall.

Robert Evans earned a considerable fortune during his life as a tanner, farmer, and miller. He was a member of the 1740 militia and a justice of the peace. His son John began the manufacture of bar iron, nails, and copper at a site across the road from the house. This and Paul Revere's copper works in Massachusetts were the only copper rolling mills in the fledgling United States and were responsible for sheathing the vessels of the U.S. Navy in the War of 1812. Several other industrial activities—iron manufacture and a hydroelectric power plant—were carried out on the Evans property during the 19th and early 20th centuries, making it a potentially important archeological site.

Eight Corner Schoolhouse (site)
c. 1820
Providence vicinity

Octagonal structures began appearing on the American landscape in the early 19th century, and each region of the country has eight-sided houses, barns, and schoolhouses. The lone octagonal structure in Cecil County was built of local fieldstone by Robert Carter on the edge of his Walnut Hill farm. It was the first school in the county to be integrated. Converted to a dwelling in 1886, it eventually fell into disrepair and was torn down.

(See chapter 5, "'Farming and improvements generally…in advance of the average in the State,'" for a photograph of this building.)

McCracken House
c. 1820, 1865
Lewisville, Pennsylvania, vicinity

As is the case with most two-story, three-bay fieldstone dwellings in northern Cecil County, a Scots-Irish builder is responsible for the construction of this house. John James McCracken is recorded as owning part of "Mount Hope" until 1831, and he is the likely builder of this stone house. It has a hall/parlor plan, with one large, nearly square room entered through the centrally located front door and an adjacent smaller room. The hall was heated with a large fireplace vented through an interior end chimney, while the parlor was unheated. A mid-19th century frame addition was attached to the east gable end. The foundations of a large barn remain in front of the house.

In the late 20th century this house was remodeled by a developer, leaving the exterior virtually unaltered but the interior very different.

Rock Spring Farm
late 18th century, 1820-30
Fair Hill vicinity

This stone house probably began as a simple story-and-a-half dwelling with a hall/parlor plan on the first floor, now part of the western end of the main block. Entrances were on the east and west sides of the former hall, which has a fireplace and an

CE-176, Rock Spring farmhouse (1994)

Rock Spring Farm springhouse (1994)

CE-758, Center School (1994)

CE-514, Scott Mill ruins (1976)

enclosed winder stair on the north end. A late 18th or early 19th century mantel with paneled pilasters is found on the west side of the south room or original parlor.

In the 1820s and '30s, the house underwent an extensive enlargement. The original story-and-a-half dwelling was raised to two stories and an ell was added to the north side to serve as the new kitchen. The house was extended three bays, adding a center hall and parlor to the east. An opening on the south facade of the old house was altered and fitted with a jib door. The new main entrance was placed at the center of the enlarged house.

The interior woodwork dates mostly from this later period and exhibits several examples of fine craftsmanship in the Greek Revival style. The mantel in the first floor parlor has fluted pilasters and a reeded frieze and center panel. The sharp, crisp lines of these pilasters and the fluted door and window architraves with bull's-eye corner blocks are features of the early Greek Revival style. The stonework of this section is exceptional. A stone springhouse also survives on the property.

House at Miller's Crossroads

c. 1820-40
Elk Mills vicinity

Standing on a corner known historically as Miller's crossroads, this 19th century stone-and-frame house was built in two stages, three bays of stone and two of weatherboard-covered frame, but the overall effect resembles any five-bay house with central entrance and flanking rooms. Two gabled dormers with arched sash windows were centered on the structure, doubtless to create a more cohesive architectural effect. The Miller family owned this property for most of the 19th century—Mrs. F. Miller is designated here on the 1858 Martenet map, while the 1877 county atlas lists an H.D. Miller. It served as the John R. Evans family tenant house; the mansion house, which stood to the east, is no longer standing.

Center School

c. 1820-40
Fair Hill vicinity

This single-story fieldstone schoolhouse has long been a favorite of local historians and preservationists. Its architectural details and construction methods indicate a second quarter of the 19th century date, which makes this schoolhouse the earliest stone schoolhouse still standing in the county. It predates the establishment of a county school system in 1850, and thus belongs to the group of subscription schools built by local residents to educate their children. By 1852 Center School had been incorporated into the county school system and designated School No. 4. Classes were held here until it closed in 1915. In the 1990s it was restored by the Maryland Department of Natural Resources.

Scott Mill Ruins

early to mid-19th century
Cowentown vicinity

Few grist- and sawmills were better known or patronized in this area than those of the Scott family of Cowentown. These mill ruins stand on the east bank of the Big Elk where the road from Andora to Cowentown ran. The site was once teeming with activity: The mill in the large four-story stone building ground flour and feed, a sawmill processed timber, a cider mill pressed juice, a bone mill ground bone for fertilizer, and, across the covered bridge, an auger factory turned out augers for drills and a blacksmith tended horses and farm

CE-772, house at Miller's Crossroads (1936, Historic American Buildings Survey)

359

CE-171, Little Elk house

CE-631, Howard Mackey house (1980)

CE-695, Providence workers' houses (1976)

equipment. The mill complex was described in 1874 as a "grist mill…of stone, four stories high with two run of burrs, driven by a Leffel wheel of great power; frame saw mill, two stories and basement with overshot wheel; bark mill, bone mill, etc. The dam is a substantial stone structure, the fall sixteen feet at the mills, and the power ample. On the mill lot there are four houses, a stone blacksmith shop, stabling, and outbuildings, also a young orchard."

This was not the first mill on the property, for in 1783 Samuel Cummings sold Henry McCoy "a piece of land adjoining the river with privilege to butt and raise a dam to pen and raise the water for the purpose of erecting water works on the east side of the river." A deed of 1796 refers to "the new slitting mill now erecting on the east branch of the Elk River." This mill slit iron bars or plate into nail rods. In 1815 James Jackson and John Bemis bought the mill; they owned it until John Scott purchased the property in 1845.

Little Elk House
2nd quarter 19th century
Rock Church vicinity

This impressive brick house on a slope of the Little Elk Creek Valley reflects the Greek Revival style popular when it was built. It is three stories tall, with six-over-six sash windows on the first two stories, three-over-three sash on the third story, and a semicircular attic window at each gable end. The house has a dentiled brick cornice on the front, a corbeled cornice on the rear, and paired gable end chimneys connected by a brick parapet. The basement contained the kitchen, scullery, storerooms, and a potato cellar. An earlier log house, no longer standing, once stood at the rear of this dwelling.

Howard Mackey House
c. 1830
Fairview vicinity

Two six-over-six sash dormers and a corbeled brick cornice suggest a late Federal period date for this stuccoed stone house. Period mantels with widely fluted pilasters and large sunburst designs, possibly carved by Robert Mackey, support this date. Two doors in the center of the front facade open into a common room with large hearth on the left and a more formal room on the right. A corner winder stair rises in the southeast corner of the common room.

Providence Workers' Houses
c. 1830-40
Providence

A number of mill workers' residences were built to house the crew of the first papermaking operation in the Little Elk Creek Valley—the Meteer (later Providence) mill. Placed in a uniform row along the east side of the creek facing the mill site, these three-story fieldstone houses were the earliest attempt at providing company-built housing for employees of the Providence Paper Mill. When the property was sold in 1874,

This hall/parlor plan is found throughout the county, and the presence of two front doors is a characteristic common in southern Pennsylvania.

CE-175, Spring Run Farm (1968)

an advertisement noted "other structures include a dwelling for the superintendent, six small stone tenents, a barn, and a carriage house." Three of these houses survived until the late 20th century, when one was destroyed by fire, leaving just two.

Spring Run Farm
c. 1830-50
Lewisville, Pennsylvania, vicinity

The Armstrong family patented this land in 1730 and owned it until 1934. The two-story, five-bay farmhouse, with its double-pile center hall plan and symmetrical facade, is a house type common throughout the county in the mid-19th century. The house, covered with stucco, has large double chimneys connected by a parapet at each gable end. The center door has a transom and paneled jambs and formerly was flanked by tall Greek Revival-style paneled shutters. The design of double inset panels on these shutters is repeated on the door and the cupboard doors of the interior. In the west room is an elliptical dividing arch similar to that at another Armstrong house by the Little Elk Creek. Most of the rest of the interior has been altered, although the east room features a fine Greek Revival mantel with Greek key molding, pilasters with reeding in a chevron pattern, a crescent-moon design on the two corner blocks, and a center panel with gouged flowers and a swag design. The stone barn on the property has round-arched doors with brick heads.

Joseph Biddle House
c. 1830-50
Cowentown vicinity

This two-story, three-bay stuccoed brick-and-stone farmhouse stands along Appleton Road just north of Cowentown. It has a boxed cornice above a bed and crown molding across the front. Most of the structure is built of brick, except the east bearing wall of the main block, which is built of local fieldstone. This difference in material may have occurred because the builder was short of brick and used that more expensive material for the front walls, leaving the less formal stone for the rear wall. An unusual element is the exposed hewn frame that supports the metal porch roof; the hewn timbers are fastened with pinned mortise and tenon joints and fixed to the brick wall with iron brackets. The Greek Revival mantel in the south room has inset paneled pilasters with corner blocks.

Meteer Mill/Providence Paper Mill
c. 1831-32
Providence

This manufacturing site, most recently known as the Kenmore Paper Mill, was used for the production of paper as early as 1835. Joseph Henderson, a mill hand who came to work at Providence on March 17, 1836, provided one of the first descriptions of the buildings. In his daily diary, which he kept through the first half of the 19th century, he noted that he was apprenticed to

CE-548, Kenmore Paper Mill (Meteer Mill/Providence Mill) (1976)

CE-786, Joseph Biddle house (1980)

CE-300, Amos Alexander house (1971)

Alexander barn (1971)

Alexander meat house (1971)

Samuel Meteer on January 8, 1803, "to learn the paper-making business." He served his apprenticeship at "Meteer's Paper Mill on the White Clay Crick ¼ of a mile from 'New Ark Village.'" He described the Providence property as follows: "This great and well built mill was erected on the Little Elk Creek, Cecil County, Maryland by Samuel and William Meteer in the years 1831-32 and is said to have cost near 40 thousand dollars. It is 101 feet long and 45 feet wide and five stories high. In consequence of the death of William Meteer, April 11, 1833, the mill did not go into operation until sometime in 1835. This mill manufactures about 6000 pounds of rag per week and has one of the best machines of the kind in America."

In 1954 the Kenmore Paper Mill was destroyed by fire; all that remains is the brick boiler house, a cluster of stone ruins, and some stone workers' houses.

Laughlin's Market
c. 1839-40
Cowentown

Cowentown is named after the Cowen family, who owned the four major buildings at this crossroads in the mid-19th century. By 1877 ownership had changed and Mrs. J. Cowen is the only family member listed in the county atlas of that year. Apparently, Mrs. Cowen held onto the main farmhouse and sold the rest of the property, including this building known as Laughlin's Market. In 1877 the structure was owned by A. J. Armstrong, who ran a local store in the frame section of the building.

Amos Alexander House
c. 1810, c. 1840, c. 1850
Fair Hill vicinity

This house appears on Cecil County maps of 1858 and 1877 associated with the name Finley, a family who seems to have owned most of the surrounding countryside for the better part of the 19th century. It was built earlier in two stone sections with an east-west axis; the frame addition to the south is modern. Each stone section has an entrance on the north elevation. On the interior, the deep window reveals of the west end curve to meet the interior wall in a smooth transition. The roof beams in this end are mortised and tenoned and pegged at the ridge. The main room on the ground level of the east end has beaded beams and a very fine mantel of about 1800-10. Extensive remodeling in the 1940s and '50s altered most of the woodwork and hardware throughout the house. This work was carried on by Henry du Pont, a son of William, consolidators of the entire Fair Hill estate.

Also on the property is a stone meat house built into a bank, giving it two levels. The two-story south elevation of the 12-foot-wide structure has a batten door with tapered iron strap hinges and pegged frame and above this a square window and small lunette filled with a stone bearing the date 1868 and set into a brick arch in the gable.

The large stone-and-frame bank barn on the property, similar in most respects to that on the neighboring Finley property, is a three-level structure on a sloping site with

CE-784, Laughlin's Market

CE-534, Pine View/Brookings house

Pine View barn (1977)

rubblestone walls on three sides. On the north, an earth ramp with stone revetments leads to a heavy board-and-batten covered timber-and-frame bridge that provides access to both the middle and upper levels. A heavy board-and-batten covered timber extension stands to the south; two other additions enlarged the structure in the 1940s.

Pine View/Brookings House
c. 1840
Rock Church vicinity

Built by Robert Carter, Sr., as a wedding gift to his daughter Mary and son-in-law Dr. Richard Brookings, this two-story, five-bay stone house commands a view of the Little Elk Creek. While symmetrical facades like this one are often seen throughout the county, Pine View is unusual for the amount of period detail that remains, including the nine-over-six sash windows with paneled shutters on the first floor and louvered shutters on the second. The front entrance is unusual and features a divided transom and flanking Doric pilasters. Below the eaves are the original boxed cornice and bed and crown moldings. The present shed porch was added during the late 19th century. Some sources suggest that Carter added the house to an existing structure—the present back wing—but this has not been proved.

Accompanying the house is a fine fieldstone bank barn that is probably its contemporary. Robert Brookings, internationally known for founding the Brookings Institution, was born here. Beside the house is the small office used by Dr. Brookings.

Boxwood
c. 1840
Cowentown

The most impressive house in Cowentown, Boxwood was built by Benjamin Cowen soon after the death of his father, William, in 1838. The main block of the house is two-and-a-half stories tall and five bays wide; a three-bay wing extends from the north elevation. The stonework is carefully laid, with keystone lintels and massive quoins. The bed molding below the boxed cornice returns at the gable ends. On both sides of the gable roof are pedimented dormers flanked by paneled pilasters with Greek *paterae*. Although much of the interior has been remodeled, surviving original elements include two Greek Revival mantels, fine period woodwork around the south entrance (with fanlight transom), and an original stair in the front hall with a heavy square baluster.

Although Benjamin Cowen at one time owned most of the land in Cowentown, by the 1870s he was nearly bankrupt. He is buried at the Head of Christiana Cemetery under a tombstone with the inscription "A friend of the poor."

The famous boxwoods that gave this house its name were sold to Longwood Gardens, a du Pont family estate in nearby Pennsylvania open to the public. One still remains on the east side of the house.

Zebley Farmhouse
c. 1840-60
Appleton Crossroads

This farmhouse is a well-preserved mid-19th century brick structure that displays some unusual masonry, including the corbeled dentiled cornice and alternating common and Flemish bond courses. The two-story, three-bay main block is one room deep with an attached contemporary kitchen wing.

CE-1385, Boxwood (1985)

CE-773, Zebley farmhouse (1980)

CE-163 & 164, Elk Forge tenements (1936, Historic American Buildings Survey)

CE-165, Lord's cotton factory at Elk Forge (1936, Historic American Buildings Survey)

CE-648, Walnut Hill (1979)

CE-546, Walnut Valley gristmill (1979)

Elk Forge Tenements (site)
1846
Elk Mills

Cecil County land records show that Daniel Lord arrived in the county from Litchfield, Connecticut, in the 1840s. He then bought the old Elk Forge property along the Big Elk Creek and built a cotton factory on the site, including two rows of three-story fieldstone workers' houses. Each house was two bays wide and one room deep, and each row contained four duplexes. The structures fell into disrepair and were torn down in the 20th century.

(An aerial photograph in chapter 4, "'An Excellent Situation' for Manufacturer and Farmer Alike," shows these buildings in situ.)

Elk Forge/Lord's Cotton Factory (site)
1846
Elk Mills

Elk Forge is the name of a series of many different kinds of mills that operated on this site from the 18th to the 20th centuries. A gristmill reputedly ground flour here for Revolutionary troops; only the mill's foundation remains. Nails were made at the Marley Mill site, and there was a sawmill. The forge made cannonballs during the Revolution before it was destroyed by the British in 1777.

In 1846 Daniel Lord erected a four-story, gambrel-roofed stone textile mill building close to an earlier structure. This mill was famous for Lord's diaper cloth and Turkey red, which was used for tablecloths and napkins. Operations continued under Lord's ownership from 1846 to 1867, when the mill was purchased by his son-in-law, William Baldwin of Litchfield, Connecticut. The Baldwin name had been associated with the textile industry in Connecticut, and William Baldwin operated this mill in Cecil County successfully until his death in the 1890s, after which it was taken over by his son William. The mill was rented to the Baldwin Manufacturing Company, also a textile manufacturer, an arrangement that lasted until the Baldwin company moved about ten years later.

(An aerial photograph in chapter 4, "'An Excellent Situation' for Manufacturer and Farmer Alike," shows this building in situ.)

Walnut Hill
c. 1790, 1841
Pleasant Hill vicinity

Walnut Hill is a large stone-and-brick house built in three sections. In 1841 local paper manufacturer Robert Carter and his wife built an Italianate mansion on the east gable wall of a small stone farmhouse that had been built circa 1790. A few years later a two-story wing was added to the rear of the main house.

The 18th century house is a two-story, three-bay stone structure with gable roof and box cornice. In the west gable wall is an interior end chimney of brick. The house has been altered inside but retains one board-and-batten door with HL hinges on the first floor.

The main part of the house is a stuccoed brick structure three stories high and four bays wide with a hip roof and box cornice supported by brackets. In the east gable end is a marble datestone, which reads "REM Carter 1841." An interior end chimney rises from each gable end. The floor plan consists of a center hall flanked by a large room on each side. Period marble mantels surround the fireplaces in these rooms. The rear wing is a two-story stuccoed stone building the Carters used as a ballroom.

Walnut Valley Gristmill
1847
Providence vicinity

This four-story, gambrel-roofed gristmill is one of only a few gristmills still standing in Cecil County. Its survival is undoubtedly due to its stone construction and its continuous operation into the second quarter of the 20th century. Construction of the mill is attributed to Robert Carter, Sr., who left his initials and the date 1847 on the west wall. Carter sold the mill in 1851 to Robert M. Sherer of Chester County, Pennsylvania, who, in turn, sold it two years later to Norris Levis. Levis operated the mill until his death in 1875, when his wife Eliza assumed control of the farm and mill. In the early 20th century the mill property was purchased by the Mackie/Mackey family, who ran the business until the 1950s.

CE-1393, Gallaher house (1994)

Gallaher store (1985)

Mackey-du Pont Farm
c. 1850
Fairview vicinity

This farm along Blake Road consists of two houses and a large barn. The farmhouse is a spacious two-story, center hall frame house with kitchen wing. A second dwelling nearby appears to have been built as a tenant house; a small two-story frame structure, it has been covered with stucco. Behind the houses stands a large circa 1900 board-and-batten covered barn.

Ewing Farm
c. 1850
Fair Hill vicinity

This house has not changed significantly since its construction. Its architectural details remain intact and the structure exemplifies the mid-19th century farm complex. A period frame bank barn stands southeast of the house. James Ewing owned this property in 1858.

Providence Mill Manager's House
c. 1850
Providence

Although the Meteers owned Providence Paper Mill, they lived in Baltimore and relied on mill managers to carry on their business in Cecil County. One manager was Joseph McCullough, who lived in this house around 1858. The two-and-a-half story, cross-gabled frame house was built on the west bank of the Little Elk on a hill that overlooks both the mill and the general area. This hilltop location was undoubtedly chosen to separate the house both visually and socially from the mill workers' housing along the creek. There is reputedly a history of Providence contained in the cornerstone.

Gallaher House and Store
c. 1855 with additions
Cherry Hill vicinity

This farmhouse, like so many others in Cecil County, has seen numerous periods of expansion. The two-story, three-bay clapboard section on the west dates from circa 1855 and was built by John Gallaher. With the entrance in the north facade, it was two bays deep and had two small rooms on each floor; the fireplace and winder stair were situated on the north side. Later, a two-story, two-bay addition was built on the rear of the original house. Another entrance was placed in the north elevation and a fireplace and enclosed stair on the west. An unusual feature of this section is a built-in cupboard with classical entablature. A one-story porch with turned posts runs across the south elevation of the addition. The late 20th century owners have added extensively to the north and east elevations and changed

CE-676, Mackey-du Pont farm (1979)

CE-1105, Ewing farm (1980)

CE-647, Providence Mill manager's house (c. 1976)

CE-1090, William Wade house (1980)

the orientation of the house to the west.

Nearby is the two-story frame Gallaher store, a farm supply store operated between 1911 and 1945. Before this store was built, the business was run from the adjacent stone-and-frame barn, which has an 1881 datestone.

Cherry Hill United Methodist Church
1858
Cherry Hill

The first Methodist church at Cherry Hill stood on land donated by Robert Carter in 1831 approximately where the present cemetery is. The second church, a two-story, three-bay, gable-roofed brick building with a center steeple, was completed in 1858 at a cost of $4,149. The plans were drawn up by local residents Joseph Miller, William Grant, and Donald Parker, and the contractor was Stephen Gallagher.

In 1859 the congregation adopted what was for them a liberal seating policy: "Resolved, that in the future, we approve of promiscuous seating in our church. Also, the first line of seats next to the door be reserved for colored people."

Melissa Mackie House
c. 1860-70
Lewisville, Pennsylvania, vicinity

This modest two-story, three-bay, single-pile house is of a form built throughout the county during the second half of the 19th century. The floor plan rarely differs: invariably, a central closed stair is flanked by one room on each side. By some mid-19th century standards, the size of this example was small, but it must have been deemed sufficient. A stone smokehouse adjoins the house.

William Wade House
c. 1860-70
Appleton vicinity

Two-and-a-half story, cross-gabled farmhouses like this one are the best representatives of late 19th century architecture in Cecil County. Other popular period architectural forms exist in various parts of the county, but residents preferred this form—the traditional, two-story, three-bay frame house. Some people added personal touches such as front and side porches, bay windows, and cross gables, but the basic form remained the same. William Wade, for example, decided to include decorative sawn fascias and a hipped roof cast-iron porch to distinguish this house. Another unusual feature is the use of window surrounds and a door frame that taper to the bottom.

Hiram Walker House
c. 1862-67
Cowentown vicinity

County tax assessments have established this five-year bracket date for the construction of this two-story, three-bay, double-pile brick house laid in common bond. Hiram Walker purchased 120 acres north of Elkton along Appleton Road in 1862, along with a dwelling valued in that year by county assessors at $2,544. By 1867 the tax list showed 116 acres and a brick dwelling valued at $6,148. This rather sizable discrepancy in value indicates the construction of this house and perhaps the sale of the other house and four acres.

CE-1383, Cherry Hill Methodist Church (1985)

CE-639, Melissa Mackie house

CE-1088, Hiram Walker house (1980)

CE-238, Big Elk Creek covered bridge (1968)

Big Elk Creek Covered Bridge
(site)
1860-80
Fair Hill vicinity

Although the exact age of this covered bridge was unknown, it was important as one of only a handful of covered bridges in Maryland and of only two in the county. Until its demise, it spanned Big Elk Creek about a mile north of Maryland Route 273. The bridge was supported by a pair of Burr arch trusses resting on fieldstone abutments. The main posts, which carried the roadbed and supported the roof, were bolted to the arch. The bridge was held together with mortise and tenon joints, and the walls rose to within a foot of the roof, leaving a clerestory the length of both sides. This bridge was rebuilt for William du Pont by William Strahorn in the 1930s.

Interior of the Big Elk Creek covered bridge

St. John's Methodist Episcopal Church
1866
Lewisville, Pennsylvania, vicinity

This imposing brick church was undoubtedly built to serve Methodists in both Maryland and Pennsylvania, since it stands within a few hundred yards of the Mason-Dixon line. As is true for most two-story Methodist churches, the sanctuary is located on the second floor with Sunday School rooms and meeting halls below. The heavily bracketed eaves and round arches are typical touches of Italianate and Romanesque design.

Baldwin House
1867
Elk Mills

William Baldwin of Litchfield, Connecticut, married the daughter of Daniel Lord, who

Grammy's Run
c. 1860-80
Fair Hill vicinity

Named for a small tributary of the Big Elk Creek, this farm also borders Maryland Route 273. The two-and-a-half story, T-shaped farmhouse and accompanying braced frame bank barn are both products of third quarter of the 19th century technology. Still in use in both structures is a system of heavy braced timber framing. While barn construction remained basically the same into the early 20th century, the framing members and building methods for a house were streamlined and standardized for what is known as balloon framing.

CE-1097, Grammy's Run (1980)

CE-640, St. John's Methodist Episcopal Church

CE-1098, Deep Run Farm (1980)

Deep Run Farm
1840, 1870
Barksdale vicinity

The rear wing of this house is of vertical plank construction. It was built soon after Jethro McCullough, who ran a bark mill on the Deep Run stream, bought the property from John and Isabelle Evans in 1840.

In 1870 the house and mill were purchased by Howard Scott, who built the two-story, three-bay, frame front section. The vertical plank house was moved to the rear, where it now serves as a kitchen; its original stone foundations are contained within the foundation of the 1870 house.

The mill was sold in 1844 to James Tweed, who converted it to a gristmill, and in 1852 to Jacob Markee, from whom Scott bought it. The mill is gone, but the millrace is still visible in front of the house.

ran a textile mill at Elk Forge. In 1867 Baldwin purchased Lord's mill and built a house nearby. The house is a two-and-a-half story, three-bay sandstone structure with a cross gable. Inside, it has a center hall flanked by two rooms on each side and typical period trim. It sits on a hill overlooking the creek and the sites of the mill buildings.

Local tradition maintains that William Baldwin built this house on the site of an earlier house; this story is strengthened by the presence of the dated 1810 stone bank barn that formerly stood just north of the house. The gable end stone walls of the barn were pierced by narrow embrasures, which ventilated the hay storage area. The overall form of the three-bay barn had definite European antecedents; similar structures can be found in northern England, Switzerland, and Germany. The datestone featured the initials RCM, along with the date 1810.

CE-166, Baldwin bank barn (1981)

Baldwin house (1981)

CE-73, Rock Presbyterian Church and session house (1980)

George Grant House
c. 1820-40, 1870-80
Fair Hill vicinity

Distinctly separate methods of construction, architectural periods, and structural placement distinguish the two sections of this fieldstone-and-frame house. The early 19th century two-story, one-room fieldstone house is built into a bank and faces fields to the north. This orientation changed with the construction of a frame addition that faced Little Egypt Road rather than the fields. It was fitted with fish-scale shingles on each end and a shed-roofed front porch.

Moore's Chapel
1871
Fairview vicinity

The inscription "Moore's Chapel, Methodist Protestant Church—1871" firmly establishes the date and builders of this simple frame church. Gabriel and Sarah Moore granted the trustees of Methodist Protestant Church at Fairview a parcel of land containing three roods and thirty square perches for this "comfortable house of public worship for their neighborhood with a suitable burying ground."

CE-1094, George Grant house (1980)

Rock Presbyterian Church (NR)
1761, 1872, 1900
Fair Hill vicinity

Rock Presbyterian Church is a rectangular building of uncoursed rubble construction, three bays wide by three deep, with a steeply pitched, slate-clad gable roof. The

CE-1106, Moore's Chapel (1980)

building was originally constructed in 1761, but its present appearance, which shows Victorian Gothic influence, is the result of renovations carried out in 1872 and 1900. The entrance—double doors in an arched opening—is centered in the south gable end and flanked on each side by a lancet window. The stained glass rose window above was added in 1900. In the peak of the gable, a shuttered lancet window is topped with a datestone reading "A Presbyterian Church 1761." The side elevations have tall lancet windows containing colored and etched glass with Gothic tracery in the upper sash. A small rectangular addition made to the north end in 1900 contains a recessed pulpit.

On the interior, a vestibule leads into the church, which has a raised gallery to the rear. The interior features rich Gothic detailing, including elaborately carved walnut trusswork, a walnut arch defining the pulpit recess, and a gallery rail with a lancet-arch motif. These elements date from the 1900 renovation, as do the pressed metal ceiling and chestnut wainscoting. The pews of grained ash with walnut trim were installed in 1872.

West of the church is a stone session house, one of the few early session houses still standing. It is a one-and-a-half story, gable-roofed building originally erected in 1762. It, too, has been altered and is a fine example of the 19th century Gothic Revival style. It has been used as a school, including several years as the Rock Academy.

Rock Presbyterian Church is important for its association with the early Scots-Irish immigrants in Maryland and the accompanying growth of Presbyterianism in the region. The congregation it serves was

CE-644, Kite's Mill (historic photograph, Scarborough Collection)

organized in 1720 as the New Erection, Elk River, at what is now Lewisville, Pennsylvania. In 1740 the congregation split into two factions, the Old and the New, and the New contingent erected a clapboard church at what is now Sharp's Cemetery, above Fair Hill. In 1761, under the Reverend James Finley, the two sides were reunited as one congregation and built this church. The third to serve the group, it reflects the efforts of a mature, established community.

Throughout the building's many renovations, the basic form of Rock Church has been preserved, allowing it to evoke a sense of association with Cecil County's early Presbyterians at the same time its updated style testifies to the continuing vitality of an active congregation.

Big Elk Chapel
1877
Fair Hill vicinity

Big Elk Chapel was erected in 1877 as a result of the religious fervor created at local Methodist camp meetings. The single-story rectangular frame building is sheathed with clapboards. The windows, three on each side, have six-over-six sash and louvered shutters. A central brick stove stack rises out of the building. The chapel is one of the least altered examples in the county, both inside and out, of this widely used church form. A horse and carriage house stands behind the chapel.

Kite's Mill
c. 1878
Providence vicinity

Kite's gristmill, now a double dwelling, is the last of several mill buildings that stood on this site. The 1858 Martenet map of the county shows a mill and five other structures known as Jordan's Rock Paper Mill. This mill was sold to Israel Day Carter and Thomas Tong and then to Mrs. Elizabeth Duckett. The Stone Paper Mill, as the Ducketts called it, operated until 1874, when it was destroyed by fire. By 1878 the property had been sold and a gristmill built by Arthur J. Alfred and Franklin T. Mackie.

Mackie had had a mill near Rock Church, which local lore records as a site subject to flooding, leading him to dismantle the mill or its workings and move the parts, using them to build what later became known as Kite's Mill. William Penn Kite purchased the property in the early 20th century from William Singerly, owner of the Providence Paper Mill. Kite owned the mill until the 1940s.

CE-630, Big Elk Chapel (1978)

CE-1101, Highlawn (1980)

CE-196, house near Pleasant Hill (1968)

Highlawn
c. 1878-90
Fair Hill vicinity

Mackie family history dates this house from the partial dismantling of the Mackie brothers' complex called the Beehive, located near the Little Elk Creek in the 1880s, and some of the stones used in its construction came from the structures at that site. The high location with its expansive view of the creek valley was probably one factor in determining the location of this two-and-a-half story, cross-gabled stuccoed fieldstone dwelling.

House near Pleasant Hill
c. 1800-20, 1880
Pleasant Hill vicinity

The fieldstone walls and large interior end chimney stack are the only exterior indications that an early 19th century house stands behind the late 19th century frame additions and porches of this dwelling. Extensively remodeled when the additions were made, the house is now an attractive example of the Queen Anne style, a popular type in late 19th century America.

Providence Boardinghouse (site)
late 19th century
Providence vicinity

The Providence boardinghouse was a large Victorian vernacular frame building. Two and a half stories tall and three bays wide, it had a two-story wing to the rear. During the late 19th and early 20th century, this was the dwelling of a man who worked in the nearby paper mill and rented rooms to other mill workers. The building burned about 1980.

Providence Row
c. 1880-1900
Providence

William M. Singerly's expansion of the Providence Mill included the construction of several new structures among Meteer's earlier buildings, as is recorded in the company's 1896 assessment, which included slightly more than 100 acres on the Little Elk Creek, a gristmill, "other buildings (site of Rock Paper Mill) purchased from the Mackeys," the main paper mill surrounded by the wash house, a carpenter shop, pump house, and machine shop, as well as a barn, "a stable and other buildings," a warehouse, a building on the side of the creek, two tenant houses, two stone houses, eight double houses, and the "large house." Of these eight double houses, four were built on the same elevation as the mill along the creek road. Each building was a separate unit, with its own stair, heating system, and kitchen.

CE-666, Providence boardinghouse (1977)

CE-645, Providence Row

CE-669 & 659, Walnut Valley store and house and Providence corner house

Walnut Valley Store and House and Providence Corner House
c. 1880-1900
Providence

This irregular looking frame building once contained both a country store and a residence for the store owners; it also served as a boardinghouse. Both parts of the building date from the last decades of the 19th century and exhibit similar architectural features, including center cross gables and two-over-two sash windows. The exact proportions of the store section were slightly compromised to make a continuous roofline, but the slopes and angles fit in well with the late 19th century attraction to asymmetry.

A three-story, two-bay, double-pile house built into a bank with its east basement fully exposed stands on a corner next to the Walnut Valley Store. The two main floors contain two back-to-back rooms;

CE-642, Brick Hill (1980)

all have separate hearths along the west end wall. The window and door frames are pegged rather than nailed together. This building, which has been remodeled but possibly dates from the late 18th century, served as a small store in the early 19th century.

Brick Hill
1751, late 19th century
Lewisville, Pennsylvania, vicinity

The David Mackey farmhouse shows how something as simple as a change in roof slope and a kitchen addition could impose a 19th century appearance on an 18th century house. Sometimes, however, owners went beyond such elementary alterations, and Brick Hill farmhouse is one of the extreme examples of a Victorian era remodeling.

In the late 19th century, the owners of this house, named for a brick kiln on the site in the 18th century, decided to transform their 18th century Flemish and common bond brick dwelling into a fashionable Queen Anne structure with a fish-scale shingled third story, cross gables, and a bay window. They also reoriented the house, redirecting its outlook from the fields to the road. Shed porches were added to each side and the chimney stacks divided to create a more rhythmic effect. The farm buildings have been modernized and the massive bank barn demolished; once the bank barn and the cross-gabled stables and cow barns southwest of the house formed one of the most impressive collections of outbuildings in the county.

CE-1394, Carter-Ness house (1985)

Baldwin Manufacturing Company
c. 1890
Elk Mills

The Baldwin Manufacturing Company was first housed in the converted Elk Forge building and the adjacent mill built by Daniel Lord in 1846. After the Baldwins sold the company in the 1890s, it was moved up the hill to these structures constructed for the company along the main line of the B&O Railroad. Built of local sandstone and covered with stucco, the buildings have brick segmental arches over the windows and clerestories lighting the interior. Textile manufacturing was conducted in these buildings through the 1960s.

As a result of the shift in location of the Baldwin Manufacturing Company, new worker housing, stores, and town services were built, which today make up the town of Elk Mills.

CE-168, Baldwin Manufacturing Company (1968)

CE-1004, Fair Hill Racetrack (1994)

Carter-Ness House
c. 1890-1900
Fair Hill vicinity

This house is an attractive example of the Shingle style, which enjoyed great popularity at the turn of the 20th century. Two projecting wings flank the narrow three-bay center section of this two-and-a-half story house. The wing on the right has a gable roof, and the gable end faces forward and is emphasized with projecting segmental-arched bargeboards. In the center a small balcony rests above the hipped-roof front portico. The left wing has a hipped roof. The entire house is covered with cedar shingles. Like the exterior, the floor plan is rambling and asymmetrical, a characteristic of this style.

Dolfinger Creamery
c. 1900-20
Providence vicinity

The Dolfinger Creamery was one of the last commercial/industrial structures erected along the Little Elk Creek spur line of the Lancaster, Cecil, and Southern Railroad. The single-story creamery building is a distinctive common bond brick pile with a towering chimney stack. The last active user was Abbott's Dairy, an operation well remembered by local residents.

CE-635, Dolfinger Creamery (1994)

Fair Hill Racetrack
1930
Fair Hill

This complex includes stables, betting windows, stands, paddocks, jockey weigh-in stations, and numerous ancillary structures. In general, the buildings are board-and-batten covered frame structures painted dark green with white trim. The races at Fair Hill have two claims to fame: the seventeen jumps of the meet make it the toughest steeplechase course in the United States, and it is the only steeplechase in the country run with parimutuel betting. William du Pont had already acquired most of the land east of Fair Hill, nearly 7,600 acres, when he began operation of the course in the early 1930s.

Horses have always been closely associated with the Fair Hill area. William du Pont hunted the entire tract and influenced the use of the land and buildings to the extent that bridges were built above roads and streams for the convenience of the fox hunters. The steeplechase races that annually take place at this track, now owned by the state, bring the area alive.

Fifth District

Mill House
early 18th century
North East

This important early gambrel-roofed frame dwelling is hidden in a remote section of North East. Three bays long and two deep, it has several interesting features. Across the west end is a large room from which the stylish paneling was removed and installed at Winterthur as the "Cecil bedroom." The back of the fireplace in this room is exposed on the exterior, where the brick is laid in Flemish bond with glazed headers. An open, narrow porch that runs the width of the room, sharing the same roof, is original to the house. Originally covered in beaded shiplap siding, the house is now covered with clapboards or weatherboards.

Attached to this house by one corner is another 18th century structure, which originally served as a kitchen and servants' quarters. This second structure is a two-story, four-bay frame building with paneled doors swinging on original strap hinges in the outer bays. A pent eave stretches around the building and connects the cornices across the gable ends. To the southeast is an addition of nearly the same size as the original structure, with matching trim.

Colonial Wharf, Warehouse, and Customs House
18th century
Charlestown

The General Assembly of the Province of Maryland enacted a law in 1742 to build a town at Long Point on the North East River—a town to be called Charlestown—and to build a wharf at the same site. The

CE-101, Mill House (1993)

wharf extended 300 feet into the river and was wide enough for the passage of three wagons. It was built of heavy log cribbing, a process involving construction of a four-sided tower that was then filled with stones. In addition to the wharf itself, an inspection house once stood here, where flour was inspected and graded before it was shipped. Grains were stored in a massive stone warehouse, three stories high and 80 feet long with walls 36 inches thick at the base. During the Revolutionary War, Charlestown was a supply depot for the Continental Army, and supplies brought here by ship and barge from the southern part of the state were stored in the warehouse.

A supplementary act established that "a person of good repute and skill in the goodness and quality of flour, wheat, and other grain should be wharfinger and store-house-keeper." The wharfinger was required to give security in the name of the Lord Proprietary in the sum of £100 in provincial currency. His duty was to keep a record of the grains that passed through his hand and report to the town commissioners. A "Viewer" or "Examiner of Flour" was to inspect the casks of flour. Each cask was branded as a mark of its quality, and no cask without a brand could be sold. For this inspection, the owners of the flour paid the examiner three pence current money per barrel. Any flour that did not pass inspection was branded with a broad arrow. The act went further to say that no flour was to be shipped from any other place on the North East River. Anyone caught violating this had either to forfeit the flour or pay a fine equal to its value; this money went toward maintaining the public wharf.

CE-127, Indian Queen Tavern (1968)

Indian Queen Tavern (NR)
c. 1740s with additions
Charlestown

In 1742, when Charlestown was chartered, the town founders drew chances for lots in the new community. One of these founders, Zebulon Hollingsworth, drew lot 82, which contains the Indian Queen. Hollingsworth was called "Innkeeper" on his deed. The Indian Queen is a two-story frame structure 30 feet square with a floor plan consisting of four rooms arranged around a massive chimney, which rises through the middle of the first floor and accommodates four fireplaces set back to back. The two fireplaces on the second floor are molded into the chimney stack with plaster-covered brick. No mantels are evident, and the bold mass of the masonry is impressive. The cellar has no fireplace and was used for storage, although the bulk of it is filled by the huge stone foundation of the chimney, which is approximately 10 feet square.

The tavern is of post and beam construction and is insulated with brick. The front and rear are covered with wide boards fitted shiplap fashion, each with a beaded lower edge. The gable ends were re-covered with weatherboards and a double-galleried porch extended across the front in the 19th century. The end walls are covered on the interior with lath and plaster, while the interior walls are made of original vertical board partitions in which the boards are usually beaded on one edge. Gunstock swells occur at the top of each of the four corner posts on the second story, adding strength to carry the massive hewn plates that crown the walls. Boards with beaded edges were used to box the exposed posts and girts.

Throughout the interior, the moldings and trim are characteristic of the mid-18th century. The hardware exhibits a great variety of period work, from crude wooden latches to neat iron box locks fitted with sophisticated brass knobs. Hinges include a range of styles from wrought HL to much later cast-iron Eastlake designs.

The roof was rebuilt in the 19th century, and the decorative jig-sawn bargeboards date from that period. The Indian Queen was restored in the 1960s using funds available through the Maryland Historical Trust, the state historic preservation agency.

Behind the tavern stands a story-and-a-half log kitchen with loft above. A two-story smokehouse, stone on the first story and brick above, stands between the Indian Queen and neighboring Red Lyon Tavern.

CE-102, St. Mary Anne's Church (1936, Historic American Buildings Survey)

St. Mary Anne's Church
1742
North East

This church was chartered by Queen Anne, although not built until some years after her death. It is a gambrel-roofed structure with clipped gables and wide, compass-headed windows. The brick is laid in Flemish bond with glazed headers on the south wall. Further enrichment is given by an unusual string course over the doors. The Georgian Revival bell tower was added in 1904 by Robert Brookings, founder of the Brookings Institute, in memory of his parents, who are buried in the church graveyard. This yard is said to hold graves of Susquehannock Indians, and some of the tombstones date from the 1770s.

Paca House
c. 1750 with additions
Charlestown

Begun by John Paca, brother of Governor William Paca, this house has undergone at least three periods of building activity. Paca's house was probably a two-story, three-bay frame building, incorporated into the east end of the present house. In plan, it has two rooms of equal size above a deep cellar. Paca sold the house in 1753 to Edward Mitchell, a commissioner of Charlestown. When the property was evaluated for Mitchell's daughter in August 1770, the house was described as a frame dwelling 20 x 30 feet.

The story-and-a-half, gambrel-roofed stone wing to the west was added later, and the two sections were connected by means of a two-bay, one-room frame

CE-111, Paca house (Colonial Charlestown)

section. Examination of the wall between the stone wing and the wooden house shows that the stone section has only three walls, evidence that it was added to the wooden house. Bevel-jointed weatherboards of the latter remain in place, showing little sign of weathering, indicating the stone addition was added soon after the second wood section was built. The weather-

CE-107, Hamilton house (1936, Historic American Buildings Survey)

boards extend behind the ends of the front and rear stone walls, a physical impossibility unless the wood construction was earlier than the stone. An obvious irregularity in the wooden walls, front and rear, from one end to the other, indicates they were originally one story high. A cellar extends under two rooms of the wooden house at the opposite end from the stone wing. It is unclear when the frame section gained its second story or when the porch was added.

Hamilton House (site)
c. 1745, c. 1751
Charlestown

Perhaps the most intriguing house in Charlestown, this structure may well have been the oldest as well. The log portion with central chimney—the one-story, two-room rear wing—had measurements that suggest it was built by John Kankey on lot 74 of the original town and was approved by the town commissioners in 1745.

Hamilton house (1936, HABS)

The Reverend John Hamilton bought the lot in 1748, and the deed refers to a standing structure. Hamilton was rector at St. Mary Anne's Episcopal Church in North East, and it is thought he bought this house and lot as a speculative venture. The town had recently been founded and was an international port; real estate in a town with such a booming present and apparently glorious future must have seemed a safe investment. It is believed

CE-128, Red Lyon Tavern/Black's Store

that Hamilton added a one-and-a-half story gambrel-roofed frame house around 1751, when he bought the adjoining lot (no. 73).

Until it was moved to Pennsylvania in the last quarter of the 20th century, Hamilton's house had not undergone a major remodeling since its construction. Most of the interior walls were board partitions, either of flush beaded boards or alternating lapped boards. Some original hardware, including door latches, a wood rim lock, and HL and strap hinges survived. The main door was made of vertical battens and may have been original. Inside, the house had a quartered floor plan that resembled that of nearby Indian Queen Tavern: The two northern rooms had corner fireplaces that shared an interior end chimney; the southeast room had a boxed winder stair. A one-story porch shaded the entire main facade.

Nathaniel Ramsey House (site)
mid-18th century
Charlestown

Nathaniel Ramsey may well have been the most notable person in Charlestown during its mid-18th century boom period. Born in 1741, he graduated from Princeton in 1767, moved to Charlestown, and was admitted to the Cecil County bar. He married Margaret Jane Peale, sister of the painter Charles Willson Peale, and was a close friend of the artist. Ramsey was a Cecil County delegate to the Maryland convention in 1775, signed the Declaration of the Freemen of Maryland, and served on a committee to encourage manufacturing in the state. In 1776 he was commissioned a captain in the First Maryland Regiment and saw action in many campaigns with George Washington. Captured by the British and released in 1780, he remained a friend of Washington's and served as a pallbearer at the general's funeral. Active in politics after the Revolutionary War, Ramsey served two terms in the U.S. Congress, and in 1794 he became officer of the Port of Baltimore, a position he held until his death. Ramsey's brick house burned in 1834, after use as a town meeting hall, church, and school.

(The Ramsey house is clearly visible in Benjamin Latrobe's 1813 sketch of Charlestown, shown in chapter 3, "Making a Plantation Out of the Woods.")

Red Lyon Tavern/Black's Store (NR)
c. 1755 with additions
Charlestown

Located on lot 96 of the original plat of Charlestown, next door to the Indian Queen, is the Red Lyon Tavern. Later known as Black's Store, the building has

CE-393, Still House (1995)

CE-186, William and Mary Veazey house (1995)

had a complex history. At its core is a room measuring 23 x 19 feet and constructed of poplar log planks, hewn square with the ends neatly fitted with intricate dovetailing. Some of the planks, which are covered with siding, are twelve inches wide and five inches thick. The siding on the front is identical to the wide shiplap planks on the front of the later, larger structure, and the lower edges are beaded in the same way. The shiplap siding on the back was applied with the beads on the upper edge of each plank. The siding on the east gable end is rabbeted; the back flange of the upper plank fits into the forward lower rabbet to create a lap that weathers the rain.

Dry-laid rubblestone walls underpin the log structure to form a cellar keeping room; the great cellar fireplace has an opening five feet wide. An archeological dig in the hearth area revealed seven occupational layers. The fourth level is the most intriguing, for it reveals a cobblestone floor in the room. Preserving, soapmaking, and winter housekeeping took place in this room, which later served as a stockroom for goods sold in Black's Store.

Circa 1830 a one-room addition was built to the west of the log room. It also stands on a rubblestone foundation but exhibits post-and-beam construction.

A second addition made to the rear of this structure contains a kitchen with a deep fireplace on the first floor.

Still House
c. 1760 with additions
Charlestown

Situated on lot 1 of the original town plat, this rambling frame structure gets its name from one of early Charlestown's leading industries, liquor distilling. Peacock Bigger announced in the *Maryland Gazette* on March 8, 1753, that he had "Erected a Distillery at Charles Town where he makes rum." An advertisement run on July 16, 1759, offering the property for sale after Bigger's death, noted that the distillery, which converted raw sugar to rum, was the only one in Maryland.

Ships carried grain and salted fish, primarily herring and shad, from Charlestown to the West Indies and returned with rum, raw sugar, European products, slaves, and immigrants, who broke their journey to the British colonies at Barbados or St. Eustatius. Charlestown's inns, at one time as many as ten, soon became renowned for their selection of rum drinks, and its citizens became known for imbibing the same. The two

one-and-a-half story portions of the Still House, each two bays wide and one room in plan, date from the period when the distillery was operated. The two-and-a-half story frame house at one end is a later addition. The house overall has been altered.

William and Mary Veazey House
1768
Oldfield Point

William and Mary Veazey's initials, a tree of life symbol, and the year 1768 are all inscribed in a slate datestone in the east gable end of this house at the end of Oldfield Point Road overlooking the Elk River. It is a two-story, three-bay brick dwelling with a double-pile center hall plan. When the British landed at Oldfield Point on their way to Elkton in 1777, the house experienced a major fire. Damage from the blaze caused extensive structural and cosmetic changes, including replacement of the roof, rebuilding of the kitchen wing, and a uniform application of stucco to cover uneven brick repairs. Inside, the main stair was added and window sash, frames, and reveals were replaced.

CE-110, Linton house (Colonial Charlestown)

CE-795, Walnut Lane Farm (1978)

Linton House
c. 1787 with addition
Charlestown

Built by Town Commissioner William Linton when Charlestown served as the county seat, this fine house stands as a reminder of that prominent time in the town's history. Samuel Hogg, a prosperous businessman from Wilmington, purchased the house in 1797 and it served as his residence until his death. George Washington recorded several stops here on his journeys along the Post Road from Philadelphia to Mount Vernon.

The two-story, five-bay Flemish bond brick house is a restrained, late example of high-style Georgian architecture, complete with brick beltcourse and molded water table on the main facade. The absence of window arches is odd, and there is some evidence that the openings may originally have been wider. The door leads to a wide center hall flanked on each side by two rooms. A modern brick garage has been added to the west gable end.

Ford House
late 18th century
North East

This two-and-a-half story frame-and-brick house was built by the Fords, a North East family prominent in local politics, education, and the Methodist church. The five-bay frame section, which sits on a fieldstone foundation with cellar and has interior end chimneys of brick, may have been the home of John Ford, who owned a tannery in the town in the late 18th century. The dormers were added to this section in the mid- to late 19th century, and it was covered with weatherboards circa 1910. Extending to the rear of this portion is a two-story, mid-19th century brick wing laid in running bond with segmental arches over the windows. The bricks on the main road side are rubbed, giving them a soft red color. A two-story, one-room plan brick outbuilding stands near the wing; it has a small one-story brick addition on the rear.

CE-734, Ford house (1995)

CE-79, Bay View fieldstone house

CE-386, Tory House (Colonial Charlestown)

CE-811, Oldfield Point Road frame house

Walnut Lane Farm
c. 1800
North East vicinity

The house on Walnut Lane Farm was built in several stages in the late 18th or early 19th century. The earliest section is a two-story, three-bay hall/parlor log house covered with weatherboards. Log houses of this date with surviving period details, as seen here, are uncommon in Cecil County. A two-story, one-bay frame addition connects the log house to a one-and-a-half story, one-room frame kitchen addition. This kitchen wing was built on an earlier fieldstone foundation, with a cellar.

Outbuildings on the property include a pyramid-roofed stuccoed stone meat house and a similar icehouse. The ruins of a braced timber frame bank barn also stand on the property.

Land records document transfer of this property back to 1692, when John Watmore sold 200 acres to William Dare for 7,000 pounds of tobacco. James Hart, a farmer from Kent County, bought "Wadmore's Neck" in 1761. In his will of 1773, he left the property to his daughter Jannett or, if she had died, to his daughter Ann. Ann married Noble Hamm, and in 1800 their daughter Ann and her husband, Lambert Foard, sold the property to Alexander Wilson. The present log house was probably built either by the Hamms, Foards, or Wilson.

Mary Palmer's Tavern
late 18th century with additions
Charlestown

Owned and operated by Mary Palmer, who was widowed by the Revolutionary War, this tavern stood conveniently by the side of the Old Post Road. It is a three-story, three-bay frame structure with side hall plan on a stone foundation. A two-story, four-bay wing extends to the rear. It has been altered significantly in the late 20th century.

Bay View Fieldstone House
early 19th century
Bay View

This two-story, two-bay, one-room stone house with a frame wing at the rear stands on the north bank of the North East Creek above Gilpin's Falls. The area is well known as an early mill site, and milling activity continued through the 19th century; ruins of a dam and millrace survive nearby. This dwelling may have been the home of a miller.

Oldfield Point Road Frame House
early 19th century with additions
Elk Neck

This house is the product of two building stages. The first period of construction appears to have produced a one-room log structure, three bays wide and two stories tall. This section was probably raised to its present two-and-a-half story height when the larger three-bay frame structure with center hall, single-pile plan was attached. The house retains much original woodwork, and the alterations that have been made are noteworthy for themselves. These alterations clearly show a progression of styles, reflecting the changes in taste from the early 19th through the early 20th century.

Tory House/107 House
c. 1750, c. 1800-10, c. 1870
Charlestown

Long thought to have been an 18th century tavern run by British sympathizers and confiscated during the Revolution, this house became known as the "Tory House." Old deeds make it clear there was an 18th century structure on this lot and mention a house built in the "Dutch" fashion, although there is no proof that the owners were Tories. It is believed the present two-

CE-398, Mary Palmer's tavern (1985)

CE-108, Cecil Hotel (Colonial Charlestown)

CE-1246, Crawford house (1980)

story, three-bay, Federal frame structure, with its side hall/double-parlor plan, was built from the remains of the earlier house. Parts of the older house are visible in the cellar, where the tavern kitchen has been restored. A circa 1870 two-story wing stretches to the south.

The house stands on lot 107 of the original, 1742 plat of Charlestown. It has been restored through the efforts of Colonial Charlestown, Inc.

Principia
c. 1800-30, 1840-50
Principio vicinity

In 1832 John Megredy sold 197 acres called "Principia" to Henry S. Stites for $3,165.60. Stites, an associate justice of the Orphans Court, and his wife Harriett sold 165 acres of the property to Jacob Kreider in 1860 for $8,254.

Construction of the L-shaped frame house was carried out in three primary stages, all before Jacob Kreider purchased it. The house is complex because of the various additions made to the original structure, which was a two-story, three-bay heavy timber frame house. A continuous gable roof with four evenly spaced dormers and single-story porches help unify the various additions.

Cecil Hotel
c. 1810 with additions
Charlestown

This two-story frame Federal structure was once a tavern that rivaled the Indian Queen. The five-bay building sits on a high stone foundation sheathed in brick. It is covered in asbestos siding, and the cornice has been removed. The front door is topped with a semicircular fanlight, and the windows appear to be original. A late Victorian porch, complete with fine scrollwork, covers the front facade. Interior woodwork is characteristic of the 1790-1825 period; the round, tapered banisters of tiger maple are especially notable.

Crawford House
c. 1820-40
Bay View vicinity

Evidence of a stone foundation is all that remains of the Crawford Woolen Mill, but some ancillary houses—the mill owner's dwelling and one stone tenant house—are still in use. The former is a two-story, four-

CE-1233, Principia (1980)

bay hall/parlor house described in equity proceedings as the "Mansion House…of stone, 34 feet by 20 feet, 2-1/2 stories; good outbuildings, conveniently located."

Mary Reynolds Stone House
c. 1830
Mechanics Valley vicinity

This two-story, four-bay hall/parlor dwelling was referred to as an "old house" in 1863, when Mary Reynolds built a new three-story house across the road and wrote her will. Distinct similarities in the arrangement of rooms and placement of doors and windows are seen in both the old and new houses. In other words, while thirty years separates their construction, the traditional building methods and arrangement of living space in the earlier house reappeared basically unaltered in the later one.

Turkey Point Lighthouse
1833
Elk Neck
Public

Built to help sailors navigate the route to and from the Chesapeake and Delaware Canal, this 35-foot stuccoed stone lighthouse stands on the 100-foot clay cliffs of Turkey Point. An automatic light and foghorn were installed in 1948, ending more than 100 years of manual operation by a salaried lightkeeper.

(For more about the lighthouse, see Chapter 4, "'An Excellent Situation' for Manufacturer and Farmer Alike.")

William Cosgrove House
2nd quarter 19th century
Principio vicinity

The William Cosgrove house is unusual architecturally for Cecil County and might seem more at home in the mountains of Virginia than it does in the hills of northeastern Maryland. Especially rare is the large exterior stone chimney base with detached brick stack above the first story. The two- or perhaps three-room plan log house measures 22 feet 9 inches by 18 feet 8 inches and contains a boxed winder stair in the northwest corner. The interior first floor partitions have been removed, but evidence indicates a lateral wall divided the first floor. Another significant construction feature is the use of hole-set locust posts to support the rear shed kitchen addition. The use of hole-set posts for support is an early construction method, and, although this example is 20th century in date, it is an important example of the continuation of this building tradition.

CE-195, Turkey Point lighthouse (c. 1980)

CE-429, Mary Reynolds stone house (1980)

CE-1240, William Cosgrove house (1980)

CE-104, Brick House (1978)

CE-549, Foster or coffin maker's house (1985)

Wesley Chapel
c. 1840
Elk Neck vicinity

Wesley Chapel is one of the earliest church buildings surviving on Elk Neck. A local craftsman attests it is of vertical plank construction, making it a particularly important structure. Tombstones dating from the early 19th century are in the adjacent graveyard.

Brick House
c. 1840
North East vicinity

The Brick House stands two miles south of North East on the Elk Neck peninsula. The first floor plan of the main block originally consisted of two rooms, one behind the other, each heated by separate fire-places, with a stair on the west wall of the back room. A shorter two-story kitchen wing is attached to the east gable end. Although the common bond brick house has seen structural alterations, it is architecturally significant as an example of the double-cell house type in Cecil County.

This house served for a time as the rectory for St. Mary Anne's parish.

Foster or Coffin Maker's House
c. 1840
North East

As the name suggests, this two-and-a-half story brick structure was once the home of North East's coffin maker Francis A. Foster, who listed himself in the 1877 Cecil County atlas as "Undertaker and Dealer in Furniture." The house is three bays wide with a gable roof running parallel to the street. The glazed bricks running in random strips across the gable ends and the graceful pilasters flanking the tall dormer windows are unusual features. The rear wing with its side entrance is a later addition and served as Foster's shop after he bought the house in 1870. The pent roof is most likely not original.

Thomas J. Gillespie House
c. 1840-50
Principio vicinity

Popular architectural designs often affected vernacular house forms, resulting in struc-

CE-815, Wesley Chapel (1978)

CE-1234, Thomas J. Gillespie house (1995)

tures that reflected hybrid mixtures of popular and vernacular building forms. The basic hall/parlor floor plan and four-bay, two-door facade of the Gillespie house are traditional features of many area houses, features that have 18th century antecedents. The third floor, with its small two-over-two sash windows, is not characteristic of the type and belongs instead to the early 19th century Federal/Greek Revival period. The stylish two-bay front porch, with its dentiled cornice and paneled square columns, is another feature derived from mid-19th century architectural patternbooks.

Mauldin-Beatty House
c. 1850
North East

CE-559, Mauldin-Beatty house (1985)

This restrained Greek Revival brick structure sits on a fieldstone foundation. It is two and a half stories tall and half of a double house. The small three-over-three windows seen here often appear in Greek Revival structures in this area. The Colonial Revival porch, with its graceful curve at the northeast corner, was added in the 20th century. A granite fence encloses the house and garden, and two small outbuildings stand to the rear of the house.

This house, its neighbor, and the pair at 221-223 Main Street in North East were constructed within a few years of each other in the 1850s, during what was undoubtedly a minor building boom in the town. Nicholas Manley bought part of a tract named "Enlargement" in 1849 and divided it into ten lots, each with 40 feet of frontage on Main Street. This house was built in the 1850s on lot 6, probably by John Mauldin. The house, along with a small drugstore on the lot, were bought in 1906 by Arthur Beatty, who operated the store for many years. The one-story frame store was later moved and became a boathouse.

Oak Grove School
c. 1850
Mechanics Valley vicinity

The Oak Grove Schoolhouse stands along Lum's Road northwest of Mechanics Valley. When the one-story, three-bay, one-room fieldstone structure received a fresh coat of stucco in 1855, the date was scratched into the north wall. The building stopped serving as a school in 1940, but except for a gabled front porch, it has remained virtually unaltered on the exterior.

Maffit Farm
c. 1850
North East vicinity

Once part of sprawling "St. John's Manor," this farm was sold to Samuel Maffit by Stephen, Mary, and Jane Hyland in March 1850; this house was probably built soon after. It is a three-story, center hall frame form that was popular in the mid-19th century in the mid-Atlantic region, although it seems unusually stylish for its location in isolated Elk Neck. The house retains much period detail.

Johnson's Woolen Mill
19th century
Bay View

Located at the base of Gilpin's Falls are the large holding pond and stone dam breast that once held and diverted water through Johnson's Woolen Mill. The stone walls of the mill are barely visible, but the millrace remains intact both above- and below-ground. Other, smaller structural foundations are also associated with the mill. In January 1854, William Johnson bought the sixty-acre Cedar Valley property along with

CE-428, Oak Grove Schoolhouse (1980)

CE-816, Maffit farmhouse (1978)

CE-555, Roney and Wells Hardware Store (1985)

CE-1244, Bay View log house (1980)

four carding machines, one picker, one 156-spindle jack, one regulator, two power looms and fixtures, and one broad loom. The Johnson family owned the mill property until the turn of the 20th century.

Roney and Wells Hardware Store
mid-19th century
North East

One of only a few structures in North East to use Port Deposit granite, this handsome old store is one of the area's most important commercial buildings. Brick is used for the side walls, front facade trim, and stepped cornice. On the main facade large glass windows flank the double entrance doors. Much of the original interior is still intact, including the counter, shelves, drawers with porcelain knobs, and an old wood stove.

Stoney Chase/Curry Stone House
c. 1855
Mechanics Valley vicinity

Joseph Curry of Butler County, Pennsylvania, and John Curry of Cecil County purchased three tracts of land between 1849 and 1860: two parcels of Stoney Chase from Ann Russell and a two-acre parcel from Joseph Lort. These gentlemen presumably were responsible for the construction of this two-story, three-bay, center hall fieldstone structure.

Bay View Log House (site)
early to mid-19th century with additions
Bay View vicinity

This log house illustrates the expansion many log buildings experienced during the 19th century. The two-story structure was apparently raised by stud frame to a higher elevation and extended on all sides by various gabled and shed additions. The V-notched structure originally formed a rectangle approximately 18 feet deep by 22 feet across.

CE-430, Stoney Chase (1980)

CE-402, Old Post Road frame house (1995)

CE-1235, Prospect Hill farmhouse (1980)

CE-1340, Mauldin double house (1995)

Old Post Road Frame House
mid-19th century
North East

The original weatherboard siding of this two-part, L-plan frame house survives beneath the asphalt shingles. The main block is four bays long beneath a steeply pitched gable roof with wide eaves. An interior chimney rises at each gable end. The five-bay wing runs east along the north end wall; it is only one room deep. Possibly of commercial use—the house is on the Old Post Road—the wing has three doors that open onto its second story porch.

Prospect Hill Farm
c. 1855
Principio vicinity

A 19th century carte-de-visite of Prospect Hill farm, made by A. L. Barry of Port Deposit, shows the house and barn from the head of the fence-lined entrance. The three-story, five-bay, single-pile frame house dates from the ownership of Benjamin Gifford, who bought the 109-acre Prospect Hill tract in April 1854 from William and Lydia Bryson of New Castle County, Delaware. The massive front block has a much shorter two-story, two-bay kitchen ell. This house is similar in form to other houses a few hundred yards to the east and west along McGrady Road.

Mauldin Double House
c. 1856
North East

This pair of two-and-a-half story Greek Revival-style brick houses has a central chimney that serves both halves. The windows have simple architraves typical of the mid-19th century. The entrances are set at opposite ends of the main facade, and each leads into the stair hall of a side hall/double parlor plan.

The building sits on part of a 19,000 square foot lot bought unimproved by John Mauldin in 1851. Mauldin subdivided the lot, built these houses, and sold one to Richard Thomas for $500. Thomas, a judge of the Orphans Court, resided from 1862 until 1888 at another house in town, so must have purchased this dwelling as an investment.

Belvidere (site)
c. 1860
Principio Furnace vicinity

This large-scale, three-story frame dwelling, which has been moved to Pennsylvania, was one of the most elaborate houses in this part of Cecil County. Its overall proportions and widow's walk could be interpreted as Federal period leftovers, but the shallow roof and rhythmic cornice suggest Italianate influences and the tracery on the one-story front porch is purely eclectic Victorian.

CE-147, Belvidere (1968)

389

CE-379, St. John's Methodist Church (1984)

CE-724, Mechanics Valley yellow house (1980)

St. John's United Methodist Church
1856
Charlestown

Exhibiting a traditional floor plan and appearance typical of other rural brick Methodist churches in Maryland, this church is distinguished by its geometric-patterned colored glass. Offices, Sunday School quarters, and meeting rooms are located on the ground floor below. The ground floor entrance is in the center of the south end wall. The heavily dentiled cornice provides a degree of decoration to the otherwise austere exterior, unrelieved by either steeple or belfry.

Gilpin's Falls Covered Bridge
c. 1859-60
Bay View vicinity

Formerly the connection between Old Nottingham Road and the town of North East, Gilpin's Bridge crosses the North East Creek just north of a precipitous waterfall. At 119 feet, it was the longest covered bridge in Maryland when it was constructed under the supervision of George Johnson in 1859-60. The roadbed and mortised-and-tenoned structural frame were hung on a pair of Burr trusses. The roof, siding, and flooring were replaced in 1958-59.

Mechanics Valley Yellow House
c. 1860-70
Mechanics Valley

Two-story porches with stick balusters on the first floor and an alternating grid pattern on the second dominate this two-story frame house with its exposed fieldstone basement. Its three-story height and expansive porch make this a larger version of the typically modest two-story, two-bay, single-pile house.

Mary Reynolds's New House
c. 1863
Mechanics Valley vicinity

Mary Reynolds's 1863 will bequeathed this property to her daughter Lydia Maria Miller: "all my real estate lying west of the two roads—the one crossing Little North East Creek and passing the new house which I now occupy and the old house which I formerly occupied...."

It is possible to make an interesting contrast between these two houses because they both still stand along Stevenson Road. This three-story, four-bay hall/parlor stuccoed building is the "new house" mentioned in the will; her "old house" stands across the road. Both houses have a hall/parlor arrangement and two central front doors, but the "new" house has a third floor, giving it an entirely new, more up-to-date appearance. Although she accepted a third story, Mary Reynolds maintained the old

CE-78, Gilpin's Falls covered bridge (1977)

CE-513, Mary Reynolds's new house (1980)

CE-1344, Italianate double house (1985)

CE-543, Griffith-Smith house (1980)

familiar room arrangement and orientation in her new dwelling.

Thomas House
c. 1830, 1860s
North East

Despite its elegant Victorian appearance, this two-story frame house is locally believed to contain a late Federal period dwelling. If so, it has been almost completely encased in alterations carried out after 1862, the year the house was acquired by Judge Richard Thomas. The five-bay main block is notable for its graceful mansard roof with bracketed eaves and highly decorative corbeled chimney stacks. Behind this section is a rear wing, much smaller in scale, with a huge brick fireplace between two small rooms; this is probably the older house Thomas bought from John McCracken.

Thomas, who was judge of the Cecil County Orphans Court, was one of the most prominent citizens of North East during the 19th century and was proprietor of the local grocery firm Thomas & Anderson. Although he owned numerous houses in town, this one served as his residence until his death in 1888.

Italianate Double House
1860s
North East

This handsome pair of two-and-a-half story brick houses, now stuccoed, appears to be later than the Greek Revival style houses father south on Main Street. The double house is distinguished by its Italianate bracketed eaves, boxed cornice, and unusual casement windows in the attic story.

Griffith-Smith House
c. 1850, c. 1865
Bay View

On May 6, 1856, an occupant of this house recorded the weather on a second story floor joist, writing "A heavy rain," along with the date. This seems to document the presence at that time, when William Griffith owned the property, of at least the shorter two-story, two-bay front block. (Land records document Griffith's purchase of three parcels of land two or three years earlier.) Edwin B. Smith probably added the substantial two-story, two-bay gable end addition when he returned to the house, which he owned, after the Civil War.

CE-399, Thomas house (1985)

CE-106, Greenhill Farm (1995)

McCullough Iron Company Office (ruin)
after 1865
North East

This small one-story stone ruin, with its tall window frames and partially stuccoed exterior, stands forlornly in a public park at the north end of the town of North East. Along with a brick chimney and several foundations located close to the railroad tracks, this office building is all that remains of the giant rolling mill operated by the McCullough Iron Company between 1865 and 1898. The company, one of the original manufacturers of galvanized sheet iron in the United States, operated the Shannon, Octoraro, and West Atwell mills in Cecil County in addition to plants in Wilmington and Philadelphia. Although it was only one of several industries in North East, the company exercised a pervasive influence in the community; Jethro McCullough, its first president, paid for the construction of the town's first Baptist church and the company probably built and owned the four stone double houses on Pennsylvania Avenue as well as the row of frame houses on Rolling Mill Road.

Industrial activity has existed in the North East area since at least 1711, when land was condemned for construction of a mill at the junction of the east and main branches of North East Creek. The Dutton Mill ironworks was built in North East in 1716, and smelting operations were carried out in one form or another until the last furnace closed in 1936.

This office building was very similar in appearance to the Whitaker Iron Company's office at Principio and featured a mansard roof and cupola.

Elk River Farm
c. 1870
Elk Neck

Gothic Revival structures are rare on Elk Neck, making this elaborate example of the style all the more significant. The three-story, five-bay frame house retains most of its exterior ornament. A three-story wing extends to the rear.

The Lake, Griffing, and Stevenson atlas

CE-807, Elk River Farm (1978)

CE-1242, Ebenezer Methodist Church (1980)

CE-810, Simpers house (1978)

indicates the farm was owned by John T. Pryor in 1877.

Greenhill Farm
c. 1760-80, 1860-80
North East vicinity

A sizable amount of time, effort, and money in the third quarter of the 19th century transformed an earlier house into this three-story, five-bay, stuccoed residence with mansard roof and center hall, double-pile plan. The entrance has double doors with a porch above; the door to the porch is topped by a small canopy of Victorian pierced fretwork.

The 18th century was not totally whisked away by a carpenter's crowbar, for the house displays a fine Chinese Chippendale trellis stair, which rises to the third floor. Paneled window reveals and seats, along with a heavy dentiled cornice also survived the Victorian alterations. The earlier house had a side hall/double parlor plan.

A one-and-a-half-story, Flemish bond brick detached kitchen and slave quarter dating from the 18th century stands to the east of the house. The two-room structure is four bays across with a separate center entrance into each room.

Ebenezer Methodist Church
1871
College Green vicinity

A circular plaque on the east gable end of the main block records that the original 1826 church was replaced in 1871 by this building. The single-story, gable-roofed frame church is dominated by a Colonial Revival temple vestibule. The pedimented front entrance is supported by Tuscan columns and has a dentiled cornice. Fluted pilasters frame the heavily molded double door entrance and colored glass transom.

Simpers House
third quarter 19th century and earlier
Elk Neck

This frame house is a good example of a type often built across Cecil County in the second half of the 19th century. This particular two-story, five-bay, cross-gabled, center hall farmhouse was built of wood with balloon frame construction. It is covered with weatherboards, except in the gables, which have decorative fish-scale shingling. Unlike many examples of the type, this house retains its Victorian period detail.

An earlier 19th century common bond brick structure is attached to the rear of this frame house. Originally one story tall, this section has been extensively altered.

The name J. Simpers is cited at this location in the 1877 atlas.

McCullough House
1870-74
North East

One of the most ornate houses in North East, this two-and-a-half story, three-bay frame house is covered with German siding. It has two-over-two sash windows with paneled shutters, round-headed attic windows, and a double door with round-headed glass inserts. The most noticeable

CE-1342, McCullough house (1995)

CE-105, North East Town Hall (1995)

CE-401, George Simcoe house (1995)

feature of the house is its decorative Victorian woodwork, including the heavy brackets below the eaves and the hipped roof porch with its jig-sawn fleur-de-lis trim and latticework posts. The porch is a carpenter's version of the ornate cast-iron porches often found in Elkton. A two-story, four-bay wing extends to the rear of the house.

This house was probably built by George McCullough after he bought the unimproved lot in 1870. The house was sold in 1874 to James Roney, who operated a store on the adjacent lot.

North East Town Hall
c. 1880
North East
Public

Although built on a small scale, the North East town hall contains many interesting details and is one of the most unusual civic buildings in the county. Constructed as the town hall and lock-up shortly after the town bought the land in 1886, it is a two-story brick cube with three-pronged turrets on the main facade, a vigorous cornice below a slate roof, and an elaborate belt-course between the ground and second stories. The variation in window shapes and sizes is also notable.

George Simcoe House
c. 1880
North East

Behind a picket fence, sheltered by young maple trees, this house is evidence of the prosperity of the little industrial town of North East in the late 19th century. It is a large, three-story frame dwelling covered with weatherboards. The main block is three bays wide below a low hipped roof with a bracketed cornice; the windows decrease in dimension from the first to the third story. A one-story period porch stretches across the front of this section.

The east wing has scallop-shaped eave trim and is probably contemporary to the main section; the rear wing has a central chimney between two rooms and may predate the rest of the house.

Converted into apartments circa 1980, this house is one of the handsomest dwellings in North East.

Victorian Double House
1880s
North East

This Victorian-era double house with its mansard roof and pressed brick facade provides an interesting contrast to the midcentury Greek Revival-style houses found elsewhere in North East and suggests that residential construction continued in the town throughout the 19th century. The house on the right retains most of its decorative features, including the paired wooden brackets below the eaves and the fish-scale slate shingling on the roof. A wooden porch with turned posts and bracketed eaves unites these two dwellings.

CE-1304, Barnes icehouse (1985)

CE-387, Perry Barnes house (1985)

Cramer House
late 19th century
North East

This well-preserved Victorian common bond brick house is two and a half stories high and has a three-story tower topped by a pyramidal roof and a finial at the southwest corner. The windows are headed with segmental arches and retain their two-over-two sash. There is decorative wood shingling in the gable ends and on the third story of the tower. An Eastlake-style wrap-around porch extends across part of three facades.

Perry Barnes House
1880s
Charlestown

This Victorian-style frame house is L-shaped and covered in clapboard. The two-story, three-bay structure faces south below a steeply pitched gable roof. The eaves are heavily ornamented with some of the most elaborate Victorian trim in Charlestown, providing an interesting contrast with the colonial-era buildings in town. The house was built by Perry K. Barnes, who operated a fishery at Carpenter's Point. Barnes's grandson Cranford Henry still lives in the house.

Barnes Icehouse
c. 1890 with addition
Charlestown

Facing a protected cove on the Charlestown waterfront, this 19th century structure was built by Captain Perry K. Barnes to serve his large commercial fishing business. The practically cubical building is sheathed entirely of 12-inch Eastern white pine planks, ship-lapped to fit, and the inner walls were filled with 18 inches of ground cork for insulation. Designed to be loaded directly from the river, the building was expanded at a later date with the addition of a shed for storing fishing nets. This section was also built of white pine planks, but here 10-inch boards were aligned vertically rather than horizontally as in the main structure.

CE-1339, Victorian double house (1985)

CE-1338, Cramer house (1995)

CE-762, Johnson Victorian house (1978)

CE-1306, Charlestown water tower (1985)

Johnson Victorian house detail (1978)

Johnson Victorian House
1898
Bay View vicinity

The success of the woolen mill industry on Big North East Creek is reflected in this two-and-a-half story frame house at Gilpin's Falls. John and Jethro Johnson are said to have built the house on the site of an earlier structure. The T-shaped dwelling is traditional in plan but unusual in detail, and the Eastlake style of the front porch is especially atypical for Bay View. A central pediment with a sunburst design of split spindles emphasizes the front steps, and the arched sunburst design is repeated on either side of this using fully turned spindles.

Water Tower
1900
Charlestown

Charlestown, although located on the banks of the North East River, has from its beginnings had a problem obtaining an adequate supply of drinking water. The town rests on a layer of clay 150 feet deep that has very few of the water-bearing gravel strata found elsewhere in Cecil County. The original town commissioners recognized this problem as early as 1743, when they were preparing the area for development, and they constructed five communal wells, two along the water's edge and three that apparently tapped small streams in the clay layer. Built as a water tower for the McKown house, this tall frame structure once stood adjacent to one of those early wells.

The tower is a two-story structure, approximately 12 feet square, that contains a large tank of thick cypress in its upper story. The cypress probably came from trees on the Eastern Shore. The framing is pegged and the siding is shiplapped, techniques not unfamiliar to Charlestown's early carpenters, most of whom were also boatbuilders. In 1978-79 members of Colonial Charlestown, Inc., arranged for the tower, which had fallen into disrepair, to be moved four blocks to a site behind the Tory house. It has been restored and is visible to the public.

McKown House/"Klondyke House"
1900
Charlestown

This fine house is an anomaly in a town otherwise lacking many Victorian houses. Because Charlestown has experienced a depression since the county seat was moved to Elkton in 1787, the funds to build this elaborate house came from elsewhere. In the late 19th century, two McKown brothers left Charlestown to make their fortune in the West. After mining unsuccessfully for silver in Nevada, they went to the Klondyke gold fields, where they decided not to mine but instead to open a gambling house. They prospered and returned to build this turreted extravaganza in Charlestown.

It seems likely that in traveling from Nevada to Alaska and then back home, the brothers would have sailed out of San Francisco. This fact seems even likelier considering the style of this house, which displays many characteristics of the 1880-1910 architecture in Nob Hill or Pacific Heights. San Francisco architecture at that time was experiencing the "First Bay Tradition," a high style characterized by a flamboyant mixture of styles, an abundance of dark stained wood, and picturesque changes in spatial and axial arrangements. Self-evident

CE-1305, Scott Jackson house (1995)

on the exterior of this house in Charlestown, these characteristics are continued on the interior with dark wood paneling that extends up two 15-foot walls. Two sets of twin sliding doors leading to the centrally placed parlor are remarkable: walnut on the parlor side, cherry with dark stain on the other. The house is virtually intact, down to such details as the massive curtain rods over all interior doors and intricately formal brass chandeliers. A hexagonal weatherboard-covered icehouse stands to the rear of the house.

One McKown brother moved to Baltimore, but Sam McKown remained in this house. His daughter Millicent then lived here with her husband, Craig Jackson of Principio.

CE-109, McKown house/"Klondyke house" (1973)

Scott Jackson House
1901
Charlestown

This house and the neighboring McKown "Klondyke" house represent an unusual degree of prosperity in otherwise financially troubled turn-of-the-century Charlestown. Scott Jackson, a contractor and decoy maker, built the house, and it testifies to his skill as a craftsman. The irregular, flowing plan, evident on the exterior, shows that Jackson was aware of the architectural fashions of his day. He displayed his artist's eye in the details of the house as shown in the interior door surrounds, which have five strings of delicate reeding in their centers. This reeding is echoed throughout the house on every possible flat surface: in the center of the panels on all the doors; in the mantels that once framed heating stoves; in the bannister; in the solid panel that covers the stepends of the stair; and in the window frames. All the wood trim in the house was executed in chestnut, a further refinement.

Gilpin's Falls Hydroelectric Plant
(site)
c. 1905-26
Bay View vicinity

In 1895 William Warburton, a county attorney, purchased several properties around Gilpin's Falls in order to fulfill his lifelong ambition of constructing a hydroelectric plant. The falls were a logical choice, as here the Big North East Creek makes a 106-foot drop in approximately 2,000 feet. Warburton had accomplished his goal by 1905, and his Elkton Electric Light and Power Company operated until 1926. The stone abutments and part of the concrete water control system are all that remain today.

CE-763, Gilpin's Falls hydroelectric plant (historic photograph)

North East United Methodist Church
1911
North East

Methodists, who organized in North East in 1781, worshiped in a succession of churches built or remodeled at various times during the 19th century, including ones dating from 1804, 1837, 1854, 1882, and 1903. The last burned in 1911 and was replaced with the present Gothic-style brick structure. The two-story, gable-roofed church is L-shaped and has a three-story bell tower with a crenelated top between the two wings. The exterior is notable for the decorative slate shingles at the two gable ends, the Tudor-arched colored glass windows that break through the flared eaves of the first story, and the Palladian-style attic windows.

CE-1343, North East Methodist Church (1985)

Sixth District

William Moore House
c. 1730s, mid-18th century, and later
Colora vicinity

This long stone dwelling was built in two stages marked by the seam between them. The original part, perhaps dating from the early 1730s, comprises the westernmost two bays of the present house and is built of fieldstone with large quoins and keystone lintels above the door and windows. The interior of this section is notable for the massive fireplace with beehive oven, exposed beaded summer beam, beaded floor joists, and enclosed winder stair with beaded paneling. The remainder of the house, four bays on the first floor, three on the second, was probably built in the mid-18th century. Although the house was extensively remodeled in the mid-19th century, the interior retains beaded beams, joists, and paneling and corbeled fireplace supports.

CE-791, William Moore house at Hilltop (1995)

Evan's Choice
1756
Richardsmere vicinity

The two-story, three-bay, double-pile main block of this house seems, at first, to resemble Graystone Manor in general form and appearance. However, the presence of a second front door west of the center door indicates an entirely different arrangement of rooms and variation in living spaces: The two front doors allow for entrance into either the cross passage on the left or the more formal parlor.

The construction of this massive stone house and bank barn is attributed to the Evans family, early Quaker settlers of the

CE-98, Evan's Choice (1980)

CE-39, John Swisher house

Nottingham Lots. The property remained in their hands until the early 1940s, and they are locally reputed to have been the last farmers to use oxen to plow their fields.

John Swisher House
1756
Rowlandsville vicinity

John Swisher of Coleraine Township in Lancaster County, Pennsylvania, purchased several tracts near West Nottingham and sold a 30-acre parcel subsequently known as "Father's Gift" to his son John Swisher, Jr., for $850. The son is the presumed builder of this two-story, cross passage/three-room plan stone house with symmetrical main elevation and two front doors. Swisher family descendants owned the property until the 1920s, and family initials are carved in a number of stones. A date carved by the front door reads June 10, 1756. Corner hearths, early moldings, and a huge fireplace with bake oven and mantel shelf are features that support a mid-18th century construction date.

Haines House
c. 1724, 1767, late 18th century
Rising Sun vicinity

This early colonial-era house just north of Rising Sun was built in three distinct stages. It is one of the earliest, if not the earliest, dated house in Cecil County.

The earliest section of the house is a two-story, three-bay structure framed with mortised-and-tenoned timbers and marked at the corners by flared posts. These posts and the front and rear girts are visible on the interior of the house. A beam marked with the date 1724 suggests one of several possible construction dates for the house. The heavily stuccoed exterior hides the early clapboard siding, although some of the original hand-split boards were found in the attic. Stone and clay nogging was used to insulate the walls. In the west gable end of the house is a large walk-in fireplace supported by a massive brick arch in the cellar.

The interior of this house, although altered, retains several significant original features. The front door frame suggests it once held a Dutch door. To the left of the fireplace is a set of winder stairs with an early feather-edged paneled door. The most

CE-216, Haines house (1983)

CE-218, Joseph Haines house/Willowdale (1979)

CE-95, Graystone Manor (1980)

unusual feature is the exposed chamfered corner posts with elaborate decorated post heads, a feature more commonly seen in New England and perhaps unique in Maryland.

In 1767 William Haines and his wife Lydia had a brick addition built that butted against the west gable of the older frame house. Among the important features of this building are the beveled brick water table, chair rail, raised panel interior doors, and corner fireplace. A tombstone-shaped datestone on the west gable end is inscribed 1767—WHL. The brick wing built on the rear of this section probably dates from the late 18th century.

The land on which the house stands was settled by a member of the Quaker Haines family before 1725. The family was one of the first to settle in the Nottingham Lots area, perhaps as early as 1701. Joseph Haines, "the settler," is mentioned in both the 1722 and 1731 tax assessments. Because it was his son William (born in 1725) who built the addition in 1767, it is believed that the elder Haines built the original house.

Moore-Reynolds Mill Property
c. 1770
Richardsmere vicinity

Joseph T. and Rebecca M. Reynolds acquired this house and the mill property along the east bank of the Octoraro Creek, in part through inheritance from William Moore's 1844 will and in part from a deed of sale from him to them. The mill no longer stands, but the mill owner's house is a two-story, three-bay stone structure with segmental arches over the windows and doors. The exact date of construction is not known, but architectural details suggest the third quarter of the 18th century. A porch spanning the front of the house dates from the period when the Nice and Addison families owned the property during the last half of the 19th century.

Joseph Haines House/Willowdale
1774 with additions
Rising Sun vicinity

In 1815 Joseph Haines willed to his son Nathan "all that plantation where I now live together with all land in both Pennsylvania and Maryland...." This remarkable two-story, cross passage/three-room plan stone house has a date plaque embellished with interlocking hearts above the Haineses'

CE-141, Moore-Reynolds Mill property (1980)

initials and the date 1774. The front entrance of the early section originally opened into the cross passage, which ran the full depth of the house; a stair with turned newel post and balusters and a molded handrail rises in the southwest corner of this rectangular room. East of the cross passage were two rooms, now combined into one, heated by corner hearths. Chimney supports in the cellar indicate the original room sizes. The floor plan and slightly asymmetrical main facade of the early house are characteristic of an early house form found in many northern areas of the county. The two-story west end, also of stone, was added as a kitchen in the 19th century.

Graystone Manor
1791 with additions
Rising Sun vicinity

Jacob Reynolds, grandson of the Henry Reynolds who was grantee of the 1,000-acre Nottingham Lots, built this solid, two-story, three-bay fieldstone house. The center passage, double-pile building included cooking facilities before the shorter two-story, two-bay service wing was added soon after initial construction. The wing contains a separate stair to bedrooms on the second floor that were used as servants' sleeping quarters; there is no access between the second floors of the main house and the wing. A datestone in one gable end of the main house records the 1791 construction date.

CE-230, Thomas Richards house (1968)

Reynolds Farm
1794, mid-19th century
Harrisville vicinity

This house was built in two stages: The two-story, two-bay, single-pile stuccoed fieldstone kitchen wing dates from 1794, as marked with a datestone in the gable. It is attached to a two-story, three-bay, stuccoed brick main block built in the mid-19th century. The house has been owned by the Reynolds family for most of its history. An eight-sided, board-and-batten covered dairy house also stands on the property.

On this farm was the "New Side" church whose congregation had split from the West Nottingham Presbyterian Church in the early 18th century. Sara Finley, wife of the Reverend Finley who founded West Nottingham Academy, is buried in the adjoining cemetery.

Thomas Richards House (NR)
c. 1795-1810 and additions
Harrisville vicinity

This house comprises a story-and-a-half, late 18th century fieldstone house and a two-story, three-bay common bond brick house added onto its east gable end. The stone section sits at a lower level, following the contours of the rolling terrain. The two sections are connected only by a narrow, enclosed winder stair.

The stone house measures 22 by 18 feet, the minimum house size set out by William Penn when the Nottingham Lots, on which the house stands, were laid out. The brick house exhibits the formal characteristics of the early Federal style. The entry hall is unusual in that it runs across the front of the house rather than through it. The four

CE-97, Reynolds Farm (1968)

CE-212, Maple Shade Farm (1980)

CE-769, Krauss's Tavern/Cross Keys Tavern (1995)

CE-229, Nathan and Susannah Harris house (1995)

fireplaces in the house exhibit woodwork ranging from an early molded mantelshelf to a finely reeded Federal mantel. Original interior woodwork, including some hardware, remains in place.

This house and an accompanying early 19th century bank barn stand on the westernmost Nottingham lot, which originally extended to Octorara Creek. Thomas Richards, Sr., purchased the 200-acre tract with the stone house in April 1797. By then called "Edminston Heights," it remained in his family for the next 130 years.

Thomas Richards's heirs included many prominent Cecil County citizens, including Dr. Hampton G. Richards, a physician, and Joseph T. Richards, an engineer. The large families of the Richardses gave the name Richardsmere to the area from Love Run to the Octorara.

A log house on the bank of the Susquehanna at Pilot Town, scheduled for demolition, was instead moved in the late 20th century and reconstructed on the south side of the brick portion of this house. The house was built of chestnut, walnut, and oak logs. The owners, copying Crooked Intention in Talbot County, are renovating the interior of the story-and-a-half building after that stylish 1750 dwelling. Consistent with this style, on the exterior the bricks behind the firebox are exposed, rather than covered with siding.

Maple Shade Farm
c. 1798 with additions
Farmington vicinity

The main house on Maple Shade Farm is not immediately recognizable as an 18th century log house because of the presence of later, oversized dormers; a five-bay, hip-roofed porch; narrow chimneys; and vinyl siding. Once inside, however, it becomes apparent that the house consists of two sections: a two-story, cross passage/three-room plan log house to the west and a 19th century gable end addition on the east. The two three-bay sections mirror each other in window and door placement. The early log house has a fully excavated fieldstone cellar. Although the interior partitions have been removed, the three hearth walls retain their fully raised overmantels and crossetted fireplace surrounds. Double-beaded joists are supported by a heavy summer beam that spans the distance between the corner hearths and the east end fireplace. An enclosed winder stair rises in the northeast corner of the cross passage.

Nathan and Susannah Harris House (NR)
1798
Harrisville vicinity

Nathan and Susannah Harris are permanently recorded as the builders of this fascinating stone house on the northwest corner of the intersection of Maryland Route 273 and the Jacob Tome Highway: A rectangular datestone is inscribed with the Harris surname above the split date and builders' initials; a heart separates the N and S, and a chevron design runs below the whole composition.

Important to the architectural history of northern Cecil County, the Harris house exhibits an adaptation of the cross passage/three-room plan, which has a more formal center passage separating the cross passage from the two rooms on the side. The centrally located righthand door opens into the hall and the door left of center opens into the cross passage or main cooking area. This definite specialization of interior space is indicative of the changes that occurred in house forms from the mid-18th century onward. The house also displays a fine collection of late 18th century woodwork and construction details. A massive principal rafter/butt purlin roof spans the 30-foot house depth.

Nathan Harris's estate was divided among his heirs in the early 19th century, and they were responsible for selling building lots south of the house, the basis for the present village of Harrisville. The bricks for these houses came from a local source, Krauss's brickyard.

Krauss's Tavern/Cross Keys Tavern
c. 1802
Harrisville

The 1858 Martenet map designates this house as the "X Keys Tavern" and places it along one of the main roads from Lancaster to Port Deposit. Major transportation routes

CE-228, West Notthingham meetinghouse

CE-371, Simeon Woodrow house (1973)

between Pennsylvania and Maryland spawned similar ventures in the county, including the Cross Keys Tavern in Calvert, the Cummings or Battle Swamp Tavern at Woodlawn, and Cather's Tavern near West Nottingham.

Built in 1802 by Leonard Krauss, this cross passage/three-room plan structure is similar to many houses in the area; a partially enclosed shed porch covers the second of two front doors. A story that Krauss was George Washington's "tailor" is based on the fact that Krauss presented the general with a suit of new clothes during one of his numerous travels through Cecil County.

Richards House
c. 1804 with additions
Harrisville vicinity

Family tradition is the source of the date for this two-story stuccoed stone house with three-room plan, built by Thomas Richards, Jr., early in the 19th century. It stands on a hilltop immediately southwest of the house of the builder's father, Thomas Richards, Sr. The western half of this dwelling is divided into two rooms heated by corner hearths. The kitchen is east of these rooms but does not extend the full depth of the house. The interior features several finely gouged early 19th century mantels and a corner cabinet. A large stone lean-to with bake oven stands on the east gable wall.

West Nottingham Meetinghouse and Cemetery (NR)
1811
Harrisville

This one-story, six-bay common bond brick structure resembles the Colora meetinghouse in Cecil County and nearby Pennsylvania Friends' meetinghouses. Known also as Little Brick Meeting House, it typically has separate entrances for men and women on both the north and south facades. The rectangular interior space is divided by sliding paneled partitions.

This brick building replaced the meetinghouse of log and frame that was constructed in 1727. The original structure was moved to Rising Sun by Benjamin Reynolds, who used it alternately as a carpenter's shop and a stable; around 1900 it was taken over by Miss Mabel Reynolds for use as a private school. The log-and-frame structure has since been moved from Rising Sun. The brick building is owned and maintained by the Cecil Historical Trust, Inc.

Members of the meeting are buried in a cemetery enclosed by an iron fence adjacent to the meetinghouse. A row termed "Roman Row" was reserved for poor families who could not afford to pay for burial.

Simeon Woodrow House
c. 1810-20
Richardsmere vicinity

County land records document the transfer of 135 acres of "Edminston's Heights" from Samuel Cookson, a native of Frederick County, to Simeon Woodrow for $2,000 in 1811. Architectural details suggest a construction date for the main block of this stone house within a decade of the 1811 purchase. The floor plan is very similar to that of the Nathan and Susannah Harris house, with a central stair hall dividing a three-room arrangement. Peculiar to this almost square house, however, is its orientation: The side facade has a symmetrical five-bay arrangement with center entrance, while the facade facing the road is only three bays wide.

CE-231, Richards house (1968)

CE-1408, Queen Street brick house (1985)

Queen Street Brick House
1st quarter 19th century
Rising Sun

This two-story, six-bay, brick-and-frame double house probably dates from the early 19th century. The south portion served as a store for several years. One of only two buildings in Rising Sun with Flemish bond brickwork, the north half of the house has a boxed cornice with bed molding, six-over-six sash windows, and a side hall/double-parlor plan. The interior of this section has retained its graceful elliptical stair at the rear of the long hall as well as Federal mantels and chair rail. A later porch stretches across the front.

James and Rachel Cameron House
1816
Principio vicinity

An 1816 oval datestone with James and Rachel Cameron's initials is set into the fieldstone gable end wall of this two-and-a-half story, side passage/double-pile house. Finely appointed architectural details appear throughout, from the pilastered and arched sash dormers to the uncommon interpretation of early 19th century mantel design. The treatment of the mantel pilasters is similar to that in the Elisha Kirk house in Calvert. The design similarities may indicate the same craftsman built both houses, since they date within a few years of each other. A shorter two-story kitchen wing is attached to the east gable end.

CE-135, James and Rachel Cameron house (1979)

Cummings Tavern
c. 1820
Port Deposit vicinity

A January 7, 1865, clipping from the *Cecil Whig* notes the court-ordered sale of this property, described as

> all that valuable tract of land, with the tavern and store, known as Battle Swamp....the improvements are a large Stone Tavern House, well known for many years as the Battle

CE-139, Cummings Tavern (historic photograph)

Swamp Tavern containing four rooms on each of the first and second floors with back building, one of the best tavern stands in the state; a large barn, with ample room for the accommodation of the horses of travelers and for all the farm purposes; corn crib, smoke house, and ice house. There are two pumps of good water, one at the kitchen door and the other at the barn. There is also a tenant house built of logs and weather boarded, with two rooms downstairs and three rooms upstairs. There are a number of fine apple and pear trees on the place….

Old photographs add to our understanding of this massive stone building; one shows a two-story porch, which explains the presence of the second floor door. An exact construction date for the tavern has not been determined, but architectural details firmly suggest the early 19th century. The tavern still stands but is in bad condition.

CE-1196, Mount Pleasant/Ewing house (1995)

McCauley Road Stone Bridge
c. 1820
Rowlandsville vicinity

Located along McCauley Road between Rowlandsville and Mount Pleasant, this stone bridge is undated but was probably built in the early 19th century before iron spans were used. A stone arch allows the passage of a tributary of the Octoraro Creek.

Mount Pleasant/Ewing House
c. 1820-30
Colora vicinity

Mount Pleasant stands atop a gentle rise that overlooks an expansive valley of small streams and runs, one of which supplied the water power for the Ewing family mills. This two-and-a-half story brick house is an 18th century form that was actually more commonly built in the 19th century. The main block has a Flemish bond facade and a kitchen wing of the same height on the rear; another kitchen building further extends this wing. Much of the late Federal/Greek Revival interior woodwork remains.

New Valley Factory
c. 1820-40
Liberty Grove vicinity

With its two gabled dormers and gable end chimney, this two-story, four-bay fieldstone structure along Basin's Run looks more like a house than a mill, and in fact the roof and dormers date to the 20th century, when the mill was converted into a residence. During its industrial era, the structure, known as New Valley Factory, stood next to another mill and across the road from the miller's house. Local oral tradition documents its last operation as a shoe peg factory. The 1858 and 1877 county maps indicate saw- and gristmills on the site.

CE-1201, McCauley Road stone bridge (1995)

CE-45, New Valley Factory (1979)

CE-1175, Trumph house (1979)

CE-136, Jehoiakim and Agnes Brickley house (1980)

Trumph House
1831
Mount Pleasant (Vinegar Hill) vicinity

This stone house combines a common Cecil County house form with some features not often seen in the county. The gable roof over the two-story, three-bay, center hall plan house extends into a hipped roof at one end to cover the integrated two-story stone porch found there. Porches such as this are more common in western Maryland, although there they are often part of a rear wing rather than the main block. The house has an 1831 oval datestone with M and R Trumph inscribed.

Stoney Batter Farmhouse
c. 1830-60
Liberty Grove vicinity

This farmhouse consists of three two-story, three-bay, single-pile hall/parlor fieldstone sections built during the second and third quarters of the 19th century. The first section is the eastern half of the main block; it dates from 1830-40 and was built by Samuel, Joseph, and Moses Nesbitt. The other half of the main block repeats the first in exterior appearance, with the addition of another three bays and a central door. The rear wing straddles the two front sections and provides an attached kitchen.

Jehoiakim and Agnes Brickley House and Mill
1834
Principio vicinity

As viewed from the mill, the Brickley stone house appears as a massive stone pile, two and a half stories high, five bays wide, and six bays deep. The house has two important facades, which are fitted with gabled dormers and porches. The main facade is distinguished by a centrally placed single-bay portico and, more important, a construction plaque reading "J & AR Brickley 1834." This facade also commands an expansive vista of surrounding mills and fertile fields; while this hill site was obviously chosen for aesthetic reasons, it also lets the house dominate the industrial site and adjacent county road. Two rooms flank the center hall, while two more rooms form the rear dining and service wing of the house. The entire structure is an excellent example of the builder's art.

Originally two mills operated on this property. The flour mill, directly across from the house, was torn down. The sawmill and gristmill remain.

CE-1177, Stoney Batter farmhouse (1995)

Haines-Reynolds Farm
c. 1830-50
Rising Sun vicinity

This two-story, five-bay Flemish and common bond brick farmhouse has a history of ownership in both the Haines and Reynolds families. The main block was built in two stages; the eastern three-bay hall/parlor house predates the two-bay kitchen addition made to the west gable end. The house remains basically untouched and is complete with corbeled brick cornices, paneled shutters, and period woodwork.

Davis-Christy Mill
c. 1840
Rowlandsville

This area, at the confluence of Basin's Run and the Octoraro Creek, has been the site of a gristmill since the early 19th century. The Rowland, Christy, and Davis families have all produced millers that operated a gristmill at this site. The 1880 manufacturing census listed the Davis and Christy firm with capital investments of $15,000 and production at $17,000 per annum, which included 1,934 barrels of flour. With three stones, the mill was doing 25 percent custom work and had a sixty-bushel per hour elevator. A 60-foot fall on Basin Run drove two turbines at 280 RPM to produce a speed of 44 horsepower.

CE-217, Haines-Reynolds farmhouse (1981)

Matthew Morrison House
c. 1840
Rowlandsville vicinity

This house stands on a tract known in 19th century land records as "Mount Montgomery." Robert and Cornelia Gerry of Philadelphia and Mary Gerry of Cecil County, widow of James, sold 100 acres of the tract to Matthew Morrison and John Graham in 1840. Graham sold parts of it to Morrison that same year and again in 1844, making it seem more likely that Morrison built this finely pointed cut-and-coursed fieldstone house. It is a two-story, four-bay structure with two center doors marking the cross passage/three-room plan often seen in this part of Cecil County. The interior retains much of its original woodwork.

Harrisville
2nd quarter 19th century

The village of Harrisville comprises several attractive brick houses situated in a straight line on the west side of the Harrisville Road north of Krauss's Tavern. Probably dating from the second quarter of the 19th century, the houses were occupied by the

CE-789, Davis-Christy Mill (1980)

CE-1181, Matthew Morrison house (1980)

CE-1123, two-story brick house in Harrisville (1980)

CE-1123, house with Victorian additions in Harrisville (1981)

Reynolds, Post, and Krauss families during the 19th century. Probably the oldest is the two-story, four-bay brick house painted white (pictured). This house features a Flemish bond facade, six-over-six sash windows with brick jack arches, two doors on the front with paneled reveals and six-panel transoms. A particularly unusual feature is the molded brick cornice.

The Steppe house features a Flemish bond facade and molded cornice and has extensive Victorian frame additions. The house at the northwest corner of the Harrisville road probably dates from the 1830s or '40s and is a two-story, L plan common bond brick house with brick sills and boxed cornice. The interior features one large room in the front wing, a steep winder stair in the southeast corner, and Greek Revival period woodwork and mantels.

The town was named for Charles Harris, a locally prominent landowner. It was once home to a number of butchers and blacksmiths, a reflection of the German heritage of several of its early settlers.

Nesbitt Stone House
c. 1830 with additions
Vinegar Hill vicinity

Thomas Patten sold eighty-six acres of the tract "Liberty Grove" to Moses Nesbitt in 1802 for £161 sterling. The property remained in the Nesbitt family until the 1890s, passing from Moses to Robert Nesbitt in 1827 and Robert to John Allison Nesbitt in 1865.

Architectural details date the first part of this house to the second quarter of the 19th century. It is a two-story, three-bay, single-pile fieldstone house built into a bank. Inside, an enclosed central stair is flanked by a room on either side. This house form is usually found in areas of the county with extensive Scots-Irish settlement, and this house is one of the very few for which the Scots-Irish background of the builders is certain. Later, a two-story, two-bay kitchen wing was attached to the west gable end, and a circa 1860-80 hipped-roof porch built across the entire facade unifies the two sections.

CE-1184, Nesbitt stone house (1979)

CE-1119, Samuel Taylor brick house

CE-1162, Independence (1995)

Samuel Taylor Brick House
2nd quarter 19th century
Harrisville

This handsome brick dwelling sits atop a prominent hill overlooking Harrisville from the north. Two stories high and five bays wide, the house is built on an L plan with Flemish bond brickwork on the south facade and glazed headers laid in strips on the east gable end. The six-panel front door is flanked by plain pilasters and topped with a classical entablature; the paneled door jambs are typical of the late Federal (1820-30) period. On the west facade is a handsome pedimented dormer with fluted pilasters and a segmental-headed window. The house was probably built by Samuel Taylor, who was listed in the Cecil County tax records as owning this house in 1841.

Independence
18th century with additions
Rising Sun vicinity

The extremely eclectic appearance of this house is due to the numerous additions and alterations it has undergone since the mid-18th century. The original house consisted of the two-story, two-bay stone section with entrances on the north and south and a fireplace and boxed winder stair on the east. In the late 18th century a two-story, gable-roofed stone kitchen wing was built at right angles to the original house; the original window and door were retained and incorporated into the new building, an additional entrance was cut into the west facade of the old section, and the roof height raised an additional story. In the 1830s or '40s an entire frame house was moved to the site and attached to the east; the weatherboards can be seen from an upstairs closet in the original section. It was also at this time that the main stair was enlarged and connected to the new frame section.

Wilson House
c. 1830, c. 1860
Principio vicinity

From the road, this house appears to be an ordinary two-story, three-bay, single-pile frame house without any unexpected architectural features. It is only from behind that the older common bond brick house is visible. This two-story, three-bay, single-pile brick house predates the frame house by thirty years and offers a rare chance to analyze a similar house form from two different

CE-1199, Wilson house, east elevation (1979)

Wilson house from the southwest (1980)

periods. The brick house faces the fields to the south, while the frame addition faces east to the road. This change in orientation coincides with the move in the mid-19th century to build houses facing the road rather than the farm or riverfront. The L shape created by the addition was a widely accepted and appealing form by the mid-19th century.

The farm was assembled around 1812-14 by William Wilson, a carpenter, who had bought two parcels of a tract called "Independence" from John Megredy.

CE-638, Colora meetinghouse

Gayley House (NR)
c. 1830-60
West Nottingham

The thirty-year bracket date listed for this house covers construction of the side passage/parlor main block and the subsequent two-story, two-bay gable end addition. Seams in the common bond brick walls and differences in interior woodwork indicate two separate building periods. Tall, lancet-shaped dormer windows flanked by pilasters add interest to the house.

A shorter two-story kitchen wing extends behind the first house; its smaller proportions, less elaborate detailing, and different floor level are typical features of kitchen wings. The bond pattern of the brick and the absence of a northeast gable end wall suggest the kitchen wing was built as part of the older house or added to it.

(This house now serves as the headmaster's house at West Nottingham Academy and is listed on the National Register of Historic Places as part of the West Nottingham Academy Historic District.)

Stoney Run
c. 1834 and earlier
Rising Sun vicinity

Although it is large and impressive, little about the exterior of the Stoney Run farmhouse hints at the Greek Revival ornamentation within. The removal of a wooden portico with Doric columns and corner pilasters left a plain exterior, but the rectangular transom and sidelights remain at the entrance on the south facade. The interior of the house exhibits decorative features common to the Greek Revival period, including corner blocks (with square rather than roundel decorations) and mantels with severely plain flat pilasters and a simple ornamental frieze. The large and spacious third floor was completed with classical motifs.

This large square house is five bays wide and two-and-a-half stories tall. It was built circa 1834, but it incorporates an earlier building. Now the kitchen, this structure has exposed beaded floor joists and a fireplace with massive stone hearth; it is believed to date from the mid- to late 18th century, and records substantiate that the Evans brothers moved into the valley northwest of Rising Sun in that time period.

Colora Meetinghouse (NR)
1841
Colora

Colora Friends meetinghouse stands in a wooded glen on land donated by Thomas Waring. The single-story stuccoed stone building was completed in 1841 at a cost of $626.62. The young men of the meeting carried out the construction under the direction of a stonemason and a carpenter

CE-705, Gayley house (1980)

CE-1118, Stoney Run (1995)

CE-1117, Rebecca Haines house (1981)

CE-1153, Cather house and tavern (1979)

with materials donated by Lloyd Balderston I, founder of the meeting. In architectural form and plan, the meetinghouse is identical to nearby West Nottingham meetinghouse, although its stuccoed exterior gives it a different appearance. The separate entrances and divided interior conform with the standard building form of the Quaker meetinghouse by the early 19th century. The interior has never been painted.

Colora Meeting was founded as a break from Nottingham Monthly Meeting, which followed the teachings of Elias Hicks, a Quaker liberal. A small group at West Nottingham who held more conservative views began Colora as a meeting affiliated with the Orthodox Friends.

Rebecca Haines House
1843
Rising Sun vicinity

Standing just north of Rising Sun, this house overlooks the once-active Haines Mill. The basic two-story, five-bay, center hall frame house was, according to local tradition, built for Mrs. Rebecca Haines in 1843. A three-bay Greek Revival front porch with full entablature and Tuscan columns dominates the south facade. The terrain slopes away from the front of the house, exposing much of the south basement wall and requiring a long flight of steps to reach the front porch.

Lloyd Balderston House/Colora Farm/Paradise
c. 1843
Colora

Very few houses are accompanied by as much family history and construction detail as this one at Colora Farm. This richness doubtless stems from the fact that the property has descended from father to son since the mid-19th century. From an architectural standpoint, the farm is important for its unusual collection of mid-19th to 20th century structures.

The house is thought to have been built two years after Lloyd Balderston moved here from Montgomery County, Pennsylvania; he purchased 104 acres of a tract called "Paradise" in 1841. Family tradition asserts that the two-bay, side passage/double-pile stone house was built with the intention of adding two more rooms on the west side of the hall. Because of the closeness of Colora Road, these plans were changed and the east gable end received the extra rooms, along with a two-story porch incorporated into the main block.

Cather House and Tavern (site)
c. 1830-80
West Nottingham vicinity

The junction of the Hopewell and Post roads southeast of West Nottingham has been known as Cather's Corner since that family acquired the property in the 1830s. Robert Cather bought 119 acres in 1834,

CE-1191, Lloyd Balderston house (1979)

CE-1171, Tosh house (1995)

CE-1160, Abrahams house (1980)

part of a tract known as "The Meadows." Not long afterward he built a two-story, three-bay, single-pile frame house similar in size and detail to hundreds throughout the county. Within the next decade, however, the house was rebuilt to be two rooms deep, and the resulting shift in roofline placed the end chimneys on the front slope of the roof. A two-bay addition was built on the west gable end, conforming to the double-pile depth and larger roof dimensions fashionable at the time.

The expansion of this house was undoubtedly undertaken in response to the booming tavern trade along this major route from Pennsylvania to Port Deposit; the structure was mentioned as Cather's Tavern as early as 1845. It was burned by the owner in 1992.

Tosh House
c. 1846
Colora vicinity

This house is another example of the house form most commonly erected by the Scots-Irish in Cecil County in the second quarter of the 19th century. The traditional plan seen here comprises an enclosed center stair flanked by a room on each side. The builder of this house was probably John Tosh, whom the 1877 atlas records as having Cecil ancestry from 1808. Other Tosh farms in the Colora area exhibit the same floor plan.

The two-story, three-bay fieldstone house stands on a hill overlooking Colora. The south facade is a semicoursed stone wall with square corners, while the other facades are more uncoursed. A shorter two-story, two-bay stuccoed fieldstone kitchen wing extends from the west gable end. The interior of the house retains period trim, mantels, and doors. A small frame meat house on fieldstone foundations, a corncrib, and barn, all dating from the 19th century, also remain on the property.

Abrahams House
c. 1840-50
Woodlawn vicinity

From the exterior, this house could date from any time from the late 18th century to the mid-19th century, demonstrating the conservatism that allowed popular house forms to continue in use for decades. However, the presence of the Greek Revival woodwork makes it possible to guess when the house was built. The side passage/double-pile dwelling was probably built by the Abrahams family, who operated the store and post office in Woodlawn.

Clendenin Farm
c. 1840-60 with additions
Cather's Corner vicinity

This dwelling presents an instructive example of house evolution, particularly of the influence the five-bay "Georgian" house form had on later additions. Begun as a two-story, three-bay stuccoed masonry house with side hall/double parlor plan, it was expanded later in the 19th century with the addition of a two-story, two-bay weatherboard-covered frame section. This was

CE-1155, Clendenin Farm (1979)

CE-373, Moore house (1980)

CE-1154, Charles Keilholtz house (1979)

CE-213, Rombecca/Gillespie house (1980)

added to the gable end by the hall, creating a symmetrical five-bay facade with center entrance. A central cross gable, covered with fish-scale shingles, was added to unify the main facade. Most of the interior woodwork dates from the time of the addition.

Moore House
c. 1850-60 with additions
Richardsmere vicinity

In 1868 Joshua M. Deaver of Lancaster County, Pennsylvania, was appointed executor of John Moore's Cecil County estate, which included 120 acres of land and this squarish side hall/double-pile house. The property was sold later that year to Amos Preston for $8,460. Such a substantial price indicates the presence of an improvement, in all probability this stone house.

The main block of the house has four rooms: a corner stair hall and a front parlor, each with a smaller room behind. The house is further extended by a contemporary kitchen ell.

Charles Keilholtz House
c. 1850
Cather's Corner vicinity

A distinctive hipped roof and rooftop balustrade differentiate this house from most two-story, three-bay, single-pile frame houses with center hall plan. Remodeled on the interior, the house is basically unaltered on the exterior. Unusual survivals on the property are a small weatherboard-covered frame workshop with a rooftop cupola and a corncrib embellished with louvered and bracketed cupolas with pyramidal roofs and lightning rods.

Rombecca/Gillespie House
c. 1850-60
Principio vicinity

A three-story elevation, double set of twin chimneys, and an early 20th century front and side porch are a few of the architectural features that separate the common bond Gillespie house from the normal two-story, center hall, double-pile dwelling. A large

mid- to late 19th century frame barn also stands on the property, which was owned by the Gillespie family for most of the 19th century; a Thomas Gillespie is cited in the 1858 Martenet map and a W. E. Gillespie in the 1877 atlas.

Cloverly/Pyle House
1853 with additions
Rising Sun vicinity

Built in two stages, this house appears as one due to its uniform white color and fancifully sawn L-shaped front porch. First to be constructed was a two-story, three-bay, side passage/parlor brick house, which was soon followed by a two-story, two-bay gable end brick addition. Together these two sections produced a full five-bay facade with center entrance. The porch addition, with its wooden gingerbread trim made to imitate cast-iron porches of the time, was probably a last touch intended to unify the whole. The two-story frame kitchen ell was built at the same time as the first house. A barn, granary, and

CE-1141, Cloverly/Pyle house (1981)

CE-1130, Marshall I. Hunt house (1981)

CE-1128, Dr. Slater B. Stubbs house (1995)

chicken house also stand on this property.

Jesse Pyle bought 71 acres from John Brickley in September 1838, but a brick house is not listed on this tract in the assessment books until 1853. The valuation jumped from $710 (probably $10/acre with no house) in 1852 to $1,573 in 1853, when a brick-and-frame house was noted on the property.

Dr. Slater B. Stubbs House
c. 1857
Rising Sun vicinity

This Italianate side passage/double-pile house was constructed by Dr. Slater B. Stubbs in 1857 on a hill overlooking Rising Sun. The Italianate house type is not uncommon in Cecil County, but this house exhibits some unusual details, including the cast-iron widow's walk with interior circular stair. The construction date can be derived from county tax assessments, which in 1857 list a new house on 50 acres assessed at $800. Dr. Stubbs, a prominent physician in Rising Sun, served both on the county Board of Elections and in the House of Delegates.

Marshall I. Hunt House
1858-59
Rising Sun vicinity

Marshall I. Hunt is listed in the 1859 Cecil County tax books as the owner of 144 acres and a frame house assessed together for $4,150. Just one year earlier his assessment had only amounted to $3,600 and there was no mention of a house. The plan of the first floor of this square three-story Italianate frame house differs from most in having a three-room floor plan with an enclosed center stair. Exterior architectural features are relatively tame in comparison to other Italianate structures. The squarish proportions, low pitched roof, three-story elevation, and bracketed cornice are, however, typical of the style.

After leaving Head of Elk in April 1781, Lafayette and his army encamped on this property and presented each of the farmer's sons with a gold coin.

CE-227, West Nottingham Presbyterian Church (1981)

West Nottingham Presbyterian Church
1800, 1857
West Nottingham

The present West Nottingham Church was constructed in 1800 and altered to its present appearance in 1857. It is a three-bay wide, four-bay long, gable-roofed granite building with sandstone trim. The two entrances on the south facade are separated by tall stone buttresses and a triple-arched

CE-1164, old school building at West Nottingham Academy (1990)

window. The wide bracketed cornice likely dates from the 1857 remodeling. The tall steeple consists of two parts: the open belfry is late Victorian (it does not show in the illustration of the church in the 1877 atlas), while the top portion, with its classical pilasters and louvered opening, is probably original. The entire composition is topped with an elaborate wrought-iron cross. The interior dates from the mid-Victorian period and features a painted cornice and a large choir loft supported by massive scrolled brackets.

The church and its two predecessors have been the center of Presbyterianism in this part of the county since at least 1724, when mention was first made of a church here in the Presbytery records. Although it falls within the Nottingham Lots, laid out by William Penn in 1702 to encourage Quaker settlement, this area also contained a large number of Scots-Irish immigrants. The rapid influx of these settlers in the early 18th century necessitated the frequent building of churches. According to one source, a frame church was built in 1729 to replace an earlier one and was roofed with clapboards; it was later enlarged to form an L plan. In 1796 the congregation resolved to build a new church on land donated by Andrew Ramsay and Captain William Johnson. Not completed until 1804, the church had a dated lintel on the west door, which was visible until covered by alterations to the church made in 1857. A chapel was built adjacent to the church in 1880 (see separate listing).

The congregation of West Nottingham was disrupted by the same "New Light" versus "Old Light" controversy that divided Presbyterianism during the second quarter of the 18th century. The New Light church at Nottingham stood so close to the old church that "each congregation could hear the other sing." In 1744 the Reverend Samuel Finley became pastor of the new congregation and founded the West Nottingham Academy for training boys for the ministry.

Old School Building at West Nottingham Academy (NR)
c. 1865
West Nottingham

One of the oldest preparatory schools in the country, West Nottingham Academy traces its origins to the school established by the Reverend Samuel Finley shortly after he became minister at West Nottingham Presbyterian Church in 1741. Founded to "educate young men for the gospel ministry," the academy boasted a number of distinguished alumni during the 18th century. Dr. Benjamin Rush, founder of Dickinson College and signer of the Declaration of Independence; Richard Stockton, also a signer; Governor Martin of North Carolina and Governor John Henry of Maryland; and several well-known Philadelphia surgeons, jurists, and religious leaders. So great was his success at West Nottingham that in 1761 Finley was elected president of the College of New Jersey, later Princeton University. The school apparently declined for a time after his departure, perhaps even closing, but in 1812 a new school was chartered and named West Nottingham Academy. Graduates of this school include Governor Austin Crothers of Maryland and Dr. Robert Brookings, founder of the Brookings Institute.

Despite the school's distinguished history, neither the log building that supposedly housed "Mr. Finley's Academy" nor the brick schoolhouse erected at West Nottingham in 1812 have survived. The latter building was destroyed by lightning in 1835 and replaced. The oldest surviving

CE-1110, James M. Evans house (1979)

CE-1152, Gillespie house (1995)

academy building, a one-story brick building with two projecting wings, round-arched windows, and a wooden belfry, was erected in 1865 to replace the 1835 building. Today the campus has expanded to include a number of nearby farmhouses and other buildings as well as structures put up in the 20th century. The campus has been listed in the National Register of Historic Places as a historic district.

James M. Evans House (site)
c. 1850-70
Richardsmere vicinity

The location in the remote northern hills of Cecil County of this stylish frame house, with its neoclassical bracketed temple form, may seem rather odd when compared to the numerous log and stone houses that surround it. But James M. Evans, who built the house, was one of a dozen wealthy landowners in the Sixth Election District and was probably familiar with popular architectural designs. Evans's wealth, coupled with his proximity to major supply routes and active sawmills, provided him with the resources needed to construct this two-story house with gable end main elevation and bracketed roof and porch. Its hillside location and elevated fieldstone foundation heightened the prominence of the house, which was burned by vandals in the 1980s.

Gillespie House
c. 1830-50, 1860-80
West Nottingham vicinity

The soaring verticality of the side hall/parlor Gothic Revival main block of this house stands in direct contrast to the earlier two-story, five-bay stuccoed masonry rear section. Although the two halves seem worlds apart architecturally, the room arrangements in both stem from vernacular building traditions. The rear wing has a hall/parlor plan with two rooms of roughly equal size. The hall contains the major entrance and originally was one of the main living spaces in the house, containing both a fireplace and the main stair. For all its exuberance, the

CE-1157, Hopewell Methodist Church (1979)

CE-368, Porters Bridge, Eckerson's gristmill (1973)

main block is based in the same tradition, although by the mid- to late 19th century the hall had been universally transformed into a more formal entrance and passage space leading to the parlor and second floor.

In this house, liberties were also taken at midcentury with the traditional two-story, three-bay house form. The addition of a steeply pitched and patterned slate roof, central cross gable with flanking dormers, sawn eave ornament, and hipped roof front porch disguise the evolving vernacular house form. On the interior, the house retains most of its period woodwork. George Gillespie is shown as the owner of this house in the 1877 county atlas.

Hopewell Methodist Church
c. 1850–80
Cather's Corner vicinity

The Hopewell Methodist congregation has worshiped at this site since the late 18th century, and this is the second structure on the site. The Romanesque Revival building is plain in comparison to other churches of its style, but the massing, asymmetrically placed pyramidal-roofed bell tower, and round-arched window and door openings are characteristic of the period. Jacob Tome, the industrialist and generous philanthropist from Port Deposit, is buried in the adjoining cemetery.

Gerry House
c. 1879
Rowlandsville vicinity

This house of cut and coursed fieldstone and granite is a fine example of the stonemason's skill. Basically unaltered, it is a typical form—a two-story, three-bay, single-pile dwelling with rear wing. The house apparently replaced earlier structures at this site, which appear on the 1877 atlas of the area. A barn and corncrib are accompanied by a most unusual plank frame workshop or slaughterhouse, which has a massive semicircular chimney base.

Ira White House
c. 1860–80
Colora vicinity

This frame house exhibits the two-and-a-half story, three-bay, center hall plan form typical of the second half of the 19th century in Cecil County and elsewhere. It is distinguished, however, by a few unusual details, including pressed metal shingles, pierced fascia, and second floor window hoods.

Ira White was listed at this site on both the 1858 Martenet map and the 1877 Lake, Griffing, and Stevenson atlas of Cecil County.

CE-1188, Ira White house (1979)

CE-1185, Gerry house (1980)

CE-1129, house by Richards's Oak (1979)

CE-1156, Nevin Orr house (1980)

Porters Bridge
mid- to late 19th century
Richardsmere vicinity

The little community known as Porters Bridge was centered around the Magraw Mill (also known as Eckerson's or Porter's Mill), built in 1862 near this crossing of the Octoraro Creek. The mill, now gone, stood on a high granite foundation and had some distinctive Victorian jig-sawn woodwork under the eaves. Built by H. S. Magraw, a native of Lancaster County, Pennsylvania, it operated well into the 20th century.

As shown in an illustration from the 1877 atlas of the county, the settlement once included a covered bridge across the Octoraro and four frame houses. The covered bridge was dismantled in 1885 and replaced with the present five-panel iron truss bridge designed by the civil engineer Charles H. Latrobe. The iron bridge rests on the same stone abutments that supported the wooden bridge. The two rowhouses that still stand at the site were probably built to house workers at the mill.

Nevin Orr House
c. 1860-80
Rising Sun vicinity

County tax assessments record a frame house on this property in the mid-19th century, but the architectural details of this structure, especially its interior woodwork, date from later in the century. Nevin Orr is listed in 1867 as the owner of a 100-acre parcel with a house and another nine-and-a-half acre tract. His livestock was valued at $252, household furniture at $40, and personal property at $307. The full assessment in that year was for $2,574.

The house is a two-story, three-bay frame structure with a two-story wing on the rear. A two-story bay window is built into each gable end.

House by Richards's Oak
c. 1877-90
Richardsmere

Richards's Oak shaded this house from when it was built until the late 20th century, when the tree finally succumbed to old age. Although basically the same as other late 19th century cross-gabled houses, this
structure strays from the norm by having a projecting central bay and gable end bay windows. The main cross gable is echoed by a smaller version on the shed-roofed front porch. This basically unaltered example of the two-story, center hall house with cross gable is a reminder of the popularity of the form, which was accepted across the county in the second half of the 19th century as a social statement of prosperity.

West Nottingham Chapel
1880
West Nottingham

West Nottingham Chapel stands just east of West Nottingham Presbyterian Church and is joined to it by a hyphen built in 1930. The

CE-226, West Nottingham Chapel (1981)

CE-1192, George McCullough house (1995)

plaque on the west gable indicates the chapel was built in "1880 by the Ladies of the Congregation aided by a bequest of Sarah E. Patterson." Both in style and general appearance, the chapel closely resembles and complements the church, which was built in 1800 but altered to its present appearance in 1857.

George McCullough House
4th quarter 19th century
Colora

This attractive Victorian farmhouse on the road from West Nottingham is thought to have been built for George McCullough, owner of the McCullough Ironworks at Rowlandsville. The house sits on a foundation of Port Deposit granite and comprises a two-story, three-bay main block with a one-story kitchen wing extending to the rear. A double door on the main facade is flanked by tall two-over-two sash windows. A shed-roofed porch with Eastlake woodwork extends across the front. The roof has a decorative bracketed cornice that is repeated on the tall dormers; the dormers have steeply pitched roofs trimmed with bargeboard and a wooden finial. Corbeled chimneys rise at each gable end. The interior displays the varnished woodwork, commodious stair, and marble fireplaces typical of the period.

Also on the grounds are an unusual and still functioning windmill, a privy, a barn, and a two-story icehouse. All are roofed, as is the main house, with metal manufactured at the McCullough Ironworks at Rowlandsville.

Liberty Grove
late 19th century

This little crossroads community at Liberty Grove and Russell roads is situated on Basin Run and includes six or seven late 19th century frame and stone houses and a church. Once served by a railroad spur, the town supported two canneries, a post office, and several stores in the late 19th century.

A stone house on Liberty Grove Road has a segmental-headed stone panel that probably once held a datestone or inscription. A large two-and-a-half story, three-bay frame house with cross gable, Victorian porch, and Gothic-arched windows on the attic level sits on a hill in the community. The old Liberty Grove School, for a time a Baptist Church and now a residence, is located on a hill above the creek and the railroad track. Built in 1880 by S. M. McCardell at a cost of $734, it is a wide frame building on a high stone cellar with the entrance on the south gable end.

CE-1186, house in Liberty Grove (1980)

CE-1186, school in Liberty Grove (1985)

CE-748, Maxwell Victorian house (1981)

Maxwell Victorian House
1894
Farmington vicinity

The Maxwell family has occupied this farm continuously since the 18th century. James H. Maxwell built this three-bay farmhouse with cross gable in 1894 to replace the 18th century brick house that stood on the property. The site of the earlier house is marked by its foundations. The present two-story frame house with shingled cross gable is typical of its period and is graced with a front porch with turned posts and pierced corner brackets that join in a series of alternating size segmental arches.

Wilson Victorian House
1890s
Rising Sun

One of a number of architecturally significant houses from the Victorian period in Rising Sun, this house has a tall gabled facade enlivened by fish-scale shingles, a polygonal bay, and a half-timbered north gable. It was built by the contractor Charles W. Wilson, who built the National Bank in Rising Sun in 1881 and the old Academy building there. Wilson was a Civil War veteran who, while stationed on the Potomac, happened to be in Ford's Theater the night Lincoln was assassinated.

Brookview Chapel
c. 1880
Rising Sun vicinity

Cemeteries often contain architectural oddities. Some give the impression of having given builders and architects a chance to exercise liberties on the drafting table that they are not always allowed when designing a house. The Rising Sun Cemetery chapel brings to mind such a situation. Although the modern funeral home has replaced the need for cemetery chapels, this strikingly designed building has been well maintained. It has a cross shape extending from a conical-roofed octagonal frame center. The windows are Gothic arched, as is the transom over the double entrance doors. The building is covered with fish-scale shingles typical of the Queen Anne shingle style.

CE-1124, Brookview Chapel (1985)

CE-264, Wilson Victorian house (1995)

CE-1450, West Nottingham Academy historic district, stone bridge dated 1877 (1990)

CE-1450, West Nottingham Academy historic district, Magraw Hall (1990)

Pleasant Meadows Schoolhouse
c. 1896
Rising Sun vicinity

School No. 1, on the corner of Route 273 and Stephens Road east of Rising Sun, is a single-story frame structure that replaced the "Old Stone" schoolhouse, built in 1780. This replacement is typical of the many schoolhouses built during the late 19th century in Cecil County. It was sold and converted to residential use early in the 20th century, and the porch was probably added in the 1940s.

Records show that the old stone one-room school was privately run, with students paying 2½ cents per day. There were no public schools in the Rising Sun area until 1854, and students who could afford it continued their education at West Nottingham Academy.

Colonial Revival House
c. 1904
West Nottingham

This dwelling exemplifies the overwhelming architectural massing given to Colonial Revival houses in the early 20th century. This house, and the movement in general, did not imitate one particular colonial form; rather, builders of the style were interested in borrowing various forms and decorative features from the colonial period and bringing them together in new designs. In this example, colonial features include a gambrel roof, Palladian window, Tuscan porch columns, and classically derived interior decorations.

West Nottingham Academy Historic District (NR)
19th and 20th centuries
West Nottingham

West Nottingham Academy, founded in 1724, is the oldest operating boarding school for boys in Maryland. It has prepared privileged boys for college life throughout its history. Well-known early graduates include Benjamin Rush and Richard Stockton, signers of the Declaration of Independence.

The academy campus today includes historic buildings dating from 1864 until the beginning of World War II, when the school had its highest enrollment. Monumental Magraw Hall, built in 1929, has heavy Georgian decoration typical of campus buildings of the period; it is one of the grandest buildings in Cecil County. The 1864 academy building and the Gayley house, now used as the headmaster's house, have separate entries in this inventory. Other historic structures include the Wiley house, Bechtel house, Hilltop House, the old gym or barn, and the stone entrance and stone bridges. Six buildings constructed after 1940 are also part of the campus.

CE-1132, Pleasant Meadows schoolhouse (1981)

CE-1165, Colonial Revival house (1995)

Seventh District

Perry Point Mansion and Mill (NR)
c. 1750s with alterations
Perry Point

This advantageous location at the mouth of the Susquehanna River was one of the first sites to be developed in Cecil County; it was, in fact, patented to John Bateman in 1658. The two-story stuccoed brick house with Georgian plan and corner fireplaces is typical of the mid-18th century; a fireback forged at Principio Furnace is dated 1771.

The house has been considerably altered, first by damage caused when Union officers were quartered here during the Civil War and then in 1918 when the federal government bought the house and surrounding ground for use as the center of a Veterans Hospital complex. On the grounds is a small gristmill, possibly from the 18th century, which at one time also served as a granary.

CE-146, Perry Point Mansion (c. 1968)

Rodgers Tavern (NR)
c. 1760-70
Perryville

Situated on the important Baltimore to Philadelphia Post Road and alongside the Lower Susquehanna Ferry, this tavern and inn lodged numerous important travelers during the 18th century. George and Martha Washington, Lafayette, Rochambeau, Jefferson, and Madison all made it a stop on their journeys; Washington's diary records more than thirty visits to "Mr. Rodgers' Tavern" between 1775 and 1798. Before 1775 it was known as Stevenson's tavern, but by 1788 John Rodgers had shrewdly acquired it as well as the ferry across the Susquehanna. After his death in

CE-129, Rodgers Tavern (1994)

CE-117, Brookland (1994)

1791, the business was operated by his widow. The building continued in use as a tavern until 1884.

The Rodgers family produced several distinguished naval leaders, including Commodore John Rodgers (1772-1839) and his son Commodore George Washington Rodgers.

The two-story fieldstone structure has a cut stone facade and rests on a raised fieldstone basement, which contains large storage rooms with brick floors. The four rooms on the main floor were heated by corner fireplaces. The impressive center stair rises to both the second and third floor chambers. In the southeast parlor is an original raised panel chimney breast with bold cornice and a dated 1771 fireback. The house underwent extensive alteration when it was bought by the Pennsylvania Railroad in 1884 and converted to a double house. Formerly owned by Preservation Maryland, it was carefully restored with the aid of a group called the Friends of Rodgers Tavern. It is now owned by the Town of Perryville.

Brookland
1735, c. 1771, 19th century
Perryville vicinity

Brookland consists of three sections: a one-story log kitchen wing, which dates from circa 1735; a central stone section, which dates from the late 18th century; and a large frame section, built in the 19th century. A fireback in one fireplace is dated 1771. The house stands on land patented in 1732 and is most famous as the home of George Gale (1756-1815). A distinguished soldier in the Revolution, Gale was both a member of the Maryland Convention that ratified the U.S. Constitution in 1788 and of the first U.S. Congress. In 1791 President Washington appointed him supervisor of distilled liquors in Maryland.

Thomas House
late 18th century
Port Deposit vicinity

Overlooking both the Susquehanna River and the old Susquehanna Canal, this two-story, gable-roofed fieldstone house dates from the Federal period. Among the late 18th century features are the two cut stone facades (front and back); the bed molding; and handsome interior woodwork, including several original chair rails, a handsome mantel with reeded columns, and an open-string stair with bracketed stepends.

The house was once owned by Phillip Thomas, who also owned Mt. Ararat south of Port Deposit.

Steel Mount
c. 1780-1800, c. 1820-30
Port Deposit vicinity

This farmhouse, on a tract of land known as "Steel Mount," is a combination of two granite-and-fieldstone structures. The older section is a two-story, three-bay, hall/parlor house; the addition is a three-bay, side hall/parlor unit that is not as deep as the original house, creating an uneven gable end on the east. This configuration appears more frequently in Pennsylvania and western Maryland, where the gap in the rectangular form is usually filled by a two-story porch. A massive late 19th century frame barn stands west of the house. The land was surveyed in 1798 and patented in 1803 by James Steel.

The Old Sorrel
before 1803
Port Deposit

This old frame building on North Main Street in Port Deposit was once an inn and consists of two parts: a four-bay structure on a high stone basement and a three-bay structure on a brick basement. As at the Gerry house, a brick sidewalk laid in herringbone pattern stretches beneath the porch. A small stone springhouse stands at the rear of the property.

According to Alice Miller, in her book *Cecil County, Maryland, A Study in Local History*, this building was alluded to in the following reference, suggesting it served as the local post office: "In 1803, mails for Brick Meeting House, Rising Sun, Unicorn, Black House and Sorrell Horse closed every Friday at 12 o'clock noon."

CE-1221, Steel Mount (1980)

CE-767, Thomas house (1980)

CE-1217, Union Hotel/Gillespie log house (1994)

CE-148, Taylor's Venture (1968)

Union Hotel/Gillespie Log House
c. 1800-20
Port Deposit vicinity

The Union Hotel building stands on a substantial rise of land east of the Susquehanna River. This site protects the property from floods and at the same time provides access to major transportation routes such as the Susquehanna Canal on the west and the road to Port Deposit from Rowlandsville to the east.

The two-story, three-bay, cross passage/three-room plan log house has been altered on the interior, but the original room plan is still evident. The south end consists of one large space, while the north is divided into two rooms with corner hearths. The early 20th century weatherboarding has been removed to expose the V-notched log construction with chinking of mud and stone. Original vertical board framing members for both doors and windows are noticeable on either side of the newer window sash and door frames. The building is currently operated as a restaurant.

Taylor's Venture
early 19th century and later
Principio Furnace vicinity

This two-and-a-half story Federal brick farmhouse stands prominently among the fertile fields on the west bank of Principio Creek and adjacent to the extensive Whitaker forest. The side passage, two-room deep house has an original two-story stone kitchen wing and a more recent single-story frame addition. On the grounds is the Taylor family cemetery dating from 1800; a 1720 map labels this "Thomas Taylor's land."

Mrs. Murphy's Hotel
1st quarter 19th century
Port Deposit

This large Federal house has a facade of cut stone laid in regular courses with quoins at each corner. Two and a half stories high and built on a high basement, it has paired six-over-six attic windows and a dentiled cornice. Late 19th century additions stand to the north of the original house.

Built as a tavern, this structure was known for many years as Mrs. Murphy's Hotel. John A. J. Creswell, postmaster gen-

CE-1415, The Old Sorrel (1986)

CE-286, Mrs. Murphy's Hotel (19th century, Carson-Drennen Collection)

CE-142, Mount Ararat/Thomas-Physick house (1968)

CE-277, Vanneman house (1985)

eral under President Grant, was born here in 1828. His nieces sold the house to Dr. G. H. Richards, who added the long frame wing in two parts and turned it into a hospital. It is now an apartment house.

Mount Ararat/Thomas-Physick House
c. 1810-30
Port Deposit vicinity

The manor house on Mount Ararat farm, like Holly Hall in Elkton, reflects the formal architectural style of the Federal period. Both are raised on an elevated foundation and covered with a hipped roof with rooftop balustrade. The tall proportions of this house are further accentuated by a steep rake to the roof, narrow chimney stacks, and twin gabled dormers. Mount Ararat also has its own special features, among them the pair of jib doors on the south facade that provides access to a porch. Philip Thomas is credited with building the house, but the property was purchased by the prominent Physick family in 1829 and remained with them until the late 19th century. From an architectural standpoint, Mount Ararat is one of the best preserved, most intact Federal buildings in Cecil County.

Gerry House
c. 1813
Port Deposit

Saved from an uncertain future and carefully restored by Port Deposit Heritage Corporation, the Gerry house stands as a proud showpiece of early 19th century architecture in Port Deposit. Three stories tall with a typical fully exposed basement and handsome cut stone facade, the double-pile house is one of the larger residences of its period in the town. Built circa 1813, it was visited by General Lafayette during his tour of the United States in 1824.

Until acquired by Port Deposit Heritage in 1981, the house had been continually occupied by the same family and was virtually unaltered on the second and third floors. Much of the original hardware and woodwork—including chair rails, interior shutters, fireplace mantels, and stairs—remain in place and are fine examples of early 19th century craftsmanship. The most notable feature, however, is the exquisite two-story Greek Revival porch with highly ornamental iron railings. The porch, supported on granite piers, features Doric columns on the first story and Ionic columns on the second. The design of the

CE-271, Gerry house (1985)

CE-1223, T. & M. Patten house (1980)

CE-713, Warwick-Tome farmhouse (1980)

railings, characterized by sheaves of wheat set between lyres, is more than decorative; it symbolizes the pride in agrarian life typical of Jacksonian democracy during the 1820s and '30s.

Vanneman House
before 1816
Port Deposit

This large, two-and-a-half story house is built with stones of various sizes on the north, south, and east facades, while the west facade is laid with cut stone in regular courses. Cut stone is also used for the jack arches with center keystones above the windows. Like many other houses in Port Deposit, the Vanneman house has a high basement and a porch on the first story with entrances on the street facade. There is also an entrance through an arched cellar door on the south facade. The boxed cornice with a molded fascia board and a bed molding below are decorative touches on an otherwise plain early 19th century house.

For many years this was the home of John Vanneman, who owned a wharf opposite the house from which lumber vessels sailed for Baltimore.

T. and M. Patten House
1818 with additions
Port Deposit vicinity

Despite the dominant late 19th century bracketed roof with gabled dormers and shed-roofed front porch, this house has a much older date, as the 1818 oval datestone with the initials of T. and M. Patten attests. The stone is set in the west gable end between two attic windows. Overall, the masonry exemplifies early 19th century coursed and semicoursed granite and fieldstone construction techniques.

Warwick-Tome Farmhouse
c. 1820
Port Deposit vicinity

The architectural massing and plan of this two-story, five-bay stuccoed stone farmhouse is similar to that of the Brickley house on Principio Creek. The major differences between the two buildings are that this farmhouse is stuccoed and the rear wing of the Brickley house is three bays longer. Both houses date from the same period and have similar interior room treatment. John Warwick is listed on the 1858 Martenet map as owner of the property; Jacob Tome had acquired the farm by 1877.

Paw Paw Building/Odd Fellows Hall (NR)
1821
Port Deposit

The Paw Paw Building was built in 1821 by the first Methodist Episcopal congregation of Port Deposit; it takes its name from two paw paw bushes that once flanked the entrance. Originally a one-story building, it had separate entrances for male, female, and black members of the congregation. Inside, there

CE-291, Paw Paw Building/Odd Fellows Hall

CE-46, Hall's Choice (1967)

CE-1213, Craig stone house (1980)

was a slave gallery against the south wall.

In 1839 Nesbitt Hall was built across the street and the Paw Paw became both a school and an Odd Fellows Hall. In 1844 the second story was added and the entire building was plastered, inside and out. The building served as the meeting place of the Harmony Lodge of Masons from 1852 to 1867. It went through several owners and gradually deteriorated until it was acquired by Port Deposit Heritage Corporation circa 1974. Expertly restored, the building is now used as a museum.

Hall's Choice
1822
Rowlandsville vicinity

This two-story, three-bay, double-pile stone house overlooks the Susquehanna River and stands on part of a tract known as "Hall's Choice." David Craig, an Irish immigrant who settled in Cecil County in 1848, appears in the 1877 atlas as owner of this house, 170 acres, and a tenant house near Liberty Grove.

Craig Stone House
c. 1820-30
Liberty Grove vicinity

This house, like many in the area, stands on a hilly site; consequently, the foundation was cut into a bank, leaving one cellar elevation fully exposed. Building with fieldstone, the mason wisely used larger stones for door and window lintels and for quoins: Two large lintels on the main facade indicate there once were two openings there, one of which has been filled in. According to the 1877 atlas David Craig owned this house along with a number of others, including his own residence, Hall's Choice.

Bella Bond House
before 1829
Port Deposit

This early stone house on North Main Street has a high basement and a steeply pitched roof with a porch built under the projecting eaves. All the windows have stone lintels. A stone addition on the rear has a cellar entrance. The house was standing when John Creswell leased the property to Ira Emmons in 1829. The lot was later subdivided and the neighboring frame double house, also on a high basement, was probably built by 1840.

Greek Revival Stone House (site)
c. 1820-40
Port Deposit vicinity

This finely cut and pointed two-and-a-half story granite house was gutted by fire and

CE-43, Greek Revival stone house (1968)

CE-1414, Bella Bond house (1994)

CE-281, brick row house, Port Deposit (1973)

CE-296, McDowell-Blackburn house (1986)

the stones reused at a property in Harford County. With a particularly well-executed Ionic front porch, it was one of the most important Greek Revival buildings in Cecil County. The 1877 atlas identifies the house as the residence of Hugh Steel, farmer and owner of 268 acres and several tenant houses.

Bromwell House
c. 1820-50 with additions
Port Deposit vicinity

Like Hillwood, the nearby Bromwell house has experienced a continuous family history and has much architectural merit. The importance of the house is not readily apparent from the exterior since it is somewhat plain. Its significance lies in its complex architectural growth: The house began as a three-bay side passage/parlor dwelling and grew to a six-bay mansion with rear wing. These architectural changes were begun by William Bromwell, a Quaker who moved to Cecil County in 1825 and added a two-story, one-room addition to the original structure circa 1827. Around 1850 an addition of approximately the same size as the original house was added to the east gable. A late 19th century frame school building was later attached to the rear of the 1850 section. Dr. Robert Bromwell practiced medicine here until he moved to Hillwood.

Brick Row House
2nd quarter 19th century
Port Deposit

This handsome row of four houses has paired chimneys at the gable ends, a pressed brick facade, granite lintels, and a granite dentiled and modillioned cornice. There are Greek style three-over-three sash windows on the third floor. Like so many other Port Deposit houses, the basement is built at ground level, with steep steps leading up to a front porch and living quarters above. This was because it was impossible to dig cellars through the granite ledge on which the town rests. As well, the living quarters were then safer from the ice gorges that came down the Susquehanna in the winter. In this case, the porch rests on massive Tuscan granite piers.

McDowell-Blackburn House
1st quarter 19th century
Port Deposit

This two-and-a-half story, gable-roofed house is one of the best examples of a Greek temple-front house in Cecil County. The two-story porch on the front has fluted Doric columns on the first story and plain Doric columns on the second. The front of this stone house is stuccoed, and there is a fine Greek Revival style entrance on the northeast corner. The windows on the second story contain large twelve-over-twelve sash.

The porch, which probably dates from

CE-770, Bromwell house (1980)

CE-1206, New Valley Factory house (1980)

CE-1224, Moore-Rea house (1980)

the 1830s, is a later addition. The stone portion of the house is reportedly one of the thirteen houses standing when Port Deposit was incorporated in 1812. Clinton McCullough built the gable-roofed frame wing in 1881.

New Valley Factory House
c. 1830-40
Liberty Grove vicinity

Located along twisting Basin's Run Road, this elevated two-story, five-bay, single-pile stuccoed fieldstone house has been associated historically with the now deserted stone mill buildings across the road. Architectural research indicates a second quarter of the 19th century date, and this is substantiated by a $4,000 mortgage in 1842 to Benjamin Fell of Lancaster County, Pennsylvania. The structure has a traditional architectural form with a center stair that divides each floor into two rooms. The exposed cellar, with ground level access under the porch, contains a cooking fireplace in the east wall.

Moore-Rea House
c. 1835
Rea's Corner
Battle Swamp vicinity

A variation in the arrangement of rooms and subtle architectural details separate this house from the many other two-story, three-bay, double-pile structures in Cecil County. The front door allows access to a corner stair hall with two doors—one leads to a formal parlor, the other to a dining room. Each room is heated by a fireplace in an end wall. Unusual exterior features include a side-lighted front entrance and second floor windows, two-story porches on either side of the service wing, and a Greek Revival front stoop.

The stuccoed stone house is associated with parts of two tracts, "Steelman's Delight" and "Consent." George F. Moore owned the farm in the 1830s and probably built the house. His estate was settled in 1852, and the property was sold to David Rea of New Orleans. The property remained in the Rea name until the early 20th century, and the junction of five roads at this point is known as Rea's Corner.

An entire complex of 19th century outbuild-

CE-112, Prinicipio Furnace (1970s)

CE-293, Nesbitt Hall (1973)

CE-285, 38 South Main Street, Port Deposit (1973)

ings once stood behind the house and was recorded in an engraving in the Lake, Griffing, and Stevenson atlas of 1877.

Principio Furnace/Whitaker Iron Company (NR)
1836
Principio Furnace

At the center of this important early industrial complex is the Principio blast furnace, a full brick structure with arches on all four sides built on stone foundations. Behind it is a large heater, which provided the blast to the furnace; the heater and blowing machine were probably built after the furnace, but the date of construction is not known. In the immediate vicinity are a number of other small buildings connected with operations at the furnace, including machine, wheelwright, and blacksmith shops; offices; worker housing; and a circular brick charcoal burner.

The present furnace was built in 1836 and

CE-381, Old Tome Bank/Jefferson Hall (1986)

is the third constructed in the general area of Principio. The Principio Iron Company, the first in Maryland, was formed in England in 1714 and began to purchase land in this area in 1721. Construction of a forge and furnace began in 1722 and by the 1750s the company had built two other furnaces in Baltimore County as well as one in Virginia. It has been estimated that of the approximately 50,000 tons of pig and bar iron exported to Great Britain from Maryland between 1718 and 1755, perhaps half came from the furnaces owned by the Principio Company. Until the British destroyed the iron-making facilities here, both cannon and cannonballs were produced here during the War of 1812.

The fourth and last furnace was constructed in 1890; when production stopped shortly after World War I, this furnace was dismantled and sold. The earlier furnaces and forges have been destroyed or dismantled. Several preliminary archeological excavations have been carried out at this site; two of the most interesting finds were pigs of iron marked with "Principio" and the dates 1727 and 1751.

Old Tome Bank/Jefferson Hall
1834, 1899
Port Deposit

The center portion of this building, at the top of a steep flight of curved steps, was once the Tome Bank and dates from 1834. The impressive Greek temple front portico, with its stuccoed brick columns, extends across the facade. The Jacob Tome Institute bought the bank building and renamed it Jefferson Hall; the two large granite classroom wings were added in 1899. Recently gutted by fire, the building has been renovated for use as an apartment house.

Nesbitt Hall
1837
Port Deposit

This handsome granite building has its entrance on the gable end and was constructed as a Methodist church in 1837. In 1872 the Methodists moved to the just completed Tome Memorial Church, and Nesbitt Hall was used by the Port Deposit Academy, a public school. It is now the church house for Tome Memorial Church, the gift of Jacob Tome's widow, Evalyn Nesbitt Tome, in memory of her parents.

38 South Main Street
1840s with additions
Port Deposit

Although this is probably an early house, it has been altered with the addition of a bold Victorian porch with Romanesque columns and heavy bracketed eaves, brackets along the cornice, and a two-story bay window with bracketed cornice at the south end. Quadruple brick chimneys rise at either end.

CE-294, Vannort house (1986)

Vannort House
c. 1840s
Port Deposit

This two-and-a-half story frame house is notable for its many Greek Revival features. The three-part windows have a flat Greek architrave. The door, set within a one-story, flat-roofed portico with Ionic columns, has an elaborate transom with diamond panes. There are an unusual false front dormer with a full entablature and dentiled cornice and a Diocletian, or thermal, window on each gable end.

149 Main Street
c. 1840-50
Port Deposit

An unusual feature of this two-story, gable-roofed house is the three-story false front that runs across the street facade. The three small shuttered windows on the upper story are false and provide the building with an impressive three-story Greek Revival appearance. The facade dates from the mid-19th century; the house itself is perhaps earlier.

Woodlands (NR)
c. 1811-14, 1840-50
Perryville vicinity

Woodlands, the ancestral farm of the Coudon family since the early 19th century, is the product of two distinct building periods. The earliest portion is a two-and-a-half story, three-bay stuccoed stone section with side hall/double-parlor plan. Built between 1812 and 1814, most of its exterior features date from circa 1840, when the two-bay stuccoed brick addition was made. The Greek Revival features that make this house so exceptional date from the second quarter of the 19th century remodeling, including the handsome south portico with fluted columns, the dormers, and much of the interior trim. Among the significant features on the interior are the delicate Federal scrolled step ends, interior columns, and locks stamped WR for William IV, King of England between 1829 and 1837.

Beaven Log House
19th century
Port Deposit vicinity

Log buildings were often enlarged when time and money permitted. This clearly occurred at the house at Forks of Run, where many additions in fieldstone and frame have rendered the initial log house invisible from the exterior. Inside, exposed

CE-145, Woodlands (1968)

CE-1417, 149 Main Street, Port Deposit (1986)

CE-1220, Beaven log house (1980)

CE-144, Ellerslie (1968)

log walls reveal the early construction. The house appears to have begun as a single-story, two-bay, one-room log dwelling with exposed basement kitchen. A one-story stone addition on the east gable end probably came next; second stories to both sections followed. J. W. Beaven may have been responsible for these alterations—and even for the log house itself—after he arrived in Cecil County from Charles County in 1848.

The Sterritt-Christie family had earlier owned the property. Captain James Christie, a Scots-Irish immigrant and veteran of the War of 1812, is buried in the adjoining graveyard.

Ellerslie
c. 1812-14, 1850s
Perryville vicinity

Both Ellerslie and nearby Woodlands were added onto and updated around the same time by different members of the Coudon family. The resulting dwellings are both Greek Revival in appearance, but they differ subtly in exterior details and interior finishes. The present appearance of Ellerslie is due to several changes executed by Joseph Coudon II, when he bought the house (according to once source built circa 1812-14) for his son in 1854.

The largest copper beech tree in Maryland stands on the lawn of Ellerslie, which once was approached on a mile-long oyster shell driveway.

Tome Carriage House
Tome Gas House
c. 1850
Port Deposit

This stone building, with its highly decorative bracketed eaves and center cupola, once served as the carriage house for the nearby Jacob Tome mansion. After Tome died, Will More operated a livery stable and taxi business here. The first floor was converted to one large room and the second floor is now an apartment.

Across the railroad tracks from the carriage house is the Tome gas house, probably from the same period. Very similar in appearance to the carriage house, this stone building also features wide bracketed eaves and a center cupola.

CE-276, Tome carriage house (1976)

CE-279, Tome gas house (1973)

CE-1205, Graham house/"The Valley" (1980)

Rock Run Mill
19th century
Port Deposit

This stone gristmill located at the northern end of Port Deposit is two stories high and three bays wide on a high basement. Because it has been used for several different purposes, the interior does not retain much machinery, but the mill is one of the few mills in good restorable condition remaining in the county.

Although of uncertain date, the present mill almost certainly succeeded the one built in 1725 and operated by John Steel in 1731, when it was described as a "Merchants' Mill." At that time a merchant mill was a large enterprise that produced flour for trade rather than just for local use. The mill was operated in the late 19th century by John and Charles Fox, later by William Nesbit, and then Rumsey Smithson, Sr. It served as a sausage factory in 1940 when recorded in the WPA *Guide to the Old Line State*. Nearby is a three-story Italianate miller's house and two frame commercial buildings.

Graham House/"The Valley"
c. 1850
Liberty Grove vicinity

This house along Basin's Run has changed little since its construction. Local tradition records the builder as a man called "Dutch Sam," who was obviously a good craftsman, although nothing else is known about him. "Dutch Sam" is also credited with building a farmhouse near Colora, and the two structures have some similarities, especially in the mantel designs. This house was owned in the third quarter of the 19th century by a Mrs. Graham and is still owned by her descendant.

Ashlawn
c. 1850 with additions
Perryville vicinity

Ellis G. Chandlee, surveyor, outlined George W. Taylor's property in 1866 and described the boundaries as being "E. Cosgrove's mill to the north and Moutton's Smith shop to the south." Taylor's two-story, three-bay frame house differs from most of its type in having a hip roof and a sturdy Colonial Revival front porch.

41 North Main Street
1850s
Port Deposit

This two-story, two-bay brick house has stone trim and a dentiled cornice. A Greek Revival period door is flanked by paneled shutters. The one-story Victorian porch, with a wealth of jig-sawn decoration, is probably a later addition.

Winchester Hotel
1850s–60s
Port Deposit

Two buildings on South Main Street make up what is Winchester's Hotel. The south building, possibly older, is a three-story, three-bay brick structure with a bracketed cornice, long side porch, and several additions to the rear. The display windows on the ground floor partially conceal two cast-iron columns. The north structure is a double dwelling with plain cornice. The buildings have been used for a variety of purposes: The south building served as a dry goods store for several years, while the north building once housed a candy-making business, restaurant, and soda fountain. The buildings now shelter apartments and a pub.

CE-1418, 41 N. Main Street, Port Deposit (1994)   CE-1227, Ashlawn (1980)

CE-1423, Winchester Hotel (historic photo)

Winchester Hotel (Carson-Drennen Collection)

CE-241, Rock Run Mill (historic photograph, Carson-Drennen Collection)

CE-1225, S. M. Jenness house (1980)

CE-44, Evans house (1980)

Evans House
1789, c. 1850-70
Port Deposit vicinity

When Robert Evans died on December 15, 1821, his 600-acre farm was devised to his three sons, James, Robert, and John. Evans's two-story, side passage/double parlor stone house was part of this farm. With the death of James and Robert, the house and farm were granted entirely to John in 1860; he was presumably responsible for the extensive alterations, possibly encouraged by his status as a doctor. He modified the original floor plan, and he added a new roof with bracketed eaves, most of the extant interior woodwork, and many farm buildings. The property passed out of the Evans family in 1884, when the Rowlands acquired the farm.

S. M. Jenness House
c. 1850-70
Liberty Grove vicinity

This house stands alongside the road that parallels Basin's Run between Liberty Grove and Rowlandsville. The plain two-story, five-bay main block was built in two stages. A turn-of-the-century, two-story frame addition extended the dwelling to the south. The house is not associated with a farm in the area and probably housed a local craftsman or mill worker's family.

Taylor's Store
1855
Battle Swamp

Taylor's Store was operated at Blythedale by several generations of the Taylor family for nearly a century before it closed its doors in 1950. At one time the Blythedale post office was housed in the building, which has an interesting stepped false front that hides the gable roof of the otherwise simple frame box. The store was moved and rebuilt at its present site and is now an antique shop. The porch posts are said to have been oars used on rafts floated down the Susquehanna River.

Holly Tree Farm
c. 1854
Perryville vicinity

Whether mid-19th century architectural pattern books influenced the design of this three-story, five-bay frame house near the Cecil County Holly Tree is unclear. However, here the traditional five-bay, single-pile form is dominated by a third floor with bracketed eave and projecting central pavil-

CE-143, Taylor's Store (1968)

CE-1228, Holly Tree Farm (1980)

ion. The projecting bay further asserts its importance with a bracketed hood over the second floor window and an arched sash on the third floor. The front porch masks the main entrance but at the same time accentuates it with a long flight of stairs framed by a projecting porch bay. The bracketed porch and projecting bay are obvious design elements that strengthen the entire building and add to the all-important porch space.

Rowland House/Presbyterian Manse
c. 1856
Port Deposit

This two-and-a-half story, three-bay Italianate building is constructed of Port Deposit granite with raised mortar joints and faces Oyster Shell Alley. The two shuttered false windows on the northeast corner were placed to achieve symmetry. The entrance has a superb colored glass transom and etched glass sidelights and is flanked by Doric pilasters; it is sheltered by a large entrance porch with bracketed cornice and column capitals created with brackets. A frame addition stands on the west side. The house was built by James Rowland and bought by the Presbyterian church in 1904 for use as a manse. About eighty years later it was sold to a private owner.

Touchstone House
c. 1857
Port Deposit

This distinguished two-story brick house sits on a high stone basement and has a long porch on the side to provide privacy in a manner often found in Charleston, South Carolina. The windows have paneled shutters on the first story and louvered shutters above, and there is a balcony with jig-sawn woodwork on the street facade. The graceful bracketed eaves are typical of the Italianate period.

CE-273, Rowland house/Presbyterian manse (1986)

CE-282, Touchstone house (1985)

CE-1212, Davis house (1980)

CE-1222, Pattersonville/Rawlings farm (1980)

Davis House
c. 1860
Liberty Grove vicinity

The 1877 county atlas cites J. A. Davis as owner of this cross-gabled frame house. He also owned property in Port Deposit and is listed on the atlas patron list as a lumber dealer. Architecturally, the house is significant because it has remained relatively untouched and much of its period trim is still in place.

Pattersonville/Rawlings Farm
c. 1860 and earlier
Woodlawn vicinity

Architectural trends did not often tempt county residents, most of whom built and lived in houses such as the one standing on the Pattersonville farm. However, some concession to style can be seen in the pierced gable bargeboard, rooftop finial, and bracketed window hood with incised S scrolls on the second floor. These few decorative touches differentiate this house only slightly from hundreds of other center hall, cross-gabled structures of the period. Liberties were taken, though, in the construction of the adjacent unorthodox stone structure, which served as a combination carriage house/workshop/dairy/wash house (see chapter 10). The frame barn on the property is decorated with Victorian bargeboards.

Hillwood
c. 1860-61
Port Deposit vicinity

An unusual combination of several outstanding architectural features, a continuous family history, and grounds filled with mature shade trees distinguish Hillwood from other two-story, cross-gabled farmhouses in Cecil County. Architecturally, this board-and-batten structure is significant as one of the best examples of mid-19th century design and plan as popularized by architectural pattern books and building manuals. Family records document the construction of the house in 1860-61 by George J. A. Coulson and his wife, Deborah Bromwell Coulson. After Coulson died, his widow occupied the house until she moved to New Jersey. After Mrs. Coulson's departure, her brother Dr. Robert Bromwell moved his family and medical practice here from an earlier house down the road.

Robert Evans House/Maplewood Farm
1861
Liberty Grove vicinity

A penciled inscription left on a chimney breast dates this house to 1861. The Gillespie Paint and Paper Company of Liberty Grove

CE-768, Hillwood (1980)

CE-1218, Robert Evans house (historic photo, collection of Mrs. Hubert Ryan)

CE-288, St. Teresa of Avila Catholic Church and rectory (c. 1934, Carson-Drennen Collection)

was apparently responsible for the interior finish of the house because company employees left their names along with the date. County tax records confirm this construction date. In 1877 Mrs. Robert Evans was cited in the county atlas as resident here, and on the atlas patrons' list she is referred to as principal of the Evandale Home School for young ladies and children.

The 19th century complex of house, barn, bell and water tower, smokehouse, and granary constitutes a rare and valuable collection of agricultural and domestic structures. Many of these buildings exhibit traditional construction and plan, although this conservatism is tempered with stylishly exuberant sawn ornament. The Kimble family bought the farm in the late 19th century and began a commercial dairy operation here under the name of Maplewood.

Whitaker Iron Company Office
1860s
Principio Furnace

The Whitaker Iron Company office is a one-and-a-half story stuccoed Victorian structure with a high mansard roof and bracketed cornice. The roof has two dormers on each of its four sides and a cupola in the center. Probably built in the 1860s, it served as the offices of the Whitaker Iron Company and later as the Principio Furnace Post Office.

The Anchorage
c. 1860-70 with additions
Perryville vicinity

In 1877 William J. Lamdin (1830-88), chief engineer for the U.S. Navy and a native of Talbot County, owned this impressive center passage frame house. His balanced and traditional five-bay house is distinguished by exuberant late 19th century details that give the structure an asymmetrical appearance. One detail especially unusual for this area is the bracketed shelf over the wide central door.

St. Teresa of Avila Catholic Church
1866
Port Deposit

Constructed of Port Deposit granite in 1866, St. Teresa's Roman Catholic Church is an attractive gable-roofed building with wide

CE-112, Whitaker Iron Company office (1968)

CE-1230, The Anchorage (1980)

CE-297, Municipal Building, Port Deposit (1973)

CE-113, Whitaker Mansion (1985)

bracketed eaves, a wooden vestibule on the gable end, round-headed windows, and a Gothic bell-cote on the rear. Before the construction of this church, Catholic services were held at the Abrahams Building and at Jefferson Hall. (The rectory next door is gone.)

Port Deposit Municipal Building
1868
Port Deposit

This three-story, flat-roofed brick building has a dentiled brick cornice, round-arched windows on the third story, and segmental-arched windows on the second story. Each has a projecting brick architrave with corbeled ends. Building construction in 1868 was financed by three groups: the Board of Town Commissioners, who owned the first floor and used it as an engine and wheel house; the School Board, who conducted school on the second floor; and the Harmony Lodge of Masons, who owned the third floor.

Tome Memorial United Methodist Church
1872
Port Deposit

With its tall granite tower, this church is one of the most impressive architectural legacies left to the town of Port Deposit by successful businessman and philanthropist Jacob Tome.

CE-290, Tome Memorial United Methodist Church (1973)

CE-278, McClenahan Mansion (1977)

CE-1204, Basin's Run Road iron bridge (1980)

Completed in 1872 at a cost of $65,999, the building is an interesting example of the North German Romanesque style. Because of limited space and the granite shelf on which the town is built, there is no adjoining cemetery; Jacob Tome and other members of this church are buried at the graveyard of Hopewell United Methodist Church.

Whitaker Mansion
3rd quarter 19th century
Principio Furnace

Although the date 1837 appears on the balustrade of a rooftop widow's walk, this large two-and-a-half story, hipped roof frame house appears to be much later in date. Standing on a hill overlooking the Principio Furnace, it was the home of George P. Whitaker (1803-1890), the last ironmaster at the ironworks. The most impressive feature of the house is the expansive porch that wraps around the east and south facades. A frame carriage house with scalloped eave trim stands to the east of the house.

Basin's Run Road Iron Bridge
c. 1870-90
Rowlandsville

After the Civil War, the Philadelphia, Wilmington, & Baltimore Railroad Company finished laying track through northwestern Cecil County. The track connected Liberty Grove and Rowlandsville, but to do so meant four crossings of Basin's Run and several cuts through hilly bedrock. This Pratt through truss bridge spans both Basin's Run and the adjacent road and is supported at one end by a rusticated granite abutment.

McClenahan Mansion
1840s, 1880s
Port Deposit

This house was built in two stages. To the rear is a two-and-a-half story, hipped roof frame house with small Greek Revival attic story windows, which dates from the second quarter of the 19th century and was moved to this site. The large three-story granite

CE-1409, McClenahan double house (1994)

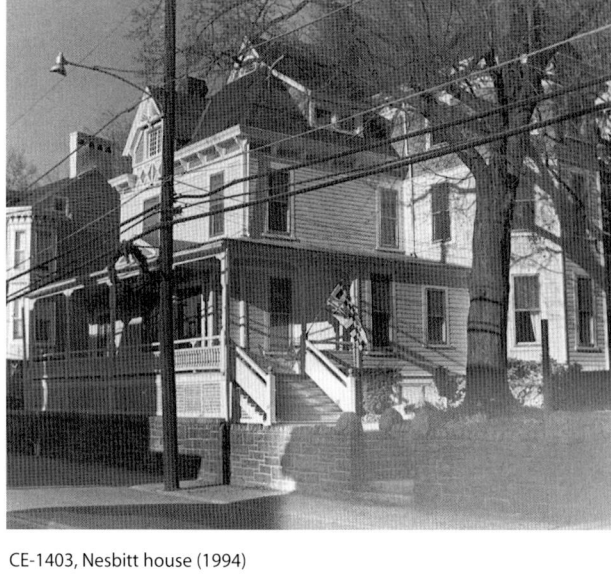

CE-1403, Nesbitt house (1994)

house that faces Main Street was built in the 1880s by the McClenahan family. This tall Queen Anne style residence has a projecting northwest bay with a hipped roof topped by decorative iron cresting. The third story is covered with fish-scale wooden shingles. The interior, consisting of sixteen rooms, has retained its 11-foot ceiling height, mahogany woodwork and mantels, oak staircases, and stained glass windows. Granite is also used for the retaining wall along the front and for the carriage mount by the sidewalk.

McClenahan Double House
1880s
Port Deposit

This large double house on South Main Street was built by John McClennahan, the north half for his son John and the south half for his daughter, Mrs. Nesbitt. Stone was used for the high basement and first floor, while the second and third stories are built of frame covered with clapboards and shingles. Both houses feature a frescoed ceiling in the front room and a curved staircase open all the way to the third floor.

Harmony Chapel
c. 1880-1900
Rowlandsville vicinity

Harmony Chapel is located along Dr. Jack Road east of Rowlandsville. It is a single-story weatherboard-covered frame block with cross gables on either side that give it a cruciform appearance. The gables are covered with fish-scale sheathing typical of the late 19th century.

Nesbitt House
1888
Port Deposit

This ornate, multigabled Queen Anne style residence on South Main Street was built in 1888 by Henry Clay Nesbitt, whose parents lived next door. Both houses were bought in 1902 by his daughter, Evalyn Tome France, widow of Jacob Tome. Mrs. France

CE-1208, Harmony Chapel (1980)

CE-1419, 88-94 N. Main Street, Port Deposit (1994)

CE-1285, Tome School for Boys dorms & gym (c. 1907)

Tome Inn (1982)

Tome School Memorial Hall (1982)

Tome School director's residence (1982)

Tome School Jackson House (1982)

added the south bay window. The house is notable for its decorative woodwork, including bracketed eaves, gable ends with sunray design, and fish-scale shingling.

88-94 North Main Street
late 19th century
Port Deposit

This four-part, two-and-a-half story row house is covered with German siding and has a high mansard roof with bracketed eaves. The pedimented dormers have decorative bargeboards, and a one-story porch with jig-sawn woodwork stretches across the front of all four units. The tall windows on the first story have triple-hung sash.

Tome School for Boys (NR)
1900-1905
Port Deposit

The Tome School for Boys was founded as a boarding school adjunct to the Jacob Tome Institute located in Port Deposit. Built on the high bluff overlooking the town and the Susquehanna River, the school complex consists of twelve buildings constructed between 1900 and 1905. This collection of structures provides an outstanding example of Beaux Arts-style architecture. The largest and most prominent structure is Tome Memorial Hall, a classroom building constructed of Port Deposit granite and Indiana limestone with a distinctive copper-roofed clock tower. Other buildings include the three dormitories

CE-1421, McClennahan Quarry Company office
(historic photograph, Carson-Drennen Collection)

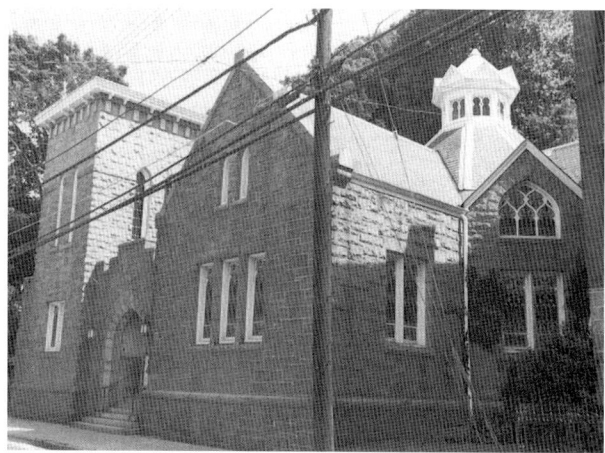

CE-283, Port Deposit Presbyterian Church (1985)

(Jackson, Harrison, and Madison houses), the director's residence, the Tome Inn and dining hall, six masters' "cottages," and Monroe Hall. All except the Harrison dormitory were designed by the New York architectural firm of Boring and Tilton, designers of the famous Ellis Island complex in New York City.

Both this school and the Tome Institute were founded and endowed by the wealthy industrialist Jacob Tome. Because it was a boarding school for students outside Port Deposit, the Tome School acquired a more prestigious reputation than the Tome Institute, but both were considered among the best schools in the state. When the school closed in 1941 after financial difficulties, the grounds of the Tome School were acquired by the U.S. Navy and incorporated into the new Bainbridge Naval Training Center.

McClennahan Quarry Company Office
1894
Port Deposit

The style of this structure, built in 1894 as the office of the McClennahan Quarry Company, is unusual. A residence since 1915, it looks like a Swiss chalet. The house contains a handsome fireplace of Port Deposit granite with a polished granite mantel and most of its original woodwork. A granite vault with 30-inch thick walls is located in the west end of the room now used as a kitchen.

CE-1412, The Steps (1985)

CE-1442, Perryville Railroad Station (1994)

The Steps
Port Deposit

Constructed to climb from Main Street to High Street and then up the cliff to the Tome School for Boys at the top, this dramatic stairway of 75 steps begins with a series of wide, ramped brick steps followed by a curving stone series leading to the first landing. They continue to a higher overlook, offering a panoramic view of the Susquehanna. Above High Street the ascent is continued to the top of the hill by a series of steps left as graduation memorials by various classes of the Tome School for Boys.

Port Deposit Presbyterian Church
1902
Port Deposit

This late Gothic church is built of Port Deposit granite and has a handsome wooden ceiling and an octagonal sanctuary topped by a cupola with eight pedimented dormers. The church was a gift of James Harvey Rowland; most of the colored glass windows are memorials.

Perryville Railroad Station
1904
Perryville

In 1904 the old railroad bridge across the Susquehanna at Perryville was rebuilt as a double-deck bridge. As part of this change the tracks were relocated, moving them away from the old Philadelphia, Baltimore, & Wilmington station. The station was rebuilt beside the new tracks on the site of the Perryville Presbyterian church. The Pennsylvania Railroad moved the church and the stone slab sidewalk beside it, giving the congregation $1,000 toward their expenses.

Construction of the new station was a major undertaking involving much regrading. Along with the sizable, modern station, wooden platforms were built for passengers and freight. Once completed, the station was a grand building, with baggage compartment and newsstand for the convenience of the passengers. It was renovated around 1990 and attracts train watchers from around the area, who come on weekend evenings to watch the trains pass through this major regional junction.

Adams Hall/Port Deposit Town Hall
1905
Port Deposit

Originally built as the gymnasium for the Jacob Tome Institute, this hall once contained an indoor pool, basketball court, and locker rooms. The stone building has typical Georgian Revival details, including the dentiled and modillioned cornice, keystone lintels, and a Palladian window arrangement on the center gable. Now owned by the town of Port Deposit, the building opened as the town hall in 1983.

CE-274, Adams Hall/Port Deposit Town Hall (1985)

CE-1229, The Crow's Nest (1980)

CE-997, Susquehanna River Bridge administration building (1980)

CE-1284, Bainbridge Naval Training Center (1982)

The Crow's Nest
c. 1840, 1913
Port Deposit vicinity

This house, once known as The Crow's Nest and now as Beechwood, primarily dates from the early 20th century and is a good example of Colonial Revival design. The symmetrical five-bay facade, dentiled cornice, gabled dormers, and classical interior details are all characteristic of the period. The need for a uniform architectural statement required the renovation of the earlier frame farmhouse, which now appears as a gable end kitchen addition.

Susquehanna River Bridge Administration Building
1940
Perryville

This finely detailed two-story building constructed of steel and concrete is an excellent example of the modern style that flourished in the United States during the 1930s. A blend of traditional structural means, elements borrowed from the International style, and some distinctive ornamental and formal characteristics (such as banding and streamlining), the building is an example of an important artistic episode in American life that is rarely seen in Cecil County.

Bainbridge Naval Training Center
1942-50s
Port Deposit

This vast complex of nearly 500 buildings served as the East Coast training center for the U.S. Navy from 1942 until 1976. Most of the buildings were constructed during the 1940s and '50s and consist of barracks, training halls, classrooms, gymnasiums, and mess halls. All were built in a simple, functional style devoid of the monumental scale and decorative features of the former Tome School, which constitutes the heart of the complex.

After the Tome School closed in 1941, it and the surrounding 330 acres were acquired by the Navy. Construction of the training facilities commenced soon after the Navy purchased an additional 740 acres in 1942. At its peak during World War II, the center housed nearly 35,000 recruits. By the time the recruiting center closed in 1957, nearly 550,000 servicemen had passed through its program. From 1943 to 1949 and 1951 to 1974, Bainbridge Center was also the site of the Naval Academy Preparatory School. By the 1970s, most of the specialized training schools had been moved elsewhere, and the center closed in 1976.

Eighth District

CE-913, Success (1936, Historic American Buildings Survey)

Success (1936, HABS)

Success (site)
mid- to late 18th century, c. 1825-40
Conowingo vicinity

Memorably photographed by the Historic American Buildings Survey in 1936, the old plantation house on Success farm was an 18th and 19th century structure distinctive for the northwestern region of Cecil County. Similar to third quarter of the 18th century plantation houses in the southern portion of the county, this timber frame house was built with a side hall/parlor plan and a gambrel roof marked by shed-roofed dormers. Although the construction date of the original house is inexact, these features are common to houses dating from the decades leading up to and following the American Revolution. Similar in some respects to the expansion of Cherry Grove in the First District, the initial side hall/parlor plantation house at Success was enlarged with a one-room plan, gambrel-roofed addition that repeated the roofline of the original house. A shed-roofed addition to the rear, also built in two sections, stretched across the back wall of the gambrel-roofed house. A final addition, erected around 1825-40, was assembled of rubble fieldstone to house an attached kitchen. This rectangular story-and-a-half structure was lighted by six-over-six sash windows on the first floor and squarish six-over-three windows on the second floor.

In her 1949 book *Cecil County, Maryland: A Study in Local History,* Alice E. Miller identifies this house as one of the historic sites in northwestern Cecil County, relating that the property descended through the Hammond and related Cromwell families, who occupied it during the second half of the 18th century. The oldest portion of

CE-38, Old Fort Smith (1978)

Fulton-Alexander House
c. 1796
Pilot Town vicinity

This two-story, side hall/double parlor coursed fieldstone house is located just outside Pilot Town on a knoll overlooking the Susquehanna River. The main facade faces what was once the busy road between Lancaster and the Bald Friar ferry.

This property includes parts of three tracts, called "Amory's Satisfaction," "Harmon's Ramble," and "Love's Rocky Bottom," patented to Alexander Fulton in 1760. The property remained in possession of various members of the Fulton family for more than 100 years before it was bought by Reuben Alexander, a successful river pilot on the Susquehanna.

Restored in the late 20th century, the house retains much 18th century woodwork, which is grander than that usually found in this corner of the county. Also on the property is a 19th century wagon shed, featuring dual corncribs and built-in nesting boxes for hens. The barn has been rebuilt on its original stone foundation.

the house was probably erected for John Hammond Cromwell and his family, many of whom were buried on the farm.

Old Fort Smith
c. 1770-90
Oakwood vicinity

A close inspection of this two-story, four-bay stone house suggests it was the "now dwelling plantation" Andrew Porter bequeathed to his son in his 1789 will: "I give and devise unto my son James Leiper Porter all my now dwelling plantation and tract of land called Smith's Fort containing 500 acres…." Just as important as the 18th century date is the early woodwork and original floor plan that survive in this house. The symmetrical four-bay main facade with two front doors signals a cross passage/three-room plan, and this house is one of the earliest of the type in Cecil County. The unusual principal rafter roof system in the house suggests a simplified version of the overbuilt roof systems common in continental European house construction.

Pembroke Farm
c. 1798-1800
Pilot Town vicinity

Edward Teague obtained a patent for this tract, called "Pembrook," in 1695. According to the Rent Rolls of Cecil County at that time, the tract was "possest" by

CE-841, Fulton-Alexander house (1978)

CE-836, Pembroke Farm (1980)

CE-854, Pilot Town, Founds house (1978)

Abraham Pennington, who probably continued to farm the land and pay rent to the Teagues until he bought it from William Teague in 1714. The land was later owned by John Graham, William Graham, Sr., and William Graham Jr., to whom the construction of this house is attributed.

Local tradition asserts that this house was built two years after its neighbor, the Fulton-Alexander house, which was constructed circa 1796. It is a two-story, two-bay braced timber frame dwelling with four-room plan. Inside, the main framing members are exposed. The presence of 18th century wrought iron nails and the survival of some late 18th century ovolo molded door surrounds and molded chair rail tend to substantiate the traditional construction date. The barrel-vaulted subterranean chamber in the basement, likely used for cool storage, is a feature similar to Pennsylvania German construction. The cooking fireplace, brick floor, and whitewashed walls here show it was used as the kitchen before the single-story kitchen wing was added to the house.

Pilot Town
19th century

Pilot Town owes its existence to two primary factors. The first is the shift of the Susquehanna crossing from the Bald Friar ferry to the town of Conowingo; the second is the mining activity in the area in the 19th century. The road from Pennsylvania to the ferry passed west of the present Pilot Town crossroads; this route predated any other southerly road in the vicinity, and the early farms and houses were, and still are, oriented toward it. For example, St. Patrick's Church, Pembroke Farm, the Moore-Love log house, and the Fulton-Alexander house all date from before the mid-19th century and all stand near or next to the early thoroughfare. Eventually, however, the treacherous descent to the ferry led to demand for an easier crossing and a covered bridge was built across the Susquehanna at Conowingo. This soon eclipsed activity at Bald Friar and led to a new route from Pennsylvania, causing traffic to shift to the east, where it formed an intersection with the east/west Mount Pleasant road. Moreover, feldspar, soapstone, and gravel were mined throughout the mid-19th century. This encouraged the construction of miners' houses and dwellings, traditional two-story frame houses seen throughout Cecil County. Despite the mining, the farming community continued as it had since the late 18th century. Pilot Town supplied its own local market and school until the 20th century.

Pilots who served on the arks and rafts brought down the Susquehanna during spring flooding often made their homes in Pilot Town, hence its name. When the canal on the west side of the river was built, many of the construction workers were from Pilot Town.

Typical of the dwellings of Pilot Town is the Founds house, a modest frame house of the late 19th century.

Rowlandsville
19th century

Rowlandsville derives its name from the Rowland family, who have lived along the banks of the Octoraro Creek since their first purchase of a tract of land called "Glass House" in 1749. A number of factors have contributed to the economic and community development of the town. Grist- and sawmills operated on both the Octoraro Creek and its tributary Basin's Run (Beeson's Run) in the 18th, as well as ironworks in the very late 18th and most of the 19th century. The McCullough Iron Company continued the manufacture of iron in mid-century after buying the property in 1859. Extensive remains of the factory attest to the important role this iron manufacturer

CE-882, Rowlandsville Hill house (1978)

CE-885, Rowlandsville, Clarke Moore house, c.1920 (1978)

CE-886, Rowlandsville, McCullough iron workers' houses (1980)

CE-884, Rowlandsville, iron bridge (1978)

played in boosting Rowlandsville to more than a gristmill community.

As in many industrial complexes, mill housing was constructed to shelter company workers and their families. Four sturdy granite and fieldstone structures once housed iron company employees along the east bank of the Octoraro Creek in the Sixth Election District. Some of the earliest mill housing in Cecil County, these units were built in the second quarter of the 19th century and stood two stories tall and three or four bays wide, either as single family houses or duplexes.

Residential and commercial structures were built on both sides of the Octoraro Creek and were connected by a late 19th century single-span Pratt through truss bridge, one of several crossing the creek. (This bridge was replaced circa 1990 with a concrete bridge.) Steep hillsides restricted town development, but construction was not contained to the relatively few flat plots of ground. Frame structures with elevated and exposed basements compensated for the drastic change in slope. Rowlandsville was also blessed with the presence of a railroad depot for the Philadelphia Baltimore Central Railroad. This asset undoubtedly provided the town the business it needed to remain vital through the 19th and into the early 20th century. The Morocto Paper Company bought the iron mill complex in 1892 and produced roofing paper until the operation burned, leaving the structures in ruin, in 1928.

Two elevated train bridges were built south of Rowlandsville to cross the Octoraro. The first was built by the A and P

CE-883, Rowlandsville, concrete train bridge over Octoraro (1978)

CE-906, William Preston house (1978)

Roberts Company at Pencoyd Iron Works, Pencoyd, Pennsylvania, in 1901. The single lane reinforced iron wall bridge with supporting granite piers runs through the mammoth reinforced concrete arches of the higher Penn Central bridge.

William Preston House
c. 1807-10
Conowingo vicinity

In March 1801 Joseph Preston of London Grove Township, Chester County, Pennsylvania, sold to his son William Preston of Octoraro 218 acres bordering the Octoraro Creek just south of the Maryland-Pennsylvania line. William Preston, along with many other Pennsylvania farmers, had moved south into this area because the farmland was less congested. By 1810 Preston had built this two-story, four-bay, three-room plan fieldstone farmhouse. Although a coat of pebbled stucco implanted with colored glass fragments covers the fieldstone, two dates were worked into the stucco on one corner of the main house. The date 1929 probably refers to the application of stucco and the 1807 date is most likely the date of construction.

William Preston's will of 1865 provides a rare documented description of his house: "It is also my will that my widow Mary Preston have and enjoy peaceably the parlor, the room we sleep in and the room over the parlor together with full priveledge for her own use also of the kitchen to do her own work in and the cellar and pump...." The house was built in three parts, the main block, an ell, and two bays that extended the original facade. The land was acquired by the Preston family in 1793. They were prominent Quakers, and William Preston donated the lot for the Octoraro meetinghouse.

The interior of this house has been modified and some detail removed.

Green's Delight
1st quarter 19th century
Kilby's Corner vicinity

The farm known as Green's Delight comprises parts of two 18th century land grants, "Bourne's Forest Addition" and "Green's Delight." Although the 112-acre farm was probably inhabited through the 18th century, the present house and barn date from the first decades of the 19th century. Joseph Moore acquired the property in 1813 from James Sims of Cecil County, while owning an adjacent farm that he had bought in 1803 when he moved south from London Grove Township, Pennsylvania. Since Joseph Moore held the property until 1836, he was probably responsible for building the present two-and-a-half story fieldstone farmhouse with its three-room plan. Now stuccoed, the house was remodeled in the 19th century, when the floor plan and woodwork were altered and a porch added. The double-pen log barn on the property was also built by James Sims, who signed his initials and the 1806 construction date on one of the foundation stones. It is an unusual survival of a once-common form.

Samuel Porter Farm/Rock Spring Farm
1790s, 1820s
Rock Springs vicinity

The Porter family had extensive holdings in the Conowingo area during the 18th century. In 1796 Samuel Porter devised to his nephew Andrew a farm that consisted of approximately 313 acres. Shortly thereafter, a one-and-a-half story fieldstone house was built on the property, with one room on each floor connected by a boxed winder stair at the northeast corner. The large cooking fireplace on the east gable end of this structure has a squared log lintel and an entrance to a beehive oven, which no

CE-34, Samuel Porter house/Rock Spring Farm (1985)

CE-918, Green's Delight (1978)

CE-867, Rock Springs Hotel (Maryland Writers Project Collection, MSA SC 908-08-00598)   CE-905, McKinney house (1978)

longer exists, on the outside wall.

In 1824 the property was sold to Lewis Thomas and, probably within ten years of this sale, the house was extensively enlarged. The roof of the old section was raised a story, an open stairway was placed in the southwest corner, and a two-story, four-bay, hall/parlor stone extension was added on the west gable end. The coursed fieldstone masonry of this section is more regular than that of the first house, featuring queen quoins at each corner. The interior woodwork, including paneled reveals and handsome late Federal mantels, dates this extension to the third decade of the 19th century.

Rock Springs Hotel
c. 1825
Rock Springs

The Rock Springs Hotel served as a stopping place for various guests throughout the 19th century, including drovers on their way to the Susquehanna River crossings. Built of uncoursed local fieldstone, the two-story tavern structure reveals how common house forms were modified for commercial use. It comprises two sections built not too far apart in time: One is a four-room plan house with center stair, and the other, to the north, a hall/parlor section. The barroom retains the early barred cage from which drinks were served. An elaborate, two-story wrought iron porch across the front is gone, and three sides of the building are covered with imitation formstone ashlar.

Numerous barns and other outbuildings once stood behind the inn.

The Rock Springs Hotel was known as Gibson's Tavern or Inn during the mid-19th century. The Lowe family sold acreage to Benjamin Gibson in 1838, and it is possible the tavern was converted from the Gibson residence.

Grubb Property
c. 1830
Pilot Town vicinity

The house on this property is a two-story, three-bay, side passage/double-parlor brick structure. Unusual for this part of the county is the retention of much original Federal woodwork, including a handrail that was executed in a very individualistic style. A two-story, one-room wing extends from the rear, and two stuccoed additions have been made to this ell.

This property includes the tract known as "Dougherty's Endeavor," which was patented to Alexander Fulton in 1762, and part of a tract called "Arbuckle Park." Thomas Grubb is shown as the owner on both the 1858 Martenet map and the 1877 Lake, Griffing, and Stevenson atlas. The Grubb family owned the property for most of the 19th century, during which time they operated a farm and ran a general store at Grubb's Corner on the Lancaster Road at the Pennsylvania-Maryland state line. W. M. Grubb and Company is listed in the 1877 atlas business directory as "Dealers in Dry Goods, Groceries, Boots, Shoes, Hats, Caps, Notions, and all articles usually kept in a General Store."

McKinney House
c. 1830
Rock Springs vicinity

This two-story, seven-course common bond brick house with corbeled brick cornices stands on property John McKinney purchased from Jonas Preston in 1830. County tax assessments valued the 50 acres at $1,800, while an adjoining 48-acre parcel McKinney purchased later was assessed at $672. This substantial difference suggests the house stood on the 50-acre tract by 1830. Architectural details and woodwork typical of the second quarter of the 19th century corroborate this date. The house

CE-33, Grubb property (1978)

CE-41, Octorara (Maryland Writers Project Collection, Maryland State Archives, MSA SC 908-08-00578)

retains most of its period woodwork and architectural details; a two-story frame addition was built in the late 19th century.

The McKinney house exhibits a plan type commonly favored by the Scots-Irish immigrants who settled in northern Cecil County durng the early 19th century. The two doors in the front elevation were a common feature of houses built in the area from the mid- to late 18th century onward, especially in nearby Pennsylvania. More in line with fashionable construction of the time were the brick walls accented with corbelled cornices, which constrasted with the fieldstone and log building techniques that were more pervasive in northwestern Cecil County.

Octorara (NR)
c. 1800, c. 1833-34
Conowingo vicinity

Commanding an expansive view of the rolling countryside northeast of the Susquehanna River, the brick-and-stone house on the Octorara farm is particularly significant for its unusual architectural qualities and its high degree of architectural integrity. The property also includes an important collection of early 19th century outbuildings.

The complex architectural development of this plantation dwelling began with a turn of the 19th century, single-story stone house that is now buried in the center of the 70-foot long dining room and service wing. Other than the heavy, mortised-and-tenoned frames with ovolo-molded backband surrounds that frame two nine-over-six sash windows and a raised six-panel door with raised panel reveals, little original woodwork from this structure survived an extensive second quarter of the 19th century expansion and restyling. The two-and-a-half story stone kitchen addition erected around 1825 against the east gable end of the older stone house completely reoriented that single-story structure. Incorporating a large cooking fireplace and a beehive oven, the stone kitchen included a narrow staircase built against the west wall. To provide a uniform appearance and hide differences in construction, the exterior was coated with a thick layer of stucco. Within ten years of this large addition, further alterations included the extension of the circa 1800 stone portion two bays to the west and the raising of its walls to two full stories; the erection of a two-story porch across the newly expanded south facade; and, most dramatically, the construction of the two-and-a-half story, four-room plan, Flemish bond brick addition that reoriented the entire house to the west rather than the south. The four-bay west elevation of the brick structure also featured a two-story porch. While the woodwork finishes of the rear stone wing are relatively plain, the interior features of the brick section reflect refinements in Federal and Greek Revival design evident in few other Cecil County houses of the time.

Accompanying this distinctive and complex house is an early 19th century stone bank barn of unusual form with a small stone outshut flanking the center entrance. Other outbuildings include a wagon house, a weatherboard-covered frame dairy with plastered interior, and the remains of an octagonal frame smokehouse.

The Hall family owned this property from the patent date in the 1670s through most of the 18th century, and the circa 1800 stone house is believed to date from the last generation of Halls to hold title to the land. Henry White Physick purchased the property in 1807 and probably executed some of the early 19th century alterations before 1820. The major expansion to the house, which included the brick addition, was accomplished during the ownership of Philadelphia physician Philip Syng Physick. Dr. Physick purchased the Octorara Creek property in 1823 and resided here periodically until his death in 1837. A substantial increase in the tax assessment valuation

CE-868, Lowe house/Clearview Farm (1978)

CE-788, Highfield (1980)

between 1833 and 1834 likely dates the brick addition to that time.

Dr. Physick was a prominent and respected physician in Philadelphia. He was well-known for inventive modernization in the field of surgical equipment, and some historians have credited him with being the "father of American surgery." Elected to the staff of Philadelphia Hospital in 1794, he held that position until 1816. After his death in 1837, the Octorara farm passed to his daughter Susan Dillwyn Conner, wife of Commodore David Conner, USN. Octorara farm remained in the Conner family until the early 20th century.

Lowe House/Clearview Farm
c. 1830-50
Rock Springs

This house just east of Rock Springs crossroads is a largely intact two-story, three-bay common bond brick structure with a center hall plan. A two-story, one-room plan wing of the same date extends to the rear.

County land records rarely substantiate construction dates of houses, but an 1865 title transfer reveals that this structure was standing at that time. In that year, Elizabeth and Jesse Lowe and Rebecca Davis transferred possession of "Huckleberry Meadow" and "Clearview" to Joshua Lowe, with this caveat:

> Excepting and reserving the aforementioned tracts or parcels of land for the use of Elizabeth Lowe sister of the said Joshua Lowe the following privileges to be held by her during her natural life, that is to say, the use of two rooms in the brick house on said premises, one room upstairs the other down, situate on the north east corner of said house with the use of garret over said rooms, and free ingress and egress along the passage and up the stairs leading to said rooms and garret, and further privileges of the front yard next to the public road and the use of as much firewood as she may need....

Highfield
c. 1840
Rowlandsville vicinity

This house is a two-story, three-bay, single-pile frame house located off Rowlandsville Road. A story-and-a-half kitchen wing extends from the east gable end. The house rests on a fieldstone foundation and is sheathed with wood shingles over weather-

CE-907, Z. T. Rawlings house (1978)

board. The center entrance has a four-light transom and sidelights, and the windows on both floors contain nine-over-nine sash.

Inside, two rooms flank the center hall. A dogleg stair rises to the second floor with a swollen newel and oval handrail. The door and window surrounds are widely fluted and are not unlike the fluted fireplace surround. A plain frieze runs under a molded and broken mantelshelf. The kitchen wing is probably log and retains its original bake oven.

A few outbuildings survive, including a five-sided pump house and a carriage house.

Z. T. Rawlings House
c. 1840-50
Oakwood vicinity

This house exhibits a house form atypical in Cecil County and, in fact, is one of only two known examples of the type in the county. The two-story, three-bay hewn log house looks ordinary enough at first, but the central brick chimney and off-center placement of the front door are a clue to its unusual form. These two features indicate the house had some continental European background. Germans did not settle in Cecil County, and the owner of the house at the time of its construction was a member of the Rawlings family, who were not of Germanic heritage. However, the 1840s deed that releases the property from Rebecca Rawlings mentions that she, Henry McVey, and Elizabeth Taggart Rawlings all came from Lancaster County,

CE-35, McVey Hotel/Old Stagecoach Inn (1967)

Alexander House
c. 1850 with additions
Pilot Town vicinity

This two-story frame house was built in two sections, both two bays wide and one room deep. The two-story, two-bay, one-room form is very common. A single-story shed addition has been added to the west side and a shed porch on the east.

The house sits on part of a tract known as "Arbucke Park." On the 1858 Martenet map it was owned by Reuben Alexander, Jr., who resided here from 1837 until 1864 and thus was likely the builder of the house.

Pennsylvania, which was heavily populated by Germans.

A modern house has been built in front of this structure.

McVey Hotel/Old Stagecoach Inn
c. 1840-50
Oakwood vicinity

This large structure, now owned by the Oakwood Rod and Gun Club, was an inn and tavern on the Baltimore-Philadelphia stagecoach route. Constructed of fieldstone on the first story and common bond brick on the second, it is two and a half stories tall and five bays wide. The two doors in the front facade lead into the two first floor rooms—a large kitchen and even larger tavern room. The kitchen fireplace and two fireplaces in the tavern room all have late Federal mantels. A narrow stair rises to the second floor, where there are two private rooms and one very large communal bedroom. A large door originally opened from the rear of the building, leading to the outbuildings. A one-story porch across the front of the building has cut Victorian brackets.

A two-story porch was to have been built in the northeast corner of the building but never was, leaving a hole at that location in the rectangular shape of the building. A house with an incorporated two-story porch is a common Pennsylvania form, so it is not surprising that this structure was built by a man from nearby Lancaster County, Pennsylvania. Henry McVey purchased the property from the heirs of Andrew Dunbar in pieces, from 1835 to 1847. In 1841 he was taxed for 214 acres on which stood a brick dwelling.

"The Tombs"/McNamee House
c. 1852
Rock Springs vicinity

This house is certainly not without duplicates, but in Cecil County at least it remains a rare example of a two-story, three-bay half fieldstone, half log house with a definite Scots-Irish background. What makes it particularly important is the extraordinary amount of original detail it retains.

Frederick McNamee bought a 70-acre tract called "Tombs" from Elizabeth Hallowel for $860 in 1852 and presumably built the present structure. The use of local building materials such as fieldstone and log is not an exclusively Scots-Irish tradition, but the culture has a long history of using indigenous materials to construct their houses. The two-room floor plan with enclosed central stair is another feature

CE-835, Alexander house (1980)

CE-900, "The Tombs"/McNamee house (1978)

CE-834, St. Patrick's Church (1978)

found in other documented Scots-Irish buildings. The house sits on an elevated stone basement, which is not uncommon in the county, especially along the Susquehanna; kitchen was housed here until the addition was built.

St. Patrick's Church
c. 1850-60
Pilot Town vicinity

This building, the only Catholic church in the area, substantiates the Irish settlement that took place here in the 19th century. A typical early to mid-19th century Greek Revival church form, St. Patrick's is a frame structure on a fieldstone foundation that retains most of its 19th century character on the exterior. A graveyard containing many area names is nearby. The land for the church was purchased in 1819 by Father Roger Smith of St. Ignatius Church in neighboring Harford County, Maryland.

Oakwood School No. 4
mid-19th century
Oakwood

This mid-19th century single-story schoolhouse is typical of such structures throughout the county. Once known as the Mount Pleasant Academy, it has (also typically) been converted into a residence.

The community of Oakwood has had other names, including Mexico and Mount Pleasant. The land was part of an early grant made to William Husbands called "Mount Pleasant."

McCullough Rolling Mill Ruins
mid-19th century and later
Rowlandsville

The extensive system of ruinous fieldstone walls that lines the west bank of the Octoraro Creek at Rowlandsville is all that remains of the McCullough Rolling Mill. The ironworks operated through the second half of the 19th century and was advertised in the 1877 county atlas as "McCullough Iron Company, Galvanized, Refined and Charcoal." The McCullough family firm had its origins in the Red City Rolling Mill in Delaware, purchased by Jethro McCullough in 1842. Five years later McCullough purchased the forge at North East and in 1853 the Westamerell plant near Elkton. Before the end of the century production at Rowlandsville had changed from iron to paper; later roofing material was produced, until the mill was destroyed by fire in 1928.

Iron was manufactured here before 1795

CE-871, Oakwood School #4 (1978)

CE-42, McCullough Rolling Mill ruins (1967)

CE-892, Keithley house (1978)

CE-891, Riley property (1978)

CE-873, Dr. David Ragan house (1978)

by John Jones and Thomas Rogers, later by John Frey, Matthew Irwin, and Joseph Roman. The McCullough Iron Company purchased the mill from Mr. Roman in 1859 and conducted a successful business until 1892. It was during this period that the first sheet iron in Cecil County was manufactured. The mill, which employed numerous county residents, made Rowlandsville one of the most prosperous communities in the Eighth Election District.

Enoch McCullough, a son of the founder, at first lived with his family in a large Federal house in Rowlandsville. Later, he built a fine residence, which he called Orkney. This well-preserved stone Victorian house stands beside the road leading from Liberty Grove to Port Deposit on a tract called "Hollands Choice." It has several interesting outbuildings.

Keithley House
c. 1850-60
Rock Springs vicinity

This two-story, three-bay, single-pile frame house was owned by William Keithley in 1877. Along with hundreds of others like it from the period, it substantiates the division of older and larger farms for an increased populace.

Riley Property
c. 1850-60
Conowingo vicinity

This property provides an unusual comparison between the main house and adjacent tenant house. The four-bay main elevation, which includes two central front doors, is repeated on the single-story tenant house. The four-bay, hall/parlor house with two central front doors is not an uncommon house type for the county, as they are found in the Fourth, Fifth, Sixth, and Eighth election districts.

Dr. David Ragan House
c. 1860
Oakwood vicinity

Popular use of floor plans that originated in the late 18th century continued well through the 19th and into the 20th century. This house is a mid-19th century example of a side hall/double-parlor house with touches of Victorian detail. (The floor plan was changed in the late 20th century, but some original woodwork remains.)

McCullough-Cummings Property
c. 1860
Pilot Town vicinity

This property just north of St. Patrick's Church contains two frame houses and several barns. The larger house is a two-story, three-bay, double-pile dwelling; the smaller, two-story, three-bay, single-pile structure is shown as an "office" in the county atlas dated 1877, at which time J. McCullough owned the property. Three generations of the Cummings family served as justices of the peace with their office at this same place.

CE-833, McCullough-Cummings office (1980)

McCullough-Cummings house (1980)

CE-911, Brown house (c. 1978)

CE-889, Gillespie house (1978)

Gillespie House
c. 1860
Oakwood vicinity

The architecture of the third quarter of the 19th century is best remembered by the proliferation of revival and eclectic styles that echoed earlier traditions in design. More pervasive, however, is the style of houses such as this, a two-story, three-bay, center hall frame house with a rear addition. Harking back to its 18th century precedents, the ever-present center hall house plan was extensively employed in the mid- to late 19th century and represents the typical house type of the period better than its elaborate contemporaries.

This exemplary two-story, single-pile frame house retains most of its period detail and is a good example of the period and type. A small, two-story frame tenant house also stands on this property, which William Gillespie owned in 1858.

Brown House
c. 1860–70
Richardsmere vicinity

Stylish mid-19th century woodwork dates this basically unaltered house to around 1860. The two-story, four-bay, three-room plan house is a late example of a modified Pennsylvania German house form widely used in the first half of the 19th century. The floor plan and arrangement of two front doors in the center of the main facade both have a history dating from the late 18th century. Although the corner fireplaces are gone and the door openings widened, the basic three-room plan remains the same. As here, these houses typically were built on the south slope of a hill.

The fieldstone springhouse on the property is a good example of a longstanding local tradition in stone masonry. Both quoins and flat keystone arches provide necessary support at the corners and a few openings.

Joshua Ewing and his half brother Nathaniel, both Scots-Irish immigrants, bought a 600-acre tract called "Dividing" in 1728. Their heirs divided the property and later, after many transfers of ownership, the part that had been Joshua's became the property of Amos Henshaw and David Brown jointly on August 6, 1833.

Crothers House
c. 1860–79
Pilot Town vicinity

The Crothers house is a two-story, three-bay, hall/parlor frame farmhouse with a two-bay addition on the west gable end. A late 19th or early 20th century shed-roofed porch extends along the south and east sides. A 20th century single-story shed addition is attached to the west gable end.

The land on which this house stands was part of tracts originally patented to Michael Helms under the names "Helmsford" and "Helmsborough," but in 1805 it was resurveyed and a patent was issued to John Swaggart with the tract name of "Leyden." Alpheus Crothers purchased this land in 1860, and it was here that Austin Crothers, governor of Maryland from 1908 to 1912, was born.

CE-838, Crothers house (1978)

CE-875, house in Mt. Zoar community (1978)

CE-877, Mt. Zoar Methodist Church (1978)

Mount Zoar
c. 1860-90

Mount Zoar is a black settlement that was founded in the third quarter of the 19th century along Mt. Zoar Road just west of Route 222. Approximately a dozen structures stand along the road. Located among the standard two-story, two-bay, one-room plan frame houses is a frame Methodist church with projecting entrance and bell tower. The two-room schoolhouse is larger than most of the school buildings in the county, which had but one room. It retains its blackboards and pot-bellied stove. Serving as a bar/taproom in the 1960s, it is now unoccupied. (For a photograph of the school, see chapter 5, "Farming and improvements generally…in advance of the average in the State.")

Bell Manor/Shadowbrook
c. 1865
Pilot Town vicinity

Bell Manor is a grand Italianate building from the mid-19th century. The basic two-story, five-bay structure is highlighted with corner pilasters, heavily bracketed eaves, and three gabled dormers. The outbuildings, both intact and ruinous, reflect a once-extensive complex. James Heriot Bell assembled the sprawling estate after retiring from a career in New York State shipping and banking in 1859. The house is presently owned by the Girl Scouts of Central Maryland, Inc.

Oakwood Crossroads Frame House
c. 1865
Oakwood Crossroads

This two-story, three-bay frame house is a basically unaltered example of the ubiquitous I house built throughout the county in the second half of the 19th century.

CE-864, Bell Manor (1978)

CE-865, Oakwood Crossroads frame house (1978)

CE-908, Johnson Road farmhouse (1978)

Johnson Road Farmhouse
c. 1870
Oakwood vicinity

This house appears on the 1877 Lake, Griffing, and Stevenson atlas and is an interesting continuation of the two-story, four-bay frame house form with two central front doors. The structure has been changed little since its third quarter of the 19th century construction date. A board-and-batten covered barn also stands on the property.

Mount Welcome/Porter House
c. 1830, c. 1880
Kilby's Corner vicinity

This two-and-a-half story stuccoed brick house overlooks U.S. Route 1. A chain of title traces the property back to Hall family ownership. When the property was auctioned in 1873, an advertisement in the local paper described it as containing 128 and a half acres with a "good BRICK DWELLING HOUSE, large frame Barn, with Carriage-house and other outbuildings." W. E. Porter had a mortgage from the Halls for this property beginning in 1870, and he purchased it in 1874. He transferred it the following year to Sarah Porter.

The Porters enlarged the house by adding four rooms with a center hall and a porch across the front. The addition was of fieldstone. A stone smokehouse and a stone vault in which a well was dug, as well as frame wagon sheds and barns, stand behind the house.

Before U.S. Route 1 was rerouted to carry traffic across the Conowingo Dam breast, a lane ran from Halls Crossroads (now Kilby's Corner) past Mount Welcome and on to Waterview, another property of the Porters. Waterview was a large frame dwelling used as a dormitory to house Maryland state prisoners who helped build the new road. It stood on a hilltop overlooking the site of the dam. The house was accidentally burned sometime after the road was completed.

New Valley School (site)
Conowingo School No. 2
c. 1882
Rock Springs vicinity

Five mid-19th century single-story frame schoolhouses served the Eighth District in 1877. The single-story weatherboard-covered frame structure that stood on this spot must have been the second school on the site since a building was located here on the 1877 atlas and this structure, according to Ernest A. Howard's history of the county schools, was built by S. M. McCardell in 1882. The school was torn down and replaced with a house in 1984.

Porter's Bridge
c. 1884-85
Richardsmere

This five-panel iron Pratt truss bridge carries Johnson Road over the Conowingo Creek outside Richardsmere. It is 188 feet long, with a 16-foot roadway and a wooden deck. Major structural members, top chords, and compression members are compound beams connected with rivets. Wrought iron bars serving as tension members are connected with pins.

In 1884 the commissioners of Cecil County, William S. Potter, Wilson D. Pierson, and Ellis Sentman, commissioned Charles H. Latrobe to prepare plans and specifications for rebuilding and/or constructing several iron bridges in the county, of which this was one. The earlier bridge at this site, a covered bridge generally referred to as Porter's bridge after the nearby mill, is pictured in a lithograph in the 1877 county atlas. Stone abutments from this earlier bridge survive near the present structure.

CE-878, Mount Welcome/Porter house (1978)

CE-902, New Valley School/Conowingo School #2 (1978)

CE-914, Porter's Bridge (1980)

CE-896, New Bridge iron road bridge (1978)

CE-874, Old Conowingo iron bridge (1978)

Old Conowingo Iron Bridge
c. 1885
Pilot Town vicinity

This is the only iron road bridge on the Conowingo Creek, but it is identical to three that span the Octoraro. Charles H. Latrobe was commissioned by the county commissioners in 1884 to prepare specifications for the substructures and superstructures for the bridges on both creeks. This single-span Pratt through truss bridge was moved upstream before the waters of the Conowingo Dam covered its earlier location at Old Conowingo.

New Bridge
19th century

A small group of late 19th century residential structures stands near the northernmost Maryland crossing of the Octoraro Creek at New Bridge. The small community developed under the influence of the once-active Sun Paper Mill along the east side of the creek. A sturdy single-span iron Pratt through truss span replaced its predecessor in the late 19th century under the direction of Charles H. Latrobe, who had been hired by county commissioners William Potter, Wilson Pierson, and Ellis Sentman. Local oral tradition links the community name of "New Bridge" with completion of the new span. The J. S. Ray store and residence is a typical two-story, three-bay frame house with a commercial bay attached to the west gable end. A store operated in the building until the early 20th century. Other structures in the immediate area are modest two-story, three-bay frame houses as well.

House from Conowingo
c. 1910
Oakwood

Residents in the area remember this house as one of those moved from the town of Conowingo before it was flooded when the Conowingo dam was constructed in the 1920s. This duplex, typical of such structures built in the early 20th century, combines elements of the Queen Anne and Colonial Revival styles. It is two and a half stories tall and four bays wide, and a two-story, shed-roofed addition extends across the rear.

CE-872, Conowingo house (1978)

Ninth District

Roger Kirk House (site)
1719
Calvert vicinity

The photograph published here is one of the few remaining images of the Roger Kirk house, one of the most significant structures to stand in the region until an arsonist's match reduced it to charred timbers in June 1980. The timber frame house was the earliest dated structure in Cecil County, documented by the date "1719" scratched on a rafter blade. Similar in construction to early New England frame buildings, the story-and-a-half dwelling was built with four stout corner posts with "gunstock" flared tops. The braced timber frame rested on a fully excavated stone cellar accessible by a winder stair of timber steps. The first floor was divided into a three-room/cross passage plan, with three additional chambers on the second floor and a garret above. A later addition doubled the size of the house.

Roger Kirk, a weaver, purchased property in the Nottingham Lots in 1714. When an inventory was made of his property on May 1 and 2, 1761, it included "two looms and harnesses for weaving." The Roger Kirk house was one of several buildings under the care and restoration of Edward Plumstead.

Brick Meeting House (NR)
1724, 1749, 1810
Calvert

Central to the history and geography of the Nottingham Lots is Brick Meeting House, now located in the center of the small crossroads village of Calvert. The lots, laid

CE-209, Roger Kirk house (1968)

out in 1701 by William Penn in an effort to expand his Pennsylvania colony southward, included a centrally located parcel of forty acres "for a Meeting House and Burial Yard, Forever," although the grant was not formalized until 1765 by Penn's sons.

The meetinghouse was constructed in two principal stages, beginning with the Flemish bond brick structure erected in 1724 to replace the first, log meetinghouse built around 1706. The two-story brick meetinghouse was doubled in size with a stone addition after a fire around 1744 gutted the brick structure. Joshua Hempstead, a New England farmer who visited his sister Lucy Hempstead Hartshore in 1749, recorded seeing the Nottingham Quaker meetinghouse,"which hath been lately burnt down & now Enlarged. the Bottom of Stone is Laid."

The expanded brick-and-stone meetinghouse, probably the largest building in the entire region, served as a hospital during the Revolutionary War. Dr. James Tilton (1745-1822) wrote for supplies from the nearby town of Newport:

> Since the first of March, I have had charge of the hospital, for the reception of sick, from General Smallwood's Division. I have just recieed a Letter from Doctr. Shippen directing me to expect my future supplies of medicine & stores from you. We have occasion of an immediate supply of Both. The stors we want are wine, coffee & tea. The enclosed List will show you the medicines we need. The hospital is just removed from this place to Nottingham brick meeting house, wehre I shall be glad to receive a supply as soon as possible.

CE-82, Brick Meeting House exterior (1936, Historic American Buildings Survey)

Brick Meeting House interior (1936, HABS)

Beside the ordinary sick of the garrison, we have about 50 recruits under Inoculation & expect a great many more.

Some of the soldiers who died here were buried in the adjacent graveyard.

Fire again ravaged Brick Meeting House in 1810, and the present interior dates from that time. Divided into two large rooms with paneled sliding doors, it contains a complete set of early 19th century grained pews and elders' benches; two 18th century benches saved from the fire of 1810 stand in the gallery. Hardware was salvaged from before the fire, as well. The massive king post, principal rafter roof system dates from the early 19th century. Builder Thomas Horton of Willistown, Pennsylvania, assisted by his brother Jesse, was responsible for the carpentry work done in 1810. The

CE-205, William and Elizabeth Knight house (1995)

CE-187, John Churchman house (1980)

plastering was performed by John and William Ray of Wilmington.

Brick Meeting, once part of Philadelphia Yearly Meeting, was then the largest Friends meetinghouse south of Philadelphia. A school was established here in 1740 and a lending library by 1783. Well-known early members of the meeting included Thomas Chalkley and John Churchman, Quaker ministers; George Churchman, founder of Westtown, the first Quaker boarding school in the United States; John Churchman III, a scientist and explorer; and Benjamin Chandlee, Sr. and his son Benjamin, Jr., early American-trained clockmakers.

William and Elizabeth Knight House
1745
Calvert vicinity

William and Elizabeth Knight's initials, three floral motifs, and the date 1745 are etched into the tombstone-shaped date plaque on the west gable end of this fine three-room brick house. Laid in Flemish bond with glazed headers, the two-story house has a chamfered water table and a two-brick belt course, which probably marks the location of a pent eave. A two-story, two-bay frame wing was later constructed on the west gable, and north of this is a one-story, 20th century addition.

The Knight house was built in the same year as the John Churchman house and a year before the Mercer and Hannah Brown house, two nearby dwellings of similar style and detail. The Knight house is an important early example of the high standard of living some Quakers had attained forty-four years after the initial settlement of the Nottingham Lots.

William Knight's will of 1783 illuminates his relationship with his wife as well as a way in which widows could be provided for in the 18th century:

> I give and bequeath unto my loving & well beloved wife Elizabeth Knight…the Northwest room of my now dwelling house with egress & regress there unto without molestation with her necessary priviledges of the Cellar and also the whole benefit of the garden adjoining of the North side of the house with sufficient of good firewood found & brought to the door & cut at a proper length for the room fireplace….

John Churchman House (NR)
1745, 1785
Calvert vicinity

Dated by a set of glazed headers spelling "1745" in the east gable end, the John Churchman house is one of a small collection of relatively intact Cecil County dwellings unquestionably built during the first half of the 18th century. The original, brick portion of the Churchman house is highlighted by carefully laid walls of Flemish bond brick, and the south and east walls further display checkerboard patterns of glazed headers. The less public north (rear) wall was laid in three-course common bond without the sophistication of a glazed header brick pattern. A molded water table defines the foundation wall, which is pierced by small window openings topped by segmental arches. The house also displays pent eaves, which provided weather protection for windows, doors, and wall surfaces. The pent eave was supported by the extended ends of floor joists protruding through the main bearing walls. The hall/parlor plan house exhibits as well fine examples of mid-18th century Georgian carpentry, with a winder stair built in a raised panel enclosure in the "hall" and an original corner cupboard in the "parlor."

This hall/parlor plan house was built during the ownership of John Churchman (1705-75), son of John Churchman "the Immigrant," who was one of the original settlers of the Nottingham Lots, acquiring Lot 16. His son John was a prominent minister who traveled extensively in an effort to spread the Quaker faith. Following his death in 1775, the East Nottingham property passed to his son George Churchman (1730-1814), who financed the construction of a large stone addition to his father's house in 1785. The double-pile stone addition, served by a large interior chimney stack with corner fireplaces, was designed with pent eaves like the older brick dwelling.

CE-88, Mercer and Hannah Brown house (1995)

CE-1260, Warburton farm (1980)

Mercer and Hannah Brown House (NR)
1746 with additions
Calvert vicinity

This property, originally 490 acres, was purchased from William Penn in 1701 by William Brown, "the Immigrant," as a gift for his son Mercer Brown, Sr. In 1746 Mercer Brown, Jr., built the present two-story, three-bay Flemish bond brick house on the central portion of the original tract. The house was laid with glazed headers on the front and one gable end, and it has a datestone in the center of the second story front. Intricately carved, the stone reads "MBH," for Mercer and his wife Hannah, "Anno Domoni [sic] 1746." Neighbors who helped construct the house carved their names and initials on the bricks, providing a rare record of the builders' names. TW, WW, JB, JD, SE, and HR apparently refer to Thomas Wilson, William White, Jeremiah Brown, John Day, Samuel England, and Hezekiah Rowls or Henry Reynolds. Benjamin Chandlee, the well-known Quaker clockmaker, carved his last name in full. The house displays features common to other houses on the Nottingham Lots, including the John Churchman house and the William and Elizabeth Knight house.

Mercer Brown, Sr. and Jr., were both ironsmiths, and surviving receipts show that they made hinges and latches for their neighbors. Some traces of their decorative craftsmanship can be seen on the few original doors of this house. Most of the paneling and hardware in the hall/parlor plan house had been removed, but Edward Plumstead, owner of the house, replaced them with material from other early houses. Of particular note is the woodwork in the first floor of the frame addition, which largely came from a house built in 1728 in Feasterville, Pennsylvania, and includes an unusual staircase and landscapes painted on panels. This owner also carefully removed stucco from the brick walls.

The framework of the two-story, three-bay frame section of the house dates from the 19th century and is partly the work of Amassa Churchman, who married Mercer Brown, Jr.'s granddaughter. The log section was constructed on the site of an earlier portion of the house using timbers from a double-pen log barn built by Mercer Brown, Jr.'s son in 1786.

Warburton Farm
1751 and later
Bay View vicinity

Several architectural features corroborate the original construction date on the inconspicuously placed datestone of this cross passage/three-room plan stuccoed fieldstone house: the arches that span the two first floor windows, the slightly asymmetrical three-bay facade with off-center entrance, and the original floor plan. Later changes were made, including raising the height of the house, marked by a change in brick color. A two-story, two-bay stone addition extends from the east gable end.

Fell Road Log House
mid-18th century, 1845
Calvert vicinity

Situated in the Nottingham Lots area on Route 272 north of Fell Road, this is an early log house built in two parts. The shorter two-story west end probably dates from the mid-18th century and has one room on each floor connected by a boxed winder stair at the northwest corner. The brick fireplace with its large hewn log lintel is flanked on the left by a full-length cupboard and on the right by a smaller cupboard beneath the stair. The east half of the house is much later, although it may predate the Greek Revival fireplace mantel on the east wall. It, too, has one room on each floor and the same cupboard-fireplace-stair arrangement.

CE-199, Fell Road log house (1976)

465

Benjamin Chandlee House
18th century
Calvert vicinity

Located about a mile west of Brick Meeting House, this house sits on lot 15 of the Nottingham Lots, which William Penn conveyed to Randall Janney in 1702. Over time, it has been called Randall's Prospect, Randall's Purchase, Rose Bank Farm, and Rosegarden Farm.

The two-story fieldstone house has undergone a number of alterations in both fenestration and floor plan. Basically it was built in two parts. The western section is a large, irregularly fenestrated, three-bay structure built over a full basement. In the basement are the foundations of two corner fireplaces at one end and a fireplace centered in the other gable end, suggesting the house originally had the cross passage/three-room plan often seen in this area. The eastern portion is shorter and smaller and has no basement.

This site is noteworthy as the home of Benjamin Chandlee, one of the first American-trained clockmakers. Chandlee was apprenticed to Abel Cottey of Philadelphia, his future father-in-law, a respected clockmaker. Cottey purchased Nottingham Lot no. 15 in 1706, and his wife and daughter Sarah and her husband, Benjamin Chandlee, moved there in 1711. Chandlee had a shop 800 feet from the house on Little North East Creek, where water power was available to help manufacture tall clocks.

Jeremiah Brown House (NR)
1757, 1904
Calvert vicinity

This property has been occupied since the settlement of the Nottingham Lots in 1702. The present house has undergone three major stages of construction: the initial frame house, a 1757 stone addition to the east, and the rebuilding of the frame house in 1904 using many of the original timbers.

The dated stone house is one of the earliest examples of a side hall/double parlor house in the county. The stone walls are built of a combination of Pennsylvania limestone and local fieldstone. On the main

CE-200, Benjamin Chandlee house (1977)

facade, on the north, the stone is laid in fairly regular courses and large squared stones serve as quoins at the corners. Narrow stones project above the window and door openings on the first story. At one time a corner fireplace heated each main room, but around 1813 these hearths were removed and new fireplaces with Federal mantels were built flush to the end wall. The stair in the southwest corner of the side passage retains its mid-18th century balustrade and paneling.

The up-to-date floor plan and careful stonework testify to the prosperity of Jeremiah Brown, an original settler on the Nottingham Lots and owner of a gristmill and a sawmill at this site. The house exhibits characteristics of the distinctive Pennsylvania building traditions brought to this section of Cecil County in the early

CE-203, Jeremiah Brown house (1995)

CE-188, Clarwyn Farm (1985)

Clarwyn Farm second house (1980)

18th century, including pent roofs and a second story door. This is one of only two houses in the county known to exhibit the initials of local craftsmen who worked on the house. Among those carved into the stonework are the initials of Morris Reese and David Linch, stonemasons.

A small 19th century bank barn stands on the property, and a reconstructed building stands on the 18th century foundations of Jeremiah Brown's mill.

Walnut Garden
mid- to late 18th century and later
Calvert

From the side, it is apparent how many changes this house near Calvert has undergone. The original two-story, three-bay brick house with Flemish bond facade dates from the mid- to late 18th century. It features a typical hall/parlor plan and much original interior woodwork. A three-story, shed-roofed frame addition later built on the west facade created the unusual roofline seen on the south end.

Clarwyn Farm
c. 1775 with additions
Lombard vicinity

The original portion of this two-story log house is the two-bay north section, which is thought to date from 1775. The floor plan, now altered, consisted of a hall with two rooms to the side and a boxed winder stair rising from the middle of the south wall. The original corner fireplaces have been removed. Much early hardware has remained, however, as has the west door with its beaded diagonal boards and long strap hinges with rounded ends. A one-story, two-bay wing, also of log, was added to the south gable end; later it was raised to two stories, at which time the boxed cornice and porch were added.

Nearby is a one-story building, probably used as a summer kitchen, which has a large cooking fireplace and buttressed chimney. The log framing is sheathed with vertical boards but exposed on the interior.

Long Green Farm
mid-18th century, 1785
Calvert vicinity

This farm has been in the Crothers family since it was first bought by the Irishman John Crothers in the late 18th century. It is not certain who built the two-story, three-bay log section, but the initials JC along with the date 1785 in the round datestone in the east gable of the two-story, three-bay stone section suggest that John Crothers was responsible for this handsome addition. The house was originally oriented toward the north, and it is this facade (now the rear) that displays the best cut stonework, along with such typically 18th century refinements as keystone lintels and queen quoins. Both entrances have paneled reveals and are flanked by fluted pilasters. The interior of this hall/parlor plan house features exceptional Federal woodwork, including reeded window reveals and mantels.

A brick necessary house on the property is one of the few remaining in Cecil.

Among the inhabitants of Long Green Farm was James Crothers, born in 1799, who became a prominent Whig and later served as Cecil County commissioner.

CE-211, Walnut Garden (1968)

CE-208, Long Green Farm (1985)

CE-81, log store/Mullen's Folly

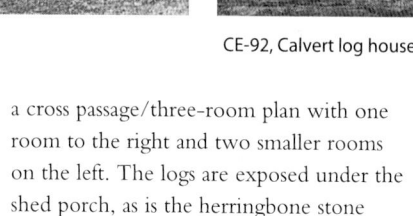

CE-92, Calvert log house (1970)

Log Store/"Mullen's Folly"
c. 1789 with additions
Calvert

Adjacent to the Rosebank Cemetery in Calvert, this V-notched log structure is reputed to have housed David Mullen's store. The building is important architecturally for its cross passage/three-room plan, exposed log construction, and 18th century details, including the nine-over-six window sash on the front facade. Later additions include a single dormer, shed-roofed front and side porches, and rebuilt roof.

Calvert Log House
late 18th century
Calvert vicinity

The exact construction date and early history of this V-notched log house with three-room plan is not known, but its architectural importance is clear. The slightly asymmetrical fenestration suggests a cross passage/three-room plan with one room to the right and two smaller rooms on the left. The logs are exposed under the shed porch, as is the herringbone stone chinking. A ruinous two-bay stone addition with large gable end hearth apparently served as a kitchen.

Milestone House
late 18th century with addition
Lombard

Although there are a number of extant log houses in the Ninth Election District, few have retained as much of their original interior appearance and arrangement as this two-part log-and-frame house east of Lombard. The east end is probably the earliest and has a hall/parlor plan with a massive fireplace with simple wood trim on the west gable end. Original batten doors hang on the enclosed winder stairs on both the first and second stories. The fireplace in the two-bay west section has been covered over but was probably much smaller. The window sash and shed-roofed porch are products of 20th century remodelings. A Mason-Dixon milestone sits directly behind this house, giving it the name "Milestone House."

Jesse Brown House
late 18th century, early 19th century
Calvert

The south gable end of this stuccoed log-and-brick house brings to mind the well-known saltbox shape so familiar in the houses of New England. The shed is an early addition to this two-story log house, while the three-bay brick section is a later 19th century extension. Three generations of the Brown family occupied this house, each practicing a trade in local iron manufacture. A double-pen log bank barn stood behind the house until it was dismantled in the spring of 1969.

CE-739, Milestone House (1980)

CE-89, Jesse Brown house

CE-189, Hebron's Gift (1968)

Cross Keys Tavern
1744, c. 1800-20
Calvert

The Cross Keys Tavern, located in Calvert along the Old Post Road that connected Philadelphia and Baltimore, has had a long history as a stopping place. Thomas Hughes, innkeeper, is known to have erected the large front portion of the structure in 1744, while his son Elisha added the rear portion in the early 19th century. The symmetrical front facade and the presence of a door on the second floor are architectural features also seen at Cummings Tavern near Port Deposit. (This Cross Keys Tavern should not be confused with the Cross Keys Tavern in Harrisville, which was built by Leonard Krauss in 1801.)

Hebron's Gift
early 19th century
Calvert vicinity

The architectural integrity of this two-story, five-bay, center hall brick house is great enough to establish Hebron's Gift as one of the finest Federal buildings in northern Cecil County. The walls are laid in Flemish bond on the south facade, and the house sits on a stone foundation. The later wing that extends to the rear incorporates an earlier structure.

Hebron's Gift was first owned by John Daye in 1739; his tanyard, east of the house, operated until the early 19th century.

William Kirk House
c. 1800-20 and later
Calvert

This house dates from the early 19th century and is notable for its handsome Federal period woodwork, including stair, chair rail, and mantels. The two-story, three-bay house, constructed of common bond brick on a stone foundation, has a side hall/double parlor plan. A two-story, late 19th century frame addition with a cat-slide roof extends to the rear.

CE-589, William Kirk house (1995)

CE-83, Cross Keys Tavern (1976)

Elisha Kirk House (NR)
c. 1810
Calvert

Strong architectural evidence and court records place the construction of this finely appointed two-story, center hall brick house during the first decade of the 19th century. An Orphans Court evaluation for the estate of Elisha Kirk, recorded on March 1, 1810, documents the lands of his children, Jonathan, William, Joseph, Rachel, Nathan, and Elisha, under the care of widow Mary Kirk. Their assessed property included a 187-acre West Nottingham farm called "Vulcan's Hall," improved by a brick dwelling, log kitchen, and double-pen log barn, and a 50-acre property in East Nottingham called the "widow's crooked lot." On this lot stood a

brick house and kitchen about forty feet by twenty five feet, with a small log barn covered with board, with a good garden boarded in and about twenty apple and peach trees and about ten acres of meadow of middling quality and about ten acres of thinly timbered woodland.

The second house described is this two-story, five-bay brick house, which stands a few hundred yards south of Brick Meeting House. It is a fine example of early 19th century plan, design, and construction. The original floor plan followed a modified center hall plan with four rooms arranged around a center stair passage. Built-in cupboards flanking the fireplace in the southwest room suggest it was used as a dining room. During restoration work, a large hearth was found in the room behind the dining room, suggesting it was probably used as an early kitchen. The reduction of the hearth size slightly later probably coincided with the construction of a separate kitchen wing. The north side of the house was originally divided into two rooms as well, and evidence on the walls and ceiling indicates where the center partition was located. Many of the rooms in the house display a particularly fine level of Federal style craftsmanship, with delicate gougework patterning across mantels and chair rails.

CE-84, Elisha Kirk house (1981)

Isaac England House (NR)
c. 1812
Calvert vicinity

A virtually unaltered example of a form common in the area during the early 19th century, this two-and-a-half story, three-bay brick house sits on an uncoursed fieldstone foundation. The main facade is laid in Flemish bond with a stringcourse between the second story windows; bed molding topped with a boxed cornice runs across the facade under the roof. Renovations in the 1940s replaced a late 19th century shed-roofed porch with the present covered stoop. The walls of the rest of the house are laid in

CE-207, Isaac England house (1978)

CE-90, Brown house (1968)

the ceiling are beaded on the lower edges.

It is believed that Isaac England built this house on the property he inherited from his father around 1812; he farmed the property until he died in 1877. In 1883, after his wife's death, the property was advertised for sale in the *Cecil Democrat*, 100 acres and a "good comfortable brick dwelling, large barn, with all other necessary outbuildings." Isaac H. England, grandson of the builder, purchased the farm for $6,500.

Brown House
c. 1810-20
Calvert

This well-proportioned, simple Federal house is two stories tall, three bays wide, and four bays deep, with doorways on both the front and one gable end. It is laid in common bond.

Ury-Fassitt Farm
1819 and later
Calvert vicinity

Thomas Fassitt, civil engineer, is cited in the 1877 Lake, Griffing, and Stevenson county atlas as owner of 150 acres near Brick Meeting House. Fassitt had bought the "Ury Farm" in the early 1870s after he moved to Cecil County from Philadelphia. The farmhouse dates from the second decade of the 19th century and is a fine example of a two-story, five-bay Federal farmhouse. On the south facade runs a fine strapwork cornice. Inside, a central stair passage divides a three-room plan. At one end is a three-story, two-bay brick wing with small windows at the attic level and a gable roof with a much longer slope to the rear; its Greek Revival form suggests it was built later than the main part of the house. Fassitt's improvements include a late 19th century frame bank barn that still dominates the rolling landscape near Calvert.

Federal Brick House
c. 1820-40
Calvert vicinity

Three bays wide and two rooms deep, this two-story Flemish and common bond brick house stands on the north side of the Old Post Road south of the Calvert crossroads. The Federal structure, with side hall plan, has seen little exterior change other than a replaced roof with extended gable end eaves and an early 20th century hipped roof front porch supported by Tuscan columns on concrete plinths. The windows have three-panel shutters on the first story and louvered shutters on the second story.

common bond; Isaac England's initials appear in a glazed header pattern on the west end. A two-story, single-pile brick wing contemporary to the house extends to the rear; in 1976 a two-story frame addition was built on the north gable end of this wing.

The main block has a single-pile center hall plan. The two first floor rooms feature Federal-style mantels and chair rail; there is a built-in cupboard in the dining room. The first floor of the wing undoubtedly served as the kitchen when the house was built; the exposed floor joists in

CE-204, Ury-Fassitt farm (1977)

CE-86, Federal brick house (1968)

CE-542, Nowland's Tavern (1980)

CE-591, Crothers's store (1977)

Nowland's Tavern
c. 1820-40
Bay View vicinity

Local tradition associates this two-story, four-bay frame structure with the operation of a tavern, and county land records and tax assessments substantiate this: Otto Nowland was assessed in 1854 for 43 acres and a frame house and tavern. The neighboring property's metes and bounds description also documents the tavern's existence, reading "beginning at a stone standing on the east side of the public road leading from Nowland's Tavern to Warburton's saw mill."

Crothers's Store
c. 1820-40
Calvert vicinity

For much of its existence, this two-story, three-bay stuccoed brick structure was known as Crothers's Store. While the builder is not known, it is assumed to be Elisha Kirk, who owned the neighboring property. One 1849 transfer of land concerning the Elisha Kirk house next door mentions a "stone near the store house door." The store operated until 1958, when it was converted to a residence.

Kirk Brick House
2nd quarter 19th century
Calvert

Standing in the village of Calvert along the once-busy Post Road, this two-story brick house has a wooden cove cornice with bed molding below and six-over-six sash windows with original paneled shutters. The floor plan consists of a room on either side of a center stair. A later frame addition extends to the rear. A two-story frame tailor shop/post office/store once stood on this property close to the north gable end of the house.

The house was probably built by a member of the Kirk family; the 1858 county map shows Abner Kirk at this location.

CE-520, Kirk brick house (1995)

CE-565, Levi Kirk house/Cedar Farm (1995)

CE-80, Abel Mearns house (1968)

CE-210, Lickingbank Farm (1995)

Levi Kirk House/Cedar Farm
1835
Calvert vicinity

A unique plaque between the two center windows on the second story not only documents the date and builder of this brick house but also reveals the stormy fate of an earlier building. The inscription reads, "Blown down and rebuilt in 1835, Levi Kirk."

The two-story, five-bay, center passage farmhouse is typical of structures from the late Federal period. It has a plain box cornice and transom and sidelights at the main entrance; the house has been stuccoed and has a rear wing.

Abel Mearns House
c. 1830–50
Zion vicinity

Cecil County estate books record the division of the deceased Abel Mearns's property in 1859 and, in so doing, note the location of this fieldstone house, a two-story, center hall structure that is extended to the rear by a shorter two-story kitchen wing. This symmetrical elevation and plan is common throughout the county, but a regional difference here is the use of fieldstone, a material common to the county's piedmont region. Two 19th century farm buildings accompany the house—a large frame bank barn and a two-level springhouse and dairy.

Lickingbank Farm
c. 1830–50
Calvert vicinity

Coats of heavy stucco once nearly obliterated the complex growth of this two-story, five-bay brick house, but its removal revealed the three periods of construction suggested previously. First to be built was apparently a large portion of the main block, an L-shaped form five bays across and two rooms deep on the south end and one room deep on the north end. In effect, the northeast corner of the house was filled in later. This fact explains the off-center placement of the north gable end chimney and the two three-over-three sash attic windows to the right of the stack; the lower window apparently lights a separate attic space. This corner was presumably filled in just before or soon after the addition of the slightly shorter two-story gable end kitchen wing.

The L-shaped form of the original house may be unusual in Cecil County, but the house type is well-known in Pennsylvania, where a two-story porch usually occupies the corner niche. The McVey Hotel near Oakwood in Cecil County is a local example of the form without the corner infill.

Bailey House
c. 1780-1800, 1840
Calvert vicinity

A smooth stuccoed exterior and a continuous mid-19th century dentiled cornice do not even hint at the construction history of this stone house. Interior construction details and woodwork firmly support an early Federal period date for the eastern half of this four-bay house. The original house was a double-cell structure, two bays across and two rooms deep. In 1840 a mirror image of the old house, dated in the east gable, was attached to the west gable end. The builder of the first house has not been definitely established, but William Bailey is a strong possibility; he bought the 108-acre tract known as "Coventry and Mount Rocky" on which this house sits in 1790.

A small two-story stone springhouse and a mortised and tenoned outbuilding remain on the property.

White Oak School
1840
Calvert

The small frame schoolhouse built in the mid-19th century was converted from academic to domestic use in the early 20th century. It has been stuccoed.

CE-597, White Oak School

Chantilly Country Club
c. 1840-50
Zion vicinity

Once centered on the extensive 295-acre Passmore family farm, this two-story, five-bay stuccoed stone farmhouse is now surrounded by the rolling fairways and manicured greens of Chantilly Country Club. In all likelihood the late Federal, center hall/double-pile farmhouse was built by E. P. Passmore, who moved here from Chester County, Pennsylvania, in 1848.

Zion Brick House
1840s-50s
Zion

This two-story, three-bay common bond brick house stands south of the main crossroads in Zion. The interior has a center stair hall with one room on each side; the room to the right of the stair features a well-crafted Greek Revival mantel. The shed-roofed porch with bracketed eaves and decorative balustrade and the wood-shingled third story cross gable date from a late 19th century remodeling.

CE-629, Bailey house (1981)

CE-221, Chantilly Country Club (1968)

CE-756, Zion brick house (1985)

CE-87, Dr. Joseph Hopkins house (1978)

Dr. Joseph Hopkins House
1850
Calvert

Cecil County tax assessments proved invaluable in documenting the owner and construction date for this traditional two-story, three-bay frame house. Dr. Joseph Hopkins is recorded on the tax lists as owning a "new house" in 1850 valued at $3,000. The "new house" exhibits a traditional center passage/single-pile form found throughout the county. The farmhouse is accompanied by an outstanding mid-19th century bank barn and privy. The barn is especially unusual for the small round window that lights the bridge house.

Hiram Clement House
c. 1850
Blue Ball vicinity

This two-story, three-bay masonry house, in poor repair, was once a fine property. As described in an advertisement for a trustee's sale in 1895, it was a "Stone and Brick dwelling, covered with slate, containing twelve rooms, well of excellent water with pump in kitchen, good cellar and milk vault; good barn 40 x 50 feet, wagon and carriage house and other outbuildings." A new house appeared on Hiram Clement's property in the Cecil County tax assessment records around 1850.

Joseph Haines House
c. 1852-53
Calvert vicinity

Cecil County tax assessments help date this two-story, five-bay, center hall brick house. This imposing structure, with double chimneys, stands on the crest of a hill southwest of Calvert and dominates the rolling countryside as seen from the Old Post Road between Brick Meeting House and Port Deposit. Joseph Haines, builder of the house, also owned a store and tavern. This property was owned by Abel T. Lincoln when an engraving was made of the house for the 1877 Lake, Griffing, and Stevenson atlas.

CE-1107, Hiram Clement house (1985)

CE-600, Joseph Haines house (1980)

CE-1256, Graystone Road frame house (1980)

CE-583, Bethel (1980)

Graystone Road Frame House
c. 1850-70
Bay View vicinity

This house exemplifies one of the most pervasive house types in Cecil County. Popular in the late 18th and early 19th centuries, it reappears in buildings that date from 1810 through 1870. Its popularity can be attributed to a conservative fondness for the Federal style and a reluctance to adopt either the Greek Revival temple form or the eclectic Victorian mixtures.

Kirk's Mill
c. 1850-70
Zion vicinity

An active grist- and sawmill business once operated out of this unassuming board-and-batten covered frame building. The structure, which stands along the level floodplain of the Great North East Creek southwest of Zion, now serves as a hay barn. W. R. Matthews, miller, originally from Bucks County, Pennsylvania, was located here in the 1877 county atlas.

Bethel
c. 1785, 1860-70
Calvert vicinity

The construction of this house is recorded in rare documents showing that carpenters John Tollum and Bill Cook built it for Ian England. Their records specify work schedules and money due. In his will, Ian England left to his son Elisha "that Plantation I have lately built on called Bethel with the meadow below Perry's divided from my other plantation…." This reference is all the more interesting because the existing structure at this site does not immediately appear so old. A thorough interior inspection and family tradition, however, verify its age as well as the extensive remodeling of the two-room log house that took place in 1860-70. The alterations included the addition of a center stair hall, a two-story kitchen wing on the rear, and front and side porches. A two-story bay window appears to be later than the other changes, as an old photograph shows the house without it. Carpenters' records credit Job, John, and Lewis England with the remodeling work, which took place after Job England arrived in Cecil County from Philadelphia in 1867.

The original two-story, three-bay house of logs laid in the saddle-notch style is the largest known residential log building in the county. Two gabled dormers are trimmed with pilasters. A small shed addition was built in the early 19th century.

Victorian bargeboards decorate the smokehouse, chicken coop, wagon shed, and large barn, which date from the mid- to late 19th century.

Dr. Mearns House
c. 1860-70
Calvert vicinity

Dr. James A. Mearns built this house after he arrived in Cecil County from Chester County, Pennsylvania, in 1857. His large, cross-gabled frame dwelling housed both his family and his office. An entry in the Brick Meeting House district business reference in the county atlas of 1877 reads, "Dr. J. A. Mearns, Physician and Surgeon, Office and Residence on Rising Sun Road ¼ mile west of Brick Meeting House." Until about 1980, a massive timber frame bank barn stood on the property.

Crothers's Victorian House
c. 1860-70
Calvert

This rather small two-story, three-bay, one room deep frame house stands in the village of Calvert. The builder used a traditional side hall/parlor plan with rear wing but added individual details that make the house

CE-220, Kirk's Mill (1968)

CE-608, Dr. Mearns house

CE-730, Crothers's Victorian house (1976)

different from other three-bay houses of this type. The small cross gable with pointed-arch window and eave decoration and the multiple-pane transom and sidelights emphasize the entrance bay. Other distinctive features include the bay window on the south side and floor-to-ceiling windows on the first story.

Zion Methodist Church

c. 1860-70
Zion
public

This church is one of the most distinctive and best preserved of the mid- to late 19th century frame churches in Cecil County. The large rectangular structure has dominated the Zion crossroads since the third quarter of the 19th century, and an old photograph reveals there has been little change. A small date plaque in the upper portion of the main facade records that the congregation was organized in 1810, when they built a log church on this site.

Kirk Stone House

1797, 1840s, 1860s
Calvert vicinity

This interesting house comprises two two-story, two-bay stone sections with a two-story, two-bay frame addition. The westernmost section has a stone with the date 1797 and the initials EKS, for

CE-759, Zion Methodist Church (1995)

CE-606, Kirk stone house (1985)

CE-617, Charles England house (1995)

Charles England house from north (1980)

Elisha and Susan Kirk. The interior woodwork of this section, which has one room on each floor, dates from an 1860s remodeling. The second stone section was added in the 1840s, and the open stair in it replaced the winder stair in the early house. In the 1860s a frame addition without a fireplace extended the house by two additional bays. The surrounding farm buildings, including an unusually large springhouse, probably also date from this period. Written records of daily work schedules and payment for the construction of this house have survived.

Levi and Amanda Mearns House/White's Plains Farm
c. 1867
Calvert vicinity

Levi Ross Mearns married Amanda Fitzallen Hilaman in 1850; seventeen years later they built this impressive cross-gabled brick house. Standing on part of "White's Plains," their house combines many of the architectural elements commonly associated with the Victorian period, including the intricate cast-iron front porch across the front and the two-story turned post porch and bay window on the rear. The polygonal bay window on the west end and the rear kitchen wing were added after 1877, because they do not appear in the engraving of the house that appeared in the county atlas published in that year. (The engraving published in the Lake, Griffing, and Stevenson county atlas appears in chapter 4, "'An Excellent Situation' for Manufacturer and Farmer Alike.")

William Cameron House
1868
Bay View vicinity

The Second Empire architectural style is well-known for its exuberant use of the mansard roof. The marble datestone on this house places its construction toward the beginning of the style; indeed, the house has one of the earliest known mansard roofs in the county and indicates the Camerons or their architect were aware of national design trends. This large farmhouse is accompanied by an equally large timber frame barn and a two-story, center passage granary.

CE-609, Levi and Amanda Mearns house (1980)

CE-1258, William Cameron house (1980)

CE-93, College Green Victorian Gothic house (1970)

CE-576, Biles house (1980)

Charles England House
c. 1840-50, c. 1860-80
Calvert vicinity

The Charles England house is instructive for several reasons. The two-story, one-room plan common bond brick house built on the property in the mid-19th century, like many houses in Cecil County, was rebuilt and reoriented in the third quarter of the 19th century. The basic one-room plan was enlarged with a stylish, cross-gabled center passage frame addition. Change made in response to the preference for popular Victorian architectural styles and formal room plans was one of the major architectural movements of the mid- to late 19th century in Cecil County.

Biles House
c. 1870
Blue Ball vicinity

The facade of this center hall frame structure is misleading; it suggests a late Federal dwelling, circa 1830, but the house actually was built much later. The conservative retention of early architectural forms is not surprising and makes it difficult to know what period a house such as this may date from without seeing the interior. In this case, each room is fitted with machine-made mantels and woodwork, placing the house in the post-Civil War period. In 1877 William Biles owned this property, the Blue Ball Tavern, and several other properties in the Fourth District of Cecil County.

Howard England Farm
c. 1870
Zion

In addition to his own house, Samuel J. England owned 237 acres, which apparently included this farm complex, still in the England family. This house is a two-and-a-half story, three-bay frame house with a cross gable containing a pointed-arch window, overhanging eaves, two-over-two sash windows, and a finely detailed period porch across the front. A two-story bay window fills the east end.

The farmhouse is accompanied by a large frame bank barn, also sporting a cross gable, as well as wagon sheds, a shop, and a privy. These farm buildings form a courtyard just behind the house.

College Green Victorian Gothic House
c. 1877-90
Calvert vicinity

The distinctively decorated cross gable, arched window sash, patterned slate roof, and decoration of the shed-roofed front porch of this house successfully evoke the

CE-1255, Howard England farm (1980)

479

CE-604, John P. Wilson house (1981)

John P. Wilson tenant house (1981)

Gothic spirit of the late 19th century. Apparently the house was built after 1877 because it is not included in the county atlas published in that year.

John P. Wilson Farm
1876-77
Calvert vicinity

County tax records help pinpoint the construction of this cross-gabled frame farmhouse on the property of John P. Wilson. The records also reveal the presence of an earlier house of log and stone, which apparently was demolished to make room for this stylish, center hall Victorian house. Physical evidence of the earlier house exists in the attic of the "new" house, which contains several 18th century paneled doors with foliated iron hinges.

The current two-and-a-half story, three-bay house is a fine example of its type, with a round-arched window in the cross gable; pairs of windows in each bay, including a pair of round-arched windows in the center of the second story; patterned shingle roof; overhanging eaves; and spindles decorating the cross gable and rising from each end of

John P. Wilson barn (1981)

CE-605, Cherry Grove School (1995)

CE-206, Chalkleys Garden/Springfield (historic photo)

the roof. A period frame bank barn stands behind this house, and a two-story, three-bay frame tenant house is also found on the property.

Cherry Grove School
1881
Calvert vicinity

Built by the Jackson brothers in 1881 for $680, this structure stands on the site of an 1847 school, and the brick and stone in its foundation were salvaged from this earlier building. The school is now a private residence.

Chalkleys Garden/Springfield
1764, late 19th century
Calvert vicinity

Dated to 1764 by surviving bills for building materials "for his new house," Samuel England's house today reflects the significant changes in architectural taste that persuaded his descendant Samuel J. England to refashion the late 18th century, Flemish bond brick structure into a stylish Victorian dwelling. The late 19th century appearance was completed with center cross gable, gable end bay windows, a turned post front porch, and two-over-two window sash. Although the Flemish bond walls and some interior trim remain from the original structure, the house is now a representative example of the tastes of a later time.

Brown's Mill (site)
1734, 1892
Calvert vicinity

A mill was built on this site circa 1734 by Jeremiah Brown, Sr., miller, and William Coale, millwright, in "Joynt and Equall Partnership." A deed to them from Mercer Brown, Jr., transferred the land for construction of a "Water Corn Mill and Gristmill." The Brown family operated the thriving mill until 1776, when it was sold to Joseph Reynolds.

In 1892 the original mill burned and was rebuilt on the same foundation by Howard Brown, who purchased the property in that year. The 1892 building was renovated in 1972 with reference to two sketches of the mill drawn by George Churchman in 1785.

CE-202, Brown's gristmill (1968)

CE-234, Pleasant View Farm main house and doctor's office (historic photograph, Miller family collection)

CE-234, early house on Pleasant View Farm (Miller family collection)

Pleasant View Farm/Grove-Miller Farm
late 18th century, c. 1840, 1896-97
Calvert vicinity

Pleasant View Farm exemplifies two centuries of Cecil architecture, combining an old log-and-brick house and a balloon frame Victorian dwelling on the same property. The earlier house faces east, away from the road and toward the fields. It consists of a two-story brick section and a shorter, two-story stuccoed log portion, probably built in the late 1790s, several decades before the brick house. The later house is a two-and-a-half story structure with multiple-gable roof and bay windows typical of the Victorian style.

This property has been farmed by the Grove-Miller families since Joseph T. Grove came to the area in 1859. The Victorian house was built in 1896-97, when Lalla Blanche Grove and Dr. Charles Francis Miller were married. Dr. Miller built an office to house his medical practice across the lane from the house; this two-room structure matched the house in style and decoration. A spacious bank barn built in 1889 stands between the two houses. The Miller family has operated the property as a dairy farm for many years.

Trinity Church
c. 1898
Calvert vicinity

Like many rural Methodist churches, this is a rectangular frame building with an entrance in the gable end. The most prominent period features are the steeply pitched gable roof and the colored glass lunette over the entrance. One of the few rural African-American Methodist congregations in northern Cecil County worships here.

CE-599, Trinity Church (1980)

Subject Index

Bold page numbers refer to captions in chapters 1-6 and to photographs in chapters 7-10 and the inventory; italic page numbers refer to sidebars in chapters 1-6.

Entries in this index are often grouped together by subject rather than individually listed. For example, look for Rodgers Tavern under "taverns" rather than under "Rodgers Tavern." This sample list of topics may help readers use the index more effectively: African-American, agricultural buildings, architects, architectural style, bridges, churches, construction, ferries, fishing, house form, housing, Indians, industry, interiors, maps, mills, newspapers, outbuildings, prehistory, railroads, roads, schools, settlement, siding, stores, taverns, tracts, transportation, walls.

Aberdeen Proving Ground 157
Abrahams house (CE-1160) **413**, 413
African-American:
   in Chesapeake City 313
   churches 314, 320, 367, 459, 482
   communities 105, **108**, 314, 459
   during Depression 146
   education **108**, 108-109
   emancipation 103-104
   free black population 51, 101, 104
   free blacks 101
   housing after Civil War 267
   "Jim Crow" laws 105
   rights after Civil War 104-105
   schools **108**, 108-109, 296, 358, 459
   slave housing 37, 53, 100, 207, 249, 264-67, **266**
   slave population 37, 51, 101, 104
   slavery in Cecil 100-101
   slaves 28, 30, 37, 39, 40, 43, 53, 105, 163, 178, 219, 264
   USO for (WW II) **156**
agricultural buildings 248-60
   bank barns 51, 250-56, 309, **369**
   barns 96, 132, 142, **201**, 207, **248**, **250-51**, 250, 256, **362**, **363**
   bridgeway or bridge house 252-53, **254**
   chicken coop 259
   corncribs 37, 250, 256, 257
   dairy houses 54, 96
   double-pen log bank barn **250-51**, 251
   German influence 250
   granaries 65, 96, 250, 256-58
   19th century improvements 257
   rebuilding of 257, 267
   silos 96, 142, **258-59**, 258-59
   springhouses **259**, 259, **358**

   stone barns 254-56
   strawhouse **253**, 253
   tobacco houses 37, 38, 96, 250
   wagon house 259
   water tank **260**, 260, 261
agricultural exhibitions 91, 93
agricultural publications 91, 92, 93, 94, 264
   Agricultural Museum 93
   American Farmer 93
   The Cultivator 96
   Elkton Press "Farmers' Register" 93
   The Plow 257
agricultural societies 91, 92-93
agriculture *see also* grain, tobacco
   circa 1900 119
   dairy farming 119, 142, 482
   diversification 37, 249, 250
   in 18th century 59
   economy and 53
   farm vs. plantation 178
   fruit cultivation 119
   hay 131, 140
   mechanization of 140, **141**
   in 19th century 61, 91-96, 113, 257
   orchards 51, 250, 264
   scientific/experimental 91-92, 93-96
   soil quality 91-92, 131, 249, 297
   subsistence 37
   tenancy 51-53, 96
   truck farming **118**, 119, 131
   after World War II 159, 160
Alexander, Amos, house (CE-300) **362**, 362-63
Alexander house (CE-835) **455**, 455
American Revolution 54, 57, 215, 240, 251, 307, 312, 330, 331, 338, 354, 355, 365, 376, 380, 381, 424, 447, 462
Anchorage, The (CE-19) **290**, 290
Anchorage, The (CE-1230) **439**, 439
Anchor and Hope farmhouse (CE-140) 212
Anglican:
   church *see also* churches, Church of England 39
   planters 40
   power in county 43
Anglican parishes:
   boundaries 43
   establishment of Cecil parishes 39-40
   North Elk **39**, 40, 332
   North Sassafras 39, 40, 302, 311
   South Sassafras 39
   St. Augustine 40
Antego (CE-1075) **339**, 339
A and P Roberts Co. 451
Apoquemene Creek 29
Appoquinimink 28, 29

archeology 381
   17th century sites 189, 309
   18th century sites 283, 358
   prehistoric artifacts **2-5**
   prehistoric sites **2**, 2, 4, 5-6
architects 224
   Benjamin, Asher 332
   Boring & Tilton 110, 444
   Burns, Charles M., Jr. 322
   Campbell, Colen 180
   Congdon, Henry 348
   Dixon & Davis 339
   Dixon, Thomas 302
   Downing, Andrew Jackson 100, 316
   Le Corbusier 149
   Malone & Williams 149
   Morris, Roger 180, 332
   Palladio, Andrea 180
   Simms, James Peacock 302
   Wright, Frank Lloyd 149
architectural publications 224, 264
   Antiquities of Athens 96
   The Architect, or Practical House Carpenter 96-97
   Architecture of Country Houses 100
   The Beauties of Modern Architecture 97
   builders' guides 227
   Cottages & Villas 100
   pattern books 96-97, 100, 191, 236, 244, 314, 332, 387, 436, 438
   Rural Architecture 253-54, 257
   Rural Architecture in the Chinese Taste **238**, 278
   Young Carpenter's Assistant 244
architectural style:
   changes after American Revolution 240
   conservative taste in 96, 191, 224, 299, 321, 323, 413, 457, 479
   mass production and **228**, 246
   prosperity and 100, 195, 236, 245-46, 374
   standardization of 217-19, 245-46
architectural styles/periods 134-36, **135**, 149-50, 160-61
   Adamesque 237, 240
   American foursquare 304
   Art Deco 149, **151**
   Art Moderne 149
   baroque classicism 235-26, 240, 241
   Beaux Arts **110**, 110, 134
   Colonial Revival 134, **135**, **137**, 151, 422
   cottage 246
   Eastlake 303
   Federal 219, 240, 241-44, 245
   French mansard 134
   Georgian 175, 178, 180-83, 236-41
   Georgian Revival 136, **137**, 142

Gothic Revival **100**, 100, 134, 246
Greek Revival **96**, 96-100, **99**, 219, 220, 224, 244-45, 246
International 153
Italianate **98**, 100, 134, 180, 246
Mission Revival 134, 136, **137**, 327
modern 149-51, **151**, 161
Palladian-inspired 181, 182, 183, 244
Queen Anne 134
Rococo 237
Romanesque 100
Second Empire 100, 246
Streamline Deco 149
Victorian 100, **135**, 478
architecture *see also* agricultural buildings, all entries beginning with "architectural," banks, churches, construction, house form, interiors, outbuildings, schools
   development of American 193
   impermanent 30, 164, 193, 194, 228, 250, 264
   rebuilding in prosperous times 30, 131-32, 164, 246, 297
   Sears, Roebuck catalog houses 134, **136**, 326
Ark and *Dove* **14**, 21
arks *see* rafts
Army Board of Engineers 78
Army Corps of Engineers, U.S. 120, 159, 310
Arundel Corporation 145
Ashlawn (CE-1227) **434**, 434
atlas of Cecil County *see* Lake, Griffing, and Stevenson atlas
Atlas Powder Co. **138**, 139
automobile *82*, 126-27, **129**, 131, 132, 149, 160, 161
   dealer 325
   Ford Motor Co. 127, **129**
Back Creek **75**, **77**, **78**, **81**, **120**
Back Creek Neck 204
Bailey house (CE-629) **474**, 474
Bainbridge Naval Training Center (CE-1284) **153**, 153, 157, 159, 444, **446**, 446
Balderston, Lloyd, farmhouse (CE-1191) **412**, 412
   icehouse 263
Bald Friar **9**, 9, 57, **67**, **145**, 449
Baldwin house (CE-166) 368-69, **369**
   barn 254-56, **256**, 369
Baldwin Manufacturing Co. *see* mills
Baltimore 43, **45**, **46**, **56**, **58**, 59, 65, 71, 73, 83, 103, **110**, 115, 119, **128**, 131, *133*, 140, 142, **143**, 145, 146, 160, 187, 245, 250
Baltimore coat of arms **35**, 331
Baltimore Co. 27, 28, 31, 32
Bank Road bill 105
banks 343
   Chesapeake City Bank building (CE-311) **323**, 323
   Elkton Bank & Trust Co. 323
   National Bank of Chesapeake City 323
   National Bank of North East 333
   Old Tome Bank **431**, 431
   Peoples Bank Building (CE-1334) **350**, 350
Baptists 146
Barnes, Perry, house (CE-387) **395**, 395
Barnes icehouse (CE-1304) **395**, 395
Basin Run 190
Bayard farm (CE-1042) **321**, 321
Bayard House (CE-119) **310**, 310
Bay View fieldstone house (CE-79) **383**, 383

Bay View log house (CE-1244) **388**, 388
Beaven log house (CE-1220) 432-33, **433**
Beehive, The (CE-72) 208, **209**, **352**, 352
Beeks, William T., house (CE-988) **298**, 298
Beeson's Branch 195
Bell Manor (CE-864) **459**, 459
Belvidere (CE-147) **389**, 389
Bennett & Karsner lumber co. 70
Bethel (CE-583) 203-204, **204**, 227, **476**, 476
Biddle house (Port Herman) 324
Biddle, Joseph, house (CE-786) **361**, 361
Big Elk Creek 17, 25, 32, 51, 89, 186
Biggs house (CE-954) **293**, 293
Biles house (CE-576) **479**, 479
Black's Store *see* taverns
Blackway house (CE-357) **303**, 303
Bloomingdale (CE-17) 180, **180**
Blue Ball 34
Bohemia (Milligan Hall) (CE-32) **53**, 53, 180, 181-82, **182-83**, 183, 187, **216**, 216, **217**, 236-40, **237-39**, 267, 278-79, **279**
Bohemia Creek 29
Bohemia Hill (CE-125) **315**, 315
Bohemia Lodge #68 IOOF 319-20
Bohemia Manor *see also* tracts 29, 30, 32, 40, 43, 159
Bohemia Manor ruins (CE-54) **309**, 309
Bohemia Manor (Bayard house) (CE-1445) 136, **137**, **142**, **326**, 326-27
Bohemia River 29, 31, 44, 53, 57, 178, 187
Bohemia Vineyards (CE-126) **316**, 316
Bond, Bella, house (CE-1414) **428**, 428-29
Boulden farm (CE-1061) **314**, 314
boundary disputes *see also* Mason-Dixon survey
   with Dutch over Delaware 25-27
   between Maryland and Pennsylvania 31-35, **33**
Bournes Forest (CE-414) 196
Boxwood (CE-1385) **363**, 363
Bradford house (CE-237) **327**, 327
Brady, Henry H., house and office (CE-122) **321**, 321
Brantwood (CE-69) **220**, 220, **313**, 313-14
Bratton house (CE-1320) **135**, **348**, 348-49
Brick Hill (CE-642) **374**, 374
Brick House (CE-104) **386**, 386
brick house, old (CE-63) **309**, 309
Brick House Farm (CE-11) **286**, 286
Brickley, Jehoiakim and Agnes, house (CE-136) **407**, 407
Brick Meeting *see* Calvert
brick row house, Port Deposit (CE-281) **429**, 429
bridges **123**, 123
   B & O Railroad 115-18, 119
   Basin's Run Road (CE-1204) **441**, 441
   Big Elk Creek covered (CE-238) **368**, 368
   Bohemia River **123**
   at Chesapeake City **120**, 120, **122**, **152**, 153
   Childs pony truss (CE-999) **350**, 350
   concrete 350
   Conowingo 103, **143**
   Conowingo, Old (CE-874) **461**, **461**
   covered **143**, **368**, 368, **390**, 390, 449
   in 18th century *82*
   Elk Forge (CE-233) **346**, 346
   Gilpin's Falls covered (CE-78) **390**, 390
   log *82*
   McCauley Road (CE-1201) **406**, 406
   New Bridge (CE-896) **461**, 461

   Pennsylvania Railroad 145
   Plum Creek (CE-1037) **348**, 348
   Porter's (CE-914) 123, 460, **461**
   Principio Creek *82*
   Rowlandsville concrete train (CE-883) **450**, 450-51
   Rowlandsville iron (CE-884) **450**, 450-51
   Scotchman's Creek (CE-1036) **305**, 305
   Susquehanna (1816-17) 67, 71
   Susquehanna (Rte. 40) 148, **151**, 151
   U.S. Route 40 over AMTRAK (CE-998) **350**, 350
   at West Nottingham Academy 422
Bristole (CE-99) **204**, 204-205, 306-307, **307**
Bromwell house (CE-770) **429**, 429
Brookings house (CE-534) **363**, 363
Brookings Institution 363, 416
Brookland (CE-117) **424**, 424
Brookview Chapel (CE-1124) **421**, 421
Brown house (CE-90) **471**, 471
Brown house (CE-911) **458**, 458
Brown, Jeremiah, house (CE-203) **187**, 187, 208, **209**, **466**, 466-67
Brown, Jesse, house (CE-89) **468**, 468
Brown, Mercer and Hannah, house (CE-88) **214**, 214-15, **465**, 465
Broxen's Point 44
builders 224, 227
   Armitage, Mr. 245
   Atmore, Mr. 219
   of Brown, Mercer and Hannah, house 215
   carpenters 163
   Conrey, Thomas 317, 319
   Cook, Bill 476
   Cook, William 203, 227, 232
   Crispin, Mr. 219
   Gallagher, Stephen 367
   Handburg, Mr. 245
   Hessey, John H. 300
   Horton, Thomas and Jesse 463
   invoices from 203-204, 232
   Jackson Bros. 303, 481
   Linch, David 467
   McCologh, Andrew 227
   McCullough, Penrose 252
   Ray, John and William 464
   Reese, Morris 467
   Strickland, Price 338
   Tollum, John 476
   Wilson, Charles W. 421
building code in 18th century Charlestown 46
Bull Line 122
Burbage-Brock house (CE-266) **335**, 335
C & D Canal *see* Chesapeake & Delaware Canal
Calvert 87, 203, 241
Calvert log house (CE-92) **468**, 468
Calvert Road 124
Cameron, James and Rachel, house (CE-135) **405**, 405
Cameron, William, house (CE-1258) **478**, 478
canals 83, 85, 119, 120
   see also Chesapeake & Delaware Canal, Susquehanna Canal
   17th century Dutch idea 29
   Susquehanna and Tidewater (Harford Co.) 67
Carpenters Point **23**, **63**
Carpenters Point Neck 25
Carter-Ness house (CE-1394) **374**, 375

Carter's Mill workers' house (CE-674) **356**, 356
Cather's Corner 413
Catholics in Cecil County:
    in Chesapeake City 321, 326
    at Old Bohemia/St. Francis Xavier 40, 282-83, 292
Cayot's Corner 136
Cecil Co.:
    creation of **27**, 27, 28
    frontier character of 24, 25, 27, 28-29
Cecil County Arts Council 317
Cecil County Council of Defense 158
Cecil County Jail (CE-1307) **342**, 342
Cecil County, Maryland: A Study in Local History 447
Cecil Hotel (CE-108) **384**, 384
Cecilton 87, 93, 216, 256, 267
Ceciltown 44
Cecil *Whig* Building (CE-1308) **344**, 344-45
Cedar Farm (CE-565) **472**, 473
Centennial Celebration of 1876 134
Chalkley's Garden (CE-206) **481**, 481
Chandlee, Benjamin, house (CE-200) **466**, 466
Chantilly Country Club (CE-221) **474**, 474
Character of the Province of Maryland 1
Charles St., 205-207, Chesapeake City (CE-502) **318**, 319
Charlestown 36, 44-49, **46**, 58, 61-62, **62**, 65, 131, 134, **135**, 214, 229, 376
    colonial fairground **46**, 46
    colonial wharf, warehouse, and customs house 376
    water tower (CE-1306) **396**, 396
Charter of Liberties (Pa.) 34
Cherry Grove (CE-50) **166**, 166-67, 195, 207, 267, **284**, 284-85, 447
Chesapeake City 70, **78**, 81, 81, **89**, **96**, 96, 119, **120**, 120, *132, 133*, **136**, 159
    boatyard buildings (CE-1328) **324**, 324
    Fire Co. 318, 325
    during World War II **152**, 153
Chesapeake City District Civic Association 317
Chesapeake City firehouse **325**, 325
Chesapeake & Delaware Canal 60, 73-81, **74-77**, **78**, **79-80**, 81, 83, 119, **120**, 120, *132, 133*, **136**, 159, 219, 310, 311
    arch across feeder canal 332, **333**
    feeder canal for 78, 332
    housing for workers 313
    pump house **78**, **311**, 311
    during World War II **152**, 153
Chesapeake & Delaware Canal Co. 73, 308
Chester Co. (Pa.) 93
Childs 345
Childs, George W., house (CE-422) **346**, 346
Childs Row (CE-667, 686, 687) **344-45**, 345
Christiana (Del.) 75
Church of England, establishment of 39, 40, 332
churches *see also* Friends meetinghouses
    Bethel A.M.E. (CE-320) **320**, 320
    Big Elk Chapel (CE-630) **371**, 371
    Boulden Chapel and cemetery (CE-1080) **342**, 342
    chapels of ease 39-40
    Cherry Hill U. M. (CE-1383) **367**, 367
    Church of the Good Shepherd (CE-263) **322**, 322
    Ebenezer A.M.E. (CE-1329) **314**, 314
    Ebenezer Methodist (CE-1242) **393**, 393
    Elkton Methodist (CE-257) **340**, 240
    Elkton Presbyterian (CE-258) **343**, 343
    First Presbyterian Church (CE-340) **315**, 315
    Hopewell Methodist (CE-1157) **418**, 418
    Moore's Chapel (CE-1106) **370**, 370
    Mt. Olivet U. M. (CE-1353) **296**, 296
    Mt. Zoar Methodist (CE-877) **459**, 459
    North East United Methodist (CE-1343) **398**, 398
    Nottingham Presbyterian meetinghouse (1749) 201
    Old Bohemia (CE-60) 282-83, **283**
    Old Leeds 334
    Port Deposit Presbyterian (CE-283) **444**, 445
    Port Herman Methodist 324
    Rock Presbyterian (CE-73) **41**, 41, 43, 208, 210, **370**, 370-71
    St. Augustine's Episcopal (CE-64) **311**, 311-12
    St. Basil's 321, **326**, 326
    St. Francis Xavier (CE-60) 282-83, **283**
    St. Ignatius (Harford Co.) 456
    St. John's M. E. (CE-640) 368, **369**
    St. John's U. M. (CE-379) **390**, 390
    St. Mark's 40
    St. Mary Anne's (CE-102) **39**, 40, 215, **378**, 378, 386
    St. Patrick's (CE-834) 449, **456**, 456
    St. Paul's Methodist (CE-23) **303**, 303
    St. Rose of Lima (CE-336) **320**, 320-21
    St. Stephen's (CE-22) 40, **302**, 302
    St. Stephen's Chapel (CE-356) **302**, 302
    St. Teresa of Avila (CE-288) **439**, 439-40
    Tome Memorial U. M. (CE-290) 431, **440**, 440-41
    Trinity Episcopal (CE-256) **348**, 348
    Trinity Methodist (CE-314) **322**, 322-23
    Trinity Methodist (CE-599) **482**, 482
    Union United Methodist (CE-1077) **341**, 341
    Wesley Chapel (CE-815) **386**, 386
    West Nottingham Chapel (CE-226) **419**, 419-20
    West Nottingham Presbyterian (CE-227) **415**, 415-16
    Zion Methodist (CE-360) **300**, 300
    Zion Methodist (CE-759) **477**, 477
Churchman, John, house (CE-187) **54**, 54, 168, 168-69, 203, **215**, 215, **230**, 230, **464**, 464
Circus Park 128
Civil War 101, **102**, 103, **108**, 114, 115, **116**, 119, 180, 190, 220, 264, 329, 349, 441
Clarwyn Farm (CE-188) **467**, 467
class:
    in colonial period 43, 53, 54, 164, 178, 195
    gentry's display of wealth 177, 180, 181, 183, 230
    middle class 132
    in 19th century 91, 100
    in 20th century 132
Clayton Building (CE-262) **339**, 339
Clearview Farm (CE-868) **454**, 454
Clement, Hiram, house (CE-1107) **475**, 475
Clendenin Farm (CE-1155) **413**, 413-14
Cloverly (CE-1141) **414**, 414-15
coffin maker's house (CE-549) **386**, 386
Cole Pier 119
Coleraine Township (Pa.) 175
College Green Victorian Gothic house (CE-93) **479**, 479-80
Colonial Revival house (CE-1165) **422**, 422
Colora 258
Colora Farm (CE-1191) **412**, 412
commerce:
    Caribbean, colonial trade with **53**, 381
    fur trade 19-23
    grain trade 65
    increased ties to Phila./Wilmington 85
    merchants **53**
    tobacco trade 23-24, 29, 37, **38**, 38, 39, 48-49, 65
    wheat/flour trade 46-48, 49, 65
communal living *see* Labadist sect
Congress, U.S. 77, 78, **104**, 104, 112, 148
Conowingo 118, **127**, 449
    Creek 17, 123
    dam **10**, 10, **145**, 145
    falls 9
    house from (CE-872) **461**, 461
Conrey, Thomas, house (CE-123) **318**, 319
construction 100, 192-225
    see also roof, siding
    balloon framing 100, **197**, 197, 201, 368
    braced timber frame 172, 190, 193, 254
    brick 53, **54**, 54, 207, 214-20
    brick nogging 190, 195, **196**, 289, 377
    central European influence 193, 201
    corner posts *see also* interiors 194, 250, 377
    cross gables **98**, **100**, 100, 419
    datestones 215
    of early dwellings 193
    English influence 193
    European cultural traditions, adaptation of 193
    fire door 203
    flounder addition 294
    of gable **198**, 203
    German influence 195
    hole-set post 194, 249, 250, 385
    industrialization, effects of 193, 220, 224, 257
    ironwork 224
    log 53, 193, 200-207, **202**, 257
    log crib 201, 202
    plank framing 197-99, **198**, 201
    porches **99**, 222-24
    post 194, 194
    post-and-plank **206**, 207
    round log 207, 267
    Scandinavian influence 201
    Scots-Irish tradition 455-56
    standardization of building materials 257
    stone 53, 110, 149, 207-14
    stone foundation 207, 228, 254
    stucco **211**, 212, 219
    technology influences 199
    timber framing 100, 193, 194, 196, 199, 201, 203, 228
    window frames **202**, 203
Cosgrove, William, house (CE-1240) **204**, 205, **385**, 385
Coulson house 100
county commissioners 43, 123,
county court 43, 44
    in Charlestown 46, 61
    in Elkton 62
county government *see* county court
county seat 62, 120-23, 146, 153

courthouse:
    first 29
    in 18th century 309
    on Elk River 201
    in Elkton 65, **146**, 146, **148**, 149, 350
Courthouse Point 43, 57, 309
Courthouse Point farmhouse (CE-1057) **242**, **309**, 309
Cowen brick house (CE-790) **357**, 357
Craig stone house (CE-1213) **428**, 428
Cramer house (CE-1338) **395**, 395
Crawford house (CE-1246) **384**, 384-85
Crisfield 84
Cromwell government 23
Cropper house (CE-307) **310**, 311
cross passage *see* house form
Crothers house (CE-838) **458**, 458
Crothers's Victorian house (CE-730) **476**, 476-77
Crow's Nest, The (CE-1229) **446**, 446
Cruikshank house (CE-31) **301**, 301
Curry stone house (CE-430) **388**, 388
dating houses 227
Davis house (CE-973) **285**, 285
Davis house (CE-1212) **438**, 438
Davis, Dr. H. V., house (CE-118) 312, **319**, 319-20
Declaration of the Freemen of Maryland 380
DeCoursey frame house (CE-1043) **322**, 322
DeCoursey house (CE-1051) **314**, 314-15
Deep Cut (C & D Canal) **77**, **78**
Deep Run farm (CE-1098) **369**, 369
Delaware 34, 41, 83, 84, 93, **142**, **159**, 159, 267
    Bay 27, 29, **78**, 193, 201
    City **78**
    Co. (Pa.) 252
    legislature 73
    River 19, 22-23, 29, 31, **75**, 81, 163, 245
    valley 41, 222
Democratic Party 104, 129
Denmark 30
Depression 145-46, 148, 151, 160
doctor's offices 365, 482
Dolfinger Creamery (CE-635) **375**, 375
Dutch West India Co. 19
Earleville 207, 217, 267
Eastern Shore 84, 85, 131, 140
Ecole des Beaux-Arts 134
economy, Cecil 96
    and agriculture 53, 249
    change after Civil War 103
    Depression 145-46, 148, 151
    and fishing 62-65
    in steamboat age 59, 61
    after World War II 159-60
education 35
    see also African-American, schools
    for blacks **108**, 108-109
    in colonial period 105
    county school system **107**, 109, 110-12
    establishment of public system 105-108, 422
    subscription schools 105, **107**, 422
electricity 142, 142-45
    Home Manufacturing Light & Power Co. 142, **143**
    power plants **138**, **142**, 142-45, **145**, 148
    Rural Electrification Administration 148
Elk Forge 123
Elk Forge Co. 51, 57, 89

Elk Landing 66
Elk Landing Farm (CE-132) **329**, 329-30
Elklands (CE-126) **316**, 316
Elk Mills 89, **90-91**, 142
Elk Neck 28, 58, 131, 132, **141**
Elk Neck State Park **60**
Elk River **opposite 1**, 16, 25, 40, 43, 57, 59, *61*, 62, 65, **75**, **78**, 78, 178, 183, 201, 249
Elk River Farm (CE-807) **392**, 392-93
Elk River House (Port Herman) **324**, 324
Elkton **46**, 57, 58, 61, 62,, 65-66, **84**, 84, 85, 87, 100, 101, **102**, 119, 124, 125, *130*, 216 131, *132, 133*, **140**, 142, **146**, 146-48, 149, **151**, 159, 251
    Armory (CE-1035) **349**. 349-50
    Diner **151**
    Electric Light & Power Co. 142
    firehouse 347
    Italianate houses on East Main St. **338**, 338-39
    Line **58**
    Main St. 100, 134, **135**, 149, **155**
    Marble & Granite Works 350
    packet **65**
    in 1795 202-203
    Town Hall (CE-1309) **347**, 347
    221-23 East Main St. (CE-157) **341**, 341
    during World War II *133*, **144**, **145**, 153-59, **154-57**
Ellerslie (CE-144) **433**, 433
Elsie books 346
Emancipation Proclamation 103
Encatada (CE-232) **330**, 330-31
England 41, **53**, 91, 92, 153
England, Charles, house (CE-617) **478**, 479
England, Howard, farm (CE-1255) **479**, 479
England, Isaac, house (CE-207) **470**, 470-71
Essex Lodge (CE-21) **98**, 100, **297**, 297
Etherington, William G., house (CE-15) **293**, 293
Europe 39
European exploration of New World 1
    John Smith voyage to head of bay 15-19
European settlement of Cecil *see also* Irish presence, Scots-Irish
    Dutch presence 19, 21, 22-23, 25-26, 29, 30, 193
    English presence 163, 169, 201, 249
    Finnish presence 33
    Scandinavian presence 193
    Swedish presence 22-23, 25, 26, 33, 37, 201, 330
Evan's Choice (CE-98) **173**, 173-75, **399**, 399-400
    barn **253**, 253, 254-55
Evans house (CE-44) **436**, 436
Evans house (CE-77) **357**, 357-58
Evans, Robert, house (CE-1218) **438**, 438-39
Ewing farm (CE-1105) **366**, 366
Ewing house (CE-1196) **406**, 406
Ewing Mill property silo (CE-1190) **259**, 259
Ewing, Patrick, house (CE-40) 179-80, **179**
fair, market **46**, 46, 65
Fair Hill Racetrack (CE-1004) **375**, 375
Fairview 189
fall line **3**, 250
falls *see also* Conowingo, Gilpin's, Smith's **6**, 16, 49, 88, 142

farming *see* agriculture
Federal brick house, Calvert (CE-86) **471**, 471
Federal Manpower Commission 154
Fell Road log house (CE-199) **465**, 465
ferries **31**, *82*
    Bohemia 48
    bridges replace 67
    Creswell's 67, 199
    at Ordinary Point 29, **31**
    railroad at Perryville 86, 103
    Susquehanna 44
    Susquehanna lower (Rodgers) 43, 85, 423
Fifteenth Amendment (U.S. constitution) 104
Fifth Maryland Regiment **102**
Finland 153
Finley, Martha, house (CE-1313) 346
firebrick companies 118
firefighting *130*, 318
First Maryland Regiment 380
Fisher diary 95-96, 219, 223-24, 236-37, 245-46, 278-79, 281, 291 252, 257-58
fisheries
    Indian **9**, 9-10, **10**, 145
    19th century 101
Fisher-Wilson house (CE-983) **164-65**, 165-66, **284**, 284
fishing:
    huts **63**, 65,
    industry 62-65, **63**, **65**,
    rafts 64, 65
    villages 64, 65
flurkuckenhaus 174
Ford house (CE-734) **382**, 382
Forman diary 178, 188, 200, 219, 245, 261, 262, 263, 264
Fort Casimir 25
Fort Christiana 22, 25
Fort Conquest 23
Fort Defiance 58
Fort Hollingsworth 58
Foster house (CE-549) **386**, 386
Fourteenth Amendment 104
Fox Harbor (CE-1348) 316, **317**
Franklin Hall (CE-120) **96**, 316-17, **317**
Fredericktown **36**, 44, 46, 48, 49, 58, 131, **159**, 159
free blacks *see* African-American
Freedmen's Bureau 104
Frenchtown 17, **56**, 57, 58, **59**, 59, **75**, **77**, 81, 83, 118, 245
Friends *see* Quakers
Friendship Stone, Elkton (CE-1311) **328**, 328
Friends meetinghouses *see also* Quakers
    Colora (CE-638) 41, **411**, 411-12
    East Nottingham (Brick) (CE-82) **33**, 35, 40-41, **54**, 54, 57, **208**, 208, 214, 215, **221**, 221-22, 462-64, **463**
    log at Nottingham 201
    Octoraro Creek 41, 451
    West Nottingham (Little Brick) (CE-228) 41, 44, **404**, 404, 412
Friends of Rodgers Tavern 424
Frisby's Delight (CE-29) **178**, 179, **289**, 289
Frisby's Prime Choice (CE-12) **217**, 217, **285**, 285
Fulton-Alexander house (CE-841) **448**, 448, 449
Fulton, William, house (CE-533) **354**, 354-55
fur trade *see* commerce
Gallaher house and store (CE-1393) **366**, 366-67

gardens 250, 262, 264, 342
    Italian at Tome Institute **110**
    at Rose Hill 291
    Victorian 295
Garrett, Thomas, house (CE-715) 356, **357**
Gassaway house (CE-321) **313**, 313
gas station *see* service station
Gayley house (CE-705) **411**, 411
Gee Funeral Parlor *see* Finley, Martha, house
General Assembly of Maryland *see also* Maryland legislature
    colonial period 37, 39, 40, 44-46, 48, 49, 50, 376
    and education 105, 106, **108**
    19th century 64, 73, 84, 103, 104,
    and roads 120, 123, **123**, **124**, 125, 126
    20th century 146, 149
General Court (Annapolis) 43
General Historie of Virginia 6, 32
Georgetown [D.C.] 93
Georgetown (Md.) 58
Georgetown University 40, 283
Gerry house, Port Deposit (CE-271) 212, 224, **225**, 426, 426-27
Gerry house (CE-1185) **418**, 418
Gibson's Green (CE-964) 295-96, **296**
    corn-crib **258**
    granary **258**
Gillespie Hotel (CE-1349) **297**, 297
Gillespie house (CE-213) **414**, 414
Gillespie house (CE-889) **458**, 458
Gillespie house (CE-1152) **417**, 417-18
Gillespie log house (CE-1217) 196, **202**, 203, **232**, 232, **425**, 425
Gillespie Paint and Paper Co. 438-39
Gillespie, Thomas J., house (CE-1234) **386**, 386-87
Gilpin house (CE-780) **342**, 343
Gilpin, John, house (CE-1348) 316, **317**
Gilpin Manor (CE-162) **340**, 340
Gilpin's Falls 142
Gilpin's Falls hydroelectric plant (CE-763) **398**, 398
Ginn house (CE-778) 195, **196**, **288**, 289
Girl Scouts of Central Maryland 459
Givens house (CE-1082) **346**, 346
gold rush in Alaska 134, **135**, 396
gold rush in Cecil 119
governor of Maryland:
    Crothers, Austin Lane **128**, 129-30, 145, 416, 458
    Henry, John 416
    McLane, Robert Milligan 278
    Paca, William 378
Graham house (CE-1205) **434**, 434
grain *see also* milling
    cultivation 49, 51, 91, 92
    as currency 49
    inspection 49, 376
    as source of wealth 164, 177
    trade 65, 249
Grammy's Run (CE-1097) **368**, 368
granite *see* quarrying, stone
Grant, George, house (CE-1094) **167**, 167, **370**, 370
Gray's Hill 57, 131
Graystone Manor (CE-95) 183-84, **184**, **401**, 401-402

Graystone Road frame house (CE-1256) **476**, 476
Gray, William, & Son (Phila.) 118
Great House (CE-65) 186-87, **187**, 234-35, **235**, **308**, 308
Greek Revival stone house (CE-43) **428**, 428
Green, B. J., house (CE-989) **299**, 299
Greenfields (CE-16) 180, 182-83, **184**, 216, **217**, **280**, 280-81
Greenhill Farm (CE-106) **392**, 393
    kitchen/slave quarter **260**, 260-61
Green's Delight (CE-918) barn **250-51**, 251, **451**, 451
Griffith house (CE-316) **318**, 319
Griffith-Smith house (CE-543) **261**, **391**, 391
Grove farm (CE-28) **288**, 289
    icehouse **263**, 263
Grove-Miller farm (CE-234) **482**, 482
Grubb property (CE-33) **452**, 452
Guenther Realty building (CE-1366) **298**, 298
Gunpowder River 27
Hacks Point 200
Hadden double house (Port Herman) 324
Hager, Henry, house (CE-309) **136**, 326, **327**
Hager-Kinter house (CE-309) **136**, 326, **327**
Haines house (CE-216) **172**, 172, 173, 193, **194**, **228**, 228, **229**, **400**, 400-401
    barn **254**, 254
Haines, Joseph, house (CE-600) **475**, 475
Haines, Joseph, house/Willowdale (CE-218) 172-73, **173**, **401**, 401
Haines, Rebecca, house (CE-1117) **412**, 412
Haines-Reynolds farmhouse (CE-217) **408**, 408
Hall's Choice (CE-46) **428**, 428
Hamilton house (CE-107) **196**, **379**, 379-80
Hance Point 28
Hancis Point *82*
Happy Harbor (CE-8) **281**, 281
Harford Co. 61, 67, 103, 145
Harland & Hollingsworth 289
Harmony Chapel (CE-1208) **442**, 442
Harris, Nathan and Susannah, house (CE-229) **176**, 176, 220-21, **221**, 240, 240-41, **403**, 403, 404
Harrisville (CE-1123) 408-409
    house with Victorian additions **409**
    two-story brick house **409**
Harvey frame house (CE-656) **342**, 342
Havre de Grace 61
Haynes house and store (CE-960) **295**, 295
Hazel property (Port Herman) 324
Head of Christiana (Del.) 41
Head of Elk **36**, 57, 62
Hebron's Gift (CE-189) **469**, 469
Hermitage, The (CE-764) 328, **337**, 337-38
Herndon (CE-9) **299**, 299
Hideaway, The (CE-5) **287**, 287-88
Highfield (CE-788) **454**, 454
Highlawn (CE-1101) 352, **372**, 372
Hillwood (CE-768) **438**, 438
Historical Society of Cecil County 130, 332
    building (CE-1355) **343**, 343-44
Historic American Buildings Survey 43, **183**, **196**, **213**, **217**, **220**, 221, **224**, **225**, **231**, **235**, **236-239**, **243**, **244**, **260**, **280**, **283**, **285**, **289**, **290**, **329**, **330**, **331**, **335**, **338**, **359**, **364**, **378**, **379**, **447**, **463**
Hollingsworth family houses, Elkton 216-17, **217**
Hollingsworth Manor **155**, 155

Holly Hall (CE-131) 242-45, **243-44**, **332**, 332, 426
Holly Tree Farm (CE-1228) **436**, 436-37
Hopewell (CE-172) 184-85, **185**, 186, **231**, 231, **351**, 351-52, 356
Hopkins, Dr. Joseph, house (CE-87) **475**, 475
horse breeding 159, **161**
hospital *see* Union Hospital
house form 163-91
    "baffle" entrance 187
    center hall, double-pile plan 180-84
    center hall, single-pile plan 170, 176-80, 204
    center hall plans, alternative 184-87
    central chimney plan 189-90, 205, 377
    changes in 170, 171, 176, 386-87
    conservative use of 191, 224, 299, 321, 323
    continental European 190
    control of space/access 174, 177, 183, 187
    cross passage 167, 168, 170, 355
    definition of 164
    dogtrot 204-205, 306-307
    double-cell plan 188
    double-pile structures 53, 164,
    English influence 163, 169
    formal space in 180, 185, 190
    German influence 174, 175-76, 185, 190
    hall-kitchen plan *(flurkuckenhaus)* 174
    hall/parlor plan 164, 167-70, 190, 203
    mass production, influence of 170
    in mid-19th century 170, 458
    one-room plan 164-67, 168
    privacy and segregation of space 167, 170, 182, 183, 187, 357
    room use 180, 181, 182, 183-84, 185, 186, 187, 261
    saddlebag 205
    Scots-Irish influence 163, 169, 186, 355, 409
    service wings 167
    side hall plan 187-88, 352-53
    single-pile structures 164
    stairs, placement of 170
    three-room/cross passage plan 170-73, 331, 352
    town house 187
    two-door cross passage plan 173-76
    two-door plans in double-pile form 184-86, 189-90
    variety built of log 203
housing:
    in 18th century **53**, 53-54, **54**, 164
    Hollingsworth Manor **155**, 155
    mill workers' 89, **90-91**, 319, 450
    rebuilding 30, 131-32, 164, 246
    slave 37, 53, 100-101
    tenant 53, 100, 146, **267**, 267, 286, 294
    after World War II 160
    during World War II **155**, 155, **156**
Howard Hotel (Elkton) **140**
Howard house (CE-68) 308-309, **309**
hundreds:
    Back Creek 222
    North Milford (Del.) *82*
    North Sassafras 39
    Bohemia 39
    Elk 39
    Worton 39
    South Sassafras 39

Hunt, Marshall I., house (CE-1130) **414**, 415
hurricane of 1786 61
Husfelt house (CE-921) **300**, 300
Ice Age 4-5
ice gorges (Port Deposit) **72**, 73
indentured servants 28, 105, 178
Independence (CE-1162) **410**, 410
Indian Range (CE-18) barn **256**, 256
Indians *see also* prehistory in Chesapeake region
  agriculture **5**, 5, 9
  Appoquinimink village 28
  conflict with settlers 1, 11, 19, 27-28
  ethnocentric European attitude toward 1-2, 11, **17**
  fishing **4**, 4, **9**, 9, 145
  fort/town on Susquehanna 16-17
  fur trade 19-23
  housing adapted by Europeans 163
  housing of **4**, **6**, 6-8
  noble savage 1, 11, **17**
  nomadic lifestyle 2-5, **3**,
  petroglyphs of **9**, 9, **10**
  presence reduced in Cecil 28, 37
  smallpox outbreak 28
  stockades **5**, 11, **13**, 17
  trade **5**, 11
  treaties of 1661 28
  treaty of 1652 23, 27
  villages **5**, 5-6, 9, 10, 17-18
  woodworking tools 4-5
Indian tribes:
  Algonquian 5, 17, 18
  Delaware or Passayunk 9, 27, 28
  Five Nations 18, 28
  Iroquois 6, 9, 18
  Massaowomek 15, 18-19
  Seneca 18, 28
  Shawnee 28
  Sickoneysinck 19
  Six Nations 28
  Susquehannock 1, **6**, 11, **13**, 13, 16, **17**, 17, 18, 19-20, 21, 22, 23, 27, 28, 378
  Tockwogh **6**, 16, 17-19, **19**
  Tuscarora 28
  Yadkin 23
Industrial Revolution 112-13, 191
industry *see also* fishing, lumberyards, milling
  bloomery 49, **50**
  brickyard, Krauss's 403
  canneries **118**, 131
  copper rolling mill 51, 358
  distillery in Charlestown 62, 381
  diversity in 65-66
  explosives 153-55, **154**, **157**, 157-58
  firebrick **118**, 118
  iron manufacture 49-51, 61, 114, 358
  in late 19th century 112-13
  munitions plants *133*
  in North East 392
  paper **116**, 118-19
  tanning 357
  timber 199-200
  woolen factory 66
  after World War II 159
inns *see* taverns
inspection *see* grain, lumber industry, tobacco
interiors, domestic 227-47
  see also house form, walls

corner posts 190, 194, **228**, 228-29
cupboards, built-in 169, 179, 182, 233, **235**, 235-36, 241
dining room 178, 179, 182, 187-88
Diocletian window 432
English influence 229, 236
exposed timber framing 203, 228-29, 241
finish, invoice for 203-204
formal space 174-75, 177
Georgian 181-82, 182-83
imported materials 245
mantels 178, 188, **236**, 236, **240-42**, 240, 241-42, **244**, 244-45, **247**
mass production and **228**,
"music room" 182, **237**, 237-40
paneling 54, 168-69, 173, 190, 232-35, **233**
plasterwork 182, 237-40, **237-38**, 245, **246**
post heads 172
social use of space 161
Venetian or Palladian window **244**, 244
wallpaper 178, 188, **226**, 245
whitewashed **196**, 196, 199
Ireland 41
Irish presence *see also* Scots-Irish
  colonial period 30, 31, 32, 105
  in late 18th century 201
iron furnace/forge 50, 50-51, 61, 66, 88, **90**
  Accokeek 51
  Kingsbury 51
  Lancashire 51
  North East 51
  Principio **50**, 50, 51
Iron Hill 27, 35
iron manufacture *see* industry
Italianate double house (CE-1344) **391**, 391
Jackson **88**
Jacksonian democracy 427
Jackson, Scott, house (CE-1305) **397**, 397
Jacob Tome Institute *see* schools; Tome, Jacob, Institute
Jamestown (Oldtown) 43
Jamestown (Va.) 15, 23-24, 105
Jefferson Hall (CE-381) **431**, 431
Jenness, S. M., house (CE-1225) 208, **211**, **436**, 436
Jesuit settlement at Bohemia 40, 282-83
"Jim Crow" laws 105
Job farm spring/smokehouse (CE-584) **259**
Johnson Road farmhouse (CE-908) **460**, 460
Johnson Victorian house (CE-762) **396**, 396
justices of the county court 43
kammer (bedroom) 190
Karsner-Wilsey house/office (CE-327) **323**, 323-24
Keilholtz, Charles, house (CE-1154) **414**, 414
Keithley house (CE-892) **457**, 457
Kelso 159, **161**
Kent Co. (Md.) **16**, 39, 51, **159**
Kent Island 23
Kieffer brick house (CE-133) **330**, 331
Kirk brick house (CE-520) **472**, 472
Kirk, Elisha, house (CE-84) **241**, 241, 405, **470**, 470
Kirk, Levi, house (CE-565) **472**, 473
Kirk, Roger, house (CE-209) 171-72, **172**, 193, 194, 207, 220, 228, 229, **462**, 462
Kirk stone house (CE-606) **477**, 477-78
Kirk, William, house (CE-589) **469**, 469

kitchens 37, 54, 165
  summer kitchen 54
  in basement 169
  in service wings 165, 166, 170, 179, 180
Klondike Gold Co. (Cecil) 119
Klondyke house (CE-109) 134, **135**, **397**, 397
Knight house (CE-956) **293**, 293
Knight, William and Elizabeth, house (CE-205) **215**, 215, **464**, 464
Knight, William, tenant house (CE-240) 166, **206**, 207
kuche (hall) 190
Labadist sect 29, 30-31, 37
Lake, Griffing, and Stevenson atlas 63, **89**, **98**, **99**, 416, 456, 475
Lake, Reuben, house (CE-1046) 169
Lancaster Co. (Pa.) 16, 28, 43, 87, 89, 190, 455
Layman house (CE-306) **310**, 310
Lewes (Del.) 19
Lewis, James A., house (CE-1044) **316**, 316
Liberty Grove 89, 190, 208, 420
  house and school in (CE-1186) **420**
Lickingbank Farm (CE-210) **473**, 473
lighthouse *see* Turkey Point lighthouse
Lincoln farm (CE-1115) barn 254, **255**
Linden Manor (CE-56) **284**, 284
Linton house (CE-110) **382**, 382
Little Bohemia Creek 178, 181, 216
Little Elk Creek 17, 41, 88, 184, 208
Little Elk Farm (CE-170) **200**, 229, **353**, 353-54
Little Elk house (CE-171) **360**, 360
Little North East Creek 31
Locust Thicket (CE-49) **286**, 286
Lofland farm (CE-975) 304, **305**
London Company 15
London Grove Township (Pa.) 175
Long Green Farm (CE-208) **467**, 467
Long Point 43, 46, 200
Long property (CE-1052) **325**, 325
Longview Farm (CE-797) **267**, 267
Lowe house (CE-868) **454**, 454
Luff's island 67
lumber industry **70**, 70, 109, 195
  see also lumberyards, raft lumber
  inspectors 200
lumberyards 101, 199
  Bennett & Karsner 70, 199
  in Chesapeake City 89
Luten Bridge Co. 305
Mackey, Col. David, house (CE-174) 353, **354**, 354, 374
Mackey-du Pont farm (CE-676) **366**, 366
Mackey farmhouse (CE-173) **353**, 353
Mackey house (CE-473) **324**, 324
Mackey, Howard, house (CE-631) **360**, 360
Mackie, Melissa, house (CE_639) **367**, 367
Mackie, Thomas, house (CE-70) 232-33, **233**, **328**, 328-29
Maffit farmhouse (CE-816) **387**, 387
Mansion House (Port Herman) 324
manufacturing *see* industry
Maple Shade Farm (CE-212) 229, **403**, 403
Maplewood Farm (CE-1218) **438**, 438
  barn **248**
  water tank **248**, **260**, 260
maps of Cecil County:
  Charlestown plat **36**
  C & D Canal **74-75**, 77

Humphreys, William [1792] **45**
Lake, Griffing, & Stevenson atlas (1877)
Martenet (1858) **86**
Susquehanna River survey **66**, **68-69**
Wilmington & Susquehanna Railroad [1835] **84-85**
maps of Chesapeake region:
    Farrer, Virginia (1651/70) **21**
    Hall, Ralph (1635) **15**
    Herman, Augustine (1673) **27**, 27
    Homann, John B. (1714) **19**
    Lewis, Samuel (1794) **36**
    Mason-Dixon line **34**
    Smith, John (1608) **6**, 6, 16, **17**
marinas 159
Martindale-Hughes house (CE-318) **312**, 312
Maryland Business Directory 131
Maryland Canal Co. 213
Maryland Clay Co. 118
Maryland Geological Survey **124**, 125, 131
Maryland Historical Trust vi-vii, 377
Maryland legislature 83, 120, 129, *130*
    see also General Assembly of Maryland
Mason-Dixon:
    line 250
    map **34**
    markers **35**, **330**, 331
    survey **34**, **35**, 35
Masons, Harmony Lodge of 440
Mauldin-Beatty house (CE-559) **387**, 387
Mauldin double house (CE-1340) **389**, 389
Maxwell Victorian house (CE-748) **421**, 421
McCleary farm (CE-521) **355**, 355
McClenahan:
    double house (CE-1409) **442**, 442
    Granite Co. 115
    mansion (CE-278) **212**, **441**, 441-42
    quarry **114-15**, 114-15, **213**
    Quarry Co. office (CE-1421) **444**, 444
McCracken house (CE-709) **358**, 358
McCullough-Cummings property (CE-833) **457**, 457
McCullough, George, house (CE-1192) **420**, 420
McCullough house (CE-1342) **393**, 393-94
McCullough Iron Co. 89, 114, 420, 449, 456
    office (CE-1337) 392
McDowell-Blackburn house (CE-296) **429**, 429-30
McIntire, Andrew, house (CE-1067) **336**, 337
McKinney house (CE-905) **452**, 452-53
McKown house (CE-109) 134, **135**, **397**, 397
McLane-Knight tenant house (CE-965) 267, **294**, 294
McNamee log house (CE-900) **170**, 170, **455**, 455-56
McVey Hotel (CE-35) **455**, 455, 473
Mearns, Abel, house (CE-80) **473**, 473
Mearns, Dr., house (CE-608) 476, **477**
Mearns, Levi and Amanda, house (CE-609) **478**, 478
Mechanics Valley 337
    yellow house (CE-724) **390**, 390
Methodist parsonage, Cecilton (CE-359) **292**, 292
Methodists in Cecil 43, 332
Milestone House (CE-739) **468**, 468
Miller's Crossroads, house at (CE-772) **359**, 359

Mill House (CE-101) **376**, 376
milling 87-89, 113-14
    flint mills 118
    fulling mills 87
    gristmills 49, 87
    merchant mills 49, 87
    paper 118-19
    oil mills 87
    sawmills 87, 199
mills 61, 66, 101, 331, 369, 383, 407
    see also McCullough Iron Co.
    Baldwin Manufacturing Co. (CE-168) 365, **374**, 374
    Bohemia Mills 89
    on Bohemia River 49
    Brickley (CE-136) **407**, 407
    Brown's gristmill (CE-202) **481**, 481
    Brown's, Jeremiah 467, 481
    Burgett sawmill **89**
    Carter's 356 *see also* Wallace-Carter
    Carter's paper, grist-, and sawmills 88
    Cecil Manufacturing Co. 334
    Cecil Paper 88, **116**, **124**, 335
    Crawford Woolen 384
    Cyclone 329
    Davis-Christy (CE-789) **408**, 408
    Dutton ironworks 392
    Eckerson's gristmill (CE-368) **418**, 419
    Elk Forge 365
    Elk Mills cotton factory 89, **90**, **364**, 365
    Elk Paper **116**
    Elkton pulp mill 124, 347
    Ewing's, Patrick **36**
    Fulton flax (CE-535) 355, **357**, 357
    Fulton's fulling 88, 357
    gristmill in North East 44
    Haines 412
    Harlan-Wilson (CE-652) **333**, 333
    at Head of Elk 49
    Hollingsworth old 88
    Jackson's **89**
    Jesuit at Bohemia 40, 282
    Johnson's Woolen 387-88
    Jordan's Rock Paper 371
    Kenmore Pulp & Paper (CE-548) 119, **361**, 361-62
    Kirk's (CE-220) **476**, 476
    Kite's (CE-644) **371**, 371
    Lord's cotton factory **364**, 365, 369
    Mackies' 88
    Magraw 419
    Marley Paper 118-19, 345, 346, 365
    McCullough Rolling (CE-42) **456**, 456-57
    Meteer 360, 361-62
    Morocto Paper Co. 450
    New Leeds Factory 88
    at Nottingham Lots 49
    Octoraro 392
    Perry Point 423
    Porter's 419
    at Port Herman 324
    Providence Paper (CE-548) 88, 118, 124, 360, 361-62, 371
    Purnell's 88
    Radner Pulp **116**
    Red City Rolling (Del.) 456
    Rock Run (CE-241) **48**, 49, 434, **435**
    Rock Spring 88

    Scott (CE-514) **359**, 359-60
    Sewall's sawmill 88
    Shannon 392
    Stone Paper 371
    Sun Paper 461
    Tyson 355-56
    Wallace-Carter (CE-71) **335**, 335
    Walnut Valley gristmill (CE-546) **365**, 365
    Warburton's sawmill 472
    West Atwell 392
    Whitaker Iron Co. 392
    Wilna 329
mill workers' housing 89, 345, 356, 360, 366, 372, 374, 450
    at Elk Mills **90-91**, **364**, 365
Mitchell house, Elkton (CE-149) 217, 330, **331**, 331
Mitchell house, Fair Hill *see* taverns, Fair Hill Inn
modern life 132-34, 149-50, 161
monument, World War I doughboy, Elkton **349**, 349
Moore house (CE-373) **414**, 414
Moore-Rea house (CE-1224) **430**, 430-31
Moore-Reynolds Mill property (CE-141) **401**, 401
Moore, William, house (CE-791) **399**, 399
Morrison, Matthew, house (CE-1181) 213-14, **214**, **408**, 408
Mount Ararat (CE-142) **426**, 426
Mount Harmon (CE-26) **38**, 93, **94-95**, 223, 236, **304**, 304
    barn 251-53
Mount Pleasant (CE-24) **288**, 288
Mount Pleasant (CE-1196) **406**, 406
Mount Welcome (CE-878) **460**, 460
Mount Zoar 105, **108**, **459**, 459
    house, typical (CE-875) 459
    Methodist Church (CE-877) **459**, 459
    school (CE-876) **108**, 459
Mrs. Forman's diary *see* Forman diary
Mullen's Folly (CE-81) **468**, 468
Murphy's, Mrs., Hotel (CE-286) **425**, 425-26
National Industrial Recovery Act 148
National Register of Historic Places 278, 280, 282, 291, 302, 304, 308, 311, 329, 331, 332, 349, 351, 353, 370, 377, 380, 402, 403, 404, 411, 416, 417, 422, 423, 427, 431, 432, 443, 453, 462, 464, 465, 466, 470
native Americans *see* Indians
natural resources:
    clay/sand/lime 118, 207, 214
    gold 119
    iron ore deposits 49, **50**, 50-51
    lumber 119, 195
    stone 115-18, 207, 213, 216
    water power 49
Naval Academy Preparatory School 159, 446
Navy Bureau of Personnel 159
Nesbitt house (CE-1403) **442**, 442-43
Nesbitt stone house (CE-1184) **409**, 409
New Amstel 25, 26, 27
Newark (Del.) **127**, 159
New Bridge **116**, 123, 461
New Castle (Del.) 32, 41, 43, **56**, **75**, 81, 83, 163, 193, 245
    Air Base 157
    Frenchtown Turnpike Co. 81, 245
New Connaught *see also* Susquehanna Manor 32

New Deal 148
New England 49, 189, 193, 229
New Garden Township (Pa.) 175
New Ireland 32
New Jersey 118, 146
New Munster *see* tracts
New Munster stone (CE-1005) **355**, 355
New Netherlands 26, 29
newspapers:
    Baltimore Evening Post 67
    Cecil Democrat **84**, 284, 316, 321, 329, 347, 471
    Cecil Democrat & Farmers Journal **65**
    Cecil Whig 133, 341, 344, 405
    Elkton Press 93, 199
    Maryland Gazette 381
    Philadelphia *Ledger* **116**, 118
    Philadelphia *Record* 119, 124
New Sweden 201
New Valley Factory (CE-45) **406**, 406
New Valley Factory house (CE-1206) **430**, 430
New York 83, 146, 159
North Carolina 93, 205, 329
North Chesapeake City **120**, 120, **152**
    row houses (CE-341) **313**, 313
North East 44, 48-49, 118, 125, *132*, 159, 260
    Town Hall (CE-105) **394**, 394
North East Creek 142
North East River 10, 16, 23, **33**, 46, 61, 62
Northern Dancer 159
Nottingham **36**, 57, 201
Nottingham Lots **33**, 34-35, 40, **41**, **54**, 163, 168, 169, 170, 171, 187, 189, 193, 216, 228, 402
nursing school *133*
Oakwood 221
Oakwood Crossroads frame house (CE-865) **459**, 459
Oakwood Rod & Gun Club 455
Observations on the Present State of Religion in Maryland 332
Octorara (CE-41) **224**, 224, **453**, 453-54
    barn **252**, 253, 453
    dairy **262**, 262
    springhouse **259**
Octoraro Creek 16, 17, 34, 89, 118, 123, 175, 179, 212
Octoraro River 31
Odessa (Del.) 28
Old Bohemia Historical Society 283
Oldfield Point Road frame house (CE-811) **383**, 383
Old Fort Smith house (CE-38) **174**, 175, **221**, 221, **448**, 448
Old Lock Pump House (CE-124) **78**, **311**, 311
Old Post Road frame house (CE-402) **388**, 389
Oldtown 43
107 House (CE-386) **383**, 383-84
Ordinary Point 29, 309
Orkney 457
Orphans Court 262
    18th century 43, 165, 166, 284-85, 194-95, 202-203, 205, 207, 222, 223, 227-28, 249-50, 256-57, 264-65, 267
    19th century 251, 263, 470
Orr, Nevin, house (CE-1156) **419**, 419
Otter Farm Italianate house (CE-823) **340**, 340
outbuildings, domestic *132*, 164, 165, 166, 196, **200**, 207, 249-50, 260-64

carriage house 263
change in mid-19th century 264
colonial period 54, 169
dairy [house] 54, 96, 258, **262**, 262
icehouse **262-63**, 262-63
kitchen 165, 190, **196**, 196, 205, 260-61
kitchen, summer 54
of log 202, 203
meat house 261, 296, **362**
multiuse 263-64, **265**
slave quarters 264-67, **266**
smokehouse 260-61, 261
wagon house 263
in wings 189
in wings, flanking 180, 183
Paca house (CE-111) **378**, 378-79
Palmer's Island **14**, 19, 21-22, **23**, 23
Paradise (CE-1191) **412**, 412
Parliament (English) 39, 48
Partridge Hill (CE-246) **217**, 230, **231**, **235**, 236, 241, **330**, 330, 331
Patapsco River 57
patents *see also* tracts 24, 25, 52
Patten, Thomas, house (CE-1223) **213**, 213, **427**, 427
Pattersonville (CE-1222) **438**, 438
Paw Paw Building (CE-291) **211**, 212, **427**, 427-28
Pearl Harbor 153
Pembroke Farm (CE-836) **448**, 448-49
Pencoyd Iron Works 451
Penn coat of arms **35**, 331
Pennington farm (CE-1001) **315**, 315
Pennsylvania 40, 64, 66, 67, **70**, 70, **77**, 88, 114, 142, 146, 154, **159**, 163, 175, 195, 199, 256
    see also boundary dispute, Lancaster Co., Philadelphia
    legislature 67, 73
Pennsylvania Germans 190
Penn, William, prescription for dwelling 171-72, 193-94
Perkins, Dr., house (CE-978) **294**, 294
Perry Point estate **138**, 139, **423**, 423
Perryville 85-87, 103, 131, *132*, **138**, 139, 145, 151, 159
petroglyphs 9, 9, **10**
Philadelphia 32, 43, **45**, **56**, 57, **58**, 67, 73, 83, 115, 118, 119, 131, 140, 142, **143**, 160, 187, 219, 244, 245
Philadelphia Agricultural Society 92
Philadelphia Electric Co. 142, **145**
Pilot Town 123, 449
    Founds house (CE-854) **449**, 449
Pine View (CE-534) **363**, 363
Piney Creek Farm **141**
Pittsburgh 83, **154**
plantations:
    in 17th century 30, 37
    in 18th century 166, 178, 180, 183, 195, 205, 227-28, 249-50, 264
Pleasant Hill, house near (CE-196) **372**, 372
Pleasant View Farm (CE-234) **197**, 197, **482**, 482
politics and government 112-13, 127-31, **129**, **129**, 347
Poor House *see* Haines house (CE-216)
population:
    census of 1712 37
    colonial period 37, 51

free black 51, 101, 104
    of Port Deposit 67
slave 37, 51, 101, 104
in 20th century *133*, 140
after World War II 160, 161
during World War II 153, **155**, 155
Port Deposit 67-73, **70**, **71**, **73**, 89, 101, **109**, 109-10, 115, 118, *133*, 145, 159, **212**, **213**, 213
    lumber industry and 199-200
    149 Main St. (CE-1417) **432**, 432
    41 N. Main St. (CE-1418) **434**, 434
    88-94 N. Main St. (CE-1419) **442**, 443
    38 S. Main St. (CE-285) **431**, 431
    Municipal Building (CE-297) **440**, 440
    Steps, The (CE-1412) **444**, 445
    terraces **71**, 73
    Town Hall (CE-274) **445**, 445
    during World War II **152**, 153
Port Deposit Heritage 426, 428
Porter house (CE-878) **460**, 460
Porter, Samuel, house (CE-34) **451**, 451-52
Porters Bridge 419
    Eckerson's gristmill (CE-368) **418**
Port Herman (CE-1054) **324**, 324
prehistory in Chesapeake region 2-11
    artifacts **2-5**
    Early Archaic **3**, 4
    Early Woodland **4**, 5
    Late Archaic **3**, 4
    Late Woodland **5**, 5-6, 9
    Middle Woodland **5**
    Paleo-Indian period **2**, 2-3
    Transitional **4**, 4-5
Presbyterian manse, Port Deposit (CE-273) **437**, 437
Presbyterians in Cecil 43, 402
    Old vs. New **41**, 41, 43, 371, 416
    Scots-Irish arrival 41
Preservation Maryland 424
Preston, William, house (CE-906) **451**, 451
Price, Ben, hotel (CE-3) **285**, 285
Price-Murphy house (CE-51) 197-99, **198**, **200**,
Price, William, house (CE-995) **295**, 295-96
Price, William IV, house (CE-1331) **306**, 306
Princeton 43, 416
Principia (CE-1233) **384**, 384
Principio 51, 89, 205
    cannon factory 58
    Company **50**, 50-51, **93**
    Creek 25, 32, 49, **50**, *82*
    Furnace 114, **430**, 431
    Iron Co. 431
Prospect Hill Farm (CE-1235) **389**, 389
Providence 124, 125
    boardinghouse (CE-666) **372**, 372
    corner house (CE-659) **373**, 373
    Mill manager's house (CE-746) **366**, 366
    Row (CE-645) 372, **373**
    workers' houses (CE-695) **360**, 360-61
Public Utilities Commission 129
pump house, C&D Canal *see* Old Lock Pump House
Pyle house (CE-1141) **414**, 414-15
Quakerism 31, 54
Quakers 30, 31, 32, 34, 35, 37, 40, 163, 168, 169, 170, 193
    Nottingham community 40-41, 49, 54, 464

population 41, 43,
quarrying 114-18, 119, 213
  see also McClenahan quarry
  Port Deposit granite 71-73, **72**, 110, 219
Queen Anne's Co. **19**, 51
Queen Anne's War 39
Queen St. brick house (CE-1408) **404**, 405
Quinn house (CE-61) **281**, 281
quitrent 24-25, 44, 46
racetrack 297
raft auger 200
raft lumber **70**, 70, 199, 200, **200-201**
rafts:
  fishing 64, **65**,
  shipping **70**, 70, **199**, 199, 200, 449
  work 81
Ragan, Dr. David, house (CE-873) **457**, 457
railroad companies:
  Baltimore Central **87**
  Baltimore & Ohio 83, 85, 115, 131
  Columbia & Port Deposit
  Frenchtown 81-83, 85
  Lancaster, Cecil, & Southern 375
  New Castle & Frenchtown Railroad 245, 336
  New Castle & Frenchtown Turnpike &
    Railroad Co. 81, 336
  Pennsylvania 131, 424
  Philadelphia 89, 119
  Philadelphia Baltimore Central 450
  Philadelphia branch 85
  Philadelphia spur 87
  Philadelphia, Wilmington, & Baltimore **81**,
    441
  Susquehanna line 87
  Wilmington & Susquehanna **84**, 85
railroads **56**, 61, 81-87, *82,* **84**, **86**, **87**, 115, **119**,
  119, 120, 125, 131, 132, **136**, 145
  during Civil War 103
railroad stations:
  Perryville (CE-1442) **445**, 445
  Principio 89
  Rising Sun **87**
Ramsey, Nathaniel, house 380
Randalia (CE-67) **308**, 308
Rawlings farm (CE-1222) **438**, 438
  multiuse carriage house 263-64, **265**, 438
  smokehouse **261**, 261
Rawlings, Z. T., house (CE-907) 190, **191**, **454**,
  454-55
Ray, J. S., house 461
Rea's Corner 430
Red Cross **157**
Red House Farm well house (CE-1065) **259**
Reed house (CE-775) **314**, 314
Rees house and office (CE-122) **321**, 321
Relation of Maryland 24
Remy, R., & Son (Phila.) 118
Republican Party 104, 145
Reynolds farm (CE-97) **402**, 402
Reynolds, Mary, stone house (CE-429) **385**, 385
Reynolds's, Mary, new house (CE-513) **390**,
  390-91
Richardsmere 123
Richards house (CE-231) **404**, 404
Richards's Oak, house by (CE-1129) **419**, 419
Richards, Thomas, house (CE-230) **402**, 402-403
Richmond (Va.) 115
Rich Neck (CE-29) **178**, 179, **289**, 289

Ricketts house (CE-232) **330**, 330-31
Riley property (CE-891) **457**, 457
Rising Sun 41, **87**, 105, 131, 132, *132, 133,*
  172, 183, 193, 201
  Cemetery 421
roads 120-31, **124**, **126**
  see also ferries
  Appoquinimink-Bohemia road 29, 30
  Baltimore Pike (U.S. 1) 145
  condition of **43**, 43-44
  early 29, *82,*
  18th century 43-44, *44,* **45**, 123
  government and 126, 127-31, **129**
  highways **128**, 131, 148
  I-95 159
  interstate system 160
  National Road 83
  19th century 120-26, **123**
  overseers 43-44
  petitions for 44, 49
  post 43, 85, 87
  Route 40, **128**, 148, 151, 159
  Route 213 **151**
  State Roads Commission **128**, 129-31, 350
  toll 81
  turnpike/railroad (Pa.) 83
  turnpikes 120, 245
  20th century 126-31
Roanoke Iron & Bridge Works 350
Rock Springs 190
Rock Springs Farm (CE-34) **451**, 451
Rock Spring Farm (CE-176) **358**, 358-59
Rombecca (CE-213) **414**, 414
roof:
  clapboard-covered 195, 202, 250
  common rafter 220
  construction of 219, 220-22
  continental European influence 448
  king post truss **221**, 221-22
  in Penn's house prescription 194
  pent 54, 203, **222-23**, 222
  principal rafter 220-21, **221**
  shingled 195, 202, 250
  shingles 37, 53
  thatched 250
Rosebank Cemetery 468
Rose Hill (CE-27) 93, **177**, 178, **218**, 219, **226**,
  245, **246-47**, 250, 261, 264, **291**, 291-92
  dairy 262
Round Island Lumber Co. 70, 200
Rounds, The (CE-55) 178-79, **178**, **282**, 282
Rowland house (CE-273) **437**, 437
Rowlandsville 89, 114, 449-51
  Clarke Moore house (CE-885) **449**
  Hill house (CE-882) **449**
  McCullough iron workers' houses (CE-886)
    450
Rudolph, Zebulon, house (CE-247) **333**, 333
Rural Electrification Administration 148
St. Augustine Manor 27, 29
St. Francis Xavier Church farmhouse (CE-994)
  292, 292
St. Francis Xavier rectory (CE-60) **283**, 283
St. Georges Creek (Del.) **75**
St. Mary's City 21, 22, 25, 26
St. Mary's Co. **38**
St. Stephen's rectory (CE-412) **297**, 297-98

Sassafras River **8**, 16, 17, 25, 26, 29, 30, 37, 43,
  44, 48, 58, 64, 93, 178, 179, 182, 201,
  219, 251
Savinton *see also* Cecilton 93
Scarborough, Joseph, house (CE-1081) **336**,
  336-67
Scarborough Mill house (CE-537) **337**, 337
schools 107-108, 263, 354, 440
  see also African-American, education
  Bohemia Academy 105, 283
  Center (CE-758) **359**, 359
  Cherry Grove (CE-605) **481**, 481
  Eight Corner or Carter's (CE-662) **106**, 358
  Evandale Home School 438
  Jesuit at Bohemia 40
  Leeds School 107
  Locust Hill Academy (CE-6) **107**, **303**, 303
  Mt. Pleasant Academy 456
  Mt. Zoar (Conowingo #5) (CE-876) **108**, 459
  New Valley (Conowingo #2) (CE-902) **460**,
    460
  School No. 7, Earleville (CE-936) 300-301,
    301
  Oak Grove (CE-428) **387**, 387
  Oakwood No. 4 (CE-871) **456**, 456
  Old Stone 105, 107
  Perryville High **112**, 119
  Pleasant Meadows (CE-1132) **422**, 422
  Port Deposit Academy 431
  Rev. Duke's log (CE-249) **332**, 332
  Rock Academy 371
  on Sassafras Neck 105
  Tome, Jacob, Institute **109**, 109-10, 115,
    213, 431
  Tome School for Boys (CE-1285) **152**, **153**,
    153, **443**, 443-44, 445, 446
  Warwick Academy (CE-992) **296**, 296
  West Nottingham Academy (CE-1164, 1450)
    41-42, 105, **106**, 402, **416**, 416- 17, **422**,
    422
  White Oak (CE-597) **474**, 474
Scots-Irish 41, 44, 163, 169, 201, 208
  arrival in northern Cecil 41
Sealark Farm (CE-9) **299**, 299
Seamon farm (CE-13) **287**, 287
  smokehouse 261
Sears, Roebuck catalog houses 134, **136**, 326
Service School Command 159
service station **127**
settlement of Cecil 24, 25, 27, 28-31, 37, 163, 249
  see also Palmer's Island
  early dwellings 163-64, 193, 227
  frontier conditions 24, 25, 27, 28-29, 30, 53
  land grants (Pa.) 35
  land grants system (Md.) 24-25, 31, 52
  mingling of European cultural traditions 193
  of northern Cecil County 31, 33-34
Shadowbrook (CE-864) **459**, 459
Sharp, Bayard, house (CE-1050) 136, **137**, **327**,
  327
Shenandoah Valley 195
sheriff 43
shipping *see* transportation
Short, Carroll, house (CE-1365) **286**, 286
showboat 322
siding:
  clapboards, riven 37, 194, 195, 250
  on log buildings 203

491

in Penn's house prescription 194
shiplap 195
weatherboards 195, 199
Simcoe, George, house (CE-401) **394**, 394
Simpers house (CE-810) **393**, 393
Simpers log house (CE-1078) **205**, 205, 336
Singerly:
   Fire Co. 130
   mansion *133*
   William M., Steam Fire Engine & Hook & Ladder Co. 130
slaves/slavery *see* African-American
Smithers, Dr., house (CE-323) **312**, 312
Smith's falls **6**, 16, 66, 67, 199
Smyrna (Del.) 95
Society of Friends *see* Quakers, Friends meeting houses
Society of Jesus *see* Jesuit
Somerset Co. (Md.) 51, 170
South Chesapeake City **120**, 120, **152**
Southern Transportation Co. **81**
Spesutie Island 25
Springfield (CE-206) **481**, 481
Spring Hills Farm (CE-1109) **201**
Spring Run Farm (CE-175) **360**, 361
Staats cottages (Port Herman) 324
stairs 229-31
   Chinese-style 182, 237, **238-39**, 278, 304
   ladders as 229, 354
   open balustered 173, 229, 230-31, 240-41
   service 183, 186
   turned baluster 203
   winder 168, 169, 172, **229**, 229-30, 267
Staples house (CE-1325) **337**, 337
state constitution:
   of 1864 104, 105, 108
   of 1867 104
State Roads Commission **128**, 129-31
steamboats 61, *82*, **110**
   Chesapeake **56**, 59
   Eagle **58**
   Elkton Line **58**
   Erikson Line 318
   Lord Baltimore **83**
   Penn **83**
steam locomotives 83
   Delaware 83
Steel Mount (CE-1221) **424**, 424
Still House (CE-393) **381**, 381
stone types in Cecil *see also* quarrying
   Port Deposit granite **212**, 213
   sandstone 213
   Wesahiggin schist 208
Stoney Batter farmhouse (CE-1177) **407**, 407
Stoney Battery (CE-52) **290**, 290
   silo **258**, 258, **290**, 290
Stoney Chase (CE-430) **388**, 388
Stoney Run (CE-1118) **411**, 411
stores:
   Black's (CE-128) 230, **234**, 234, 377, **380**, 380-81
   Bowen & Boulden 317
   Childs (CE-661) **344**, 345
   Crothers's (CE-591) **472**, 472
   Gallaher (CE-1393) **366**, 367
   Haynes (CE-960) **295**, 295
   Laughlin's Market (CE-784) **362**, 362

Mullen, David, log store/Mullen's Folly (CE-81) **468**, 468
Port Herman 324
Ray, J. S. 461
Reed, J. M. (CE-121) **318**, 318-19
Rees's (CE-322) **325**, 325
Roney and Wells Hardware (CE-555) **388**, 388
Slicher (CE-308) **310**, 311
Taylor's (CE-143) **436**, 436
Thomas & Anderson grocery 391
Wallace, Michael 352
Walnut Valley (CE-669) **373**, 373-74
Strawberry Hill (CE-59) **282**, **283**
Stubbs, Dr. Slater B., house (CE-1128) **415**, 415
stube (parlor) 190
Success (CE-913) **447**, 447-48
Summit (Del.) **78**
Susquehanna:
   Canal 66-67, **67**, 73, 85, 203, 212, 213
   Canal Co. 67
   Manor *see* tracts
   River 3, **6**, 9, **9**, **10**, 11, **14**, 16, 17, 18, 19, 23, 28, 32, 37, 40, 49, 57, 64, **65**, 66, **67**, 67, **70**, **72**, 85, 103, 105, **110**, 110, 145, 190, 212, 213
   River Basin Commission 159
   River Bridge Administration Building (CE-997) **151**, 151, 445-46, **446**, 446
   and Tidewater Canal *see* canals
Swan Harbor (CE-20) **292**, 292-93
   carriage house 263, **265**
   icehouse **262**, 262-63
   quarter **267**, 267
   summer kitchen, meat house **262**
Swisher, John, house (CE-39) **175**, 175, **400**, 400
Talbot Co. 92-93
taverns:
   Black Rock (CE-1310) **346**, 346-47
   Blue Ball (CE-191) **43**, **352**, 352-53
   Cather's (CE-1153) 404, **412**, 412-13
   in Charlestown 62, 381
   Chick's 317
   Cross Keys (CE-83) 404, **469**, 469
   Cummings or Battle Swamp (CE-139) 404, **405**, 405-406
   early inn in Elkton 43
   Fair Hill Inn (CE-74) **43**, 208, **211**, **352**, 353, 354
   Fountain Inn 149, **236**, 236
   Gibson's 452
   Hollingsworth Tavern (CE-255) **330**, 330, 331
   Holly Inn (CE-255) **330**, 330
   Indian Queen (CE-127) **43**, **189**, 190, **228**, 229, **377**, 377
   Krauss's or Cross Keys (CE-769) **403**, 403
   licenses for 43
   Nowland's (CE-542) **472**, 472
   Old Sorrel (CE-1415) 424, **425**
   Old Stagecoach Inn (CE-35) **455**, 455
   Mary Palmer's (CE-398) **383**, 383
   Red Ball (CE-76) **186**, 186, **356**, 356
   Red Lyon (CE-128) 230, **234**, 234, 377, **380**, 380-81
   Rock Springs Hotel (CE-867) **452**, 452
   Rodgers (CE-129) **43**, 43, 212, **423**, 423-24
   in 17th century 30, 163
   Stevenson's 43, 423

Union Hotel (CE-1217) 196, **202**, 203, **232**, 232, **425**, 425
taxes 32, 33, 43, 49, 105, 107
   see also quitrent
   for established church 39, 46
tax records 165, 207
Taylor house (CE-1317) **347**, 347
Taylor, Samuel, brick house (CE-1119) **410**, 410
Taylor, Samuel, house (CE-1066) **232**, 232
Taylor's Venture (CE-148) **425**, 425
technology *see also* electricity, telephone
   and dairy farming 142
   domestic innovations in 132,
   innovations in 19th century 61
   water system *130*, 142, 155, **156**
telephone 132, *132*
   Bell Telephone Co. *132*
   Cecil Farmers' Club Telephone Co. *132*
   Diamond State Telephone Co. *132*
telescope house 287
tenancy *see also* housing, tenant
   in colonial period 25, 40, 51-53
   in 19th century 96
Thomas house (CE-399) **391**, 391
Thomas house (CE-767) **424**, 424
Thomas-Physick house (CE-142) **426**, 426
Thompsontown *see* Frenchtown
timber industry *see* lumber industry
tobacco:
   cultivation 37-39, 51, 91, 92
   as currency 39, 43, 46, 48, 49, 201
   houses 37, 38, 96,
   inspection 48-49
   prise 38
   as source of wealth 163-64, 177, 249
   trade 23-24, 29, 37, **38**, 38, 39, 48-49, 65, 250
Tombs, The (CE-900) **455**, 455-56
Tome, Jacob, Institute 444
   see also schools
   Adams Hall (CE-274) **445**, 445
   Italian garden **110**
   Tome Memorial Hall **110**, 110, **443**, 443
   Washington Hall **109**, 109-10
Tome, Jacob, mansion 213, 433
   carriage house (CE-276) **433**, 433
   gas house (CE-279) **433**, 433
Tome schools *see* schools
Torbert, Henry, house (CE-153) **341**, 341
Tory House/107 House (CE-386) **383**, 383-84
Tosh-Basham house (CE-1121) 170, **171**
Tosh house (CE-1171) **413**, 413
Touchstone house (CE-282) **437**, 437
Town Point Farm, DeCoursey house (CE-1051) **314**, 314-15
towns *see also* town names
   development of 44-49, 61-62, 65-66, 67-70, 131
   development and industry 88-89, **93**
   development and railroad 85-87
   pubic space in 46
tracts:
   Alexandria 222
   Amory's Satisfaction 448
   Arbuckle Park 452, 455
   Bateman's Tryall 286
   Bethel 203
   Bohemia Manor 27, 163, 308
   Bohemia Manor Chapel 311

Bourne's Forest Addition 451
Bristole 204
Bullens Range 314
Chamber's Venture 355
Clayfall 49
Clearview 454
Consent 355, 430
Coventry and Mount Rocky 474
Dividing 458
Dougherty's Endeavor 452
Edminston Heights 403, 404
Father's Gift 175, 400
Frisby's Forest 286
Glass House 449
Goshen 162
Green's Delight 451
Hall's Choice 428
Happy Harbor 281
Harmon's Ramble 448
Helmsborough 458
Helmsford 458
Hispaniola 314
Hog's Tract 251
Hollands Choice 457
Hopewell 231, 352
Huckleberry Meadow 454
Independence 411
King's Arm 286
Labadist 186, 308
Leyden 458
Liberty Grove 409
Little Bohemia (Middle Neck) 27
Little Venture 353
Love's Rocky Bottom 448
Meadows, The 413
Mount Hope 358
Mount Montgomery 408
Mount Pleasant 288, 456
New Munster 32, 163, 169, 186, 355
Painter's Rest 284
Paradise 412
Pembrook 448
Price's Adventure 330
St. John's Manor 387
Sligo 222
Smith's Fort 448
Steelman's Delight 430
Steel Mount 424
Susquehanna Manor 31, 32, 49, 163, 169
Wadmore's Neck 383
Ward's Knowledge 296
Welsh Tract 35, 337
White's Plains 478
Worsell Manor 280
tractor 113, 140, **141**
trade *see* commerce
trade routes *see* transportation
transportation *see also* automobile, ferries,
    railroads, roads, steamboats
  of building materials 219, 245, 246
  via C & D Canal **81**
  colonial period 29, *82*

early road network 43, 61
  improvement in 245
  market routes 83, **124**, 125, 131
  between Pennsylvania and South 56, 57, 62, *82*
  stagecoach **56**, 61
  waterborne commerce **56**, 59, 61, **65**, 81, **119**, 119
Transtown *see* Frenchtown 17
Triumph Industries 153-55, **154**, **155**, **156**, 157-58, 159
Trumph house (CE-1175) **407**, 407
Turkey Point 23, *61*
Turkey Point lighthouse 60, *60-61*, **385**, 385
Tyson Mill house (CE-1100) **169**, 169, **355**, 355-56
Tyson-Torbert house (CE-152) **334**, 334
Underwood house (CE-222) **188**, 189, 356-57, **357**
Union Church 205
Union Hospital *133*
Union party 103, 104
United Service Organizations *see* USO
University of Delaware 354
Upland (Chester) (Pa.) 32, 34
Upper Wickwire (CE-929) **299**, 299-300
Ury-Fassitt farm (CE-204) **471**, 471
USF *Constitution* 153
USO *see* World War II
U.S. Constitution 424
U.S. senator
  John A. J. Creswell **104**, 104
Valley, The (CE-1205) **434**, 434
Vanneman house (CE-277) **426**, 427
Vannort house (CE-294) **432**, 432
Veazey, William and Mary, house (CE-186) **381**, 381
Victorian double house (CE-1339) 394, **395**
vineyard 316
Virginia Company 19, 24
Vulcan's Rest (CE-59) 282, **283**
Wade, William, house (CE-1090) **367**, 367
Walker, Hiram, house (CE-1088) **367**, 367
walls:
  beaded board partitions 190
  clapboard partitions 195, 231
  insulated 190, 195-96, **196**, 289
  lath and plaster 199
  raised paneling 232-35, **233**
  vertical board partitions 203, 231-32, **232**, 241
  Walworth house (CE-4) **298**, 298
Walmsley barn 249, 250
Walnut Garden (CE-211) **467**, 467
Walnut Hill (CE-648) 358, **365**, 365
Walnut Lane Farm (CE-795) **382**, 383
Walnut Valley store and house (CE-669) **373**, 373-74
Warburton farm (CE-1260) **465**, 465
Ward's Knowledge (CE-57) **296**, 296-97
War of 1812 57-58, **59**, 61, 67, 288, 358
War of the Spanish succession 39
Warwick 36, 87, 207
Warwick-Tome farmhouse (CE-713) **427**, 427

Washington, D.C. 115, 160
water ram 259
Waterview 460
Watts house (CE-829) **337**, 337
WAVES 159
weaving room 172
wedding business **146**, 146-48, **148**
Welch Point **77**, 78
Welsh Baptist miners 35, 37
West Indies 23, **46**, 49, 62,
wheat/flour trade:
  in colonial period 48, 49
  in 19th century 65
Wheeling (Va.) 83
Whitaker Iron Co. 89, **93**, 431
  office (CE-112) **439**, 439
Whitaker Mansion (CE-113) **440**, 441
White House 112
White, Ira, house (CE-1188) **418**, 418
Whiteoak Farm 325
White's Plains Farm (CE-609) **478**, 478
Wickwire (CE-30) **287**, 287
Willowdale (CE-218) 172-73, **173**, **401**, 401
Wilmington 22, **58**, 85, 103, 131, *130*, *133*, 160
Wilna (CE-181) **329**, 329
Wilson double house (CE-178) **334**, 334-45
Wilson house (CE-985) 267
Wilson house (CE-1199) **410**, 410-11
Wilson, John, house (CE-177) **334**, 334
Wilson, John P., farm (CE-604) **480**, 480-81
  barn **480**, 481
  tenant house **480**, 481
Wilson-Quinn house (CE-1350) **288**, 288
Wilson tenant house (CE-985) **294**, 294
Wilson Victorian house (CE-264) **421**, 421
Winchester Hotel (CE-1423) **434**, 435
Windfields Farm 159
Winterthur 376
Wirt, John, house (CE-1315) **347**, 347
Woodlands (CE-145) **432**, 432
Woodlawn (CE-25) **295**, 295
Woodrow house (CE-1214) 190, **191**
Woodrow, Simeon, house (CE-371) **404**, 404
Woodstock Farm 159
Works Progress Administration 148
World's Columbian Exposition 134
World War I **126**, 131, 134, 136, **138**, 139-40, **140**, **141**, 349
World War II 60, *133*, **136**, 136, 140, **141**, *146*, **152-57**, 153-59, **159**, 160, **161**, 349, 445
  see also Chesapeake City, Elkton, Port Deposit, Triumph Industries
  Operation Elkton *146*
  USO **156**, 158-59
Worsell Manor (CE-58) 180-81, **181**, 184, 187, **279**, 279-80
Wright house (CE-1354) **301**, 301
Wright, Lana, house (CE-304) **306**, 307
York Co. (Pa.) 109
Zebley farmhouse (CE-773) **363**, 363
Zion brick house (CE-756) 474, **475**

Name Index

Bold page numbers refer to captions in chapters 1-6 and to photographs in chapters 7-10 and the inventory; italic page numbers refer to sidebars in chapters 1-6.

Abraham the Finn 26, 201
Abrahams family 413
Adams, James 322
Addison family 401
Alexander:
   family 329
   Reuben 448
   Reuben, Jr. 455
   Robert 328, 338
   Samuel 315
Alfred, Arthur J. 371
Allen:
   Lewis 253, 257
   Margaret 16-17
   Samuel 177
Alsop, George 1, 28
Antigua:
   Moses 219
   Philip 219
Argall, Samuel 24
Armitage, Mr. 245
Armstrong, A. J. 360
Asbury, Francis 332
Atmore, Mr. 219
Bacon, Francis 25
Bailey, William 474
Bainbridge, Comm. William 153
Balderston, Lloyd 412
Baldwin:
   family 374
   John 278
   William 365, 368-69
Barnes:
   George W. **63**
   Harry **63**
Barry, A. L. 389
Bateman, John 423
Bayard:
   family 309
   Mary Sophia 322
   Richard 312
   Richard H. 310, 322
   Sen. Thomas F. **142**, 326
Beaston:
   Charles 310
   Sara 310
Beatty, Arthur 387
Beaven, J. W. 433
Becker, Bishop Thomas 321
Beeks:
   John L. 298
   William T. 298
Bell, James Heriot 459
Bemis, John 360
Benjamin, Asher 97, 332
Beverly, Robert 9

Biddle:
   family 324
   Noble 307
   Noble T. 316
   Owen 244
   Thomas 207, 257
Bigger, Peacock 381
Biggs, Joseph 293
Biles, William 479
Black, William 51
Blackburn family 429
Blackway family 303
Bladen, Gov. Thomas **46**
Blake, George A. *133*
Bland, William 284
Boden, Marguerite du Pont de Villiers 304
Booth, Ebenezer 165
Bordley, John Beale 91, 92
Bouchell, Peter 263, 315
Boulden:
   Alonza 318
   family 317
   James A. 321
   Thomas, Jr. 307
   William W. 314
Bowen family 317
Bownas, Samuel 31
Bradford:
   Henry 327
   Phoebe George 93
Brady, Henry H. 321
Bragg, Gen. Braxton 329
Bratton:
   Daniel 346
   family 338
   Howard **135**, 348
Brickley:
   Jehoiakim and Agnes 407
   John 415
Brinton, Daniel 9
Bromwell:
   Dr. Robert 429
   William 429
Brookings:
   Dr. Richard 88, 363
   Dr. Robert 416
   Robert 363, 378
Brown:
   David 458
   family 468
   Howard 481
   James **33**, 40
   Jeremiah 208, 215, 465, 466-67
   Jeremiah, Sr. 49, 481
   Mercer Jr. 465, 481
   Mercer Sr. 465
   Mercer and Hannah **33**, 214-15, 465
   William 40, 201, 208, 464
Bryan:
   Charles A. 318
   Richard 318

Bryson, William and Lydia 389
Burgett
   H. **89**
   Harvey 319
Burns, Charles M., Jr. 322
Burnside, Thomas *82*
Burr, Theodore *82*
Byers, John S. & Annie E. *133*
Calvert:
   Cecil 355
   Cecilius 27, 31
   Charles 46
   family 21, 23, 24
   Gov. Leonard 22
   Gov. Philip 28
Cameron, William 478
Camlin, James 165
Campbell, Colen 180
Carpenter, William 25
Carroll:
   John 40, 283
   Charles 40
   Charles of Carrollton 283
Carter:
   Charles Lee 335
   family 356
   Israel Day 335, 371
   Robert 88, **107**, 335, 358, 365, 367
   Robert D. 335
   Robert Sr. 363, 365
Cather, Robert 412
Caulson, Jacob 28
Chalkey, Thomas 40, 464
Chandlee:
   Benjamin 215, 465, 466
   Benjamin Sr. and Jr. 464
   Ellis G. 434
   Sarah 466
Chaytor, Osborn R. *130*
Chick:
   Mrs. Mary 316
   Peregrine 316
Childs:
   George **116**, 118
   George W. 345, 346
Christie, Capt. James 433
Christy family 408
Churchman:
   Amassa 465
   George 464, 481
   John **54**, 54, 168, 464
   John "the Immigrant" 464
   John III 464
Claiborne, William 19, 21-22, **23**, 23
Clausen, Baron von 57
Clayton, Col. Joshua 314
Clement, Hiram 475
Coale, William 49, 481
Cockburn, Rear Admiral George 57
Congdon, Henry 348

Conner:
    Comm. David 454
    Susan Dillwyn 454
Conrey:
    family **96**
    Thomas 317, 319
Cook:
    Bill 476
    William 203, 227, 232
Cookson, Samuel 404
Cooling, Walter **81**
Cosgrove:
    E. 434
    William 205, 385
Cottey, Abel 466
Coudon:
    family 432
    Joseph II 433
Coulson:
    Deborah Bromwell 438
    George J. A. 438
    Dr. Robert 438
Cowen:
    Benjamin 357, 363
    Mrs. J. 360
    William 357, 363
Craig, David 428
Crawford family 384
Creswell:
    John 428
    John A. J. **104**, 104, 340, 424
Cristie, Mr. 88
Cromwell:
    family 447
    John Hammond 448
    Oliver 23
Cropper:
    Absalom 318
    Capt. Kendall 311
    Kendall 318
    William 318
Crothers:
    Alpheus 458
    Gov. Austin Lane **128**, 129-30, 145, 416, 458
    James 467
    John 467
Cruikshank:
    Dr. H 298
    family 297
    Francis B. 299
Cummings:
    family 457
    Samuel 360
Curry:
    John 388
    Joseph 388
Danckaerts, Jasper 29, 30, 163, 227, 249
Dare, William 383
Davis:
    David **46**
    family 285, 408
    H. C. **127**
    Dr. Henry V. 320
    J. A. 438
    John Ward 296
    Rebecca 454
Day, John 215, 465
Daye, John 469

Deaver, Joshua M. 414
DeCoursey:
    family 322
    Samuel W. 314
Denorritees, John 202
Dixon:
    Jeremiah **34**, 35, 331
    Thomas 302
Donahoo, John *60*
Downing, Andrew Jackson 100, 245, 316
Duckett, Mrs. Elizabeth 371
Duke, Rev. William 332
Dunbar, Andrew 455
du Pont:
    family 363, 366
    Henry 362
    Mrs. Richard 159, **161**, 310
    William 362, 368, 375
Dutton, Robert 49
Early, Gen. Jubal 103
Ellis, Francis 107
Ellsbury, Benjamin 264
Emmons, Ira 428
England:
    Charles 479
    Elisha 203, 227, 232, 476
    Howard 479
    Ian 476
    Isaac 471
    Isaac H. 471
    Job 476
    John 50-51, 476
    Lewis 476
    Samuel 203, 215, 465, 481
    Samuel J. 479, 481
Enos, Samuel B. *130*
Epinette, Father Peter 321
Etherington:
    Bartholomew 205
    Elizabeth 205
    family 53, 228, 264
    John 205
    John Ward 205
    Susannah 205
    William G. 293
Evans:
    brothers 411
    family 399
    James 436
    James M. 417
    John 51, 357, 358, 436
    John and Isabelle 369
    John R. 359
    Robert 357-58, 436, 438
Ewing:
    family 406
    James 366
    Joshua 458
    Murray J. **129**
    Nathaniel 458
    Patrick **36**, 178
Farrer, Virginia **21**
Fassitt, Thomas 471
Fell, Benjamin 430
Finley:
    family 360
    Rev. James 371
    Martha 346

    Rev. Samuel 41, 43, 416
    Rev. and Sara 402
Fisher:
    Charles Henry 284
    Sidney George 93-96, **94, 95,** 219, 223, 236, 245-46, 251-52, 257, 278, 281, 284, 291, 304
Fleet, Henry 19
Foard, Lambert 383
Footner, Hubert 149
Ford:
    Henry **127**
    John 382
Forman:
    Gen. Thomas Marsh 93, 177, 187-88, 200, 291, 219, 245, 264
    Martha Ogle 93, 177, 187-188, 291, 196, 200, 219, 245, 250, 261, 262, 263, 264
Foulks:
    Benjamin S. 315
    William S. 315
Fox, John and Charles 434
France, Evalyn Tome 442
Franklin, Maj. Gen. William B. 103
Frey, John 457
Frisby:
    family 285
    James 31
    Mr. 29-30
Fullerton, Hugh 200
Fulton:
    Alexander 448
    Thomas 354
    William 354, 357
Furst, Frank
Gale, George 424
Gallagher, Stephen 367
Gallaher, John 366
Garfield, Pres. James, wife of 333
Garrett, Thomas 356
Gassaway, Robert 313
Gayley family 411
Geddes, James *60*
George:
    Joshua 53, 267
    Sidney 94, 205
    Sidney, Jr. 304
Gerry:
    family 418
    James 408
    Mary 408
    Robert and Cornelia 408
Gifford, Benjamin 389
Gillespie:
    George 41, 418
    Samuel 297
    Thomas 4
    W. E. 4
    William 458
Gilmor, Maj. Henry 103
Gilpin:
    family 340, 343
    John *82,* 316
Ginn family 289
Givens family 346
Gough, Harry Dorsey 92
Graham:
    John 408, 449

495

William Jr. 449
William Sr. 449
Grant:
    William 367
    Gen. U. S. 103
    Pres. U. S. 104, 340, 426
Gray, Robert 11
Green, B. J. 299
Griffith:
    Araminta 319
    William 391
Grove:
    family 289
    Joseph T. 482
    Lalla Blanche 482
Hadden family 324
Hager, Henry **136**, 326
Haig, William 32
Haines:
    family 408
    Joseph 401, 475
    Nathan 401
    Rebecca 412
    William and Lydia 401
Halfpenny, William and John **238**, 278
Hall:
    Andrew 165
    Elihu 195
    family 453, 460
    Ralph **13**
Hallowel, Elizabeth 455
Halsey, Admiral *146*
Hamilton:
    Dr. Alexander 249
    Rev. John 379
Hamm:
    Ann 383
    Noble 383
Hammond family 447
Handburg, Mr. 245
Harlan:
    George 333
    John 333
    John [Jr.] 333
Harlon, Mr. 88
Harriott, William 310
Harris:
    Charles 409
    Nathan and Susannah 403
Hart:
    Ann 383
    James 383
    Jannett 383
Hartshore, Lucy Hempstead 462
Harvey family 342
Hauducoeur, Christian 67, 67, **69**
Haynes, William 295
Hazel family 324
Hedrick, Joseph 320
Helms, Michael 458
Hempstead, Joshua 48, 51, 201-202, 208, 462
Henderson, Joseph 361-62
Henricks, John 17
Henry, Gov. John 416
Henshaw, Amos 458
Herman:
    Augustine **27**, 27, 28, 29, 31, 32, 163, 193, 201, 227, 308, 309, 311, 324, 326, 327

Caspar 29
E. A. 201
Ephraim 29, 31
Hessey, John H. 300
Hicks, Elias 411
Hilaman, Amanda Fitzallen 478
Hipple, Edward 316
Hogan, Thomas 264
Hogg, Samuel 382
Holland, John 48
Holliday, John 165
Hollingsworth:
    family 66, 216-17
    Col. Henry 330, 334
    Henry 250
    Stephen 352
    Zebulon 165, 190, 330, 377
Holt, Isaac 227
Holy, Robert 352
Homann, John B. **19**
Hopkins:
    Dr. Joseph 475
    W. F. **146**
Horton:
    Jesse 463
    Thomas 463
Howard, Ernest A. 460
Howe, Gen. William 57, 330
Hudson, Henry 19
Hughes:
    Elisha 469
    Capt. James 312
    Thomas 469
Hunt, Marshall I. 415
Husbands, William 456
Husfelt, Daniel 300
Hutton:
    family 259
    Francis Clopper 131
Irwin, Matthew 457
Jackson:
    Andrew 278, 338
    brothers 303, 481
    James 360
Jeffers, Herman *130*
Jefferson, Thomas 334, 423
Job, Andrew 352
Johnson:
    Arthur 125
    Col. Bradley T. 103
    family 227, 388
    George 390
    Henry 31
    Gen. Joseph 329
    Thomas 91
    Capt. William 416
    William 387
Johnston, George 332
Jones:
    Daniel 293
    Edward 31
    Comm. Jacob 290
    John 457
    John L. K. 223, 256
    Thomas 223, 256, 257, 281
Judd, Maj. Henry B. 103
Kankey, John 379
Karsner, Dr. William C. 323

Keilholtz, Charles 414
Keithley, William 457
Kennedy, Pres. 159
Kent, James 65
Kershaw family 142
Key:
    Francis **46**
    Francis Scott **46**
Kilvington, Samuel 357
Kimble family 438
King Charles II 31, 328
King Georges 179
King James 24
King James II 32
King William and Queen Mary 34, 39
King William IV 432
Kinter family 326
Kirk:
    Elisha 470
    Elisha and Susan 478
    George **107**
    Jonathan 470
    Joseph 470
    Levi 473
    Mary 470
    Nathan 470
    Rachel 470
    Roger 172, 207, 462
    William 469, 470
Kite, William Penn 371
Knight:
    Charles D. 316
    family 297
    William 267, 293, 294
    William and Elizabeth 215, 464
Krauss:
    family 409
    Leonard 404, 469
Kreider, Jacob 384
Labadie, John 308
Lafayette 57, 331, 353, 411, 423, 426
Lafever, Minard 97
Lamdin, William J. 438
Latrobe:
    Benjamin Henry **14**, **31**, **46**, **56**, **59**, **67**, 67, 73-78, **75**, **77**,, 332
    Charles H. 123, 419, 460, 461
    John H. B. ii, **199**
Layman, Capt. Firman 310
Layton, Bishop 322
Le Corbusier 149
Lee, Gen. Robert E. 103
Leffler, F. H. *130*
Levis, Norris 365
Lewis:
    James A. 316
    Mr. 88
    Samuel 36
Linch, David 467
Lincoln:
    Abel T. 475
    Pres. Abraham 103
Linton, William 382
Lofland, W. H. 304
Logue, Ephraim 194
Long, John 325
Lord, Daniel 89, **90**, 332, 365, 368-69, 374

Lord Baltimore 22, 24, **27**, 27, 31-32, 34, **35**, 44, **46**, 46, 48, 195, 308
Lort, Joseph 388
Louttit, Mary 304
Lowe:
  Elizabeth and Jesse 454
  Joshua 454
Lusbie, Miss 281
Lusby:
  Elizabeth *60*
  John 281
  Robert *60*
Lyle, Peter 316
MacArthur, Gen. *146*
Machaloha 17
Mackall:
  Richard 329
  Dr. Richard 329
  William 329
Mackey:
  Col. David 352, 354
  family 324, 365, 366, 372
  Howard 360
  Capt. James 352, 354
  James 352
  Sgt. James 353
  Robert 352, 353, 360
  1st Lt. William 354
Mackie:
  family 351, 365, 372
  Franklin T. 352, 371
  Thomas 328
Madison, James 57, 423
Maffit, Samuel 107
Magraw, H. S. 419
Malone:
  Andrew 222
  John 222
Manley, Nicholas 385
Markee, Jacob 369
Markham, William 32
Martenet, Simon J. *82*
Martin, Gov. 416
Martindale, Martha 312
Mason, Charles **34**, 35, 331
Matthews, W. R. 476
Mauldin, John 387, 389
Maxwell, James H. 421
McCardell, S. M. 420, 460
McCauley, James 107, 339
McCleary:
  John 355
  Thomas 355
  William 355
McClenahan:
  Ebenezer 115
  family **212**, 213
  John 442
McCologh, Andrew 227
McCoy, Henry 360
McCracken:
  John 391
  John James 358
McCullough:
  Clinton 430
  Enoch 457
  George 420
  J. 457

Jethro 369, 392, 456
Joseph 366
Penrose 252, 253
McDowell:
  Rev. Alexander 354
  family 429
McIntire:
  Andrew Jr. 337
  Andrew Sr. 337
McKinney, C. W. **124**
McKown brothers 134, **135**
McLane:
  Louis 278, 294
  Robert Milligan 278
McNamee, Frederick 455
McQulkin, George 335
McVey, Henry 455
Mearns:
  Abel 473
  Dr. James A. 476
  Levi Ross 478
Megredy, John 384, 411
Meteer:
  family 366
  Mrs. Hannah 88
  Samuel 362
  William 362
Meisel, Adam *130*
Menendez, Pedro 15
Menendez-Marques, Pedro 15
Merrick, Samuel V. **78**
Meyors, Peter 28
Mifflin, Benjamin 214
Miller:
  Abraham 165
  Alice E. 447
  Benjamin 165
  Dr. Charles Francis 482
  Mrs. F. 359
  H. D. 359
  Joseph 367
  Lydia Maria 390
Milligan:
  George **53**, 53, 216, 278
  Robert 278
Mitchell:
  Dr. Abraham 331, 353
  Edward 378
  Col. George Edward 353
Mitchels, Mr. 208
Moll:
  Herman **19**
  John 163, 227
Money, Jesse 207
Moody, John 227
Moon, W. R. 146
Moore:
  Clarke 449
  Gabriel and Sarah 370
  George F. 430
  John 414
  William 399, 401
More, Will 433
Morgan, James 205, 249
Morris:
  Robert 332
  Roger 180
Morrison, Matthew 408

Moutton family 434
Mullen, David 468
Murphy, Mrs. 425
Nairne, Thomas 37
Nesbitt:
  Henry Clay 442
  John Allison 409
  Joseph 407
  Mrs. 442
  Moses 407, 409
  Robert 409
  Samuel 407
Nesbit, William 434
Nice family 401
Niles, Hezekiah 67
Norwood, Colonel 6
O'Dwire, Edwin 32, 355
Onion, Stephen 50
Orr, Nevin 419
Paca:
  John **46**, 378
  John B. and Juliana *60*
  Gov. William 378
Painter:
  Mr. 252
  Nicholas 328
Palmer:
  Edward 19, 105
  Mary 383
Parker, Donald 367
Partridge, John 87, 357
Passmore, E. P. 474
Patten:
  Thomas 213, 409
  T. and M. 427
Patterson, Sarah E. 420
Peale:
  Charles Willson **46**, 380
  Margaret Jane 380
Pearce, Anna 196
Penn:
  family 354
  William 17, 31-32, **33**, 33, 34, **35**, 163, 171, 193, 355, 402, 416, 462, 465
  Admiral William 31
Pennington:
  Abraham 449
  family 315
  Hyland B. 286
Perkins, Dr. 294
Physick:
  family 426
  Henry White 453
  Dr. Philip Syng 453-54
Pierson, Wilson D. 123, 346, 460, 461
Pinna 28
Plowden, Sir Edward 24
Plumstead, Edward 462, 465
Pocahontas 23
Porter:
  Andrew 448
  Benjamin 166, 223
  James Leiper 448
  Sarah 460
  W. E. 460
Post family 409
Potter, William S. 123, 346, 460, 461
Preston, Amos 414

497

Price:
    Ben 285
    Hyland 195, 249
    Mary 207
    Noble 207
    William 295, 329
    William IV 306
Prins, Governor 26
Printz:
    Gov. Johan 201
    Johan 22
Pryor, John T. 393
Pulfield, George 31
Pyle, Jesse 415
Queen Anne 378
Quexos, Pedro de 15
Quinn family 281, 288
Ragan, Dr. David 457
Ramsay, Andrew 416
Ramsey, Nathaniel **46**, 380
Randal, John, Jr. 308
Randel, John, Jr. 78, 336
Rawlings:
    Elizabeth Taggart 454
    family 190, 438
    Rebecca 454
    Z.T. 454
Ray:
    J.S. 461
    John and William 464
Rea, David 430
Reed:
    John M. 318
    Mrs. 314
Rees, Ralph H. 321, 325
Reese, Morris 467
Revere, Paul 358
Reynolds:
    Benjamin 404
    family 402, 408, 409
    Henry 401, 465
    Jacob 401
    Joseph 481
    Joseph and Rebecca 401
    Mabel 404
    Mary 385, 390
Richards:
    Dr. G. H. 426
    Dr. Hampton G. 403
    Joseph T. 403
    Thomas Jr. 404
    Thomas Sr. 403
Richardson:
    Joseph 257
    Richard 257
    William 257
Rickards, Mr. (Mt. Harmon) 95, 252
Ricketts:
    family 330, 331
    Dr. John *82*
Riley family 457
Ritchie, Gov. Albert 145
Rochambeau, Comte de 57, 423
Rodgers:
    Comm. Geo. Washington 424
    Commodore John 424
    John 43, 423
Rogers, Thomas 457

Rolfe, John 23, 24
Rolls, Hezikiah 215
Roman, Joseph 457
Roosevelt, Franklin Delano 148
Ross, Eliza 310
Rousby, Christopher 33
Rowan, W. P. 289
Rowland:
    family 408, 436, 449
    James 437
    James Harvey 445
    Madison 199
    Stephen 175
Rowls, Hezekiah 465
Rudolph:
    Maria 333
    Tobias 333
    Zebulon 332, 333
Rumsey family 282
Rush, Dr. Benjamin 43, 416, 422
Russell:
    Ann 388
    Thomas 50
    William 50
St. Rose of Lima 321
Salter, Mrs. C. W. (Fannie) **61**, *61*
Sartin family 313
Savin, William 195
Scarborough, Joseph and Sarah 336
Schultz, James 318
Scott:
    family 359
    Howard 369
    John 360
    Joseph 65
Seamon family 287
Sentman, Ellis 123, 346, 460, 461
Sewall:
    Gen. James 333
    James 242, 332
Shade, Sebastian **67**, *67*
Sharp:
    Bayard 327
    Rodney 136, **137**
Sharpe, Governor 10
Sherer, Robert M. 365
Short, Carroll 286
Simms, James Peacock 302
Simpers:
    J. 393
    Mrs. 205, 336
Singerly:
    William 119, 124, *130*, 371
    William M. 372
Skinner, John S. 93
Slicher, Andrew 311
Sloan, Joseph H. 349 or 350 [ck final]
Sluyter, Peter 29, 30, 31
Smith:
    Capt. 200
    Edwin B. 391
    John 310
    John (saddler) **46**
    (Capt.) John 1, **6**, 6, 15-16, **17**, 17-19, 32, 66, 207, 249
    Father Roger 456
    Thomas 21
    William 49

Smithers, Dr. 312, 318
Smithson, Rumsey, Sr. 434
Spelman, Henry 6
Staats family 324
Staples:
    Louise 337
    Seth 337
Starr:
    Jeremiah 314
    Mary Ann 314
Steel:
    Hugh 429
    James 424
    John 434
Steele:
    J. **120**
    John 201
    Joseph H. 320
Steelman, John Hanson 17, 330
Steppe family 409
Sterritt-Christie family 433
Stewart, James 165
Stites, Henry S. 384
Stockett, Capt. Thomas 28
Stockton, Richard 416, 422
Strahorn, William 368
Strawbridge, John 353
Strickland:
    Price 338
    William 78
Stubbs, Dr. Slater B. 415
Stump:
    family 139
    Thomas 64
Stuyvesant, Peter 26
Swagart, John 458
Swisher:
    John 400
    John, Jr. 400
Tailler, Thomas 32
Talbot, George 31, 32-34, 49, 355
Taylor:
    David M. 313
    family 347, 436
    George W. 434
    Samuel 410
    Thomas 424
Teague:
    Edward 448
    William 449
Tesla, Nikola 142
Thomas:
    Philip 67, 424, 426
    Judge Richard 391
    Richard *130*, 389
    Robert 324
    William 43
Thompson:
    Richard 315
    Robert 200
Thorowgood, Cyprian 10, 16, 21, 249
Tilton, Dr. James 462
Tollum, John 476
Tome:
    Evalyn Nesbitt 431, 442
    Jacob **109**, 109-10, **110**, **213**, 213, 418, 427, 431, 440-41, 442, 444
Tomkins, John 21-22

Tong, Thomas 371
Torbert:
 Henry R. 341
 Martha 334
 William 341
Tosh, John 413
Towne, John H. **78**
Trumph, M. and R. 407
Tucker, John M. 131
Tully, Edward **46**
Turner, Jan 25, 201
Tweed, James 369
Tyson:
 Levy 334
 Matthias 356
Underwood, John G. 357
Ury family 471
Utie, Col. Nathaniel 25
Valenzuela, Ismail **161**
van Bibber:
 Isaac 49
 Matthias 352
Vanderbush, Rev. Mr. 39
Van der Donck, Adriaan 19
Vanneman, John 427
Vannort family 432
Van Sant, George R. 295
Vaughan, Robert 21-22
Vaux, Calvert 100
Veazey:
 Edward 284
 family 290, 297
 Dr. John Thompson 289
 Thomas Ward 166, 267

William and Mary 381
Verazzano, Giovanni de 1, 15
Villiger, Father George 292
Wade, William 367
Walker, Hiram 367
Wallace:
 family 329
 Matthew 355
 Michael 335, 352
Walmsley, Benjamin 249
Walworth family 298
Warburton, William 142, 398
Ward:
 Col. John 281
 Henry 31
 John 166
 Joshua 223
 Peregrine II 281
Waring, Thomas 411
Warren, Joseph 356
Warwick, John 427
Washington:
 Augustine 51
 George 57, 330, 380, 382, 404, 424
 George and Martha 423
Wasyczuk, Paul 326
Watmore, John 383
Watts family 337
Weld:
 Isaac 44, *44*
 Isaac, Jr. 200, 203
Wetherill, Alfred 340
Whitaker, George P. **93**, 441
White:

 Ira 418
 William 215, 465
Whitefield, George 41
Wiley, Rev. David 93
William and Mary *see* King William
Williams, Frank 318
Williamson, James 264
Williar, H. D. 350
Wilsey, Dr. Edward 324
Wilson:
 Alexander 383
 Charles W. 421
 family 288
 Hannah 334
 John 333, 334
 John P. 480
 Rev. John 334
 Thomas 465
 William 284, 294, 411
Wirt, John 347
Woodrow, Simeon 404
Wright:
 Frank Lloyd 149
 Lana 307
 Lawrence 301
Wroth, James 205
Wye, Rev. William 46
Young:
 Edgar P. 142
 Jacob 49
 James 251
 Col. Samuel 105
 William 251

Index by Inventory Number

Bold page numbers refer to captions in chapters 1-6 and to photographs in chapters 7-10 and the inventory.

3	Price, Ben, hotel **285**, 285	21	Essex Lodge **98**, 100, **297**, 297	34	Rock Springs Farm **451**, 451
4	Walworth house **298**, 298	22	St. Stephen's Church 40, **302**, 302	35	McVey Hotel **455**, 455, 473
5	The Hideaway **287**, 287-88	23	St. Paul's Methodist Church **303**, 303	35	Old Stagecoach Inn **455**, 455
6	Locust Hill Academy **107**, **303**, 303	24	Mount Pleasant **288**, 288	38	Old Fort Smith house **174**, 175, **221**, 221, **448**, 448
8	Happy Harbor **281**, 281	25	Woodlawn **295**, 295	39	John Swisher house **175**, 175, **400**, 400
9	Herndon/Sealark Farm **299**, 299	26	Mount Harmon 38, 93, **94-95**, 223, 236, 251-53, **304**, 304	40	Patrick Ewing house 179-80, **179**
11	Brick House Farm **286**, 286	27	Rose Hill 93, **177**, 178, **218**, 219, **226**, 245, **246-47**, 250, 261, **262**, 264, **291**, 291-92	41	Octorara 224, 224, **252**, 253, **259**, **262**, 262, **453**, 453-54
12	Frisby's Prime Choice **217**, 217, **285**, 285	28	Grove farm **263**, 263, **288**, 289	42	McCullough Rolling Mill **456**, 456-57
13	Seamon farm 261, **287**, 287	29	Rich Neck/Frisby's Delight **178**, 179, **289**, 289	43	Greek Revival stone house **428**, 428
15	William G. Etherington house **293**, 293	30	Wickwire **287**, 287	44	Evans house **436**, 436
16	Greenfields 180, 182-83, **184**, 216, **217**, **280**, 280-81	31	Cruikshank house **301**, 301	45	New Valley Factory **406**, 406
17	Bloomingdale 179-80, **180** [ck revised]	32	Bohemia (Milligan Hall) **53**, 53, 180, 181-82, **182-83**, 183, 187, **216**, 216, **217**, 236-40, **237-39**, 267, 278-79, **279**	46	Hall's Choice **428**, 428
18	Indian Range **256**, 256			49	Locust Thicket **286**, 286
19	The Anchorage **290**, 290	33	St. Stephen's Church 40, **302**, 302	50	Cherry Grove **166**, 166-67, 195, 207, 267, **284**, 284-85, 447
20	Swan Harbor **262**, 262-63, 263, **265**, **267**, 267, **292**, 292-93	33	Grubb property **452**, 452	51	Price-Murphy house 197-99, **198**, 200,
		34	Samuel Porter house **451**, 451-52	52	Stoney Battery **258**, 258, **290**, 290
				54	Bohemia Manor ruins **309**, 309
				55	The Rounds 177-78, **178**, **282**, 282

499

56 Linden Manor **284**, 284	119 Bayard House **310**, 310	205 William and Elizabeth Knight house **215**, 215, **464**, 464
57 Ward's Knowledge **296**, 296-97	120 Franklin Hall **96**, 316-17, **317**	
58 Worsell Manor 180-81, **181**, 184, 187, **279**, 279-80	121 Reed, J. M., Store **318**, 318-19	206 Chalkley's Garden **481**, 481
	122 Rees house and office **321**, 321	206 Springfield **481**, 481
59 Vulcan's Rest 282, **283**	122 Brady, Henry H., house and office **321**, 321	207 Isaac England house **470**, 470-71
59 Strawberry Hill 282, **283**		208 Long Green Farm **467**, 467
60 Old Bohemia Church 282-83, **283**	123 Conrey, Thomas, house **318**, 319	209 Roger Kirk house 171-72, **172**, 193, 194, 207, 220, 228, 229, **462**, 462
60 St. Francis Xavier Church 282-83, **283**	124 Old Lock Pump House **78**, **311**, 311	
60 St. Francis Xavier rectory **283**, 283	125 Bohemia Hill **315**, 315	210 Lickingbank Farm **473**, 473
61 Quinn house **281**, 281	126 Bohemia Vineyards **316**, 316	211 Walnut Garden **467**, 467
63 old brick house, St. Augustine **309**, 309	126 Elklands **316**, 316	212 Maple Shade Farm 229, **403**, 403
64 St. Augustine's Episcopal Church **311**, 311-12	127 Indian Queen **43**, **189**, 189-90, **228**, 229, **377**, 377	213 Gillespie house **414**, 414
		213 Rombecca **414**, 414
65 Great House 186-87, **187**, 234-35, **235**, **308**, 308	128 Red Lyon 230, **234**, 234, 377, **380**, 380-81	216 Haines house**172**, 172, 173, 193, **194**, **228**, 228, **229**, **254**, 254, **400**, 400-401
67 Randalia **308**, 308	128 Black's Store 230, **234**, 234, 377, **380**, 380-81	
68 Howard house 308-309, **309**		217 Haines-Reynolds farmhouse **408**, 408
69 Brantwood **220**, 220, **313**, 313-14	129 Rodgers **43**, 43, 212, **423**, 423-24	218 Willowdale/Joseph Haines house 172-73, **173**, **401**, 401
70 Thomas Mackie house 232-33, **233**, **328**, 328-29	131 Holly Hall 242-45, **243-44**, **332**, 332, 426	
	132 Elk Landing Farm **329**, 329-30	220 Kirk's Mill **476**, 476
71 Wallace-Carter Mill **335**, 335	133 Kieffer brick house **330**, 331	221 Chantilly Country Club **474**, 474
72 The Beehive 208, **209**, **352**, 352	135 James and Rachel Cameron house **405**, 405	222 Underwood house **188**, 189, 356-57, **357**
73 Rock Presbyterian Church **41**, 41, 43, 208, **210**, **370**, 370-71	136 Brickley Mill **407**, 407	226 West Nottingham Chapel **419**, 419-20
	136 Jehoiakim and Agnes Brickley house **407**, 407	227 West Nottingham Presbyterian Church **415**, 415-16
74 Fair Hill Inn **43**, 208, **211**, **352**, 353, 354		
76 Red Ball Tavern **186**, 186, **356**, 356	139 Cummings or Battle Swamp 404, **405**, 405-406	228 West Nottingham (Little Brick) Friends meetinghouse 41, 44, **404**, 404
77 Evans house **357**, 357-58		
78 Gilpin's Falls covered **390**, 390	140 Anchor and Hope farmhouse 212	229 Nathan and Susannah Harris house **176**, 176, 220-21, **221**, **240**, 240-41, **403**, 403, 404
79 Bay View fieldstone house **383**, 383	141 Moore-Reynolds Mill property **401**, 401	
80 Abel Mearns house **473**, 473	142 Mount Ararat **426**, 426	
81 Mullen's Folly **468**, 468	142 Thomas-Physick house **426**, 426	230 Thomas Richards house **402**, 402-403
81 David Mullen log store **468**, 468	143 Taylor's Store **436**, 436	231 Richards house **404**, 404
82 East Nottingham (Brick) Friends meetinghouse **33**, 35, 40-41, **54**, 54, 57, **208**, 208, 214, 215, **221**, 221-22, 462- 64, **463**	144 Ellerslie **433**, 433	232 Encatada/Ricketts house **330**, 330-31
	145 Woodlands **432**, 432	233 Elk Forge bridge **346**, 346
	147 Belvidere **389**, 389	234 Pleasant View Farm/Grove-Miller farm **482**, 482
	148 Taylor's Venture **425**, 425	
83 Cross Keys Tavern 404, **469**, 469	149 Mitchell house, Elkton 217, 330, **331**, 331	237 Bradford house **327**, 327
84 Elisha Kirk house **241**, 241, 405, **470**, 470	152 Tyson-Torbert house **334**, 334	238 Big Elk Creek covered bridge **368**, 368
86 Federal brick house, Calvert **471**, 471	153 Henry Torbert house **341**, 341	240 William Knight tenant house 166, **206**, 207
87 Dr. Joseph Hopkins house **475**, 475	157 221-23 East Main St., Elkton **341**, 341	241 Rock Run Mill 49, **49**, **434**, 435
88 Mercer and Hannah Brown house **214**, 214-15, **465**, 465	162 Gilpin Manor **340**, 340	246 Partridge Hill **217**, 230, **231**, 235, 236, 241, **330**, 330, 331
	166 Baldwin house 254-56, **256**, 369, 368-69	
89 Jesse Brown house **468**, 468	168 Baldwin Manufacturing Co. 365, **374**, 374	247 Zebulon Rudolph house **333**, 333
90 Brown house **471**, 471	170 Little Elk Farm **200**, 229, **353**, 353-54	249 Rev. Duke's log schoolhouse **332**, 332
92 Calvert log house **468**, 468	171 Little Elk house **360**, 360	255 Hollingsworth Tavern/Holly Inn **330**, 330, 331
93 College Green Victorian Gothic house **479**, 479-80	172 Hopewell 184-85, **185**, 186, **231**, 231, **351**, 351-52, 356	
		256 Trinity Episcopal **348**, 348
95 Graystone Manor 183-84, **184**, **401**, 401-402	173 Mackey farmhouse **353**, 353	257 Elkton Methodist Church **340**, 240
97 Reynolds farm **402**, 402	174 Col. David Mackey house 353, **354**, 354, 374	258 Elkton Presbyterian **343**, 343
98 Evan's Choice **173**, 173-75, **253**, 253, 254-55, **399**, 399-400		262 Clayton Building **339**, 339
	175 Spring Run Farm **360**, 361	264 Wilson Victorian house **421**, 421
99 Bristole **204**, 204-205, 306-307, **307**	176 Rock Spring Farm **358**, 358-59	266 Burbage-Brock house **335**, 335
101 Mill House **376**, 376	177 John Wilson house **334**, 334	271 Gerry house 212, 224, **225**, **426**, 426-27
102 St. Mary Anne's Church **39**, 40, 215, **378**, 378, 386	178 Wilson double house **334**, 334-45	273 Presbyterian manse, Port Deposit **437**, 437
	181 Wilna **329**, 329	273 Rowland house **437**, 437
104 Brick House **386**, 386	186 William and Mary Veazey house **381**, 381	274 Adams Hall, Tome Institute/Port Deposit Town Hall **445**, 445
105 North East Town Hall **394**, 394	187 John Churchman house **54**, 54, **168**, 168-69, 203, **215**, 215, **230**, 230, **464**, 464	
106 Greenhill Farm **260**, 260-61, **392**, 393		276 Tome carriage house **433**, 433
107 Hamilton house **196**, **379**, 379-80	188 Clarwyn Farm **467**, 467	277 Vanneman house **426**, 427
108 Cecil Hotel **384**, 384	189 Hebron's Gift **469**, 469	278 McClenahan mansion **212**, **441**, 441-42
109 Klondyke/McKown house 134, **135**, **397**, 397	191 Blue Ball **43**, **352**, 352-53	279 Tome gas house **433**, 433
	196 Pleasant Hill, house near **372**, 372	281 brick row house, Port Deposit **429**, 429
110 Linton house **382**, 382	199 Fell Road log house **465**, 465	282 Touchstone house **437**, 437
111 Paca house **378**, 378-79	200 Benjamin Chandlee house **466**, 466	283 Port Deposit Presbyterian Church **444**, 445
112 Whitaker Iron Co. office **439**, 439	202 Brown's gristmill **481**, 481	285 38 S. Main St., Port Deposit **431**, 431
113 Whitaker Mansion **440**, 441	203 Jeremiah Brown house **187**, 187, 208, **209**, **466**, 466-67	286 Mrs. Murphy's Hotel **425**, 425-26
117 Brookland **424**, 424		288 St. Teresa of Avila Church **439**, 439-40
118 Dr. H. V. Davis house 312, **319**, 319-20	204 Ury-Fassitt farm **471**, 471	290 Tome Memorial U. M. Church 431, **440**, 440-41

291	Paw Paw Building **211**, 212, **427**, 427-28	549	coffin maker's house **386**, 386	780	Gilpin house **342**, 343
294	Vannort house **432**, 432	555	Roney and Wells Hardware Store **388**, 388	784	Laughlin's Market **362**, 362
296	McDowell-Blackburn house **429**, 429-30	559	Mauldin-Beatty house **387**, 387	786	Joseph Biddle house **361**, 361
297	Port Deposit Municipal Building **440**, 440	565	Kirk, Levi, house **472**, 473	788	Highfield **454**, 454
300	Amos Alexander house **362**, 362-63	565	Cedar Farm **472**, 473	789	Davis-Christy Mill **408**, 408
304	Lana Wright house **306**, 307	576	Biles house **479**, 479	790	Cowen brick house **357**, 357
306	Layman house **310**, 310	583	Bethel 203-204, **204**, 227, **476**, 476	791	Moore, William, house **399**, 399
307	Cropper house **310**, 311	584	Job farm **259**	795	Walnut Lane Farm **382**, 383
308	Slicher Store **310**, 311	589	William Kirk house **469**, 469	797	Longview Farm **267**, 267
309	Henry Hager/Kinter house **136**, 326, **327**	591	Crothers's Store **472**, 472	807	Elk River Farm **392**, 392-93
311	Chesapeake City Bank building **323**, 323	597	White Oak School **474**, 474	810	Simpers house **393**, 393
314	Trinity Methodist Church **322**, 322-23	599	Trinity Methodist Church **482**, 482	811	Oldfield Point Road frame house **383**, 383
316	Griffith house **318**, 319	600	Haines, Joseph, house **475**, 475	815	Wesley Chapel **386**, 386
318	Martindale-Hughes house **312**, 312	604	Wilson, John P., farm **480**, 480-81	816	Maffit farmhouse **387**, 387
320	Bethel A.M.E. Church **320**, 320	605	Cherry Grove School **481**, 481	823	Otter Farm Italianate house **340**, 340
321	Gassaway house **313**, 313	606	Kirk stone house **477**, 477-78	829	Watts house **337**, 337
322	Rees's Store **325**, 325	608	Dr. Mearns house 476, **477**	833	McCullough-Cummings property **457**, 457
323	Dr. Smithers's house **312**, 312	609	Levi and Amanda Mearns house **478**, 478	834	St. Patrick's Church 449, **456**, 456
327	Karsner-Wilsey house/office **323**, 323-24	609	White's Plains Farm **478**, 478	835	Alexander house **455**, 455
336	St. Rose of Lima Church **320**, 320-21	617	England, Charles, house **478**, 479	836	Pembroke Farm **448**, 448-49
340	First Presbyterian Church **315**, 315	629	Bailey house **474**, 474	838	Crothers house **458**, 458
341	North Chesapeake City row houses **313**, 313	630	Big Elk Chapel **371**, 371	841	Fulton-Alexander house **448**, 448, 449
356	St. Stephen's Chapel **302**, 302	631	Howard Mackey house **360**, 360	854	Founds house **449**, 449
357	Blackway house **303**, 303	635	Dolfinger Creamery **375**, 375	864	Shadowbrook/Bell Manor **459**, 459
359	Methodist parsonage, Cecilton **292**, 292	638	Colora Friends meetinghouse 41, **411**, 411-12	865	Oakwood Crossroads frame house **459**, 459
360	Zion Methodist Church **300**, 300	639	Melissa Mackie house **367**, 367	867	Rock Springs Hotel **452**, 452
363	Church of the Good Shepherd **322**, 322	640	St. John's M. E. Church 368, **369**	868	Clearview Farm/Lowe house **454**, 454
368	Eckerson's gristmill **418**, 419	642	Brick Hill **374**, 374	871	Oakwood School No. 4 **456**, 456
371	Simeon Woodrow house **404**, 404	644	Kite's Mill **371**, 371	872	house from Conowingo **461**, 461
373	Moore house **414**, 414	645	Providence Row 372, **373**	873	Ragan, Dr. David, house **457**, 457
379	St. John's U. M. Church **390**, 390	648	Walnut Hill 358, **365**, 365	874	Conowingo, Old, bridge 461, **461**
381	Jefferson Hall **431**, 431	652	Harlan-Wilson Mill **333**, 333	875	Mount Zoar house **459**
386	107 House **383**, 383-84	656	Harvey frame house **342**, 342	876	Mount Zoar school **108**, 459
386	Tory House/107 House **383**, 383-84	659	Providence corner house **373**, 373	877	Mt. Zoar Methodist Church **459**, 459
387	Barnes, Perry, house **395**, 395	662	Eight Corner or Carter's School **107**, 358	877	Mount Zoar Methodist Church **459**, 459
393	Still House **381**, 381	666	Providence boardinghouse **372**, 372	878	Mount Welcome **460**, 460
398	Mary Palmer's **383**, 383	667	Childs Row 1 **345**, 345	878	Porter house **460**, 460
399	Thomas house **391**, 391	669	Walnut Valley store and house **373**, 373-74	882	Hill house **449**,
401	George Simcoe house **394**, 394	674	Carter's Mill workers' house **356**, 356	883	Rowlandsville concrete train bridge **450**, 450-51
402	Old Post Road frame house **388**, 389	676	Mackey-du Pont farm **366**, 366	884	Rowlandsville iron bridge **450**, 450-51
412	St. Stephen's rectory **297**, 297-98	686	Childs Row 2 **345**, 345	885	Clarke Moore house **449**
414	Bournes Forest **196**	687	Childs Row 3 **344**, 345	886	McCullough iron workers' houses **450**
422	George W. Childs house **346**, 346	695	Providence workers' houses **360**, 360-61	889	Gillespie house **458**, 458
428	Oak Grove School **387**, 387	705	Gayley house **411**, 411	891	Riley property **457**, 457
429	Reynolds, Mary, stone house **385**, 385	709	McCracken house **358**, 358	892	Keithley house **457**, 457
430	Curry stone house **388**, 388	713	Warwick-Tome farmhouse **427**, 427	896	New Bridge bridge **461**, 461
430	Stoney Chase **388**, 388	715	Thomas Garrett house 356, **357**	900	The Tombs **455**, 455-56
473	Mackey house **324**, 324	724	Mechanics Valley yellow house **390**, 390	900	McNamee log house **170**, 170, **455**, 455-56
502	Charles St., 205-207, Chesapeake City **318**, 319	730	Crothers's Victorian house **476**, 476-77	902	New Valley (Conowingo #2) School **460**, 460
513	Reynolds's, Mary, new house **390**, 390-91	734	Ford house **382**, 382	905	McKinney house **452**, 452-53
514	Scott Mill **359**, 359-60	739	Milestone House **468**, 468	906	William Preston house **451**, 451
520	Kirk brick house **472**, 472	746	Providence Mill manager's house **366**, 366	907	Z. T. Rawlings house 190, **191**, **454**, 454-55
521	McCleary farm **355**, 355	748	Maxwell Victorian house **421**, 421	908	Johnson Road farmhouse **460**, 460
533	William Fulton house **354**, 354-55	756	Zion brick house 474, **475**	911	Brown house **458**, 458
534	Pine View **363**, 363	758	Center School **359**, 359	913	Success **447**, 447-48
534	Brookings house **363**, 363	759	Zion Methodist Church **477**, 477	914	Porter's bridge 123, 460, **461**
535	Fulton flax mill 355, **357**, 357	762	Johnson Victorian house **396**, 396	918	Green's Delight **250-51**, 251, **451**, 451
537	Scarborough Mill house **337**, 337	763	Gilpin's Falls hydroelectric plant **398**, 398	921	Husfelt house **300**, 300
542	Nowland's **472**, 472	764	The Hermitage 328, **337**, 337-38	929	Upper Wickwire **299**, 299-300
543	Griffith-Smith house **261**, **391**, 391	767	Thomas house **424**, 424	936	School No. 7, Earleville 300-301, **301**
546	Walnut Valley gristmill **365**, 365	768	Hillwood **438**, 438	954	Biggs house **293**, 293
548	Providence Paper Mill 88, 119, 125, 360, 361-62, 371	769	Krauss's or Cross Keys **403**, 403	956	Knight house **293**, 293
548	Kenmore Pulp & Paper Mill 119, **361**, 361-62	770	Bromwell house **429**, 429	960	Haynes house and store **295**, 295
549	Foster house **386**, 386	772	Miller's Crossroads, house at **359**, 359	960	Haynes Store **295**, 295
		773	Zebley farmhouse **363**, 363	964	Gibson's Green **258**, 258, 295-96, **296**
		775	Reed house **314**, 314		
		778	Ginn house 195, **196**, **288**, 289		

965	McLane-Knight tenant house 267, **294**, 294	1129	Richards's Oak, house by **419**, 419	1256	Graystone Road frame house **476**, 476
973	Davis house **285**, 285	1130	Hunt, Marshall I., house **414**, 415	1258	William Cameron house **478**, 478
975	Lofland farm 304, **305**	1132	Pleasant Meadows School **422**, 422	1260	Warburton farm **465**, 465
978	Dr. Perkins house **294**, 294	1141	Cloverly **414**, 414-15	1284	Bainbridge Naval Training Center **153**, 153, 157, 159, 444, **446**, 446
983	Fisher-Wilson house **164-65**, 165-66, **284**, 284	1141	Pyle house **414**, 414-15		
		1152	Gillespie house **417**, 417-18	1285	Tome School for Boys **152**, **153**, 153, **443**, 443-44, 445, 446
985	Wilson house 267	1153	Cather's 404, **412**, 412-13		
985	Wilson tenant house **294**, 294	1154	Keilholtz, Charles, house **414**, 414	1304	Barnes icehouse **395**, 395
988	William T. Beeks house **298**, 298	1155	Clendenin Farm **413**, 413-14	1305	Jackson, Scott, house **397**, 397
989	B. J. Green house **299**, 299	1156	Orr, Nevin, house **419**, 419	1306	Charlestown water tower **396**, 396
992	Warwick Academy **296**, 296	1157	Hopewell Methodist Church **418**, 418	1307	Cecil County Jail **342**, 342
994	St. Francis Xavier Church farmhouse **292**, 292	1160	Abrahams house **413**, 413	1308	Cecil *Whig* Building **344**, 344-45
		1162	Independence **410**, 410	1309	Elkton Town Hall **347**, 347
995	Price, William, house **295**, 295-96	1165	Colonial Revival house **422**, 422	1310	Black Rock Tavern **346**, 346-47
997	Susquehanna River Bridge Administration Building **151**, 151, 445-46, **446**, 446	1171	Tosh house **413**, 413	1311	Friendship Stone, Elkton **328**, 328
		1175	Trumph house **407**, 407	1313	Martha Finley house 346
998	U.S. Route 40 over AMTRAK bridge **350**, 350	1177	Stoney Batter farmhouse **407**, 407	1315	John Wirt house **347**, 347
		1181	Morrison, Matthew, house 213-14, **214**, **408**, 408	1317	Taylor house **347**, 347
999	Childs pony truss bridge **350**, 350			1320	Bratton house **135**, **348**, 348-49
1001	Pennington farm **315**, 315	1184	Nesbitt stone house **409**, 409	1325	Staples house **337**, 337
1004	Fair Hill Racetrack **375**, 375	1185	Gerry house **418**, 418	1328	Chesapeake City boatyard buildings **324**, 324
1005	New Munster stone **355**, 355	1186	house and school in Liberty Grove 420		
1035	Elkton Armory **349**, 349-50	1188	White, Ira, house **418**, 418	1329	Ebeneezer A.M.E. Church **314**, 314
1036	Scotchman's Creek bridge **305**, 305	1190	Ewing Mill property silo **259**, 259	1331	Price, William IV, house **306**, 306
1037	Plum Creek bridge **348**, 348	1191	Colora Farm **412**, 412	1334	Peoples Bank Building **350**, 350
1042	Bayard farm **321**, 321	1191	Balderston, Lloyd, farm 263, **412**, 412	1337	McCullough Iron Co. office 392
1043	DeCoursey frame house **322**, 322	1191	Paradise **412**, 412	1338	Cramer house **395**, 395
1044	Lewis, James A., house **316**, 316	1192	McCullough, George, house **420**, 420	1339	Victorian double house 394, **395**
1046	Lake, Reuben, house 169	1196	Mount Pleasant **406**, 406	1340	Mauldin double house **389**, 389
1050	Sharp, Bayard, house 136, **137**, **327**, 327	1196	Ewing house **406**, 406	1342	McCullough house **393**, 393-94
1051	DeCoursey house **314**, 314-15	1199	Wilson house **410**, 410-11	1343	North East United Methodist Church **398**, 398
1051	Town Point Farm, DeCoursey house **314**, 314-15	1201	McCauley Road **406**, 406		
		1204	Basin's Run Road bridge **441**, 441	1344	Italianate double house **391**, 391
1052	Long property **325**, 325	1205	The Valley/Graham house **434**, 434	1348	Gilpin, John, house 316, **317**
1054	Port Herman **324**, 324	1206	New Valley Factory house **430**, 430	1348	Fox Harbor 316, **317**
1057	Courthouse Point farmhouse **242**, **309**, 309	1208	Harmony Chapel **442**, 442	1349	Gillespie Hotel **297**, 297
1061	Boulden farm **314**, 314	1212	Davis house **438**, 438	1350	Wilson-Quinn house **288**, 288
1065	Red House Farm 259	1213	Craig stone house **428**, 428	1353	Mt. Olivet U. M. Church **296**, 296
1066	Samuel Taylor house **232**, 232	1214	Woodrow house 190, **191**	1354	Wright house **301**, 301
1067	Andrew McIntire house **336**, 337	1217	Union Hotel 196, **202**, 203, **232**, 232, **425**, 425	1355	Historical Society of Cecil County **343**, 343-44
1075	Antego **339**, 339				
1077	Union United Methodist Church **341**, 341	1217	Gillespie log house 196, **202**, 203, **232**, 232, **425**, 425	1365	Carroll Short house **286**, 286
1078	Simpers log house **205**, 205, 336			1366	Guenther Realty building **298**, 298
1080	Boulden Chapel and cemetery **342**, 342	1218	Maplewood Farm **248**, **260**, 260, **438**, 438	1383	Cherry Hill U. M. Church **367**, 367
1081	Joseph Scarborough house **336**, 336-67	1218	Evans, Robert, house **438**, 438-39	1385	Boxwood **363**, 363
1082	Givens house **346**, 346	1220	Beaven log house 432-33, **433**	1393	Gallaher Store **366**, 367
1088	Hiram Walker house **367**, 367	1221	Steel Mount **424**, 424	1393	Gallaher house and store **366**, 366-67
1090	William Wade house **367**, 367	1222	Pattersonville/Rawlings farm (CE-1222) **261**, 261, 263-64, **265**, **438**, 438	1394	Carter-Ness house **374**, 375
1094	George Grant house **167**, 167, **370**, 370			1403	Nesbitt house **442**, 442-43
1097	Grammy's Run **368**, 368	1223	Thomas Patten house **213**, 213, **427**, 427	1408	Queen St. brick house **404**, 405
1098	Deep Run farm **369**, 369	1224	Moore-Rea house **430**, 430-31	1409	McClennahan double house **442**, 442
1100	Tyson Mill house **169**, 169, **355**, 355-56	1225	Jenness, S. M., house 208, **211**, **436**, 436	1412	Steps, The, Port Deposit **444**, 445
1101	Highlawn 352, **372**, 372	1227	Ashlawn **434**, 434	1414	Bond, Bella, house **428**, 428-29
1105	Ewing farm **366**, 366	1228	Holly Tree Farm **436**, 436-37	1415	Old Sorrel 424, **425**
1106	Moore's Chapel **370**, 370	1229	The Crow's Nest **446**, 446	1417	149 Main St., Port Deposit **432**, 432
1107	Hiram Clement house **475**, 475	1230	The Anchorage **439**, 439	1418	41 N. Main St., Port Deposit **434**, 434
1109	Spring Hills Farm **201**	1233	Principia **384**, 384	1419	88-94 N. Main St., Port Deposit **442**, 443
1115	Lincoln farm 254, **255**	1234	Gillespie, Thomas J., house **386**, 386-87	1421	McClennahan Quarry Co. office **444**, 444
1117	Haines, Rebecca, house **412**, 412	1235	Prospect Hill Farm **389**, 389	1423	Winchester Hotel 434, **435**
1118	Stoney Run **411**, 411	1240	Cosgrove, William, house **204**, 205, **385**, 385	1442	Perryville railroad station **445**, 445
1119	Taylor, Samuel, brick house **410**, 410			1445	Bohemia Manor 20th c. house 136, **137**, **142**, **326**, 326-27
1121	Tosh-Basham house 170, **171**	1242	Ebenezer Methodist Church **393**, 393		
1123	Harrisville 408-409	1244	Bay View log house **388**, 388	1450	West Nottingham Academy 41-42, 105, **107**, 402, **416**, 416-17, **422**, 422
1124	Brookview Chapel **421**, 421	1246	Crawford house **384**, 384-85		
1128	Dr. Slater B. Stubbs house **415**, 415	1255	England, Howard, farm **479**, 479		

975.2 BLU   EIK
Blumgart, Pamela James
At the head of the bay : a
cultural and architectural